T0301457

THE JAPANESE AND GERMAN ECONOMIES IN THE 20TH AND 21ST CENTURIES

BUSINESS RELATIONS IN HISTORICAL PERSPECTIVE

Kudō Akira

Renaissance Books Distinguished Asian Studies Scholars – Collected Writings series. Vol. 1

The Japanese and German Economies in the 20th and 21st Centuries

BUSINESS RELATIONS IN HISTORICAL PERSPECTIVE

By

Kudō Akira

Professor Emeritus, University of Tokyo (Institute of Social Science)

RENAISSANCE BOOKS

RENAISSANCE BOOKS DISTINGUISHED ASIAN STUDIES SCHOLARS:
COLLECTED WRITINGS SERIES. Volume 1 ISSN 2515-0626

THE JAPANESE AND GERMAN ECONOMIES IN THE 20TH AND 21ST CENTURIES
BUSINESS RELATIONS IN HISTORICAL PERSPECTIVE

First published 2018 by
RENAISANCE BOOKS
PO Box 219
Folkestone
Kent CT20 2WP

Renaissance Books is an imprint of Global Books Ltd

© KUDŌ Akira, 2018
ISBN 978-1-898823-69-8 [Hardback]

British Library Cataloguing in Publication Data
A CIP catalogue entry for this book is available
from the British Library

Set in Garamond 11 on 12 point by Dataworks
Printed and bound in England by CPI Antony Rowe, Chippenham, Wilts

Contents

❖

Preface

THE MAIN PURPOSE of this volume is to shed some light on the state of Japanese-German business relations throughout the whole of the twentieth century and at the beginning of the twenty-first. A further aim is to provide some clarification on the structures and processes of the world economy in the same period, while retaining a focus on Japanese and German, as well as European business, and attempting to give a clear picture of the Japanese and European 'national' and business economies.

Globally, Germany has long been significant. It was a major player in the two world wars in the first half of the twentieth century, and in the latter half – particularly at the end of the century and the beginning of this one – it was the driving force behind European integration and remains the most important partner of the United States in Continental Europe. For Japan, its relationship with Germany has long been important, while Japan has been a nation, which is indeed impossible for Germany to ignore. In political and diplomatic relations in the first half of the twentieth century, the two nations both came into conflict, with the 'Japanese-German War' in 1914, which was one facet of the First World War, as a representative example; and also cooperated, as symbolized by the conclusion of the Tripartite Pact in 1940. Simultaneously, in the realm of the economy (both business and national) there was both competition between Japanese and German companies in the world market, and collaboration through, for example, technological licensing. The relationship between the two countries, needless to say, included the study of Germany by Japan. This study was both broad and deep, encompassing the formation of the state system, science and technology, and reaching into the realm of ideology.

After the Second World War, both nations continued to remain important to each other, most of all in economic relations (both business relations and national economic relations), and their relationship developed while both their competition and their collaboration expanded.

In this period, unlike the one before, Germany began to study Japanese business management and technology. More significant than this, however, are the clear parallels between the steps both countries have taken: that is to say, the parallels between defeat as allies, post-war occupation, reform and reconstruction and becoming 'economic powers'.

Over the past twenty years, these parallels have taken on new forms, and are particularly clear in their economies. As a result of the trend towards globalization in the world economy – something, which it might be better to call Americanization to a large extent – various parallels and similarities have come to be recognized in both nations' economies. As a result the Japanese and German economies have frequently been lumped together in discussions, whether it be as the nations criticized as the slowest to adapt to globalization, or Americanization, in contrast to the American economy or the Anglo-Saxon economic pattern; or those praised as expected standard-bearers of anti-globalization.

In the histories of Japanese-German relations, which developed under the influence of these types of studies and parallels, research on economics and diplomatic relations has flourished, focusing on the first half of the twentieth century, but the history of economic relations over the entire period is still in its infancy. On the other hand, there is a great deal of research focused on the parallels which have been recognized between the Japanese and German economies after the Second World War, and in particular over the last twenty years. Given this, the parallels should now be clear, based on both the transition in economic relations between the two countries in this period, and also the history of both countries' economic relations up to the middle of the twentieth century. With these issues in mind, this book will ask what sort of relationship the economies of both Japan and Germany (both business and national) have developed, aiming to clarify its history and current circumstances. An additional theme will be the comparison of the Japanese and German economies in the light of their mutual interrelationship. As a result of this, its perspective will naturally broaden from Western Europe, to East Asia and then to the world.

Part I, *Japanese-German Business Relations*, will explore the history of business relations between Japan and Germany in the period from the twentieth to the twenty-first centuries. Part II, *Trajectory of Japanese-German Business Relations*, while being based on this relationship history, will focus on Japanese and German, and also European business. Part III, *The Japanese and European Business and Economies*, will attempt to explicate the nature of the Japanese and European business and national economies, while also aiming at contributing to the discussion of the structure and processes of the world economy.

This book is my second in English, following on from *Japanese-German Business Relations* (Routledge, 1998). Even though the main topic – the history of Japanese-German economic relations (national economic relations and business relations) – is the same, in comparison to the previous volume this book has a weaker focus on the history of the relationship. I believe this to be unavoidable, because the studies assembled here were written for various purposes (publications, conferences, and others) over a period of more than twenty years. To a greater or lesser degree, however, all were written with the intention of clarifying the history of Japanese-German economic relations, and they were written because I wished to raise the important issue of the history of Japanese-German economic relations internationally, and not just in Japan. I am not claiming that in this work I will be able to explain the entire history of Japanese-German economic relations throughout the entire twentieth and early twenty-first centuries. However, I do feel that by demonstrating the main points of contention, attempting to explain them, and clarifying the meaning which it is possible for this type of research to have, I will be able to provide a point of departure for further in-depth study. It is for these various reasons that I believe there is merit in publishing these papers as an 'introduction' to the history of Japanese-German economic relations.

Finally, I should like to record my thanks to all those who have assisted in the publication of this book. First, although I am unable to mention everyone individually, my warmest thanks to all those who assisted in the original publication of the various works collected here. Next, I should like to express my deepest appreciation to my esteemed colleague, Philipps-University Marburg Professor Erich Pauer, who has provided me with the benefit of his experience from this project's inception to its conclusion. Professor Pauer was my co-editor on *Japan and Germany: Two Latecomers to the World Stage, 1890–1945*, which was published in three volumes by Global Oriental in 2009, and it came as a complete surprise to me when he, on behalf of the managing director of Global Oriental, Mr Paul Norbury, suggested the publication of my collected works in English, immediately after the latter book was published. I hesitated briefly, but came to think that this would be a good opportunity to inform people of the significance of the history of Japanese-German economic relations – something which I have been engaged in for the past twenty-five years – and in addition, that the work could be positioned as an introduction to the publications on the history of Japanese-German economic relations which are currently in preparation, and so I replied to Paul Norbury and Erich Pauer that I would gladly follow their suggestion. Furthermore, I would like to express my profound thanks to Gakushūin University Professor YUZAWA Takeshi, former President of the Business History Society of Japan, who has kindly written a splendid foreword to the book's contents. In addition, I should like to thank Dr Thomas McAuley from the School of East Asian Studies, University of Sheffield, who undertook the work of translating my sections of the above-mentioned three volume collection on Japan and Germany, and who has once again assisted me with this work. Finally, I should like to express once more my gratitude to the publisher, Mr Paul Norbury, for his determination in overseeing the publication of both works.

Addendum

For various reasons, publication of this work has been delayed. My words above were originally drafted in late 2010 in anticipation of the book appearing in print the following year. However, although it now has a 2018 imprint, I am delighted to affirm what I believe to be the ongoing relevance of its pages – a view which I trust will be shared by my colleagues and those accessing it for research purposes.

KUDŌ Akira
Tokyo, September 2017

Foreword

Professor Kudō Akira's Work and its Historical Background

Yuzawa Takeshi, Professor Emeritus of Gakushūin University, Tokyo

1. INTRODUCTION

On 22 April 2011, the House of Representatives in the Japanese Diet resolved to promote the friendship between Japan and Germany on the celebration of the 150th anniversary of the amity treaty between Japan and Prussia in 1861.[1] The resolution stressed that the newly-founded Germany in 1871 became a model for the Japanese modernization during the Meiji period. And, although Japan and Germany fought each other in the First World War, both countries were allies in the Second World War – launching an aggression, which caused unparalleled human suffering and material damage in their neighboring countries but ultimately resulted in their own defeat and destruction. However, both Japan and Germany miraculously succeeded in rebuilding their country from the ruins and reviving their economies. Having reflected on the war they caused and its consequences, both countries are now cooperating for the peace and prosperity of the world. There is now an active and steady interchange between the Japanese and the Germans in various fields, with both respecting each other's culture and values. The House of Representatives declared on this occasion that Japan will contribute to the realization of world peace based upon the reliable partnership with Germany. Based on this declaration, various events in both countries took place nationwide on official and private levels. This occasion provides a good opportunity to consider the relations between Japan and German from a historical perspective.

There are many books on the relationship between Japan and Germany, especially on diplomatic history and the comparison of types of economic development. One of the main concerns in the field of economics and business deals with the characteristics of the Japanese and German economies compared with the Anglo-Saxon ones.[2] Given the growing weight of the Anglo-Saxon economic and business models on the one hand, and the frequency of global economic crises starting in these economies on the other, a historical analysis of the economy and business in Japan and Germany might provide us with some clues for alternative models.

I am, therefore, very glad that Professor KUDŌ has published this collection of his articles written over the last quarter of a century on Japan's business and economic relations with Germany as well as with the EU and Asia. The book begins with an analysis of the historical relationship between Japanese and German companies. His early works concentrate on IG Farben and the German chemical industry as a whole. Regarding IG Farben's strategy for Japan, KUDŌ examined the negotiation process between IG Farben and Japanese companies. His interest subsequently spread to the role of the German economy within the EU, to business relations between Germany and Japan, and to wider issues on Japanese business and economy, including the possibility of Asian economic integration.

In this short Foreword, I would like to consider the significance of this book from historical backgrounds. First, it will be useful to reconsider the German involvement in the modernization of Meiji Japan. Then I will depict simply how much Japan owed to German academics, especially in the field of history, and how Japanese academic bodies were developed to maintain a high level of research. KUDŌ's works are a product of these academic traditions in Japan, in addition being based on his long connection with German academics. Lastly, I would like to consider the meaning of his works and their contribution to our studies.

2. GERMAN INVOLVEMENT IN JAPANESE MODERNIZATION

As is well known, Germany was a comparatively late industrializer in Western Europe, and then rushed to catch up through strong government leadership and the development of close relationships between financial and economic agents. At the time of her opening to foreign countries, Japan was in a situation similar to that of the NIEs (newly industrializing economies) in recent years. Japan in the middle of the nineteenth century was an underdeveloped country, and needed to introduce the Western economic and social system, and high technologies as well. Germany provided a good template for Japanese industrialization, in Professor KUDŌ's words, 'Germany was a good teacher and Japan was a good student.'

In spite of Japan's isolation during the Edo era, the Tokugawa government had collected information about the West through Dutch and Chinese connections. At the time of the Meiji restoration in 1868, the Japanese government recognized that world leadership had switched to Britain and France rather than the Netherlands and set its mind on learning from them. During the last stages of the Tokugawa government, consultations were held on military matters with French advisers given Napoleon Bonaparte's great achievements in Europe. But after the Franco-Prussian War of 1870–71, the newly established Meiji government adopted the German military system instead.

More generally, the government pursued modern industrialization under the slogan of 'the promotion of industry and the encouragement of new industry' – and in as short a period as possible. One of the most feasible ways to realize modernization was the employment of the so-called *o-yatoi* (lit. 'hired foreigners'). These were Westerners with particular knowledge of modern technology and know-how who were hired both by central and local government as well as the private sector – often at high salaries. They introduced Japan to superior technologies thereby contributing to her modernization. Some took the role of advisers for the development of the constitution, industry, the military and so on. They also took a leading role in the modernization of education. The 'hired foreigners' were contracted usually for three or five years, enabling the Japanese to absorb a considerable amount of knowledge from them, especially in the technological fields.[3]

The number of 'hired foreigners' employed by Japanese public and private institutions ranged from 1500 to 2000. The largest number (928) came from Britain, followed by the United States (374), France (259), China (253), Germany (175), and the Netherlands (87). Although the number of Germans among the 'hired foreigners' was not necessarily as large as from other Western countries, Japan was particularly interested in Germany's experience as a latecomer to industrialization and her ability to emerge as a powerful nation within Europe in a comparatively short period of time. Germany was a model for Japan 'to enrich the country and to strengthen the military'[4] and her experience proved particularly valuable in the fields of legislation, the military, medicine, and history education.

Itō Hirobumi, the first prime minister, drafted the Meiji constitution of Japan under the influence of Rudolf von Gneist of the University of Berlin and Lorenz von Stein of the University of Vienna, both of whom suggested that Japan should adopt a German-style constitution. In addition, the Meiji government asked *Generalfeldmarschall* (field marshal) Helmuth Karl Bernhard Graf von Moltke to send an adviser to help create a modern Japanese army. Jacob Meckel was dispatched from Germany and succeeded in laying the firm foundations of the modern Japanese army system, though he stayed in Japan for only three years (1885–88). He educated students at the Japanese Army War College, and acted as an adviser to the Ministry of Army.[5]

German influences were also clearly visible in the field of medicine. It was essential to improve the level of Japanese physical strength, not least to maintain a strong army. After the bombardment of Kagoshima, Satsuma province succeeded in combating anti-Western perceptions to such an extent that British culture, technologies and British medicine became popular there. However, after the Meiji Restoration the government decided to invite German military medical personnel to Japan, even though many core members in the new government came from Satsuma where British medicine was familiar. Theodor Eduard Hoffmann and Benjamin Carl Leopold Müller were sent to Japan in 1871 for three years. They were military doctors, and educated at a medical school. They contributed significantly to the establishment of modern Japanese medicine.[6] Erwin von Bälz was invited to found Japan Tokyo-Medical School (later the Faculty of Medicine, University of Tokyo) in 1876. He stayed in Japan for 27 years, contributing greatly to the advancement of Japan's medical community.[7] Indeed, German was the official language among doctors up to recent times.

3. DEVELOPMENT OF ECONOMIC AND BUSINESS HISTORY IN JAPAN

The theory of the Historical School of Economics advocated by Friedrich List was attractive to underdeveloped countries like Japan during the Meiji period, particularly his idea of 'developmental stages of economies'. The first academic to introduce Western historiography to Japan was Ludwig Riess who had studied at the University of Berlin under Leopold von Ranke. He arrived in Japan in 1887 and taught for five years at Tokyo Imperial University, where he presented Ranke's methods of historical research and introduced European archival materials. He promoted the establishment of The Historical Society of Japan (Shigakukai) launched in 1889 and the creation of *Shigaku Zasshi* (Journal of Historical Science), the oldest academic journal of history in Japan.

The first economic historian in Japan was FUKUDA Tokuzō who was dispatched by the Ministry of Education to study in Germany in 1898. He studied at the University of Leipzig and the University of Munich, and was strongly influenced by Karl Bücher and Lujo Brentano. On Brentano's recommendation and at the age of twenty-six he presented his Ph.D. thesis to the University of Munich in 1900 entitled *Die Gesellschaftliche und wirtschaftliche Entwicklung in Japan.*[8] He subsequently became a professor at the Tokyo Higher Commercial School (now Hitotsubashi University). Next was SAKANISHI Yoshizō, who was taught by Fukuda at the Tokyo Higher Commercial School, and was also dispatched to Germany to study the history of commerce and the theory of commerce under Brentano at the University of Munich from 1906 to 1910. After he returned to Japan, he lectured on economic history at the Kōbe Higher Commercial School (now Kōbe University). Another graduate of the Tokyo Higher Commercial School, MIURA Shinshichi was sent by the Ministry of Education to Leipzig University in 1903 to study under Karl Gotthard Lamprecht. He returned in 1912 and taught economic, cultural and commercial history at the School. And another student of Fukuda, UEDA Teijirō, was taught economic history at Birmingham University under W.J. Ashley, the first professor of economic history in England.[9] NOMURA Kentarō of Keiō University introduced to Japan the theory of Heinrich Rickert, before turning his attention to economic history. Nomura visited W.J. Ashley in 1923, who recommended him to J.H. Clapham at Cambridge University. He studied under Clapham and in 1928 published *Ei-koku shihon-shugi seiritsu-shi* (The Establishment of English Capitalism). Those pioneers, first under strong influence from German, and then British scholars, made a great impact on traditional Japanese historians and they moved to organize academic bodies in Japan.

By the 1920s there was already a strong tide of opinion in favor of economic historians organizing their own academic organization, spurred by the establishment of the Economic History Society in the UK in 1926. *Shakai-keizai-shi gakkai* (originally translated as The Social and Economic History Society, now The Socio-Economic History

Society) was inaugurated on 27 December 1930. The name change reflected the fact that the German Society was called *Gesellschaft für Sozial- und Wirtschaftsgeschichte* and that, although the UK society was formally known as the Economic History Society, its major purpose was to promote the study of social history as well as economic history. It seemed natural therefore that the Japanese initiative should call itself the Socio-Economic History Society, and about fifty scholars from major universities participated in it. By the time of the first annual conference, held in November 1931, the number of members had increased to about 500. Since then, the Socio-Economic History Society has remained the largest body in the field of economic history in Japan. It currently has a membership of about 1,300, and organizes an annual conference and publishes its own journal entitled *Shakai-keizai-shigaku* (The Quarterly Journal of the Social and Economic History Society, now Socio-Eco-nomic History). In the first issue of the journal, HIRANUMA Yoshiro of Waseda University, representative of the Society, stressed how much the German publication, the *Vierteljahrschrift für Social- und Wirtschaftsge-schichte*, first published in 1903, had inspired Society members to pub-lish a similar academic journal in Japan.[10]

There is an additional academic society for economic history in Japan, which used to be strongly linked to Marxism and the left wing movement. This society, called Tochi-seido shigakukai (Agrarian His-tory Society), was established under the guidance of YAMADA Moritarō in 1948. At the time of the establishment of the society, agricultural land reform was one of the most important and controversial political and social issues of the day.[11] It started to publish a journal, *Tochi-seido shigaku* (The Journal of Agrarian History) from 1958, which mainly focused on economic theory, current economic conditions, agriculture, and economic history. Its editorial policy resembles *Past and Present* in Britain. The Society changed its name to Seiji-keizai-gaku – keizai-shi gakkai (Political Economy & Economic History Society) in 2002, and accordingly its journal changed its name to *Rekishi to keizai* (Journal of Political Economy & Economic History).

The latest academic body in this field is the Japan Business History Society, which was established in 1964 during the period of high eco-nomic growth. It was promoted by NAKAGAWA Keiichirō who returned to Japan from the Harvard Business School in 1960 and launched a small study group on business history, which finally developed into the Society. The membership of the Society is composed mainly of scholars from economic history and business and management studies.

It is worth reflecting on some of the differences between the Japanese Business History Society and those in the USA and in Europe. Japanese business history started later than in the USA and differs in its organizational and financial background. In the United States, the first journal in the world for the study of business history, *The Bulletin of the Business Historical Society*, has been published since 1926 by the Harvard Business School. It was renamed *Business History Review* in 1954. That same year, an association, the Business History Conference (BHC) held its first meeting. It has been publishing the proceedings of its meetings since 1962 under the title *Business and Economic History* (now available only on-line), but only established its own academic journal, *Enterprise & Society*, in 2000.

In Britain, the journal *Business History* was first published from Liverpool University in 1958. Although many prominent business historians were involved in the editorial board of the journal, there was no formal society as such to promote its interests. The first British business history research centre, called the Business History Unit, was established at the London School of Economics (LSE) in the University of London in 1978. The Unit was not formally associated with the national Economic History Society and lacked to some degree the financial and personal links to enable it to become a national center for business history in the UK. The Unit temporarily took over editorial control of *Business History* from the University of Liverpool, but responsibility for the journal soon moved to the University of Reading. Eminent scholars were invited to join the journal's editorial board to help sustain quality but no national academic body emerged to undertake responsibility for publishing the journal. The Association of Business Historians (ABH) was founded in the UK in 1990, but it had no claim to publish Business History or any direct links with the Business History Unit. The journal and the research center already existed before the ABH.

The Business History Society in Japan is different from these bodies. First, it is run by an executive committee based at one of its members' offices with a temporary secretary. Membership of the Society is currently about 800. Basically, the Society is financed by membership fees with some support from companies. An Annual General Meeting approves the plans of the executive committee, and a yearly budget. The Society organizes a two-day annual conference and also separate monthly meetings in the Kantō and Kansai regions, and workshops in Tōhoku, Nagoya and Kyūshū.

Second, the Society's major publication *Keiei-shigaku* (Japan Business History Review) (in Japanese) is issued quarterly and sold to the public through bookshops. Apart from this journal, the *Japanese Yearbook on Business History* (in English) has been published since 1984, following the example of the German *Yearbook on Business History*, which began publication in 1981. The *Japanese Yearbook on Business History* changed its title to *Japanese Research in Business History* from 2004 and is now mainly distributed to the members of the Society. In addition the Society occasionally undertakes commemorative publications such as *Keiei-shigaku no 20-nen* (Twenty Years of Japan Business History Society), *Nihon Keiei-shi no kiso-chishiki* (Business History in Japan: Basic Facts and Concepts), *Gaikoku keiei-shi no kiso-chishiki* (Business History in the World: Basic Facts and Concepts), and *Keiei-shigaku no 50-nen* (Fifty Years of Business History in Japan).

Third, an International Conference on Business History has been held by the Society since 1974. This was supported financially by the Taniguchi Industrial Foundation to commemorate the tenth anniversary of the Society. The first occasions of this conference took place at the foot of Mt Fuji and it was subsequently known as the Fuji Business History Conference (FBHC). Prominent scholars from foreign countries were invited to the gatherings and the proceedings were published by the University of Tokyo Press (and later Oxford University Press). The first conference focused on 'Strategy and Structure of Big Business', in which A.D. Chandler and Charles Wilson participated. From the start, the principal concern of the conference was to encourage international comparative work centred on Japan. Japanese scholars were provided with excellent opportunities to discuss matters of mutual interest with foreign scholars and vice versa, investigating especially the differences and the similarities in business development within Japan and Western industrialized countries. One series was composed of five yearly conferences.

Professor Kudō, a specialist on German business history, is one of the active members of the FBHC, and took the chair for the fourth series committee of the FBHC. At the time of his chair, University of Tokyo Press refused to publish the series thereafter and then he approached Oxford University Press, which eventually agreed to take on the responsibility. As a result, FBHC became renowned worldwide by publishing the series with a prestigious publisher. However, the Taniguchi Industrial Foundation terminated their previous crucial support and eventually FBHC could not continue either the conference or publication as before. In addition, during the long-term depression of the Japanese economy in the early 1990s, it became quite difficult to find other financial support from within the business community.[12]

FBHC was fortunate to produce as one of its by-products another international conference, a Japanese-German business history workshop, which was designed to discuss more in detail the topics, which had originally featured in FBHC. The first conference was held in 1979 in Berlin, and the second one in 1981 in Tokyo. Thereafter, Japanese-UK, and Japanese-French workshops were also held, providing valuable occasions for the discussion of comparative business history with participants from each country. Professor KUDŌ has been one of the most active promoters of the Japanese-German business history workshop. He published with Matthias Kipping and Harm G. Schröter, *German and Japanese Business in the Boom Years*[13] as the result of the third Japanese-German Business History Conference in Tokyo in 2000.

4. FROM COMPARATIVE BUSINESS HISTORY TO THE HISTORY OF BUSINESS RELATIONS AND BEYOND

After the Second World War, one of the big issues among economic and business historians was the comparison of Japanese politics, economy and society with the Western ones. Scholars pointed out the backwardness of democracy, bureaucratic control over the economy, restricted media activities etc. – ideas that were strongly influenced by Marxism. ŌTSUKA Hisao was one of the leaders of economic history, who analyzed the process of the dissolution of feudalism in England, and industrialization through emerging manufacture in the rural areas.[14] In the mid-1950s, he already proposed the idea of proto-industrialization, which is now popular among economic historians. His studies made a great impact on the Japanese economic historians as well, who debated hotly about what kind of definition to give to the Meiji Restoration, and whether a civil revolution occurred in Japan or not. There were lots of arguments about the comparison of history between Japan and Britain. It was thought by Japanese academics that Japan industrialized very quickly with immature democracy and imperfect markets, and that the rapid industrialization accompanied by the close ties among politics, business and the military eventually pushed Japan into the war. There were also many scholars involved in German history, which had a historical background similar to Japan. Fascism closely connected with a monopolistic economy was seen as key to explain the characteristics of Japan and Germany before the Second World War.

After the War, Japanese scholars seriously reflected upon the backwardness of the Japanese economy and business, and stressed how to transfer US American style business into Japanese firms.[15] While Japanese firms were struggling to introduce the US American model, Japanese firms, though persisting in the traditional management, could succeed in rapid economic growth. There occurred a big question why Japanese companies could achieve a high performance with traditional Japanese management, which had been severely criticized by these scholars. James Abegglen proposed a clue to solve this question in his epoch making book *The Japanese Factory* published in 1958.[16] This book evaluated the traditional Japanese management, which was identified by these scholars as a hindrance to the modernization of business. This book had a great impact not only in academia, but also on business people, and many scholars changed their view and tended to follow his opinion. Now Japanese management was no longer considered as backward, and was positively appreciated instead. Japanese business and management were 'hot' issues from the 1960s to 1980s, with many international comparisons, and it was transferred to foreign countries.[17]

From 1980 onward, one fashionable trend has been to study business relations between two countries. One excellent book entitled *Nichi-Bei kankei keiei-shi* (Competition between Japanese and American companies), with comparative studies between Japan and the US was edited and published by Professor SHIOMI Haruhito and Professor HORI Ichirō.[18] It picked up major companies among the same industrial sectors in Japan and US, which were competing with each other at the time of high economic growth in Japan, while the American economy was confronting a severe economic recession. The historical case studies explained the reasons why Japanese companies were successful with the Japanese management system. Ten years later, Professor SHIOMI edited with Professor KIKKAWA Takeo *Nichi-Bei kigyo no gurobaru kyōsō senryaku* (Competitive Strategy for Globalization between Japanese and American Companies),[19] which also compared the weakness and strength of the companies in both countries after Japan had entered what is now called the 'lost decade', since the early 1990s. It also considered the applicability of the Chandlerian model to companies at this time, and his contribution to their competitiveness in the global market.

On the relation between Japanese and British companies, Professor NAGURA Bunji started to write articles on Vickers and Armstrong's strategy of branching into Japan, and also published *Heiki tekko-kaisha no Nichi-Ei kankei-shi* (Anglo-Japanese Relations in the Case of Vickers and Armstrong*)*.[20] He analyzed in detail the shareholdings of Nihon Seikō-sho, a subsidiary of Vickers and Armstrong, between 1907 and 1952. He also published a book with other members on the Siemens incident, which developed into a serious scandal in politics in the early twentieth century.[21] It examined the severe rivalry between Vickers and Siemens in the Japanese armaments market from various aspects.

We can also find a rich literature on the history of business relations between Japan and Germany. Professor WATANABE Hisashi started early to analyze the relationship between Siemens and the Furukawa Zaibatsu in Japan in an article entitled *Fuji Denki seiritsu katei* (The Creation of Fuji Electric).[22] He also wrote another article on Fuji Electric, which explained the second and third stages of Fuji Electric at the time of establishment. He investigated in detail the negotiation process between Siemens and Furukawa when Siemens branched into the Japanese market.[23]

Professor TAKENAKA Tōru also picked up the topic of Siemens entering into Japan in the Meiji era in his book titled *Jiimensu to Meiji Nippon* (Siemens and Meiji-Japan) in 1993.[24] He analyzed the negotiation process between Siemens and Furukawa with the cultural differences in both countries.

5. CONCLUDING REMARKS

Professor KUDŌ contributed tremendously to the new stages of economic and business history. He started his business history of IG Farben, and extended it to the German chemical industry as a whole. His main concern was the relationship between the companies of the two countries rather than their comparison. He energetically conducted his research on the relations between the companies and the relations between the two countries, because the relationships between the companies were deeply affected by the policies of the two nations. While he belonged to the Institute of Social Science of the University of Tokyo, he organized various projects, and edited and published books like *Haken no henyō to fukushi-kokka* (The Changing World Hegemony and the Welfare State) in 1995, and *Gendai Nihon kigyō* (Contemporary Japanese Enterprise) with KIKKAWA Takeo and Glenn D. Hook, 3 vols., in 2006. They are mainly the products based upon the projects within the Institute of Social Science, but he developed his main concerns by organizing a team with Professor TAJIMA Nobuo, a specialist of diplomatic history between Japan and Germany, to prepare the highly successful three-volume work entitled *Nichi-Doku kankei-shi 1890– 1945* (The Relations between Japan and Germany 1890–1945) published in 2008,[25] also published in English in 2009. This will be one of the epoch-making publications on the relationship between Japan and Germany bringing together relevant scholars in the fields of economic, political, social and military history.

Finally, I would like to highlight three points, which emphasize the importance of Professor KUDŌ's work. First, with Professors WATANABE and TAKENAKA, he explored a new field, the history of Japanese-German business relations, and this is quite important for business history as well as comparative history. Many other case studies in different countries should be conducted with international cooperation, and they will elucidate business practice from these multilateral aspects.

Second, Germany and Japan are thought to be latecomers in modern industrialization, and they had common characteristics, which were different from the Anglo-Saxon business model. The Anglo-Saxon economy is dominated by financial powers, seeking profit as much as possible in the short term. But Germans and Japanese are aiming for a different business model though they are under strong pressure from the Anglo-Saxon business model. In the recent crisis of the world economy, it might be a good opportunity to reconsider what German and Japanese business tried to look for, and what kind of ideas could be taken from them to solve the current economic problems.

Third, the role of Germany in the EU is quite important in the current economic crises among member countries, and it will be quite useful to reconsider the characteristics of German business from a historical perspective, especially regarding the business relations with Japan. Japan also has an obligation to contribute to the development of the Asian economies, and to promote their integration. In this respect, Japan might be able to benefit from the know-how and experience of Germany as a teacher, just like it did during the Meiji era.

REFERENCES:

Abbegglen, James C., *The Japanese Factory: Aspects of its Social Organization*, The Free Press, 1958.

Abo Tetsuo (ed.), *Hybrid factory: the Japanese production system in the United States*, Oxford Univ. Press, 1994.

Bälz, Toku, *Erwin Bälz. Das Leben eines deutschen Arztes im erwachenden Japan*, Stuttgart: J. Engelhorns Nachf., 1930.

Dohi Tsuneyuki, 'Taishō-ki no Ōshū keizai-shigaku to Fukuda-gakuha' (The 'Fukuda School' and European Economic History Studies in Taishō Japan), in *The Hitotsubashi Review* vol. 132 (2004), no. 4.

Dore, Ronald P., *Stock Market Capitalism: Japan and Germany versus the Anglo-Saxons*, Oxford: Oxford University Press, 2000.

Fukuda Tokuzo, *Die Gesellschaftliche und wirtschaftliche Entwicklung in Japan*, Stuttgart: J.G. Cottasche Buchhandlung Nachfolger, 1900.

Hiranuma Yoshirō, 'Shakai-keizai shigaku no sōkan ni saishite' (Some Remarks on the Publication of the Journal of the Social and Economic History Society), *Shakai-keizai shigaku (The Quarterly Journal of the Social and Economic History Society)* vol. 1 (1931), no. 1.

Jones, H.J., *Live Machines, Hired Foreigners and Meiji Japan*, Tenterden, Kent: Paul Norbury Publications, 1980.

Kraas, E. and Hiki Y. (eds), *300 Jahre deutsch-japanische Beziehungen in der Medizin*, Berlin/Heidelberg: Springer Verlag, 1992.

Kerst, Georg, *Jacob Meckel. Sein Leben und sein Wirken in Deutschland und Japan*, Göttingen: Musterschmidt-Verlag, 1970.

Kumon Hiroshi and Abo Tetsuo (eds), *The Hybrid Factory in Europe: The Japanese Management and Production System Transferred*, London: Palgrave Macmillan, 2004.

Kudō Akira, *Haken no henyō to fukushi-kokka* (The Changing World Hegemony and the Welfare State), Tokyo: Tokyo Daigaku Shuppan-kai, 1995.

Kudō Akira, Matthias Kipping and Harm G. Schröter (eds), *German and Japanese Business in the Boom Years: Transforming American Management and Technology Models,* (Routledge International Studies in Business History), London: Routledge Chapman & Hall, 2003.

Kudō Akira, Kikkawa Takeo and Glenn D. Hook (eds), *Gendai Nihon kigyō* (Contemporary Japanese Enterprise) with KIKKAWA Takeo and Glenn D. Hook, 3 vols., Tokyo: Yuhikaku, 2005.

Kudō Akira and Tajima Nobuo (eds), *Nichi-Doku kankei-shi 1890 – 1945* (The Relations between Japan and Germany), 3 vols., Tokyo: Tokyo Daigaku Shuppan-kai, 2008.

Kudō Akira, Tajima Nobuo and Erich Pauer (eds), *Japan and Germany: Two Latecomers to the World Stage 1890–1945*, 3 vols., Folkestone: Global Oriental, 2009.

Nagura Bunji, *Heiki tekkō-kaisha no Nichi-Ei kankei-sh*i (Anglo-Japanese Relations in the Case of Vickers and Armstrong), Tokyo: Nihon Keizai Hyōron-sha, 1998.

Nagura Bunji, Yokoi Katsuhiko and Onozuka Tomoji (eds), *The Nichi-Ei heiki sangyō to jiimensu jiken. Buki iten no kokusai keizai-shi* (Japanese and British Armament Industry in the Naval Race – Economic History of Arms Transfer and the Vickers Kongo Case in 1910), Tokyo: Nihon Keizai Hyōron-sha, 2003.

Ōtsuka Hisao, *Ōtsuka Hisao chosaku-shū* (Collected Works of Ōtsuka Hisao), Tokyo: Iwanami Shoten, 1969.

Shiomi Haruhito and Hori Ichirō (eds), *Nichi-Bei kankei keiei-shi* (Competition between Japanese and American Companies), Nagoya: Nagoya Daigaku Shuppan-kai, 1998.

Shiomi Haruhito and Kikkawa Takeo (eds), *Nichi-Bei kigyō no gurōbaru kyōsō senryaku* (Competitive Strategy for Globalization between Japanese and American Companies), Nagoya: Nagoya Daigaku Shuppan-kai, 2008.

Takenaka Tōru, *Jiimensu to Meiji Nippon* (Siemens and Meiji-Japan), Tokyo: Tōkai Daigaku Shuppan-kai, 1993.

Takenaka Toru, *Siemens in Japan: Von der Landesöffnung bis zum Ersten Weltkrieg*, Stuttgart: F. Steiner, 1996.

Umetani Noboru, *The Role of Foreign Employees in the Meiji Era in Japan*, Tokyo: Institute of Developing Economies, 1971.

Umetani Noboru, *O-yatoi gaikoku-jin gaisetsu* (Overview of the 'Hired Foreigners'), Tokyo: Kajima Shuppan Kenkyū-kai, 1975.

Watanabe Hisashi, 'Fuji Denki seiritsu katei' (The Creation of Fuji Electric), in *Kigyōsha katsudō no shi-teki kenkyū* (Historical Studies on Entrepreneurship – Festschrift for NAKAGWA Keiichirō), Tokyo: Nihon Keizai Shinbun-sha, 1981.

Watanabe Hisashi, 'A History of the Process Leading to the Formation of Fuji Electric', in *Japanese Yearbook on Business History*, 1984.

Watanabe Hisashi, 'Fuji Denki no sōritsu katei – dai2, dai3 dankai wo chūshin to shite' (The Creation of Fuji Electric – Its Second and Third Stages), in *Kigyō keiei no rekishi-teki kenkyū* (Historical Studies on Business and Management – Festschrift for WAKIMURA Yoshitarō), Tokyo: Iwanami Shoten, 1990.

Yamamura Kozo and Wolfgang Streeck, *The End of Diversity? Prospects for German and Japanese Capitalism*, Ithaca, NY: Cornell University Press, 2003.

Introduction

KUDŌ Akira

IN ORDER TO clearly explain the starting point for the major exploration of Japanese-German economic relations in the twentieth and twenty-first centuries, which I am commencing with this work, I should like to briefly review my own research to date.

My initial research was focused solely on German economic and business history, and the point at which I turned to studying the history of Japanese-German economic relations came in the early summer of 1985, when I visited the Hoechst Company Archives in Frankfurt am Main. There, in addition to materials on the dissolution of IG Farben after the Second World War, which was the object of my research at the time, I found a wealth of materials, of a better quality, and in greater quantity, than I had imagined would have been possible, on the German chemical industry's Japan strategy, and hastily added them to the list of documents I wished to read and copy. Subsequently, I was blessed with similar good fortune in the BASF archives in Ludwigshafen, and after returning to Japan, I also surveyed the materials held by several Japanese companies, which were mentioned in the German documents. Then for six months in 1988, I ventured to study more than twenty German archives, and was able to read many more Japanese company records after I returned home. Thus my first steps on the road to studying the history of Japanese-German economic relations began with the history of relations between companies.

The results of these two data gathering visits to Germany, and the follow-ups in Japan, were published as a number of articles in both Japanese and English. Then, viewing the reality of German unification from the sidelines, in 1992 I was able to combine these articles into two volumes: *Nichi-Doku kigyō kankei-shi* (The History of

Japanese-German Business Relations) (Yūhikaku) and *Ii-Gee faruben no tai-Nichi senryaku: senkan-ki Nichi-Doku kigyō kankei-shi* (IG Farben's Japan Strategy: A History of Japanese-German Business Relations in the Inter-war Period) (University of Tokyo Press). During this time, in addition to the work represented by these two volumes, my interests and studies developed in three separate directions. First, I became interested in Japanese companies as a key to Japanese-German relations; second, Japanese-European economic relations, which became a topic of interest as trade frictions were extensively debated at that time; and finally, I became interested in the economy of East Asia.

Since the publication of the two works in 1992, I have continued to research the history of Japanese-German business relations, and have continued to publish in both English and German, mainly on the subject of IG Farben's relations with Japan. In addition, I have continued to focus attention on the history of Japanese-European economic relations and the East Asian economy. More recently, I have also attempted to compare the Japanese and German economies, and analyze European integration. During this time, I have been editor or one of the co-editors of the following works: *International Cartels in Business History* (University of Tokyo Press, 1992, Co-ed.: HARA Terushi), *Doitsu tōitsu to Tō-Ō henkaku* (The Unification of Germany and Changes in Eastern Europe) (Minerva Shobō, 1992, Co-eds: SUMIYA Kazuhiko and YAMADA Makoto), *Nijusseiki shihon-shugi II: haken no hen'yō to fukushi kokka* (Twentieth Century Capitalism II: The Changing World Hegemony and the Welfare State) (University of Tokyo Press, 1995), and *Gendai Yōroppa keizai-shi* (Modern European Economic History) (Yūhikaku, 1996, Co-ed.: HARA Terushi). In addition to these books, as part of the continuation of my interest in companies, I contributed to a company history, *Kaō-shi hyaku-nen (1890–1990)* (One Hundred Years of Kaō (1890–1990)) (Nihon Keieishi Kenkyūjo, 1993, Co-authors: YUI Tsunehiko and TAKEDA Haruhito).

In 1998, I compiled my articles in English to date, and published them as *Japanese-German Business Relations: Cooperation and Rivalry in the Inter-war Period* (Routledge). The contents of this work matched closely with those of the two Japanese books I published in 1992. The following year, I was able to assemble the results of my research on German companies and German capitalism, which I had studied prior to beginning the examination of the history of Japanese-German economic relations and the history of Japanese-German business relations in particular, into two volumes: *Gendai Doitsu kagaku kigyō-shi:*

IG faruben no seiritsu-tenkai-kaitai (The History of Modern German Chemical Companies: The founding, development and dissolution of IG Farben) (Minerva Shobō, 1999) and *Nijusseiki Doitsu shihon-shugi: kokusai teii to dai-kigyō taisei* (The 20th-Century German Capitalism: International orientation and the big business system) (University of Tokyo Press, 1999).

I considered the two books I produced in 1999 to be a form of preparation for once more, and at long last, taking a fresh look at the history of Japanese-German economic relations. My plans were, however, somewhat disrupted since I have, quite unexpectedly, continued to be asked to edit a variety of volumes: *Doitsu keizai: tōitsu-go no jūnen* (The German Economy: Ten years since Unification) (Yūhikaku, 2003, Co-eds: TOHARA Shirō and KATŌ Ei'ichi), *German and Japanese Business in the Boom Years: Transforming American Management and Technology Models* (Routledge, 2004, Co-eds: Matthias Kipping and Harm G. Schröter), *Gendai Nihon kigyō (zen sankan)* (Modern Japanese Enterprise (3 vols)) (Yūhikaku, 2005–06, Co-eds: KIKKAWA Takeo and Glenn D. Hook), *Kigyō bunseki to gendai shihon-shugi* (Corporate Analysis and Modern Capitalism) (Minerva Shobō, 2008, Co-ed.: IHARA Motoi), and *Gendai sekai keizai no kōzu* (Structure of the Modern World Economy) (Minerva Shobō, 2009, Co-ed: BABA Hiroji). Other than these, I also edited the conference proceedings published as *Approaches to Corporate Governance* (Institute of Social Science, University of Tokyo, Research Series, No. 3, 2002). In addition, during this period as well as the chapters included in the above mentioned edited works, I also published articles on regional integration, globalization/Americanization and a survey of research on the history of international business.

While engaged in these editorial works, I was also able to begin a thorough study of the history of Japanese-German economic relations, with the result being that the scope of my research has broadened from the history of company relations to encompass the business system, with a focus on legal framework for business activities, and to have an international orientation, with a focus on the intricacies of commerce and tariff policy. I intend to publish the results of this as quickly as possible as *Nijusseiki Nichi-Doku keizai kankei-shi* (The History of Japanese-German Economic Relations in the Twentieth Century) and a number of other works. In the process of writing these manuscripts, a number of issues have arisen which have excited my interest. These have included: diplomatic relations, military relations, Japanese and German relations with China, issues of race and ethnicity, and the mutual awareness Japan and Germany have had of each other. Clearly, this was too broad a range of topics for me to adequately analyze alone, and thus I arranged with Tajima Nobuo, who has conducted ground-breaking research in political history with his studies of Japanese-German relations, to call upon researchers with proven track records in these various areas, and co-edit and publish *Nichi-Doku kankei-shi, 1890–1945, zen sankan* (A History of Japanese-German Relations, 1890–1945 (3 vols)) (University of Tokyo Press, 2008). Simultaneously, I was also able to publish *Japan and Germany: Two Latecomers to the World Stage, 1890–1945, 3 vols* (Global Oriental, 2009, Co-eds: Tajima Nobuo and Erich Pauer). The English work included a number of new chapters by German scholars and the contents differed by about a third from the Japanese version.

Through the process of editing these works, the issue of the business system within Japanese-German relations, as well as its international orientation, has come to my attention, and I have come to feel strongly that it is essential to examine the role of China in order to properly study Japanese-German relations. Thus, my editorial work has given a strong impetus to my own research, and my sole desire at present is to press ahead with the publication of the complete history of Japanese-German economic relations. As a precursor to this history, however, I strongly desired to assemble the various articles I have produced to date into one volume, and so resolved to publish the current work. I took an editorial decision to make the heart of the book papers I had already published, and also, exceptionally, to include unpublished discussion papers. In line with the stages of development of my research to date, I have incorporated work demonstrating my interest in Japanese business, and the development of the history of Japanese-European economic relations, while still retaining a focus on the history of Japanese-German business relations. I am unfortunately, however, not yet able to include the results of my interest in East Asia.

For my part, I hope this book will provide a firm first step towards providing a thorough analysis of the history of Japanese-German economic relations, and in this sense, it is a transitional work, but I hope that it is able in some small way to shed some light on the significance of research on the issue.

Prologue
[1]

Why Study the History of Japanese-German Relations?

Kudō Akira

Over Twenty-five Years have passed since 1992, when two of my books on the history of Japanese-German business relations were published.[1] Here, I would like consider the significance of the history of Japanese-German relations, and why the subject should be studied.

First, I would like to pose six propositions, which I have derived from a number of practical examples in the history of Japanese-German relations, about comparison and studying a relationship as two methods of revealing the actual historical circumstances:

1. Knowledge of an object is based upon conscious and unconscious comparisons with other things.
2. Attempting conscious comparisons is important, and in such cases, one must be aware of the method one is using.
3. There is a tendency for comparisons to become arbitrary, because either the method of comparison, or the basis for making it, is vague, or because a conception of how things should be is at work.
4. Making a comparison while also addressing the relationship between two things is one method of eliminating arbitrariness from the comparison.
5. It is important to attempt to clarify the relationship, because things, which could not be seen in the comparison alone can become apparent by doing so.

6.   One must proceed from knowledge of the relationship, to knowledge of the whole, including the relationship.

The six propositions above have occurred to me in the course of dealing with various issues in the history of Japanese-German relations. While I consider them to be self-evident, that may not be the case to others. Thus, as an illustrative example, I should like to demonstrate proposition (5) by citing some instances from the early post-war history of Japanese-German economic relations.[2] It might be considered that the pre-war period would be more appropriate for my purposes, however, today, I am going to choose the early post-war period, when relations between certainly Japan and Germany continued to be tenuous, because, in my view, relations at this time have yet to attract much attention, while comparisons between the two nations have been frequently made.

1. 'SOCIALIZATION' AND ARISAWA HIROMI

Japan and Germany fought the Second World War as allies, were defeated and occupied, and under occupation both nations experienced reform – occupation reforms – across all facets of their politics, economies and societies. Comparisons of the reforms to Japan and Germany have been made in various ways: for example, the presence or absence of 'socialization' has been suggested as one point of comparison on one important element of the reforms: labor reform, and in particular labor relations reform. In West Germany – henceforth we will limit our consideration to that nation – the West German government itself (of course, while having limited state sovereignty) made minor revisions to the Weimar Socialization Act (*Sozialisierungsgesetz*) of 1919 and re-enacted it, while in Japan, by contrast, most studies argue socialization was not a decisive issue and democratization laws were compulsorily introduced by the occupation forces.

Of course, it is not wrong to make this comparison, and doing so is something that can provide major suggestions about similarities and differences between the situations in Japan and Germany. From the viewpoint of the history of Japanese-German relations, however, we should remember that Weimar period socialization was adopted as a model to follow in Japan by part of the Japanese leadership. One member of this group was Tokyo University Professor ARISAWA Hiromi, who was active both as a major thinker on the left wing of the Socialist

Party, and as an economic technocrat who crossed party boundaries. He emphasized socialization, while also being aware of the limits of the Weimar version from a left-wing perspective. The left wing of the Socialist Party, too, claimed a vague form of socialization to be one of its political objectives. This should be seen as being a secret, in the case of ARISAWA, or vague, in the case of Socialist Party, alternative plan to adoption of the American Model of industrial relations.

ARISAWA entrusted the realization of these dreams to the Economic Reconstruction Conference (*Keizai Fukkō Kaigi*), which was established in February 1947. This national organization attempted to reconstruct the Japanese economy, which was suffering from stagnant production and rising inflation, through labor-management cooperation. After barely a year had passed, however, in April 1948, the Economic Reconstruction Conference dissolved without being able to achieve its objectives, and this sadly ended ARISAWA's dreams of socialization in Japan.

This fact has an importance beyond that of being the unfulfilled dream of a single intellectual who had participated in politics. With ARISAWA as its most important theorist, the left wing of the Socialist Party, having plans for the actual economic reconstruction of Japan, was certainly a powerful actor in the revived party politics. Worthy of further attention is the fact that the experience of Weimar Germany – particularly in inflation, its resolution and then industrial rationalization – was a frame of reference for many political actors submitting policy proposals, from ARISAWA and the ŌUCHI Hyōe group to which he was attached, to ISHIBASHI Tanzan, who was the finance minister in the Liberal Party cabinet of YOSHIDA Shigeru during 1946–47. The socialization model of labor relations was one part of the wider Weimar model.

It is certainly strange that Weimar Germany became a frame of reference for such major political actors after twenty years had passed and, moreover, under what were clearly different global and national contexts. From today's perspective, it would be easy to dismiss this as an historical oddity; however, from the perspective of the history of Japanese-German relations, there is merit in attempting to re-examine the Japanese political economy under the occupation, with a focus on the role of the Weimar model, which was implemented in various policy proposals. This will make it possible to emphasize the dynamism of the period – something, which it is not possible to do through static comparisons.

2. THE JAPANESE-GERMAN TRADE AGREEMENT

As stated above, the two nations of Japan and Germany experienced the parallel histories of alliance, defeat, and occupation, and under that occupation had their political and economic relations with the other interrupted. In October 1949, however, while both were still under occupation, through the good offices of their occupying forces they concluded a Japanese-German Trade Agreement, which linked them in a managed trade relationship. Furthermore, in August 1951, just before Japan regained its sovereignty, the two nations concluded a slightly more liberal trade and payment agreement, although it was still intended to link them in a system of managed trade. Thus, the resumption of economic relations preceded that of foreign relations, as it was more than three years after this, in 1954–55, that the two nations, having resumed diplomatic relations, exchanged ambassadors.

The revival of economic relations also saw memories of the pre-war situation revived, meaning that in West Germany the image of the Japanese economy as overwhelming the world market with the weapon of low wages re-appeared. This was the so-called 'social dumping' theory. What revived these memories were, first, the international negotiations over Japan's accession to GATT, which took place in September 1955, a little less than four years after West Germany's accession, and then, the GATT-negotiations over the so-called 'German Problem', which occurred when West Germany achieved currency convertibility and pressed for the elimination of several of the restrictions on its trade. During the GATT negotiations, West Germany strongly advocated, and eventually achieved, item-by-item limits on the quantity of goods, which could be imported into it from Japan. The objects of these limits were first textile goods and ceramics, then glass, sewing machines, sea-shell buttons and toys. There were causes for the desire for these restrictions in the post-war situation, such as the fact that the manpower for textile production in West Germany was largely composed of refugees, but it was memories of the pre-war situation, which were more strongly at work behind them. In addition, the fact that Britain, having its own pre-war memories of Japan, continued to object strongly to Japan's GATT accession, may have revived memories in West Germany, which supported the accession itself.

The history of quantity restrictions on imports from Japan continues long after that, entangled with the establishment of the European Economic Community (EEC). If one traces that history, one is obliged to make certain revisions to the image of Ludwig Erhard as a standard bearer of free trade, and of the Ministry of Economics, which he headed, as a bastion of free trade. For example, not only leaders of economic organizations such as the Federation of German Industries (*Bundesverband der Deutschen Industrie*), but also leaders of labor organizations such as the Confederation of German Trade Unions (*Deutscher Gewerkschaftsbund*), were invited to meetings in the Ministry of Economics, which set the policy on Japan and thrust of the negotiations. West German trade union leaders at the time firmly believed in the 'Social dumping' theory. It may be possible to say that in this period West Germany surpassed Japan – although the situation in Japan is not clear due to only a limited amount of historical data being available – in the degree of maturity of organized capitalism. In any case, however, as far as can be seen from the Economics Ministry archives, it was only at the end of the 1970s that the ministry's bureaucrats' views on the Japanese economy clearly began to change.

3. THE 'ERHARD DISPUTE'

The historical parallels between both countries, which had continued in defeat and during occupation, continued thereafter with economic recovery and high-speed growth. There was a roughly five-year time lag in these parallels – the four-year difference in accession to GATT is simply one example of this – and as a result the growth and revival in the German economy was much admired in Japan. Erhard himself was a key focus of this admiration, although readers who expected a key to unlocking the secrets of the social market economy in his writings were also discouraged, finding that they did no more than repeat the benefits of free trade. At any rate, for a long period there were plans to invite him to Japan, but it was in October 1958 that these were finally realized. In contrast to the enthusiasm in Japan, for Erhard Japan was only one of many Asian countries, and the main purpose of his trip to Asia was to attend a meeting of the IMF and World Bank in New Delhi, with his visit to Japan included as one of a number of calls on South East Asian countries.

Reflecting the enthusiasm and admiration felt for him in Japan, Erhard, economics minister and deputy-chancellor, was treated as a semi-guest of the nation. Throughout his stay he candidly repeated the same statements. In outline, these were: first, that Japan's wages were too low; second, that Japan's market price for the yen was too low; and finally, that the export price of Japanese goods was too low. The first was an extension of the aforementioned 'social dumping' argument, and the second was a natural assertion to make for West Germany, which had re-valued the mark. Thus, his final point was a natural conclusion following on from his first and second points, and was the most vital one for West Germany, which had firmly continued to demand and implement import quantity restrictions on Japanese products, as previously mentioned. The remarks also systematically laid out his own views, strengthened through studies he had made and briefings he had received prior to visiting Japan, and so he felt confident in making them.

In contrast to this, Japanese politicians, business managers and scholars who had respected Erhard, criticized him for his remarks, while also feeling somewhat perplexed. For many of them, the remarks were an indication of a misinterpretation of the Japanese situation. Some, such as ARISAWA, explained Japan's cheap currency and low exchange rate by its low economic development and argued for asking Erhard for a brief delay before Japan should address these issues. As a result of this 'Erhard Dispute', the image of Erhard in Japan as a standard bearer for free trade was strengthened further, but of course the feelings of veneration for him weakened. Simultaneously, the West German social market economy continued to be understood as focusing on the uninterrupted market economy, and there was almost no attention paid to its welfare state aspects – social housing and pensions reform.

This view of the West German economy in Japan can be described as focusing on its Americanization, while simultaneously one can see in it a reflection of the self-awareness in Japan of the nation's own economy, which had Americanized broadly and deeply. By this point, 1958, the German model was not even considered as a secret alternative to the American model. Studies of the German business system had come to an end, and Erhard's visit to Japan and the 'Erhard dispute' may have put the final seal on German studies.

On the other hand, Erhard 'discovered' through his visit that Japan, unlike the other Asian countries, had already reached a high economic level, but, of course, he felt no need to revise his view of the Japanese economy, and thus he did not. The negotiations on concluding a new, more liberal, trade agreement were beginning at the time of his visit to Japan – the agreement was concluded in July 1960. Erhard, as the major German negotiator, was confronted constantly with anti-Japanese demands opposed to liberalization, from the textiles industry among others, and so had no intention of revising his view of the Japanese economy, which formed the basis of his negotiation strategy.

The negotiations between Japan and Germany aimed at concluding this trade agreement were a continuation of those over Japan's accession to GATT as well as over the 'German Problem' in GATT. The largest point of contention was quantity import restrictions on Japanese products. The expression 'social dumping' had already ceased to be used, but Japan was regarded first as a 'low-wage state', and then also as a 'low price state', and thus literally not a suitable partner for free trade.

Thus, faced with these types of assertions by the West Germans, the trade agreement negotiations had a difficult journey. Further causes of difficulties, other than the above, were the attenuation of American will and ability to intervene in Japanese-German relations in support of Japan, and also the inauguration of the EEC, which had founding nations, such as France and Italy, that were distinctly more protectionist than West Germany, meaning that West Germany was obliged to negotiate with Japan, having the claims of other EEC member states in mind.

4. CONCLUSION

Above, I have given a rough sketch of one portion of Japanese-German relations in the early post-war period. From this, I feel that proposition (5) on comparing and learning about a relationship, 'It is important to attempt to clarify the relationship, because things which could not be seen in the comparison alone can become apparent by doing so', has to some extent been demonstrated. At the very least, one can understand how many topics there are yet to be studied which have not yet been addressed in the flourishing field of Japanese-German comparative research.

If propositions (4) 'Making a comparison while also addressing the relationship between two things is one method of eliminating arbitrariness from the comparison', and (5) are correct, we can proceed believing in the value of the history of the Japanese-German relations for its own sake. Furthermore, if proposition (6) 'One must proceed from knowledge of the relationship, to knowledge of the whole, including the relationship' is also correct, we must proceed to study the history of the Japanese-German relations, aiming at producing explanation of the entirety of it.

Whatever we do, there are many themes and materials in the field of the history of Japanese-German relations, which as yet remain unexplored. Thus, while I have provided, in a somewhat rough form, six propositions on knowledge, the methodology of relationship history, too, is an important topic for consideration in the future, and the entry of more researchers into this field is certainly to be expected.

Prologue
[2]

A Personal Historiography of
Japanese-German/Euro-Asian Relations

Kudō Akira

When My First two books, *Nichi-Doku kigyō kankei-shi* (A History of Japanese-German Business Relations) and *Ii-Gee-faruben no tai-Nichi senryaku* (IG Farben's Japan Strategy) were published in 1992, there were three major sentiments which leapt out from the book reviews and personal communications I received. First, some remarked that my work 'lent itself to publication in foreign journals'. to which I could only reply that that very well might be the case. Another sentiment similar to the first but tinged with condescension – or at least that is how it felt to me – was that my work 'was aimed at a niche audience.' To this I could only respond with a wry grin. The third sentiment was the one, which rang truest to me: 'So you have studied the history of Japanese-German relations. What's next?' Nearly twenty years have passed since then and I have come to ponder what would happen if I attempted to respond to this query again. The following is a synopsis of my answer.

1. MY INTEREST IN THE HISTORY OF
JAPANESE-GERMAN/EURO-ASIAN RELATIONS

First, let me discuss why I have studied the history of Japanese-German relations and why the study thereof poses challenges. In essence it is two separate questions, why Germany and why Japan? When answering the former question, several replies immediately come to mind. Germany, economically and otherwise, is an important country, it has been a driving force of European integration, and it is the United States' most important partner in continental Europe. But at the same time I think that as research subjects everything (not just nations) throughout history are equally deserving of attention, and an idea that comes to mind is that things only become unequal by way of a researcher's interest in an issue. If this is true, then I am obliged to explain my interest.

This obligation also applies to the question of why Japan. In fact, it applies even more so. Although I am a researcher who was born and raised in Japan and thinks in Japanese, it obviously does not necessarily follow that I should deal with Japan. Here, the nature of the interest I have in the issues is called into question even more sharply. If this is the case, then why Germany and why Japan are not the right questions to ask. Rather, I think I should reply to the original query of 'Why Japanese-German relations?' My immediate reply to this question – or should I say the reply I have pondered repeatedly over the years – is as follows.

First, Japan and Germany developed an important partnership starting in the mid-nineteenth century and continuing through the twentieth century. With regard to politics and diplomacy, there was both confrontation, as typified by the Siege of Tsingtao (China) in 1914 – known then as the Japanese-German War – and cooperation, as seen with the conclusion of the Tripartite Pact in 1940. One might say that this relationship of confrontation and cooperation was more significant for Japan than for Germany and that this significance declined after the Second World War, but that is a separate issue. What I will stress here is simply the importance of Japanese-German relations in the realms of politics and diplomacy.

As for economic ties, there was competition between Japanese and German companies in the global marketplace – Germany often accused Japan of 'social dumping' both before and immediately after the war – and collaboration via technology licensing. In the high-growth era after the war, the direction of transfers was from Germany to Japan, but technology later began to flow in the reverse direction. Here, too, the issue that this bilateral economic relationship of competition and collaboration grew comparatively weaker at some point after the war arises, and if one looks back to before the war, one could also note that the relations between the two countries were fragile then. In either case, I will leave this issue – which is thought to relate to the existence of a hegemonic United States – on the back burner.

My second reason for focusing on Japanese-German relation is, in a few words, the parallelism evident between the histories of the two nations. Much emphasis has been placed on the shared political and economic backwardness of both countries from the mid-nineteenth century until the middle of the twentieth century, with various examples drawn from the study of Japanese history in particular. I feel strongly that the theories about this backwardness must be re-examined with a focus on the nations' bilateral relationship because time lags make it hard to define this situation as a case of parallelism, but I will leave this point aside for the time being. In any case, the historical parallels after the war were plain as day: both countries lost the war as Axis nations, were occupied thereafter, and reformed and rebuilt into economic powers. Some might say that this post-war parallelism faded away at some point – again this is thought to pertain to the rise and fall of American hegemony – but let us just leave it at that.

The third reason is the record of the two nations studying each other. For well over a century, various actors have studied a wide range of sectors in the other nation. It goes without saying that from the late nineteenth century and throughout the twentieth century this primarily took the form of Japan studying Germany. Without question, the German or Prussian models were vital to the establishment of the Meiji state. In the field of scholarly thought alone, the study of Germany progressed steadily from *Staatslehre* and *Sozialpolitik* to Marxism. Meanwhile, German companies also served as models for Japanese companies. For example, when the Mitsubishi zaibatsu launched a chemical company in the 1930s, its slogan was 'Bound to be the IG Farben of the East.' Here, some may say, and rightfully so, that Japan's study of Germany was replaced by its study of the United States, and for a time after the war, there is evidence – albeit limited to the fields of business and economics – of the study of Japan by Germany. In any case, let us leave this issue aside for the time being.

While not entirely orderly, the paragraphs above constitute my initial answer to the question of 'Why Japanese-German relations?' However, several more questions, some of them, which I pose myself, immediately arise therefrom. The first question is whether my interests are limited to nations and their bilateral relations. My answer to this is a resounding 'No'. At some point after the war there was a staged progression toward regionalization in the form of European integration, and this gave rise to the issue of 'Europeanizing' Germany. European integration led to the incorporation of Japanese-German

relations into Japanese-European relations. Meanwhile, regionalization
also spread through Asia despite the region's differences from Europe.
It was not possible for Japan to remain immune to this trend. Regionalization was a global phenomenon and a situation emerged which
could be considered the relativization of nations. This is how Japanese-German relations came to be one facet of Euro-Asian relations.
Therefore, if one takes an interest in the history of Japanese-German
relations, one has no choice but to expand one's interests to include
Euro-Asian relations.

This is not to say that my research is restricted to inter-regional and
bilateral ties either. My ultimate interest is in depicting a wider picture
of the world economy, especially during the twentieth century. I believe
that understanding the history of Japanese-German/Euro-Asian relations is one approach to that end. Moreover, I maintain that understanding Japanese-German/Euro-Asian relations is absolutely essential for understanding the world economy of the twentieth century,
in which the hegemony of Great Britain was followed by that of the
United States. Earlier in this article when I mentioned the importance
of Japan's partnership with Germany dating back to the mid-nineteenth century, I was referring to the importance of their relationship
with regard to understanding its impact on the world economy. While
I do not have time to go into details, this understanding is also related
to the recognition that private companies are the primary shapers of
structures and processes in the world economy.

2. FRAMING THE HISTORY OF JAPANESE-GERMAN
RELATIONS IN THE TWENTIETH CENTURY

In the previous section I have attempted to answer the questions, be
they self-posed or otherwise, of why I have researched Japanese-German
and Euro-Asian relations. So what exactly am I attempting to elucidate
about Japanese-German/Euro-Asian relations? I would have to sketch
an outline of my analytical framework, but I do not have enough time
or space to do that here. Let me get straight to the point of Japanese-
German relations in the twentieth century. First, I must explain briefly
that for the purposes of my argument here, the twentieth century refers
to the time period from 1914 to 1990. The starting point of 1914
requires no explanation, as it is the year in which the First World War
erupted. Aside from 1914, 1890 and 1868–71 could be alternative
starting points, but I would like to focus on the irreversible impact of

the First World War. I chose 1990 as the end point because it is the year
the Cold War ended. One issue with these dates is that they do not correspond to events in Asia, as clearly as they delimit European history,
but if one assumes the end of the Cold War was a globally transforming
event then once again differences among regions should be discussed to
develop our understanding of events as a whole.

The next question is why I choose to focus on the history of economic relations. As I mentioned earlier, my personal interests play a
large part in this, of course, but that is not the only factor. The history
of Japanese-German relations has many more ups and downs politically
than it does economically and, in light of this, more research has been
conducted on the political history of the relationship than its economic
history. I try to incorporate the outcomes of political history research
into economic history in order to further develop a political-economic
history of relations between the two nations.

To achieve this I am currently preparing to publish a two-volume
work entitled *Nijusseiki Nichi-Doku keizai kankei-shi* (The History of
Japanese-German Economic Relations in the Twentieth Century, vol.
I: International Orientation, vol. II: Business Systems) and a number of
other books. I began working on these books immediately after I published *Nijusseiki Doitsu shihon-shugi* (20th Century German Capitalism) and *Gendai Doitsu kagaku kigyō-shi* (The History of Modern
German Chemical Companies) in 1999. In my forthcoming work,
I define Japanese-German relations in terms of international orientation
and business systems, picking up where I left off in my earlier work on
business relations. In the end the work grew to encompass three volumes.
I have not reached a final conclusion on how to integrate the separate
strands of inter-state relations and business relations, an issue that I touched
on earlier. Therefore, I have not decided whether or not I will incorporate
business relations into my aforementioned book on twenty-first century
Japanese-German economic ties. In addition, I plan to publish *Japanese-
German/European Economic Relations*, a collection of the papers that I have
presented in English, as well as a collection of papers on the methodology
of relationship history. Now I must also develop these projects, and every
day I am reminded of the old proverb, 'Art is long, life is short'.

Be that as it may, ten years have passed since I began these projects
and I was not able to finish them before retiring from the University of
Tokyo's Institute of Social Science. Although I kept busy in the meantime co-editing volumes such as *Doitsu keizai* (The German Economy, co-edited with TOHARA Shirō and KATŌ Ei'ichi, 2003), *German*

and Japanese Business in the Boom Years (co-edited with Matthias Kipping and Harm G. Schröter, 2004), *Gendai Nihon kigyō, zen sankan* (Modern Japanese Enterprise, 3 vols, co-edited with KIKKAWA Takeo and Glenn D. Hook, 2005–2006), *Kigyō bunseki to gendai shihon-shugi* (Corporate Analysis and Modern Capitalism, co-edited with IHARA Motoi, 2008), and *Gendai sekai keizai no kōzu* (Structure of the Modern World Economy, co-edited with BABA Hiroji, 2009), I feel now I was neglectful.

Meanwhile, while I was preparing to publish the three volumes of *Nijusseiki Nichi.-Doku keizai kankei-shi*, more topics that piqued my interest came to light. These included diplomatic relations, military relations, Japan and Germany's respective relationships with China, race issues, and mutual recognition between Japan and Germany. It also became clear that researching these topics was more than I could handle on my own, so I enlisted the help of TAJIMA Nobuo, the pre-eminent researcher of the political history of Japanese-German relations. Together we called on a host of researchers with significant achievements pertaining to these topics and co-edited *Nichi-Doku kankei-shi, 1890–1945, zen sankan* (The History of Japanese-German Relations: 1890–1945, 3 vols, 2008). Several reviews have been written about this collection, and as far as I can tell by reading these, the reviewers grasped the objective of this project, and assessed all of the chapters as high-quality work. Tajima and I are now planning to publish two collections of papers, *Ō-A kankei-shi, 1890–1945* (The History of Euro-Asian Relations: 1890–1945) and *Sengo Nichi-Doku kankei-shi* (The History of Post-war Japanese-German Relations) as extensions – although they are more than extensions since both works cover new issues – of *Nichi-Doku kankei-shi, 1890–1945*. For this reason alone, we are very grateful for the positive reviews of the three-volume work.

Furthermore, Tajima and I, together with Erich Pauer, one of the contributing authors of *Nichi-Doku kankei-shi, 1890–1945*, have recently published *Japan and Germany: Two Latecomers to the World Stage, 1890–1945*, 3 vols (Global Oriental, 2009). This English language compilation contains several new chapters by German authors, and approximately one-third of the content differs from the original Japanese version. We would also like to publish English versions of *Ō-A kankei-shi, 1890–1945* and *Sengo Nichi-Doku kankei-shi*. Besides, quite some time has passed since I last published in English (*Japanese-German Business Relations: Cooperation and Rivalry in the Interwar Period*, 1998). For these reasons, I hope that *Japan and Germany: Two Latecomers* is as well received as its Japanese version was.

PART I

Japanese-German Business Relations

Source: *The Making of Global Enterprise* (Geoffrey Jones (ed.)), London: Frank Cass, 1994, pp. 159–183.

1

I.G. Farben in Japan: The Transfer of Technology and Managerial Skills

I

THIS CHAPTER DEALS with the technology and management transfer from the German to the Japanese chemical industries during the 1920s and 1930s.[1] Before 1945, I.G. Farbenindustrie Aktiengesellschaft (hereafter referred to as I.G. Farben), the giant German chemical firm, exported goods such as dyestuffs and nitrogenous fertiliser to Japan, and licensed its synthetic ammonia process to Japanese companies. It also made direct investments in Japan, both in manufacturing and in sales outlets. Through these three forms of international business activities – export of products, licensing, and direct investment – I.G. Farben transferred to the Japanese chemical industry, intentionally or not, its production technology and managerial skills. Its technology and management transfer also produced far-reaching effects on other facets of the Japanese chemical industry, including its distribution system. In fact, I.G. Farben was one of the two German companies which affected business management in Japan most profoundly, the other being Siemens in the electrical machinery industry.[2]

This article divides the period under study into the 1920s and the 1930s, the two decades when the Japanese market took on significantly different characteristics. This will be followed by a brief overview of the activities of I.G. Farben during the two decades, with a review of the technology and management transfer which was effected by its business activities. Throughout, the focus is on production technology, marketing policy, the distribution system,

3

and personnel management. Financing issues are omitted due to the shortage of available information.

II

It is necessary to begin with a brief outline of the Japanese market for chemical products from 1910 through the 1920s. In pre-First World War years, the major German chemical companies were already exporting their products to Japan on a considerable scale. Dyestuffs were an important export item, particularly synthetic indigo, which was especially favoured in the Orient. Each company had its Japanese agent; BASF established its agent in 1881 and Bayer changed its agent in 1891.[3] By 1913, immediately before the First World War, the Japanese market had become very important for German dyestuff producers. In that year Japan ranked as the eighth largest export market for German dyestuffs, importing 15.83 million marks' worth of the products, or 4.9 percent of total German dyestuff exports of 321.20 million marks. Among the eight German dyestuff manufacturers, the largest three, BASF, Bayer and Hoechst, overwhelmed the others in export sales to Japan, with two of the three, BASF and Hoechst, dividing between them as much as two-thirds of the exports to Japan. In addition, the two companies had stronger interests in the Japanese market than the six other German dyestuff producers. They saw Japan not only as an important export market in itself but also as a sales base for East Asian markets, including China. In fact, Japan with its political stability and communications infrastructure had become an important foothold for business activities in the large Chinese market.[4]

With the outbreak of the First World War, the German chemical manufacturers were denied access to the Japanese market. In an attempt to fill the suddenly created vacuum, many small dyestuff manufacturing firms cropped up, and, also, large firms like the Mitsui Mining Co. began to undertake dyestuff manufacturing operations. The trend was further accelerated by the Japanese government, which, in an effort to foster a modern chemical industry, promulgated the Law for Promoting Dyestuff and Medicine Production and other laws, and established the government-owned Nihon Senryo Seizo Kabushiki Kaisha (Japan Dyestuff Manufacturing Co. Ltd, hereafter referred to as Nihon Senryo). Thus the First World War marked the birth of a modern chemical industry in Japan.

After the war, the Japanese market became even more important for the German chemical industry. The rapidly developing Japanese textile industry was in need of ever-increasing quantities of dyestuffs. Also, the spread of fertiliser-intensive farming methods in the agricultural sector was creating a lucrative export market for the German nitrogen industry with its newly developed synthetic ammonia process. In addition, the Chinese market, following the revolution of 1911 that overthrew the Ch'ing dynasty, seemed ready to grow by leaps and bounds. Thus, it was only natural that the German chemical firms were greatly attracted by the Japanese market, and competed fiercely with each other in order to get their pre-war sales networks back into shape, regain their export shares, and capture the newly expanding segments of the market.

In the immediate aftermath of the war, the Japanese demand for dyestuffs and nitrogenous fertiliser was met to a large extent by supplies from the United States and other European countries, but, before long, German products began to dominate the market. This was because the newborn Japanese chemical industry was not yet competitive enough to dominate the domestic market, while the German chemical industry had a significant competitive edge over its international competitors in chemical production as a whole, even though the degree of its supremacy varied from one product to the next.

Moreover, the Japanese government had not yet adopted a protectionist policy effective enough to stem the inflow of foreign chemical products. To be sure, the government felt the need to protect the country's infant chemical industry, on the one hand, but, on the other hand, it also found it imperative to serve the interests of the textile industry and agriculture by allowing them access to cheaper chemical products imported from abroad. As a result, the government adopted what could basically be characterised as a 'weak protectionist policy', or a policy of selective protection of the infant chemical industry, one which kept the import tariffs at relatively low levels, while fostering sentiments of economic nationalism by encouraging the population to 'buy Japanese'. Direct investments by foreign chemical firms were also welcomed, in principle, for the same reason, even though the government was reluctant to allow the investing foreign companies to gain control of management of the joint ventures, and the Japanese partners of the joint ventures, too, were insistent on keeping them under their own control.[5]

Despite its 'weak protectionist' stance, the government sometimes took bold steps to sustain sections of the domestic chemical industry under threat from foreign competition. For instance, it enforced, in June 1924, an import licence system to protect the dyestuff industry which was badly in need of protection. This system was, in effect, meant to discriminate against German goods. One of the countermeasures devised by the German dyestuff industry was reorganisation of its distribution outlets within Japan.

At the time, major German dyestuff companies belonging to an industry-wide *Interessengemeinschaft* (community of interests) were being pressed hard to rationalise their business organisations in response to the subsiding post-war hyperinflation. And the consolidation of their sales outlets outside Germany was one of the most important and difficult tasks, because each member company considered its own traditional sales outlets, trade rights and trade marks as too precious to be subjected to reorganisation and reshuffling. Nevertheless, the effort to consolidate the German sales outlets in Japan was completed relatively smoothly, most likely because each German company took a serious view of the growth potential of the Japanese industry's production capabilities and the adverse effects of the discriminatory import licensing system.

Interestingly enough, in the course of deliberation on the consolidation of sales organisations in Japan, BASF presented a plan which called for an immediate and complete integration of the sales branches of all the German companies concerned, while Hoechst proposed an export quota system and Bayer suggested a partial integration as a compromise between the two. This conflict of plans preceded and anticipated a dispute at the top management level concerning the reorganisation of the community of interests, namely, a conflict between a merger plan proposed by Carl Bosch of BASF and a shareholding plan by Carl Duisberg of Bayer. Eventually, the immediate integration measure won its day. In December 1924, the Doitsu Senryo Gomei Kaisha (German Dyestuff Co.) was established at 37 Akashi-cho, Kobe, as the sole representative for the community of interests with the exception of Cassella. Established with a capital outlay of 300,000 yen, the office was staffed by two employees from BASF, and one each from Hoechst, Bayer, Agfa, and Griesheim-Elektron, with Richard Veit of Bayer appointed as chief manager. It was just one year after this that Bosch's plan was accepted and, as a result, I.G. Farben was established back in Germany.

Much the same pattern of reorganisation took place in other fields. For fertiliser products like nitrogenous fertiliser, H. Ahrnes & Co. Nachf., located in the Yaesu Building at Yaesu-cho, Kojimachi-ku, Tokyo, was established as the sole representative for the community of interests from the outset. As shown in Table 1.1, sales organisations for medicine, photographic products and titan were reorganised or newly established one after another.

As a consequence of this reorganisation, a strategy of the community of interests in Japan was to be carried out through a set-up composed of three strata. Situated at the top was a council of the community of interests composed of the chief executives of the eight participating companies. This council would directly involve itself in making decisions on matters of crucial importance. Placed directly subordinate to this council was the Japan Commission (later renamed East Asian Commission), charged with the task of devising the community's strategy toward Japan and carrying it out with the council's consent. Hermann Waibel of BASF was appointed as the first chief of this commission. At the bottom of the hierarchy were sales organisations, such as Doitsu Senryo, each responsible for directly handling the sales of a specific variety of goods in Japan. This hierarchical set-up was basically kept intact even after the establishment of I.G. Farben.[6]

Table 1.1 I.G. Farben's Direct Investment in Japan as of 1945

Company	Place	Purpose of establishment	Capital (million yen)	Shareholding ratio (%)
Asahi Bemberg Kenshi Kabushiki Kaisha	Osaka	Rayon manufacturing	46.00	1.81
Nihon Tokushu Seizo Kabushiki Kaisha	Tokyo	Pesticide manufacturing	1.00	10.00
Bayer Yakuhin Gomei Kaisha	Kobe	Sales of medicine	0.15	100.00
Doitsu Senryo Gomei Kaisha	Kobe, Tokyo	Sales of dyestuffs	0.30	26.23
H. Ahrens & Co. Nachf.	Tokyo	Sales of nitrogenous fertiliser	0.20	100.00
Agfa Gomei Kaisha	Tokyo	Sales of photographic products	0.10	100.00
Titan Kogyo Kabushiki Kaisha	Tokyo	Sales of titan	3.50	4.17

Source: Finance and Accounting Section, I.G. Farben Control Office of the Office of Military Government for Germany (US), *Survey*, 1947, Hoechst-Archiv.

It is hardly necessary to emphasise the significant place I.G. Farben occupied, not simply in the German industry, but in the world chemical industry as a whole. Naturally, for the newborn Japanese industry, I.G. Farben was a formidable giant. It was capitalised at 650 million marks (some 300 million yen) at its establishment, whereas the Mitsui Mining Co., the largest Japanese mining company which was diversifying into chemical production, was capitalised at only 52.50 million yen, and the government-owned Nihon Senryo at a mere eight million yen.

The Japanese dye industry and the government repeatedly requested technical co-operation and/or licensing from I.G. Farben. Although I.G. Farben did not openly reject these requests, it was tacitly following a policy of not granting such requests. One well-known example of I.G. Farben's tacit refusal to grant such requests involved the transfer of technical know-how about the Haber-Bosch process. The patent for this process was confiscated by the Japanese government during the First World War, and the exclusive right to use the patent was sold to Toyo Chisso Kumiai (Oriental Nitrogen Association) established by major *zaibatsu* groups. However, Japanese chemical firms, including those of the *zaibatsu* groups, had no knowledge of how to put this process to commercial use. As soon as the war was over, therefore, some companies contacted BASF in the hopes of acquiring the necessary know-how. BASF, however, demanded an outrageous fee of 68 million yen, and the Japanese firms had to give up the idea of acquiring the technology from BASF. Indeed, by quoting the prohibitively high fee BASF made it known that it had no intention of offering licensing or technical co-operation. It should be kept in mind that the term 'licensing' here is used in a broad sense, because BASF's patent was still under confiscation by the Japanese government when this episode took place.[7]

Another illustration of I.G. Farben's lack of interest in offering technical co-operation is found in the reaction of the top executives of the community of interests to a proposal for technological co-operation which Fritz Haber made to them in 1924 upon his return from a trip to Japan. Haber possessed great prestige at BASF and the community of interests because of the remarkable success of the Haber–Bosch process, and he proposed that the community should offer technological co-operation to Japan in the field of inorganic chemistry as an indispensable means of compromise to entice the Japanese government into abolishing the import licence system for German chemical products. However, the community council flatly rejected his proposal. Especially obstinate in opposing Haber's proposal was Carl Bosch, the very person who had worked closely with Haber in the development of the Haber–Bosch process, and who was then chairman of the board of directors of BASF and one of the leading figures of the community. Bosch maintained that, if the community started co-operating with the Japanese in the field of inorganic chemistry, the Japanese would then press hard for co-operation in the field of dye production as well. Calling attention to *'der fast krankhafte Ehrgeiz der Japaner'* (the almost morbid ambition of the Japanese), Bosch asserted that 'our objective, under any circumstances, ought not to be to offer any help whatsoever to the Japanese in their efforts to build up a profitable chemical industry, and in particular, a dye industry of their own, but rather to slow their progress in these efforts as long as possible, and moreover to reduce these efforts into a failure as best as we can'.[8]

Moreover, when Jiro Inabata, managing director of Nihon Senryo, made a tour of Europe, visiting Kuhlmann (Compagnie Nationale de Matières Colorantes et Manufactures de Produits Chimiques du Nord réunies Etablissements Kuhlmann) and St Denis (Société Anonyme des Matières Colorantes et Produits Chimiques de St Denis) of France, and Durand & Huguenin AG of Switzerland to look into the possibility of securing technological co-operation, his efforts were frustrated by I.G. Farben, which informed Inabata through Ciba (Gesellschaft für chemische Industrie in Basel) that no company that was a member of the German–Swiss–French three-party dyestuff cartel could give technological assistance to Japan without the consent of the other members.[9]

It is true, however, that there were some occasions when I.G. Farben gave positive consideration to offering technological co-operation. For instance, it considered offering technological co-operation to Nihon Senryo in the field of rayon and aluminium production as a means of discouraging the latter from developing synthetic indigo. It should be pointed out, however, that I.G. Farben brushed the idea away as soon as it discovered that Nihon Senryo was not competent enough to develop synthetic indigo.[10]

I.G. Farben's strategy can be understood in the light of the fact that it is usually difficult for a leading firm in the chemical industry, unlike its counterpart in the electrical machinery industry, to maintain its technological supremacy over its competitors by using its patents as a leverage. It should also be recalled that the Japanese government had requisitioned German patents during the First World War, and that in April 1921 the government promulgated a Revised Patent Law which made chemical material ineligible for patent protection.

In some fields of chemical production, such as nitrogenous fertiliser, Japanese firms introduced the necessary technologies from France and Italy after these had been diffused from Germany during the First World War, while in other fields they used technologies devised by themselves. In the field of dyestuffs, Japanese firms were trying hard to develop the products for themselves by copying German products. Mitsui Mining's effort to develop synthetic indigo and Nihon Senryo's to develop naphthol dyestuffs were two outstanding examples. Needless to say, the lifting of patent protection in itself did not immediately guarantee that high-technology products could be casily developed. There are a wide variety of intricate details that had to be learned or discovered before the previously patented information could be put to practical application. Nevertheless, there is no denying that these developmental efforts posed a serious threat to I.G. Farben.

Thus, in order for I.G. Farben to protect its technology, which became ineligible for patent protection, it had no choice but to deny licensing to Japan. Not only that, I.G. Farben even went so far as to dump its synthetic indigo products in the Japanese market in the hope of discouraging Mitsui Mining's effort to develop these.[11] It also had recourse to a number of other measures, including reorganisation of its sales base in Japan, as mentioned already, and readjustment of its sales policies, to be explained shortly. In addition to these, I.G. Farben concluded a series of bilateral agreements with individual Japanese firms and with the Japanese industry as a whole as a means of securing its outlets.

One such agreement signed in the field of dyestuffs was a gentlemen's agreement of August 1926 on German dyestuff export to Japan between I.G. Farben and the Japanese dyestuff industry – known as the Saito–Waibel Agreement after the representatives who signed it. The agreement stipulated, in essence, that in exchange for the Japanese government's abolishing its current import licence on German products, I.G. Farben would voluntarily restrict exports to Japan of those products which the Japanese were capable of producing domestically. Put differently, the agreement implied that I.G. Farben was free from any import restriction on products currently not being produced in Japan, like indigo. The arrangement envisioned by the agreement was a kind of international division of labour between the chemical industries of the two countries. Incidentally, it was not until the agreement was concluded that the two governments signed a new Japanese–German Commerce and Navigation Treaty, which they had been negotiating. This reveals the important place dye products occupied in trading between the two countries. The Saito–Waibel Agreement, which came into effect in April 1928, was finalised far quicker than other bilateral agreements between the two countries. This was because the import licence system, introduced by the Japanese government as one of the measures to pursue selective protection, was restraining I.G. Farben's activities. Thus, the conclusion of this agreement, which obliged the Japanese government to lift its current import licence system, and allowed German indigo and other expensive dye products free access to the Japanese market, was basically a welcome accomplishment for I.G. Farben.[12]

In the field of nitrogenous fertiliser, on the other hand, the Japanese market still had some room to absorb imports, despite the rapid growth of domestic production. As shown in Figure 1.1, nitrogenous fertiliser became, by 1929, Germany's single most important chemical exported to Japan, far surpassing other chemicals, including dyestuffs. Partly because Japan was designated by the international fertiliser cartel as a market for open competition, foreign companies in the late 1920s competed fiercely against each other for larger shares of the Japanese market, giving rise to a phenomenon called, 'gaian dumping' (gaian meaning foreign ammonium sulphate). It was against this backdrop that in December 1930 I.G. Farben, acting on behalf of the CIA (Convention Internationale de l'Azote), consulted with the Japanese fertiliser industry, and worked out a draft agreement called the Fujiwara–Bosch Draft Agreement which was meant to put an end to the heated price competition. It called upon the Japanese industry to refrain completely from exporting its nitrogenous fertiliser, and upon the foreign industries to curtail their exports to Japan in exchange for this, but it miscarried because of strong domestic opposition. Several months later, in April 1931, a Tentative Agreement on Domestic and Foreign Ammonium Sulphate was signed, but this, too, failed to come into effect.[13] It was only in the 1930s that agreements between the international cartel and the Japanese chemical industry began to materialise.

Figure 1.1 German Chemical Exports to Japan, 1929–36

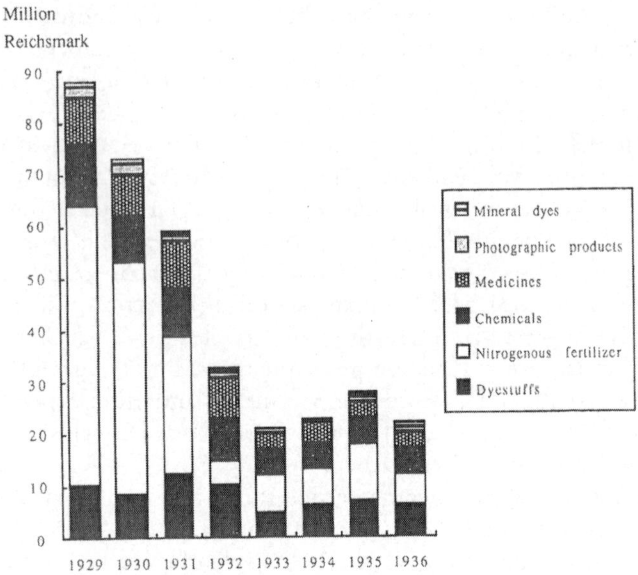

Source: Die Chemiewirtschaft Japans, S. 25, BASF-Archiv.

III

The rapid growth of the Japanese market continued well into the 1930s. However, German exports to the Japanese market were seriously thwarted by the collapse of the international gold standard and by the fragmentation of the world economy into several economic blocs. As is evident from Figure 1.1, German chemical exports to Japan in 1932 decreased to less than half of those of 1929, with a significant drop in nitrogenous fertiliser export.

There were two factors underlying this decrease in exports. One was the emergence of 'strong protectionism' in Japan, prompted by the fall of the yen and the rise in import tariffs. The other was the continued gain in the productivity attained by the Japanese chemical industry. In the field of dyestuffs, Japanese firms expanded their production so rapidly as to account for 3.2 percent of the total world-wide sales by 1938. In the same year, Mitsui Mining had a 20 percent share of the domestic market, Nihon Senryo 60 percent, Mitsubishi Chemical Industries ten percent and others ten percent.[14] In the field of fertilisers, Japanese firms continued to invest in plants and equipment even during the world depression, when manufacturers abroad were foreseeing a glut in the market. In pharmaceuticals, the great progress made by the Japanese industry and the introduction of a licence system by the government led to a decrease in German exports. In fact, I.G. Farben named Kitazato Institute as a potentially strong competitor in the field of serum.[15] Thus, the chemical industry became an early cornerstone of industrialising Japan, the forerunner of what are now known as 'Newly Industrialising Economies' (NIEs).

The Manchurian Incident of September 1931 marked a turning point for the Japanese government's policy toward foreign capital, with the previous policy of welcoming foreign capital investment replaced by that of rejection. Foreign capital was to be either phased out or Japanised, and foreign firms were prevented from exercising control over the management of their joint ventures.[16] As shown in Table 1.1, I.G. Farben's direct investments in manufacturing firms, if not those in distribution firms, were seriously restricted, with the result that its participating ratio in Asahi Bemberg, a rayon manufacturer, remained no more than 1.81 percent in 1945, and that in Nihon Tokushu Seizo, an insecticide manufacturer, as low as ten percent.

I.G. Farben's response to this policy change was, for the time being, to pursue the strategy devised in the 1920s, trying to conclude bilateral agreements with the Japanese chemical industry. With the advance of Japanese products, which were capturing ever greater shares of the market, it was becoming increasingly difficult to keep the market open for free competition among members of the international cartel. On the other hand, however, the international cartel had grown stronger, making it possible for I.G. Farben to carry out negotiations with the Japanese to its own advantage through collaboration with the participating companies of the international cartel. In the field of dyestuffs, where the Saito–Waibel Agreement had been reached early, I.G. Farben concluded in the early 1930s, either on its own or on behalf of the international cartel, agreements with Mitsui Mining, which had developed synthetic indigo, and with Nihon Senryo, which had developed naphthol dyestuffs.

The international cartel in the field of dyestuffs had its origin in the German–French agreement of 1927. In 1928 it grew into a three-party cartel with the participation of Switzerland. February 1932 saw the establishment of a four-party cartel, consisting of the dyestuff industries of Germany, France, Switzerland and Great Britain. This cartel was further expanded with the conclusion of separate agreements with the industries of the United States, Italy, Czechoslovakia and Poland.

In May 1935, six parties of the international cartel – consisting of I.G. Farben, Swiss companies, French companies, ICI (Imperial Chemical Industries) of Britain, Du Pont and Nacco (National Aniline & Chemical Co.) of the US – signed the Mitsui Indigo Agreement with Mitsui Mining. This agreement stipulated that Mitsui export its products only to China (including Manchuria, Hong Kong and Dalian) and within the bounds of a quota to be assigned to it. In return, the six parties concerned were to accept quotas for their exports to Japan. The distribution of the Japanese market including Korea and Formosa was 85 percent for Mitsui and 15 percent for the six parties. The prices in the Japanese and Chinese markets were also set at the same time.

I.G. Farben also signed for itself an agreement with Nihon Senryo in March 1931, called the Variamine Blue Agreement. There were several patent disputes between I.G. Farben and Nihon Senryo concerning Variamine Blue B, Naphthol AS, and their equivalents. The agreement was to solve these disputes and to restrain competition. Nihon Senryo agreed to honour the patents of I.G. Farben and not to export its products outside China. In exchange for this, both sides agreed to divide up the Japanese market between themselves, with I.G. Farben enjoying a 68 percent share and Nihon Senryo 32 percent for Variamine Blue B. Concurrently, it was also agreed that both sides would sell their products at the same prices in the Chinese market.[17]

In addition, I.G. Farben, acting on behalf of the six parties of the international cartel, concluded a sales and price agreement on sulphur black dyes exports to China with Mitsui Bussan (Mitsui & Co.) in 1931. And, in October 1931, I.G. Farben alone signed the Alizarine Blue Agreement with Mitsui Bussan, which represented Mitsui Mining. This latter agreement stipulated that I.G. Farben would have a 60 percent share of the Japanese market, and Mitsui the balance.[18] In February 1934, I.G. Farben concluded the Astraphloxine Agreement, again with Nihon Senryo, restricting the latter's export of the product and specifying the two parties' shares of the Japanese market.[19]

In the field of nitrogenous fertiliser, the Fujiwara–Bosch Draft Agreement had failed to materialise, as noted earlier, owing to a large extent to the collapse of the CIA. The CIA was re-established in July 1932. In March 1934, the CIA succeeded in concluding an Overall Ammonium Sulphate Agreement with the Japanese nitrogenous fertiliser industry through I.G. Farben. This was followed by the signing of the second agreement in February 1935, and the third agreement in November 1935. I.G. Farben was satisfied by these three agreements because they imposed a quota on Japanese exports to China, and so was the Japanese industry because they reduced or eliminated German exports to Japan and China.[20]

By the mid-1930s, I.G. Farben had to acknowledge that the Japanese market had been saturated with Japanese products. Of the two alternatives to product export which were theoretically available, namely, direct investment and licensing, the former was virtually out of the question since the Japanese government was bent on rejecting the inflow of foreign capital. I.G. Farben thus opted to change its strategy, beginning to offer Japanese firms the licences to use its know-how for the production of dyestuffs and nitrogenous fertiliser, and to export plants to the licensees. The new strategy seems to have much in common with those which advanced countries of today adopt in their relations with NIEs. However, in the case of synthetic oil, the situation was different. I.G. Farben could not export the product to Japan, and it was ready from the outset to respond positively to enquiries about licensing arrangements for synthetic oil production.

Concurrently with the adoption of the licensing strategy, I.G. Farben began to emphasise intelligence activities in Japan and East Asia. To be sure, German marketing subsidiaries in Japan, such as Doitsu Senryo, had been fairly active in collecting information,[21] but they became far more active as the licensing issue developed. For instance, Max Ilgner, executive chief of the Public Relations Office of I.G. Farben, made a tour of inspection in East Asia from 1934 to 1935, and wrote a detailed three-volume report entitled 'Report of the Far Eastern Tour, 1934–35'.[22] Several other reports, including 'The Japanese Chemical Industry', were also compiled, most likely by the Research Division.[23]

In the field of dyestuffs, there is a record suggesting that in 1934 or thereabouts, I.G. Farben concluded a licensing agreement with Nihon Tar Industries (later renamed Mitsubishi Chemical Industries). But the agreement did not seem to bear much fruit: when an engineer from Mitsubishi visited I.G. Farben's plants, I.G. Farben deeply suspected him of being an industrial spy.[24]

In sharp contrast to this, the licensing strategy proved quite successful in the field of fertilisers, where the Japanese market's vigour continued well into the 1930s, assuring high profit rates and enticing new entrants into the industry. Although the fertiliser producers had already

been using the Casale process and the Claude process, they were eager
to introduce I.G. Farben's Haber–Bosch process. This zeal to introduce
the process must have derived, at least partly, from its having been rated
by Japanese specialists to be the best. It should be pointed out, moreover, that Japanese curiosity and inquisitiveness, which astonished an
I.G. Farben engineer, must have also contributed to the introduction of
the process. This engineer observed that 'Japanese mentality is always
in quest of something new, and it matters little whether the "new"
thing is really superior to the older one or not'.[25]

The patent for the Haber–Bosch process had expired by then, so
the arrangements made between I.G. Farben and Japanese fertiliser
manufacturers were for technological guidance, to be specific, but
in a broad sense they might be regarded as licensing arrangements.
I.G. Farben offered licences to a total of five companies, beginning
with a licensing arrangement made with Taki Seihisho (Taki Fertiliser
Works) in Hyogo Prefecture in May 1935. The four other licensees
were Yahagi Industries (later renamed Toa Chemical Industry), Nihon
Tar Industries, Dainippon Tokkyo Hiryo (later renamed Nitto Chemical Industry) and Dainippon Sugar Manufacturing.[26]

In the field of synthetic oil, I.G. Farben started to negotiate with
Japanese companies earlier than it did in the field of nitrogenous fertiliser. In the early 1930s, it approached South Manchurian Railways,
and later contacted more than a dozen companies including the Mitsubishi Mining Co. and Ogura Petroleum. However, no licensing
agreement resulted from these contacts. The most important reason
for the failure of these efforts seems to have been the stiff opposition
mounted by the Japanese Navy, which developed its own process and
was interested in seeing private companies put this into commercial use.
I.G. Farben continued trying to sell its synthetic oil technology to Japan
even after the outbreak of the Pacific War. However, it was not until
January 1945, when the Second World War was drawing to an end, that
I.G. Farben was able to conclude with the Japanese Army what became
its first and last licensing contract on synthetic oil production.[27]

IV

Since I.G. Farben made little direct investment in manufacturing in
Japan, its technological transfer to Japan was limited in scope. Nonetheless, its technological influence was not insignificant in the fertiliser
industry where it licensed the Haber–Bosch process to five companies.

The case of Taki Fertiliser Works, the manufacturer of superphosphate fertiliser in Hyogo and the first of five companies to receive technological assistance from I.G. Farben, is instructive. The technological agreement stipulated as follows. First, I.G. Farben would provide all the drawings and specifications necessary for building the plant and equipment and all the other pertinent information necessary for putting these into operation; second, I.G. Farben would provide engineers and foremen to train the operators of Taki Fertiliser; and, third, I.G. Farben would assume the responsibility for placing orders for and supplying machinery, equipment and apparatus. In short, I.G. Farben committed itself to offering not only the licence for the Haber–Bosch process for use in the production of synthetic ammonia but also peripheral technology as well as the know-how for ammonia sulphate production, all in one package. Taki Fertiliser Works at the time was trying to diversify from the production of calcium superphosphate, which did not require much technological expertise, into the technologically more sophisticated area of synthetic ammonia production, and, as such, the company must have been in need of securing technological co-operation in as comprehensive a manner as possible.

It should be kept in mind, however, that the contents of the contract signed by Nihon Tar Industries, a member of the Mitsubishi *zaibatsu*, were similar to that of Taki Fertiliser, except that Nihon Tar Industries adopted the state-of-the-art Winkler reactor as a means of generating hydrogen gas. It is plausible that Nihon Tar Industries, with its avowed intention to become 'an I.G. Farben of the Orient', concluded the agreement on terms as comprehensive as possible with the intention of learning the most from I.G. Farben. It can be presumed, however, that the comprehensive nature of the technological transfer agreement should be interpreted as reflecting the wide technological gap between Germany and Japan rather than the intent of Nihon Tar Industries.[28]

I.G. Farben did send a team of its engineers, chemists and foremen to Japan to supervise the building and operation of the plants. Though only five of them (two engineers and three foremen) stayed for an extended period of time, the team consisted of 12 members at its peak (two engineers, two chemists and eight foremen). From a historical point of view, they were like a large number of foreign advisors who assisted in Japan's modernisation in the early Meiji period. Unlike the famous foreign advisors of the earlier time, who were mainly government employees, these I.G. Farben technicians were a group of unknown foreign advisors dispatched at a private level to supervise the construction of chemical plants.

Of all the machinery procured for the sake of implementing the technological licensing agreement with Taki Fertiliser Works, I.G. Farben's own products consisted only of high-pressure apparatuses, pipelines and fittings, and measuring instruments. I.G. Farben procured the rest from other companies: specifically, these consisted of high-pressure compressors and gas circulating pumps from Borsig, water gas plants and conversion plants from Bamag, high-pressure centrifugal pumps and rotary vacuum pumps from Klein, Schanzlin & Becker, Cu-lye pressure pumps from Hydraulik, ammonia hydraulic pumps from Balke, free jet turbines from Escher Wyss, transformers for electric heaters from Siemens-Schuckert, centrifuges from Gebr. Heine, saturators from Schütze, and synchron motors from AEG. This list is a virtual exhibition of German machinery, with the exception of the products of Escher Wyss, a Swiss firm.[29]

Under the supervision of the German engineers, the German-made machines were assembled and installed. This process by which the German engineers trained Japanese junior engineers into supervisors constituted an important aspect of technology transfer, understood in a sense broader than the transfer of technological know-how itself. The training was provided at the site of construction, and along the line of command and supervision which stretched down from the German chief engineer at the top, to the German engineers and foremen below him, to a group of young Japanese junior engineers. The Japanese junior engineers, through their daily contacts with the Germans, learned not only about engineering skills but also about how to supervise their own subordinates, the Japanese foremen and rank-and-file workers.[30]

The Taki Fertiliser plant and equipment, which embodied the Haber–Bosch process, was later taken over by a joint venture with Sumitomo Chemical Industries and produced ammonium sulphate in the early post-war period. The imported facilities at other companies followed a similar fate after the war.

There were several other instances of technology transfer. In the field of dyestuffs, the activities of research laboratories and their travelling engineers were instrumental in the transfer of German dyestuff technology. More specifically, the 1930s saw dyestuff manufacturers' associations in several localities establish syndicated plants and laboratories and invest in technology improvement. These moves were a concerted response to I.G. Farben's activities.

German exports also played an important role in transferring German technologies to Japan. Mitsui Mining's synthetic indigo and Nihon Senryo's naphthol dyestuffs, both modelled after I.G. Farben's products, were the products of unintended technology transfer. In the case of synthetic oil, the contacts that companies had with I.G. Farben in the process of negotiating on licensing contracts provided them with channels for technology transfer, such as experiments with crude coal, written estimates, and factory tours. Moreover, the factory tours and the access to drawings granted to visiting Japanese scholars, government officials and military officers also served as an important channel for technology transfer.

I.G. Farben affected the marketing practices and the distribution system of the Japanese chemical industry primarily through export of its manufactured goods, but the establishment of its sales bases also amplified these effects. In the summer of 1927, the head of the East Asian Commission and *Japan-Herren* (personnel responsible for business in Japan, actually employees of Doitsu Senryo) met at I.G. Farben's headquarters to discuss I.G. Farben's overall strategy in Japan. The main purpose was to re-evaluate the company's marketing policy and distribution system in Japan, and the discussions allow an insight into the influence I.G. Farben exerted on the distribution system.[31]

Let us first look at the re-examination of the distribution system. The history of the German dyestuff distribution system in Japan in the period from the late nineteenth century to the outbreak of the Second World War may be divided into three phases. The first period was from the early Meiji era to immediately before the outbreak of the First World War, the period when imports from Germany were handled by agents. Products manufactured by German companies were imported by foreign-owned or Japanese-owned sales agents, and were then sold to Japanese dyestuff wholesalers which were franchises of the German companies. The second period was from the eve of the First World War to its conclusion, or the period of 'direct import' when the sales agents came under direct management of the German firms. With this change, the route along which imported dyestuffs were distributed also changed, so that products manufactured by the German firms were imported by their respective agents or branches under their direct management, and were then sold to the franchised wholesalers. The first of such direct sales agencies was Friedrich Bayer & Co. Gomei Kaisha, established by Bayer in Kobe in 1911. Other German companies followed suit, reorganising their sales agencies and franchised wholesalers on a large scale. The third period started in 1924, when the sales agencies under direct German control were consolidated into Doitsu Senryo Gomei Kaisha.[32]

As mentioned above, the German dye companies which were consolidated into I.G. Farben expanded their distribution networks in Japan by nurturing large wholesalers into their special agents or franchises. In other words, they built a franchise system, drawing upon the existing wholesale system. In this sense, German dyestuff companies had the effect of accelerating the stratification of the dyestuff wholesalers, and, in effect, reinforced the traditional Wholesale system.

Even before the establishment of I.G. Farben, the German dyestuff companies had been talking about the need to reorganise the franchise system drastically. The most serious drawback of this system, it was argued, was that it was unavoidably accompanied by increased distribution costs. The minutes of the aforementioned meeting contain several interesting figures showing the high distribution costs in Japan. At the level of Doitsu Senryo, the distribution costs, inclusive of handling fees and warehouse charges of five percent, amounted to as much as 9.08 percent of gross revenues. When clerical and other handling charges of 1.77 percent due in Germany were added to this, the total cost percentage rose to 10.85 percent, an exceptionally high ratio by international standards. At this meeting, the possibility of abolishing the special agent system and replacing it by a direct sales system was discussed. However, the meeting concluded that a drastic change of this sort would be extremely difficult to implement. Ironically enough, the existing system had grown so firmly rooted that it could not easily be discarded.

Textbooks on Japanese business history usually point out that the pre-war market, in which a wholesale distribution system was dominant, was quite different from the American or European system.[33] One observation of the dyestuff market points out that in the period from the turn of the century to the 1920s, when non-traditional manufactured goods started to flow in, the market was sometimes affected more profoundly by European companies than by American companies. This was particularly true in already highly segmented markets, such as dyestuffs, in which the situation was closer to that of European countries, and in their efforts to adapt themselves to the Japanese market, European companies made the characteristics of that market all the more conspicuous. The viability of this hypothesis cannot be demonstrated here. However, unlike the distribution system for automobiles and electric appliances, which were formed under the influence of American companies, the dyestuffs distribution system seems to have been strongly affected by European companies.

The summer 1927 meeting also discussed marketing policy. It was decided, for instance, that in order to meet the various demands of Japanese users, company engineers, be they Japanese or German, were to participate in *Reisetätigkeit* (tours of production centres) across the country. This measure was linked to the reorganisation of laboratories which was implemented simultaneously. One objective of sending specialists on these tours was to investigate firsthand the competitive situation, but another, more important, objective was to help customers solve their problems by providing advice on dyeing and printing technologies. Through these activities, the specialists were expected to help promote the sales of new and expensive dyestuffs like naphthol, indigo paste, and indanthren.

In order to accommodate its marketing practice to swift changes in customer tastes, a peculiar trait of the Japanese market, the meeting decided that special *Musterkarten* (brochures of samples) specifically targeted to the market should be prepared. Unlike the existing, voluminous and comprehensive brochures, these compact brochures were designed to cater for the needs of selected strata of customers, could be produced at lower costs, and could prove more effective. It would also make sense to leave out some of the dyestuffs which were not being imported to begin with. The meeting also decided that samples be explained in Japanese, and that the brochures be produced in Japan.

This line of thinking on the marketing policy was based on the understanding, gained through experience, of the nature of the Japanese market. The minutes of the meeting stated that 'only through a ceaseless and thoroughgoing study of the Japanese market, the one which is exposed to violent changes in fashions and tastes, can we hope to fully open up the prospects for expensive dyestuffs with new uses to be accepted there'. It was also pointed out that

> considering the particular situation of Japan, it is urgently necessary to see to it that information on our new products, sample brochures and handling methods be disseminated among customers promptly, and that the introduction of new products, as long as they can attract interest in the Japanese market, be executed and monitored carefully.

Another improvement in marketing practice was to cut down inventories. Previously, inventories had tended to pile up, partly because of the frequent changes in the dyeing and printing methods brought about by sudden changes in trends, and partly because of the need to prepare for the possibility of a sudden imposition of import bans. The meeting concluded on the one hand that while it was definitely impossible to abide by the company's policy of maintaining inventories of six-month supplies the inventories should not be allowed to exceed an eight-month supply. At the same time, the meeting deliberated on the means of reducing inventories and found it essential that products of a low-to-medium price range, which were being supplied in increasing volumes by Japanese manufacturers, should be sold in the Chinese or other markets nearby, or shipped back to Germany, or even disposed of. The meeting agreed, furthermore, that new additions to inventories should be prevented by all appropriate means, for instance by keeping closer watch on the market and accurately forecasting the demand in the coming season. Here again, how to cope with the rapidity of fashion changes was the most crucial issue.

The meeting also re-examined the marketability of each product in detail. For instance, there was deliberation on sulphuric dye, a black dye much in demand for its use in school uniforms. The attempt to introduce powdery indanthren black BB as a substitute for sulphur black dye had turned out to be unviable because of the proposed product's lack of price competitiveness. Indian carbon was a better choice. But the existing CL variety of Indian carbon left something to be desired in terms of its colour shades, and the SN variety was not pure enough. A mixture of Indian carbon composed primarily of the CL variety but with improved colour shades was desirable. This combination, argued the meeting, would yield a reasonably priced dyestuff. The headquarters of I.G. Farben should send a telegram to Doitsu Senryo informing it of this decision, and instructing it to develop this new Indian carbon. With this substitute for sulphur black, I.G. Farben would be able to expand its sales and regain much of the share it had lost in the sulphur black market.

On the whole, this re-examination was geared not so much to applying I.G. Farben's marketing policy directly to the Japanese market as to re-adapting it to the Japanese realities. Nevertheless, the revised policy was quite different from those being followed by its Japanese competitors. As such, the new policy must have exerted some influence on the Japanese industry, and have been copied by it gradually, although this remains to be confirmed by evidence. At any rate, there is no denying that I.G. Farben's approach was radically different from those of Japanese firms. To take Nihon Senryo, for instance, it was not until after Katsutaro Inabata became president in 1926, when the company began to divest itself of its earlier characteristic as a semi-government corporation and become a more genuinely private entity, that the company launched a campaign to advertise its products to plants and laboratories, resuming distribution of its samples and brochures.[34]

It was the German dyestuff industry that had introduced innovative marketing policies to the Japanese market in the pre-First World War days. Take, for instance, an observation of the policy for marketing indigo products adopted by H. Ahrens & Co. Nachf., BASF's sales agent in Japan, as excerpted from a document compiled by an association of dealers in painting and dyeing materials in Osaka. This observation is revealing of how active and aggressive German dyestuff manufacturers were in their approach to the Japanese market. BASF's agent made

> ... very strenuous efforts to promote BASF products. Not only did it prepare a very detailed brochure and distribute it widely, it also sent specialists all over the country to visit indigo dye works, literally door to door, instruct the owners of the works on the use of the products, and explain details of their advantages and disadvantages in comparison with natural indigo.

It was also the German industry that introduced the practice of cash transactions, as attested to by the same document:

> Under the traditional practice of indigo transaction in Japan, which was based on consignment, customers used to settle their bills only after three to six months following delivery, by which time they would have mostly used up the dyestuffs. We found this practice undesirable, and so, when we began to deal in synthetic indigo, we decided to follow the advice of German trading houses and to stick fast to cash transactions from the beginning despite all the difficulties.[35]

The meeting of 1927 did not simply re-examine the company's marketing policy and distribution system in Japan, but also considered reducing its staff of local employees. According to the minutes of the meeting, the main objective was to discharge older Japanese employees who were 'not competent enough' but were 'becoming an increasingly heavier financial burden for Doitsu Senryo', and thereby to 'rejuvenate' the local staff as a whole. On the surface, this personnel rejuvenation scheme appears to have been dictated by the management's concern for cost curtailment.

Much the same concern seems to have underlain the discussion on the method for paying severance allowances to the employees to be discharged. At the time the payment of lump sum retirement allowances for white-collar workers was beginning to take root in Japan, and in fact Doitsu Senryo was advised by outsiders to pay the retirement allowances as a lump sum. The management of the company, however, was reluctant to follow this advice, and tried to negotiate payment by a long-term instalment or retirement pension plan.

When looked at from a different angle, the two episodes above may be interpreted as manifesting I.G. Farben's willingness to introduce the German practice, that is, the corporate pension system, to Japan. Unfortunately, little is known about how the personnel rejuvenation scheme was actually carried out and how the retirement allowances were actually paid. Even if these were known, their effects on the Japanese personnel management practice must have been negligible. Nevertheless, the fact that these possibilities were actually discussed at a time when the retirement allowances for white-collar workers were not firmly established in Japan deserves special attention.[36]

V

The First World War gave rise to a modern chemical industry in Japan. In the post-war period, the government adopted a policy of selective, or limited, protectionism to nurture this infant industry. Given the growing importance of the Japanese market, I.G. Farben first re-established its sales outlets in Japan and then undertook their reorganisation, which resulted in the establishment in 1924 of Doitsu Senryo as the sole agent of the German dyestuff industry in Japan. During the 1920s, I.G. Farben refused to agree to Japanese companies' requests for licensing arrangements, and its strategy toward Japan was basically formed around product export. In pursuing this strategy, I.G. Farben tried to conclude several bilateral agreements. The only agreement concluded during the decade was the Saito–Waibel Agreement on dyes, which enabled I.G. Farben to gain a foothold in the Japanese market in exchange for voluntary restrictions on exports.

In the 1930s, 'strong protectionism' emerged in Japan, making the market less accessible to I.G. Farben's exports. Meanwhile, the strengthening of the international cartel enabled the company to conclude several agreements with Japanese companies on market share and prices, either on its own or as a member of the international cartel. The agreement with Mitsui Mining on indigo and the Agreement on Domestic and Foreign Ammonium Sulphate were two examples. In the late 1930s, when the prospects for further expansion of its product export to Japan were foreclosed, I.G. Farben eventually changed its Japanese strategy to one oriented towards licensing. It made at least one licensing agreement in dyestuffs and five licensing agreements in synthetic ammonia and nitrogenous fertilisers.

Through its technology and management transfer during the 1920s and 1930s, I.G. Farben exerted significant influence on the production technology, marketing policy, and distribution system of the Japanese chemical industry. Much technology was transferred to Japan in the course of implementing agreements in the field of nitrogenous fertiliser, through the dispatch of I.G. Farben's engineers and foremen to Japan, and through I.G. Farben's procurement of plants and equipment from Germany. It is also worth noting that these employees of I.G. Farben played an important role in training Japanese junior engineers not only in engineering but also in supervisory skills. In marketing practices, too, I.G. Farben introduced several innovations, such as sales activities by travelling engineers and improvements in sample brochures, which sought to cope effectively with the rapidly changing fashion trends in Japan and with specific requirements of users. As for the distribution system, I.G. Farben nurtured large Japanese wholesale dealers as its special agents, and consequently reinforced the traditional wholesale distribution system.

Source: *The German Chemical Industry in the Twentieth Century* (John E. Lesch (ed.)),
Dordrecht and Boston: Kluwer Academic Publishers, 2000, pp. 243–283

2

Dominance through Cooperation: I.G. Farben's Japan Strategy

THIS CHAPTER DEALS with the Japan strategy of I.G. Farben, a giant German chemical firm which dominated the world market in the inter-war period.[1] In that era, I.G. Farben was a technological as well as organizational leader in the world chemical products market. For I.G. Farben, Japan was both an opportunity and a challenge: the Japanese market supplied a new business opportunity, and Japanese chemical companies were new challengers to its world dominance.

The Japanese economy in the inter-war period can be characterized by its high growth rate. It experienced an annual growth rate of more than 4 percent, among the highest in the world at that time.[2] Moreover, the speed of Japan's industrialization was remarkable, matched only by some small East European countries. Japan seized the opportunity of the First World War to begin development of its heavy industry and chemical industry, the pace of which did not slacken even during the World Depression of the 1930s. Japan can claim to be among the first Newly Industrializing Economies (NIE).

The key feature of the Japanese economy during the inter-war period, however, was economic nationalism in its tariff, commercial, and foreign capital policies, although these differed between the 1920s and 1930s in both structure and severity. In the 1920s, as in most other countries, the trade policy line followed was one of relatively free trade, although policy measures to protect domestic industries, such as imposition of custom duties and limits on the quantity of imports, were implemented. The prevalent attitude toward European and American firms was one that welcomed their direct investment in line with the liberalization policy followed since the turn of the century. The gold standard was established around the turn of the century; it was abandoned at the outbreak of the First World War, but reintroduced in January 1930. Also the Commercial Law Act was enforced, and foreigners acquired the right to deal in real estate and make direct investments. Various restrictions, however, were placed on the management control that could be assumed by European and American firms over their subsidiaries based in Japan. In general, the 1920s were a time of relatively weak economic nationalism.

The 1930s brought rapidly increasing protectionism in Japan, such as tariff increases on imported industrial products, as well as the promotion of domestic products and the replacement of imports with domestic products. The tone of the Japanese government's foreign capital policy also changed to one that favored the exclusion of direct investment in Japan, a move influenced by the increased political intervention of the military.[3] Against this background of growing economic nationalism, Japanese firms, which formed the backbone of Japan's emergence as an early NIE, began strongly asserting their independence from European and American firms in both technical and managerial terms. Moving from domination of the domestic market to advance into Asian markets, these Japanese companies became new challengers to the old order of the international cartels.[4]

In short, Japan was an early NIE characterized by a high growth rate as well as growing economic nationalism. This situation raises a number of questions. How did I.G. Farben perceive the Japanese market and companies, especially the Japanese market for chemical products and the Japanese chemical industry? How did it position them in its world strategy? What kind of business organization did it build up toward Japan following its observation and strategy? What kind of entry strategies did it adopt for the Japanese market? What kind of business activities did it pursue in Japan? What were the results of those activities? The case of I.G. Farben provides us with a good example of the strategy of Western big business toward Japan in particular as well as toward NIEs in general.

OVERVIEW

Japanese market and companies

The Japanese market for chemical products had already developed to some extent and was developing further around the end of the nineteenth and beginning of the twentieth century, along with the development of the textile industry and agriculture in Japan. Import items included dyestuffs, dyeing assistants, fertilizer, and pesticides. A modern chemical industry, represented by those products, had not yet emerged in Japan. Japan was, therefore, mostly dependent on imported chemical products. It was in those years that German chemical companies began to advance into the Japanese market. German dyestuffs companies, the ancestors of I.G. Farben, began to export their products to Japan on a full scale around 1890, and pharmaceuticals entered on a considerable scale from around 1900.

It was during the First World War that the modern chemical industry, especially the dyestuffs industry, began in Japan with the emergence of many small firms, the establishment of one large company, and diversification attempts by existing firms in other industries. This can be seen as a part of the worldwide diffusion of technology and production capabilities in the industry with the war as a turning point. Thereafter, the share of those new products in the production and exports of the Japanese chemical industry rose, while traditional products such as vegetable wax and peppermint oil lost their importance. The importance of the chemical industry in the Japanese industrial structure also increased: its share in the production value of the manufacturing sector, which was less than 10 percent just before and during the First World War and stayed at this level in the 1920s, rose to 15 percent in the 1930s. It constituted a part of Japan's development of the heavy and chemical industry sectors.[5]

In the 1920s, however, the newborn Japanese modern chemical industry suffered from international competition. Most new products remained import items: dyestuffs, nitrogenous fertilizer, and chemicals were representative. The industry was always threatened by imported products, especially by those sold at low prices. One of the main reasons for the imports at low prices was a change in Europe after the war: the development of a division of labor in the European chemical industry, which made major exporting nations of chemical products also major importers. On the other hand, most European nations strengthened their protectionist tariff and trade policies, focusing on dyestuffs and nitrogenous fertilizer. As a result, they rushed into the Asian market, where the indigenous chemical industry was underdeveloped, with low prices. In fact, the Asian market, especially the Chinese and Japanese markets, absorbed 15 percent of world imports of chemical products in those years and became the largest market, replacing the United States which had been largest before the war.

The rapid growth of the Japanese market continued well into the 1930s. European exports to the Japanese market, however, were seriously affected by the collapse of the international gold standard and the general fragmentation of the world economy into several economic blocks, as well as by the December 1931 re-imposition of the ban against gold imports, the fall of the yen, and the rise in import tariffs thereafter in Japan in particular. As is evident from Figure 2.1, German chemical exports to Japan in 1932 decreased to less than half those of 1929, with a significant drop in nitrogenous fertilizer exports, and then stagnated through the 1930s.

There was another factor underlying this decrease in exports in addition to the emergence of strong protectionism in Japan, prompted by the fall of the yen and the rise in import tariffs, namely the continued gain in the production capabilities attained by the Japanese chemical industry. In the field of dyestuffs, Japanese firms expanded their production so rapidly that they accounted for 3.2 percent of total worldwide sales by 1938.[6] In the field of fertilizers, Japanese firms continued to invest in plants and equipment even during the World Depression, when manufacturers abroad were producing a glut in the market. In pharmaceuticals, the great progress made by Japanese industry and the introduction of a license system by the government led to a decrease in German exports. In fact, I.G. Farben named the Kitazato Institute as a potentially strong competitor in the field of serum.[7] Thus, the chemical industry became an early cornerstone of industrializing Japan.

The German chemical industry, the biggest exporter in the world market, focused on the European market. In the 1920s, West Europe remained the largest market for German exports of chemical products, accounting for almost 40 percent of its total exports. The importance of the non-European market, however, should not be neglected. The Asian market, especially the Japanese market, was important. Japan's share in German exports of chemical products was 8.4 percent in the middle of the 1920s, ranking third after the United States and the former Austro-Hungarian empire.[8] This was also true for I.G. Farben. In 1913, Japan ranked seventh among I.G. Farben's export markets, accounting for 19.2 million marks. After the First World War, the importance of Japan as an export outlet increased. In 1926, exports to Japan accounted for 4.1 percent of I.G. Farben's total sales, including sales in the domestic market, making Japan the second largest market outside Europe after China (5.0 percent). It ranked third with a share of 3.0 percent in 1929 and second with a share of 3.5 percent in 1932. Its importance decreased only after the middle of the 1930s, ranking sixth with a share of 1.0 percent in 1938.[9]

The balance of trade in chemical products between the two nations continued to show an enormous excess of German exports. In 1929, German exports to Japan were 92 million reichsmark and imports from Japan were only 3 million reichsmark. The German surplus, therefore, amounted to 89 million reichsmark. Even in 1935, when German exports to Japan decreased as shown in Figure 2.1, the surplus was 27 million reichsmark with exports of 28 million reichsmark and imports of 1 million reichsmark.[10]

Regarding the contents of German chemical exports to Japan, dye-stuffs were most important in the earlier years. In 1913, dyestuffs had an 83 percent share of I.G. Farben's exports to Japan, the rest being held by pharmaceuticals (9 percent) and chemicals (8 percent).[11] As shown in Figure 2.1, however, nitrogenous fertilizer became, by 1929, Germany's single most important chemical exported to Japan, far surpassing dyestuffs and other chemical products. Important items other than nitrogenous fertilizer in the same year were chemicals, pharmaceuticals, and dyestuffs in that order.

This export structure of the German chemical industry roughly reflected that of I.G. Farben. The Japanese market was quite important for I.G. Farben, not only in dyestuffs and fertilizers, as discussed below, but also in other products. Its export of chemicals to Japan in 1926 accounted for 2.1 percent of its total sales, including domestic sales, making Japan seventh as an export market. Japan's share was 3.2 percent in 1932, ranking second. In pharmaceuticals, Japan was ranked the second largest export market of I.G. Farben after the United States in 1932. In photographic products, too, Japan was ranked second after the United States in 1926 with a 6.1 percent share of total sales, with lesser importance in later years.[12]

The features of the bilateral trade, as shown in the balance of trade and in the trade items mentioned above, clearly reflect the discrepancies

Figure 2.1 German Chemical Exports to Japan, 1929–36

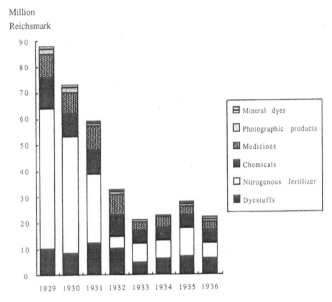

Source: Die Chemiewirtschaft Japans, S. 25, BASF-Archiv.

in the development of each nation's chemical industry. The one-way flow of technology and direct investment from Germany to Japan also reflects the backwardness of the Japanese chemical industry.

It is hardly necessary to emphasize the significant place I.G. Farben occupied, not simply in German industry, but in the world chemical industry as a whole. Naturally, for the newborn Japanese industry, I.G. Farben was a formidable giant. It was capitalized at 650 million reichsmark (some 300 million yen) at its establishment, whereas Mitsui Kozan Kabushiki Kaisha (Mitsui Mining Co., Ltd), the largest Japanese mining company which was diversifying into chemical production, was capitalized at only 52.50 million yen, and the government-owned Nihon Senryo Seizo Kabushiki Kaisha (Japan Dyestuff Manufacturing Co., Ltd., hereafter referred to as Nihon Senryo) was capitalized at a mere eight million yen.

As factors in the background of I.G. Farben's Japan strategy, however, we should point out not only the backwardness, but also the development and aggressiveness of the Japanese chemical industry. The Japanese chemical industry grew so rapidly as to almost dominate the domestic market and moved into exports in the 1930s. Its exports increased at the enormously high rate of 17.3 percent from 1932 to 1937, ahead of Canada (11.3 percent), Britain (5.1 percent), the United States (4.0 percent), Italy (4.0 percent), and Germany (3.4 percent). Its share in the world market also almost doubled from 1.7 percent in 1932 to 3.2 percent in 1937. Japan ranked ninth in 1937, though still far behind the three major exporting nations: Germany (25.4 percent), Britain (13.6 percent), and the United States (12.9 percent.[13]

Moving from domination of the domestic market to advance into the Asian market, Japanese companies became the new challengers to the old order of the international cartels. At the same time, they began to assert their independence from European and American firms, in both technical and managerial terms, against the background of growing economic nationalism, although they maintained a strong desire to introduce technology and management skills from European and American companies.[14]

I.G. Farben strategy and organization toward Japan

How did I.G. Farben appraise the Japanese market for chemical products and the Japanese chemical industry? It seems that I.G. Farben through its business organization, was able to assess the Japanese market and Japanese industry with some accuracy, as will be discussed below. How then did I.G. Farben position the Japanese market and competition in its world strategy? In brief, it attached importance to advancing into the growing Japanese market, and it also tried hard to respond to ambitious Japanese chemical companies.

I.G. Farben saw Japan not only as an important export market in itself but also as a sales base for East Asian markets, including China. In fact, Japan with its political stability and communications infrastructure had become an important foothold for business activities in the large Chinese market.

Ultimately, I.G. Farben used all three forms of international business activities toward Japan, namely export of products, licensing of technologies, and direct investment. It exported its products such as dyestuffs and nitrogenous fertilizer to Japan, and licensed its technologies such as the Haber-Bosch process for synthetic ammonia to Japanese companies. It also made direct investments in Japan, both in manufacturing and in sales outlets, but mainly in the latter. At first, however, I.G. Farben was extremely reluctant to pursue anything but an export strategy.

The Japanese chemical industry and the Japanese government were eager to introduce advanced technologies from European and American firms. They repeatedly requested technical cooperation with, or licensing from, I.G. Farben. I.G. Farben was tacitly following a policy of not granting such requests, for example in the case of technical information about the Haber-Bosch process and technologies in the dyestuffs field, which are discussed below.

An extreme illustration of I.G. Farben's lack of interest in offering technical cooperation is found in the reaction of the top executives of the Community of Interests (Interessengemeinschaft) to a proposal for technological cooperation that Fritz Haber made to them in 1924, upon his return from a trip to Japan. Haber possessed great prestige at BASF and the Community of Interests because of the remarkable success of the Haber-Bosch process, and he proposed that the community should offer technological cooperation to Japan in the field of inorganic chemistry as an indispensable means of compromise to entice the Japanese government into abolishing the import license system for German chemical products. The community council, however, flatly rejected his proposal. Especially obstinate in opposing Haber's proposal was Carl Bosch, the very person who had worked closely with Haber in the development of the Haber-Bosch process, and who was then chairman of the board of directors of BASF and one of the leading figures in the community. Bosch maintained that if the community started cooperating with the Japanese in the field of inorganic chemistry, the Japanese would then press hard for cooperation in the field of dye production as well. Calling attention to „der fast krankhafte Ehrgeiz der Japaner" (the almost morbid ambition of the Japanese), Bosch asserted that "our objective, under any circumstances, ought to be not to offer any help whatsoever to the Japanese in their efforts to build up a profitable chemical industry, and in particular, a dyestuffs industry of their own, but rather to slow their progress in these efforts as long as possible, and moreover to reduce these efforts into a failure as best as we can."[15]

It is true that there were some occasions when I.G. Farben gave positive consideration to offering technological cooperation. For instance, it considered offering technological cooperation to Nihon Senryo in the field of rayon and aluminum production as a means of discouraging the latter from developing synthetic indigo. It should be pointed out, however, that I.G. Farben brushed the idea aside as soon as it discovered that Nihon Senryo was not competent enough to develop synthetic indigo.[16]

I.G. Farben's strategy can be understood in light of the fact that it is usually difficult for a leading firm in the chemical industry, unlike its counterparts in the electrical machinery industry, to maintain technological supremacy over its competitors by using patents as leverage. It should also be recalled that the Japanese government had requisitioned German patents during the First World War and that in April 1921 the Japanese government promulgated a Revised Patent Law that made chemical materials, but not processes, ineligible for patent protection.

In some fields of chemical production, such as nitrogenous fertilizer, Japanese firms introduced the necessary technologies from France and Italy after these had been diffused from Germany during the First World War, while in other fields they used technologies devised by themselves. In the field of dyestuffs, Japanese firms were trying hard to develop the products for themselves by copying German products. Mitsui Mining's effort to develop synthetic indigo and Nihon Senryo's to develop naphthol dyestuffs were two outstanding examples. Needless to say, the lifting of patent protection in itself did not immediately guarantee that high-technology products could be easily developed. There were a wide variety of intricate details that had to be learned or discovered before the previously patented information could be put to practical application. Nevertheless, there is no denying that these developmental efforts posed a serious threat to I.G. Farben.

In order for I.G. Farben to protect its technology, which became ineligible for patent protection, it had no choice but to deny licensing to Japan. In addition I.G. Farben even went so far as to dump its synthetic indigo products in the Japanese market in the hope of discouraging Mitsui Mining from developing these.[17] It also had recourse to a number of other measures, including reorganization of its sales base in Japan, as mentioned below, and readjustment of its sales policies. In addition, I.G. Farben concluded a series of bilateral agreements with individual Japanese firms and with the Japanese industry as a whole as a means of securing its outlets.

In the 1930s, when strong protectionism emerged in Japan, I.G. Farben concluded several agreements with Japanese companies either on its own or as a member of international cartels so that it succeeded in securing a stable share in the Japanese market as well as in the Chinese and other Asian markets. I.G. Farben, however, had to acknowledge that meanwhile the Japanese market had been saturated with Japanese products. Of the two alternatives to product export that were theoretically available, namely, direct investment and licensing, the former was virtually out of the question, even apart from the growing political instability in East Asia, since the Japanese government was bent on rejecting the inflow of foreign capital.

Table 2.1 I.G. Farben's direct investment in Japan as of 1945

Company	City	Purpose of establishment	Capital (million yen)	Shareholding ratio (%)	Year established
Asahi Bemberg Kenshi Kabushiki Kaisha	Osaka	Rayon manufacturing	46.00	1.81	1929
Nihon Tokushu Seizo Kabushiki Kaisha	Tokyo	Pesticide manufacturing	1.00	10.00	1941
Bayer Yakuhin Gomei Kaisha	Kobe	Sales of pharmaceuticals	0.15	100.00	1927
Doitsu Senryo Gomei Kaisha	Kobe, Tokyo	Sales of dyestuffs	0.30	26.23	1924
H. Ahrens & Co. Nachf.	Tokyo	Sales of nitrogenous fertilizer	0.20	100.00	1869
Agfa Gomei Kaisha	Tokyo	Sales of photographic products	0.10	100.00	1925
Titan Kogyo Kabushiki Kaisha	Tokyo	Sales of titanium	3.50	4.17	1936

Source: Finance and Accounting Section, IGFC, *Survey,* 1947, HA.

The Manchurian Incident of September 1931 marked a turning point for the Japanese government's policy toward foreign capital, with the previous policy of welcoming foreign capital investment replaced by a policy of rejection. Foreign capital was to be either phased out or Japanized, and foreign firms were prevented from exercising control over the management of their joint ventures.[18] As shown in Table 2.1, I.G. Farben made direct investment more in sales outlets and less in manufacturing. Only three companies in which I.G. Farben made investments, Asahi Bemberg, Nihon Tokushu Seizo, and Titan Kogyo, were manufacturing companies. Its direct investment in manufacturing firms, though not in distribution firms, was seriously restricted as before, with the result that its participation ratio in Nihon Tokushu Seizo remained at 10 percent and that in Asahi Bemberg, as low as 1.81 percent in 1945.

I.G. Farben thus opted to change its strategy, beginning to offer Japanese firms licenses to use its techniques for the production of dye-stuffs and nitrogenous fertilizer, and to export plants to the licensees. The new strategy seems to have much in common with those advanced countries of today adopt in their relations with NIEs.

In the 1920s, despite its weak protectionist stance, the Japanese government sometimes took bold steps to sustain sections of the domestic chemical industry under threat from foreign competition. For instance, in June 1924 it enforced an import license system to protect the dye-stuffs industry, which was badly in need of support. This system was, in effect, meant to discriminate against German goods. One of the countermeasures devised by the German dyestuffs industry was reorganization of its distribution outlets within Japan.

At the time, major German dyestuffs companies belonging to the industry-wide Community of Interests (Interessengemeinschaft) were being pressed hard to rationalize their business organizations as the post-war hyperinflation in Germany was brought under control. Consolidation of their sales outlets outside Germany was one of the most important and difficult tasks because each member company considered its own traditional sales outlets, trade rights, and trade marks as too precious to be subjected to reorganization and reshuffling. Nevertheless, the effort to consolidate the German sales outlets in Japan was completed in relatively smooth fashion, most likely because each German company took a serious view of the growth potential of the Japanese industry's production capabilities and the adverse effects of the discriminatory import license system.

Interestingly enough, in the course of deliberation on the consolidation of sales organizations in Japan, BASF presented a plan that called for an immediate and complete integration of the sales branches of all German companies concerned, whereas Hoechst proposed an export quota system, and Bayer suggested a partial integration as a compromise between the two. This conflict of plans preceded and anticipated a dispute at the top management level concerning the reorganization of the Community of Interests, namely, a conflict between a merger plan proposed by Carl Bosch of BASF and a shareholding plan by Carl Duisberg of Bayer. Eventually, the immediate integration measure won the day. In December 1924, Doitsu Senryo Gomei Kaisha (German Dyestuff Company) was established in Kobe as the sole representative for the Community of Interests with the exception of Cassella. Established with a capital outlay of 300,000 yen, the office was staffed by two employees from BASF and one each from Bayer, Hoechst, Agfa, and Griesheim-Elektron, with Richard Veit of Bayer appointed as chief manager. It was just one year after this that Bosch's plan was accepted and, as a result, I.G. Farben was established back in Germany.

Much the same pattern of reorganization took place in other fields. For fertilizer products, such as nitrogenous fertilizer, H. Ahrens & Co. Nachf. was established in Tokyo as the sole representative for the Community of Interests from the outset. As shown in Table 2.1, sales organizations for pharmaceuticals, photographic products, and titanium were reorganized or newly established in succession.

As a consequence of this reorganization, the strategy of the Community of Interests in Japan was to be carried out though a setup composed of three strata. Situated at the top was a council of the Community of Interests composed of the chief executives of the eight participating companies. This council would directly involve itself in making decisions on matters of crucial importance. Placed directly subordinate to this council was the Japan Commission (Japan-Kommission), later renamed East Asian Commission (Ostasien-Kommission), charged with the task of devising the community's strategy toward Japan and carrying out that strategy with the council's consent. Hermann Waibel of BASF was appointed the first chief of this commission. Later, after the establishment of I.G. Farben, this commission was abolished. Waibel remained responsible for East Asian business and regularly attended meetings of the Sales Commission, one of three commissions directly subordinate to the top management, as well as of the Patent Commission, making reports and proposals regarding business in Japan, China, Manchuria, and other East Asian regions. He also regularly attended the Arbeitsausschuß (the inner circle of the board of directors) to give reports on East Asian business.[19]

At the bottom of the hierarchy were local sales organizations, such as Doitsu Senryo and H. Ahrens, each responsible for directly handling the sales of a specific type of goods in Japan. Those organizations can be seen as an extension abroad of business divisions of I.G. Farben. There was no regional headquarters in Japan or in East Asia. This hierarchical setup was basically kept intact despite partial revisions even after the establishment of I.G. Farben.[20]

Concurrently with the adoption of a licensing strategy in the mid-1930s, I.G. Farben strengthened organizations to foster Japanese and

East Asian business. The Arbeitsausschuß of October 1935 decided to establish an Ostasienausschuß according to Bosch's proposal. The reason was to strengthen business activities in East Asia and especially to respond to increasing competitive pressure from Japan. Waibel remained the head of the commission.[21]

I.G. Farben also began to emphasize intelligence activities in Japan and East Asia. To be sure, German marketing subsidiaries in Japan, such as Doitsu Senryo, had been fairly active in collecting information, but I.G. Farben became far more active as the licensing issue developed. For instance, Max Ilgner, executive chief of its public relations office, made a tour of inspection in East Asia from 1934 to 1935 and wrote a detailed three-volume report entitled "Report of the Far Eastern Tour, 1934–35." In 1937 and 1938, Anton Reithinger, the head of the Research Division (Volkswirtschaftliche Abteilung), also made a research tour in Asian countries.[22] Several other reports, including "The Japanese chemical industry," were also compiled, most likely by the Research Division.[23]

What kind of business activities, then, did I.G. Farben pursue in Japan, and what were their results? I will try to answer these questions by taking up three major businesses: dyestuffs, nitrogenous fertilizer, and synthetic oil.

EXPORT STRATEGY – DYESTUFFS

German dominance and the Japanese challenge in the 1920s

As mentioned above, in the period before the First World War, the major German chemical companies, which dominated the world dyestuffs market, were already exporting their products to Japan on a considerable scale.[24] Dyestuffs were an important export item. By 1913, immediately before the First World War, the Japanese market had become significant for German dyestuffs producers. In that year, Japan ranked as the eighth largest export market for German dyestuffs producers, importing 4.9 percent of total German dyestuffs exports.[25]

With the outbreak of the First World War, however, the world market for dyestuffs experienced a shift from a German monopoly to greater competition. European nations and the United States adopted policies aimed at protecting and fostering their dyestuffs industries, and they continued and strengthened those policies after the end of the war. German and Swiss producers lost their market shares while manufacturers in the United States, Britain, and France gained better positions. Moreover, companies from Italy, the Soviet Union, Czechoslovakia, and Poland emerged in the world market.

The First World War also brought about profound changes in the Japanese market and in the Japanese dyestuffs industry. With the outbreak of the war, Japanese imports of dyestuffs from Europe, especially from Germany, became impossible, and a vacuum was created within the Japanese dyestuffs market, which had formerly been dominated by German products. This led to a sudden large increase in the number of smaller indigenous dyestuffs producers. A single exception was the establishment of Nihon Senryo, which was set up as a state-owned company with share capital of 8 million yen (about 4 million U.S. dollars) under a government policy of fostering the domestic dyestuffs industry. Moreover, one of the largest mining companies in Japan, Mitsui Mining, which was one of the main manufacturing companies of the Mitsui zaibatsu enterprise group with share capital of 52.50 million yen (about 26 million U.S. dollars) and which had already experimentally diversified into the dyestuffs business shortly before the war, began operations on a commercial scale at this time.[26]

Immediately following the end of the war, imports into Japan were begun once more. Not only German but also Swiss and American products began to flow into the market. It was the German products that managed to regain their dominant position, however, because of their superior quality. The German dominance led the Japanese Ministry of Agriculture and Commerce (which was divided in March 1925 into two ministries: the Ministry of Agriculture and the Ministry of Commerce and Industry) to set up an import license system in June 1924. This system gave the ministry the power to ban importing of those goods that could be produced domestically. It targeted German products and functioned, in effect, as a selective barrier against German imports. The effectiveness of the import license system proved remarkable. Imports from Germany were reduced as planned, for the time being, although imports from Switzerland and the United States took their place.[27] This proved a blow for the German dye-stuffs companies, which had, by the end of 1925, joined forces to create I.G. Farben.

I.G. Farben entered into negotiations with the Japanese Ministry of Commerce and Industry and the Ministry of Foreign Affairs, which ministries represented Japanese dyestuffs manufacturers, especially the smaller ones.

Two years of tough negotiations produced the signing of an agreement between I.G. Farben and Japanese dyestuffs makers in August 1926. This was later called the Saito-Waibel Agreement after the representatives who signed it (Ryoei Saito was an official of the Ministry of Foreign Affairs; Hermann Waibel, a director of I.G. Farben who was responsible for Japan and East Asia). The main points contained in this agreement were:

- abolition by the Japanese government of its current import license system for German products;
- in exchange, imposition by I.G. Farben of voluntary restrictions on its exports to Japan of those dyestuffs that the Japanese were capable of producing domestically;
- as a general rule, unrestricted exports to Japan by I.G. Farben of all other products, such as synthetic indigo, that the Japanese were unable to produce.

The agreement thereby provided for a kind of international division of labor between the Japanese and German producers. The main reason for I.G. Farben's signing of this agreement at a comparatively early stage of Japanese industrial development was the fact that the Japanese government had early on put into effect an import licensing system that targeted German products.[28] Subsequently, the agreement became the basis for the reconstruction of Japanese-German economic, as well as political, relations with the conclusion of the Japanese-German Commerce and Navigation Treaty in July 1927.

Japanese strategy of the international dyestuffs cartels

With the implementation in April 1928 of the Saito-Waibel Agreement between I.G. Farben and the Japanese dyestuffs industry the import license system became invalid. From that time on, I.G. Farben concentrated its efforts on those products, such as synthetic indigo, that had not yet been commercially developed in Japan, while at the same time it did its best to hinder the efforts of Japanese firms to develop new products.

One of the most powerful weapons it had to frustrate the Japanese was a low-price policy, which was criticized by Japanese firms as no more than a form of dumping. Another powerful weapon was I.G. Farben's refusal to provide technical assistance to Japanese firms, despite the repeated requests to it and other European companies from the Japanese dyestuffs industry and government for technical cooperation and help. Although I.G. Farben did not openly reject these requests, it was tacitly following a policy of not responding to them in order to maintain its competitive edge.

Then, in April 1929, German, Swiss, and French dyestuffs produc- ers concluded an international cartel. This was called the three-party cartel. German producers had come together through the establish- ment of I.G. Farben as early as 1925, while three leading Swiss compa- nies, Ciba (Gesellschaft für chemische Industrie in Basel), J.R. Geigy AG, and Chemische Fabrik vorm. Sandoz, had formed a Community of Interests dating back to the First World War. French companies had also been concentrated into a dyestuffs union, CMC (Centrale des Matières Colorantes). In addition, these companies of the three coun- tries had already concluded bilateral agreements. In April 1929 they signed a new trilateral agreement, while renewing their bilateral agree- ments. This international cartel held an 80 percent share of total world exports of dyestuffs products. The distribution of its total sales was 71.67 percent for Germany, 19.00 percent for Switzerland, and 9.33 percent for France. Whereas other international dyestuffs cartels had previously been formed on the basis of individual products and expe- rienced a history of formations and collapses, the three-party cartel in 1929 became one of the most powerful international cartels of its time due to its scheme of distributing its total sales and because of its large share of the world market. The three parties used the same letterhead (the logo consisting of the figure "3" in a triangle) for their mutual cor- respondence, symbolizing their close cooperation. Their Japan strategy was no exception to this pattern of cooperation.[29]

Even before the formal establishment of the three-party cartel, a united front of European and American producers had been formed against Japan. In October 1928, a half year after the effectuation of the Saito-Waibel Agreement, most Western producers simultaneously raised the export prices to Japan of all kinds of dyestuffs by a uniform 5 percent. This concerted action was proposed by I.G. Farben and was followed by Swiss and American companies. In fact, Swiss companies were at first opposed to this action, partly for the technical reason that the different export prices of each company's products made it difficult to raise prices uniformly. A more important reason for their initial oppo- sition was that the Swiss companies were afraid that Japanese compa- nies, especially Nihon Senryo, in an attempt to dominate the Japanese market, would not follow the Western companies' price increases. The fear of the Swiss producers became a reality: Japanese firms did not follow suit. As a result, while the market share of the three-party cartel fell, that of the Japanese firms rose. Moreover, Japanese exports, mainly to the Chinese and other East Asian markets, exceeded 1,000 tons.[30]

Other evidence exists for the development of cooperation between European producers in their Japan business. At the beginning of 1929, I.G. Farben had been negotiating through its agent in Japan, Doitsu Senryo, with Nihon Senryo for the conclusion of a comprehensive market agreement. Ciba, the leading Swiss company, learned of this and, at first, feared I.G. Farben's exclusive cooperation with Japanese producers. It called the attention of I.G. Farben and Swiss partner companies to the necessity of cooperation in business with Japan. I.G. Farben admitted that negotiations were taking place with Nihon Senryo, but added that any agreement would not be comprehensive.[31]

Details of the negotiations are unknown. It is, however, certain that although the three-party cartel wanted a comprehensive agreement with the Japanese, on the Japanese side, both Nihon Senryo and Mitsui Mining adopted a strategy of concluding individual or special agreements rather than comprehensive ones with their Western competitors. "When manager Voigt [of I.G. Farben] held occasional discussions with some leading representatives of Nihon Senryo and the Ministry of Commerce and Industry, the Japanese side repeated that they were prepared to negotiate for comprehensive regulations on dyestuff problems with the German side in principle, but that it was still premature to begin these negotiations."[32]

The reason for their attitude is clear. The Japanese dyestuffs industry was still developing. It suffered from a lack of production lines in some principal dyes such as synthetic indigo, as well as from limited areas of export. The Japanese side was therefore afraid that it would tie its own hands if it concluded a comprehensive agreement. It preferred instead to conclude a series of partial agreements and to aim at developing new products while expanding its production capabilities and widening its export areas from China to Indochina and British India. The tactics of I.G. Farben as well as those of the three-party cartel were entirely different from those of the Japanese side. The Western firms wanted to contain the Japanese production capabilities. I.G. Farben's explanation to the Swiss companies mentioned above may, therefore, have concealed its own real aims. What is certain, in any case, is that I.G. Farben endeavored to obtain the consent of the Swiss companies.

These moves toward cooperation were promoted through the formation of the three-party cartel. At the same time, I.G. Farben, leader of the three-party cartel, tried to obtain the agreement of the cartel's other member companies concerning its Japan strategy. For example, I.G. Farben reached an accord with three Swiss firms, its partners in the three-party cartel, not to provide technical assistance to Japan. Jiro Inabata, managing director of Nihon Senryo, made a tour of Europe, visiting Kuhlmann (Compagnie Nationale de Matières Colorantes et Manufactures de Produits Chimiques du Nord réunies Etablissement Kuhlmann) and St. Denis (Société Anonyme des Matières Colorantes et Produits Chimiques de St. Denis) of France, and Durand & Huguenin AG of Switzerland to look into the possibility of securing technical cooperation or assistance, but his efforts were frustrated by I.G. Farben, which informed Inabata through Ciba that no company that was a member of the three-party cartel could give technical assistance to Japan without the consent of the other members.[33]

In February 1932, the British company ICI (Imperial Chemical Industries, Ltd) joined the three-party cartel that had been composed of German, Swiss, and French companies. Thus, a four-party cartel was established. This international cartel dominated almost 90 percent of the world's total exports; sales were distributed according to the following ratio: 65.602 percent for I.G. Farben, 17.391 percent for Swiss I.G., 8.540 percent for French CMC, and 8.467 percent for British ICI. The logo on its common letterhead was changed to the figure "4" in a circle. Around that time, the international dyestuffs cartels had included all the main producers in Europe in their network. The three-party and, later, the four-party cartel had concluded individual or special agreements with dyestuffs producers in Italy, Poland, Czechoslovakia, the Netherlands, and other nations. Their member companies had participated in, and concluded, inter-firm agreements with firms in those nations. Thus, only producers in the United States and Japan remained outside their network in the world market, and only the Asian and South American markets remained as areas of free competition.[34]

The Asian region thus became a focal point as one of the last remaining non-cartelized free markets, with Japanese companies, which were expanding rapidly in this region, considered as outsiders by the international cartels.

I.G. Farben, the leader of the four-party cartel, implemented its Japan strategy with the agreement of the other member companies of the four-party cartel, in the same way as it had done during the life of the three-party cartel. Its strategy for Japanese companies was different from that for other outsider companies, such as those in the United States. There were several reasons for this. First, while the U.S. market absorbed one-fourth of the total global output of dyestuffs and was the largest market for German producers, the Japanese market ranked eighth in importance for Germany. Second, although European companies had undertaken direct investment in the United States (for example, I.G. Farben in General Aniline and Film Corporation and the Swiss companies in Cincinnati Chemical Works, Inc.), they had no direct investment in the manufacturing sector in Japan.[35] Third, the governments of Japan and the United States differed in their attitudes toward international and domestic cartels: the American situation was prohibitive, while the Japanese one was tolerant or even promotive.

The strategy of the international cartels toward one influential outsider, L.B. Holliday and Company, in the British market where ICI was dominant, gives us some basis for another comparison. Holliday held a 25-percent share of British exports. Even with the depreciation of the pound sterling after September 1931, the firm did not raise its prices, but pegged them in order to increase its market share. This price policy greatly resembled that of Japanese dyestuffs producers in 1928. Responding to this, I.G. Farben and ICI took the ingenious measure of cutting prices, on the one hand, and stopping the supply of intermediate chemicals to Holliday, on the other. This approach was also similar to that of I.G. Farben toward Japan. In contrast to I.G. Farben's situation in Japan, however, in Britain I.G. Farben had an alternative to direct investment. In fact, I.G. Farben drew up a plan to purchase Holliday in league with ICI, and, when that failed, it established a joint venture with ICI to compete with Holliday.[36]

During this time, the exports of European firms to Japan were showing a downward trend. I.G. Farben's exports to Japan fell sharply from 1,138 tons in 1932 to 630 tons in 1933, due mainly to the fall of the yen following the re-imposition of a ban on the export of gold in December 1931. Moreover, the amendment of import tariffs in May 1932 added 35 percent to the dyestuffs tariff.[37] Meanwhile, however, Waibel of I.G. Farben reported in February 1932 that the company still enjoyed steady sales in Japan due to its cooperation with American companies as well as its emphasis on higher-quality products. He also made the optimistic observation that the company could improve its relations with Japanese companies and that it could, for the time being, minimize the negative effects of the depreciating yen through an appropriate response.[38] Reality, however, later showed such optimism to be wrongly placed. The Japanese side observed that it "soon became impossible" to import those items listed in the Saito-Waibel Agreement, and that the agreement "appeared to have become merely nominal."[39]

The falling yen not only made it more difficult for I.G. Farben and other members of the four-party cartel to export to the Japanese market, it also threatened the companies with Japanese competition in the Chinese and other Asian markets. Subsequently, the Japanese dyestuffs industry, protected by the depreciation of the yen and other measures, enjoyed a second boom period, peaking in 1939. Japanese output capacity increased further, and Japan held a 3.2-percent share of total world sales in 1938. Its share of the Asian market was even higher, reaching 10.5 percent in 1938. According to an estimate made by I.G. Farben, in the same year, Nihon Senryo had a 60 percent share of the domestic market; Mitsui Mining, 20 percent; Nihon Tar Kogyo (Japan Tar Industries, Ltd, later renamed Nihon Chemical Industries, then Mitsubishi Chemical Industries), 10 percent; and other firms 10 percent.[40]

Conclusion of special market agreements

Although I.G. Farben targeted Japanese firms as a group, it concentrated on two leading companies that had the potential to develop new products. One was Nihon Senryo, which was putting its efforts into the development of a broad range of products centering on naphthol dyestuffs. The other was Mitsui Mining, which was developing alizarin dyestuffs, azo dyestuffs, and indanthrene dyestuffs with the express purpose of developing synthetic indigo. Thus, the international cartel and its member companies were forced to find new ways to deal with a challenging situation. One way was by intensifying their efforts to conclude a series of bilateral agreements with individual Japanese firms, and with the Japanese industry as a whole, as a means of securing their outlets.

I.G. Farben's response was to pursue a strategy devised in the 1920s that aimed at concluding bilateral agreements with Japanese industries. With the advance of Japanese products, which were capturing ever-greater shares of the market, it was becoming increasingly difficult to keep the market open for free competition among members of the international cartel. On the other hand, the international cartel had grown stronger, making it possible for I.G. Farben to carry out negotiations with the Japanese to its own advantage through collaboration with its allies.

The first individual, or special, market agreement concluded between I.G. Farben and Nihon Senryo was that regarding naphthol dyestuffs. I.G. Farben had already recognized the necessity of some kind of cooperation with Nihon Senryo on naphthol dyestuffs in the summer of 1927.[41] At the beginning of 1931, Nihon Senryo put onto the market Blue Salt-NSV to compete directly with I.G. Farben's Variamine Blue-B, while at the same time putting in an application for a process patent in Japan. I.G. Farben immediately voiced a protest over this. The two sides entered into a patent dispute. In the end, I.G. Farben, recognizing the fact that a patent dispute would take a long time to resolve in Japan, chose to compromise in order to avoid a renewed price war. Thus, in March 1931, the so-called Japan Variamine Blue Agreement with Nihon Senryo was tentatively concluded.[42]

Under the agreement, Nihon Senryo agreed to honor the patents of I.G. Farben in Japan (including Korea and Formosa), to pay license fees to I.G. Farben, and not to export identical products to the Asian market outside China. In exchange, I.G. Farben recognized the right of Nihon Senryo to sell Blue Salt-NSV in the Japanese market. Moreover, an accord was reached on sales quotas for the Japanese market; for Variamine Blue-B of I.G. Farben (or Blue Salt-NSV of Nihon Senryo), I.G. Farben was allotted a 68 percent share and Nihon Senryo, 32 percent, and for Naphthol-AS of I.G. Farben and the equivalent Naphthoid-AS of Nihon Senryo, which were dyeing assistants, I.G. Farben was allotted a 32 percent share and Nihon Senryo, 68 percent. At the same time, the sales prices for the Chinese market were to be the same.[43]

The agreement in March 1931 was a tentative one, and later a formal agreement was signed. It was concluded by I.G. Farben without any previous discussion within the three-party cartel. Three Swiss firms, partners in the three-party cartel, at first criticized I.G. Farben, saying that it should have requested their prior consent and that it made excessive concessions to the Japanese side, but in the end, they consented to the formal agreement.[44] This agreement was renewed in March 1935 and later automatically extended several times, until it expired in 1941.[45]

I.G. Farben also concluded the so-called Japan Astraphloxine Agreement, again with Nihon Senryo, in February 1934. The main points of this ran parallel to the Variamine Blue Agreement. In return for relinquishing exports, Nihon Senryo got a 50 percent share of the Japanese market and I.G. Farben, the remaining 50 percent. Sales prices were to be the same. This agreement was also renewed and lasted until the end of 1939.[46]

I.G. Farben concluded the two agreements independently. This time, however, it obtained the consent of its partners in the international cartel. Thus, those individual or special agreements, on individual items as well as by individual companies, represented the means by which the international cartel could include the Japanese outsiders in their network.

It was also I.G. Farben that led the international cartel in negotiations with Mitsui Mining, the other leading dye producer in Japan. The first agreement covered sulphur black dye, for which, by 1928, Japan had almost attained self-sufficiency. Among producers, Miike Dyestuff Works of Mitsui Mining was the leader, holding a 70-percent share of the market. For Mitsui Mining, too, sulphur dye was the most important item at that time.[47] In April 1931, the three-party cartel concluded an agreement regarding the sales and prices of exports to China with a leading trading company, Mitsui Bussan Kabushiki Kaisha (Mitsui & Co., Ltd), as Mitsui Mining's representative. British ICI and two leading American firms, National Aniline and Chemical Co. (Nacco) and E. I. Du Pont de Nemours and Company, were also drawn into this agreement. Mitsui Mining was awarded a 17.5 percent share of exports to the Chinese market.[48] When the agreement expired at the end of 1933, it collapsed because of Mitsui Mining's withdrawal, while the agreement among the six parties (the three-party cartel, ICI, Nacco, and Du Pont) was extended.

After the agreement of the six parties with Mitsui collapsed, I.G. Farben began to reconstruct the agreement.[49] On the one hand, it had to readjust its relations with Du Pont, which was planning direct investment in China together with ICI and was opposed to an automatic extension of the six-party agreement. On the other hand, it had to negotiate not only with Mitsui Mining, but also with all other Japanese producers of sulphur black, following the collapse in March 1934 of a Japanese domestic cartel that had been formed in October 1931. The competition among Japanese producers became keener than before, and their response to I.G. Farben's proposal became disunited. Mitsui Mining, the leading company in this field in Japan, failed to show any interest in an agreement. Nihon Senryo was opposed to any restrictions on exports, although it agreed to cooperation in principle. Some other producers were in favor of an agreement.[50] In the end, a new agreement was not concluded, partly because of Du Pont's disturbing behavior, and mainly because the position of the many competing Japanese producers was not united.

Meanwhile the Japanese producers of sulphur black were keen to export to China, Manchuria, and Dutch Indochina. Some firms even directly invested in China. This represented a new threat for European exports to China.[51]

Apart from the agreement on sulphur black dye, in October 1931 I.G. Farben concluded an agreement with Mitsui Bussan, which was to be the sole representative of Mitsui Mining, with regard to alizarin blue. This agreement concerned the division of the Japanese market; at first this was apportioned at a ratio of 60 percent to I.G. Farben and 40 percent to Mitsui. The agreement was, however, repeatedly revised until its termination in 1940, when market shares were in fact reversed to 40 percent for I.G. Farben and 60 percent for Mitsui.[52]

Mitsui indigo agreement

Among the market agreements that I.G. Farben, the three-party cartel, and the four-party cartel concluded with the Japanese producers, the agreement with Mitsui Mining on synthetic indigo was the most important.

In 1925, Japanese imports of such dyestuffs amounted to 974 tons or 2.62 million yen (approximately 1.3 million U.S. dollars), which accounted for 31.8 percent in volume or 35.9 percent in value of the Japanese total imports of dyestuffs. Synthetic indigo ranked second in importance after aniline. I.G. Farben was dominant in the export of synthetic indigo to Japan with a 72.7-percent share, although Swiss, French, and American producers had already succeeded in commercializing the product after the First World War. For I.G. Farben, too, synthetic indigo was its second principal export item to Japan after aniline.[53]

The history of Mitsui Mining's attempts to synthesize indigo dates from the First World War. The company was unable to introduce the production technology from Germany and other nations and had to develop the production process by itself. In April 1926, after several years of trial and error, the company finally managed to achieve its aim of indigo production, but only within the laboratory. Therefore, it was natural that the Saito-Waibel Agreement of August 1926 did not list synthetic indigo as one of the items whose export was to be voluntarily restricted by I.G. Farben. Development and production of the dye-stuffs were not subsidized until October 1929, when Mitsui Mining finally managed to obtain a government subsidy. Construction of a new factory began in February 1931, being completed at the beginning of 1932. The factory's output finally found its way into the market in the latter half of 1932. By 1933, Mitsui Mining became the largest supplier of indigo in the Japanese market, and it began to export to China.[54]

Meanwhile leading European and American producers of indigo were expanding their network of oligopolistic agreements in the Asian market. Two leading American companies, Nacco and Du Pont, which had embarked in rapid succession on ventures of indigo exports to the Far East, strengthened their efforts. At the beginning of 1931, the three-party cartel and ICI concluded an agreement with these two American companies, concerning the sales ratio and prices of indigo and other products in the Chinese market. This agreement was called the China Six-Party Dyestuffs Agreement. Later the six parties added Aziende Colori Nazionali Affini of Italy and Dow Chemical Co. of the United States to the agreement.[55]

On the basis of these agreements concerning the Asian market, the six parties concluded an agreement regarding indigo with Mitsui Bus-san, the representative of Mitsui Mining, in February 1934. This con-cerned cooperation over the sales price and market share within the Japanese market, which was to be 25 percent for the six parties and 75 percent for Mitsui Mining. This was a temporary agreement that remained valid until July 1934.[56]

Soon after, negotiations were begun for the conclusion of a formal agreement. The biggest issue of contention was the regulations govern-ing Japanese exports to China, especially the decision on the Japanese quota for the Chinese market. I.G. Farben perceived that these negotia-tions offered a unique opportunity to protect the Chinese market from a recurrence in the fall of product prices. It thus prevailed upon its cartel partners with the argument that, should the agreement be imper-fectly concluded, Mitsui Mining would undoubtedly be able to exert a fairly strong influence on the price levels of not only the Japanese, Chinese, and Manchurian markets, but others as well. Because I.G. Farben held the largest share in the Asian market, which it wanted to keep, it took the initiative in these discussions with the other partners, in order to try and maintain the *status quo*.[57]

Hermann Waibel of I.G. Farben prepared a draft proposal, to which the other members of the four-party cartel, as well as Nacco and Du Pont, gave their consent. Subsequently, Waibel energetically negotiated with Mitsui Mining. During the negotiations, he had to revise his original draft at least twice in order to get Mitsui's consent. Finally, in May 1935, one year after the lapse of the tentative agreement, a settlement was reached in the negotiations in line with the latest of Waibel's revised points.[58]

The formal agreement, which I.G. Farben called the Mitsui Indigo Agreement, stipulated that Mitsui export its products only to China (including Manchuria, Hong Kong, and Dalian) and held the Japanese exports of 20 percent-purity indigo to China at a three-year total of 96,300 piculs. As compensation for this, the six parties were limited in their exports to Japan. The distribution of the Japanese market, including Korea and Formosa, was 85 percent for Mitsui and 15 percent for the six parties. The prices for the Japanese and Chinese markets were set at the same time.[59]

The formal Mitsui Indigo Agreement was to expire at the end of 1937. Mitsui Mining was fully satisfied with its performance within the Japanese and Chinese markets and, therefore, with the agreement as it stood. As it did not want to have to accept new restrictions, which would inevitably be imposed by the uncertainties of the prevailing political climate, in the Far East due to the outbreak of the Sino-Japanese War in July of the same year, it welcomed the agreement's extension. Its foreign competitors also agreed to extend the agreement. The agreement was therefore extended unchanged until the end of June 1938.[60]

Upon the agreement's expiry, the member companies of the international cartel had in mind a further extension. Mitsui Mining agreed, but it made requests for the abolition of, or at least a change in, the restrictions on the areas of export, and for the carrying over of the unused quota amount for 1937 to the next year. The international cartel reexamined what course it should take in the negotiations. The result was that it decided to compromise regarding the requests from the Mitsui side, that is, to change the existing stance limiting Mitsui Mining's exports to China and Manchuria, and to allow exports of indigo to Dutch and British Indochina, with a ceiling. I.G. Farben, as the representative of the four-party cartel, began negotiations with Mitsui Mining on the basis of the decision, while at the same time obtaining the agreement of the two American indigo producers, Nacco and Du Pont. Even with the willingness of the international cartel to compromise, however, the negotiations proved tough and lengthy, especially because Mitsui

Mining had, meanwhile, gone so far as to demand the total abandonment of the quota system. Moreover, when the Japanese side eventually agreed to the continuation of the quota system, they thrust a request before the international cartel, asking to be allowed to carry out exports to some areas on a scale far exceeding the expectations of the cartel.[61]

The reason it took so long to reach a conclusion was not only Mitsui Mining's requests, however, but also the fact that opinions were divided within the cartel regarding the demands made. A confrontation arose between I.G. Farben, on the one hand, and the Swiss, French, and British firms, on the other. The former faction was in favor of making concessions to Japan, while the latter wanted to take a tough stance.[62]

In the end, the international cartel made large-scale concessions to the Japanese side, approving Japanese exports not only to China and Manchuria, but also to Dutch and British Indochina, the Philippines, Thailand, the Straits Settlements, Iran, Egypt, Belgium, and Mexico. Moreover, an agreement was reached in April 1939 on the removal of quotas from the Japanese market.[63] This agreement was extended until the end of 1940, but the war in Europe began before it had expired, and thus ICI broke the agreement.[64]

Meanwhile, Mitsui Mining had increased its production to enable it to dominate the Japanese market and, moreover, to advance into the Asian market throughout the latter half of the 1930s. At the same time, the international cartel sought to maintain a foothold in the Asian market by cooperating with American firms as well as by making concessions to Mitsui Mining. I.G. Farben showed itself more willing than the other cartel member firms to cooperate, and the other firms followed I.G. Farben's lead while secretly opposing its stance. In the end, the international cartel as a whole made concessions to Mitsui Mining.

Thus, there was no confrontation great enough to cause a collapse of the cartel until September 1939, when the Second World War broke out. In other words, despite the increased tensions, which reflected international political conflicts, the four-party cartel succeeded in coordinating both the economic interests of the members and its relations with the American companies. Thus, on the face of it, the attempts to include the Japanese developer of indigo, Mitsui Mining, in the sphere of influence of the international cartel succeeded. The real situation, however, was that the international cartel was forced into an immediate backdown when faced with Mitsui Mining's demands.

Few market agreements on dyestuffs were dissolved before the outbreak of the Second World War. The 1931 agreement between I.G.

Farben and Mitsui Mining on the export of sulphur black to China was a rare case. Most international dyestuffs cartels did not weaken until the outbreak of the war, and most achieved great success in regulating the volume and prices of exports in the world market.[65] The Mitsui Indigo Agreement between Mitsui Mining and the six parties was one such representative case. The success, however, was achieved only through a series of concessions by the international cartel to Japanese firms.

Based on examination of the strategy employed by international cartels *vis-à-vis* the Japanese market, the following conclusions can be made. First, the international dyestuffs cartels, including the three-party and four-party cartels, pursued a comprehensive agreement with the Japanese producers. The leader of the international cartels, I.G. Farben, was more willing to compromise with the Japanese than were the other member companies, which followed the lead of I.G. Farben with some criticism and hesitation. Second, the Japanese side wanted a series of individual or special agreements in order to keep its hands free in developing new products such as naphthol dyestuffs and indigo. Third, through negotiations, the international cartels or their member companies, especially I.G. Farben, concluded a series of individual or special agreements with individual Japanese firms as well as with the Japanese dyestuffs industry as a whole. The Japanese firms, who were the toughest competitors among firms outside the cartels, became partially drawn into the international cartels. Fourth, however, the Japanese firms proved to be troublesome members, so much so that I.G. Farben and the other cartel members were forced to make successive concessions. Fifth, although the international cartels succeeded in including the Japanese firms in their networks, they failed to restrain the ambitions and capabilities of the Japanese firms in developing new products. Finally, the Japanese firms, led by Mitsui Mining and Nihon Senryo, succeeded in introducing and exploiting European and American technologies as well as management skills, concluding a series of special or individual agreements with the international cartels led by I.G. Farben.

LICENSING STRATEGY:
SYNTHETIC AMMONIA AND SYNTHETIC OIL

Licensing of the Haber-Bosch process

The worldwide diffusion of the Haber-Bosch process.[66] was largely occasioned by the requisition by the allied countries belligerent to Germany during the First World War of the patented process. Following this, development of similar manufacturing methods took place in a number of countries, including France, Italy, and the United States.[67] Japan was no exception to the process of global diffusion of the Haber-Bosch process. After the introduction of the Casale process in 1923 by Nippon Chisso Hiryo (Japan Nitrogenous Fertilizer), a succession of processes for ammonia synthesis, including the Claude, Fauser, Mont Cenis (Uhde), and NEC processes, were introduced into Japan. Development and commercialization of the Tokyo Industrial Institute process was carried out in Japan. Regarding this situation, one cannot help but feel a strong sense of agreement with the following remark made by the I.G. engineer stationed in Japan: "The Japanese mentality is always in quest of something new, and it seems to matter little whether the 'new' thing is really superior to the older one or not."[68] The development of the Japanese ammonium sulphate industry in the 1920s was supported technologically by this energetic introduction of technology

The patent for the Haber-Bosch process was confiscated by the Japanese government during the First World War, and the exclusive right to use the patent was sold to Toyo Chisso Kumiai (Oriental Nitrogen Association), established by the major zaibatsu groups. No Japanese chemical firms, even among the zaibatsu groups, had knowledge of how to put this process to commercial use, however. As soon as the war was over, therefore, some companies contacted BASF in the hope of acquiring the necessary expertise. BASF, however, demanded an outrageous fee of 68 million yen, and the Japanese firms had to give up the idea of acquiring the technology from BASF. Indeed, by quoting a prohibitively high fee, BASF made it known that it had no intention of offering licensing or technical cooperation. It should be kept in mind that the term "licensing" here is used in a broad sense, because BASF's patent was still under confiscation by the Japanese government when this episode took place.[69]

The reason why only the Haber-Bosch process had not been introduced, in contrast to the numerous other processes for ammonia synthesis, is to be found, above all, through an analysis of I.G. Farben's strategy. I.G. Farben did its utmost to refrain from employing the alternative strategies of licensing or direct investment where expansion of exports was at all possible. This position was not only adopted *vis-à-vis* Japan but was employed worldwide.

In the 1920s, in the field of nitrogenous fertilizer, the Japanese market still had some room to absorb imports, despite the rapid growth of domestic production. As shown in Figure 2.1, nitrogenous fertilizer became, by 1929, Germany's single most important chemical exported to Japan, far surpassing dyestuffs and other products. Partly because Japan was designated by the international fertilizer cartel as a market for open competition, foreign companies competed fiercely against each other in the late 1920s for larger shares of the Japanese market, giving rise to a phenomenon called "gaian dumping" ("gaian" meaning foreign ammonium sulphate). A second equipment investment boom in the ammonium sulphate industry in Japan, continuing from the first one of the early 1920s, was experienced in the period from the end of the 1920s to the early 1930s. This exactly coincided with a period of worsening global overproduction as the worldwide depression deepened. For I.G. Farben, the equipment investment boom in the Japanese ammonium sulphate industry meant the loss of the Japanese market and posed a threat to the Chinese market.

It was against this backdrop that in December 1930 I.G. Farben, acting on behalf of the international nitrogen cartel (Convention Internationale de l'Azote, or CIA) established with firms in continental Europe, Britain, and Chile, consulted with the Japanese fertilizer industry and worked out a draft agreement called the Fujiwara-Bosch Draft Agreement, which was meant to put an end to the heated price competition. It called upon the Japanese industry to refrain entirely from exporting its nitrogenous fertilizer and called upon the foreign industries to curtail their exports to Japan in exchange for this, but the agreement miscarried because of strong domestic opposition in Japan as well as the collapse of the CIA. Several months later, in April 1931, a Tentative Agreement on Domestic and Foreign Ammonium Sulphate was signed, but this, too, failed to come into effect.[70]

The CIA was reestablished in July 1932. In March 1934, the CIA succeeded in concluding an Overall Ammonium Sulphate Agreement with the Japanese nitrogenous fertilizer industry through I.G. Farben. This was followed by the signing of the second agreement in February 1935 and a third agreement in November 1935.[71]

I.G. Farben was successful in limiting Japanese exports to China through these agreements but, in return, was forced to limit its own exports to Japan and China. Consequently, as an alternative to exports, I.G. Farben began to consider licensing. Moreover, the vigorous growth of the Japanese market for ammonium sulphate in the early 1930s had resulted in a succession of new Japanese entrants and expansion plans by existing competitors aimed at ensuring a share of the high profit margins. A number of these firms sounded out I.G. Farben as to the possibility of the introduction of the Haber-Bosch process.

Although the Japanese fertilizer producers had already been using the Casale process and the Claude process, they were eager to introduce I.G. Farben's Haber-Bosch process. This zeal to introduce the process must have derived, at least partly, not only from the Japanese curiosity and inquisitiveness mentioned above, but also from its having been rated by Japanese specialists to be the best. I.G. Farben was offered extremely favorable conditions because of the strong desire for introduction, and the high potential for plant exports was also attractive. This situation prompted a change in I.G. Farben's strategy The patent for the Haber-Bosch process had expired by then, so the arrangements made between I.G. Farben and Japanese fertilizer manufacturers were strictly speaking for technological guidance, but in a broad sense they might be regarded as licensing arrangements.

At this time, I.G. Farben was considering a change in strategy not only as regards Japan, but also for Finland, Egypt, and Spain. It was also considering a plan for direct investment in Japan via a joint venture to be set up with the Mitsubishi zaibatsu. I.G. Farben's choice of licensing seems quite natural, however, in view of the rapid development of the Japanese market.

As can be seen from Table 2.2, five Japanese firms were involved in the importing of the Haber-Bosch technology at this time. They were Taki Fertilizer Works, Yahagi Kogyo, Nippon Tar Kogyo, Dai Nippon Tokkyo Hiryo, and Dai Nippon Seito. Of these, only Dai Nippon Seito and Taki Fertilizer Works were listed among the 200 largest firms for 1930, with Dai Nippon Seito being ranked in eighth position. Nippon Tar Kogyo had not yet been established in 1930.[72]

The case of Taki Fertilizer Works was, in fact, among the world's first cases of actual licensing of the Haber-Bosch process, following only the politically forced licensing by BASF to a French firm in Toulouse during the chaotic post-war years and the licensing in 1927 by I.G. Farben to the Norwegian subsidiary Norsk Hydro-Elektrisk Kvaelstof AS.[73]

In 1935, Taki Fertilizer was a phosphate fertilizer manufacturer with a paid-up capital of 3.5 million yen (approximately one million U.S. dollars); it had approximately 800 employees in 1938.[74] It was ranked 159th among the 200 largest Japanese firms in 1930 as regards assets.[75] Although not a small firm, it could not be regarded as representative of the large-sized firms of this period. Also, the calcium superphosphate sector was an area of the chemical industry that was not

Table 2.2 Introduction of the Haber-Bosch process in Japan

Company	Later name	Location	Location	Contract signed	Oper. start	Scale (amm sulphate tons/year)	Hydrogen production method	Payment (yen)
Taki Seihisho	Sumitomo Precision Chemicals	Befu, Hyogo Prefecture Prefecture		1935	1938	50,000	Aqueous	2,579,000
Yahagi Kogyo	Toa Gosei Kagaku Kogyo	Nagoya, Aichi Prefecture	Mitsubi-shi Shoji	1935	1938	50,000	Winkler	2,390,000
Nippon Tar Kogyo	Mitsubi-shi Kasei Kogyo	Kurosaki Fukuoka Pref.	Mitsubi-shi Shoji	1936	1939	80,000	Winkler	4,109,395
Dai Nippon	Nitto Kagaku	Yokohama, Kanagawa Pref.	Mitsubi-shi Shoji	1937	1939	50,000	Aqueous	unknown
Tokkyo	Kogyo							
Hiryo Dai Nippon Seito	Nitto Kagaku Kogyo	Hachinohe, Aomori Pref.	Mitsubi-shi Shoji	1937	1940	50,000	Aqueous	unknown

Source: Mainly from records in the BASFA.

especially sophisticated. The very fact that such a firm should enter into a contract at this early date for technology transfer with I.G. Farben, the world's largest chemical firm at the time, and that it should undertake the challenge presented by the high technical standards of ammonia synthesis, is of considerable interest.

An analysis of these five cases, covering the steps involved from the initial approaches, to the signing of technology transfer agreements, up to start of operations, while showing a number of differences in individual cases, reveals several more or less common points.[76] For example, one common point evident is the positive effort made on the Japanese side for obtaining the contract. Moreover, the Japanese firms competed with each other in efforts to achieve contracts. This would seem to be a kind of bandwagon effect. A second point was that the question of plant supply became the main point of dispute in negotiations. I.G. Farben wanted to ensure a commission in the form of the export of German equipment, but Japanese firms desired supply to be carried out domestically wherever possible. The actual contract drawn up, however, and this is the third common point, stated that equipment supply was to be largely from Germany. Furthermore, responsibility for activities, from planning, equipment installation and test runs, on to operations, was to be taken by I.G. Farben engineers and foremen dispatched to the site. Fourth, in many cases, technical problems developed, and these gave rise to disputes between I.G. Farben and the Japanese parties. These disputes were largely caused by the reluctance of the Japanese parties to entrust operations completely to I.G. Farben, including those of a technological nature, and the desire of the Japanese to participate actively. It is fair to highlight the difference between this arrangement and the full turnkey basis generally adopted today in technology transfer to developing countries. Finally, despite the various problems, a number of Japanese firms went on to draw up expansion plans based on a greater scale of equipment.

Licensing of the I.G. Process for synthetic oil

By the mid-1930s, I.G. Farben was taking steps to license its synthetic oil production process and to export the necessary equipment to foreign customers.[77]

In 1923, BASF had decided to use the Bergius hydrogenation process to try to produce large quantities of synthetic fuel oil. I.G. Farben was formally established in December 1925, and six months later it began construction of a facility that could produce 100,000 tons of synthetic oil using the I.G. process, itself a refinement of the Bergius process. In April 1927, the firm began operating high-pressure reaction chambers. Thereafter, technical problems prevented I.G. Farben from achieving any sort of economies of scale; this fact, and the fact that the German economy was obviously worsening, led a commission report presented at the firm's board of directors in June 1929 to call for a temporary halt to synthetic oil production. Production did continue, but I.G. Farben was not able to solve its problems until December 1933, when the firm reached an agreement with the Nazi government to supply it with synthetic oil, and in so doing secured both a price and a market for its product.

Over time, however, I.G. Farben's ties with the Nazi government became more a burden than a blessing, largely because of its increased payment and the emergence of competing operations. At this point, the firm began to move uncertainly in several directions. One of these was the attempt to license its I.G. production process and profit from the resulting licensing fees; another was to invest in firms that had moved into synthetic oil production, expecting to receive a substantial dividend income; and a third was the adoption, as part of the firm's participation in the second Four-Year Plan in October 1936, of a policy of plant expansion and product diversification.[78]

I.G. Farben's initial attempts to market its I.G. process were thus made in the mid-1930s, about the same time it began selling its expertise in the Haber-Bosch process, and at a time when synthetic oil production in Japan was very much in its infancy.

The Japanese government did not begin to formulate a synthetic oil production policy until after the Manchurian Incident in September 1931, when it moved from simply encouraging research into coal liquefaction technologies to promoting large-scale production projects in this area.[79] Following Japan's withdrawal from the London Disarmament Conference in January 1936, the government issued a set of guidelines for fuel production in July of the same year. The guidelines attempted to foster the large-scale development of alternative fuels; they cited the need for legislation to this end and for the subsidization of firms engaged in coal liquefaction, synthetic gasoline research, or low-temperature carbonization.[80]

The following year, the Ministry of Commerce and Industry formulated its own plans to promote synthetic fuel production. The plans called for an annual production level of 2 million kiloliters to be achieved within seven years. The figure included production by low-temperature carbonization, which, if achieved, would represent a self-sufficiency rate of 50 percent. The ministry estimated that achieving this goal would require a capital expenditure of about 750 million yen. It also expected that coal liquefaction would account for half the synthetic fuel produced. The legal support for this endeavor was given in August 1937 with the issuance of the Synthetic Fuel Production Law and a law establishing the Imperial Fuel Industry Co., Ltd., both of which went into effect in January 1938.[81] In May 1937, the Ministry of Commerce and Industry had set up its own Fuel Bureau, one of the express functions of which was to promote synthetic fuel production. Managers for the bureau were commissioned naval and army officers, and synthetic fuel production was put under the direction of a naval officer.[82] War with China began two months after the bureau was established.

The aforementioned laws were milestones in the development of government policy with regard to synthetic fuel production. The Synthetic Fuel Production Law established procedures for licensing production in this area. Licenses could only be issued to companies where a majority of stockholders, executive positions, capital, and voting positions were held by Japanese nationals or Japanese corporations. The law also required that licensed companies annually produce at least 10,000 kiloliters of synthetic fuel. For these companies, the law made provisions for the expropriation of land, allowed the companies exemption from taxes, and gave them startup money, among other measures, in addition to setting prices for their products and guaranteeing them a market.[83] Imperial Fuel Industry itself was to be a national enterprise, half the capital being government-owned. The government guaranteed it special privileges as well as the requisite technical expertise and also planned to supply fully half the funds the company was expected to need over the seven years to follow.

In February 1936, Ruhrchemie AG contracted to license its Fischer-Tropsch synthetic fuel process to Mitsui Bussan.[84] By this time, considerable work was already being done in Japan on developing processes of hydrogenation, for which the I.G. process was a prototype. Research as well as trial production of coal hydrogenation was being carried out at thirty locations, including the South Manchurian Railway's Central Research Institute, the Ministry of Commerce and Industry's Fuel Institute, the Institute of Physical and Chemical Research, and Mitsubishi Mining's Research Institute. Coal hydrogenation was clearly the major focus of research during this time.[85] Within I.G. Farben itself, due note of all this activity was made, and the firm's interest in Japan increased accordingly.[86]

Table 2.3 Enquiries from Japan for which permissions to export were not
granted (as of 25 January 1941)

Enquiry year	Enquirer or intermediary	Subject item	No. of pipes	Total amount (reichsmark)
1937	Mitsubishi Shoji	Boiler drum	1	40,000
	"	"	3	120,000
	"	"	3	140,000
	"	"	3	96,000
	"	"	1	17,000
	Okura Shoji	"	4	150,000
1938	Mitsubishi Shoji	"	1	33,540
	Manchurian Fuel Liquefaction	Reaction pipe	24	10,000,000
	Japanese Navy	"	30	8,000,000
	Ogura Oil	"	10	800,000
	Toho Gas	"	5	750,000
1939	Uhde	Reaction vessel	1	61,250
	Sumitomo Chemical	Conversion plant	1	42,360
	I.G. Farben	High-pressure reaction pipe	6	444,600
	Uhde	Reaction vessel	1	89,000
	Nissho	High-pressure reaction pipe	8	3,000,000

Enquiry year	Enquirer or intermediary	Subject item	No. of pipes	Total amount (reichsmark)
	"	"	9	144,000
	"	"	6	132,500
	"	"	6	174,510
	"	"	9	198,150
	Takata Shokai	Reaction vessel	3	112,500
1940–42	Mitsubishi Shoji	Boiler drum	4	196,000
	"	Reaction vessel	22	1,920,700
	Japan Nitrogenous	High-pressure	6	2,722,000
	Fertilizer	reaction pipe		
	"	"	12	4,020,222
	Lemke	"	4	414,200
	"	Nitrogen reaction pipe	12	1,242,600

Sources: Aufstellung über abgelehnte Auslandsgeschäfte; Neue Auslandsprojekte, die vorsichtlich auch in vollem Umfange abgelehnt werden müssen, HA (Historisches Archiv) Krupp, WA 51 /v 1071. Also similar tables that included figures for domestic enquiries (i.e. Aufstellung der Anfragen auf geschmiedete Druckbehälter am 24 Jan 1941, HA Krupp, WA 51 / v 1071 and Anfragen auf Hohlkörpern am 27 Jul 1938, HA Krupp, WA 51 / v) were used.

From the start, there was almost no thought on I.G. Farben's part concerning direct investment in Japan, either in the form of a joint venture or as an exclusive operation. I.G. Farben had had no experience in actual materials production in the Far East and was undoubtedly wary of the political and economic hazards such an undertaking might involve. Even in Eastern Europe, the firm invested almost nothing through 1939. Its interest, therefore, was mainly in licensing its production process and selling the equipment needed for the process. At least this was the case as of the middle 1930s.

As shown in Table 2.3, I.G. Farben expended a good deal of effort in trying to license its production processes and export its equipment to Japan, but in the end this effort was unsuccessful. Examination of the steps I.G. Farben undertook, and consideration of the firm's own analysis of the situation,[87] makes it possible to ascertain some of the reasons for the lack of success. I.G. Farben faced several problems: the lack of cooperation from International Hydrogenation Engineering and Chemical Co. (IHEC), an international joint venture that held patent rights to all hydrogenation processes; the inflexible nature of the firm's own negotiating tactics; and the opposition of the Japanese navy.

IHEC certainly served as a check on I.G. Farben's freedom of action. This was most apparent in the negotiations with South Manchurian Railway. IHEC, however, thereafter became more interested in licensing Japanese firms but continued to differ with I.G. Farben on how licenses should be given. This disagreement had the effect of increasing the cost of licenses, although it did not make their acquisition or sale impossible. Similarly, IHEC took a cautious approach in shipping equipment to Japanese customers, noting that British and American steel producers would stop shipping to Japan if they lacked the support of the major oil companies, specifically Royal Dutch Shell and Standard Oil Company (NJ).[88] In both of these areas, then, IHEC affected I.G. Farben's operations. On the other hand, IHEC had no influence on German equipment manufacturers, and whatever checks IHEC applied to I.G. Farben, at least as of the middle of 1939, it had not completely circumscribed the firm's ability to function in Japan.

The terms I.G. Farben offered to customers in Japan were quite prohibitive. To Mitsubishi Mining, for example, it presented a bid for equipment of almost 22 million yen, which was much more than Mitsubishi Coal Liquefaction's share capital of 20 million yen. To make the situation worse, Japan's foreign currency reserves began to decline quite rapidly after 1937. In fact, government officials only allowed Ogura Oil enough access to foreign currency to cover part of its project. Under the circumstances, I.G. Farben's high bids must have dampened the enthusiasm of potential clients. But they were not high enough to eliminate interest altogether. This is clear, for example, in the reminiscences of Ogura Oil's top manager, Nobuhei Nakahara.[89] In addition, I.G. Farben was fully prepared to help finance the operations of clients such as the North China Project and Nissan Chemical.

Another factor affecting I.G. Farben's fortunes in Japan was the opposition of the Japanese navy, which had already done some research into hydrogenation processes. H. Ahrens' Hermann Bosch had perceived early on that by acquiescing in the purchase of expertise in I.G. Farben's process, the navy would in effect be admitting its own failure in this area.[90] In fact, the navy's opposition doomed Ogura Oil's plans, as well as those of the army. The Synthetic Fuel Production Law had guaranteed prices and markets for producers. But since this meant that the government would be the major consumer of the product, the guarantee was meaningless even if synthetic fuel producers were successful, as long as the navy, which accounted for the greatest source of demand, remained opposed. The navy was even able to influence the companies in which Imperial Fuel Industry invested and to which it loaned the funds at its disposal. Thus, the navy decisively affected the ability of Ogura Oil and others to obtain funding and outlets for their products. In this context, then, the passage of 1938 laws designed to encourage synthetic fuel production actually had the effect of reducing the chances for the success of firms like I.G. Farben. Through the middle of 1939, it was the opposition of the Japanese navy, much more than IHEC's position or the terms that could be offered to clients, that had the greatest adverse effect on I.G. Farben's fortunes in Japan.

CONCLUSION

The First World War gave rise to a modern chemical industry in Japan. In the post-war period, the Japanese government adopted a policy of selective, or limited, protectionism to nurture this infant industry. Given the growing importance of the Japanese market, I.G. Farben advanced actively into the market. It reestablished its sales outlets in Japan and then undertook their reorganization, which resulted in the establishment in 1924 of Doitsu Senryo as the sole agent of the German dyestuffs industry in Japan

During the 1920s, I.G. Farben refused to agree to Japanese companies' requests for licensing arrangements, and its strategy toward Japan was basically formed around product export. In pursuing this strategy, I.G. Farben tried to conclude several bilateral agreements. The only agreement concluded during the decade was the Saito-Waibel Agreement on dyestuffs, which enabled I.G. Farben to gain a foothold in the Japanese market in exchange for voluntary restrictions on exports.

In the 1930s, strong protectionism emerged in Japan, making the market less accessible to I.G. Farben's exports. Meanwhile, the strengthening of international cartels enabled the company, the core member of the cartels, to conclude several agreements with Japanese companies on market share, prices, and export territories, either on its own or as a member of the cartels. The agreement with Mitsui Mining on synthetic indigo and the agreement on domestic and foreign ammonium sulphate are two examples.

By the mid-1930s, I.G. Farben had to acknowledge that the Japanese market had been saturated with Japanese products and that prospects for further expansion of its product exports to Japan were foreclosed. Of the two alternatives to product export that were theoretically available, namely, direct investment and licensing, the former was virtually out of the question, even aside from the growing political instability, since the Japanese government was bent on rejecting the inflow of foreign capital. I.G. Farben thus opted to change its strategy, beginning to offer Japanese firms licenses to use its expertise in the production of dyestuffs and nitrogenous fertilizer, and to export plants to the licensees. In the case of synthetic oil, the situation was different. I.G. Farben could not export the product to Japan, and it was ready from the outset to respond positively to enquiries about licensing arrangements for synthetic oil production.

I.G. Farben made at least one licensing agreement in dyestuffs. There is a record suggesting that in 1934 or thereabouts I.G. Farben concluded a licensing agreement with Nippon Tar Kogyo. But the agreement did not seem to bear much fruit: when an engineer from Mitsubishi visited I.G. Farben's plants, I.G. Farben suspected him of being an industrial spy.[91]

In sharp contrast to this, the licensing strategy proved quite successful in the field of fertilizers. I.G. Farben offered licenses to a total of five companies, beginning with a licensing arrangement made with Taki Fertilizer Works in May 1935. In the field of synthetic oil, I.G. Farben started to negotiate with Japanese companies earlier than it did in the field of nitrogenous fertilizer. In the early 1930s, it approached South Manchurian Railways, and later it contacted more than a dozen companies including the Mitsubishi Mining and Ogura Oil. No licensing agreement resulted from these contacts, however. The most important reason for the failure of these efforts seems to have been the stiff opposition mounted by the Japanese navy, which developed its own process and was interested in seeing private companies put that process into commercial use.

Source: *Business History and Business Culture* (Andrew Godley and Oliver M. Westall (eds)), Manchester: Manchester University Press, 1996, pp. 241–255.

3

Cultural Barriers Facing Exporters to Japan: German Business in the Inter-war Period

THE INTERNATIONALISATION OF business in recent years has highlighted increasingly cultural aspects of business activities. Concepts such as cultural contact and cultural exchange, cultural co-operation and cultural friction, as well as cultural learning, have become more popular. Often culture is seen as a certain kind of barrier or hurdle to be overcome in international activities. Those businesses that are engaged in international business observe that it is difficult, or even impossible, for them to understand, manage and overcome such barriers or hurdles. Perhaps it is even the case that they call anything which is incomprehensible, unmanageable or unconquerable a cultural barrier or hurdle.[1]

Recent examples of businesses trying to enter the Japanese market show that they have often blamed the 'closeness' of the Japanese market for their lack of success, usually pointing to the uniqueness of Japanese business culture. Often accused are the *Keiretsu* system, which allegedly excludes foreign firms, and the *Shotengai,* that is the shopping street, which allegedly excludes foreign products, as well as more obvious forms of government protectionism. On the other hand, Japanese businessmen in the European market are also facing difficulties which they often find are intimately associated with the cultural nature of European countries. Some Japanese companies are even moving towards the establishment of their own world-wide corporate identities. For example, Canon has adopted the motto 'a business culture which can be accepted not only by indigenous, but also by world citizens'.

The awareness of cultural differences and, in particular, cultural barriers is not a new phenomenon in business. Businesses that confronted difficulties in foreign markets whilst in the process of the internationalisation of business activities have left an ample record.[2] In the current light of such vociferous criticism from the United States of Japanese business practices and alleged cultural barriers to imports, it is important to focus on the experience of German exporters before 1939. German businesses then, as American ones today, were convinced that there were significant cultural differences which impeded their effective penetration and dominance of the Japanese market.

The following chapter charts the experiences of the most important German exporters to Japan, such as Krupp, Siemens and IG Farben, and shows what the specific cultural context of Japan did indeed do to some German firms experiencing disappointment. However, cultural factors were not always disadvantageous to German firms. On occasion German exporters found that Japan's unique culture presented not just barriers to be negotiated but opportunities to be exploited.[3]

All Western firms have traditionally found the Japanese market difficult to penetrate. German firms were no exception.[4] Before the Second World War a number of German companies began to enter the Japanese market through their normal tried and tested strategies. They found it unexpectedly difficult to enter and even more so to fulfil their normal goal of market domination. There were several reasons for this failure. Japanese companies seemed unreliable partners in the German attempts at direct investment and licensing agreements. The Germans often saw these difficulties for successful entry and operation as being rooted in Japanese business culture. They sometimes claimed that the Japanese violated the rules of the game, or exhibited uncontrollable ambition, as a result of a distinct and different value system governing business relations. Of course, justifying their failure in Japan by pleading cultural barriers might have simply been seeking easy excuses then, as it may be now. It is important to see whether German firms genuinely did face abnormal difficulties in Japan. If so, were they caused by some unique features of the Japanese socio-economic system, including Japanese business culture? Or was it simply strategic failure on behalf of German exporters?

It is conventional nowadays to separate the influence of culture on business into two different dimensions. The first is that on the national or regional level, and can be called the environmental culture, which refers to cultural features of the environmental conditions for business activities. The general cultural climate for business was not constant in

Japan during the inter-war period – far from it. The inter-war period 1919–1939/41 was the era of economic, political and military nationalism which grew against the background of the disintegration of the multilateral international economy. The Japanese market was influenced, especially in the 1930s, by phenomena such as the 'Buy Japanese Movement' and the 'Promotion of Domestic Production Movement'. These trends in the wider political economy most certainly contributed to the cultural context of Japanese–German business relations in the inter-war period. The second dimension of business culture is called corporate culture, which consists of the cultural features of businesses themselves. These two dimensions of business culture were of greater or lesser importance for German entrants according to the manner of entry. Environmental culture influenced all German firms. Japanese corporate culture was only a significant factor for those firms needing partners in their licensing agreements or investment plans. It was less important for those firms which were merely exporting to Japan.

ENVIRONMENTAL CULTURE: THE JAPANESE MARKET

Environmental culture is discussed relatively frequently these days, as it was before 1939. In cases of German businesses in Japan, the differences in Japanese marketing and distribution were, and are, usually commented on. Production and technology, or personnel and labor management, or financial differences, were rarely mentioned for the obvious reason that most German (and Western) companies took exporting as their primary strategy for entering the Japanese market, rather than direct investment or licensing. Little direct investment and licensing made the other aspects of the Japanese business system seem less important. Exporters in foreign markets have often been punished for their ignorance of the local cultural values that bear on the presentation or wording of the product. But German exporters found that the Japanese market represented a much more significant challenge than merely getting the marketing mix right. In particular, German businesses found Japanese consumers to have rapidly changing tastes. What was fashionable one year was impossible to sell the next.

A further barrier faced by German exporters was the extremely complicated Japanese distribution system. Whilst in itself an institutional feature, rather than directly one of cultural value, the distribution system was reinforced by deeply rooted conservative values which hindered German attempts to change or bypass the distribution network.

Finally, German firms could not understand the intense competitiveness in the Japanese business system.

Rapid change of tastes and fashions

German businesses that were engaged in business in Japan often regarded the rapid change of consumers' tastes and fashions as a peculiar trait of the Japanese market. One of the most representative examples would be the case of IG Farben in the dyestuffs business.[5] IG Farben, the massive German combine of BASF, Bayer and Hoechst, was exporting over 10 million RM of dyestuffs to Japanese textile firms each year in the late 1920s and early 1930s. It had become increasingly apparent that Japanese demand for specific colors was extremely volatile. In the summer of 1927 the head of the East Asian Commission and the Japan–Herren, the personnel responsible for business in Japan, met at IG Farben's headquarters and concluded that it was 'only through a ceaseless and thoroughgoing study of the Japanese market, which is exposed to violent changes in fashions and tastes, can we hope to fully open up the prospects for expensive dyestuffs with new uses to be accepted there'. They tried to accommodate their marketing practices to these swift changes and altered their normal approach to entering a foreign market. For example, they decided to prepare special brochures of samples specifically targeted for the Japanese market. According to their observations, unlike the normal rather voluminous and comprehensive brochures, these compact brochures could cater for the needs of selected strata of customers, could be produced at lower costs, and would prove more effective. It would also make sense to leave out some of the dyestuffs which were not being imported. They decided that samples should be explained in Japanese, and that the brochures should be produced in Japan.

Another improvement in the marketing practice was to cut down inventories. Previously, inventories had tended to pile up, partly because of the frequent changes in the dyeing and printing methods brought about by sudden changes in trends, and partly also because of the need to prepare for the possibility of a sudden imposition of import bans. The meeting concluded that, on the one hand, while it was definitely impossible to abide by the company's policy of maintaining inventories of six-month supplies, the inventories should not be allowed to exceed an eight-month supply. At the same time, they deliberated on the means of reducing inventories and found it essential that products of low-to-medium price range, which were being supplied in increasing volumes by Japanese manufacturers, should be sold in the Chinese or other markets nearby, shipped back to Germany, or even disposed of. The meeting agreed, furthermore, that new additions to inventories should be prevented by all methods available: for instance, by keeping a closer watch on the market, and by accurately forecasting the demand in the coming season. How to cope with the rapidity of fashion changes was the most crucial issue.

They also pointed out that:

> considering the particular situation of Japan, it is urgently necessary to see to it that information of our new products, sample brochures and handling methods be disseminated among customers promptly, and that the introduction of new products, as long as they can attract interest in the Japanese market, be executed and monitored carefully.[6]

IG Farben saw the rapidly changing tastes of consumers, and the changing dyeing and printing methods that followed as a result, as barriers to be overcome and regarded these as having cultural origins. They applied aggressive marketing policies, modifying them, and succeeded, in principle, in overcoming those barriers.

Complicated distribution system

IG Farben was less successful in overcoming the problems of the distribution system in Japan. Textbooks on Japanese business history usually point out that the pre-war market, in which a wholesale distribution system was dominant, was quite different from the American or European system.[7] The dyestuffs industry was a typical example of this.[8]

The history of the German dyestuff distribution system in Japan in the period from the late nineteenth century to the outbreak of the Second World War may be divided into three phases. The first period was when imports from Germany were handled by agents. Products manufactured by German companies were imported by foreign-owned or Japanese-owned sales agents, and were then sold to Japanese dyestuff wholesalers, who were franchises of the German companies. The second period was the period of 'direct import' when the sales agents came under direct management of the German firms. With this change the route along which imported dyestuffs were distributed also changed. Products manufactured by the German firms were imported by their respective agents, or by branches under their direct management, and were then sold to the franchised wholesalers. The third period started in 1924, when the sales agencies under direct German control were consolidated into one subsidiary.

The most serious problem for the German dyestuff makers, and later for IG Farben, was the increasing power of the Japanese franchised wholesalers. Japanese wholesalers could handle both imported products and indigenous products. This, against the background of the emergence of indigenous production after the First World War, meant that the Japanese wholesalers could enjoy countervailing power against the German-owned sales agencies and controlling power over smaller local retailers. Here IG Farben found a barrier. Ciba, the big Swiss chemicals company, also suffered from the same barrier. James Brodbeck-Sandreuter, later a top' manager of Ciba-Geigy, reported to his headquarters as follows:

> According to my investigation, dyestuff business in Japan is quite different from business in Continental Europe or other overseas markets, in so far as domestic dyestuff merchants should be taken into account in Japan. Associations of dyestuff merchants in Japan have an enormous influence over the whole market, which cannot be eliminated even through the direct control of sales agencies.[9]

The most serious drawback of the special agent system was that it was unavoidably accompanied by increased distribution costs. An internal document from the same 1927 meeting of IG Farben's Japanese representatives contains several interesting figures showing the high distribution costs in Japan. At the level of a single direct-controlled sales agency, the distribution costs, inclusive of handling fees and warehouse charges of 5 percent, amounted to as much as 9.08 percent of gross revenues. When clerical and other handling charges of 1.77 percent due in Germany were added to this, the total cost percentage rose to 10.85 percent of gross revenues. This was an exceptionally high ratio by international comparison within IG Farben's activities.

IG Farben tended to see the problem of its distribution system as an institutional one initially, and, indeed, it reviewed the possibility of abolishing the complicated special agent system and replacing it by a direct sales system. However, it had to conclude that a drastic change of this sort would be extremely difficult to implement. Ironically enough, the existing system, the establishment of which the German dyestuff companies had contributed to beforehand in order to expand their own sales networks, had grown so firmly rooted that it could not be easily discarded. The problem was not just overcoming the established and costly institutional network, but also overcoming the whole Japanese value system as it related to the hierarchy of special agents in the distribution system. Buyer–seller relationships were different in Japan from those in the West. In Japan the buyer has a much higher status than the seller. These Japanese cultural values ensured that the wholesalers maintained their supremacy over manufacturers, both foreign and domestic. As a result, the special agent system remained as a barrier.[10]

Excessive competition

The conventional image of the Japanese market is one of widespread collusion. German businesses by contrast, however, sometimes complained of excessive competition in Japan, especially among Japanese companies. The dyestuffs market is, again, a good example. IG Farben realised that the Japanese dyestuffs market was extraordinarily unsound because of excessively strong competition among wholesalers. It even pointed out the fact that sometimes the selling price of wholesalers went below their buying price.[11] Another example is the case of the electric machinery market. Here too, what was thought to be excessive competition among Japanese manufacturers meant German companies suffered, especially Siemens. Siemens was bored with cutthroat competition in the Japanese market and consistently expected some way of restricting competition to emerge, such as the establishment of price agreements, mergers or holding companies. It even tried to persuade its subsidiary, Fuji Electric, to co-operate with its other Japanese competitors on the one hand and work with General Electric, Westinghouse and the other members of the international electric machinery oligopoly to force a truce on the other.[12] The efforts of exporters to Japan to enforce international cartels were complicated by the Japanese drive to protectionism after the Manchurian incident in 1931. In general, German big business succeeded in bringing about co-operation among Japanese companies through expanding the networks of international cartels into Japan, but it was noticeably less successful than elsewhere in the world.[13]

CORPORATE CULTURE: JAPANESE COMPANIES AS PARTNERS

In comparison to environmental cultural differences, corporate cultures were rarely mentioned by foreign businesses in Japan. This is hardly surprising when bearing in mind how foreign such a concept would have been to the businesses of the inter-war period. But its reality was nonetheless felt. The German incomprehension of the Japanese reluctance to collude has already been mentioned. German business strategy was usually to seek profit-sharing partnerships with their major rivals which enabled all parties to exploit monopoly rents. Competition within cartels was restricted to product differentiation, which in turn favored incremental innovation and the pursuit of technical excellence rather than any technological breakthroughs. These were the accepted methods of conducting international business in German eyes.[14]

Japanese firms appeared to work to different rules. These were acknowledged as being a product of Japanese culture. They operated in three distinct areas: first, it was felt that Japanese firms showed a remarkable fascination for modern technology; second, the Japanese firms dealing with foreign technology were seemingly consumed by the ideal of matching and improving the imported technology with their own efforts; and finally, Japanese firms showed a zeal for taking managerial authority in any joint venture or licensing agreement.

Japanese fascination with modern technology

German businessmen sometimes pointed out the eagerness of Japanese to introduce new technologies through licensing agreements. This eagerness led to the continual introduction of advanced, even experimental, technologies and consequently a resulting diversity of technological processes. Krupp's Renn process is a good example of the licensing of experimental technology. The Renn process was a method of utilising iron ore with a low iron content and was introduced into Japan by four Japanese companies, including Mitsubishi Mining and Kawasaki Shipyard, within only a few years of its development by Krupp. The transactions provided Krupp with remarkably large profits so soon after its development.[15] Another example is the IG Farben's Winkler process to produce hydrogen gas for synthesizing ammonia. This was also licensed into Japan by two Japanese companies, Yahagi Kogyo and Nihon Tar Industries (later renamed Mitsubishi Chemical), after only a few years of its development in Germany,[16] resulting in what were very welcome profits to its licenser so soon after its development.

Synthetic oil provides another example. Two major processes developed in Germany, the Ruhrchemie's Fischer-Tropsch process and the IG process, were objects of Japanese curiosity. The former process was introduced into Japan by Mitsui Mining, while the latter failed to be licensed in spite of much interest from almost a dozen Japanese companies.[17]

The Japanese eagerness to introduce technology which had never before been used in Japan resulted in the introduction of a wide range of different processes into Japan. The most illustrative example of this is the case of the process for manufacturing nitrogenous fertilizer. The Casale process was the first one to be introduced in Japan. The licence was given to Nihon Nitrogenous Fertilizer. This was followed by the introduction of various methods, including the Claude process by Miike Nitrogen (a subsidiary of Mitsui Mining), the Fauser process by Dainihon Artificial Fertilizer, and the NEC process by Sumitomo Fertilizer (later renamed Sumitomo Chemical Industries). Regarding this situation, one cannot help but agree with the following remark made by one of IG Farben's engineers stationed in Japan: 'The Japanese mentality is always in search of something new. However, it does not seem necessarily important whether the novelty be superior to what precedes it.' The Japanese market was a profit-promising one for many Western companies. IG Farben was one of the beneficiaries from the curiosity of Japanese companies, licensing its Haber-Bosch method of ammonia synthesis to a total of five companies including Nihon Tar Industries of Mitsubishi *zaibatsu*.[18]

German businessmen seem to have interpreted the curiosity of the Japanese in a cultural context, as illustrated in the observation of the IG Farben's engineer cited above. At all events, German firms found business opportunities rather than just business barriers to be a consequence of the specific cultural context of the Japanese market.

Ambition towards technological independence

German businesses noticed that their Japanese partners were ambitious for technological independence. Here again, the case of the Krupp's Renn process gives us an illustration. An engineer of Kawasaki Shipyard, one of the companies which introduced the process, recollected that:

> Mr Nishiyama inspired us, insisting that we should pay every effort to master the technology for ourselves during the introduction period. He also said, 'it would be certainly easier for us to learn from Germans, but then we would have only an imitated technology, not our own one. Try to solve problems for ourselves'.[19]

They mastered the technology almost through consulting specialist literature alone.

Mitsubishi Mining, another licensee of the Krupp's Renn process, also expressed a very strong desire to build the facilities, using its own technology and production ability as far as possible in the installation of the new foundry. For example, Mitsubishi insisted in a change to the numbers of foremen and workers to be sent from Germany to its building site; it considerably altered some of Krupp's original drawings; it wanted to produce some spare parts for itself; it wanted to produce the kiln bricks for itself; and it wanted to solve a serious problem at the initial stage of operation for itself. Mitsubishi wanted to stick to its own ideas and skills as far as possible, and even to develop its own technologies. Each attempt of Mitsubishi to be more independent caused a technical difficulty. This drive for independence also caused conflict between Krupp and Mitsubishi. Even though Krupp tried to exploit the improvements made by Mitsubishi, it suffered, mainly because it did not always rely on the technological ability of Mitsubishi.

Moreover, Mitsubishi wanted to operate the facilities as soon as possible, and forced Krupp's engineers and foremen to leave Mitsubishi's factory for Germany as soon as could be justified, although it later needed their further technical assistance. A leading engineer of Krupp pointed to the 'ambition of Mitsubishi men', which caused the Germans a whole catalogue of burdens and problems.[20]

This kind of Japanese ambition towards technological independence from German licensers sometimes enabled Japanese licensees to absorb German technology fully and then to go on and make a series of incremental improvements, and even achieve the ideal of independence. For German licensers, however, it usually caused technological problems and managerial headaches.

The case of Siemens' telephone equipment provides us with another example. Siemens established a subsidiary, Fuji Electric, as a joint venture with Furukawa Electric. The latter constantly insisted on the localisation of production, that is, the production of telephone equipment, especially automatic switchboards, by Fuji Electric in Japan, stressing the importance of increasing price competitiveness. Siemens was eventually forced to hand production over to Fuji Electric. Fuji Electric later established its own subsidiary, Fujitsu, whose main business was to produce telephone equipment including automatic switchboards, the main competitor of which was Siemens.

Although Fujitsu remained as dependent on the technology of Siemens as Fuji Electric, its president, Manjiro Yoshimura, dared to give the following instructions: 'We should not be content with the introduction of excellent technology from Germany. We need to make research of our own.' A leading engineer of the company recollects, 'we were often rather childishly in high spirits, arguing, "Because we are not monkeys, we do not imitate" '. This ambition for technological independence led to the localisation of production, with lower costs but lower quality. It also forced the German firm to face a new problem, that is, competition from its own granddaughter company.[21]

Siemens was rather tolerant in licensing its technology to Japanese partners, and certainly so when compared to IG Farben in dyestuffs production. The Japanese were as ambitious in the dyestuffs industry as in other industries. They had to recognise, however, the need for foreign technological assistance in some products. The Japanese dyestuffs producers and the government, therefore, repeatedly requested technical co-operation and domestic licences from IG Farben. It is true that IG Farben did not openly reject these requests and that on some occasions it gave a positive consideration to offering some sort of technological co-operation. It was, however, tacitly following a policy of not granting such requests. In order for IG Farben to protect its technology, which became ineligible for patent protection, it had no choice but to deny licensing to Japan. Not only that, IG Farben went even so far as to dump its synthetic indigo products in the Japanese market, in the hope of discouraging Mitsui Mining's effort to develop these.

Carl Bosch, chairman of the board of directors of BASF, as well as later of IG Farben, was strongly antagonistic to Japanese ambition. He once maintained that, if German dyestuffs companies had started co-operating with the Japanese in the field of organic chemistry, the Japanese would then press hard for co-operation in the field of dye production as well. Calling attention to what he called 'the almost morbid ambition of the Japanese' or their strong 'vanity', Bosch asserted that 'our objective, under any circumstances, ought not to be to offer any help whatsoever to the Japanese in their efforts to build up a profitable chemical industry, and in particular, a dye industry of their own, but rather to slow their process in these efforts as long as possible, and moreover to reduce these efforts to a failure as best as we can'.[22]

In some cases, this ambition of the Japanese led to a German firm failing to license its technology. This can be illustrated through the case of the IG process for synthetic oil. Here, the opposition of the

Japanese navy, which had already conducted some research into the hydrogenation processes in synthesizing oil from coal tar, played a decisive role in IG Farben's failure. In fact, the navy's opposition doomed Ogura Oil's plan, as well as those of the army to import this technology. A representative of a Japan-based subsidiary of IG Farben predicted such a failure on the assumption that by acquiescing in the purchase of the know-how of the IG process, the navy would in effect be admitting its own failure in this area. Such a loss of face could never be tolerated in the heady atmosphere of the late 1930s.

Germans tended to regard such enthusiasms of the Japanese as cultural. At any rate, suffering from the consequences of this untrammelled Japanese ambition, Germans sought to cover the growing risks of losing their proprietorial rights, when licensing their technologies to Japanese firms, by charging higher fees. Japanese licensees refused to pay the higher fees, however. For them it was a matter of losing face. If such a process were so valuable then Japanese firms would develop the technology independently, it was believed. Occasionally the Germans succeeded in finding effective tactics to deal with Japanese ambitions and ensure they earned their risk premium. For instance, an engineer of IG Farben noticed that the Japanese engineers, such as those in the navy, usually resisted the idea of paying licensing fees as a matter of pride. However, they were often perfectly willing to pay high prices for German-made equipment. He could, therefore, propose the inclusion of part of the actual licensing fee in the equipment price, as a way of dealing with the problem of national ambition and pride.[23]

The drive for independent managerial authority

The modes of entrance for German businesses in the Japanese market varied, but there were fewer cases of direct investment and more cases of licensing. There were reasons for this bias to licensing on both sides. German firms were, in principle, reluctant to make direct investments in Japan. If they decided to invest in production, then they preferred joint ventures with Japanese partners, mostly with *zaibatsu*-owned big firms. The Germans had learnt from their painful experience of losing their external assets during and after the First World War, and so developed strategies which maximised security and avoided risks in international trade. Besides, they saw Japan as 'the remotest place on the earth' in both geographical and psychical terms. If they were interested in East Asia, they gave priority to China rather than Japan. On the other hand, where the introduction of technology was concerned, Japanese firms generally preferred a strategy of importing their competitors' products and then learning how to produce similar goods from dead copy to the other options of licensing and direct investment. If they had to rely on direct investment or licensing, they preferred the latter. The result of these factors was that German firms were not as committed to maintaining managerial authority overseas as they might have been. Japanese firms were, by contrast, very aware of the need for managerial control. Even in the few cases of direct investment by German firms, the Japanese side wanted a joint venture style of operation, and they also wanted to maintain the controlling right of management for themselves. Ultimately they wanted independence from their German partners. The case of Siemens offers us a good example among the few incidences of direct investment. As referred to above, Siemens' daughter company, Fuji Electric, established its own subsidiary, Fujitsu, with 100 percent ownership. The establishment was implemented in spite of the resistance and even the disagreement of Siemens. Fuji Electric even selected a German member of the board of directors without getting the agreement of Siemens in advance. Siemens could hardly understand the ambition of the Japanese side and was obliged to make concessions and eventually give up their controlling right in Fujitsu.[24] Japanese insistence on managerial control cost Siemens dear.

CONCLUDING REMARKS

German big business in Japan found cultural barriers which, they felt, constrained their business activities in areas such as dyestuffs and telephone equipment. Equally in other cases, such as iron and steel, and nitrogenous fertilizer, there seemed to be few cultural barriers. Sometimes, however, they were able to overcome the barriers and opportunities in the unique cultural context of the Japanese market. By employing specific marketing strategies, or exploiting the demand for sophisticated technology, or new technology, German firms were able to overcome the very real cultural differences between the two nations. In areas where they failed, it would seem that poor business strategies were at least as much at fault as insurmountable cultural barriers. This is a feature of the Japanese market which has continued with similar consequences for foreign firms trying to enter today.

Source: Institute of Social Science, University of Tokyo, Discussion Paper Series, F-98, 2002, pp.1–18.

4

Search for Stability:
Siemens in Inter-war-period Japan

1. INTRODUCTION

PRIOR TO THE Second World War, foreign direct investments by German companies in Japan were mostly aimed at establishing sales and distribution organization, with only a small portion going to local production. Investment made by Siemens, a giant electrical engineering company, was the largest one made for local production. The company established Fuji Electric Manufacturing Co. Ltd as a joint venture with the Furukawa business group.[1]

Siemens started its business activities in Japan at an early stage. Export activities began in the 1860s. Siemens was exporting various types of products, from heavy electric machinery to light electric appliances. For this reason, sales agencies were first set up in Japan, and local affiliates were established after that. A plan to make direct investments in Japan to set up local production had already been put in place before the First World War. Local production then entered its initial stage.[2]

But the plan by Siemens to make direct investments in Japan materialized in earnest only after the First World War. Competition among foreign and Japanese companies on the Japanese market intensified under conditions in which, spurred by the First World War, electric machinery companies experienced further development, trade practices were again relaxed, and capital liberalization policies continued to be implemented in Japan. Confronted by this situation, on August 22, 1923, Siemens established Fuji Electric as a joint venture with

Furukawa Electric Industry, which was a member of the Furukawa business group.[3]

The aim of this paper is to discuss the position Siemens occupied in Japan as a multinational enterprise operating in a dictatorial environment, and to determine how Siemens perceived this environment, what strategies it developed, what types of structures it put in place, how it developed its business, and what results it ultimately achieved.

2. PRELIMINARY CONSIDERATIONS

Before delving into this case any further, I would like to put forth some preliminary considerations regarding the issues covered in this workshop.

First, we need to establish the facts concerning the direct investments made by Western companies in Japan during the inter-war period.

Increased foreign direct investment in Japan is a relatively recent phenomenon, and the investments existing prior to the Second World War were extremely modest by modern standards. This, however, does not mean that no foreign direct investments at all were made in Japan. Nor does it mean that Japan continued to shut its door to foreign capital. In fact, the Japanese government maintained a policy of accepting inward direct investment from around 1900 to 1930, causing robust growth in investment by foreign companies.

Around 1900, the Japanese government put a lot of effort into the unresolved issue of rescinding unequal treaties in the context of industrial development on the one hand and the improvement of external political position made possible by Japan's victory in the Sino-Japanese War in 1894–95 on the other. The manifestation of this effort was the Treaty Revision, which was aimed at abolishing extraterritorial rights and reinstating tariff autonomy. The government set down the following preconditions in order to achieve this goal. First, the Commercial Code was revised, patent law was established, and other legislative measures were introduced. The government also embarked on liberalizing inward foreign direct investment, and hence set up measures aimed at easing land ownership rules for foreign nationals. It also set out to join the international gold standard system. The Treaty Revision program was completed by 1911, but the program aimed at liberalizing inward foreign direct investment continued up to around 1930. From around 1930, and particularly since the Manchurian Incident in September 1931, the Japanese government reversed its policy regarding inward foreign direct investment and gradually introduced a variety of progressively tighter regulations against the investment. This was accompanied by a sharp drop in direct investment by Western companies in Japan and their continued withdrawal from Japan.[4]

Second, it is necessary to determine the position of German companies, and Siemens in particular, in the overall picture of Western companies making direct investments in Japan in the period between 1900 and 1930.

German companies were reluctant to make foreign direct investments after the First World War because of their losses of foreign assets and rights as a result of the war. Naturally, this reluctance was particularly pronounced with respect to the remote region of the Far East. Many German companies emphasized exporting as the business development mode for Japan, and even when other modes were adopted, licensing was often preferred over foreign direct investment.[5]

The same applied to I.G. Farben, which was very active in terms of pursuing business development in Japan. In the 1920's, I.G. did not have any specific plans to make direct investments in Japan. The company was thinking about establishing local production of nitrogen fertilizers in Korea, but nothing specific was in the works. I.G. had lost its chance for direct investments by the 1930s. At that time, Japanese companies had already gained control of the expanding internal Japanese market and East-Asian market in the fields of dyestuffs and nitrogen fertilizers. For this reason, I. G. directed its efforts at strengthening international cartels and subsuming Japanese companies into them, and also adopted a licensing strategy. There were no opportunities for direct investment, however. The company made some licensing attempts in the field of synthetic oil, but no direct investments were made.[6]

For German companies, the emphasis was on China rather than on Japan in terms of foreign direct investment. With the increase in the export of industrial products, several large German companies started developing plans to make direct investments in China in order to establish local production. There is evidence that I.G. was seriously considering making direct investments in China for dyestuffs production. It also planed to manufacture synthetic oil by coal liquefaction.[7]

As a result, German companies constituted only a small proportion of the Western companies with foreign direct investments in Japan around 1930:

According to a survey on foreign direct investment conducted by the Ministry of Commerce and Industry in 1931, eighty-eight foreign-affiliated manufacturing companies were operating in Japan, excluding trading and insurance firms. Of these, thirty-six were American, twenty-one British, seventeen German, three Swiss, two Chinese, and one each for France, Luxembourg, and Czechoslovakia, with six of unknown origin. Germany was thus ranked number three following the United States and Britain.[8]

Among these, Siemens was an exception:

Thirty-nine foreign-affiliated manufacturing companies are listed by Masaru Udagawa, whose research represents the most up-to-date and comprehensive data about foreign companies in pre-war Japan. Although foreign manufacturing companies are listed as manufacturers, however, that does not mean that they carried out local production in Japan. Udagawa's list contains companies of which more than 10 percent of the capital was owned by foreigners at the establishment of the joint venture. These include five German companies, namely, Siemens-Schuckert Denki (Siemens-Schuckert Electric), Goto Fuundo, Asahi Silk Fabrics, Fuji Electric, and Nihon Bemberg Kenshoku (Japan Bemberg Silk Fabrics). The most active foreign corporations were in the four industrial areas of oil, heavy electric machinery, tires, and automobiles. The only German company active in these areas was Fuji Electric.[9]

In the 1920s, although Japan welcomed foreign capital, German companies preferred an export strategy, and their strategy vis-à-vis Japan was generally cautious, as we saw earlier. The number of cases and amount of direct investment were small, mostly being for the purpose of the setting up of sales and distribution networks. For distribution, the majority used the agency system. Direct investment for production was very rare. The most important exception was Fuji Electric, which Siemens jointly established with Furukawa Electric Industry in 1923, with about 30 percent of the capital provided by Siemens. This is a very rare example of direct investment in local production by a German firm, and the most important example of German direct investment prior to 1945.[10]

In making direct investments in Japan, Siemens was atypical of German electric machinery firms. For example, Allgemeine Elektricitäls-Gesellschaft (AEG), a comparable firm to Siemens, formed an agency arrangement with Okura Shoji (Okura Trading), and pursued a policy of exporting rather than direct investment in Japan. Robert Bosch (which became a limited company in 1937), although also pursuing international promotion of its proprietary technologies (first low-pressure, then high-pressure magnetic plugs), including to Japan, maintained a policy of licensing rather than direct investment. Another company, Felten & Guilleaume Carlswerk, exported wire rods, electric wire, and cables to Japan from before the First World War. But although Japan became one of its most important overseas markets, this company did not make any direct investments. Thus, Siemens' establishment of Fuji Electric was an unusual case, and it was among the largest direct overseas investments made by a German company in Japan prior to the Second World War.[11]

Third, political dictatorship must be tentatively defined.

As is well known, the political regime existing in Japan following the Meiji Restoration can be defined in several ways. A tentative definition is that the establishment of the Takashi Hara cabinet in September 1918 marked the beginning of a multiparty system within the framework of parliamentary democracy, and that a dictatorship was created as a result of the parliamentary democracy and the multiparty system being overrun by the military. Then, several indicators can be offered for this transition to a dictatorship. Examples include the Manchurian Incident in September 1931, the May 15 Incident in May 1932, the February 26 Incident in February 1936, and the start of the Sino-Japanese War in July 1937. The following events can also be cited as examples of the political interference by the military during this period: the abrogation of the Washington Treaty in March 1932, withdrawal from the League of Nations in March 1933, and the signing of the Anti-Comintern Pact between Japan and Germany in November 1936. Thus, political interference by the military gradually grew in scope and became decisive after July 1937. After that, although some civilians became prime ministers, the military dictatorship became irreversible.

I would like to offer another, slightly different explanation here. It deals with an observation of the business environment around Western companies which entered Japan through direct investment, that is, an analysis of the established legal system and foreign capital policies *vis-à-vis* the companies' proprietary rights, management rights, business scope, range of functions, structure, and other issues. In this case, both a democracy and a dictatorship can be interpreted as factors that determine such an environment. For Western companies in Japan, the business environment could change, and did indeed change, irrespective of whether the change was effected by a democracy or a dictatorship. In fact, restrictions on foreign companies were strengthened by the Osachi Hamaguchi cabinet in July 1929, which was a period of parliamentary democracy and multiparty system. It was, however, after the Manchurian Incident in September 1931 that the restrictions on foreign capital were instituted in earnest, so it was a dictatorial regime in this case. In this paper, a point of view in line with this interpretation is emphasized, and the inter-war period is divided according to the point of view.

Fourth, risk-related preliminary considerations must be taken into account.

One of the factors determining the strategy of a company expanding into a foreign market has to do with how the company perceives the environment in which the expansion is taking place and how it thinks this environment may change in the future. Risk has to do with any greater-than-expected, unforeseen changes in such an environment. Most of the risk is believed to have political character. A scholar of business management says that about 90 percent of the changes in a business environment are due to political factors.[12] He goes on to say that it is necessary to carefully examine the political and economic conditions of the host country, the financial situation of your trading partners, the hidden motives behind requests for technical cooperation, and other factors, and that the strategy has to be periodically reviewed on the basis of thoroughly collected and analyzed information. Some of his other statements: "In international business, the outcome of an enterprise depends on the abilities of managers to identify changes in the business environment, to define them in a certain way, and to devise a responding strategy," and "Since risk is inherently present in any plan based on an erroneous interpretation of conditions, it is too late to do anything once the risk is actually revealed."[13]

Based on the above consideration for the third point, the inter-war period is divided into two sub-periods according to the changes in the foreign capital policies, Our goal is to determine how Siemens perceived the environment in which it found itself in Japan, how it was able to predict any changes in this environment, what strategies, business ventures, and organizational structures were established to deal with these changes, and what results were achieved.[14]

3. PERIOD OF LIBERAL ENVIRONMENT

Ever since it was founded in 1923, Fuji Electric was plagued by a series of misfortunes. The Great Kanto Earthquake occurred on September 1, 1923, which was the day the new company started operations. Fortunately, the personnel escaped unharmed and there was no damage to the structures of the corporate headquarters in the Yaesu district of Tokyo. Since the company took over import service from Siemens, there was still some inventory available, and some products were left over from before the transfer. The company was thus able to operate normally. In addition, demand for electric machinery had skyrocketed because of the post-earthquake recovery, and the inventory was quickly sold out.[15]

Problems still persisted, however:

At the time of Fuji Electric's founding, it was concerned only with the import and sale of Siemens products. The products to be imported included everything from large-scale generating equipment to small gauges. In April 1925, the Kawasaki factory commenced operations. The products made in-house included distributing boards, electric motors, transformers, and generators. Later, the drive to make in-house products intensified, and, by 1931, in-house products accounted for more than half of total sales: 58 percent versus only 42 percent for imports. However, Fuji Electric's financial results were disastrous. [As we saw in table 9–5], after a minimal profit in 1927, the following years showed losses. In particular, the loss in 1931 of 125,000 yen brought the cumulative deficit to over 1.3 million yen.[16]

Initially, the capital stock of 10 million yen was too small. Since Siemens invested with kind, that is, technology, Furukawa had to raise all the capital. But Furukawa had suffered tremendous losses as a result of their disastrous soybean gamble in Manchuria. A senior Siemens executive, Carl Köttgen, said at the time, "Japaner hat kein Geld"(The Japanese have no money). For this reason, Furukawa had difficulty coming up with the capital. So it was that the initial payment was only 2.5 million yen, small payments were continued to be made over time, and the payment of 9 million yen was finally delivered in late 1930s.[17]

To offset the deficit, Fuji Electric had borrowed from several banks. The loan reached a total of 2.6 million yen in March 1925, and another 1.8 million yen was borrowed after that.[18]

The payments of Fuji Electric due to Siemens reached over 2 million yen by early 1927. Fuji Electric entered into negotiations with Siemens in May of the same year and was extended a loan worth 1 million US dollars at 7.5 percent interest. [19]

In addition to the transfer of technology in the form of investment in kind, Siemens had also dispatched a former Siemens Brothers factory manager, Emil Otto Kiefer, as the first factory manager, and provided a second factory manager as well. Initially 25 or 26 Germans had been dispatched to fill positions below that of plant manager, and this number peaked at 29 in 1925. As their contract expired, many were sent back home to cut costs, so a much smaller number remained after that, although eight people were still there in 1931.[20]

Such managerial difficulties experienced by Fuji Electric confirmed the worst expectations of Siemens.

In 1930, when the country entered the Showa Depression as part of the Great Depression, Fuji Electric found itself in an even deeper financial crisis. Fuji Electric consolidated its management and made staff cuts. In May 1930, 205 employees, or 16 percent of all employees, were terminated, and the company embarked on a program to cut wages and salaries. A second wave of layoffs occurred in September 1931.[21]

There were also changes at the top:

> In May 1931, Fuji Electric's Wasaku Natori resigned from his position as president to take a job as special advisor to the firm, and moved to the Jiji Shinpo newspaper. His successor was Manjiro Yoshimura, who had been both a director of Fuji and a senior managing director of Furukawa Shoji (Furukawa Trading). At the same time, Hideo Kajiyama and Tsunesuke Wada were internally promoted to the position of director. In the company's official history, this change of president was treated simply as a personal decision by Natori in response to Jiji Shinpo's entreaty, but as we have already seen, Natori was at that time warning about Furukawa Electric Industry's plan to absorb Fuji Electric, and he had contacted Siemens about the idea of a merger with Mitsubishi Electric as a countermeasure. That plan soon became known to the executives of Furukawa Electric Industry, and this perhaps resulted in friction between them and Natori. Natori's sudden retirement, in fact, was probably something closer to dismissal. In any event, the change in presidents was sudden. Toranosuke Furukawa – the head of the founding family – himself informed Carl Friedrich von Siemens of this.....[22]

Meanwhile, the headquarter of Siemens recognized the situation and pursued the following strategy:

> During this period of instability, Siemens adopted a defensive business strategy. It discontinued diversification into fields such as automobiles, and it concentrated its business resources in areas of traditional strength such as electric equipment. If we consider these results and strategies of Siemens, it is clear that during this period Siemens had little incentive or motivation, or financial resources, to undertake foreign direct investment. Even more out of the question was direct investment in the distant Far East.[23]

Consequently, Siemens implemented the following measures to cope with the financial crisis at Fuji Electric:

> Siemens was, as we have seen, frightened at the fierce competition in the Japanese market, and it consistently placed its hopes in measures that would achieve the restraint of competition, whether it be in the form of pricing agreements, corporate merger, or a holding company. Therefore, Siemens basically gave its approval to the pricing agreement as well as to the idea of merging Fuji Electric and Mitsubishi Electric, and of the merger of the big four heavy electric companies. Toward that end, it even worked directly to persuade General Electric and Westinghouse. In particular, Siemens atten-

tively examined the merger proposal of the Temporary Industrial Rationalization Board. In the end, the merger did not come about. However,
the movement toward cooperation bore fruit in the May 1931 agreement
among the big four relating to sales quotas, pricing, and distribution channels. This was undoubtedly a great relief to Siemens.[24]

In this way, Siemens found itself involved in a network of international
cooperative agreements in both the heavy and light electric fields. Within
Germany, there were even repeated discussions between 1925 and 1933
aimed a t a union of Siemens and AEG, Against this background, it seems
only natural that Siemens should have been distressed by the excessive competition in Japan and looked toward greater cooperation.[25]

4. PERIOD OF RESTRICTIVE ENVIRONMENT

In July 1929, a tighter financial and monetary policy and a set of economic measures aimed at returning to the gold standard were adopted
at the same time as the Hamaguchi cabinet was formed. Import restrictions and a domestic production stimulus package were announced as
part of this policy. Issue of foreign loans was encouraged at the same
time. In January 1930, the gold embargo was lifted and the country returned to the gold standard. Import was further restricted and
domestic production additionally encouraged. Due to the start of the
Showa Depression, however, the gold export ban was reintroduced, that
is, the gold standard suspended, under the subsequent Inukai cabinet
in December 1931. The yen exchange rate then plummeted, exports
increased as a result, and domestic economy was on its way to recovery.

Meanwhile, with the Manchurian Incident of September 1931 as
a turning point, the foreign capital policy of the Japanese government
gradually turned restrictive, and ultimately became prohibitory.

Such changes in the business environment manifested themselves in
the following manner for Fuji Electric:

In January 1930, the Hamaguchi cabinet removed the gold embargo, and
with that the Encourage Japanese Manufacturing and Buy Japanese movements accelerated. In July, the Communications Ministry enacted regulations aimed at the encouragement of domestic manufacturing and the
rationalization of purchasing. The objectives were the exclusion of foreign
management and profits, effectively, the expulsion of foreign capital, a
withdrawal from dependence on foreign technology, and technological self-
sufficiency. At around the same time, the navy's desire to maintain secrecy
led to the removal of foreigners from military-demand-related factories, and
it demanded that foreigners should, as far as possible, be removed from Fuji
Electric's Kawasaki factory.[26]

Fuji Electric rebounded. Sales expanded. The share of factory products in the overall sales volume increased sharply. It was 50 percent in 1929, but reached 90 percent in 1934–35. The principal products manufactured at the main plant in Kawasaki included electric motors, engines, distributing boards, searchlights, and transformers.[27] Plant expansion, machinery additions, and job growth followed.

Although the financial report for 1933 showed that the company was still in the red, this was the year when the company bottomed out, and business performance rapidly improved after that. All the carryover losses were eliminated. A dividend of 6 percent was realized in the second half of 1934. It was the first time such a result was achieved since the founding of Fuji Electric. The dividend rate was subsequently raised to 8 percent, and then to 9 percent.

The following record can be found in Fuji Electric's company history:

> Considering the hardship the company had gone through in the first ten years of its existence, these results indeed seemed like a dream come true. This unusual development was undoubtedly due to the increased orders for materiel brought about by the arms race, as well as the demand for the equipment and materials needed for the development of Manchukuo as a national entity, the surging demand for electrical machinery spurred by the development of power resources in Japan, and other factors.[28]

The capital situation also improved in this period, and the entire amount of 10 million yen was finally paid off in March 1932. The capital increased to 15 million yen by October of the same year.[29] Fuji Electric was thus able to pay off its loan to Siemens:

> The burden of the outstanding 750,000 -US-dollar balance of the one-million-US-dollar loan from Siemens increased as a result of the yen's depreciation, however, and the loan became difficult to repay. But, as a result of Furukawa Electric Industry's guarantees and financing from the Industrial Bank of Japan, Fuji was able to purchase the US-dollar loan from Siemens under par in New York and eliminate it. Fuji was able to realize a dividend of 6 percent in the second half of 1934 for the first time since the start of its operations.[30]

One of Fuji Electric executives has the following memories from that era:

> A hint of insincerity had permeated the air up to that point because of the unresolved problem of debt repayment between our company and Siemens,

but as soon as we were free and clear, the companies became increasingly friendlier with each passing day. For example, our best employees were soon traveling to Germany one after another for training and technology transfer, which significantly contributed to our subsequent development.[31]

We can see that Siemens was happy with this situation. In stark contrast to pre-1933, Siemens was now able to receive dividends and to recover its receivables.

On the other hand, Siemens had gradually lost its managerial control over Fuji Electric. The telephone switchboard business can be cited as an extreme example. In this field, Siemens had acceded to local production by Fuji Electric and had allowed Fuji Electric to set up Fuji Tsushinki Seizo, currently Fujitsu, a wholly owned subsidiary of Fuji Electric. Some at Siemens were strongly opposed to the founding of Fujitsu. Despite this, Fuji Electric went ahead with the founding.

The author has previously performed a detailed analysis of the events that followed the start of local production of telephone switchboards by Fuji Electric and led to the establishment of Fujitsu. The results are as follows.

Siemens' establishment of Fuji Electric is the most important among the rare cases of direct overseas investment by German companies before the Second World War that went as far as local manufacturing. Here we have traced the transition in Siemens' Japanese telephone business, while considering Siemens' strategic choices.

Before the First World War, the American company Western Electric had pioneered direct investment in local manufacturing in Japan in the field of telephone equipment. By contrast, Siemens continued its policy of exporting. Siemens, according the Japanese market a minor status, had made an agreement with Western for market division and technology cooperation in the Japanese market.

After the First World War, however, Siemens decided to begin local manufacturing of electric machinery products in Japan, including telephone equipment, while renewing its pre-war agreement with Western. At the same time, Siemens concluded a joint-venture contract with Furukawa Electric Industry and included telephone equipment in the activities of the new company. However, this contract contravened the agreement with Western. Once it realized that, Siemens attempted to revise the terms of its memorandum with Furukawa. The result was that telephone equipment was removed from the list of activities of the joint-venture company Fuji Electric, which was established in 1923. With regard to telephone equipment, Siemens thus continued its export strategy as before. However, rather than being a positive strategic decision, this strategy may be termed a "coerced export strategy," since Siemens adopted it in spite of its manifest desire to manufacture locally.

The Great Kanto Earthquake brought about a rapid expansion of the Japanese telephone equipment market, and it was a major turning point for the Japanese telephone equipment industry. In response to Fuji Electric's demands, Siemens transferred its telephone equipment sales rights to Fuji, but Siemens did not agree to the localization of production of automatic switchboards. Meanwhile, a fierce battle for orders erupted between Fuji Electric's SH-type automatic switchboard, and Western/NEC's Stroger-type switchboard. Although strong in the Osaka – Kobe area, Fuji was vanquished overall by Western Electric/NEC. Furukawa Electric Industry saw lack of price competitiveness as the cause, but another factor was the Buy Japanese movement. As a result, Furukawa tried to persuade Siemens to switch to local manufacturing. But Siemens, in negotiations in 1929, once again refused.

Siemens' compliance with Furukawa's demand to embark on local manufacturing of automatic switchboards had to wait for Fuji Electric's management crisis and the Communications Ministry's strengthening of its plan for promotion of domestic manufacturing. Fuji dealt with its management crisis by implementing reorganization and personnel reductions. Furukawa also pressed Siemens to strengthen Fuji's independence. On the other hand, Siemens planned a restructuring that would strengthen its control over Fuji's business, and Siemens endeavored to ensure the preservation of its investments in the form of loans to Fuji. Moreover, given the background of its international cooperation agreement, Siemens came to look to the restriction of competition in the Japanese market. In particular, Siemens supported a plan for the merger of Fuji Electric with Mitsubishi Electric. Thus, for the time being, the plan for localization of automatic switchboard manufacturing was frozen.

With the coming of the global depression in 1929, Siemens' profitability also deteriorated, and it had neither the incentive nor the financial resources to undertake overseas direct investment. But from the perspective of Fuji Electric and Furukawa, the limited product line-up, and above all the lack of manufacturing rights for automatic switchboards, were cause for impatience – particularly since their competitors were at this time beginning to undertake local manufacturing. In 1931, when Yoshimura became president, he, on the one hand, implemented a second personnel reduction, but, on the other hand, he once again implored Siemens to allow local manufacturing of telephone switchboards. This request was based on the need to respond to the Encourage Japanese Manufacturing movement as well as on the desire for diversification, premised on price cooperation in the Japanese market. Yoshimura argued that automatic switchboard manufacturing was the key to overcoming Fuji's management crisis.

This plan of Yoshimura's was in complete opposition to that of Siemens, which called for the curtailment of Fuji Electric's business and the reversion to a strategy based on exports by Siemens. However, having promised the Communications Ministry – without Siemens' approval – that it would begin local manufacturing, Fuji Electric made a last-ditch attempt to persuade Siemens, and this time Fuji was successful. The main reason why Siemens was forced to accept local manufacturing was the Communications Ministry's Encourage Japanese Manufacturing plan. Once Fuji Electric embarked on local manufacturing, the increase in orders from the Communications Ministry resulted in rapid growth.

In a move related to the agreement between Siemens and Western Electric, Fuji Electric and NEC entered into an agreement that divided the Japanese market based on a 70 percent share for NEC and 30 percent for Fuji Electric in addition to implementing cross-licensing. Siemens confirmed this agreement after the fact. Moreover, Fuji Electric also entered into a cooperation agreement with wireless manufacturer Tokyo Electric. Once again, Siemens confirmed the agreement. The result of the agreement with Tokyo Electric was the creation of a communications equipment manufacturing company, Fujitsu, with Siemens being forced into a position of separation from this company. From the point of view of ownership and management, this new company was overwhelmingly under the shadow of Fuji Electric, and even in the area of technology, it aspired to independence from Siemens.[32]

Thus, to summarize one more time, we can conclude that Siemens was dispossessed of its managerial control:

> Ultimately, the basic picture of Siemens' Japanese telephone business, and above all its automatic switchboard business was, first, adherence to an export strategy; second, local manufacturing under pressure from the Communications Ministry and Furukawa; and, third, a similarly forced separation from its Japanese subsidiary. The basic trend was toward the relinquishing of managerial control by Siemens over its Japanese subsidiaries and related companies.[33]

My interpretation of the telephone switchboards history as that of relinquishing managerial control is also true to a certain degree for the entire

Fuji Electric business. The founding of Fujitsu as a maker of telephone switchboards can be viewed as an extreme example, Although such loss of managerial control has also been experienced by the American company Western Electric, parent company of NEC, the fate of Siemens, which was different in that it was a company of a political ally, was the same.

With the subsequent breakout of the Sino-Japanese War in July 1937, the Japanese economy was placed on a war footing. To manage external economic relations, trade and foreign exchange controls were implemented by the adoption of the Provisional Financial Regulation Law and the Law on Provisional Regulation of Export, Import, and Others in September 1937. The Ammunition Industry Mobilization Law was enacted in January 1938, and the National Mobilization Law took effect in April 1938.

Fuji Electric's Performance improved dramatically. Production, sales, and profit rose at a fast clip. The dividend rate increased to 10 percent. The main Kawasaki plant was expanded. Because of difficulties in obtaining mechanical equipment and securing trained personnel, there were also plans to acquire and develop contractor factories. Such factories were set up in Nagoya, Yokkaichi, and Osaka, and Fuji Electric provided the capital, made financing available, offered equipment subsidies, gave technical guidance, and provided other kinds of support. The volume of import transactions gradually decreased because of the tight supply in Germany and the difficulties associated with delivering goods from Germany. "Despite all this, orders continued to pour in from Manchuria and the Japan war machine."[34]

5. REMAINING PROBLEMS

In conclusion, let me recount the problems that still need to be addressed to resolve the issues raised by the organizers of this workshop.

First, this paper leaves unanswered questions such as what assessment Siemens had of the situation existing at the time, and, moreover, what Siemens thought about the future changes that might occur in the business environment. No archive materials directly related to this issue can be found if we limit ourselves to the materials on telephone equipment business circulated at the time within Siemens.

The second question is related to the first one and deals with how Siemens viewed or anticipated the Japanese economy's conversion to a system geared to a total war. Together with AEG, its competitor, Siemens had experienced the totality of the First World War. Japan, on the other hand, had not experienced it, as pointed out by Nobutoshi

Hagiwara. The Japanese government and military establishment have unwittingly entered into a new total war without realizing its gravity. This was in marked contrast to Germany's position. Nazi Germany had tried to avoid a full-scale war by launching a blitzkrieg, and was forced to engage in all-out warfare only when its strategy was unsuccessful. The question is how Siemens viewed this lack of strategic thinking on the part of the Japanese government and military establishment.

The third remaining question is related to the economic spheres dominated by Japan and Germany. Siemens continued supplying Japan with high-performance, oversize equipment that could not yet be manufactured locally, and also continued exporting its products to Korea and Manchuria.[35] This situation presents two problems. The first is related to the linkage between the Great Asia Co-prosperity Sphere and the Greater Nazi Economic Sphere. Although Japan and Germany had been conflicting over China for a long time, they finally reached agreement when the government of Nazi Germany recognized Manchukuo in May 1938. But these two spheres remained plagued by the lack of free foreign exchange, and the cooperation had failed to produce any tangible results. One question is how this reality reflected itself in the business practices of Siemens in the Far East and Central and Eastern Europe. The next question concerns a comparison between the two economic spheres. It is believed that Siemens preferred conducting its business within the European economic sphere than in the distant Far East, and the question is how this strategy manifested itself in reality. It would be also of significant interest to compare the business development practices pursued by Siemens in the distant lands of the Far East and South America.

Fourth, we need to establish what post-Second World War history teaches us. In 1945, Siemens possessed 30 percent of the entire Fuji Electric stock – that is, up to the last moment Siemens continued to have a controlling share of Fuji Electric stock despite its relinquishing managerial control. The Siemens' share was subsequently seized as the asset of a hostile country under a completely different kind of dictatorship – the General Headquarters (GHQ) of the Allied Forces – in the period between August 1945 and April 1952. After Japan regained its independence, in June 1952, Siemens again offered a broad range of technologies to Fuji Electric and Fujitsu, and invested in Fuji Electric. However, Siemens' stake was only 5 percent at the end of 1956. The questions are what this much lower share tells us about the pre-war strategy of Siemens *vis-à-vis* Japan, and whether it can be that Siemens had initially been less prejudiced in terms of share percentage.

PART II

Trajectory of Japanese-German Business Relations

Source: *International Cartels in Business History* (co-authored with Hara Terushi) (Kudō Akira and Hara Terushi (eds)), Tokyo: University of Tokyo Press, 1992, pp. 1–24.

5

International Cartels in Business History

I. INTRODUCTION

This chapter examines the evolution of international cartels by focusing on the process of organization as well as rationalization of manufacture and sales in corporations in different countries through the international cooperation and competition that took place. As a definition of cartels we propose the following: "Cartels have been defined as voluntary agreements among independent enterprises in a single industry or closely related industries with the purpose of exercising a monopolistic control of the market."[1] The United Nations, Department of Economic Affairs, gives the following definition of international cartels: "International cartels are of the same nature and serve essentially the same purpose [as national cartels], with the qualification that the contracting parties are located in two or more countries and may be either single firms or groups of firms already combined into national cartels."[2]

Within international cartels, there are both raw materials cartels and manufactured goods cartels. An examination of manufactured goods cartels or, more precisely, industrial cartels is undertaken because raw materials cartels are in many cases affected by the geographical, political, and diplomatic factors of the countries where the raw materials are produced. In contrast, manufactured goods cartels are more strongly influenced by operational factors, such as production technology and terms of sale. Therefore, manufactured goods cartels prove more suitable for a historical analysis of the management of international cartels.

We have limited ourselves to international cartels from the inter-war period, the 1920s and 1930s, because it is within the process of economic reconstruction after the First World War, in the 1920s, that the full-scale establishment of international cartels can first be observed. Moreover, this was the period when the world economy began to be reorganized through competition and cooperation on an international level. One of the factors behind the emergence of the international cartels was the imbalance that arose between production and consumption. This was due to the accumulation of surplus production power exceeding demand, caused by the construction or enlargement of production facilities to meet the urgent demand that arose during the war. The international nitrogen and dyestuffs cartels are two examples of cartels that arose in this way. Additionally, with the progressive internationalization of economic activity, a number of international agreements concerning patent rights and production method exchanges were made. Therefore, international cartels were set up in order to assist in the implementation of these international agreements. The incandescent electric light bulb cartel is representative of this type. Furthermore, corporations in various countries, confronted with the intensification of international competition, set up international cartels in order to preserve their domestic markets for domestic producers. The railroad materials cartel is one such example. In terms of the research that has been carried out up to now, analysis that has been done on the managerial history of the international cartels remains insufficient. Full-scale research on this theme remains a task for the future. However, on the basis of the little research that has actually been done, we wish to consolidate what basic knowledge is available to enable debate to take place at this conference.[3]

II. SOME SELECTED TOPICS ON INTERNATIONAL CARTELS

1. Geographical Distribution

There are no conclusive figures available on the number of international cartels in the inter-war period. Haussmann and Ahearn emphasized that from 1929 to 1937 42% of all international trade was under the control of international cartels.[4] Hexner considered that the ratio of major products under the control of international cartels in 1937 was more or less the same.[5] At this stage, we cannot specify the total number of international cartels, but we can offer conjectures on the situation as regards their ratio by location, through an understanding of the regional distribution of trade. The ratio by area of export of industrial raw materials, semimanufactured and manufactured goods for 1926, 1929, and 1935 is shown in Table 5.1. According to this, the percentage of manufactured goods exported in 1935 was 70% for Europe, 13% for America, and just over 17% for the rest of the world. This is, therefore, the reason for the international cartels being centered in Europe at this time.[6] The importance of the European countries becomes even clearer if we look at the number of cartel members by country, as shown in Table 5.2.[7]

Table 5.1 Share of Europe and the United States in the Total Value of World Exports of Industrial Products, 1925, 1929, and 1935 (%)

Area	Raw materials and semi-manufactured goods			Manufactured goods		
	1925	1929	1935	1925	1929	1935
Continental Europe	24	29	31	47	49	49
Great Britain	5	5	6	25	20	21
Total (Europe)	29	34	37	72	69	70
United States	20	18	15	14	18	13
Rest of the World	51	48	48	14	13	17
Total (World)	100	100	100	100	100	100

Source: United Nations, Department of Economic Affairs, *International Cartels* (New York, 1947), p. 3.

2. Membership and Administration

By classifying the international cartels according to differences in the form of membership, the following three forms emerge. The first is where participation was by individual corporations from different countries; the alum cartel, which was set up in 1901 and re-established in 1926, is an example of this type. The second form is where participation was by domestic cartels of different countries; the iron and steel cartel is one such example. The third is where participation was by various

Table 5.2 Number of International Cartel Member Corporations by Country

Country	No. of Participants		
	Direct	Indirect or Partial	Total
France (and colonies)	67	2	69
Germany	57		57
Great Britain	31	9	40
Switzerland	25		25
Holland	20		20
Belgium	20		20
Czechoslovakia	17	3	20
Norway	16	1	17
Sweden	16		16
Austria	15	3	18
Italy	15	1	16
Poland	13	2	15
Finland	10	1	11
Yugoslavia	9	1	10
Hungary	8	3	11
United States	8	3	11
Japan	2	2	4

Source: Laurence Ballande, *Essai d'Elude Monographique et Slatistique sur les Ententes Economiques Internationales* (Paris, 1937), pp. 312–13.

forms of organizations, such as domestic cartels, domestic or foreign trusts and/or individual corporations; the potassium and rayon cartels are examples of this form.[8]

The administration of the international cartels was entrusted either to a body formed of representatives from the member corporations or to an organization legally independent of the member corporations and their agreement. In the first, day-to-day business was dealt with by the organization's executive office in accordance with decisions made at regular meetings of the members' representatives. More important business was decided at general meetings. This was a system that worked as far as the fixing of minimum price levels and the protecting of domestic markets and such matters were concerned. However, where it had to deal with production quotas, apportionment of orders, and other matters relating to accounting or indemnity payments, the fact that the adjudicators were also, as representatives of the member corporations, interested parties, made impartial administration difficult. This was where the second administrative form, where administration was carried out by groups that were more or less legally independent from the member companies, was more effective. The Société Anonyme Suisse of the aluminum cartel and the Société Allemande GmbH of the rayon cartel are two examples of this. Moreover, within the second form there were cases of centralized consolidated control organs, such as Phoebus of the incandescent electric light bulb industry, being formed by the international cartels so as to be able to perform the administrative functions required. There were also cases of joint sales organizations (comptoir de vente), such as the Convention Internationale de l'Azote in Basel, being set up.

3. Functions of International Cartels

These agreements can be classified on the basis of the following five functions. (1) Agreements regarding production, where a fixed standard rate was set for production; such methods as the individual enterprise production quota, the banning of installation of new equipment in factories, and the payment of compensation to firms whose production had been cut were all used to achieve this. (2) Agreements regarding sales, which were first of all designed to protect the domestic markets of the member corporations and block the advance of foreign corporations into them. The methods used to achieve this can also be said to have served as substitutes for the setting up of import quota systems and protective tariff duties by governments. Furthermore, the export markets were divided among the cartel's member companies. This could be done either by area or amount of exports, but usually a combination of the two was used. In other words, it became a system whereby the export volume and the export markets of a said product were distributed among the cartel members. Where these sales agreements went further, joint sales organizations (comptoir de vente) were set up. These organizations collected together the orders received and distributed them among the member corporations. (3) Price adjustment agreements, which used the methods of compulsory price-setting and indicative price agreements. These agreements included export price-setting, market price-setting by country, and price-setting for specific markets, etc. In addition to this, the method used for distribution of profits between member corporations can be thought of as having the same effect as indirect price adjustments. (4) Agreements concerning inventories, which included cases of buying in of stock by the cartels or stockpiling by member companies, used in order to prevent price falls caused by excess production. (5) Agreements concerning product quality and rationalization, which provided for patent and technology exchanges, joint surveys, and the creation of research bodies.[9]

4. Legal System

If we take a look at cartel legislation, we can see that in the 1930s European countries, which were restricted by the size of their domestic markets in comparison with the American one, showed a fairly tolerant attitude regarding international cartels. In the majority of countries, rather than trying to actually make the cartels illegal, attempts were made to prevent abuses of the system in advance. Additionally, when abuses did occur, efforts to eradicate them were made.[10] Against this background, the most important historical fact to be noted is that in European countries in the 1930s, the general trend was not just to approve the setting up of domestic cartels, but going a step further, to in fact make it compulsory. This change in stance from prohibiting to allowing, and then enforcing, the setting up of domestic cartels, can be said to be what caused the acceleration of the formation of the international cartels.

Before 1930, only Germany and Norway had special cartel laws. But in the 1930s, the following countries set up cartel enforcement laws: Japan (1931), Italy and Hungary (1932), Czechoslovakia and Poland (1933), Yugoslavia (1934), Belgium and Holland (1935), Bulgaria (1936), Romania and Denmark (1937). Additionally, in Germany the 1923 Cartel Law was revised in 1933, and a cartel enforcement law was set up. In France in 1935, a motion for the Code Marchandean was adopted by the Chamber of Deputies. This organization of markets by each country, through the legal enforcement of cartels, certainly facilitated the formation of international cartels.[11]

5. The Economic Effects

The economic effects of international cartels fall into three categories, as defined by research done by the United Nations, Department of Economic Affairs, namely: effects on cost, effects on price, and effects on trade.[12] International cartels, in contrast to multinational corporations, were formed through agreements between independent corporations and as such did not include a unified cost policy. The membership in cartels of high-cost producers meant that profit had to be obtained by the distribution of markets and price-setting. For lower-cost producers, the elimination of these inefficient producers would have been more beneficial, but as long as they remained members of the international cartels, this proved difficult. Therefore, within those industries in which cartels were formed, high costs were generally maintained. However, at the level of individual enterprises, this was not necessarily the case. Even where temporary price-setting was carried out, those companies that had the desire and capacity to do so tried to reduce costs in order to increase profitability. They usually did so through the implementation of technical advances. Moreover, the economies on advertising through elimination of competition, the reduction of transportation expenses through the distribution of markets, the setting up of joint sales bodies, and so on also had cost-saving effects. International cartels promoted technical progress through the exchange of patents, licenses, and research data. Examples can be seen of international cartels trying to spread new technology and technological improvements among their member corporations as rapidly as possible. These cost-saving effects first became possible where the international cartels had set up central organs from which directives could be given. In the cartel industries as a whole, however, the general result was one of rising costs.

Following this, let us consider the effect on prices. This differed according to whether the international cartel possessed export quotas that were not accompanied by a regional division of the export markets, or whether they were market distribution cartels. International cartels that had export quotas in most cases had a common price policy. The ways of determining sales prices varied. One was to impose a uniform export price on the markets of all member corporations (as in the case of aluminum, mercury, tin plate, phosphate, etc.), while another was to fix the sales price in each export market separately (as in steel cartels). Alternatively, the desired price level could be brought about not by directly fixing the sales price, but by production policies. Within cartels in general, sales prices showed a constant tendency to rise in order to cover the costs of the highest cost producer.

The effect on sales prices of cartels that operated on a market distribution system is as follows. Within these cartels, the system used was one of dividing domestic markets among domestic producers and export markets among the member corporations. The decision on the sales price in the apportioned export market was left up to each individual enterprise; there was no existence of a common price policy. Therefore, according to the degree of monopoly enjoyed by the cartels, price differences arose.

Finally, we have the effects on trade. First, there were cases where international cartels protected internal markets for their domestic producers and prevented the entry of products from other countries' cartels. In such cases, domestic markets were even better protected than through the imposition of tariffs, and the monopolistic position of domestic corporations was further strengthened. Second, we have cases where import quantity limitation agreements were combined with licensing systems, thereby allowing for technical exchanges. Third, agreements over distribution of export markets strengthened the monopoly of corporations in the markets which had been apportioned to them. The countries that were on the receiving end of this, however, suffered difficulties as regards domestic production, and this created unfavorable conditions for their domestic consumers. Fourth, export quota cartels, since competition in terms of product quality remained among the member corporations, in many cases pursued technical innovation rather than aimed for mass production enabling price competition. Finally, if we look at the connection between international cartels and tariff barriers, we can see that corporations from newly industrializing nations in some cases used the threat of protective tariff barriers in their negotiations over membership of the cartels.[13]

6. Subjects Discussed at the Conference

We propose the following subjects concerning international cartels for study and analysis in this volume.

(1) We must describe as accurately as possible the actual facts relating to the research subject of each paper presented here, namely, the various international cartels. In other words, the production agreements, sales quota agreements, price agreements, technological agreements, and other concrete matters relating to international cartels and their methods of administration.

(2) We need to analyze the relationship between domestic and international cartels. In other words, how domestic industries responded to international cartels, the process by which domestic corporations were organized into domestic cartels, and how the latter participated in the international cartels; or in contrast to this, the process by which domestic companies banded together against the international cartels.

(3) There is a need to analyze the effect of the international cartels on the management of domestic corporations. There is also a necessity to clarify the kind of influence not only domestic but also international cartels had on the running of individual companies, illustrating our points as far as possible with actual examples.

(4) There is a need to explain the response of legal systems, governments, industry, and the labor force of each country to international cartels. In addition, it is also necessary to examine the effects of the policies prohibiting cartels in some countries and allowing and regulating them in others, plus the endemic differences in each country's business climate on the management of corporations.

(5) There is a need for an analysis of the effectiveness of international cartels, as well as a requirement to show clearly how the production, sales, technical improvements, etc., of a country changed with the setting up of the cartels.

(6) We must examine not only the cooperative relationships between the corporations of countries within the cartels' areas, but also the competitive aspects of the free market and cartel-free areas.

III. INTERNATIONAL CARTELS AND JAPAN

The above is thus a consolidation of basic facts known about international cartels in the 1920s and 1930s, including the work of past scholars. While fully recognizing that they were above all a European phenomenon, we wish to examine themes concerning the international cartels as looked at from the point of view of Japan, at that time a newly industrializing nation.

1. Regional Characteristics – Japan, the First NIE

A high economic growth rate was one of the characteristic features of modern Japan. Between the two world wars, Japan's annual growth rate surpassed 4%, which was the highest growth figure for any country in the world at that time. Moreover, in terms of speed of industrialization, Japan, together with the countries of Eastern Europe, also stands out. It seized the First World War as an opportunity to begin heavy and chemical industrialization, and the pace of this did not slacken even during the Depression. Japan can thus be said to be the first NIE.[14]

The second salient feature was the strength of economic nationalism. In the 1920s, in Japan, as in other countries, the policy line followed was one of relatively free trade, and the prevalent attitude was one that welcomed direct investment by European and American firms. However, at the same time, policy measures to protect domestic industries, such as imposition of customs duties and limits on the quantity of imports, were also implemented. Moreover, various restrictions were placed on the management rights that could be assumed by European and American companies with respect to enterprises based in Japan. Moving into the 1930s, we find increasing trade protectionism, and the tone changes to one favoring exclusion of direct investment in Japan.[15] Against this background of increasing economic nationalism, Japanese corporations, which formed the backbone of Japan in its emergence as the first NIE, began to strongly assert their independence, both technically and in managerial terms, of European and American corporations. Moving from domination of the domestic market to advance into the Asian market, these Japanese companies became the new challengers to the old order of international cartels.

2. Industrial Characteristics – The Chemical and Electrical Equipment Industries

Taking the chemical and electrical equipment industries as examples of the new industries, even at first glance we can see the existence of distinct differences between the two. First of all, within the chemical industry the protection of technology by a patents system proved rather ineffective. Therefore, enterprises in this industry sought to achieve overseas expansion by exports and licensing rather than by direct investment. In connection with this came the spread of the comprehensive international cartel network worldwide. European companies were the main force in this with I.G. Farbenindustrie (I.G. Farben) at the center, to which were added American corporations.

In contrast to this, within the electrical equipment industry, in addition to exports and licensing, fairly active direct investment and production overseas were carried out, backed up by a viable patents system. American corporations were drawn into the international cartels within this industry too, but these cartels did not have the power of their counterparts in the chemical industry. This was related to the fact that General Electric and the other American corporations within the industry were in fact ahead of the European companies.[16]

3. Vertical Type and Horizontal Type

As well as considering the characteristic features of the country and the two industries, we would now like to give a typology of the kinds of relationships that existed between the international cartels and the Japanese market and Japanese corporations.

Figure 5.1 Vertical Type and Horizontal Type

In one type of relationship, international cartels and/or a few members of international cartels made individual agreements or settlements with Japanese companies. This is called the vertical type. (See Figure 5.1.) This type can often be observed in the chemical industry. It did not involve direct investment, but instead the spreading of the intricate net of the international cartels still wider. European and American corporations made individual agreements with leading Japanese companies with respect to the Japanese and Asian markets so that they could gain supremacy in the Japanese market by using these firms and at the same time apply the brakes to Japanese exports to the Chinese and, more broadly, to the East and Southeast Asian markets.

On the other hand, in the electrical equipment industry, where direct investment played a more important role, relations with Japanese companies were more or less governed, or at least regulation was attempted, through direct investment channels. Consequently, within this industry, vertical-type agreements regarding Japanese corporations and the Japanese market do not have much significance. But there were cases of European and American companies reaching accords over the Japanese and Asian market without the inclusion of Japanese companies. These were either in the form of links in the international cartel structure or separate special agreements. They were in both cases of the horizontal type.[17]

In other words, vertical-type agreements were those formed with Japanese companies with regard to the Japanese and Asian markets, and horizontal-type agreements were those concerning the Japanese market formed between the international cartels' member companies. Actually, there were also agreements that were a mixture of the two types. Provided that the agreements can be recognized as deriving from one type or the other, they have been included here.

4. Seven Case Studies

Presented here as case studies within the chemical industry are dyestuffs, fertilizers, soda, and synthetic oil; and, within the electrical equipment industry, incandescent light bulbs, heavy electrical equipment, and telephones. These have been selected as being the most important examples both quantitatively and qualitatively, as well as the most representative from within their industries. Moreover, in all cases an international cartel or corresponding structure existed within the relevant industry. (For each case, see Figure 5.2.)

Dyestuffs. In August 1926, a gentleman's agreement was made between I.G. Farben and the Japanese dyestuffs industry. This was named the Saitō-Waibel Agreement after its signatories. The main points contained in this agreement were the banning in principle of exports to Japan of products that could be domestically produced, and the free export, as a general rule, of those products such as indigo that could not. The agreement thereby laid down a kind of division of labor within the industry. Thus an agreement had been drawn up between

Figure 5.2 Seven Cases

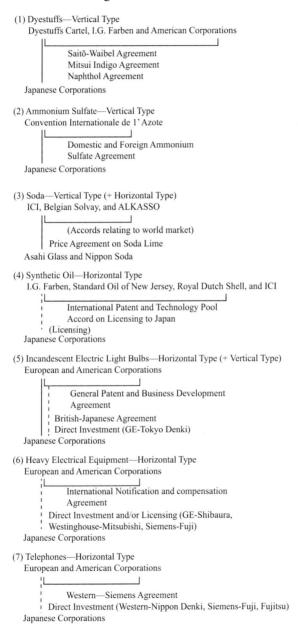

(1) Dyestuffs—Vertical Type
　　Dyestuffs Cartel, I.G. Farben and American Corporations

　　　　　　　　　Saitō-Waibel Agreement
　　　　　　　　　Mitsui Indigo Agreement
　　　　　　　　　Naphthol Agreement
　　Japanese Corporations

(2) Ammonium Sulfate—Vertical Type
　　Convention Internationale de l'Azote

　　　　　　　　　Domestic and Foreign Ammonium
　　　　　　　　　Sulfate Agreement
　　Japanese Corporations

(3) Soda—Vertical Type (+ Horizontal Type)
　　ICI, Belgian Solvay, and ALKASSO

　　　　　　　　　(Accords relating to world market)
　　　　　　　　Price Agreement on Soda Lime
　　Asahi Glass and Nippon Soda

(4) Synthetic Oil—Horizontal Type
　　I.G. Farben, Standard Oil of New Jersey, Royal Dutch Shell, and ICI

　　　　　　　　　International Patent and Technology Pool
　　　　　　　　　Accord on Licensing to Japan
　　　　　　　(Licensing)
　　Japanese Corporations

(5) Incandescent Electric Light Bulbs—Horizontal Type (+ Vertical Type)
　　European and American Corporations

　　　　　　　　　General Patent and Business Development
　　　　　　　　　Agreement
　　　　　　　British-Japanese Agreement
　　　　　　　Direct Investment (GE-Tokyo Denki)
　　Japanese Corporations

(6) Heavy Electrical Equipment—Horizontal Type
　　European and American Corporations

　　　　　　　　　International Notification and compensation
　　　　　　　　　Agreement
　　　　　　　Direct Investment and/or Licensing (GE-Shibaura,
　　　　　　　Westinghouse-Mitsubishi, Siemens-Fuji)
　　Japanese Corporations

(7) Telephones—Horizontal Type
　　European and American Corporations

　　　　　　　　　Western—Siemens Agreement
　　　　　　　Direct Investment (Western-Nippon Denki, Siemens-Fuji, Fujitsu)
　　Japanese Corporations

I.G. Farben and Japanese companies with regard to the Japanese market. This agreement was an individual one made by I.G. Farben, but, if we take into consideration the fact that the company held by far the largest share in the world dyestuffs trade, this agreement can be considered as a vertical-type one. The real reason that I.G. Farben had independently entered into this agreement with the Japanese, and at an early stage in comparison with those developments in other industrial sectors, was closely linked to the fact that the Japanese government had promptly put the import permit system targeting German products into effect early on.[18]

Meanwhile, in Europe, following the German-French agreement made in November 1927, an agreement between Germany, France, and Switzerland was made in April 1929, thereby establishing a three-party international cartel.[19] This cartel very rapidly joined in concerted action with relation to Japan. In October of the same year, the export price to Japan was raised uniformly by 5%. However, Japanese corporations did not follow suit. This was because the growth of the Japanese dyestuffs market, affected by a domestic financial crisis in 1927 and the Depression in 1929, had exhibited a slowdown. Under these circumstances, Japanese dyestuff corporations were able to compete even more vigorously for a share of the market. As a result of this, the share of the three-party cartel fell. Thus it was made clear that in circumstances such as these, the ability of even an international cartel to cope was limited.[20]

At this time exports of European companies to Japan were showing a downward trend. This was caused by the fall of the yen following the re-imposition of a ban on the export of gold in December 1931. In addition, one after the other, Nihon Senryō Seizō (Japan Dyestuffs Manufacturing Co.) and Mitsui Mining Co. were successful in developing new products. Thus the international cartels and their member corporations were forced to find new ways to deal with the situation. One way was by intensifying efforts to form vertical-type relationships through the concluding of agreements with Japanese corporations. In March 1935, I.G. Farben concluded the Variamine Blue Agreement with Nihon Senryō Seizō. This was later ratified by three Swiss firms. By this agreement, Nihon Senryō Seizō recognized I.G. Farben's patent and agreed not to carry out exports of identical products. As vicarious compensation, an accord was obtained on sales quotas for the Japanese market; for Naphthol AS the share was I.G. Farben 32% and Nihon Senryō Seizō 68%, while for Variamine Blue-B the figures were reversed. At the same time, the sales price was to be equal. Thus a vertical-type agreement came into being. This agreement lasted until 1941.[21]

I.G. Farben also made the Astraphloxine Agreement with Nihon Senryō in February 1934. The main points of this ran parallel to those in the Variamine Blue Agreement. In return for relinquishing exports, Nihon Senryō Seizō got a 50% share of the Japanese market and I.G. Farben the remaining 50%. This agreement lasted until the end of 1939.[22]

A vertical-type relationship was formed also between I.G. Farben, the international dyestuffs cartel, and Mitsui Mining. First, with regard to sulfur black dye, in April 1931 the three-party cartel made an agreement with Mitsui Mining's representative, Mitsui & Co., Ltd., regarding the quantity and price of exports to China. The American corporation Nacco (National Aniline and Chemical Co.) and Du Pont de Nemours & Co. were also drawn into this agreement, which lapsed as early as the end of 1933.

In addition, in October 1931, I.G. Farben concluded an agreement with Mitsui & Co., which was henceforth to be the sole representative of Mitsui Mining with regard to alizarine blue. The agreement concerned the division of the Japanese market, and at first this was apportioned at a ratio of 60% to I.G. Farben and 40% to Mitsui & Co. This agreement was revised again and again, and, although it lasted until 1940, during its term the market ratio was in fact reversed to I.G. Farben 40%, Mitsui & Co. 60%.[23]

The biggest problem remained indigo. In April 1926, Mitsui Mining finally managed to achieve its aim of the industrialization of indigo production. Then, in October 1929, the company managed to obtain a subsidy for the promotion of dyestuffs manufacture. Thus construction of a factory was begun in February 1931. Its products were finally put on the market in the latter half of 1932. Meanwhile, Nacco and Du Pont, which had already succeeded in the development of indigo immediately after the First World War, now embarked in rapid succession on export ventures to the Far East. The four-party cartel concluded a six-party agreement with these two corporations concerning the sales ratio of the Japanese, Chinese, and Far Eastern markets.[24]

In addition to this, the six corporations concluded an agreement with Mitsui Mining in February 1934. This concerned cooperation over the sales price within the Japanese market and the sales ratio, which was to be 25% for the six corporations and 75% for Mitsui

Mining. This was a temporary agreement valid until July 1934. Soon after, discussions for the conclusion of a formal agreement took place.[25] At last, in May 1935 a settlement was reached. The formal agreement held Japanese exports to China of indigo (20%) to a three-year total of 96,300 piculs. As vicarious compensation, the six corporations were limited in their exports to Japan.[26] This agreement was extended several times in favor of Mitsui Mining until the end of 1940, but war in Europe broke out before it had expired, and thus Imperial Chemical Industries (ICI) broke the agreement.[27]

Ammonium Sulfate. In the first half of the 1920s, the first plant and equipment investment boom occurred in Japan, for which Nippon Chisso Hiryō (Japan Nitrogen Fertilizer Co.) and Denki Kagaku Kōgyō (Electrochemical Industries) were mainly responsible, and thus an ammonium sulfate industry was established in Japan. At the end of the decade, there was, on the one hand, a second plant and equipment investment boom, and on the other, an increasing aggressiveness in the export offensive by European and American companies. In August 1930, the Convention Internationale de l'Azote (CIA) was set up, and European firms began to revise their relationships with Japanese companies accordingly. As a result, in December 1930 a proposal for an agreement, known as the Fujiwara-Bosch Agreement Proposal, which mainly concerned sales, was drawn up, but this was not in fact put into effect. Later, in April 1931, a proposal for a Domestic and Foreign Ammonium Sulfate Agreement, with more or less the same contents as the previous agreement, was made, but this also was not put into effect.

In July 1932, the CIA was set up once more, and through this, in March 1934, an agreement regarding domestic and foreign ammonium sulfate was able to at last be made. In it limits were placed on exports to Japan by enterprises belonging to the CIA, while restrictions were also placed on exports by Japanese corporations in terms of quantity, price, and area. This was a vertical-type agreement. It was subsequently renewed twice. However, I.G. Farben, which considered that exports to Japan would not increase any further, agreed to provide the technology for the Harber-Bosch method to Taki Seihisho (Taki Fertilizer Works) in May 1935. It subsequently agreed to do the same for Nihon Tāru Kōgyō (Japan Tar Industries, now Mitsubishi Chemical Industries) and a number of other companies.[28]

Soda. In 1920, an international alkali cartel was organized, mainly by Belgian Solvay, with the participation of Brunner, Mond & Co., and United Alkali Co. As a result of this, market-control rights over the European mainland were given to Solvay and over all other areas to the two British companies, which in December 1926 became Imperial Chemical Industries, ICI. However, in 1919, the ALKASSO Alkali Export Union was set up by American corporations, mainly those using the Solvay process, thereby forcing competition on the British companies in the world market. Both sides engaged in a desperate struggle to capture markets outside of Europe until a truce was finally called in February 1924.

The most important markets for Brunner, Mond–ICI were the Asian market centering on Japan and the South American market. Between 1921 and 1924 dumping of magadi soda and soda lime was carried out in competition on the Japanese market, from which Brunner, Mond came out successful. Therefore it made a truce with ALKASSO at about the same time, and they were thus able to face their other competitors in unity. In 1929 they came into confrontation over dumping with the Japanese companies Asahi Glass Co. and Nippon Soda Co.

Meanwhile, in 1929, sales quotas for the world market were decided on between ICI and ALKASSO, and interests were balanced with Belgian Solvay. In 1930, when the Japanese government was making preparations for the application of an antidumping law, ICI entered into a price agreement over soda lime with Asahi Glass and Nippon Soda. As a result, a vertical-type relationship was formed. However, this agreement collapsed almost immediately, and dumping began once more, finally ceasing some time after the re-imposition of a ban on the export of gold. Thus a vertical-type relationship was not in fact able to be re-established.

In 1936, ICI, ALKASSO, and Belgian Solvay came to an accord over regional distribution and sales quotas for the world market. Within this the Japanese soda lime market was divided between ICI and ALKASSO at a ratio of 65% and 35%, respectively, thereby establishing a horizontal-type agreement. However, it must be noted that in 1937 imports to Japan fell to zero and thus the quota agreement did not in fact have any substance.[29]

Synthetic Oil. In 1927, I.G. Farben and Standard Oil of New Jersey made the first agreement over the exchange of hydrogenation processing technology, and the scope of this was considerably extended in November 1929. Later on, Royal Dutch Shell and ICI also entered into this agreement. Moreover, in the early 1930s Standard Oil and Royal Dutch Shell set up the International Hydrogenation Patents Co., Ltd. (IHP), thereby forming an international patents pool. I.G. Farben was eager to provide licenses to Japan, whereas the British and American companies, taking into account the political situation at the time, did not welcome this development. However, they did not express strong opposition in the period up until the summer of 1939. In fact, in July 1939 I.G. Farben and IHP came to an accord regarding licensing to Japan (fixing licensing fees and determining obligations regarding the exchange of know-how), thereby establishing a kind of horizontal relationship. Thus for a time it seemed as if I.G. Farben would succeed in its licensing plans. However, opposition was demonstrated to this by the Japanese Navy, which was developing its own production method. Starting with the failure of talks with South Manchurian Railways Co. in 1935, I.G. Farben faced many frustrations until it managed to hold negotiations with Ogura Oil Co. from 1938 to 1939. Furthermore, Standard Oil and Royal Dutch Shell took the chance given them by the outbreak of the war in Europe to harden their stance against Japan. Thus provision of licenses by I.G. Farben became an absolute impossibility.

For I.G. Farben, the directives of the German government to cooperate with Japan held more importance than I.G.'s consideration with regard to the British and American corporations. Thus at the end of the war, in January 1945, it finally managed to conclude some kind of contract for the provision of technology with the Imperial Japanese Army. But this contract proved to have very little basis in reality, and this was the end of this particular episode.[30]

Incandescent Electric Light Bulbs. In 1924 an incandescent electric light bulb international cartel was formed through the General Patent and Business Development Agreement. During the Depression, four business groups in this industry were set up one after the other in Japan, thereby organizing most of the small-to-medium-sized companies in Japan into some kind of grouping. In October 1933, these joined to form the Japan Electric Light Bulb Industrial Association Federation. The largest corporation outside of this federation, Tokyo Denki (Tokyo Electric Co., General Electric Co.'s subsidiary), finally joined it in November 1934. Following this, the organization continued to grow.

From about 1931, Japanese exports began to grow rapidly, through the efforts of the smaller enterprises (Tokyo Denki was forbidden by an agreement made with General Electric in 1919 from exporting to countries other than China), and thus trade friction arose in various parts of the globe. In May 1934, an agreement was made with certain British companies, the main point of which was the restriction of exports to Britain to 33.8 million units for a one-year period starting in February 1934. In fact, the actual figures went far in excess of this limit. In February 1935, Phoebus, a syndicate set up in 1924, made an application to join the international cartel; in spite of negotiations, this never came to pass. Therefore, the vertical relationship formed within this industrial sector did not develop fully. Moreover, one of the characteristics of the relationship that developed here was that it had tried to limit Japanese exports more than in the other cases examined.[31]

Heavy Electrical Equipment. The international arm of General Electric Co., namely, International General Electric Co. (IGE), made an agreement with its subsidiary company in Japan, Shibaura Seisakusho (Shibaura Manufacturing Co.) in 1919, thereby recognizing the latter's exclusive rights with regard to the Japanese market. Siemens and Westinghouse Electric & Manufacturing Co., on the other hand, concluded an agreement in 1924 over exchange of patents, technology, and division of markets. Through this agreement, Siemens took the markets of Germany, Austria, and the three Baltic states, while Westinghouse took America and Canada. All other areas were to be open to competition. Regarding the Japanese market, the exclusive rights of the various subsidiary companies, including Fuji Denki Seizō (Fuji Electric Manufacturing Co.), established in August 1923, and Mitsubishi Denki (Mitsubishi Electric Co.), which had made a patent agreement with Westinghouse in November 1923, were recognized. Thus the respective subsidiaries of General Electric, Siemens, and Westinghouse in Japan, Shibaura Seisakusho, Fuji Denki, and Mitsubishi Denki, were all able to obtain exclusive rights within the Japanese heavy industrial equipment market. However, on the other hand, Japanese subsidiaries were still limited to the Japanese market in the context of "export terms." Control over the Japanese market was thereby exercised mainly by direct investment.

During the period of the Depression, in December 1930, General Electric, Westinghouse, Allgemeine Elektrizitäts-Gesellschaft, Siemens, plus the British firm English Electric Co., Ltd., and the Swiss company Brown Boveri and Cie. entered into a global sales agreement, which went under the name of the International Notification and Compensation Agreement (INCA). Japan and Southern Manchuria were areas not covered by this agreement, and therefore it did not have any direct influence on Japanese companies. However, the markets into which Japanese enterprises had finally begun to advance, namely, China,

India, Soviet Asia, and Southeast Asia, were put under the control of the European and American companies. By carrying out direct investment, certain European and American companies had managed to spread the web of control over the Japanese market through an ambiguous form of horizontal-type agreement.

Around this time, General Electric, Westinghouse, Siemens, etc. flinched from engaging in fierce competition within the Japanese market. They hoped that Japanese companies would cooperate by price agreements, corporate mergers, and holding companies. Particular attention was given to the examination of a proposal for a merger by the Special Bureau for Industrial Rationalization of the Ministry of Commerce and Industry. This was not in fact put into effect. Efforts towards cooperation, however, achieved success in May 1931 through the achievement of an agreement on sales quotas, prices, and market outlets between Shibaura Seisakusho, Mitsubishi Denki, Fuji Denki, and the wholly Japanese Hitachi Seisakusho (Hitachi Manufacturing Co.). This proved to be a great relief to the European and American companies.[32]

Telephones. The Japanese telephone industry and telephone equipment market began to expand around the turn of the century. In response, the American company Western Electric Co. set up Nippon Electric Gōshi Kaisha (NEC) in 1898, and thus began production in Japan of telephone equipment, using the company's own technology. Nippon Electric was incorporated in the following year, with Western Electric having a stockholding ratio of 54%.[33] In contrast to this, the German company Siemens continued its response in the form of exports. This caution owed to the fact that the company occupied only second place in the telephone equipment field, as well as to the fact that it felt Japan to be in psychological terms as well as in actual distance, "the furthest place on earth."[34]

Before the First World War, Western Electric and Siemens had made an agreement regarding division of the Japanese market and technical cooperation. This was eventually renewed by the two companies after the war, in 1921. The main points of the revised agreement were, first, the division of the Japanese market at a ratio of 10% to Siemens and 90% to Western Electric, to be achieved by the end of 1925. The second point concerned technical cooperation including cross-licensing. The third point was that this agreement was treated as a link in the two companies' global cooperation strategy, and it was thus to run until the end of 1935.[35]

Although this agreement did not allow for diversified expansion, as would have been the case had an international cartel been formed by the two companies, it can be included within the definition of horizontal relationships as given here. Western Electric was in fact carrying out direct investment in Japanese companies, and Siemens upon tying up the agreement also plunged straight into a course of direct investment at the beginning of the 1930s. So direct investment took the place of exports as the way of entering into the Japanese market. Thus it can be assumed that it was hoped that a horizontal-type agreement would play a role in achieving direct investment.

Of the seven examples given here, the agreements within the dye-stuffs, ammonium sulfate, and soda industries fall mainly into the vertical-relation category, whereas those in the incandescent electric bulb, heavy electrical equipment, telephone, and synthetic oil industries fall largely into the horizontal-relation category. Therefore, apart from the case of synthetic oil, the chemical industry was made up of vertical and the electrical equipment industry of horizontal relationships. The reasons that the relations in the synthetic oil industry were of the horizontal type are that in this case exports had virtually no significance and an international patents pool existed within the industry, as was the case in the electrical equipment industry.

IV. INTERNATIONAL CARTELS AND DIRECT INVESTMENT

The typology of horizontal and vertical relations was evolved through a perception of the features characterizing the Japanese market, namely, rapid growth and the rise of economic nationalism, and the industrial characteristics of the chemical and electrical industries. Taking a different perspective, this could be said to represent the two responses of the European and American companies to Japan's challenge through high growth and nationalism. These responses were the vertical relationship as represented by international cartels and the horizontal relationship as represented by direct investment. If we judge the effectiveness of the responses from the above analysis, we can arrange the data as in Table 5.3. In the 1920s, the Japanese challenge was intensified due to a high economic growth rate against which the horizontal response proved effective, whereas the vertical response was not. The vertical-type response of international cartels should have been effective against the challenge of economic nationalism, but the situation in Japan in the 1930s was a combination of high growth and economic nationalism, where both vertical and horizontal responses were rendered ineffective.

Table 5.3 Challenge and Response

Challenge/Response	Vertical Type	Horizontal Type	Case
A High Growth Rate	Ineffective	Effective	Japan 1920s
B Economic Nationalism	Effective	Ineffective	
A + B	Ineffective	Ineffective	Japan 1930s
Case	Chemical Ind.	Electrical Ind.	

To paraphrase this, in order to deal with the breaking up of the control networks of the multinational companies, especially those of German origin, due to the cataclysmic movements of the world economy caused by the First World War, a need arose for the reformation of the international cartels based in the West, or rather Western Europe, in the 1920s. The high growth rate and rise of companies in the peripheral area, namely, the East, especially Eastern Europe and East Asia, posed a challenge to the old order of the international cartels. In response to this, the Western European companies tried to draw American corporations, on the one hand, and the companies of the Eastern European nations and Japan, on the other, into the international cartel net.

As a part of the "Eastern world," the Japanese market was mainly treated as a freely competitive and cartel-free zone. Therefore, within the Japanese market competition with European and American companies was added to the competition between Japanese firms. The former practiced putting external pressure on and dumping against the Japanese heavy and chemical industry corporations, which had suddenly expanded during the First World War. However, these corporations had the power to survive such offensives.

The Western companies had two ways of dealing with this. In the case of the electric industry, in which there was direct investment in Japan, the response was for Western companies to establish agreements among themselves with regard to the Japanese market, thus creating a horizontal relationship. This was, in fact, successful. In the case of the chemical industry, in which there was virtually no direct investment, the response was for international cartels to make separate agreements with Japanese companies, in other words to seek to achieve cooperation through a vertical relation. However, this achieved no success in the 1920s. Within the dyestuffs industry, the Saitō-Waibel Agreement could be said to be an exception to this. But even in this case, when the international cartel raised its export prices in 1928, the Japanese corporations did not follow suit. Thus the cartel's share of the market fell. This clearly shows us that the power of control that international cartels could exercise over the Japanese corporations had its limitations.

In the 1930s, economic nationalism, as well as a high growth rate, had a hand in the challenge posed by Japan. The Japanese market became restricted and systematized by economic nationalism. In response to this, the international cartels that had achieved steady success in the West tried to make or actually made individual agreements with Japanese corporations. However, these companies, using a high growth rate as their weapon, enlarged their share of the market and were not in fact drawn into the net of the international cartels. An illustration of this situation is shown in the dyestuff industry. Even in industries such as the electrical industry, which had been subject to direct investment, faced with the pressures of nationalism and the desire for independence of subsidiary companies in Japan, foreign companies were forced to make a gradual retreat.

We have examined the relationships that emerged between the Japanese corporations and international cartels as they were formed within the wider context of relations between Japan and European and American corporations. Moreover, we have divided these relationships into horizontal and vertical types. In view of our emphasis on this definition, we must first discuss why these two types came into being and how these caused differences to arise in the business performances of individual corporations. More detailed research is necessary to determine whether this is an appropriate perception of the facts and to determine the reasons for the emergence of differences. Finally, there is a need to examine the relations between multinationals and international cartels. More research still needs to be done on determining whether the two were complementary and whether they possess interchangeable elements or not.

Source: *Asia Pacific Business Review*, Vol. 2, No. 1, 1995, pp. 20–36.

6

Western Multinationals in Japan: Missed Opportunities and Lessons from Inter-war Business History

INTRODUCTION

THE JAPANESE-EUROPEAN UNION relationship has experienced trade imbalances since the 1970s, alongside consecutive Japanese surpluses. The relationship is now seeing a kind of new imbalance: that is, the imbalance of direct investment. Currently, the volume of Japanese direct investment in the EU is more than ten times that of the EU's investment in Japan. Certainly, the Japan–US relationship has also experienced investment imbalances, but, without doubt, to a lesser degree. The new focal point of economic relations between Japan and the EU, as well as between Japan and the US, seems to be shifting from trade imbalance to investment imbalance. The most decisive reason for the investment imbalances seems to be the 'underinvestment' of Western firms in Japan. As a result, there is a growing tendency to consider direct steps which might discourage Japanese investment in Western countries or encourage Western investment in Japan. If it were preferable to discourage Japanese investment, voluntary investment restrictions (VIR) might be introduced following the example of voluntary export restrictions (VER). If the aim is to promote Western investment in Japan, and attain a future balance, then, it is argued, political, social and cultural hurdles need to be removed in Japan; the competitiveness of Western companies needs to be enhanced; or alternatively the strategies of non-Japanese firms with the requisite competitive advantages will have to be reviewed. It is the third option which is most likely able to produce the quickest and most decisive results. In other words, the strategic failures of Western multinationals and their ability to seize opportunities in Japan might have been the key reason for their 'underinvestment'. The aim of this paper is to provide some evidence to support this proposition, by looking at the inter-war period when Western multinationals could have adopted long-term strategies by which permanently to enter the Japanese market. Yet they failed, for a variety of reasons, to exploit fully the competitive advantages which they possessed.

OVERVIEW

Direct Investment and International Cartels

The inter-war period saw the development of Western multinational companies, which continued to invest globally in spite of the growing difficulties caused by economic nationalism. As Table 6.1 shows, the Japanese market was no exception. The inter-war period also saw international cartels flourish as an alternative to foreign direct investment by Western multinationals. International cartels emerged in a wide range of business activities – from the primary sector to manufacturing industry – and they varied in their aim and structure as well as in their performance. These cartels, especially those in manufacturing sectors, emerged against the background of increasing protectionist policies, maturing oligopolies and developing domestic cartels in Europe, the United States, and other parts of the world.

Most international cartels in the manufacturing sectors emerged first in Europe, and then spread worldwide, as can be seen in Table 6.2.[1] They usually had hierarchical internal structures of organization, and their core components in Europe. For example, international dyestuffs cartels had their core components in Germany and their semi-core components in France as well as Switzerland, placing other countries in the periphery.[2] In most international cartels, American companies remained uneager partners or even outsiders, mainly because of restrictions raised through the Sherman Antitrust Act.[3] Among other main players which stood in the periphery of international cartels were Japanese companies.

Japan as the First NIE

The Japanese economy in the inter-war period experienced rapid economic growth with an annual rate of more than 4 percent, which was among the highest in the world economy at that time.[4] Moreover, the speed of Japan's industrialization was remarkable, matched only by some small East European countries. It seized the opportunity of the First World War to begin heavy and chemical industrialization, the pace of which did not slacken even during the world depression of the 1930s. Japan can claim to be the first NIE (Newly Industrializing Economy).

The Japanese economy in the inter-war period can also be characterized as economically nationalist in its tariff, commerce and foreign capital policies, although these differed in both structure and strength between the 1920s and the 1930s. In the 1920s, as in some other countries, the trade policy line followed was one of relatively free trade, although policy measures to protect domestic industries, such as the imposition of custom duties and limits on the quantity of imports, were implemented. The prevalent attitude toward Western firms was one that welcomed their direct investment in line with the liberalization policy followed since the turn of the century. At that time, the gold standard was established, the Commercial Law Act was enforced, and foreigners acquired the right to deal in real estate and make direct investments. Various restrictions were, however, placed on the management control that could be assumed by Western firms over their subsidiaries based in Japan.[5] In general, the 1920s were a time of relatively weak economic nationalism.

Table 6.1 Foreign Firms in Japan (1931) by Type of Ownership and Management

	USA	UK	Germany	Others	Total
Foreign Firms (Sales office only)	15	5	5	4	29
Firms under Japanese Law: Fully owned and operated by foreigners	6	5	2	0	13
Mostly owned and operated by foreigners	6	2	2	0	10
Jointly owned by foreigners and Japanese and operated by Japanese	9	9	8	10	36
Total	36	21	17	14	88

Source: Gaimusho, Tokubetsu Shiryobu (Special Resource Center, Ministry of Foreign Affairs), *Nihon niokeru Gaikoku Shihon (Foreign Capital in Japan)* (Tokyo, 1948).

Table 6.2 Number of International Cartel Member Firms by Country (c.1935)

	Full members	Indirect members	Total
France (and colonies)	67	2	69
Germany	57	0	57
Great Britain	31	9	40
Switzerland	25	0	25
Netherlands	20	0	20
Belgium	20	0	20
Czechoslovakia	17	3	20
Norway	16	1	17
Sweden	15	3	18
Australia	15	3	18
Italy	15	1	16
Poland	13	2	15
Finland	10	1	11
Yugoslavia	9	1	10
Hungary	8	3	11
USA	8	3	11
Japan	2	2	4
Total	349	31	380

Source: Lawrence Balland, *Essai d'Etude Monographique et Statistique sur les Ententes Economiques Internationales* (Paris, 1937).

Moving into the 1930s, we find rapidly increasing protectionism in Japan, such as tariff rises on imported industrial products, as well as the promotion of domestic products and the replacement of imports with domestic products. The tone of the Japanese government changed to one that favored the exclusion of direct investment into Japan, a move influenced by the increased political intervention of the military.[6] Against this background of growing economic nationalism, Japanese firms, which formed the backbone of Japan in its emergence as the first NIE, began to assert strongly their independence from Western firms, both technically and in managerial terms. Moving from domination of the domestic market to advance into the Asian market, these Japanese firms became the new challengers to the old order of the international cartels. On the other hand, especially in the 1920s, the Japanese market remained mostly a non-cartelized market for free competition among member companies of international cartels. Even in the 1930s, in some industrial sectors, Japan was among the last markets left unorganized by international cartels. Negotiations for international arrangements among Western multinationals as well as between Western multinationals and their Japanese competitors were always serious and tough. Japanese firms, which at first were mostly ambitious outsiders, then concluded agreements with Western multinationals, and became troublesome members in these international arrangements.

Typology

The main aim of this paper is to clarify the following two points: first, the process by which Western multinationals tried to incorporate their Japanese competitors into their networks of direct investment and international cartels, and the results of those endeavors; second, the process by which they tried to penetrate the Japanese market (and other East Asian markets) through direct investment and international cartels, and the results of those endeavors. In short, the analysis here is focused on the motives, strategies and performance of Western multinationals towards Japanese firms and Japanese and other Asian markets in the inter-war period.

Concerning the forms of multinational activities, four modes of entrance into the foreign markets were possible depending on the combination of foreign direct investment (FDI) and international cartel (IC): (1) FDI + IC, (2) FDI + non-IC, (3) non-FDI + IC, and (4) non-FDI + non-IC. Bearing in mind the proliferation of international cartels in the inter-war period, we will investigate the following two types: (1) FDI + IC and (3) non-FDI + IC, taking the case of the telephone equipment industry as representative of type (1), and the case of the dyestuffs industry for an illustration of type (3).

FOREIGN DIRECT INVESTMENT AND INTERNATIONAL
CARTELS: THE CASE OF TELEPHONES

Generally speaking, within the electrical equipment industry, fairly active direct investment and overseas production was carried out in addition to exports and licensing, as the industry was backed up by a viable patent system. International cartels played a considerable role in this industry, drawing in even American firms. These cartels, however, did not have the power of their counterparts in the chemical industry. This was related to the fact that leading American firms within the industry, such as General Electric, were in fact ahead of European companies.[7] The case of the telephone equipment industry in Japan was not exceptional. Rather, it provides the most representative case of early direct investment by Western firms in Japan.

The Agreement between Western Electric and Siemens

The Japanese telephone industry and the telephone equipment market began to expand around the turn of the century. In response, Western Electric, a leading American player in this field, set up a Japanese subsidiary, Nippon Electric Goshi Kaisha (NEC), in 1898, and thus began production in Japan of telephone equipment, using the company's own technology. NEC, which was recorded as the first manufacturing subsidiary of a foreign firm in Japan, was incorporated in the following year, with Western Electric having a stockholding interest of 54 percent.[8] In contrast to this, Siemens, a leading German player, continued with its export strategy. This caution mainly stemmed from the fact that the company occupied only second place in the worldwide telephone equipment field, and also from the fact that it felt Japan to be, in psychological terms as well as in actual distance, 'the furthest place on earth'.[9]

On the eve of the First World War, Western Electric and Siemens had made a contractual agreement regarding the division of the Japanese market and technical cooperation, a kind of international cartel. This was eventually renewed by the two companies soon after the war, in 1921. The main points of the revision were, first, the division of the Japanese market in a ratio of 10 percent to Siemens and 90 percent to Western Electric, to be achieved by the end of 1925. From 1926, Siemens was given the possibility of increasing its share. However, the punitive measures to be taken if this quota was exceeded were not stipulated. The second point of the post-war revision concerned technical cooperation including cross-licensing between the two companies. The third point was that this agreement was treated as a link in the two companies' global cooperation strategy, which was to run until the end of 1935.[10]

As the runner-up in the field, Siemens avoided any strategy of active assault on the market. The motivation behind the company's willingness to settle for a meagre 10 percent share of the market can be explained as follows. Before the First World War, Siemens accounted for more than a third of the total world production of electrical equipment, and approximately half of all electrical equipment exports. During the war, it came under particular pressure from the production capacity generated by the sudden rise of the newly industrialising nations. Sales warfare ensued and adversely affected the company which had suffered after the end of the war from the loss of foreign assets such as sales networks and patents, the forfeiture of foreign markets, difficulties in obtaining raw materials, and financial problems. Therefore, as it judged the opportunities of expansion into the remote Japanese market as small, it was reasonable that Siemens should have seen the political and economic risks involved in direct investment in Japan as too great. The fact that Germany had been a nation at war with Japan, coupled with the after-affects of the Navy bribe affair in Japan on the eve of the war (the so-called Siemens Affair), had left the company with psychological barriers which it could not overcome [11]

Direct Investment in Japan

The Great Kanto Earthquake of September 1923 proved one of the greatest turning points for the Japanese telephone and equipment industries. Japan's telephone service infrastructure suffered devastating damage in the earthquake. Using the opportunity offered through efforts to recover from the disaster, the Ministry of Communications spelled out a plan for the automation of telephone exchanges. At this time, it was the American Stroger type, mainly manufactured by Western Electric and its associated firms, which held the leading place in the automatic switchboard field. Actually, in terms of exports to Japan, too, the Stroger type outrivalled the Siemens-Halske (SH) technology. Moreover, Western Electric was ahead in terms of overseas production. Its subsidiary company in Japan, NEC, stole a march on its rivals by delivering a 2,800 circuit switchboard for public use to the Nakano

Telephone Office in Tokyo. Then Oki Denki Kogyo (Oki Electric Industry Co.), which until then had stood for all-domestic manufacture in terms of capital and technology, began production through the introduction of technology from Britain's GEC, and began deliveries to the Ministry of Communications in 1929.[12]

In August 1923, just before the Great Earthquake, Siemens had launched Fuji Denki Seizo (Fuji Electric Manufacturing Co.) as a joint venture with Furukawa Denki Kogyo (Furukawa Electric Industry Co.), but the production and sale of telephone equipment was excluded from the company's main business. This was where Siemens suffered from the limitations put on it through the agreement it had made with Western Electric. In other words, if direct investment and production in Japan were begun, there was a danger that its own technology could be leaked to the subsidiary company of its rival, NEC, under the commitment it had made with Western Electric regarding technical cooperation and cross-licensing. Thus, at this point, Siemens retained the telephone equipment business including automatic switchboards under the jurisdiction of its sales branch in Japan.[13]

Faced with the growth of the Japanese telephone market, especially the automatic switchboard market, following the Great Earthquake, Siemens found both its exports and direct investment shackled by its agreement with Western Electric. As long as the company was bound by this, it could hope for nothing more than a minor position for its exports and production in Japan. Siemens might have made a mistake in signing this agreement. It could do nothing but resign itself to the fact.

However, it was too much for Furukawa Electric, Siemens' partner, and Fuji Electric, Siemens' daughter company, to let their chance slip away before their very eyes. In particular, an even stronger request was made by Fuji Electric for it to be allowed to add telephone equipment, especially automatic switchboards, to its line of business. As a result of this, Fuji Electric was able to involve itself in the sale of these switchboards from 1925, although the products were to be imported from Germany as before. Moreover, Siemens was to retain power over the sales price.[14] Furukawa Electric then put pressure on Siemens to allow domestic production. At last, in 1927, Siemens agreed to negotiate on this issue. However, the restrictions contained within Siemens' agreement with Western Electric remained valid, and Siemens continued in its negative stance regarding production in Japan. The company was in fact opposed to this in principle.[15]

In contrast to Siemens' vacillations, progress was achieved to a certain extent in cooperation between Japanese firms and European and American companies in the telephone equipment field. As part of the general cooperation within the telephone sector, deals with General Electric, Association Telephone and Telegraph Co. (ATT), and the British company, International Automatic Telephone Co. (Autelco), were made. Relations with the Siemens subsidiary in Britain, Siemens Brothers & Co., which had been severed during the First World War, were restored in 1929 by the mutual exchange of shares and a technical agreement in the telephone field, which provided for an exchange of licenses to use patented inventions, the results of research, and technical expertise. In 1929, the Siemens-Halske company made the so-called Zuricher contract with Autelco and Siemens Brothers. Thereafter, discussions continued, aimed at cooperation in the light electrical field, especially regarding provide sector demand and exports.[16] Within this context, the judgement that it was advisable not to do anything rash with regards to the distant Japanese market may have had some influence. On top of this, the concern expressed about the level of Japanese technology was not a mere excuse.

As a result of the discussions held from the end of 1931 to the beginning of 1932, Siemens finally decided to allow production in Japan. The main reason for this was the plan of the Japanese government for the procurement of domestically manufactured products. In 1933, Fuji Electric began production of automatic switchboards.[17]

Gradual Withdrawal from the Japanese Market

The two Japanese competitors, NEC and Fuji Electric, came to some kind of agreement by the beginning of 1934. Importantly, the Japanese market was divided between them at a ratio of 70 percent to NEC and 30 percent to Fuji Electric. This was approved in principle at a discussion of chief executives held at Siemens' head offices.[18] It is presumed that the same thing occurred on the Western Electric side. This accord, which aimed at conciliation, was designed to adjust the 90 percent to 10 percent ratio that had been stipulated in the 1921 Western Electric-Siemens agreement to the then current market situation. But an even greater change than this was undertaken in an accord between two subsidiary companies. In effect, their agreement took the place of that between their parent companies. Behind this lay the 'Japanization' of the subsidiaries as a result of the rise of economic nationalism in Japan.

In NEC's case, the process of Japanization was as follows. When the company was incorporated, Western Electric's initial shareholder ratio was 54 percent. Western Electric's overseas expansion plan had originally been to set up 100 percent subsidiary companies. In the case of Japan, however, it decided from the start to use a form of joint venture, while maintaining a majority control of the company. The shareholder ratio rose at one point to 59 percent, and subsequently, after increasing nationalistic pressure in Japan, Western Electric asked for the Sumitomo zaibatsu's participation in the company in 1932. At this point, it reduced its share to below 50 percent, but it did not relinquish its control rights. By 1938, this fell further to 37 percent under the pressure of growing Japanese economic nationalism, as well as through the strategic decision of the company to withdraw from the Japanese market. In 1941, just before the start of the Pacific War, its share declined further to just 20 percent. When the war began, it was subjected to the law regarding the requisition of enemy property.

In the case of Tokyo Denki (Tokyo Electric Co.), a subsidiary company of General Electric, the shareholder interest held by GE's overseas affairs controlling company, International General Electric (IGE), was once presumably more than 50 percent. In 1931, this was cut to just under 50 percent, and in 1934 it fell to 33 percent. Thus, in this case too, the company experienced much the same fortunes as NEC.[19] The German company, Siemens, also yielded to the pressures of economic nationalism. Its joint venture with Furukawa Electric, Fuji Electric, pursued the idea of cooperation with GE's subsidiary, Tokyo Electric, and made an agreement for the division of sectors in 1935. The main points of this were: (1) The exclusive manufacture and sale of wire communications equipment was to go to Fuji Electric, and of wireless communications equipment to Tokyo Electric. They were not to encroach upon each other's business sectors, and they were to work towards mutual profitability; (2) Both firms were to set up new companies to carry out the aforementioned manufacturing and sales; (3) The firms were to hold 20 percent of the shares of each other's newly formed company, and they were also to exchange executives.[20] There was opposition within Siemens to this proposal by its subsidiary.[21] However, Fuji Electric insisted that it went ahead.

As a result, in June 1935, the new Fuji Tsushinki Seizo (Fuji Communications Equipment Manufacturing Co.), now Fujitsu Co., was set up. Fujitsu was a daughter company of Fuji Electric and therefore a granddaughter of Siemens. This company took over the entire trade rights and capital related to the manufacturing of communications equipment including telephones, which until then had been a part of Fuji Electric's business. It was thus able to begin the manufacture of telephone exchanges and other telephone and communications equipment.[22] Fujitsu could make use of Siemens' technology, and on the other hand, as a 100 percent subsidiary of Fuji Electric, it was almost completely free of management interference from Siemens. It is true to say that here, too, the shadow cast by the increased economic nationalism of the Japanese government had an effect. But, against this background, the Japanese firms themselves also showed a strong determination to achieve the aim of administrative and technical independence from foreign dominance. Moreover, Siemens' resistance against the establishing of Fujitsu was too weak. Siemens continued to take a rather cautious attitude toward the Japanese market. The result was another type of 'Japanization', the establishment of Fujitsu.

To sum up, cooperative relations between European and American firms in the telephone equipment sector continued to progress. Within the Japanese market, the largest foreign electrical corporations occupied positions of control through direct investment. However, against the background of increasing economic nationalism in Japan, the subsidiaries which had grown by benefit of this direct investment, were now aiming at independence. Most Western firms made the strategic decision to withdraw from the Japanese market and allow their subsidiaries to pursue independence. As a result of this, although Western firms remained important in terms of their technological contribution, they gradually gave up ownership and managerial control.

AN INTERNATIONAL CARTEL WITHOUT FOREIGN DIRECT INVESTMENT: THE CASE OF DYESTUFFS

Within the chemical industry in the inter-war period, the protection of technology by patents proved rather ineffective. Therefore, enterprises in this industry sought to achieve overseas expansion by exports and licensing rather than by direct investment. Thus came the worldwide spread of a comprehensive international cartel network. European firms were the main force in this with IG Farbenindustrie (hereafter referred to as IG Farben) at the center, to which were added American firms. The case of the dyestuffs industry, where one of the most successful international cartels existed, gives us a typical example.[23]

Voluntary Export Restriction

With the outbreak of the First World War, a vacuum was created in the Japanese dyestuffs market, which had formerly been dominated by German products. This led to a sudden and sharp rise in the number of Japanese dyestuffs companies. Moreover, Mitsui Kozan (Mitsui Mining Co.) began to operate its dyestuffs enterprise. As part of a government policy for the fostering of the industry, Nihon Senryo Seizo (Japan Dyestuffs Manufacturing Co.) was set up as a state-owned company. Immediately following the end of the war, imports to Japan began once more, and not only German but also Swiss and American products began to flow into the market. However, it was the German products that managed to regain supremacy. In 1924, the Japanese government set up an import licensing system targeting German products, instituting selective safeguards and denying the Ministry of Agriculture and Commerce (later the Ministry of Commerce and Industry) permits for those items which could be produced domestically.

The effectiveness of the import licensing system was remarkable. Imports from Germany were curbed for the time being, and goods from Switzerland and the United States took their place. This proved a serious blow for the German dyestuff industry. Meanwhile, they joined forces to create IG Farben at the end of 1925, which then entered into negotiations with the Japanese Ministry of Commerce and Industry as the representative of the Japanese dyestuff industry. In August 1926, a gentlemen's agreement was finally signed, which was called the Saito-Waibel Agreement after its signatories. The main points contained in this agreement were: (1) the banning in principle of *exports* to Japan that could be domestically produced; and (2) the free *export,* as a general rule, of those products such as synthetic indigo that could not be produced domestically. The agreement thereby provided a voluntary export restriction on the side of IG Farben, laying down a division of labor within the industry. It was an individual agreement made by IG Farben, but, if we take into consideration the fact that the company held by far the largest share in the world dyestuffs trade, it can be considered as a more general one between Western and Japanese firms.[24]

The Saito-Waibel Agreement became effective from April 1928, and at the same time the import licensing system became invalid, as scheduled. From this time on, IG Farben concentrated its efforts on products, such as synthetic indigo, which could not yet be produced in Japan, while at the same time attempting to hold back the efforts of Japanese enterprises to develop new products. One of the most powerful weapons used in achieving this was a low-price policy, which was criticized by the Japanese firms as being merely a form of price dumping. Another powerful weapon was its refusal to provide technical cooperation. In relation to the latter, in May 1929, for example, IG Farben came to an accord with Swiss firms not to provide technical assistance to Japan.[25] As far as IG Farben was concerned, its target was not Japanese firms as a whole, but rather two main companies. One was Nihon Senryo, which was attempting to develop a broad range of products centering on variamine blue dye, and the other was Mitsui Mining, which was trying to develop synthetic indigo.

International Cartels and the Japanese Market

Meanwhile, in Europe, following a German-French agreement made in 1927, an agreement between Germany, France and Switzerland was made in 1929, thereby establishing a three-party international cartel.[26] This cartel very rapidly joined in concerted action against Japan, raising the export price to Japan uniformly by 5 percent in October of the same year. Japanese firms did not follow suit. The growth of the Japanese dyestuffs market, affected by a domestic financial crisis in 1927 and the world depression in 1929, had shown a slowdown. Under these circumstances, Japanese dyestuff firms were able to compete even more vigorously for a share of the market. Consequently, the share occupied by the three-party cartel fell. Thus, it was made clear that in circumstances such as these, the ability of even an international cartel to cope was limited.[27] At this time, exports of European firms to Japan were showing a downward trend, especially because of the fall of the Japanese yen following the reimposition of a ban on the exports of gold in December 1931. In addition, following in quick succession, Nihon Senryo and Mitsui Mining were able to develop new products. The international cartel and its member companies were forced to find new ways to deal with the situation. One way was to intensify efforts to conclude agreements with Japanese counterparts.

Agreement between IG Farben and Nihon Senryo

At the beginning of 1931, Nihon Senryo put a product onto the market to compete directly with IG Farben's Variamine Blue, while at the same time putting in an application for a patent. IG Farben immediately voiced a protest against this, and the two sides entered into a patent dispute. In the end, IG Farben, recognising the diminishing of the power of its technology as a negotiating weapon, chose to compromise and avoid a price war. Thus, in 1935, IG Farben concluded the Japan Variamine Blue Agreement with Nihon Senryo. Later, this was ratified by three Swiss firms. By this agreement, Nihon Senryo recognised IG Farben's patent and agreed not to carry out exports of identical products. As compensation, an accord was obtained on sales quotas for the Japanese market; the share was 68 percent to IG Farben and 32 percent to Nihon Senryo. The sales price was to be equal. This agreement lasted until 1941.[28] IG Farben also concluded the Japan Astraphloxine Agreement with Nihon Senryo in 1934. The main points of this ran parallel to those in the Variamine Blue Agreement. In return for relinquishing exports, Nihon Senryo got a 50 percent share of the Japanese market and IG Farben the remaining 50 percent. This agreement lasted until 1939.[29]

Agreement between IG Farben, the International Cartel and Mitsui Mining

A similar relationship was also formed between Western firms and Mitsui Mining. First, with regard to sulphur black dye, in 1931 the three-party cartel made an agreement with Mitsui Mining's representative, Mitsui Bussan (Mitsui & Co.), regarding the quantity and price of exports to China. Two American firms, National Aniline and Chemical Co. (Nacco) and Du Pont de Nemours & Co., were also drawn into this agreement, which nevertheless lapsed as early as the end of 1933. In 1931, IG Farben concluded another agreement regarding alizarine blue with Mitsui & Co. as the sole representative of Mitsui Mining. The agreement concerned the division of the Japanese market, and at first this was apportioned at a ratio of 60 percent to IG Farben and 40 percent to Mitsui. This agreement was revised continuously and lasted until 1940. Meanwhile, the market ratio was in fact reversed to IG Farben 40 percent, Mitsui 60 percent.[30] The biggest problem remained synthetic indigo, which was the most popular dyestuff in the East Asian countries and sold well. In 1926, Mitsui Mining finally managed to achieve its aim of fully commercializing its synthetic indigo production. Then, in 1929, the company managed to obtain a government subsidy for the promotion of dyestuffs manufacture. Thus, construction of a factory was begun in 1931. Its products were finally put on the market in 1932.

Meanwhile, Nacco and Du Pont, which had already succeeded in the development of indigo immediately after the First World War, now embarked in rapid succession on export ventures to the Far East. The four-party cartel, which emerged through the participation of Great Britain in the three-party cartel, concluded a six-party agreement with these two American firms covering the sales ratio of the Japanese, Chinese and Far Eastern markets.[31]

In addition to this, the six Western parties concluded an agreement with Mitsui Mining in 1934. This concerned cooperation over the sales price within the Japanese market, and the sales ratio, which was to be 25 percent for the six Western parties and 75 percent for Mitsui Mining.[32] This was a temporary agreement. Soon after, discussions for the conclusion of a formal agreement took place. The biggest point of contention here was the regulations governing Japanese exports to China. IG Farben perceived that these discussions offered a unique opportunity to protect the Chinese market from a recurrence in the fall of prices. It prevailed upon the other cartel partners with the argument that, should the agreement be imperfectly concluded, Mitsui would undoubtedly be able to exert a fairly strong influence on the price levels not only of the Japanese, Chinese and Manchurian market, but also of others as well. As IG Farben held the largest share in the Asian market, which it wanted to keep, it took the initiative in its relations with the other partners, in order to try and maintain the *status quo*.[33] At last, in 1935, a settlement was reached. The formal agreement held Japanese exports of indigo (with the purity of 20 percent) to China to a three-year total of approximately 100,000 piculs. As vicarious compensation, the six Western firms were limited in their exports to Japan.[34]

Successive Concessions by the International Cartels

The formal agreement was to expire at the end of 1937. However, due to the outbreak of the Sino–Japanese War and the accompanying uncertainty regarding the situation in the Far East, the two sides agreed to extend the agreement unchanged until June 1938. Mitsui Mining was in principle satisfied with the agreement as it stood. The Western firms also welcomed the extension, as they did not want to have to accept the new restrictions which would inevitably be imposed by the uncertainties of the new political climate. The Western firms had in mind the re-extension of the agreement.[35] Mitsui Mining agreed to re-extension by the end of 1938, but made requests for the abolition of, or at least a change in, restrictions on areas of export.[36] The international cartel re-examined what course they should take in preparation for the discussions. The result was that they were prepared to compromise on the requests from the Mitsui side; in other words, to change the existing stance limiting Mitsui Mining's exports to China and Manchuria, and to allow some exports of 100 percent indigo to Dutch and British Indochina.[37] IG Farben, as the representative of the four-party cartel, began discussions with Mitsui Mining on this basis while at the same time obtaining agreement from Nacco and Du Pont.

Even with the willingness of the international cartel to compromise, the negotiations were tough going. This was partly because the Mitsui Mining side went so far as to demand the total abandonment of the quota system. Moreover, when it had eventually agreed to the continuation of the system, it thrust a request before the international cartel, asking to be allowed to carry out large-scale exports to other areas. However, the reason why it took so long to reach a compromise was not only Mitsui Mining's requests, but also the fact that opinions within the international cartel were divided. A confrontation arose between the two factions: on the one hand, IG Farben was in favor of making concessions to Japan, and, on the other, the Swiss, French and British firms were in favor of taking a tough stance. In the end, IG Farben managed to persuade its partners and the international cartel made large-scale concessions to the Japanese side, approving Japanese exports not only to China and Manchuria, but also to Dutch and British Indo-China, the Philippines, Thailand, the Straits Settlements, Iran, Egypt, Belgium and Mexico. Moreover, an agreement was reached in 1939 on the removal of quotas from the Japanese market.[38] This agreement was extended until the end of 1940, but war in Europe broke out before it had expired, and Imperial Chemical Industries (ICI) broke the agreement.[39]

As a result, Mitsui Mining increased its production to enable it to dominate the Japanese market, and to advance into the Asian market. Meanwhile, the international cartel sought to maintain a foothold in the Asian market through cooperation with American firms, while at the same time negotiating with Mitsui Mining. IG Farben showed the most enthusiasm of any to cooperate, and the other cartel member firms followed IG Farben's lead while secretly opposing its stance. There was no confrontation great enough to cause a collapse of the cartel until September 1939. On the face of it, the attempts to include the Japanese developer of synthetic indigo, Mitsui Mining, in the sphere of influence of the international cartel succeeded. However, the real situation was that the international cartel was forced to immediately back down when faced with Mitsui Mining's demands.

WESTERN MULTINATIONALS AND JAPANESE POLICY TOWARDS FOREIGN CAPITAL

Direct Investment and International Cartels in Japan

In conclusion, as for the type of FDI + IC illustrated in the case of the telephone equipment industry, the main motive of Western multinationals was to dominate the Japanese market (and other East Asian markets) through direct investment. They chose to enter Japan by establishing manufacturing subsidiaries, and utilised the international cartels as a complementary device, formed between themselves and without Japanese participation. In terms of performance, their manufacturing subsidiaries could dominate the Japanese market when industrialization in Japan was at its early stage, and they also benefitted from the rapid growth of the Japanese market. At a later stage, however, they were obliged to make concessions to their Japanese counterparts, and even chose the strategy of withdrawal from the Japanese market in response to the growing anti-foreign capital policy of the Japanese government. As illustrated in the case of the dyestuffs industry, the Western multinationals wanted to dominate the Japanese market through international cartels, that is non-FDI + IC. Keeping with this approach, they tried to integrate Japanese outsiders into the network of international cartels. They also used technological cooperation as a weapon in negotiations. Concerning their performance, European and American multinationals, which were members of the international cartels, could not catch up with the growth tempo of their Japanese counterparts, because international cartels were originally defensive weapons, and were forced to make concessions successively, losing their stake in the Japanese and Asian markets.

A Missed Opportunity

What should be emphasized here is the fact that Western multinationals had a rare opportunity to make investments, to take their stand and to become dominant in the Japanese market during the period 1900–1930. The Japanese government changed its policy toward international foreign direct investment around the turn of the century, from a closed-door to an open-door policy, and it kept the door open for foreign direct investment in the country until around 1930, even though some industrial fields were never opened or only briefly and partially opened. However, during the years of 1900–1930, most Western multinationals were reluctant to invest in the Japanese market, with some exceptions such as electrical appliances, automobiles, rubber, and oil.[40] Even in those cases, some players were rather inactive, as illustrated by the case of the German firm Siemens. The reason for their reluctance to invest in Japan can be found first in their geographical and psychological distance from Japan. German companies were especially risk-averse, because they found themselves deeply damaged by the First World War in which they lost most of their pre-war foreign assets – manufacturing units and marketing networks – through seizure by the Allied nations (including Japan).[41] A second main reason can be found in the fact that most Western companies were satisfied with considerably high revenues from the export of products or technologies to Japan which were promoted particularly through international cartel arrangements, including the agreement between Western Electric and Siemens in the telephone equipment industry. Some could enjoy their own stake in the Japanese or East Asian markets through arrangements with their Japanese competitors (either allocating the Japanese market, or restricting Japanese exports to East Asian markets). Others could enjoy higher free payments for technology exports, especially because Japan was eager to introduce new technologies.

Around 1931, the Japanese government changed its foreign capital policy drastically once more. A few Western multinationals, which dared to invest in Japan, were discouraged by the antagonistic policies taken by the government, and they took the strategic decision to withdraw or to be Japanized.[42] If they had maintained their foothold and had been more long-term in their outlook, they would have had chances to come back to Japan after the end of the Second World War rather more smoothly than they did. IBM and some oil companies were exceptions.[43] In short, most failed to evaluate correctly the long-term growth potential of Japanese firms and the market. They lacked a long-term perspective. As a result of those failures, they lost a rare opportunity to benefit from the high speed growth of the Japanese economy, while they helped Japanese firms pursue a strategy to introduce technology and management skills without losing the right of control. On the other hand, assisted through the strategic failure of Western competitors, Japanese challengers could pursue the 'Japan-model',[44] preferring licensing to internal direct investment, which Asian NIEs tried subsequently to follow under the different conditions. After the end of the Second World War, two other opportunities presented themselves to Western multinationals, one soon after the end of the war and before the enactment of the laws on foreign exchange as well as on foreign capital, and one later in 1970 when the Japanese government launched a renewed liberalisation policy for foreign capital.

Nevertheless, most Western multinationals missed the opportunities in the early years after the war in the steel, electrical machinery, petrochemical and automobile industries, and only a few met with any success, like IBM Japan.[45] IBM's success lay not only in the advantages it held because its Japanese subsidiary escaped Japanization (as it was a marketing, not a manufacturing company) but also because it exhibited a wise and tough attitude before, during and after the war.[46] We should recognize once more the fact that most Western firms failed to evaluate correctly the long-term growth potential of Japanese business and the Japanese market.

Despite the other opportunities that have accompanied the liberalization policies of the Japanese government since 1970, the imbalance of direct investment between Western and Japanese enterprises still remains. We hear all kinds of complaints from Western businessmen about the alleged closed nature of the Japanese market, the so-called 'cultural barrier'. In reality, however, the Japanese market today is sufficiently open to Western multinationals, and there is no 'Fortress Japan' any more than there is a 'Fortress Europe'. An attempt to rebuild a 'Fortress Japan' of the 1930s would be the death of the Japanese economy. There remain some, though not many, success stories.[47] Successful foreign firms need only to have a long-term perspective, a deliberately conceived investment strategy and, last but not least, tenacity in the struggle with bureaucrats in Tokyo who are every bit as tough as their counterparts in Brussels and Washington.

Source: *Annals of the Institute of Social Science, University of Tokyo*, No. 37, 1996, pp. 51–75.

7

Japan's Technology Transfer and Business Management: An Analysis from the Standpoint of Business History

I. INTRODUCTION

1. Definition of the Theme

How SHOULD WE locate Japan's technological development in modern world history? What are the major features of technological development in Japan? And how and to what extent have such features molded the characteristics of business management in Japan? My purpose in this essay is to map out what needs to be done to address these questions properly from the standpoint of business history. I will do so by drawing upon relevant works available in the field of business history.[1]

Given the fact that business history is an academic discipline which concerns itself with the history of business management, and in particular the process of decision-making by the management strata, any meaningful treatise of problems pertaining to technological development from the standpoint of business history should focus its attention on the relationship between technological development and business management, and on the process of decision-making on matters related to technological development. Before focusing my attention on these factors, I would like to point to several hypothetical propositions that underlie the subsequent discussion.

One proposition concerns the relationship between technological development and technology transfer. It is my understanding that technological development is possible only when technology transfer, or, more specifically, international technology transfer, takes place continuously. Another proposition is that technology transfer in most cases is closely related to, and is accompanied by, the transfer of management skills, in the sense that the international transfer of management skills takes place only through the transfer of technologies. Put differently, normally it is technology transfer that affects or dictates the transfer of managerial skills, but not the other way around.

Furthermore, I believe that the development of management skills, just like the development of technologies, is possible only when these are transferred internationally on a continuous basis. These perceptions mean that an analysis of the relationship between technological development and business management should involve an inquiry into the transfer or exchange of technologies, as well as into the transfer of management skills.

I am using the term "transfer" to mean not only the importation or introduction of technologies or management skills from abroad, but also their exportation abroad. A firm can develop its technologies and management skills not only through their importation, but also through their exportation. A case in point here is the lesson left by the American company RCA, whose life as a corporate entity ended when it ran out of technologies it could export overseas. In this essay, however, I will mainly address the question of how Japanese firms have behaved as introducers/receivers of technologies and management skills from abroad, and will limit myself to mentioning, in the closing section, some of the problems these firms face as exporters/suppliers of technologies and management skills, problems that require a further inquiry.

Another thing that should be pointed out at the outset is that the following discussion is tentative in nature, and cannot do more than present some working hypotheses for further studies at best. This is not to say that these hypotheses are totally unfounded; on the contrary, having been derived from my empirical work, they have some supporting facts. Nonetheless, the facts cited are no more than illustrations or corroborations for the hypotheses, which remain to be fully substantiated by a more full-fledged analysis.

In what follows, I will concentrate exclusively on international, not domestic, transfer of technologies and management skills between, not within, firms. A few more words about terminology are in order. I will use the word "transfer" not only in the sense intrinsic to it, but to carry the meaning "diffusion," "dissemination," or "propagation" as well.

The expression "introduction" or "adoption" should be understood to mean the "transfer" perceived by the receivers/users of the technologies. The word "technologies" is used primarily in the sense of production technologies, as distinct from various management and administrative technologies which are referred to as "management skills," "managerial expertise," or simply "management."

2. The Analytical Perspective of International Business History

It seems safe to say that among other approaches to the study of technology and management transfer, the business history approach is characterized before all else by the emphasis placed on firms as the most important agent of the transfer. Technologies and managerial skills are transferred not simply by private firms, but also by various other economic actors, such as individuals, government organizations, and non-profit organizations. However, in business history, we place firms at the center both as the suppliers and receivers of technologies transferred. To put it differently, we are concerned primarily with inter-firm transfers of technologies.

For business history to focus its attention on firms as the most important vector of technology and management transfer derives from the discipline's very nature as one concerned with the history of corporate behavior. But, aside from this basic fact, it is also important to note that firms are at once the most important vector of technologies and the most important developer of technologies and management skills in a national economy. Looked at in this light, firms should not be understood merely as conveyors of technologies and management skills, but also as their creators and transformers.

In essence, technologies and management skills can be construed as a kind of information; but they are more than that, because they also carry with them the characteristics of knowledge. Unlike pieces of information, knowledge is not simply transmitted, collected, or stored, but is also processed, accumulated, put to use, and moreover, incorporated into an organization. As Alfred D. Chandler, Jr., emphasizes in connection with his comments on Japanese firms in his introduction to the Japanese edition of *Scale and Scope* (though his comments seem to reveal the limitations of the book), firms are organizations that are involved with knowledge rather than with information.[2] Unlike physical facilities, technologies (or at least some part of them) and management skills are embodied in human beings, and it is as organizations of such human beings that firms are formed.

Technologies and management skills, broadly defined as pieces of knowledge, are put to use by firms, while at the same time they are accumulated within corporate structure, to be reprocessed, reformulated, or refined for repeated use. Such a process of involving technologies and management skills can be characterized as one of learning by firms as organizations, or one of organizational learning by firms.

This understood, it becomes clear that studies in technology transfer carried out within the framework of business history ought to satisfy several requirements. First, technology and management transfer by firms should be interpreted as constituting a part of the knowledge accumulation process, or a part of the organizational learning process by firms, in the sense defined above (see Figure 7.1). Second, given the fact that technology transfer is inseparably related with the transfer of management skills, as already pointed out, what has been said with regard to technologies applies also to management skills. In studying technology transfer from the standpoint of business history, therefore, it is imperative that technology transfer be considered in close reference to the transfer of management skills (see Figure 7.1 again). And third, as can be directly reduced from the foregoing two points, the transfer of technologies and management skills is inseparably related to the management of firms. This means that the question of technology and management transfer ought to be considered always in relation to corporate management. In undertaking such a consideration, moreover, it is imperative that we analyze not simply the background against which, or the environment in which, the transfer takes place, as well as its motivations and results, but also the very process by which the transfer is actually carried out. Indispensable for such a scrutiny is to probe explicitly into the strategies and organizations adopted by the firms concerned. Depending on the nature of corporate strategies being pursued, technologies and management skills can sometimes flow from a firm low on the scale of development ladder to one positioned at a higher level. This is quite indicative of how decisive business strategies can be to the transfer of technologies and management skills.

One point I would like to underline premised on the foregoing is that we must put in our purview the business management of both the suppliers and the receivers of the technologies and management skills being transferred, and that, in order to do this, it is desirable for us to use the historical records on both sides (especially in-house records of the firms concerned). The transfer of a specific technology or management skill across national borders involves at least two firms which

Figure 7.1 Transfer and Development of Technology and Management

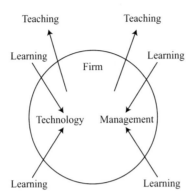

negotiate with each other as the supplier and the receiver, conclude an agreement, and execute the agreement. The firms, in their capacities as the supplier and the receiver, also compete with each other on some issues, but cooperate on other issues. Indeed, we might say that technology and management transfer takes place where the strategies and organizations of one firm intersect or cross with those of another across the national borders (see Figure 7.2). We can also liken the process of such a transfer as a game played by two players, one being the supplier firm of technologies or management skills, and the other being the receiver firm. If the government(s) of the country or countries concerned is/are also involved, we can see the transfer process as a three- or four-player game. Either way, the game takes place where the recognitions and decisions of the two parties intersect. The researcher views this game or process as a third party from the outside, as one whose role it is to observe its development from his/her vantage point as an outsider with an access to the pertinent pieces of information on both sides. If the transfer is to be considered one form of inter-firm relations, or a kind of inter-firm transaction, this approach is an obvious requirement.

This standpoint is closely related to a new analytical perspective being proposed in the field of business history, namely the perspective of the business history of international relations, or the history of international business relations. This perspective has been advocated in Japan by several business historians, notably Nakagawa Keiichiro, in their effort to overcome the limitations of the theory or history of multinational corporations. As such, this perspective proposes to

Figure 7.2 Transfer process of Technology and Management

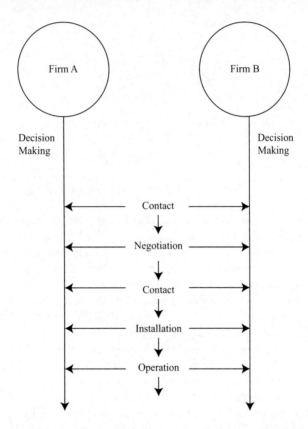

reassess the history of business management by placing it in the context of international business relations. I, too, have carried out case studies of technology and management skills transfer between Japan and Germany in the inter-war years (1919–1939/41).[3] This analytical perspective, the history of international business relations, is what will inform my subsequent discussion.

In the fields of business history and socioeconomic history, interest has been on the increase not only in the international technology and management transfer, but also in the international transfer of social-economic institutions and customs, and even of economic and business cultures. In the discussion of technology and management transfer, increasingly greater emphasis has come to be placed on the roles played in the transfer by relevant factors, including, in particular, educational systems, training regimes, employers' associations, engineers' associations, patenting systems, and immigrant workers. These factors affecting technology and management transfer have much to do with the transmission of civilization. Indeed, encounters and conflicts between the technologies and management skills introduced from abroad on the one hand, and the indigenous institutions, customs, and cultures of the receiver country on the other, have been serving as an unavoidable gateway to the transfer of institutions, customs, cultures, and even civilization. We could say that technology and management transfer has been occupying the most pivotal position for cross-national interactions at the wider social and economic level. Thus, only by probing more thoroughly into the process and structure of technology and management transfer can we hope to start gaining a better understanding of transfer at the level of the society and economy, and also of cross-national interactions between civilizations.

3. TECHNOLOGY AND MANAGEMENT TRANSFER TO JAPAN

There is already a large accumulation of studies on technology and management transfer undertaken in Japan in the field of business history. Without constant and dynamic transfer of technology, technological development, industrialization would have been impossible in the past and will be impossible in the future, both for an individual country or region and for the world as a whole. It is little wonder that the theme of technology transfer should have attracted undying attention in business history. To begin with, as various studies on civilization transfer have made clear, even Western Europe, which is regarded as the source of development of modern technology, would have been unable to accomplish technological development, if it had not first received the once advanced technologies of the Asian and Islamic worlds. More so Japan, which was a late developing country in the modern era. Japan managed to attain its rapid business and economic development thanks, to a significant extent, to the technologies and management skills imported from the more advanced countries of the West.

At this juncture, it is worth our while to take note that the three requirements pointed out earlier also apply to studies on Japan's technology and management introduction. First, during the period from the mid-nineteenth century to the mid-twentieth century, when Japan pursued modernization, it was private firms that acted as the main agent of the transfer. In Europe and the United States, this period saw private firms, especially larger ones, go multinational and become increasingly active in the exportation of technologies and management skills. On the Japanese side, the major receptacles of technologies and management skills changed from government organizations and government-run enterprises to a limited number of large private firms, and subsequently – as heavy and chemical industries grew both in depth and width – to a larger number of private firms. Second, the impact of newly imported management skills, along with that of technological imports, was enormous. Contrary to what the recent interest in the superb performance of Japanese business management and its unique features would lead us to believe, it is important to note that Japanese firms during this period imported management skills from European and American firms with great enthusiasm. And third, the transfer of technologies and management skills from Europe and the United States to Japan was inseparably related to business management (or management strategies and organizations) of Western and Japanese firms.

As I have already emphasized, it is important to view the processes of technology and management transfer as an interplay between business management of both the supplier and receiver firms. In fact, studies fulfilling this requirement are lately on the increase as the analytical perspective of the history of international business relations has gained influence and has been refined further. Studies on the introduction of technologies and management skills from the West during the late Tokugawa and the early Meiji eras began to be carried out relatively early on. But research interests subsequently expanded to cover the turn of the century, and then the inter-war years. And more recently, the years after World War II have come into the focus of studies in business history. Needless to say, it was quite rare for Japanese firms to supply technologies abroad in the pre-World War II years,[4] but studies covering the postwar period, especially the period since the early 1970s, often find it unavoidable to deal with Japanese firms not simply as receivers, but also, and increasingly, as suppliers of technologies and managerial skills.

Listed in the bibliography given at the end of this paper are studies dealing with Japan in the first half of the twentieth century, most of them undertaken in Japan. In compiling the bibliography, I have interpreted the discipline of business history as broadly as possible. Though limited in its coverage and far from exhaustive, the list may hint at the intensity of recent research interests in the question of technology transfer.[5]

I would, however, like to emphasize that fulfilling the requirements mentioned earlier is not easy. One cause of difficulties for this research concerns methodology, or issue orientation. Studies on the transfer of technology and management in Japan have tended to view Japanese firms primarily, or exclusively, as receivers of technologies and management skills imported from abroad, and thus to fail to deal properly with the transfer as an interaction between suppliers and receivers.

One reason underlying this drawback (aside from the limited access to pertinent historical documents, a question to be referred to below) can be traced to a very rigid traditional division of labor which has been drawn in the Japanese academic world between studies on Japan and those on the West. (And the history of international business relations has been aimed at overcoming this division of labor.)

Another reason, in my view, is a mistaken assumption that commodities called technologies and management skills were available from foreign firms in unlimited quantities. There is no denying that advanced firms of the West (misled partly by their underestimation of the growth potential of the Japanese economy and firms) were very eager to market their technologies and management skills in Japan, and this fact seems to have led to an understanding that Japanese firms were able to purchase technologies and management on the open market with relative ease. Even so, managers of firms who had to make actual inter-firm transactions when importing technologies and management skills had the potential of freeing themselves from such a misconception. But researchers, perhaps because of their preoccupation with the results of transfer, have failed to pay sufficient attention to the process of the transfer, and to the strategies and organizations on the part of the supplier firms of the West.

The second possible source of difficulties is the limited availability of historical documents. In order to undertake studies on technology and management transfer, proper access to historical documents of both the supplier and receiver firms, and in particular their internal documents, is desirable, or rather indispensable. Even though these basic documents have become somewhat more accessible than previously, the degree of accessibility remains far from ideal. And, regrettably, this seems to be the case more often with documents of Japanese firms than with those of Western firms. Moreover, research is seriously hindered by the fact that internal documents from the postwar period, if not those from the prewar period, are often very difficult to access.

To sum up the foregoing observations, we cannot paint a rosy picture for the future of studies on technology and management transfer without major improvements in the accessibility to historical documents and the betterment of researchers' methodology or their understanding of the nature of the issues at hand.

II. THE PROCESS

1. "Whole-hearted" Adoption

Historically speaking, the process of the adoption of technology and management in modern Japan seems to have been characterized before all else by the great vigor with which the firms (at least during the period under consideration here) tried to import technologies and management skills from the West. Even though this characteristic was shared to one extent or another by all the late developing countries, even including those of the West, the Japanese interest in technology and management importation seems to have been exceptionally keen.

Let me discuss this phenomenon at two different levels, i.e. at the level of the national economy and at the level of individual firms. Regarded at the level of the national economy, there was virtually no discrepancy that separated one constituent group of the economy from another in terms of the attitude toward the adoption of Western technologies and management skills. In other words, almost all the constituents were in favor of technology and management imports. The government promoted this through its policies on trade, foreign capital imports, industrialization, and science and technology. Private firms, almost without exception, were also eager to import technologies and management skills. A wide strata of people shared a strong curiosity of, and a strong eagerness to learn about, commodities and cultures introduced from the advanced countries of the West. In most of the late developing countries of the West at the time, firms were sharply divided into two opposing camps, one in favor of technology and management imports from more advanced countries, and the other harshly opposed to such imports; but firms of the latter kind were virtually non-existent in Japan, with a predominant majority favoring adoption at least in theory, if not in practice (see Figure 7.3).

To cite one example from the prewar years, even Hitachi Ltd., a major electric machinery manufacturer known for its pursuit of independence and autonomy and its manifested policy of "manufacturing the second and subsequent units of everything domestically," imported technologies from abroad. The eagerness to learn from abroad was spurred by a strong desire to nurture indigenous industries, a desire entertained so strongly by both the government and private firms that one top executive of a German firm called it the "almost pathological ambition of the Japanese." Similarly, after the end of World War II, it was something like a national conviction, a dictum admitting of no doubt, that Japan ought to import and absorb technologies and management skills from the West, especially from the United States. In contrast, in West Europe at around the same time, there were still some firms that were cautious or negative about importing technologies and especially management skills from the United States (see Figure 7.4).

An examination of the history of Japan's adoption of technologies and management skills seems to warrant a hypothesis that the cultural barriers to the adoption have been low and thin. This may also be called

Figure 7.3 J-Model

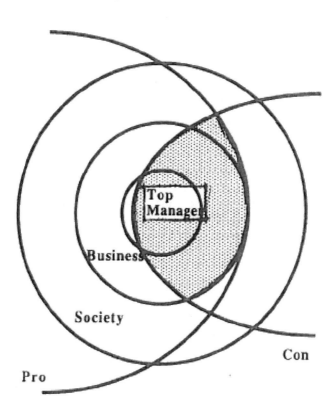

Figure 7.4 E-Model

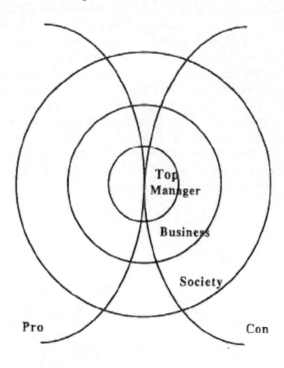

a hypothesis of Japan's vulnerability to foreign civilizations, or flexibility in the importation of civilizations.[6]

Much the same holds true at the level of individual firms. The willingness of firms to import technologies and management skills manifested itself in their attitude to do so in as profound and extensive a manner as possible. To be more specific, when a firm tried to introduce a certain technology (whether formally by signing contracts or informally without contracts), it often showed keen interest in importing the related technologies or in learning the management skills employed by the supplier firm as well; and when it tried to import a certain management skill, it similarly often showed interest in the related skills. In this sense, the importation was an "extensive" endeavor. On the other hand, it was not uncommon for firms, when importing technologies or management skills, to try to comprehend them as thoroughly as possible. There were even cases where firms tried to understand the technologies and management skills by going down to their scientific basis. In this sense, the importation was undertaken in a very "thorough" manner, as a "whole-hearted" adoption.

2. Resistance

Nevertheless, several case studies on individual firms suggest that a strong momentum was also at work in the opposite direction. Resistance, an attitude totally opposite to the one described above, was also manifest when introductions were made. This resistance took the form of a desire to cling fast to the technologies or management skills already in use by the firm, or even, and perhaps in a majority of cases, took the form of management's desire to cling fast to their managerial prerogatives in order to safeguard existing technologies and managerial skills (compare Figures 7.3 and 7.4 once again).

The intensity of the resistance at work inside the receiver firms had much to do with the fact that, in Japan during the first half of the twentieth century, importation through licensing arrangements was strongly preferred to other avenues of importation (and has remained to be so even after the mid-century, though to a lesser extent). Technology and management transfer can take place through one of three main modes, or avenues, of international exchange/expansion of corporate activities: the importation of goods (i.e. materials and/or completed machinery or equipment), direct foreign investment, and licensing. The word "licensing" is used here in a broad sense, connoting a wide range of activities pursued by a firm across national borders, unaccompanied by direct foreign investment. At first, Japanese firms showed a keen interest in learning technologies and management skills primarily through the importation of goods. This typically took the form of imitation of foreign technologies through dead copies or still blueprints, or learning by reverse-engineering. Also important was the introduction of advanced technologies and managerial skills from abroad through licensing arrangements. In terms of the number of arrangements made for technology and management importation, licensing arrangements were far in excess of the arrangements for direct foreign investment. Although accurate statistics on these matters are unavailable for the pre-World War II years, the number of arrangements made in the prewar years for licensing seems to have been several times that for direct foreign investment.[7]

The strong preference for licensing arrangements as a viable avenue for technology and management imports may be ascribed to several factors. For one thing, the prohibitive or restrictive government policies on direct foreign investments in Japan were certainly an important factor. (These policies were pursued from the early Meiji era until the end of the nineteenth century, from the early 1930s until Japan's defeat in World War II, and in the post-war era until 1970 when the Foreign Exchange and Foreign Trade Control Law of 1949 and the Foreign Investment Law of 1950 were in place.) For another, we might point out, firms of the West made strategic errors in the sense that, having underestimated the growth potential of the Japanese market, they were overcautious in pursuing the strategies of direct investment. We might also count as an important factor the above-mentioned attitude of resistance that prevailed within Japanese firms against technology and management introductions. In the world at the time, there was a network for the transfer of technologies and management skills that had been formed by multinational firms in their roles as providers of technologies.[8] Japan was, so to speak, a niche left uncovered by that network.

The strong resistance mounted by some quarters of the manufacturing industry against technological imports may be explained by several factors. One was that the technological and management skills already acquired by firms met a certain known standard. This gave the firms a certain amount of confidence that they were capable of developing the expertise further still on their own. Other plausible reasons included the nationalist mentality, and the fact that business carried a heavier influence in society than in foreign countries (for instance, in Britain).

What is important to remember here is that the resistance to the introduction of technologies and management skills was, at its base, premised on the strong interest in the introduction, an attitude that prevailed in society at large. The resistance was forward-looking, not backward-looking, in nature, as it were. In fact, many firms, in importing technologies and management skills from abroad, were not so much interested in merely imitating foreign models as eager to make improvements and innovations, which they did by relying on the technologies and management skills they had already acquired. At times, firms pursuing such ambitious goals took upon themselves challenges that were well beyond their own capabilities, and not a few of these firms ended up accomplishing results that were little better than mere imitations. The results of these frustrated attempts give the impression that the efforts at technology and management introduction were very imitative in orientation.

In sum, even though society as a whole was very receptive to the introduction of technologies and management skills, the response to the introduction at the level of individual firms was somewhat more complex. The very same firms that showed an interest in introducing technologies and management skills also displayed strong resistance to the introduction. Thus there were two opposing strong momentums at work within the receiver firms, one favoring the introduction, and the other resisting it. The strong desire to make a "whole-hearted" adoption of foreign technologies and management skills mingled with a strong sense of opposition, underpinned by the wish to retain the firms' own technologies and management skills. In Europe, there were some cases of resistance mounted by firms to technology and management adoption, but such cases of resistance seem to have been much fewer than in Japan.

3. In Two Minds

To proceed with my hypothetical argument, the receiver firms of technologies and management skills managed to quell the strong momentum of resistance, at least for the time being. The decision Toray, a major textile and chemicals manufacturer, made in the early post-World War II years to introduce nylon manufacturing technologies from Du Pont, together with the latter's management skills, and to shelve its project for the development of similar technologies, was a case in point. It was a decision made with a resolve of "nothing ventured, nothing gained." And decisions of this sort had the effect of lending credibility to the view that such "whole-hearted" introduction of technologies and management skills was imitative. Needless to say, the mitigation of the resistance to the introduction of technologies and management skills was dictated above all else by an awareness of the severe gap in technology and management competence that separated Japan and the West. And this awareness, in turn, reflected the high capability of self-assessment by the firms themselves.

Even though Japanese firms once denied their own technologies, and sometimes even their managerial practices, their denial at the end turned out to be not total or irrevocable. Within the ranks of corporate managers were the strong desire to make the introductions and the equally strong attitude of resistance. And given the way managers were integrated in the corporate system, as I will explain shortly, the strife between the two conflicting views was reproduced in a condensed manner within individual managers, and most notably within the psychological make-up of the most senior managers. To put it somewhat figuratively, managers of the receiver firms of foreign technologies and management skills were of two minds. Analyzing how such a conflict between the two opposing attitudes translated into a concrete decision of a firm is a very challenging question to be tackled by business historians, one which will have to be addressed with the use of analytical concepts developed in other disciplines, including cognitive science.[9]

III. STRUCTURE

If Japanese firms that introduced skills and management from abroad were "whole-hearted" in their intention, while simultaneously displaying a mixture of enthusiasm and reluctance (the "two minds" concept), it is to be wondered what factors generated this strife and dictated its dynamism. To answer the question comprehensively, we should take into account a number of factors, including the inter-firm relationships of competition and cooperation between the supplier firms and the receiver firms, and the relationships between these firms and the governments of their respective countries. In this section, however, I will limit myself to commenting only on the organizational structure of the receiver firms.

If we try to delineate the defining features of technology and management introduction by Japanese firms in reference to the organizational structure of these firms, we might be able to point out the integrative nature of the corporate structure – working both at the level of management strata and at the level of industrial relations – as being crucially important. Let me first explain how the integrative bind imposed on managers by the corporate structure could affect an individual firm's decisions on technology and management introductions. As I have pointed out already, firms are the most important actor of accumulating, processing, and utilizing technological and management skills as knowledge. Within specific firms, it is the management strata which bears the central responsibility for accumulation and organizational learning of technologies as knowledge, and for making final decisions as to which piece of knowledge should be imported and which rejected.

In many cases of technology and management introduction, the wish to introduce new technologies was held by all the managers, and each was involved with the introduction. They also shared a certain sense of resistance. However, opposition to introductions was rare and low-key. Instead, within the mind of each manager, there was a juxtaposition of acquiescence and opposition; at times this spilled forth as dissension within the entire management strata.

One crucial prerequisite for the introduction process is the existence of managers who possess the ability to choose and apply the necessary technologies and management skills. This prerequisite must be satisfied both at the level of society as a whole, and at the level of individual firms. First, society taken as a whole must be endowed with at least a certain number of managers having this ability, regardless of whether they are owner-managers or salaried/professional managers. Second, at the level of individual firms, these managers of competence ought to have a certain amount of a say in the management of the firms. What counts here is the question of the positions and roles of salaried/professional managers. In undertaking concrete case studies on technology and management introduction, it is crucially important that we closely examine their ability to select and apply the necessary technologies and management skills to be imported. And indispensable for such inquiries is research to ascertain basic data, such as the total number of engineers and their status and functions in the managerial hierarchy at a specific point in time.[10]

The integrative nature of the corporate structure at the level of managers, understood in the sense explained above, was underpinned by the fact that a conspicuously large percentage of managers were generalists in type, as opposed to specialists, and they were educated and trained as such. Of course, certain managerial jobs were held by specialists, but Japanese managers on the whole have been different from their Western counterparts, who are predominantly of the specialist type. On closer examination, there were and are a variety of patterns in the organizational structure of management, including: the "conciliatory pattern," where managers of the generalist type are common; the "dictatorial pattern," where managers of this type are few in number and occupy the position of chief executive officer; and the "mediated pattern," where an individual manager as an embodiment of the firm's accumulation of technological and management knowledge is vested with authority and is supported by the chief executive officer. The specific pattern of management structure adopted by an individual firm could vary depending on the combination and division of power and authority. In any of the patterns of management structure, however, the role to be performed by managers of the generalist type was significantly large.

Moreover, the greater the technological and managerial gap between Japan and the West, the greater the role the managers had to perform in the decision-making process. Historical comparisons of the introductions of technologies and management skills suggest that the roles played by managers, especially top managers, tended to be greater in the earlier periods, when Japan was at the dawn of industrialization, when certain industries began to emerge, or when firms were just established, than at later points in time. At first, the right to make and execute decisions on technology and management introduction were a part of the chief executive officer's prerogative, but this right was gradually delegated to lower echelons and made into matters of routine.

The second important feature of the corporate structure is the integrative nature of labor relations. The adoption of technologies and management skills cannot be carried out by managers alone. It is into the factories and offices that the technologies and management skills are introduced, and in order to make the introduction a success, there must be a mutual understanding and cooperation between management and employees at these sites of work. This means that both management and employees must share the perception about the importance of the introduction, and share the willingness to make it a success. These are the key factors that crucially affect the results of the introduction. Generally speaking, labor and management in Japan have seldom quarreled with each other over the question of technology and management introductions. Both in society at large, and within individual firms, workers have mounted little resistance to introductions. Their general receptiveness to technology and management imports seems to have had something to do with labor unions' eagerness to achieve a parity between blue-collar and white-collar workers, and also with the fact that workers have not developed their own specific job culture. We might also be able to mention in-house unionism and company-sponsored welfare programs as factors underlying the willingness of workers to collaborate with the introductions.

Analyzed at a more profound level, the integrative nature of industrial relations seems to be ascribable to the fact that in plants and offices of Japanese firms (and especially in plants), the very sites where imported technologies and managerial skills were put to use, close relationships of cooperation were established between engineers (some of whom belonged to the management strata) and workers, who interacted with each other as functional equals. Close working and cooperative relationships could exist in Europe between engineers inside factories and those at research facilities. But what I am referring to here is the important meaning of the establishment of the cooperative relations between engineers and production workers working in the same plant, or the establishment of what Okuda Kenji and Morikawa Hidemasa call "factory floor-ism" or "shop-floor-orientedness," or what Sasaki Satoshi calls "the cooperative relations between production control engineers and skilled workers in leadership positions." This cuts a stark contrast to the reality of shop floors in Germany, for instance, where during the same period the "foreman's empire" was being replaced by the "chief engineer's empire."[11] This particular feature of the Japanese shop floor took its shape and grew ever more prominent through the continuing process by which engineers were educated in accordance with the principle of "factory floor-ism" or "shop-floor-orientedness," and received further training on the shop floor by working in close cooperation with production workers, especially through the process of technology and management introductions.

IV. OUTCOME

The juxtaposition of the strong interests in the adoption of technologies and management skills from the West and the resistance to the adoption, as well as the continuing strife between these two opposing attitudes, rendered Japanese firms' efforts to learn from abroad beyond the level of imitation; it inspired them to make further improvements on what they imported or even to make their own innovations. The process of introducing technologies and management skills from abroad had a logic built in itself that compelled the receiver firms to improve on what they imported, and to go even further ahead in pursuit of their own innovations (proceeding from process innovation on to product innovation). Put differently, the efforts to catch up with Western firms were also characterized, from the very beginning, as efforts to leap-frog these same firms. Looked at in this regard, we might say that the resistance to technology and management introduction was of a creative nature, and so was the strife between the pros and the cons to the introduction.

The dynamics of the interaction among the momentums of imitation, improvement, and innovation that characterized the process of technology and management introduction constituted the core factor explaining the dynamics of the development of technologies and management skills. It is normal for technologies and management skills to be transformed through the process of transfer. This is natural when the economic, social, and cultural climate of the receiver country is different from that of the supplier country, and also when the receiver firms are motivated to introduce them for purposes other than what they were originally developed for by the supplier firms. I have the impression, however, that this transformation was stronger still in Japan, where the actor involved with the transfer was itself driven by both a desire to make and the aversion to enact the introduction.

Such a transformation could prove successful only when everything developed in the receiver firm's favor. If things did not work well, the introduction would end up as a failure, or as an imitation at best. Even when everything was apparently working well continuously, the firm could get caught in a pitfall, i.e. it could make the mistake of overestimating its technological and managerial competence. Living through the dynamics of imitation, improvement and innovation could entail the risk of having one's evaluation of one's own technologies and management blurred, or having the standards of evaluation themselves blurred. This risk could be present not only at the level of individual managers or engineers, but also at the level of business management, and even at the level of a national economy. I would say that the government and many firms under the economic and militaristic nationalism of the 1930s committed mistakes exactly of this nature; they became so oblivious of the dictum that technologies and management skills could be developed only through transfer, that they overestimated their own technological and managerial competence. The much-propagated argument of the time that identified technologies as the basis for Japan's nation-building, and the argument that emphasized the nation's qualitative superiority were but typical manifestations of the blurred perception.[12]

V. CONCLUDING REMARKS

I have pointed out some of the distinguishing features of Japan's introduction of technologies and management skills in the first half of the twentieth century. Although based on case studies, this discussion has been tentative, aimed at outlining some working hypotheses. Even taken as such, the hypotheses presented here need much further clarifications. Moreover, my contentions in this paper, only illustrated or corroborated by a very limited number of case studies, remain to be tested by more full-fledged empirical studies.

As to the process of the strife between the enthusiasm for and the opposition to adopting foreign technologies and management skills, my observations seem to leave much to be desired, as my attention has been focused a bit too narrowly on manufacturing industries. It remains to be examined whether the discussion of this paper also holds true for other managerial functions, such as marketing, personnel management, and public relations. Still more important and requiring a thorough reexamination is the question of to what extent the hypotheses postulated in this paper on the process, structure, and outcome of the technology and management introduction were applicable only to Japan, and to what extent they were of more universal applicability. The term "factory floor-ism" or "shop-floor-orientedness" will have to be replaced by one of greater universal applicability, and the integrative nature of industrial relations in Japan expressed by this term will have to be redefined in a more universal context.

As to the cultural factors underlying the resistance to introduction, too, much needs to be considered. In this paper, I have focused my attention primarily on the resistance within management, but an analysis of cultural backgrounds to the resistance remains a task for the future. This question is linked to the above-mentioned question of ascertaining the uniqueness and universality of Japan's experience. It is also related to the question of evaluating the ability of Japanese firms as suppliers of technologies and management skills.

Commenting on the last point, Kobayashi Tatsuya points out that "Japan's experience is Japan's alone. It may be taught as one lesson, but there are many areas in the world where it cannot be translated into real policies." He also says: "In considering the question of the industrialization of developing countries, even if the model of Japanese civilization closely identified with its culture may serve as an object lesson, it is not something that can lay claim to any particular universality. I believe it will become more important in the future to lay our expectations in the civilization of new generations than to extract from the existing Japanese civilization some factors of possible universal applicability."[13]

Kobayashi's perceptive insight is supported by his rich experience in the field. Personally, I would like to emphasize the universality of Japanese experience, but to do so, it is essential to develop further our understanding of cultural factors. I also believe a fuller assessment of Japan's experience calls for comparisons not only with countries of the West, but also with Asian NIEs, such as South Korea and Taiwan, which have succeeded as followers of the Japanese model, and for that matter with ASEAN countries and China, as well. Such comparative studies can be an important test in determining whether Japan's experience is of a universal nature or not. Here, I would like to stress again that such international comparisons should take up the perspective of the history of international business relations.

I would like to conclude with the following remark by Uchida Hoshimi on the present state of the studies on technology transfer, which applies equally to management transfer as to technology transfer:

> The problem with historical work until recently is that it has been dominated by a view that takes Western technological development as a universal historical law, and that interprets the introduction of Western technologies into Japan merely as an inevitable process of overcoming a time-lag. This view has led to a failure to fully grasp the world historical significance of this phenomenon. Research that looks afresh at the history of Western technology transfer since the Meiji era, in its relationship with indigenous technologies, and as a successful case of technology transfer between different cultures, has made its start in earnest only recently.[14]

BIBLIOGRAPHY

Daito Eisuke and Kawabe Nobuo (eds) (1993), *Education and Training in the Development of Modern Corporations. The International Conference on Business History, 19,* University of Tokyo Press.

Fruin, Mark (1992), *The Japanese Enterprise System: Competitive Strategies and Cooperative Structures,* Oxford: Oxford University Press.

Hashimoto Juro (1995), "Gijutsu Donyu to Gembashugiteki Gijutsusha Yosei: Nihon no Keiken kara" (Technology Introduction and Shop-floor-oriented Training of Engineers: The Japanese Experience), in *Shakai Kagaku Kenkyu* (Journal of Social Science, Institute of Social Science, University of Tokyo), vo.46, No.5.

Hayashi Takeshi (1986), *Gijutsu to Shakai: Nihon no Keiken* (Technology and Society: The Japanese Experience), University of Tokyo Press.

Jeremy, David J. (ed.) (1990), *International Technology Transfer: Europe, Japan and the USA, 1700–1914,* Aldershot: Edward Elgar.

—— (ed.) (1992), *The Transfer of International Technology: Europe, Japan and the USA in the Twentieth Century,* Aldershot: Edward Elgar.

Kiyokawa Yukihiko (1984), "Obei, Gijutsu no Juyo wo meguru Shomondai: Nihon no Keiken wo Do Toraeruka" (Problems concerning the Acceptance of Western Technology: How Should Japan's Experience Be Assessed?), in *Shakai Keizaishi-gaku no Kaiko to Tembo* (Socio-Economic History, Its Past and Future), Yuhikaku.

—— (1995), *Nihon no Keizai Hatten to Gijutsu Fukyu* (The Japanese Economy: Its Development and Technology Diffusion), Toyo Keizai Shimposha.

Kobayashi Tetsuya (1981), *Gijutsu Iten – Rekishi kara no Kosatsu: Amerika to Nihon* (Technology Transfer in Historical Perspective: The United States and Japan), Bunshindo.

—— (1990), "Nihon no Gijutsu Iten: 'Ukete' no Jidai, 'Okurite' no Jidai" (Japan's Technology Transfer: The Era of Japan as "Receiver" and the Era of Japan as "Supplier"), in *Heisei Gannendo Sangyogijutsu no Hatten to Shakaiteki Juyo Hosaku ni tsuite no Chosa Kenkyu* (The 1989 Survey of Measures for the Development and Social Acceptance of Industrial Technology), Japan Science Foundation.

Kudō Akira (1990), "Sekiyu Kagaku" (Petrochemical Industry), in Yonekawa Shin'ichi, Shimokawa Koichi and Yamazaki Hiroaki (eds), *Sengo Nihon Keieishi, II* (Business History of Post-war Japan, II), Toyo Keizai Shimposha.

—— (1992a), *Nichi-Doku Kigyo Kankei-shi* (A History of Japanese-German Business Relations), Yuhikaku.

—— (1992b), *IG Farben no Tainichi Senryaku: Senkanki Nichi-Doku Kigyo Kankei-shi* (I.G. Farben's Japan Strategy: A History of Japanese-German Corporate Relations in the Inter-war Period), University of Tokyo Press.

—— (1994a), "I.G. Farben in Japan: The Transfer of Technology and Managerial Skills," in *Business History*, Vol.36, No.l.

—— (1994b), "The Transfer of Leading-edge Technology to Japan: The Krupp-Renn Process," in *Japanese Yearbook on Business History*, Vol.11.

Kudō Akira and Hara Terushi (eds) (1992), *International Cartels in Business History. The International Conference on Business History, 18*, University of Tokyo Press.

Minami Ryoshin and Kiyokawa Yukihiko (eds) (1987), *Nihon no Kogyoka to Gijutsu Hatten* (Industrialization and Technological Development of Japan), Toyo Keizai Shimposha.

Morikawa Hidemasa (1981), *Nihon Keieishi* (A Business History of Japan), Nihon Keizai Shimbunsha.

—— (1988), "Nihon Gijutsusha no 'Gemba-shugi' ni tsuite: Keieishiteki Kosatsu" (On the 'Shop-Floor-Orientedness' of Japanese Engineers: An Observation from Business History), in *Yokohama Keiei Kenkyu* (Yokohama National University Business Review), Vol.8, No.4.

—— (1991), "The Education of Engineers in Modern Japan: A Historical Perspective," in Howard F. Gospel (ed.), *Industrial Training and Technological Innovation: A Comparative and Historical Study,* London and New York: Routledge.

Nakagawa Keiichiro (1981a), *Hikaku Keieishi Josetsu* (An Introduction to Comparative Business History), University of Tokyo Press.

—— (1981b), "Keiei shigaku ni okeru Kokusai Hikaku to Kokusai Kankei" (International Comparisons and International Relations in Business History), in Tsuchiya Moriaki and Morikawa Hidemasa (eds), *Kigyosha Katsudo no Shiteki Kenkyu* (Historical Studies on the Activities of Entrepreneurs), Nihon Keizai Shimbunsha.

Nakaoka Tetsuro, Ishii Tadashi and Uchida Hoshimi (1986) *Kindai Nihon no Gijutsu to Gijutsu Seisaku* (Technology and Technology Policy of Modern Japan), Tokyo: United Nations University.

Nishikawa Koji (1989), "Kigyo nò Paradaimu Tenkan ni kansuru Hikakushi-teki Kosatsu: Ford Shisutemu to Toyota Seisan Shisutemu no Keisei Katei" (A Comparative Historical Analysis of Paradigm Changes Undertaken by Firms: The Formative Processes of the Ford System and the Toyota Production System), in *Keizai Keiei Ronshu* (Ryukoku University Journal of Economics and Business), Vol.29, No.3.

—— (1993), "Hogaki Nihon Itagarasu Sangyo no Renzokushi-teki soku-men to Danzokushi-teki Sokumen: Kyotsu-teki Chishiki Ninshiki Taikei no Sonzai Kanosei ni tsuite" (Historically Continuous and Discontinuous Features of the Japanese Plate-glass Industry in Its Embryonic Stage: On the Possibility of the Existence of a Common Knowledge Recognition System), in *Keieigaku Ronshu* (Ryukoku University Journal of Business Management), Vol.32, No.4.

Okochi Akio and Uchida Hoshimi (eds) (1980) *Development and Diffusion of Technology: Electrical and Chemical Industries. The International Conference on Business History, 6,* University of Tokyo Press.

Okuda Kenji (1985), *Hito to Keiei* (Human Resources and Management), Tokyo: Manejimentosha.

Oshio Takeshi (1989), *Nitchitsu Kontserun no Kenkyu* (A Study on Nitchitsu Konzern), Nihon Keizai Hyoronsha.

Pauer, Erich (ed.) (1992), *Technologietransfer Deutschland–Japan von 1850 zur Gegenwart,* München: iudicium-Verlag.

Sasaki Satoshi and Nonaka Izumi (1990) "Nihon ni okeru Kagakuteki Kanriho no Donyu to Tenkai" (The Introduction and Development of Scientific Management Methods in Japan), in Hara Terushi (ed.), *Kagakuteki Kanriho no Donyu to Tenkai: Sono Rekishiteki Kokusai Hikaku* (Comparative and

Historical Studies on the Introduction and Development of Scientific Management Methods), Kyoto: Showado.

Takenaka Toru (1991), *Siemens to Meiji Nihon* (Siemens and Meiji Japan), Tokai University Press.

Uchida Hoshimi (1985), "Gijutsushi" (Technology History), in *Keiei shigaku no 20-nen* (20 Years of Business History), University of Tokyo Press.

—— (1988), "Gijutsusha no Zoka Bumpu to Nihon no Kogyoka: 1880–1920 no Tokeiteki Kansatsu" (The Increase and Distribution of Engineers and Japan's Industrialization: A Statistical Investigation, 1880–1920), in *Keizai Kenkyu* (Hitotsubashi University Journal of Economics), Vol.39, No.4.

—— (1990), "Gijutsu Iten" (Technology Transfer), in Nishikawa Shunsaku and Abe Takeshi (eds), *Nihon Keizaishi, 4; Sangyoka no Jidai, 1* (Japanese Economic History, 4: The Age of Industrialization, 1), Iwanami Shoten.

—— (1991a), "Kokusaiteki Gijutsu Iten: Rekishiteki Kaiko" (International Technology Transfer: A Historical Reflection), in *Heisei Ninen Sangyogijutsu no Hatten to Shakaiteki Juyo Hosaku ni tsuite no Chosa Kenkyu* (The 1990 Survey of Measures for the Development and Acceptance of Industrial Technology), Japan Science Foundation.

—— (1991b), "Japanese Technical Manpower in Industry, 1880–1930: A Quantitative Survey," in Howard F. Gospel (ed.), *Industrial Training and Technological Innovation: A Comparative and Historical Study*, London and New York: Roudedge.

—— (n.d.), *Nihon Gijutsushi Kogi* (Lectures on Japanese Technology History), n.p.

Yamazaki Hiroaki (1975), *Nihon Kasen Sangyo Hattatsushi Ron* (A Study in the History of the Development of the Japanese Chemical Fiber and Textile Industry), University of Tokyo Press.

Yuzawa Takeshi and Udagawa Masaru (eds) (1990), *Foreign Business in Japan Before World War II. The International Conference on Business History, 16*, University of Tokyo Press.

Source: Institute of Social Science, University of Tokyo, Discussion Paper Series, F-99, 2002, pp. 1–79.

8

The Political Process of IG Farben's Dissolution

SECTION 1: CONTROL BY DIVISION

1. Seizing Assets and Control by Division

(1) Occupation and Asset Seizure

THE POLITICAL PROCESS surrounding the dissolution of IG Farben began with the end of the Second World War, or, more properly, immediately after the end of the battle in Europe, which was a part of the war.[1] The battle in Europe ended with Germany's signing of an unconditional surrender either on 7 May 1945 in Reims or on 8 May in Berlin. At that point IG Farben's activities as a single, unified firm stopped almost completely. Even before that time the United States military had occupied IG Farben units within Germany and across Europe one after another and had seized their assets. The value of IG Farben assets seized in German territory reached about 1 billion Reichsmark, even without fully incorporating the assessed value of patents and trademarks. The total value of IG Farben's assets in German territory, according to balance sheets at the end of 1944, had reached 1.947 billion Reichsmark, excluding capital participation in other firms.

As Figure 8.1 shows, a 57.9% majority of IG Farben's assets in German territory were in the Soviet Zone when Germany was divided by the four occupying powers (the U.S., Britain, France, and the Soviet Union). The remaining 42.1%, or about 1 billion Reichsmark's worth, was in the occupation zones of the Western powers. A breakdown of the latter figure shows 18.3% of assets at the former BASF Ludwigshafen site, 8.5% at the former Bayer Leverkusen site, 6.8% at the former Hoechst site in the place of the same name, and 8.5% of assets in other locations.[2]

Figure 8.1 Locations of Principal Plants of Former IG Farben in Occupied Germany (1945–1949)

In the Western occupation zone, the former BASF Ludwigshafen factory near Mannheim was occupied by U.S. forces in late March 1945 and was placed under the administration of the U.S. military government.[3] The former Bayer plant at Leverkusen near Cologne was also occupied by U.S. forces in April but was placed under British military administration in June.[4] Occupation by the U.S. military began for the Hoechst factory in Frankfurt am Main as well in late March. Quite exceptional among IG Farben's main factories, the Hoechst plant was almost undamaged, having never been the target of Allied strategic bombing. The IG Farben headquarters building in Frankfurt also escaped bombing, and had been seized by the U.S. military by the end of March.[5] After July of 1945, the U.S. military government handed over the former BASF plant in Ludwigshafen to the French military government after the redrawing of the boundaries of the French and U.S. zones of occupation.[6]

The three main IG Farben plants incorporated into the Western zone of occupation were thus each placed under the administration of a different military government. The former BASF Ludwigshafen plant was under French military administration, the former Bayer Leverkusen factory was under British military control, and the former Hoechst plant in the town of the same name was under U.S. military government. As this paper will later examine in detail, this period laid the groundwork for the future dissolution of IG Farben in the Western zone of occupation into the BASF, Bayer, and Hoechst groups.

(2) Control by Division

Initially, each military government in the Western zone of occupation managed IG Farben's assets independently, based on orders that were issued by each military government and were effective from July through November 1945. These orders were the U.S. General Order Number 2, dated 5 July, that implemented Military Government Law Number 52;[7] the French military government general order dated 24 July; and the British military government's General Directive Number 2, dated 18 November. These orders dissolved IG Farben's board of auditors and board of directors, removed some managing staffs including executives (both members of the audit board and members of the board of directors) and non-executives from key decisions, and in some cases fired or purged these managing staffs. In the U.S. zone, all managing staffs were purged, regardless of whether or not they had been executives. The right of stockholders to dispose of assets or decide on their management (Verfügungsrecht) was suspended, and the sale or purchase of IG Farben stock was prohibited.

Meanwhile, seizure and control of IG Farben assets by military government order was also proceeding in the Soviet zone of occupation. Plants in eastern Germany were dismantled, destroyed, or confiscated without compensation to become enterprises owned by the Soviet Union. Some plants in Polish territory were also dismantled, and the physical assets then transported to the USSR.[8]

It was not that the Allied powers did not attempt to coordinate the control of IG Farben's division among themselves as this process got underway. The Allied Control Council did make such an attempt. This body, established in Berlin on 5 June 1945, was the supreme organ for the Allied administration of Germany. It consisted of the supreme commanders of the militaries of the U.S., Britain, France, and the Soviet Union. It announced the Allied Control Council Law Number 9 of 30 November 1945 that had the objective of coordinating the four countries' control policies toward IG Farben. The law's preamble made clear its purpose by stating that it had been promulgated in order "to render impossible any threat by a future Germany toward neighboring countries or to world peace" based on the recognition that "IG Farben essentially and demonstrably participated in the expansion and maintenance of Germany's war-making potential." Paragraph 3 of the law indicated measures to be taken to achieve this goal, including use of IG Farben facilities as reparations, destruction of facilities devoted to production of war materiel, division of property rights in remaining facilities, decartelization, control of research activities, and restriction of production activities. These stipulations clearly shared the underlying idea of the July 1945 U.S. General Order and the 2 August 1945 Potsdam Protocol. In any event, this law transferred the authority for controlling IG Farben's assets from the hands of each country's military governments to the Allied Control Council.

The Council set up a Four Power Committee (Viermächte-Ausschuβ) (Law Number 9 Paragraph 2), consisting of one representative of each occupying power, to control jointly IG Farben assets and to coordinate the measures being planned separately in each of the four zones for the dissolution of the enterprise.

The Four Power Committee made public its plan for controlling IG Farben assets. The plan stipulated that each former IG Farben plant must be a completely independent enterprise, that transactions among the plants must accordingly be made by market rather than internal prices, and that various Konzern relationships (capital ownership) must be prohibited. It is safe to say that the plan envisioned a thorough dissolution of IG Farben into individual factory units. The plan also stipulated that implementation of the dissolution should be delegated to those in charge of controlling IG Farben in each zone of occupation.[9]

In actuality, however, the activities of the Four Power Committee were nearly paralyzed from the start for two reasons. First, its higher organization, the Allied Control Council, did not have the capacity to enforce compliance with its own decisions. Second, there was hardly any agreement on policy visible within the Council itself as the contemporary division between Eastern and Western camps became clearer. Actual control of IG Farben thus fell to the military governments of the occupying powers, as had been the case previously.[10]

2. The Reality of Control by Division

As 1(2) of this section showed, the control of IG Farben's dissolution on the ground in each zone of occupation shared some common attributes, including measures to dissolve the boards of auditors and directors and to fire or purge managing staffs. In other respects, though, control differed in each zone as a reflection of the differences in each power's overall occupation policy.

(1) The U.S. Zone: Strict Dissolution Plan and Dismantling

The policy of the U.S. military government towards IG Farben was extremely strict, as was apparent in the aforementioned General Order of July 1945. It also accorded with the basic line of Allied policy towards Germany from the Potsdam Declaration in August 1945 to the Allied Control Council's Law No. 9 in November of that year. Were one to trace the source of U.S. policy, one would probably arrive at classical American legal thinking on antitrust after the Sherman Antitrust Act of 1890. It is probably also safe to say that the extremely critical view of IG Farben that developed from the U.S. Senate's Kilgore Committee in the 1930s was projected onto U.S. IG Farben policy.[11]

U.S. military government appointed one German custodian (Treuhänder) for each former IG Farben factory. These custodians managed each factory against a backdrop of the U.S. military government, understanding as though each factory were an independent firm. This management method not only applied to the production system but prevailed in accounting as well. For each individual factory that had previously been managed as part of the single firm of IG Farben, and especially for the small- and medium-sized plants, this practice was an extremely harsh one. For example, each plant had to work for additional investment to compensate for what was lost due to the cut-off of production technology links with other factories.[12]

The U.S. military government further planned a thoroughgoing division of the Hoechst plant, a main IG Farben facility, and its surrounding factories. The most extreme element of this plan was first the dissolution of the Hoechst plant itself along product lines into five independent firms, and further to create a total of 52 independent firms from the 48 factories scattered throughout the Maingau region that included the Hoechst site.[13] The first actual step toward the dissolution of the Hoechst plant occurred in January 1946. The officials in the decartelization–IG Farben control section of the U.S. military government's economic division indicated the need for dissolution of the Hoechst plant. In response, the legal affairs division proposed dividing the Hoechst factory into three parts: heavy chemicals, dyes, and pharmaceuticals (including, in some cases, synthetic resins). The plant's German executives opposed this plan on the basis that a breakup of Hoechst factory into multiple firms would interfere with the supply of raw materials to each individual factory. The U.S. military government moved ahead, however, with its dissolution policy, and aimed to divide Hoechst into three parts – acetic acid, fertilizer, and dyes and pharmaceuticals – or, with the addition of sulfuric acid, four parts.[14]

The U.S. military government dissolution proposal was an extremely severe one for the Hoechst plant. This severity was manifest in the area of removal of factory facilities as well. Leaving aside the Soviet zone, the U.S. zone was the earliest among the Western occupied zones for the initiation of plant removal. The U.S. military government began the removal of equipment from the Hoechst plant in the winter of 1947–48.[15] Removal began much later in the other two zones: in November 1949 at the Ludwigshafen plant in the French zone, and in October 1949 at the Leverkusen plant in the British zone.[16]

Along with the U.S. military government, the so-called "socialization" (Sozialisierung) movement in the state of Hesse, where the Hoechst factory was located, also affected the fortunes of that plant. Socialization was a political issue after the Second World War as the First World War in Germany, and the Hoechst plant's home state of Hesse was a mecca for the issue. On 29 October 1946, the Hesse state constitutional convention approved by majority vote a draft state constitution. In the majority were the Social Democratic Party (SPD), the Christian Democratic Union (CDU), and the Communist Party (KPD); only the Liberal Democratic Party (LDP, later the FDP) found itself in the opposition. Article 41 of the new constitution extolled the virtues of socialization of industry, and extended not only to public utilities but to a broad range of industries, including mining and manufacturing as well as finance. Even the conservative Christian Democrats had come around to supporting the draft constitution containing this socialization provision. In the Ahlen party program adapted in February 1947, the party promised socialization of the mining and manufacturing sector. This action symbolizes starkly the contemporary political conditions in Germany. Even before the constitution was approved there had been proposals for the conversion of Hoechst to state ownership. In July 1946, the German trustee of the Hoechst factory conferred with representatives of the state governments of Hesse and Bavaria about the issue of transferring ownership of the factory at the Hesse state economic ministry in the state capital of Wiesbaden. At the meeting both Hesse and Bavaria expressed interest in having the Hoechst plants turned over to them.[17] It is safe to say that this development also conveys the political atmosphere at that time.

The U.S. military government opposed the socialization statute, and it requested that the statute be subject to a special referendum when the constitution was put to a referendum for the approval of the constitution. The referendum was conducted in February, 1947, and the statute received a 72% vote in favor.[18]

Some of those within the U.S. military government who were directly charged with managing Hoechst accepted the moves toward socialization and argued for shifting the firm to public ownership. They held that the U.S. authorities ought to respect the desire for public ownership of basic and pivotal industries that was expressed in the referendum, that management by the current German custodian was really a transitional measure, and that the state government of Hesse should consider Hoechst's conversion to public ownership.[19] The top levels of the U.S. military government, however, consistently opposed socialization, including this kind of conversion to public ownership. In August 1947, General Lucius D. Clay, the deputy chief of the U.S. military government, said "The U.S. military government in Germany has no intention of imposing its opinions on Germany. But at a time when America is expending such huge sums to assist Germany, the U.S. military government has a right to express its opinions and to disapprove of this kind of experiment."

The movement toward socialization in Hesse thus met with the refusal of the U.S. authorities and was thwarted. Although the

Social Democratic Party, which had argued the most forcefully for socialization, continued to espouse socialization, its October 1947 socialization bill rejected nationalization because of the evils of bureaucratism and centralization, and it gradually softened its stance to a goal of creating a "social community."[20]

(2) The British Zone of Occupation: Lenient Policy

In contrast to the U.S. military government, the British military government was lenient in its policy toward IG Farben. As in the U.S. zone of occupation, the German custodian appointed by the military government was in charge of actual factory management, under the supervision of British control personnel. The group of former Bayer factories was, however, entrusted to a single custodian.[21] This was quite different from the situation in the U.S. zone, in which one custodian was named for each factory. Moreover, the British military government policy should be termed "laissez faire." "Except for an extremely small number of exceptions, the British control personnel left the old control format for the organization as it was, and hardly interfered in the administration of the company." Research activities in the British zone were also resumed early on. Permission to resume production was granted relatively early, and permission to use the former Bayer name was granted effective July 1947.[22]

Furthermore, the British military government never considered dividing up the former main Bayer plant at Leverkusen. On the contrary, they worked out a plan to reorganize the Bayer plants, including the former Bayer relatively large scale plants around Leverkusen, into a single firm. This too stands in stark contrast to the policy of the U.S. military government.

Despite the lenient British military government policy, those on the German side were always concerned that a strict dissolution policy might be formulated. This was of course true for management, but it was also true of the labor unions. The chemical workers' unions (Industriegewerkschaft Chemie, Papier, Keramik, or IG Chemie), German Confederation of Labor (Deutscher Gewerkschaftsbund or DGB) and the works councils in the British zone issued a statement against the division of the former main Bayer plants in Leverkusen, Elberfeld, Dormagen, Ürdingen, Knapsack, and Troisdorf.[23]

Voices demanding socialization were, although not as strident as in Hesse, also strong in the British zone. Unlike the U.S. military government, the British military government initially showed a tolerant attitude toward these as well. A statement by the Labor Government's foreign minister Ernest Bevin in October 1946 even accelerated the movement toward socialization. But as the integration of the U.S. and British zones of occupation proceeded, the Americans exerted pressure, and from the summer of 1947 the British military government also made clear its negative attitude regarding socialization.[24]

(3) The French Zone of Occupation: A Strict Repatriation Plan

Unlike in the U.S. or British zones, in the French zone a French factory custodian (Sequesterverwalter) rather than a German one was appointed by the July 1945 order. So formally it may be said that direct control by the French military government was instituted. In reality, though, it was acknowledged that German managers might continue to manage "under the authority and control" of the French custodian. Although the system was revised several times, this essentially indirect control continued throughout the occupation.[25]

It is not clear what sort of control plan the French government and the French military government had for the plants in the Ludwigshafen area. Whether or not there was a plan for dividing them up is also unclear.[26] After some initial attempts to confiscate equipment at the Ludwigshafen plants, such plans were suspended. As will be discussed below, it was not until November 1949 that the French authorities began full-scale removal, almost two years later than in the U.S. zone.

The removal plan of the French military government was thorough, and called for the removal of DM40 million, or 70% of the DM57 million (in 1938 prices) worth of equipment covering nitrogen, synthetic oil, synthetic rubber, aluminum, and many other products. There were plans to ship the confiscated equipment not just to France, but to the Netherlands, Belgium, Yugoslavia, Greece, India, and elsewhere. Out of the existing nitrogen equipment, which had an annual production capacity of 270,000 tons (pure nitrogen equivalent), for example, the French authorities planned to dismantle 120,000 tons' worth of equipment and thereby reduce the production capacity of the Ludwigshafen plant to 150,000 tons annually. Plans were also made to move the confiscated equipment to the government nitrogen corporation, the Office National Industriel de l'Azote (ONIA). ONIA was a state-owned enterprise established after the First World War to initiate nitrogen production under the Haber-Bosch process. It goes without saying that BASF resisted this removal plan while emphasizing the importance of nitrogen fertilizer production to the national economy.[27] Ultimately the removal plan met with the concerted resistance of both management and labor on the German side and was relaxed at a level at which major damage could be averted. Before that point, at the end of July 1948, a large-scale explosion occurred at the Ludwigshafen plant, but production kept expanding nonetheless after that.[28]

In the end division of plants failed to move forward in the French zone of occupation, and the main Ludwigshafen plant did not become a target for dismemberment. Traces of intervention may be discerned, however, in the leasing out of the relatively small-scale plants at Rottweil and Rheinfelden to Franco-German joint ventures controlled by French firms.[29]

(4) The Soviet Zone of Occupation: Confiscation

As noted in 1(1) of this section, the majority of IG Farben assets on German soil were located in the Soviet zone of occupation. The Leuna plant, the largest and most important plant among these assets, fell under U.S. occupation in April 1945, but was subsequently placed under the occupation of the Soviet military as it moved in to replace the U.S. military when it withdrew in July. Production resumed under the Soviet military, and they put into effect plans for denazification and democratization of the management (a purge of war criminals), as well as for the removal. The Leuna plant was converted into a "soviet joint stock corporation (sowjetische Aktiengesellschaft)" in July 1946. After the establishment of the German Democratic Republic (East Germany), in January 1954, the plant became Volkseigener Betrieb, or VEB, or, in other words, a state-owned enterprise.[30]

After the U.S. military withdrew in July 1945, the Wolfen plant was seized by the Soviet Union's occupation forces. Like the Leuna plant, it was converted into a "soviet joint stock corporation" in July 1946.[31] Various other plants, including Bitterfeld, shared a similar fate.

With the end of the war in May 1945, IG Farben was thus placed under the divided control of the Allied powers. During the sharpening standoff between East and West, the factories in the Western zone of occupation and those in the Soviet zone suffered completely different fates. The three major factories located in the Western zone, Ludwigshafen, Leverkusen, and Hoechst, fell into the French, British, and U.S. zones, respectively. The U.S. military government actively intervened in the management of the Hoechst plant, and prepared a strict plan for the division of the firm. The British military government adopted a lenient attitude toward the Leverkusen plant, and its dismemberment plan was also mild. The French military government showed more stringency than the Americans, in terms of their strict removal plan draft, but the implementation of the plan was frustrated.[32]

The policy in each of the Western zones toward IG Farben thus differed. It may be argued that this situation reflects the fact that the East-West confrontation had not yet sharpened enough to necessitate the integration of occupation policies by the West. After December 1946 moves began toward the economic integration of the U.S. and British zones, and these came to fruition with the establishment of the Bipartite Control Office (BICO) in June 1947. Differences still remained, though, between U.S. and British policy regarding the control of IG Farben. Meanwhile, France continued to adopt its own control policies.

In the Western zone of occupation, thus, IG Farben was *de facto* divided into and managed as three companies or business groups: BASF, Bayer, and Hoechst. This stands in sharp contrast to the fate of iron and steel firms. Most iron and steel firms were located in the Ruhr district and fell under the British zone of occupation. They thus were placed under the relatively mild British occupation policy.

The following section will trace the political process related to the dissolution of IG Farben in the Western zone of occupation.

SECTION 2: SOLIDIFICATION OF DISSOLUTION PLANS

1. Changes in the Political and Economic Environment

As detailed above, there was no concrete progress on the dissolution of IG Farben for more than three years after the end of the war, regardless of the policy for breaking apart the single firm of IG Farben presented in Allied Control Council Law Number 9. The turning point was in the summer of 1948, when a panel on the dissolution of IG Farben composed of German specialists was established in the combined U.S.-British zone of occupation. This measure was taken at about the same time as two major events, the implementation of currency reform and the handing down of the verdict in the Nuremberg Military Tribunal. Even if these two events had no direct causal relationship with the turn-around in the IG Farben dissolution process, they were subtly related.

The chief element of the June 1948 currency reform (Währungs-reform) was the introduction of the new currency unit, the Deutsche mark. This established the framework for West Germany's economic recovery. It led at the same time to West Germany's re-emergence as a divided state. In September 1948 a constitutional convention was established in Bonn. After repeated negotiations with the Allied pow-ers, the convention adopted a fundamental law equivalent to a con-stitution on 8 May 1949. On the basis of this fundamental law, the new state carried out elections for its federal parliament in August, and the Federal Republic of Germany (West Germany) was launched in September. The first government was led by the Christian Democratic Union (CDU) under Konrad Adenauer. Following hot on the Federal Republic's heels, the German Democratic Republic (East Germany) was established in the Soviet zone in October of the same year.[33]

Although there have been attempts to "demythologize" the currency reform, it cannot be denied that the reform was of decisive importance for the economic reconstruction of West Germany.[34] The currency reform also provided an opportunity for new departures for the factory groups under the umbrella of the former IG Farben. But it was the ver-dicts in the Nuremberg Military Tribunal that had an even more direct connection to the turnaround in the IG Farben dissolution process.

The Nuremberg Military Tribunal referred to here was carried out by the U.S. military government alone, being separate from the Inter-national Military Tribunal conducted by the Allies with respect to the leaders of the Nazi regime. Twelve courtrooms were set up, and one of them was for persons connected to IG Farben. Based on Allied Con-trol Council Law Number 10, effective 20 December 1945, the U.S. military government indicted 23 former IG Farben officials, including directors, in August 1947. The charges included planning, preparing, and executing a war of aggression, expropriation, employing forced labor, and cooperating with the SS (Schutzstaffel). Verdicts came out at the end of July 1948. Although 13 defendants were found guilty of expropriation and using forced labor and were sentenced to prison for definite terms, the defendants were found innocent on the other charges. Essentially the verdicts were close to innocent, and the trials were in general taken at that time to be a victory for the defendants. At root the outcome of the trials was not something of a character which would directly affect in any way the dissolution and control of IG Far-ben by the Allies. More than anything else, what was on trial were the individual former IG Farben officials, not IG Farben the firm. But the verdicts provided the occasion for voices to rise within Germany that demanded changes in the actual control of IG Farben and in the policy regarding its dissolution.[35]

The following is an example of this development. "Thus, if we were to say that now it has been proved that IG Farben's management (Lei-tung) did not in fact participate actively in preparing for and leading an aggressive war, and, like other German businessmen, did not belong to the circle that knew of Hitler's plans, then the preamble to Law Number 9 (Allied Control Council Law Number 9 - A. K.) would lose its meaning, because it would mean that no causal relationship existed between the business policies of IG Farben's managers and 'Germany's threat to neighboring countries and to world peace'."[36] If this argu-ment is extended, then IG Farben was not singled out for dissolution on a special legal basis but was merely made an object of decarteliza-tion at most. In fact, a while later, Alexander Menne, the Chairman of the Chemical Industry Association (Arbeitsgemeinschaft Chemische Industrie) did make such an assertion. Menne said that the "special measures" with respect to IG Farben under General Order 2, imple-menting U.S. Military Government Law Number 52, as well as Allied Control Council Law Number 9, were not only rendered moot by the Nuremberg verdicts, but also Law Number 9 itself had lost its effect and that IG Farben had hereafter merely become a target of the decar-telization mandated by U.S. Military Government Law Number 56 of 12 February 1947, which proscribed concentration and prohibited cartels.[37]

With the Nuremberg trial verdicts on the former IG Farben officials as well as the domestic reaction to them in the background, the follow-ing changes occurred in the process of IG Farben's dissolution.

2. Establishment and Selection of the German Panel

(1) The Panel's Establishment

On 5 August 1948, immediately after the verdicts were issued in the Nuremberg Military Tribunal, the Bipartite I.G. Farben Control Office (BIFCO) and the Bizonal I.G. Farben Dispersal Panel (FARDIP) were both established under the Bipartite Control Office (BICO) of the combined American-British zone of occupation. BIFCO was purely a part of the Allied control apparatus and was composed of military government personnel. FARDIP was an advisory committee that was supposed to consist of German specialists, and it was set up under BIFCO. It too thus constituted part of the Allied control apparatus.

Both organizations, BIFCO and FARDIP, were placed under the Bipartite Control Office, and they fell directly under the Decartelization Bureau. The Decartelization Bureau had been established along with the Bipartite Control Office in June 1947. The fact that the section and the panel handling IG Farben's dissolution were placed under the Decartelization Bureau meant that the dissolution of IG Farben formed a part of decartelization policy. It also meant that the dissolution would continue to be handled differently from decartelization in general. IG Farben's dissolution continued to be a special case that could not be understood as a part of decartelization.

FARDIP, the panel of German specialists, initially was given the mandate of overall control of IG Farben's assets. The fact that the organization was blessed with a name containing the word "dispersal" rather than "dissolution" is probably connected with that mandate. But later, before the panel's members could be finally selected, its mandate changed. It was now to prepare a proposal for IG Farben's dissolution, as well as proposals for the treatment of stockholders and creditors and for the settlement of the company's remaining assets. FARDIP was then to report these plans directly to its supervisory body, BIFCO.[38]

(2) Selection of the Panel

The Bipartite Control Office (BICO) issued one directive to BIFCO on the day it set up the panel, 5 August. The directive will be discussed below. At this point, the members of the panel had not yet been selected. The first job for the Bipartite Control Office and its subordinate agencies was to select the members of the panel. On this issue alone did the German side have the right to speak and it could enter into negotiations with the Bipartite Control Office.

Indeed, with this membership issue as the principal agenda item, the German side held several meetings over the period from late August to early September. Attending these meetings were members of the Administrative Council (Verwaltungsrat), including Hermann Pünder; members of the Economic Council (Verwaltung für Wirtschaft), including Ludwig Erhard; and members of the Chemical Industry Association, including Ulrich Haberland. The first two councils were administrative agencies in occupied Germany. It suggested that the panel's existence was regarded as important. The Chemical Industry Association was at that time the sole trade group representative of managerial interests. Haberland was a former Bayer official, and after the war he had been designated custodian of Leverkusen and all the other principal plants in the British zone of occupation.[39]

At its first meeting, the German side united on the understanding that "the dissolution of IG Farben must be viewed as one of the most important economic policy issues at present." In that context they agreed that the proposed panel should be composed of first-rank specialists in the areas of chemistry, law, finance, and economics. They also agreed during their discussions that "persons who were struck with a political brand" ought not to be appointed to the panel. In early September they sent the following list of candidates to BIFCO.[40]

Hermann J. Abs	Deutsche Bank
Hermann Bücher	former chairman of the board of directors, AEG
Ernst Engelbertz	
Oskar Loehr	formerly of IG Farben Leverkusen
Karl Friedrich Müller	Rütgerswerke official
Rudolf Müller	attorney, former Hesse Economics Minister
Ernst Vieths	Glanzstoff official

The Allied side studied the candidate list and objected to some of the candidates. Various conjectures then flew back and forth.[41] The German side once again submitted a list in November with Abs' name removed; the Deutsche Bank's Abs had worked before the war as a member of the board of auditor for IG Farben and was at that time already an important figure in financial circles. It was conjectured that one of the reasons for dropping Abs was the fact that membership on the panel had to be full-time.[42] The panel's membership was finally fixed as follows in December 1947.[43]

Hermann Bücher	former chairman of the board of directors, AEG
Gustav Brecht	former chairman of the board of directors, Rhein-Braun
Arnold Burghartz	former official, Karlos-Magnus mine
Egon von Ritter	formerly of IG Farben Munich

Oskar Loehr	formerly of IG Farben Leverkusen
Eugen Möhn	formerly of IG Farben Hoechst
Franz Blücher	Liberal Democratic Party

Only two people, Bücher and Loehr, were left from the initial candidate list, leading to suspicions that the Allied side had forcefully intervened. Former AEG Chairman Bücher was named chairman of the panel.[44] One of the members, Blücher, soon resigned because he was too busy. Three of the remaining six places on the panel were occupied by those who had been connected with IG Farben, including labor union representative Möhn. Later, Brecht would be welcomed as a member of the board of auditors, and Loehr named a director, at Bayer.[45]

FARDIP was thus an organization that could reflect the interests of the German side. Up until that point, there had not existed an organization on the German side that was capable of representing the interests of IG Farben's former managers, stockholders, and creditors. The panel, then, was the first formal mechanism for doing so. Thus, IG Farben stood in stark contrast to firms likewise slated for dissolution in other industries such as coal and steel, or banking, because in these two sectors boards of auditors and boards of directors had continued to exist under German law throughout the whole post-war process and had carried the responsibility for enterprise management. After a time stockholder meetings had even been held. In contrast, IG Farben "was, for an abnormally long period, a zone of what may be termed extra-territoriality for the Allied powers."[46] The establishment of the panel therefore had landmark significance in IG Farben's dissolution process.

But Allied "extraterritoriality" did not lapse with the establishment of the panel. The panel was, ultimately, subordinate to the Allied Control Council, and was no more than an advisory body. The following event is one that illustrates the limits to the panel's authority. In 1949, after the panel had begun its activities, the U.S. military government made clear its intention to sell off Kalle & Co. AG, a wholly owned subsidiary of IG Farben, as "a test case." There was no notification to the panel with regard to this intention, nor, of course, was there an advance hearing. The sell-off proposal ended without seeing the light of day primarily because of the opposition of the British military government, but the episode is sufficient to show the stature of the panel in the eyes of the Allied side, and especially the U.S. military goverment.[47] In addition, there were scattered representatives of German interests aside from the panel, including German employees within BIFCO as well as the custodians at each factory. It was noted that, relative to these, the panel had little authority and limited contact with the Allied side.[48]

3. The German Dissolution Proposal

(1) Principles for the Dissolution

FARDIP began its activities in December 1948. Its point of departure was the directive from the Anglo-American Bipartite Control Office (BICO). BICO issued a single directive to the panel on 5 August 1948, before the final determination of the panel's membership.

BICO's directive read as follows. "In preparing its recommendations, the panel must observe the principles of keeping units (Betriebe) as small as possible, integrating them geographically as much as possible, and, notwithstanding the foregoing, giving appropriate consideration to technological and economic efficiency." "Each... 'independent unit' must be operated as an independent firm. BICO will allow only normal relationships, which accord with commercial practices and which normally exist among competitive firms, between these independent units and other factories that were formerly under the umbrella of or management of IG Farben."[49] The directive thus envisioned that up to approximately 50 plants would become "independent firms."[50]

The panel interpreted the directive as follows. "The IG Farben dispersal panel is convinced that the directive emphasizes technical as well as economic efficiency (Leistungsfahigkeit). To the extent possible, competitive firms ought to be created. The degree of dissolution, or, in other words, the scale and degree of domestic and international competitiveness of independent units to be newly created from the once unified concern of IG Farbenindustries AG are therefore decisive issues, and are of the utmost concern to the IG Farben dispersal panel."[51] Here the panel emphasizes ensuring the competitiveness, both domestic and international, of the independent units created by the dissolution. This was indeed a clever interpretation which had been pulled toward the panel's own set of assumptions. One of the panel's members, Oskar Loehr, said of the panel's principal task, "we were to draw up the principles and proposals of economic policy while seeking a constructive solution that would ensure the international competitiveness of the German chemical industry" and while avoiding "problematic politicization."[52] For the panel the nucleus of the dissolution task lay in ensuring international competitiveness.

(2) Proposals for Three-way Division

Based on this sort of interpretation, the panel began work to prepare concrete proposals. At the end of June 1950, nearly two years after its inception and a year and a half after it began its activities, the panel put together its report and submitted it to its directly supervisory agency, BIFCO. In its report the panel presented the following principles relevant to the dissolution:

1) The fruits of the rationalization already achieved through consolidations of the firms which had been affiliated with the former IG Farben should be preserved, inasmuch as it is possible.
2) In deciding the scale of each firm, consideration should be given not only to domestic and international competitiveness but also to ensuring research and development, which are indispensable in the chemical industry.
3) Assets of the former IG Farben must not be sold off under disadvantageous conditions.
4) As long as it is deemed economically necessary, jointly controlled firms and joint sales organizations should be maintained even into the future.

From this perspective, the panel proposed the establishment of the following mutually independent firms:

1) Ludwigshafen
2) Niederrhein (including Leverkusen, Ürdingen, Elberfeld, and, if possible, Dormagen)
3) Maingau (Hoechst, Griesheim, Naphthol Chemicals, Bobingen, Cassella, and Knapsack)

What was proposed here was division into the three large firms (BASF, Bayer, and Hoechst) that had been integrated into IG Farben in 1925. The report also recommended an existence independent of that of the big three firms for thirteen smaller firms, including Hüls, Kalle, Wacker Chemicals, and Homburg Chemicals, which had been affiliated with IG Farben. The report also said that these firms should not be sold off because the recovery of capital markets had not made progress. Of the other 162 various remaining assets, the report recommended disposing of 156 of them through either sale or liquidation.

In addition, the panel said that dissolution must be achieved on the basis of the law-governed country. More specifically, the panel asserted that the consent of the yet-to-be-established Federal Government and of the stockholders of former IG Farben would be necessary, and that procedures that accorded with German law were indispensable. In order to guarantee the dissolution's legality in this sense, the report proposed the appointment of a liquidator in accordance with German law as well as the protection of former IG Farben stockholder profits through the exchange of former IG Farben shares for shares in its successor companies.[53]

The panel's proposal meant, in short, the division of IG Farben into three large firms as well as dissolution subject to consent of the German side and based on German law. It was nothing other than the greatest common factor of profits and claims on the German side. The proposal was thus later often reviewed or cited by various actors on the German side during the subsequent dissolution process. It provided, more or less, the prototype for subsequent German proposals.

4. The Delay in Dissolution and the Reasons for It

As described above, FARDIP, subordinate to the Bipartite Control Office (BICO), submitted its report at the end of June 1950. In it there at long last appeared a concrete proposal for the dissolution of IG Farben as a company. This concrete proposal was a landmark, even though it of course had to wait for the approval procedures on the Allied side, because it was a product of German hands. Still, five years had already elapsed since the promulgation of Allied Control Council Law Number 9 concerning the dissolution of IG Farben. During that period, the four great powers had proceeded to seize and control separately the assets of IG Farben plants without adopting any sort of concrete measures pertaining to IG Farben's dissolution as a firm. It is safe to say that IG Farben's dissolution had been delayed.

What were the causes for this delay? While it is possible to cite German resistance or the technical difficulties in drawing up a dissolution plan, the main cause of the delay was, more than anything else, the rivalry over policy within the Western Allied camp. Differences over policy between the U.S. and Britain were especially important. Until 1947 former IG Farben assets had been controlled separately in the British and U.S. occupation zones, and the differences in control policy, corresponding to differences in occupation policy, were clear. After the integration of both zones in 1947, the disparities in IG Farben dissolution policy itself went unresolved.

According to Douglas Fowles, the British military government official in charge of the IG Farben dissolution, responsibility for the delay lay exclusively with the U.S. military government. In his view, from 1945 through 1946, the policy of the U.S. authorities was in complete agreement not with that of Britain but rather with that of the Soviet Union. The U.S. military government also adopted an extremely strict policy in its planning for the subdivision of the Hoechst plant, for example. Once 1948 began, however, the Americans reversed themselves completely and adopted a policy of delegating everything to the Germans. According to Fowles, the British opposed each of these U.S. policy extremes and ultimately succeeded in getting the Americans to withdraw these policies, although the process only ended after much time and effort had been wasted.[54] Although this ultimately may be merely the opinion of an official in the British military government, Anglo-American conflict may be seen as an important cause of the delay in IG Farben's dissolution.

The existence of differing and opposing currents within the U.S. military government may also be cited as a cause for delay. The rivalry between believers in the Morgenthau plan for reducing a vanquished Germany to the status of an agrarian state and the forces opposing it were a part of that dynamic. If it is the case that the U.S. military's policy lacked consistency, then that lack is probably tied to the orientations of these internal conflicts as well.[55]

SECTION 3: THE ALLIES' NEW POLICIES

1. Changes in the Political Environment

As described above, the dissolution process for IG Farben looked as though it had entered a new stage at the end of June 1950 with the submission of the FARDIP report. Despite the fact that the panel was a German organization and was, moreover, merely advisory, its report had constituted the first concrete proposal concerning IG Farben's dissolution. Expectations, or perhaps hopes, were high on the German side that the report would be studied and approved and then be implemented by Allied organizations. These hopes and expectations were, however, neatly negated by the presentation of new Allied policies in August 1950.

Before examining the meaning and significance of the new Allied policies, this section will first give an overview of the changes in the political environment that surrounded IG Farben's dissolution and that occurred between FARDIP's establishment and the issuance of its report in June 1950.

First, there were changes in the circumstances of the occupation. The launching of the Federal Republic of Germany (West Germany) in September 1949 meant the end of direct occupation by the military governments of the Allied powers in the Western zone of occupation. On 10 April 1949 the Western Allies promulgated the Occupation Statute (Besatzungs-Status), which led to the establishment of the Federal Republic of Germany in September of the same year. But the sovereignty of the new state was to be limited, and the country's occupied status was to continue. The change went no further than a transition from direct to indirect rule.

On the basis of the Occupation Statute, the Allied High Commission (Alliierte Hohe Kommission) was established in Bonn as the agency of the occupation. It was the successor, in the Western zone, to the Allied Control Council, in which the Soviet Union had also participated. It realized the transition from direct to indirect government and from occupation by military governments to occupation by a civilian agency. The United States, Britain, and France each appointed one High Commissioner for Germany, and they formed the Allied High Commission, as shown in Figure 8.2. The Chairmanship of the Commission's top body, the Council, was filled by rotation.[56] Based on a recommendation from Assistant Secretary of State William Draper, the United States named John J. McCloy, former Assistant Secretary of Defense and former World Bank President, to serve as its High Commissioner.[57]

Figure 8.2 Basic Structure of the Allied High Commission (1949–1952)

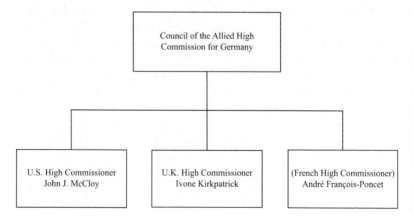

Despite these changes in the nature of the occupation, the right to make decisions on IG Farben's dissolution remained in the hands of the Allied powers. Paragraph 23 of the Occupation Statute clearly stipulated that authority pertaining to decartelization was reserved to the Allied powers. The objects of decartelization in this case included not just cartels but business concerns in general; IG Farben was of course an object of the statute. Not only that, but the authority to control former IG Farben plants remained in the grip of the Allied side.[58] There was fundamentally no real change, at least with respect to IG Farben's dissolution, and this fact symbolized that West Germany was nothing other than an "occupied ally."[59]

Nevertheless, in the Western zone at least, dissolution and control authority moved from the hands of the Allied Control Council to those of the High Commission. The handling of laws concerning IG Farben's dissolution that had been promulgated by the council thus became problematic once again. This led the Allies to present a new policy.

The second change in the political environment was the end of the system of divided occupation. The integration of the American-British zone and the French zone had been tied up and prolonged by the Saar problem and the Ruhr international control problem but was finally achieved in April 1949. There were accompanying changes in the agency charged with handling the Allied dissolution of IG Farben. In August 1949, BIFCO was reorganized and the Tripartite IG Farben Control Office (TRIFCO) was established. Approximately in tandem with this, the United States, Britain, and France began work on publishing an official list of IG Farben assets. Work on control and dissolution that had been carried out zone by zone up until this point at long last started moving in the direction of integration. The three countries thus began preparing a new draft law to implement Allied Control Council Law 9, but the new law was still conceived as a Control Council law.[60]

Here the narrative will jump ahead just a bit concerning the development of occupation zones, policies, and the consequent integration of IG Farben dissolution policy. TRIFCO's name was changed to the Tripartite IG Farben Control Group (TRIFCOG) after the announcement of the new Allied policy (which will be discussed below). TRIFCOG, like TRIFCO, was made a sub-organization of the High Commission's Decartelization Bureau. TRIFCOG established its office in Frankfurt am Main and became the organization directly in charge of the dissolution of IG Farben in the Western zone of occupation and subsequently in all of West Germany once the Federal Republic was established. Within the French zone, though, there remained a dual system of authority like the one that had existed before, in which there was joint Allied control and control by the French alone. Because the chief person responsible for control of IG Farben and the members of the control office or control group were different, the authority of the latter was limited.[61]

These changes in the system of divided occupation put limits on the significance of the FARDIP proposals discussed in Section 2.3(2). Because integration of the three zones was achieved after the panel had submitted its report, the need arose to study once again the issues taken up by the panel and its report, which had been limited solely to the U.S. and British zones. Inside the Allied countries critical opinions about the report and about the panel itself remained, and the need arose to address these as well.

Third were changes in the international political environment, or more precisely the outbreak of the Korean War and the consequent exacerbation of East-West conflict. FARDIP submitted its report on 29 June 1950, and the Korean War erupted directly before that, on 25 June. With the outbreak of the war Europe also became more tense politically and militarily. The United States keenly felt the need to strengthen the European system of collective defense and started to see the incorporation of West Germany into the Western alliance relationship and the remilitarization of West Germany as issues of the utmost urgency. British Prime Minister Winston Churchill proposed the establishment of a "European Army" including West Germany. Faced with these developments, West German Chancellor Adenauer decided that a good opportunity had arrived for the ending of the occupation and the complete recovery of sovereignty. Adenauer, with a "Memorandum on National Security" in hand, proposed the creation of a "Federal Police Corps" as a self-defense force and made it clear that West Germany would be prepared for participation in the "European Army" for which Churchill had called. It goes without saying that this move on the part of the West German government brought forth not only domestic and international praise but harsh criticism as well.[62]

It is easy to interpret that these changes in the international political environment had the effect of accelerating the IG Farben dissolution and made the dissolution a gentle process. It is rare, though, for history to move in such a linear fashion. In actuality the IG Farben dissolution process was about to negotiate another bend.

2. High Commission Law Number 35

As noted previously, after the U.S., British, and French occupation zones had been integrated, the three countries began working to publicize an official list of IG Farben assets and prepare a new draft law to implement Allied Control Council Law Number 9. The newly established Allied High Commission continued these tasks. With the aforementioned changes in the political environment directly or indirectly impinging upon the IG Farben dissolution, and especially in light of the outbreak of the Korean War, the Allied High Commission hurried the work along. Behind this haste was the desire of the Allied powers, particularly the United States, to hurry the incorporation of West Germany into the Western alliance. So even while differences remained in U.S., British, and French policies, the three powers anew issued a basic policy concerning the dissolution of IG Farben, Allied High Commission Law Number 35 on the "Dispersion of Assets of I.G. Farbenindustrie AG." The law was prepared with a date of 17 August 1950, signed by U.S. High Commissioner McCloy on behalf of the High Commission Council, and published in the official registers of the Western Allies on 28 August. The law took effect on 1 September 1950.[63]

According to its provisions, Allied High Commission Law Number 35 was supposed to supplement Allied Control Council Law Number 9 promulgated in November 1945. It was, in other words, intended to enable the Western Allied powers to achieve the goal of dissolving IG Farben that was indicated in Allied Control Council Law Number 9. Law Number 35 again confirmed that all authorities pertinent to IG Farben's dissolution were in the Allies' hands, and it stipulated in detail the assets that were to be subject to dissolution or liquidation as well as the technical procedures for dissolution and liquidation. The Allies concluded FARDIP's mandate and ordered the panel dissolved by the end of 1950. In its place the Allies set up the IG Farben Liquidation Committee (I.G. Farben-Liquidationsausschuß), to be composed of three German members.[64]

The law's basic policy on dissolution, though, was just the stipulation that IG Farben be divided into "a fixed number of economically viable independent firms (Gesellschaften)" (Article 1, Paragraph 4). Basic issues, such as specifically what sort of firms IG Farben should be divided into, were left undecided. It was not that the Allies had failed to undertake any concrete studies; there had already been a Bipartite Control Office directive on the issue (Section 2.3(1)). But the Allies had not finished putting together a policy internally, and did not have a plan specific enough to counter the FARDIP proposal. Law Number 35 had the character of a reconfirmation of Allied opinions and desires concerning the dissolution of IG Farben. In that sense High Commission Law Number 35 may be seen as corresponding to High Commission Law Number 27, which ordered the dissolution of firms in the iron and steel industry and which was issued on 16 May 1950.[65]

If one observes it in the light of actual political processes, Law Number 35 was a negative answer to the IG Farben dispersion panel's proposal, which had incorporated German preferences. The FARDIP proposal was laid to rest, and the basic policy for the dissolution had come under renewed study. In a sense, the clock was moved back in time to the point at which Allied Control Council Law Number 9 was promulgated in November 1945.

As may be seen below, the reaction in West Germany was, with the exception of some labor unions, obviously extremely strong.

One of the factors that amplified the German reaction was a change in U.S. personnel. On 30 June 1950 (the same time that FARDIP was submitting its proposals), Randolph H. Newman was appointed as the U.S. Control Officer for I.G. Farbenindustrie AG. As Figure 8.3 shows, Control Officer was the post with the greatest responsibility within the U.S. organization directly in charge of the dissolution. Newman was a Jewish German who had been born in Berlin and had fled to the United States in 1939. He acquired U.S. citizenship in 1945, and from 1946 through 1948 served as a prosecutor at the Nuremberg Military Tribunal that had been conducted by the U.S. military government and that had tried IG Farben officials.[66] In response the German side voiced its opposition out of a concern that a strict dissolution policy would be formulated. The High Commission was also besieged by a letter-writing effort that seemed to have been part of the anti-Newman campaign. One of the letters was from Arnold Burghartz, a member of FARDIP. The letter said that, in light of the anti-Semitism of German industrialists, the appointment of a Jewish refugee would lead to difficulties for the IG Farben dissolution plan.[67] There were those within the High Commission, too, who had doubts about Newman, but High Commissioner McCloy went ahead with the appointment under the justification of the "democratic principles which govern the relationship between a United States citizen and the United States Government."[68]

Figure 8.3 Organization of the U.S. IG Farben Control Office (1948)

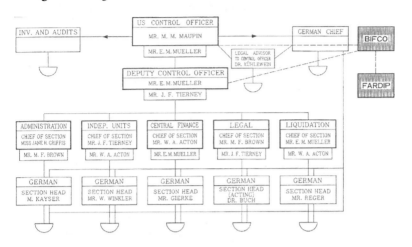

Sources: Box 327, File 11 11–15, Decartelization and Deconcentration, OMGUS. National Archives, Washington, D. C.

3. Resistance from the German Side

(1) Managers

The fate of IG Farben's managers changed greatly with Germany's defeat in 1945. Because of the divided occupation on the part of the four Allied powers, IG Farben had ceased to exist as an actual, unified enterprise, and the company had become the target for dissolution even in the Western zones. The board of auditors and board of directors had ceased to exist. Even at the level of each individual factory, some managers had been subject to accusations or purges as war criminals, and management suffered a decline. Thus, as discussed earlier, the ultimate management authority within each plant was in the grip of the Allied powers, not only under direct occupation but even under the indirect occupation that occurred after the establishment of the Federal Republic in 1949.

Even under these conditions, though, the managers at the former IG Farben plants, and especially at the big three plants, were directly in charge of management as custodian or under some other title. The top managers of the big three plants were as follows. It goes without saying that each one was a salaried manager:

Former BASF Ludwigshafen plant: Carl Wurster became district chief.
In the pre-war period he had already served as an IG Farben director and
as chief of the Ludwigshafen district, and as a result was indicted at the
Nuremberg Military Tribunal. He was found innocent, though, and later
was returned to his post as district chief.

Former Bayer Leverkusen plant: Ulrich Haberland was custodian not
only of the Leverkusen plant but of the neighboring Ürdingen, Dormagen,
and Elberfeld plants as well. He had already served during the war as the
chief of the Leverkusen plant.

Former Hoechst plant: Michael Erlenbach was named custodian by the
U.S. military government. He had entered IG Farben in 1928 and had
consistently worked as a chemist in the pesticide division. Unlike the two
managers above, Erlenbach had not risen to the position of factory chief
before the war.[69]

In early September 1950, immediately after the announcement of
High Commission Law Number 35, the managers or custodians of
the big three former IG Farben plants (Ludwigshafen, Leverkusen, and
Hoechst) paid a visit to the Economic Ministry, which had jurisdiction
over them, and held talks with the official directly in charge of their
sector, Felix-Alexander Prentzel, the chief of the chemicals, lumber, and
paper section of the commerce and industry bureau.[70] According to
Prentzel, they "judged the situation coolly and objectively," and determined that "even if the Allies were to try to solve the complicated problem of dissolving IG Farben on their own, on the basis of Law Number
35, they would certainly be doomed to fail immediately." Even while
they reacted harshly to Law Number 35, they at the same time coolly
determined that the Federal Government alone should be the party to
negotiate with the Allies and that IG Farben personnel, including legal
and technical specialists, should not be out in front.[71]

The managers at the big three plants subsequently repeated their
contacts with the Economic Ministry and conferred on a response.
They did not, however, appear out in front in public opinion work
or in negotiations with the High Commission. After High Commission Law Number 35 was announced, the Chemical Industry Association (Arbeitsgemeinschaft Chemische Industrie des vereinigten
Wirtschaftsgebietes) as a business group initially represented managers.
This business group rallied chemical firms in the U.S. and British zones
and was established in 1946. It later became the Chemical Industry
Federation (Verband der Chemischen Industrie). At the end of September, its chairman, Alexander Menne, demanded that the High

Commission revise Law Number 35 in accordance with the "norms of the rule of law." He also demanded that the Federal Government demonstrate leadership on the German side and that the interests of stockholders, employees, pensioners, and others be respected.[72] These assertions were in line with FARDIP's proposals. Menne was, however, optimistic about the prospects for agreement with the Allied powers over a basic dissolution policy. He did not acknowledge clearly the importance of German government participation. These differed from the understanding of German managers.

(2) Stockholders

The Association of the Private Securities Ownership Protection (Arbeits-gemeinschaft der Schutzvereinigungen für den privaten Wertpapierbe-sitz) represented the interests of former IG Farben stockholders. Its history is not clear, but it was formed in or around 1948 to advocate respect for private property and stockholder rights *vis-à-vis* not only IG Farben but all firms. According to its chairman, Carl C. Schmid, the association held the proxies of 80,000 IG Farben stockholders, whose stock had a face value that totaled 500 million Reichsmark.[73] The association forged a consensus among major domestic stockholders, obtained the support of foreign stockholders and creditors, and broadly represented the interests of stockholders. It also maintained contact with managers and tried to represent their claims as well.[74]

Immediately after the announcement of Law Number 35, Chairman Schmid criticized the inaction of the Federal Government and demanded that it immediately enter into negotiations with the Allied powers. He then asserted that the FARDIP report ought to form the basis for the negotiations.[75] Subsequently, he frequently repeated that same argument. Schmid stated that negotiations with the High Commission should be a roundtable discussion in which not just the Federal Government but the spectrum of interested parties on the German side would participate.[76] This was an argument for broad German participation, not for delegat-ing the negotiations to the Federal Government. On this point the atti-tude of the stockholders differed from that of the managers.

(3) Labor Unions and Works Councils

The response of labor unions to Law Number 35 was at once both despondent and resistant. According to newspaper accounts, the position of the unions was that, first, they opposed in principle any form of dissolution, including division into three big firms, in terms of protecting employment. That notwithstanding, they felt that in light of current circumstances the division into three large firms was unavoidable. Second, however, the unions opposed division into more than three firms from the standpoints of international competitiveness, profitability, and research and development. The unions then criticized as unclear the concept of "excessive concentration of economic power" in Law Number 35 (Article 1, Paragraph 2). Third, they cited the political dangers caused by excessive concentration. As a measure to resist those dangers, they argued for labor's participation in firm management, i.e. co-determination.[77]

The main labor union in the chemical industry was the Chemical, Paper, and Ceramic Labor Union (Industriegewerkschaft Chemie, Papier, Keramik, or IG Chemie), the so-called Chemical Workers Union.[78] The vice chairman of that organization, Eberhard Esser, stated, "We are shocked and angry at Law Number 35. The spirit of Potsdam and of Morgenthau live on even now in this law... Our union says that the dissolution of IG Farben should be carried out at the hands of a German trust corporation (Treuhandgesellschaft), so that we may stop the meaningless destruction of business units that are economically viable."[79] The Chemical Workers Union again repeated these same claims in its 1949–50 annual report in the following terms. The union gave four "principal reasons why Germany objects." First, the dissolution was being pursued despite the lack of responsible cooperation on the German side. Second, the meaning of "economically viable firm" had not been made at all clear. Third, the treatment of demands by employees, pensioners, and stockholders had been left to the discretion of the Allied powers. Finally, the successor firms were to remain under the control of the Allied powers.[80]

Along with its umbrella group, the German Confederation of Labor (Deutscher Gewerkschaftsbund or DGB), the Chemical Workers Union put together its proposals into a document which they then publicized and sent on to the High Commission and to the Federal Government. The main points of these letters were, first, that the liquidation and the reorganization of IG Farben should be kept clearly segregated. The connotation here was that liquidation was tied up with problems of property rights and socialization and was thus expected to take a long time, so that by splitting liquidation off, reorganization ought to move forward. Second, a trust association (Treuhandverband) should be established, on the model of the steel industry (Allied Control Council Law Number 75), as the organization in charge of the dissolution. This organization was to be composed of Germans and was to be the sole official German agency in charge of the dissolution. It goes without saying that the union organizations argued for the participation of union representatives. Third, they demanded the participation of labor on both the boards of audit and boards of directors of the new, post-dissolution companies, i.e. co-determination.[81] The German Office Employees Union (Deutsche Angestellten-Gewerkschaft or DAG) also expressed regret at the one-sided measures proposed by the allies and stated that it did not recognize any basis for Allied claims that there was a risk of monopolistic abuse of IG Farben assets.[82]

Former IG Farben's works council (Betriebsrat), which had been reconstituted after the war, argued for the particpation of the works council and labor unions in the dissolution and liquidation processes, for the creation of competitive factories of optimal scale on the basis of cooperation of the works council and labor unions, and for guarantees of labor rights and social rights for employees.[83]

Thus, in terms of arguments for German participation in the dissolution process, the labor unions and works council put themselves in the same position as the organizations representing managers and stockholders. Because they had also made demands for their own participation, for co-determination, and even for socialization, though, they incurred the corresponding amount of opposition among managers and stockholders.[84]

(4) Government

Once the system of direct occupation by military governments had ended and both the High Commission and the Federal Republic had been established, the German Federal Government became the party with whom the Allies, or rather the High Commission, directly negotiated concerning the IG Farben dissolution issue. The agency directly in charge was the Economic Ministry. Ludwig Erhard, who had been chief of the Economic Council prior to the Federal Republic's establishment, was named Economic Minister. Chancellor Adenauer himself often intervened directly on the issue. Figure 8.4 shows conceptually the Allied and German parties to the negotiations.

Figure 8.4 Structure of IG Farben Dissolution Negotiations (1950–1952)

Germany		Allies
Federal Government		Allied High Commission
Chancellor/Secretariat	← dissolution negotiation →	High Commissioner
Economic Minister/Ministry		Economic Committees
IG Farben Liqui-dation Committee	← delegation of liquidation authority advice concerning liquidation →	TRIFCO
IG Farben Liquidators		

Sources: Der Volkswirt, Beilage: Chemische Industrie, 3 April 1954.

The content of High Commission Law Number 35 was conveyed in advance of its publication to Adenauer and the Federal Government.[85] On 30 August, immediately after the law was announced, Economic Minister Erhard conferred with High Commission officials and touched upon several issues, including the Anti-Cartel Law, along with the problem of IG Farben's dissolution. While he wanted assurances from the Allies that they had no intention of enacting anti-cartel legislation, since the German side was making progress on the legislative work (in actuality, the legislation met with resistance in business circles and was delayed, and the Competition Restriction Prevention Law was not enacted until 1957), on the question of Law Number 35, Erhard

> ... expressed on behalf of the Chancellor his extremely great reservations concerning IG Farben, and referred to the increase in negative public opinion. He stated quite strongly his opinion that the law had been prepared in the spirit of 1945, not 1950, and that various German influences had been totally excluded. Erhard stated that Germans did not have the right to advise in an extremely too important area not to advise, and that the law ran contrary to German notions concerning the law and legal foundations. He said that Germans had no influence whatsoever over the scale or make-up of the new business units, their use, the value of or restrictions on former property rights, and the legal basis for the new corporations. He clearly hinted that the High Commission had betrayed them, in that there had been no advice from Germans prior to the law's promulga-

tion pursuant to Bipartite Control Office's opinion concerning FARDIP.
According to Erhard, both he and the Chancellor believed that it be
immediately necessary to revise the law. He asked for the establishment
of a joint Allied-German working group and for either the addition of
Germans when the law is implemented or the "dredging" of parts of the
current law.[86]

In response the High Commission stated that it "remained in command" of the issue. Erhard reported the results of his conference at
a cabinet meeting the following day, 31 August 1950.[87] According to
newspaper reports, he said that Law Number 35 most definitely "was
not born from the spirit of reconciliation of 1950," and he "characterized it as an expression of a policy of revenge that was totally incomprehensible at this point in time."[88] The issue was once again taken
up at a cabinet meeting on 27 September. The words "IG Farben dissolution. Encroachment on our competitiveness" may be found in a
memo about that cabinet meeting.[89] This was probably the most suc-
cinct expression of the fact that the problem really lay in ensuring the
international competitiveness of the German chemical industry.

According to a memo by Prentzel, the section chief in the Economic
Ministry directly in charge of the issue, the decision of the Federal
Government for the purpose of achieving the dissolution of IG Farben
while ensuring international competitiveness was that "Law Number 35
indicated the extremely serious political and economic problems." The
"political problems" here meant none other than the need for Federal
Government intervention. Prentzel also said that the Chancellor himself
ought to intervene. The memo stated that the issue was one of the most
serious for the Federal Government. The "economic problems" were the
scale and implementation of the dissolution, and this fell within the
purview of the Economic Minister. The memo then reflected on the
experience of FARDIP, "which, although it was composed of top-flight
people, was unable to produce any results, aside from the preparation of
a voluminous amount of documents," and noted the risk of "delegating
the handling of economic problems to a committee of experts in the
absence of clear direction from the Federal Economic Ministry." The
memo recognized a necessity for strong intervention by the Economic
Ministry. It indicated that there existed a "sense of mistrust" toward
Germany among the Allies, and said that Germany should counter
that with sincerity and should constantly bear in mind respect for legal
procedures. "Only through consistent leadership and unified policy

decisions on the part of the Economic Ministry will it be possible to achieve the goal of an ideal reorganization of all of IG Farben." This was the verdict of the Federal Government on Law Number 35.[90]

The Federal Government decided that the IG Farben dissolution was a highly political issue that required the intervention of the Federal Government and even intervention at the level of the Chancellor. This German government decision was based on the repeated arguments by German managers, stockholders, and labor unions asking for German participation and leadership. But the industrial associations (the Chemical Industry Association), the stockholders (as represented by the Association of Securities Ownership Protection), and the labor unions each strongly asserted its own claim to intervention. They remained unclear on the point that negotiations with the High Commission ought to be the responsibility of the Federal Government. Their perception of the issue therefore did not necessarily agree with the Federal Government's judgment. Managers, conversely, pushed themselves into the background and chose to leave the matter of negotiations with the High Commission to the government; this judgment alone most conformed to that of the Federal Government.

4. Resistance Solidifies

High Commission Law Number 35 was exposed to the almost unified criticism of German actors from the moment it was made public. The newspapers reacted very sensitively to the issue, and all the dailies reported on Law Number 35 in the issues of 29 August. Most articles were filled with a tone of disappointment, indignation, and denial.[91] Among them the *Frankfurter Allgemeine Zeitung* made a sweeping criticism under the headline "The IG Farben Law of the 1945 Spirit." Its core argument ran as follows. "The entire law overflows with the spirit of 1945. If this were 1945, there would probably be no one who was surprised at this law. But today, five and a half years from the end of the fighting, such a law is suspect... All legitimate hopes, such as the hope that Control Council Law Number 9, which placed IG Farben under special control, would be scrapped; that the reorganization of this central part of our country's chemical industry would finally be entrusted to German hands; that the dissolution would be proceeded according to the German stock law; that the rights of shareholders, creditors, bondholders, and pensioners would once again be completely fulfilled; and that IG Farben stock, once a blue chip stock on the German exchange, could once again be traded, have all been turned into disappointments."[92] Specific criticisms, including criticism of the unclear notion of competitiveness, followed. It is safe to say that the article put forth all of the issues surrounding Law Number 35. Articles that assembled the issues so comprehensively and so soon after the announcement of the law were nowhere else to be seen. The *Frankfurter Allgemeine* article thus made a major contribution to the formation and crystallization of public opinion against Law Number 35.[93]

The papers then opened up a campaign, the spearhead of which was aimed at Randolph Newman, as shown in 2 of this section, who had been appointed at the end of June as TRIFCOG's U.S. Control Officer for I.G. Farbenindustrie AG. The campaign had the appearance of personal attack that was tinged with anti-Semitic feelings, criticism of a defector, and enmity toward the Morgenthau Plan.[94] The papers then became full of articles telling of resistance on the part of managers, stockholders, labor unions, and the Federal Government. Two weeks after the announcement of the law, the journalistic leader of the criticism campaign, the *Frankfurter Allgemeine Zeitung*, could triumphantly write the following. "The High Commission's new IG Farben legislation has found unified rejection throughout German society such as has never been faced before by any Allied measure. This rejection started with governmental and parliamentary representatives and has extended to labor unions, shareholders and pensioners who would be directly affected by this law, employees of IG Farben factories, workers, and even to public opinion at large."[95]

One of the reasons that this "unified rejection" came into being was procedural problems with the dissolution. The German side was in agreement on its claim for participation, criticizing the fact that the law disallowed any decision-making participation by the German side. Another reason was a judgment on the results of a dissolution. The law trumpeted the birth of "a certain number of economically viable independent firms" as a result of the dissolution, but the lack of clarity in this provision met with unified resistance on the part of the Germans, who argued for ensuring competitiveness. It may be said that the "unified rejection" was based completely on these two points. In other words, High Commission Law Number 35 invited unified German resistance and increased the pressure which could be exerted by the German side in negotiations. In this sense it seems that the law, quite counterintuitively, acted as a catalyst to accelerate the IG Farben dissolution process, which had up to this point been retarded.[96]

Even though the Germans had shown "unified resistance" on the issues of the necessity for German participation and the maintenance of competitiveness, there existed, as shown previously, two different currents related to the form of German participation. In one were the Chemical Industry Association as the business group and the Association of Securities Ownership Protection (representing the interests of shareholders), who continued arguing for their respective interests through means such as the distribution of literature, press conferences, and demonstrations, while at the same time attempting to serve, to some extent, as the advocates for the opinions of managers. It is probably safe to add labor unions and works councils to this current in terms of their powerful announcement of their own interests and their demands for their own participation in the dissolution process. In the other current were the managers directly concerned with the management of former IG Farben plants, who avoided publicizing their own opinions and who took the route of conveying those opinions to the government through close contact with the federal authorities, especially the Economic Ministry. They left the resolution of the issue to active government intervention, including direct participation by the Chancellor.[97]

The German government itself realized the need for strong intervention in the form of "clear leadership by the Federal Economic Ministry." That is to say, the Federal Government aligned its understanding with that of managers regarding policy for negotiations with the High Commission. Given the backing of broad public opinion in Germany and the unified understanding it had with managers, the Federal Government entered formal negotiations with the High Commission. The Economic Ministry and its leader, Erhard, were in charge of the negotiations, and Chancellor Adenauer often participated directly. As this transition occurred, the activities of the Chemical Industry Association, the Association of Securities Ownership Protection, and the unions lost their bloom, and their role diminished.

SECTION 4: NEGOTIATIONS BETWEEN THE GERMAN GOVERNMENT AND THE ALLIED POWERS

1. The German Government Proposal

High Commission Law Number 35, announced on 28 August 1950, suffered from problems involving the selection of supervising personnel and elicited stiff resistance from the German side. Under these conditions, tension-filled negotiations began between the Allied countries and the German government. The German side already had in hand a concrete proposal in the form of the FARDIP draft. Thus it was not the Allies but rather the Germans, or the German government, who had the initiative in the negotiation process.

As noted earlier (Section 3.3(4)), a conference took place between the High Commission and Economic Minister Erhard on 30 August, just after Law Number 35 was announced. The High Commission reviewed the results of the conference the following day. Following the German position, the British argued that a joint working group ought to be established. The French expressed their concern over the tone of Erhard's criticism. The Americans worked out a compromise between the British and the French and proposed studying whether or not to establish a joint working group. Britain and France accepted the American proposal.[98]

Meanwhile the German government also made motions on the basis of the 30 August conference. The High Commission had requested that the attendee, Erhard, submit a written opinion regarding Law Number 35.[99] The Economic Ministry then took up the task of preparing the documents. While Erhard met with Chancellor Adenauer, he was plotting the timing for the submission of the document. "The Chancellor held off (the submission of the document – A. K.) in light of the foreign ministerial talks in New York."[100] The American-British-French foreign ministerial conference referred to here was held in New York in mid-September. The conference took up Churchill's proposal and decided to establish a "European Army" and to include West Germany in it. The conference also recognized the Federal Republic government as the sole legitimate government of Germany and decided to effect an early end to the (indirect) occupation.[101] Although the establishment of a European army would take many twists and turns as the European Defense Community, the actions of the conference would at any rate be explained by the High Commission at its periodic conference with the German government on 23 September. In a letter handed over at that meeting, the High Commission, referring to Law Number 35, stated its policy of swiftly completing the dissolution of IG Farben.[102]

The definitive decision by the High Commission to bring the occupation to an early close accorded with the expectations of the German government, which wanted to establish its own position. The German government had also hoped to strengthen its own position with regard to the IG Farben dissolution issue and to obtain an early settlement on terms favorable to the German side. The High Commission's letter was thus very encouraging. The German government at that point decided to submit the documents requested at the 30 August meeting to the High Commission.[103]

There were two documents. One set forth the basic position of the German government, and the other incorporated specific proposals for the dissolution. The former took the shape of a letter dated 2 October from Adenauer to the High Commission. As noted earlier (Section 3.3(4)), it took the form of a letter under Adenauer's name because the German government had made it a policy to involve the Chancellor in this issue. The letter detailed criticisms of High Commission Law Number 35. Adenauer first expressed regret that the Federal Government had not received advance communication concerning the law's promulgation. Next, the letter stated that the German government agreed concerning the need for IG Farben's dissolution and reorganization and expressed praise for the law's objective of creating economically viable units "having domestic and international competitiveness." It probably bears repeating that the stipulation "having domestic and international competitiveness" was the German government's interpretation of the text of Law Number 35. Adenauer went on to note that the fact that the law gave no consideration whatsoever to working together with the German government was an extremely serious issue, in light of the great significance this issue held for the German economy as a whole. In this way the letter asserted the German government's right to joint decision-making. More than anything else, assertion of this right was the necessary basis for deciding the "extent of an economically meaningful dissolution." The specific proposals in the letter included starting the work of jointly investigating existing dissolution proposals, appointing committees of experts on both sides, and assisting in the law's implementation with a German government implementation order.[104] It is almost certain that Adenauer had in mind the FARDIP proposals as the "existing proposals" in the letter. Overall, Adenauer's letter re-stated the basic position of the German government.

The other document, dated 18 October, incorporated concrete proposals regarding the dissolution. In the aftermath of the reconfirmation of Germany's basic position expressed in the Adenauer letter, the second document made the following specific proposals concerning the "extent of an economically meaningful dissolution" that had been stressed anew in the letter:

1) Make the Ludwigshafen and Oppau plants into an indepedent
    BASF firm; the Leverkusen, Dormagen, Ürdingen, Wupper-
    tal-Elberfeld plants into an independent Bayer firm; and the
    Hoechst, Griesheim, Mainkur, Cassella, and Offenbach plants
    into an independent Hoechst firm.

2) Give the following 8 companies independent status: Hüls
    Chemicals, Nobel Dynamite, Kalle, Wacker Chemicals, Wolf
    Chemicals, Homburg Chemicals, Viktoria Mining, Wacht-
    berg Lignite Mining.

3) Study the prospect of establishing 15 plants, including Agfa
    Camera (Munich), as independent enterprises.

4) Leave pending the decision on whether or not to give 8 cases,
    including Knapsack, Rottweil, and Rheinfelden, independent
    status.[105]

The new proposal took as its framework the division of IG Farben into
three big firms, and in that regard it clearly continued in the vein of the
proposals in the FARDIP report. But it may also be seen as proposing
an even finer subdivision. In addition to the three large firms, the FAR-
DIP report proposed the independence of 13 firms. The new proposal,
though, was to make 8 firms independent, study independence for a
further 15 companies, and leave 8 cases undecided.

Erhard handed over the two documents to the High Commission
on 19 October. At that day's conference there was some discussion
concerning Adenauer's letter, and the High Commission promised
to study the specific proposals in the second document. In reference
to the Adenauer letter's expression of regret that Law Number 35 had
been promulgated without prior notification of the German government, Gordon Macready, British Economic Advisor at the High Commission, promised to carry out advance discussions in the future even
while emphasizing the supremacy of the High Commission over the
German government. At this point Macready made it a condition that
the German government represent all interested parties on the German
side and that it alone be party to the negotiations with the High Commission.[106] The German government was satisfied with this response.
That it had been named the sole party to the negotiations should itself
have been welcome, and the German government could expect to
be able to use this response as a lever to settle the disagreements that
still remained among the various German actors. This fundamental
High Commission position was reconfirmed in a letter from British

High Commissioner Ivone Kirkpatrick to Adenauer dated 26 October. The letter said that the High Commission would in the future contact the German government in advance and give its opinion a hearing regarding important measures concerning the IG Farben dissolution.[107] As promised, the High Commission began studying the German government proposals. During this process the Commission publicized the Kirkpatrick letter along with two letters to Adenauer about decartelization and enterprise dissolution.[108] These were calculated to soothe an indignant German public and were intended to yield acceptance for Commission plans. After 10 November, German government proposals were also reported in the newspapers.[109] Meanwhile, on the German government side, Erhard prepared a report about the 19 October conference for Adenauer at the end of that month.[110]

2. Allied Proposals

The High Commission had already begun work to draft a new bill during late 1949 and early 1950. The Allied powers were short on concrete ideas for the dissolution and were compelled to give the lead on that point to the German government. Policy conflicts among the U.S., Britain, and France, however, remained unresolved. This conflict came at the tail end of conflicts and differences among military governments during the period of divided occupation. Even so, by April 1950 the conflicts within TRIFCO and other organizations had been resolved through compromise by their superiors at the Economic Advisor level, and the work to create a concrete draft continued.[111] Ultimately, though, time ran out before a specific draft could be put together, and the drafters were met with the August 1950 promulgation of High Commission Law Number 35.

Even when the law had been promulgated, there were conflicts over such things as the selection of the U.S. personnel in charge of the dissolution at the High Commission. Puzzlement spread in response to the harsh, nearly unanimous resistance on the German side to Law Number 35, and it affected internal conflicts as well. The internal conflicts continued as before at the TRIFCO (later TRIFCOG) level. U.S. Control Officer Newman and British Control Officer Fowles, in particular, were at loggerheads on every issue concerning the position of TRIFCO within the High Commission. The French Control Officer, J. de Fouchier, would sometimes join with the Americans and sometimes with the British, according to the issue.[112]

Anglo-American conflict even arose on the interpretation of High Commission Law Number 35. Newman held that dissolution should be pursued under TRIFCO's authority, regardless. Fowles, in contrast, believed that a certain level of German participation ought to be permitted. On this issue, de Fouchier took Newman's side. The conflict took on a structure pitting Britain against the U.S. and France. The parties to the conflict conceived of it as "a matter of principle."[113] The conflict between Newman and Fowles grew and developed into a personal quarrel.[114]

Even so, the Allies' specific dissolution proposal was nearly complete by September. The proposal was known within the High Commission as the experts' draft and was prepared by three specialists, Erwin H. Amick (U.S.), George Brearley (Britain), and Leon Denivelle (France). The proposal was generally known as the "ABD draft" after the specialists' initials.[115]

The draft's main point was the division of IG Farben into the following nine companies:

1) Ludwigshafen-Oppau
2) Leverkusen, Ürdingen, Elberfeld
3) Leverkusen film plant, Agfa Camera
4) Dormagen, Rottweil, Bobingen
5) Titanium Industries
6) Hoechst, Griesheim, Offenbach, Behring Chemicals, Knapsack
7) Cassella
8) Hüls Chemicals
9) Rheinfelden.[116]

While this was formally a nine-part proposal, it was essentially a three-part proposal that divided IG Farben into three companies: BASF, Bayer, and Hoechst. The proposal from the U.S. military government for the thoroughgoing dissolution of Hoechst had burned out, and the proposal only said that Cassella should be split off from Hoechst as an independent firm.

There were problems, though, with the handling of the Bayer factory complex. First, the proposal called for the Leverkusen film plant to be split off and made independent. The Dormagen, Rottweil, and Bobingen plants were also to be split off and set up as a single independent firm. Titanium Industries (in the Leverkusen region) was also to receive this treatment. In short, Bayer was to be split into four. This was harsh treatment for Bayer. British Control Officer Fowles, in fact, issued an objection to it. He especially opposed the handling of the Leverkusen film plant. The expert dispatched from Britain, Brearley, gave his assent to the treatment, though.[117] The U.S.-French proposal ultimately came to envelop and penetrate the British specialist. American predominance over Britain within the High Commission could be glimpsed in the outcome of this case.

Notwithstanding its formal nine-part division of IG Farben, the ABD draft was basically in agreement with the German position put forth in the FARDIP proposal, in terms of the main provision dividing IG Farben into three large firms. On this point it is safe to say that the ABD draft constitutes the greatest event in the political process of IG Farben's dissolution. Hermann Bücher, former FARDIP chair, praised the draft's basic acceptance of IG Farben's division into three large firms as "essential progress."[118] It had taken more than five years from war's end to reach this point.

The ABD draft was taken to mean a *de facto* three-way division on the High Commission side as well. Because the Commission had seen broad consensus on this point on the German side, it took an optimistic view of future negotiations in the belief that the draft would be accepted by the German side with little difficulty. A letter sent at about this time from the High Commission to the Federal Government read as follows: "The High Commission notes with satisfaction that there has been broad agreement on the matter of establishing three main firms, according to asset value, at the Leverkusen, Maingau (indicating Hoechst – A. K.), and Ludwigshafen factories."[119] But this understanding was overly optimistic. Negotiations between the High Commission and the German government would still continue.

The High Commission decided to transmit the documents containing this proposal to the Federal Government with a date of 23 November, but they were handed over to Erhard the preceding day. Upon going through them Erhard was shocked at the formal nine-part division. But since it was essentially a three-way division, his criticism on this point was not as strong as it had been. The parts other than the three-way division were what Erhard viewed more seriously. Of the nine companies in the proposal, only two (leaving aside the three big factory complexes) were companies whose independence had been envisioned in the Federal Government draft. Those two companies were supposed to have been Agfa Camera (Munich) and Hüls Chemicals.

Erhard found problematic the independence of the other companies – the Leverkusen film plant, Dormagen, Rottweil, Bobingen, Titanium Industries, Cassella, and Rheinfelden. He had particularly strong reservations about the separation and independence of the Leverkusen film factory, Titanium Industries, and Cassella.[120]

In a document addressed to Adenauer, Erhard again indicated that the four-way division of the Leverkusen district would be "a loss to the national economy" which "must be fought with all our might." He then added there was trustworthy information that the British Control Officer opposed the High Commission draft, and that the French were also leaning in the direction of supporting Germany's objections. The British Control Officer here is probably Fowles. Erhard was hoping for an intensification of the conflict within the High Commission.[121]

On 18 December the German government sent the High Commission a document detailing its opinion with regard to the High Commission draft.[122] Its content was on the same lines as Erhard's reactions described above. During the process of preparing the document, the government had heard the opinions of interested parties (see subsection 3 below).

At the same time, the German government sent yet another document, incorporating its opinion on liquidation procedures, to the High Commission. This document concerned the establishment of the IG Farben Liquidation Committee. The establishment of liquidation procedures was a longstanding issue, and a proposal concerning the IG Farben liquidation committee and the selection of its three German members was set out in a High Commission letter (separate from the division proposal) dated 23 November.[123]

The High Commission conceived of establishing an expert committee to study, from its perspective, the proposals coming from the German side. The High Commission proposal was thus handed over to Erhard at his meeting with the High Commission on 22 November. At that time the High Commission confirmed that the liquidation committee was to be a purely Allied agency. In terms of the conflict within the High Commission, this was in accord with American and French arguments. Erhard, even while expressing regret over this point, praised the committee for possessing independent responsibility, and agreed with the selection of the three German committee members.[124] A German government document of 18 December confirmed this view. The document went on to add, however, a request that the liquidation committee be granted the status of liquidator under German securities law.[125]

3. German Government as Coordinator

(1) Vis-à-vis Stockholders, State Governments, and Parliament

With the submission of the High Commission's ABD draft, the Allied Powers and Germany were in basic agreement on the division of IG Farben into three big firms. But conflict still remained on the independent firms other than the big three, especially on the group of former Bayer factories at Leverkusen and the former Hoechst factory complex.

The German government, using the High Commission's demand that it be the sole negotiator for the German side as leverage, would resolve the remaining conflicts among German actors and then face the prospect of negotiations with the High Commission.

There was little need for adjustment *vis-à-vis* the Association of Securities Ownership Protection, which had come to the fore as the organization representing the interests of IG Farben stockholders. Its chairman, Carl Schmid, had attended conferences with the High Commission, and had flamboyantly cultivated public opinion. But he had not swerved from the lines of the old FARDIP proposal, and he agreed with the government draft. At the same time, Schmid was affirmative in his assessment that the High Commission counterproposal ought to serve as the foundation for future negotiations. Even while he voiced his opposition to the division of Leverkusen, he did not have the materials for a concrete statement of his own regarding the specific shape of the division. The government thus felt almost no need to make adjustments for Schmid.[126]

The Economic Ministry made contact with and heard the opinions of the state governments concerned, especially the Hesse state government. The state government in Hesse, in which the Hoechst complex was located, originally had the intention of negotiating directly with the High Commission. Even after the German government had issued its draft, Hesse stated this intention to Adenauer. Adenauer responded that he would thoroughly study Hesse's request, but it seems that he would not budge even a little on the unification, within the Federal Government, of Germany's negotiation contact points *vis-à-vis* the High Commission.[127] The Hesse state government argued directly against the High Commission draft in favor of the absorption of Cassella into Hoechst.[128]

The strategy to use with parliament was also a matter for the Economic Ministry. The Economic Ministry's Prenztel called on federal legislators to submit written questions to the government at the stage prior to the government's issuance of its draft. The gist of the written questions was to ask about the policy for realizing German participation and to find out whether or not there had been preparations for submission of a government draft. The purpose of the written questions was to make clear the legislature's support for the position of a Federal Government that was facing negotiations with the High Commission. Initially only the ruling parties, i.e. the Christian Democratic Union (CDU), Christian Social Union (CSU), the Free Democratic Party (FDP), and the German Party (DP), participated in the submission of written questions. Subsequently, the opposition parties, i.e. the Social Democratic Party (SPD), the Bavarian Party (BP), the Centrist Party (Zentrum), and the Economic Reconstruction League (WAV), also took part, and the written questionnaire became a suprapartisan document. The Economic Ministry's legislative strategy had succeeded.[129]

The problems were now the managers, who stated their objections on specific issues against both the government draft and the High Commission draft, and labor unions, which opposed both drafts on principle and advocated co-determination.

(2) Vis-à-vis Managers

As indicated earlier (Section 3.3(1)), managers were essentially in agreement with the Federal Goverment in their judgments on Law Number 35. It goes without saying that they basically gave their consent to the Federal Government proposal and its division of IG Farben into three large firms. On other points, though, they had criticisms. It is not possible to confirm the opinions of BASF and Bayer managers toward the German government plan in the documentary record, but it probably is not an overstatement to say that there were basically no objections. The case that does become clear in the documentary record is that of Hoechst.

The custodian of the Hoechst plants, Michael Erlenbach, sent a letter to the Economic Ministry section chief in charge of the dissolution, Prentzel, and criticized the fact that the opinions of plant managers were not being adequately reflected in the German government's negotiations with the High Commission. Erlenbach specifically criticized the fact that Knapsack had not been integrated with Hoechst but had been left undecided. In response, Prentzel confirmed that the German government should fully convey the understandings of each affected party to the Allied side. Prentzel also replied that the reason Knapsack's fate was left undecided was that there was not enough material to support a judgment, and he stated that there had been no intention of ignoring Hoechst's desires in making decisions.[130]

The handling of Knapsack also became a problem between Hoechst managers and the Chemical Industry Association. Hoechst's Erlenbach reacted strongly to a number of issues, including the involvement of Chemical Industry Association Chairman Menne in the position of representing, on his own authority, the interests of Hoechst; Menne's failure to convey information; and the insertion of Knapsack onto the "undecided" list in the government draft. Erlenbach hinted Hoechst might as a result drop out of the Chemical Industry Association. Furthermore, it came out that Knapsack's placement on the "undecided" list in the government draft had in fact been due to a request by Chairman Menne himself.[131] In interpreting High Commission Law Number 35, Menne had originally interpreted the division into "economically viable, competitive units" as guaranteed, and had determined that there were no fundamental differences between the German and Allied sides. He was certainly more optimistic than the managers and more so even than the German government.[132] Menne had always tended to the optimistic, but here this tendency was laid bare. Erlenbach's anger at Menne likely reached its peak. Menne called on Erlenbach at the Hoechst plant and had to promise to keep in close contact with Erlenbach in the future concerning issues "related to various important circumstances, especially where the Chemical Industry Association is the spokesman."[133] At precisely this time Menne made a turnabout and used the opportunity of a conference with the High Commission's McCloy to propose, "as an absolute demand," that Knapsack be absorbed into Hoechst.[134] The Chemical Industry Association had moved closer to the side of the managers.

The opinion of the managers toward the High Commission counterproposal, i.e., the ABD draft, must now be examined. Managers of the former BASF did not raise any particularly important objections and were satisfied insofar as their own interests were concerned.[135] The former Bayer Leverkusen managers were an extreme contrast to this and reacted vehemently. Ulrich Haberland, the custodian of Leverkusen and the surrounding factories, met with the official in charge at the Economic Ministry and conveyed that, while he could accept the splitting off of Titanium Industries, he was opposed to the separation of the Leverkusen film plant and Dormagen.[136] According to an explanation by Leverkusen management, there was a risk that Leverkusen would lose 30% of its sales, 21% of its equipment, and 5,600 employees if the High Commission proposal were to be implemented.[137]

Hoechst's management was satisfied about the fact that the ABD draft, unlike the German government draft, had designated Knapsack as belonging to Hoechst. It stated its intention to oppose, however, the separation and independence of Cassella and Bobingen.[138]

Even while the Chemical Industry Association's Menne sympathized with these managers' opinions, he evaluated the High Commission draft more affirmatively. For example, even though he opposed the separation of Cassella, he said that it would be regrettable if the negotiations concerning this question were to delay the overall resolution.[139] Former FARDIP Chairman Bücher also had an opinion similar to Menne's, and praised the High Commission draft as "essential progress" in its basic acceptance of IG Farben's division into three large firms.[140]

But around this time Knapsack managers themselves publically expressed concerns about absorption into Hoechst. These concerns were based on the fact that the production relationship between the Knapsack plant and Hoechst was only partial.[141] Also, Knapsack had been incorporated into the British zone of occupation, whereas Hoechst had been located in the American, so that in fact Knapsack's connection to Bayer's Leverkusen plant had deepened. The Knapsack issue took on the character of a conflict between its management and Hoechst's.

Erhard clearly stood on the side of the Hoechst managers on this issue. "If we acknowledge Knapsack's independence, then stopping the division of Leverkusen will almost certainly be endangered, because the Allied side is attaching much importance to the fact that the scale of the three big successor firms is to be about equal."[142] His was a tactical consideration based on the importance the German government persistently placed on the principle of a three-way division.

In January 1951, the federal legislature's economic policy committee held hearings on the IG Farben dissolution issue, and invited representatives from management and the Chemical Workers Union, as well as the responsible officials from the Economic Ministry. The committee invited the executives in charge of Knapsack, in addition to those in charge of the three big plants, to represent management. The bulk of the committee's time was thus taken up with the Knapsack issue. As a result, all of the committee's members (save one whose employment history was said to have included time as a Knapsack employee) indicated their intentions to oppose the separation and independence of Knapsack.[143] The government's policy had been accepted.

(3) Vis-à-vis the Labor Unions

The labor unions were the only actors who did not agree with the government proposal on the basis of principle, in that they demanded co-determination. Persuading them was, accordingly, a problem. The Economic Ministry was at the center of effecting a persuasion strategy. On 10 November Prentzel met with representatives from the German Confederation of Labor, the Chemical Workers Union, and the Office Employees Union, and explained the progress of the negotiations with the Allied powers. At the meeting Prentzel emphasized the High Commission's intention of making the Federal Government the sole negotiating partner and the consequent need for the unions to transmit their opinions through the government to the High Commission. He then asked the unions for their sympathetic cooperation and criticism.[144] On 20 November Erhard conferred with Labor Confederation officials and Chemical Workers Union Chairman Wilhelm Gefeller. The agenda was not limited to the IG Farben dissolution issue and covered many items. On the dissolution itself, both sides reiterated their respective positions, and the meeting concluded.[145]

The Labor Confederation and Chemical Workers Union each expressed its respective rejection, in principle, of the government draft in a letter from Gefeller to Erhard dated 24 November and in a Chemical Workers Union memorandum dated 23 November. They demanded, first, the establishment of a German committee charged with the liquidation and reorganization of all of IG Farben's assets, as well as union participation on such a committee. Second, they demanded employee participation on the boards of directors and boards of auditors of the firms that were to be newly set up after the dissolution. Third, they demanded respect for the parliamentary resolution regarding the issue of property rights in IG Farben assets. The third demand was related to socialization. These demands were simply a restatement of the unions' philosophical positions up to that point.[146]

The labor unions of course strongly opposed the High Commission's counterproposal. Labor Confederation Chairman Hans Böckler sent a letter with this message to the High Commission. He then transmitted this intention to Prentzel at the Economic Ministry as well.[147] The Office Employees Union also followed suit.[148]

Erhard made clear the government's stand of "rejecting" these labor union demands.[149] He then attempted to coordinate relations with the unions under this policy. Tripartite talks among government, labor, and management were held on 20 December. Adenauer and Erhard attended from government side, Chemical Workers Union Chairman Gefeller and an Office Employees Union representative attended from the labor side, and from the employer side, the Chemical Industry Association's Menne attended the meeting. Even the tripartite discussion did not result in any particular changes in the position of the unions.[150]

In a letter to Adenauer at the end of January 1951, Gefeller again reiterated his call for co-determination and requested negotiations to that end. This effort was inspired by a recently realized agreement concerning co-determination in steel firms.[151] Following this letter, many works councils reached similar decisions.[152] Labor unions thus did not change their basic philosophical argument. But since there was no decisive conflict on the dissolution plan itself between the union position and the government proposal, they entrusted the dissolution plan to the government's negotiations with the High Commission. As a consequence, union claims regarding co-determination did not interfere with the government's negotiations with the High Commission.

Led by Economic Minister Erhard as well as Chancellor Adenauer, the Federal Government effected a powerful coordination of German interests. Although the government had not eradicated all of the conflicts of opinion on the German side, it had removed the impediments to the progress of negotiations with the High Commission. To that extent the government's coordination strategy was a success.

4. The Allied Powers' Second Proposal

With the fruits of the above coordination efforts in hand, the German government faced another round of negotiations with the High Commission. Basic agreement had already been achieved between the High Commission and the German government on the division of IG Farben into three large firms. The most important remaining issues were Knapsack, the handling of Cassella, and especially the four-way division of Leverkusen.

Replacing Adenauer and Erhard as the German government representatives in the final negotiations were lower-level players, Prentzel, the Economic Ministry section chief in charge of the dissolution, and von Rospatt. Menne of the Chemical Industry Association, the Deutsche

Bank's Abs, and former FARDIP Chairman Bücher participated as government advisors. From the High Commission came Newman (U.S.), Fowles (Britain), and de Fouchier (France) of TRIFCOG. A total of four meetings were held for the renegotiations over the course of two weeks starting 11 January 1951. During the process the Germans handed over a memorandum.[153] At the meetings the German side spoke exclusively, while the High Commission side sat and listened.

The issues taken up at the meetings were the four-way division of Leverkusen, the separation and independence of Cassella from Hoechst, and the incorporation of Knapsack into Hoechst, all of which had been broached in the High Commission proposal.

Representatives from the German side, the Economic Ministry's Prentzel and the Chemical Industry Association's Menne, one after the other stressed the appropriateness of incorporating Cassella into Hoechst.[154] But a representative of Cassella, who attended the final meeting at the request of the High Commission, emphasized that Cassella's independence was possible.[155]

Prentzel agreed to Knapsack's incorporation into Hoechst as laid out in the High Commission proposal. He then made a specific proposal, at the fourth meeting, to merge the former IG Farben oxygen plant into Knapsack and then make the resulting company a wholly-owned subsidiary of Hoechst. This proposal meant that the German government was making a compromise with the Knapsack managers' claims to independence, based on the High Commission proposal that incorporated Knapsack into Hoechst.[156] Hoechst's Erlenbach, who attended the meeting at the request of the High Commission, expressed his belief that the representatives of both Knapsack and the oxygen plant would agree to this proposal.[157]

The pattern whereby the German side presented its opinion and the High Commission listened continued for both the Leverkusen and Knapsack issues. The High Commission side hardly spoke, and so there was little concrete progress at this venue.[158]

On the basis of the January negotiations, the High Commission started preparing a revised draft. The Commission notified the Federal Government about the revision on 17 April. Like the previous draft, its main point was, formally, a division of IG Farben into nine companies, as follows:

1) Ludwigshafen-Oppau
2) Leverkusen, Ürdingen, Elberfeld

3) Agfa Camera
4) Dormagen
5) Titanium Industries
6) Hoechst, Griesheim, Offenbach, Behring Chemicals, Knap-
    sack
7) Cassera
8) Hüls Chemicals
9) Rheinfelden

Despite the revision's outward appearance, its content had changed. With respect to Bayer, the Leverkusen film plant was no longer to be split off. Although there had been no change to the plan to separate Agfa Camera and make it independent, it was made into an entity whose "continuing control by Bayer" through stock ownership "had been accepted." The prospect of not separating Rottweil and Bobingen would now be studied.[159] The policy of not splitting off Knapsack was affirmed. It is safe to say that on these points, the revision largely reflected the opinions of the German side in the January negotiations.

The German government expressed its "satisfaction" with the second proposal in the name of Chancellor Adenauer.[160] This indicated the general opinion of actors on the German side. The newspaper Die Welt reported the High Commission's revised draft under the headline "A Generally Satisfactory Resolution." Gefeller of the Chemical Workers Union appraised the revised proposal as "an essentially appropriate resolution."[161] The government, however, pointed out that separating Dormagen and making it independent from Leverkusen was the sole remaining issue. It emphasized that separation and independence were impossible, both technically and economically. The High Commission, in the name of High Commissioner McCloy, presently responded to the German suggestion in the negative. The German government again sent a letter repeating its assertion. The resolution to the problem was not to come until January 1952, when the High Commission accepted the German government's argument and consented to the incorporation of Dormagen into Leverkusen.[162]

IG Farben was thus finally broken up into the following eight companies:

1) Ludwigshafen-Oppau
2) Leverkusen, Ürdingen, Elberfeld, Dormagen
3) Agfa Camera

4)   Titanium Industries
5)   Hoechst, Griesheim, Offenbach, Behring Chemicals, Knapsack
6)   Cassera
7)   Hüls Chemicals
8)   Rheinfelden

The managers' insistence on a three-way division had essentially been realized.

SECTION 5: IMPLEMENTING THE DISSOLUTION

Once the revised High Commission proposal had been made in April 1951, the Commission and the Federal Government studied plans for establishing provisional successor companies with capital funds of 100,000 Deutsche mark each.[163] Because negotiations dragged on, though, the plan did not move into implementation until more than half a year had elapsed, in December 1951 and January 1952. First, Hoechst (Farbwerke Hoechst vormals Meister Lucius & Brüning AG) was established, after a name change, on 7 December 1951. Bayer (Farbenfabriken Bayer AG) followed on 19 December, and BASF (Badische Anilin- und Soda-Fabrik AG) was established on 30 January 1952. Each firm's capitalization was only DM100,000, as in the plan. The founding incorporators were selected based on the consensus of the High Commission and the German government.[164] The High Commission also intervened in the appointment of members to the boards of auditors and boards of directors.

All of those inaugurated as chairmen of the boards of directors had held the top leadership positions at the various plants through the post-war period; at BASF, this was district chief Carl Wurster, and at Bayer it was the custodian, Ulrich Haberland. Initially the office of chairman of the board of directors had not been established at Hoechst, and a then official at Knapsack Nitrogen Fertilizer (AG für Stickstoffdünger, Knapsack), Karl Winnacker, rather than the custodian Michael Erlenbach, was named the *de facto* top manager. Erlenbach took a position as a director. This personnel decision was quite proper, though, because even though Winnacker had been purged from the Hoechst plant after the war by the U.S. military government, he was a powerful figure who had already distinguished himself during the IG Farben era.[165]

The first step in IG Farben's dissolution was the establishment of provisional companies, where the German side had many expectations of the process. The provisional companies had been established in accord with German law, and the German side expected to increase its own influence during the subsequent dissolution process.[166] The position and power of managers was acknowledged publicly, in a sense, through the establishment of the provisional companies. Thus, even in a public venue, the firms no longer needed the advocacy of the Chemical Industry Association or the Association of Securities Ownership Protection. At the same time that the provisional companies were established, the three German members of the IG Farben liquidation committee were appointed as liquidators under the German stock law. The German request had been implemented (see Section 4.2). From this point forward all measures were based on both High Commission and German statute.[167]

The next step was the formal establishment of successor companies. By an implementing order pursuant to Law Number 35, the High Commission gave advance notice in May 1952 of the establishment of a total of twelve successor firms (including the three big successors) and the enterprises under their respective ownership.[168] In June the High Commission permitted the trading of IG Farben stock, subject to the requirement that buyers and sellers be registered.[169]

But then the formal establishment of successor firms was delayed. One of the reasons for this was the time required for the technical work for the dissolution. It was essential to work to prepare starting balance sheets for each of the successor firms that listed obligations, taxes, pensions, and the division of assets, including intangible assets. Another factor giving rise to the delay, once the dissolution entered its final stages, was efforts by the managers of the three big firms to assemble under their ownership the enterprises slated to be split off and made independent. BASF was attempting to acquire Viktoria Mining, Bayer was attempting to get Agfa Camera, and Hoechst was trying to acquire Kalle and Wacker Chemical. The German government incorporated such requests into a government proposal which it submitted to the High Commission. The High Commission rejected the proposal in December 1952, but Adenauer and Erhard would not relent, and the High Commission ultimately sanctioned the acquisition of one company for each of the three big firms. Only Hoechst gave up in its acquisition of Kalle. Otherwise, the big three firms managed to gather Viktoria Mining, Agfa, and Wacker under their respective umbrellas.[170]

In December 1952 the three big firms and Cassella were made the new successor companies to IG Farben, and their capitalizations were determined. That determination was made by means of a conference of the three big firms' chairmen, liquidators, as well as the board of auditors for I.G. Farbenindustrie AG in Liquidation, which had inherited the assets of the former IG Farben (see Figure 8.4, preceding). On one hand, these conferees had to consider compensation for former stockholders and the productive capacity of the newly established firms, and they had to agree on a total capitalization for the three big firms, plus Cassella, of over DM1 billion. On the other hand, each firm needed to avoid the risks of overcapitalization, and each fought desperately to start off with as small a capitalization as possible.[171]

In March 1953, the final series of procedures was completed, and the successor companies concluded asset transfer agreements with I.G. Farbenindustrie AG in Liquidation. The provisional companies thereby shed Allied control, and asset transfer, including capital participation share, moved into implementation. On 23 March the High Commission announced the completion of IG Farben's dissolution.[172] With this the successor companies were formally established. Bayer was established on 24 March with a capitalization of DM387.7 million and real assets of DM380 million. Hoechst followed on 27 March with a capitalization of DM285.7 million and real assets of DM203 million, and BASF was established on 28 March with a capitalization of DM340.1 million and real assets of DM317 million. Cassella, another successor company, had already been established on 19 December 1952 with a capitalization of DM34.1 million and real assets of DM 20 milllion. There had been no changes in top management since the provisional companies had been set up, and Hoechst even formally seated Winnacker as chairman of the board of directors.[173]

The exchange of former IG Farben stock for stock in successor companies began on 1 October 1953. Former IG Farben stock with a face value of 1,000 Reichsmark was made equivalent to stock worth DM285 in Bayer, DM250 in BASF, DM210 in Hoechst, and DM25 in Cassella, for a subtotal of DM770. To this was added Hüls stock worth about DM60 and Rheinstahl AG stock worth about DM50, for a grand total of approximately DM880. The exchange ratio was thus about 10 to 9.[174] Stock in the successor companies was unofficially priced on the bourse starting 2 October and officially priced starting 22 December. The market prices followed a rising trajectory and reached a level 35% higher than the stocks' initial prices by March 1954.[175]

High Commission Law Number 84, the so-called "Liquidation Ending Law" (Liquidations-Schlußgesetz) dated 21 January 1955, took effect on 6 February, and abolished all Allied authority concerning the IG Farben dissolution.[176] In the meantime, an actual peace treaty, the German Treaty, was signed on 26 May 1952. Because France never acceded to this treaty, the Treaty of Paris was signed on 23 October 1954, bringing to a formal close the occupation of Germany by the United States, Britain, and France. Occupation Statutes lost their effect, and the High Commission was abolished. On 5 May 1955 the Treaty of Paris came into effect and Germany finally recovered its sovereignty. On 27 May I.G. Farbenindustrie AG in Liquidation held its first general stockholder's meeting.[177] Ten years had passed since the end of the war.

SECTION 6: CONCLUSION

This paper has traced the Allied occupation and divided control of IG Farben factories, the development of enterprise dissolution policy, and the response of German actors, especially former IG Farben company managers, to that policy. This section will summarize the paper while supplementing the foregoing with some observations.

The political process of IG Farben's dissolution began with Germany's unconditional surrender in May 1945 and ended with the establishment of IG Farben's successor companies in March 1953. That eight year process may be divided into the following three periods:

1) May 1945 through to the Allied announcement of a new policy in August 1950
2) August 1950 through to the fixing of the dissolution framework in May 1951
3) May 1951 through to March 1953.

This paper's analysis has focused on the second period, from August 1950 to May 1951, which was period of only 10 months. It was precisely during that period that the interplay of the various actors involved in IG Farben's dissolution was most concentrated, that the independent response of former IG Farben management may be followed most clearly, and that the outlines of the dissolution were determined.

The result was the division of IG Farben into three large firms: BASF, Bayer, and Hoechst. Then what were the factors that resulted in IG Farben's dissolution into three big firms?

First of all, the dissolution was delayed, and with that delay the importance of the *de facto* three-way division of IG Farben increased. During the delay of the dissolution, which had started in May 1945, the three large plants that had been incorporated separately into three zones of occupation gradually began to follow independent fates. As a result of its seizure, its designation for dissolution, the dissolution of its board of directors and board of auditors, as well as the purge and war-crimes indictments of its officials, IG Farben lost its unity as an enterprise. The managers at each of its plants, conversely, saw their power increase as they grasped the right to manage (given the dispersed nature of the joint stock ownership structure) while they continued to garner support from the Association of the Private Securities Ownership Protection, a stockholders' group, and the Chemical Industry Association, a trade group. The result was that the revival of the three major plants led to the *de facto* three-way division of IG Farben.

Then why was the dissolution delayed? Some German actors were of the opinion that Allied tactics were the factor that brought on the delay. One newspaper criticized United States Control Officer Newman and called him "the father of stall tactics."[178] But, first of all, by the time Newman entered the scene as Control Officer in 1950, the dissolution had already been quite delayed, and so it is clear that this fact does not amount to an explanation. The causes for the dissolution's delay have to be found in the political environment, especially that existing through 1950, which had been characterized by various conflicts accompanying the Allies' joint occupation, a lag in integrating the occupation zones and policies, and a consequent delay in ending the occupation.

The second factor that resulted in the dissolution of IG Farben into three large firms was the strategy of the German government and the managers at the three big ex-IG Farben factories. When High Commission Law Number 35 was promulgated in August 1950, the actors on the German side unanimously reacted against it. The German Federal Government and the managers of the three big plants set a goal of a three-way division, and adopted a policy of waiting for a favorable turn of events in the international environment and then getting resolution through Federal Government negotiations with the High Commission. While it kept close ties with the managers, the government faced negotiations backed by the cooperation of the industry association, stockholders group, and labor unions. As a result, it reached a basic agreement with the High Commission concerning a three-way division. In a speech on the occasion of the formal establishment of Hoechst, its first Chairman of the Board of Directors, Karl Winnacker, thanked the Federal Government for its "speedy intervention," thanked Chancellor Adenauer for his "decisive, instantaneous, and personal intervention," and particularly emphasized his appreciation for the "extremely effective support during the never-ending negotiations" on the part of Economic Minister Erhard and those involved from his ministry.[179]

In this emphasis, this paper's view agrees with that of Kreikamp, who emphasized the "influence of the German industrialists concerned who acted in unison with the Federal Government to oppose the Western Allied plan." This paper, though, has attempted to trace this phenomenon through the entire dissolution process. Unlike Kreikamp, it therefore places most of its emphasis on the process during the half year from the promulgation of Allied High Commission Law Number 35 through December 1950.[180]

To the extent that it was delayed and that it basically realized the division proposal of its managers, the dissolution of IG Farben took on more of the color of an application of general decartelization policy rather than the dissolution of a corporate war criminal.[181]

On 28 March 1953, the day of BASF's formal establishment, a BASF manager let slip the following emotion: "When we look back upon the long, difficult months and years of the IG Farben dissolution from the standpoint of today, it is good to recognize that, while the delay was often uncomfortable for the Germans involved, it was not at all disadvantageous. The reasons for this were that, during the delay process, changes in the world's political situation gradually exerted an influence even on the IG Farben dissolution. As a result, instead of the initial Allied plan whose goal was pure destruction, there gradually emerged a solution which agreed, to at least a certain extent, with German wishes and demands."[182]

The dissolution that assaulted IG Farben after the war was certainly a harsh fate. Its boards of auditors and directors were forcibly dissolved, and each of its constituent plants had to continue operating independently. The delay in the dissolution also had a profound effect on the activities of the factories under the former IG Farben umbrella. Each factory had to find its own way independently, but many of the conditions necessary to do so were lacking. None of the factories enjoyed legal independence. In other words, they were not enterprises under the law. Each plant thus suffered from a variety of disadvantages. Because the trading of former IG Farben stock had been prohibited, for example, the road was closed to raising funds in capital markets.

In rebuilding an export network too, the lack of legal independence was a handicap, and it did not help with the rebuilding of domestic sales organizations either. In addition, various restrictions were placed on research and development activities, which indeed determine life or death for a chemical company. The factories suffered other disadvantages as well, including the lack of legal standing to sue and the burden of Allied management costs.[183] The hardships of IG Farben stockholders, creditors, and pensioners were also magnified by the delay. The occupation authorities had not only prohibited trading in former IG Farben stock but also repayment of IG Farben debt incurred during or before July 1945. The freezing of major assets in the corporate pension coffers also continued.[184]

The delay in the dissolution was also, conversely, a blessing for the factories affiliated with the former IG Farben, for their managers and employees, and thus for the stockholders, creditors, and formers employees as well. In those five years, the factories were restarted, their management was rehabilitated, and the German polity and economy were reborn. Germany's negotiating strength during the political process of the IG Farben dissolution was thus enhanced. The delay provided some spare time in which the *de facto* three-way division in the Western zone of occupation could become an established reality.

In later years Hoechst Chairman Winnacker aptly reminisced, "By the time the diagnosis had finally been handed down and we had prepared a proposal (indicates the FARDIP proposal – A. K.) to respond to it, two years had of course passed. But this was an advantage for Germany. In that time West Germany had become much more solid both economically and politically, and the IG Farben dissolution had taken on much greater importance in German eyes. If the Allies had previously seen agreement of opinion among their own independent views on a final decision, then there would have been an extremely strong possibility that the dissolution's provisions would have been stupid."[185] Winnacker recalled an image of management (Winnacker included) and the German state forming a harmonious whole. It is therefore safe to say that he admitted quite honestly that the delay of the dissolution was a stroke of good fortune for IG Farben's management, employees, stockholders, creditors, and pensioners.

Source: Institute of Social Science, University of Tokyo, Discussion Paper Series, F-92, 2002, pp. 1–43.

9

Second Trial for Catching up: The Introduction of German Technology and the Emergence of the Petrochemical Industry in Post-war Japan

THIS PAPER DEALS with the catching up process of the Japanese chemical industry with those of the Western nations, especially with German and West German industry, in the time period 1925–1960, focusing on the post-war years 1955–1960, the early and decisive years of the Japanese petrochemical industry from the business history view point.[1]

I. TRIALS FOR CATCHING UP

1. The first trial for catching up: 1925–1945

The modern coal chemical industry began to emerge in Japan at the latest around the turn of the century, when a variety of private companies including coal mining firms, gas companies, and electricity companies entered into this new field. It then found its decisive step in the unique conditions during the First World War, when the import of main chemical products from abroad became almost impossible, the export opportunities for the infant Japanese industry were opened abruptly, and the Japanese government took the initiative to foster the catching up process by enforcing laws for promoting the development of the domestic industry and by establishing a national owned and subsidized company, which became later privatized. This was the beginning of the first trial of the Japanese chemical industry toward the catching up to Western advanced industries, especially to German industry.

After the end of the war, those Japanese enterprises, private or state-subsidized, having faced the recurred competitive conditions in the world market, made every effort, including new product development through imitating Western products, to maintain their footholds on the Japanese market. The government also tried to protect the Japanese market for domestic producers by its tariff policy as well as direct import restriction and restriction against inward direct investment, although those policies were not comprehensive, but selective, and were enforced with time difference according to the sectors.

The German chemical firms, led by IG Farben, which was established in 1925, responded to the emerging Japanese competitors by bilateral market agreements with them on the base of international cartels by sectors, where IG Farben took the lead and the core member, and by rejecting in earlier years the repeated proposals from Japanese firms for technology transfer agreements.[2]

Toward the end of the 1930s, the Japanese companies succeeded in raising their scale of production as well as in widening their scope in product lines, and thus succeeded not only in maintaining their own footholds on the domestic markets, but also in moving into the Asian market, which previously the member countries and companies forming international cartels dominated. Realizing the success of the Japanese competitors and the vanishing hope of dominating the Japanese market as well as other Asian markets, and also facing the patents conflict with the Japanese, IG Farben with other cartel members decided to tighten its market agreements with the Japanese, and also to sell its technologies to them such as the Haber-Bosch process for synthesizing ammonium and the IG Farben process for hydrogenating coal. The Japanese chemical industry at last succeeded in introducing German advanced technologies.[3]

However, the success of the Japanese companies had its narrow limitation, especially in technological terms. The technological gap between Japan and Western nations, especially Germany, was enormous at the beginning of the European War and then the Pacific War. Moreover, the discontinuation of introducing advanced Western, especially, German, technologies hindered the Japanese technological development profoundly during the Second World War. The Japanese failed to develop new products and processes for herself, or failed to move from imitation to innovation.

The technological gap between the Japanese and German chemical industries at the end of the wars can be clearly concluded by perusing the chemical industry sections of the United States Strategic Bombing Survey reports on Japan and Germany. The survey was carried out directly after the end of the war in both nations at the almost same timing, with the same purpose to measure the effects of strategic bombing, and by mostly overlapping investigating members.[4] In brief, especially concerning synthetic oil industry, the Americans still admired the German technologies, while they simply looked down upon the Japanese ones. Compared with Germany, in 1945, Japan's chemical manufacturing technology was strikingly inferior.

This was a comparison conducted on the coal chemistry. Petrochemicals did not yet exist in pre-war Japan. At that time, the only country in which petrochemicals had developed was the United States. It is undeniable that it appeared as a new post-war industry also in Germany; in Germany, however, in a background of autarkic policies, the development of technologies such as synthetic fibers and synthetic resin, which were directly related to petrochemical manufacturing, was phenomenal. Among all the technologies developed in the 1950s, similar ones – though not entirely perfected – were found in pre-war Japan, including high-pressure polyethylene (of Japan Nitrogen Fertilizers), ethylene oxide, and ethylene glycol (of Japan Catalytic Chemical Industry and Japan Soda). For these companies, the development efforts were discontinuous and peripheral, and synthetic rubber, ethylene, and others were never industrialized. Vinyl chloride, being developed domestically, was able to make progress only after the war.[5]

The technological gap between Japan and Western nations was enormous at the end of the war. In this attempt, the first trial of the Japanese chemical industry to catch up with Western front-runners, especially Germans, by introducing German technologies, half-failed at the end.

2. Preparing for a second trial: 1945–1955

In the years 1945–55, the Japanese chemical industry struggled in disastrous conditions such as shortage of materials, chaos in traffic, lack of money, lack of appropriate demand for survival and rebirth. There was no technological development, nor technology introduction, although Japanese engineers and chemists were eager to absorb foreign technologies. Main tools for absorption were literature and product analysis. Among literatures, the so-called PB Reports, German chemical companies' technical documents, which were seized by the Allied powers and disclosed in Japan by the occupation authorities, were the most important. As late as in the beginning of the 1950s, the Japanese chemical industry began to enjoy expansion, enjoying also the improvement of external conditions such as materials, traffic, and markets, for which the change of the occupation policies of the Allied Nations, i.e. the United States, was also influencial. The expansion was, however, only quantitative and they saw no signs for qualitative development.[6]

After a post-war period of disarray the chemical industry began planning for conversion from coal chemicals to petrochemicals. One of the preconditions of this change was the lifting of bans against oil refineries' activities on the Pacific Sea coast previously made by the occupying power. Though some were partially realized, the early plans were piecemeal. The only concept with some degree of comprehensiveness in the earlier years after the war was that of Nippon Soda; however, this project never reached fruition. The government itself also formulated measures to promote the petrochemical industry, but also these never amounted to more than partial remedies.

3. The second trial for catching up: Early phase: 1955–1960

In July 1955, the Japanese petrochemical industry at last made its epochal start: MITI (Ministry of International Trade and Industry) launched its industrial policy toward the chemical industry. The policy triggered the shift of the raw materials of Japanese chemical industry from coal to petroleum, and, moreover, its shift from coal chemistry to petroleum chemistry in technological terms. At the same time, this shift meant the second trial of the Japanese chemical industry to catch up with the Western front-runners, after the first failed one in the pre-war years.

To put it more concretely, a MITI departmental council created what is known as the Policy for Promoting the Petrochemical Industry. The purpose was commercialization of the petrochemical industry in order:

(1) to sustain the rapid and promising development of synthetic fiber and synthetic resin industries, which lacked adequate

supplies of such primary resources as benzole, coal acid, acetone, etc.;

(2) to produce petrochemical products domestically, such as eth-ylene products, for which Japan was entirely dependent upon foreign imports; and

(3) to increase the international competitiveness of Japan's chemi-cal and related industries, as well as the sophistication of the industrial structure.

The government tried to achieve these objectives by approving only those petrochemical projects of private firms that it recognized as being appropriate and important. Its criteria were determined by technological as well as accounting standards. Plans that obtained approval became promoted projects. Concrete measures for promo-tion included:

(1) the appropriation of funds for capital equipment from the Japan Development Bank;

(2) approval of special redemption funds;

(3) approval for introducing necessary foreign technology;

(4) application of provisions for exemption from corporate taxa-tion; and

(5) securing foreign currency allotments as well as exemption from import taxation for necessary imported equipment.[7]

Being based on this promotion policy, quite a few projects were approved by the government one after another. In September 1955, the Mitsubishi-Monsanto and Asahi-Dow projects were approved. Both projects concerned importing styrene monomer and manufacturing polystyrene. In October 1956, the projects of three petroleum com-panies and three chemical companies were approved; Maruzen Petro-leum, Japan Petrochemicals, Mitsubishi Petroleum, Sumitomo Chemi-cal Industries, Mitsui Petrochemical, and Mitsubishi Petrochemical. Moreover, in February 1957, the project of Showa Electric Industry, that of Furukawa Electric Industry, and the polyethylene project of Mitsubishi Petrochemical were also approved. Japan Petrochemicals undertook its ethylene-butadiene project in May of the same year. These projects made up what was later known as the "commercializa-tion of the petrochemical industry – the first period plan," as shown in Table 9.1.

Table 9.1 The First Period Plan of Petrochemical Industry Commercialization

District	Company	Products	Facility Scale (tons per year)	Operation Start
Kawasaki District	Asahi Dow	styrene monomer	18,000	Oct 59
		polystyrene	10,200	Feb 57
	Showa Petrochemical	polyethylene	10,000	Dec 59
	Japan Petrochemical	ethylene	25,000	Jul 59
		isopropyl alcohol	4,000	Aug 57
		acetone	4,500	Aug 57
		isopropyl ether	500	May 58
		butadiene	6,000	Jul 59
	Furukawa Chemical Industry	polyethylene	9,000	Jun 60
	Mitsubishi Petroleum	benzene	4,440	Feb 58
		toluene	9,360	Feb 58
		xylene	7,800	Feb 58
	Japan Catalytic Chemical	ethylene oxide	1,800	Jun 59
		ethylene glycol	3,840	Jun 59
	Japan Zeon	SBR	2,400	Aug 59
		NBR	2,400	Aug 59
		high styrene rubber	3,600	Aug 59

District	Company	Products	Facility Scale (tons per year)	Operation Start
Shikoku District (Niihama)	Sumitomo Chemical Industry	ethylene	12,000	Mar 58
		polyethylene	11,000	Apr 58
Shikoku District (Matsuyama)	Maruzen Petroleum	benzene	3,000	Jan 59
		toluene	9,600	Jan 59
		xylene	9,600	Jan 59
Kinki District (Shimotsu)	Maruzen Petroleum	secondary butanol	2,400	Apr 57
		methyl ethyl ketone	2,400	Nov 57
Chugoku District (Iwakuni)	Mitsui Petrochemical Industry	benzene	6,960	Feb 58
		toluene	11,640	Feb 58
		xylene	11,640	Feb 58
		aromatic solvent	6,000	Sep 58
		terephtalic acid	14,400	Dec 58
		ethylene	19,800	Feb 58
		ethylene oxide	6,000	Mar 58
		ethylene glycol	9,600	Apr 58
		polyethylene	12,000	Mar 58
		phenol	12,000	Aug 58
		acetone	6,900	Aug 58

District	Company	Products	Facility Scale (tons per year)	Operation Start
Yokkaichi District	Mitsubishi Petrochemical	ethylene	22,000	May 59
		ethylene oxide	2,700	Apr 60
		ethylene glycol	3,000	Apr 60
		styrene monomer	22,000	May 59
		polyethylene	10,000	Jul 59
	Mitsubishi Monsanto Chemical	polystyrene	7,200	Jan 57
	Japan Synthetic Rubber	butadiene	33,500	Apr 60
		SBR	45,000	Apr 60

Among the initial projects mentioned above, four were comprehensive in that they centered on ethylene, offered a possibility of product diversification, and presented a possibility of constituting a petrochemical complex. The four were the project in Iwakuni, in which Mitsui Petrochemical took a central role; Mitsubishi Petrochemical's project in Yokkaichi; Sumitomo Chemical Industries' single project in Niihama; and a Japan Petrochemicals-centered project in Kawasaki. Sumitomo's project, aimed at converting ethylene to polyethylene, initially lacked comprehensiveness. This deficiency was, however, soon remedied thanks to the use of ethylene from the beginning.

The four companies comprised by the complex were the first so-called general petrochemical companies in Japan. These companies established themselves as general petrochemical companies by producing key products: ethylene and polyethylene. Ethylene was the most basic product in the product line of a general petrochemical company. This point is clear in the following statement: "If ethylene plants can obtain governmental permission, then it would mean that the petrochemical industrial complex has, in principle, been recognized."[8]

Polyethylene continued to be the most representative wide-use resin product. Moreover, the introduction of its production technology supplied one of the most important conditions for the founding of a general petrochemical company, as will be described later. For that reason, manufacturing technology for ethylene and polyethylene was of great significance to the establishment of general petrochemical companies.

Table 9.2 summarizes the product lines of the four advanced general petrochemical companies and the origins of their technology introduction. It clearly shows that those who supplied technology to the Japanese companies at that time were not as varied as is generally imaged. We could say that they were approximately equal. For ethylene, all four companies unanimously adopted the S & W process from Stone and Webster Company. This was also the case for acetone, ethylene oxide/ethylene glycol, and the aromatic compounds. Technology did not demonstrate its wide range of choices or "department store" appearance until later. Even then processes for ethylene, such as the Lummus process, were few in number.

Table 9.2 Suppliers of Major Technologies to Four Leading General Petrochemical Companies during the First Period

	Mitsui Petrochemical	Mitsubishi Petrochem	Sumitomo Chemical	Japan Petrochem.
ethylene	S&W	S&W	S&W	S&W
butadiene				Esso Research
polyethylene	Ziegler/Mitsui Chem.	BASF	ICI	
acetone	Distillers/S&W			Distillers/S&W
ethylene oxide/ethylene glycol	SD	SD		
aromatic compounds	UOP/Japan Volat. Oi	UOP/Japan Volat. Oil		
Terephtalic acid/DMT	SD			
styrene monomer		Shell		

On the contrary, for polyethylene production, each of the three companies that produced it from the beginning adopted a truly different process. Polyethylene products directly illustrate the truly great variety of foreign technologies that characterized the later period, as can be seen from Table 9.3.

Table 9.3 Polyethylene Technologies of Each Company

Company	Supplier	Year	Initial Facility Scale (tons per year)	Process
Sumitomo Chemical	ICI	Dec 55	11,000	high pressure
Mitsubishi Petro-chemical	BASF	Mar 57	10,000	high pressure
Mitsui Petrochemical	Ziegler	May 56	12,000	low pressure
Showa Electric Industry	Phillips	Feb 57	10,100	medium pressure
Furukawa Chemical	Standard N.J.	Feb 57	9,000	medium pressure
Mitsui Polychemical	Du Pont	Nov 60	24,500	high pressure
Nitto Unicar	UCC	Dec 60	27,000	high pressure
Asahi Dow	AGFO	Jan 62	25,000	high pressure
Ube Kosan	Rexhall	May 63	20,000	high pressure
Toyo Soda	National Distiller	Nov 66	34,000	high pressure
Mitsui Polychemical	Du Pont	Oct 65	45,000	high pressure
Sumitomo Chiba Chemical	ICI		55,000	high pressure
Japan Petrochemical	Rexhall	Aug 65	30,000	high pressure
Mitsui Petrochemical (Chiba)	Ziegler		24,000	low pressure
Kasei Mizushima	Own technology		20,000	low pressure

Why did these similarities and differences emerge in introduced technologies? In what ways were these related to common characteristics as well as to individual features of the companies? In the following section, these points will be clues to the analysis of those pioneering companies as well as to the way they manufactured according to key technologies. This paper will examine the development of these pioneering general petrochemical companies, especially the decisions concerning their first steps forward.

Keeping these questions in mind, I wish to examine the process by which each firm introduced technology, especially the process through which top managers made their decisions. This entails an analysis of company histories based on internal documents of those companies as well as on first-hand information from interviews with managers involved in the initial introduction of technology at the start of this industry or at the years of "commercialization of the petrochemical industry – the first period plan".

II. CASES: ESTABLISHING GENERAL PETROCHEMICAL COMPANIES AND INTRODUCING WEST GERMAN TECHNOLOGIES

Japanese companies introduced selectively technologies from various nations and companies. American technologies played most significant roles without doubt. West German and other European technologies as well as companies also played a role.

The important roles played by West German technologies are mostly well exemplified in the case of Mitsui Petrochemical of introducing the Ziegler process as well as in the case of Mitsubishi Petrochemical of introducing the BASF process, both of which were processes for producing polyethylene. Polyethylene was one of the most important products derived from ethylene, and the manufacturing process for polyethylene was one of the focal points in introduction. Moreover, the two companies, Mitsui Petrochemical and Mitsubishi Petrochemical, were among the first four major companies and took the most significant role even among the four at the early phase of the emerging petrochemical industry in Japan. Therefore, it is appropriate for us to focus on these two cases for the purpose of dealing with the introduction by Japanese companies of West German technologies.

The following schema is used to analyze the technology introduction process. This is a revised version of Hoshimi Uchida's schema, focusing on the process to concluding contracts.[9]

(a) Origins: How can we characterize the first information channels of Japanese companies? Did they depend upon the movement of people or upon written documents? Did trading companies intervene in any way?

(b) Negotiations: Who were the parties concerned? How might we characterize the concerned foreign companies' strategies and tactics including related restrictions, such as the monopoly of patents? What were the strategies and tactics of Japanese companies including the criteria for deciding what technologies would be introduced? What were the issues involved?

(c) Contracts: What was the role of trading companies at the time of the conclusion of the contracts? On what sections of these contracts should we focus (i.e. production scale, production processes, design, supplies of machinery and equipment, supplies of supplementary material, payment values, whether or not the concerned foreign companies sent employees to Japan, etc.)?

(d) How was the funding for payments allocated?

(e) What, if any, were the technological or managerial difficulties prior to the opening of operations?

(f) Were there any technological or managerial difficulties preceding the start of operations? Was any additional technology introduced? Or, on the contrary, was there a supply of technology from Japan?

1. Mitsui Petrochemical: A bold challenge and the introduction of the Ziegler process

(1) The introduction of Ziegler process

In the early 1950s, there were a few projects to launch a petrochemical industry among the Mitsui business group, the successor of the pre-war Mitsui zaibatsu group. In 1952, Miike Synthetic Industries, a subsidiary of Mitsui Mining, which was the core company of the group, drew up a plan to launch petrochemical industrialization. At the center of the engineers leading this drive was the director of the technology division, Noboru Nakajima. One decisive condition for realizing the plan was the sale by the government of the site of the Imperial Army's Iwakuni fuel depot. Because Miike Synthetic's project was an independent one without any related companies, however, the

Ministry of International Trade and Industry (MITI) took no interest in it. Nonetheless the company's desire to develop as a petrochemical company never waned. In 1954, Nakajima was even sent to the United States to observe the industry there.

Mitsui Chemical, a chemical company affiliated with the Mitsui business group, also increased its enthusiasm for petrochemical production. In 1953, it showed interest in Tokyo Gas's project to separate ethylene from oil gas through mixing it with coal gas. Because Tokyo Gas was a public utilities company, however, this project was neither permitted nor ever realized. From late 1953 to early 1954, the director of technology department, Yasuharu Torii, visited the British chemical giant, ICI, hoping to obtain technology for producing herbicides, and observed its polyethylene manufacturing equipment.[10] In summer 1954, an executive from ICI came to Japan to sell high-pressure polyethylene technology and visited Mitsui Chemical's Omuta factory as well as Sumitomo Chemical's Niihama factory. The technology division director, Torii, wanted to introduce ICI's technology for high-pressure polyethylene.[11]

After the projects of its daughter and sister companies failed, Mitsui Mining itself took the first step for commercializing the petrochemical industry. In November 1954 Takeshi Ishida, then vice-president of Mitsui Mining and president of Mitsui Chemical, left for an inspection of industries in Europe and the United States. The major objective of Ishida's trip was to learn more about the Fischer process of West Germany for higher alcohol. His trip was not limited to inspection of the Fischer process for higher alcohol, however. It also included other interests such as the cumene process for phenol and ICI's polyethylene technology.

Ishida called attention especially to the Fischer process for higher alcohol in the development of coal chemistry. In 1937, before the Second World War, Mitsui Mining had introduced the Fischer process for synthetic oil and tried industrial-scale coal liquefaction. According to Nakajima, the director of the technology division of Miike Synthetic Industries, their pre-war attempts were "similar to today's petrochemical techniques... These included producing isoolefin from gaseous hydrocarbon, thickening olefin and oil to make lubricating oil, resolving paraffin to make alphaolefin that could in turn be made into various derivatives, and producing fatty acid from oxidized hydrocarbon." This pre-war experience was continued by the post-war interest with the Fischer process for higher alcohol.[12]

Ishida called attention to the West German Fischer process in the field of coal chemistry. Nonetheless, in the results, this was a starting point for petrochemicals, as will be shown below.

As stated above, in November 1954, Ishida left for Europe and the United States to investigate the Fischer process for higher alcohol, the cumene process for phenol, ICI's polyethylene technology, and other technology. Both companies of the Mitsui group in which Ishida held top executive rank were to have a stockholders' meeting at the end of the month; Ishida, though, wanted to improve conditions at Mitsui Mining, so he did not wait for this meeting but hastily left on his trip to the West.[13]

One chance event leading to of the opportunities for his inspection was in 1953, the previous year, when the chief secretary of the German Coal Association, Rehring, had come to supervise the rationalization of coal mining in Japan and to visit Omuta in Fukuoka Prefecture, Kyushu, where Mitsui Mining had its main coal mine and Mitsui Chemical's main factories were located. So, Ishida first of all visited West Germany to meet Rehring. His main purpose was to investigate the Fischer process for higher alcohol. As mentioned above, Mitsui Mining had experience with this technology for synthesizing oil and had tried commercialization of it. After the Second World War, Miike Synthetic also continued in the same direction to research higher alcohol. Ishida thought this process to be the most advanced in the field of coal chemistry, and he was convinced that introducing it would contribute to structural improvements in Mitsui Mining and Mitsui Chemical.

Unexpectedly, however, Rehring expressed a negative opinion concerning the future of the Fischer process for higher alcohol and introduced Ishida to Karl Ziegler of the Max Planck Coal Institute. Ziegler had by then developed his own process for manufacturing low-pressure polyethylene. In November 1953, he had applied for a patent, and he had just given a speech at a conference in October 1954. Later, in 1963, Ziegler won the Nobel Prize for this technological achievement.[14]

Thus, Ishida paid a visit to Ziegler. Ishida received an explanation of the Ziegler process technology directly from Ziegler himself and was able to witness a demonstration in the laboratory. He was convinced that this technology had wide applications. He thought that it was held in high esteem for its technological reliability because Hoechst, one of three big successors of IG Farben in West Germany, had adopted it, as had a few American companies. He also observed that, as it was new, all the firms concerned could compete from the same starting point. One announcement by Ziegler also had some effect on Ishida's decision: "I received proposals from the president of Monsanto and then from Mitsubishi of Japan, which are both attempting to establish contracts. Consequently, the preference period for contracts will end on January 7th. If you are late, you cannot participate."[15]

In early January 1955, Nakajima paid Ziegler a visit to have the technology explained to him as well as to observe an experiment with it. He examined it and reported a positive answer to Ishida in London: "We'll go with it."[16]

Nakajima advised Ishida to adopt both the high-pressure technology, presumably of ICI or BASF, and low-pressure technology. Because of limited funds, however, Ishida said their only choice was to adopt just one of the two. Nakajima chose the low-pressure process. His reason was: "The Ziegler polyethylene is better for producing polyethylene with greater molecular weight. Future demand for polyethylene will be mainly for the hard type, and he hoped that if we could develop the Ziegler chemistry we could also produce polyethylene with lower molecular weight."[17] Takeshi Hirayama, a manager, states: "At that time, we thought that using a high atmospheric pressure of 1000 would cost 4 billion yen for the construction of a plant that could turn out 1000 tons a month."[18]

Until then, Walter Reppe, the developer of the Reppe process and at that time an adviser for Mitsui Mining, "had strongly recommended for purchase of the BASF high-pressure process rather than the Ziegler process." Ishida refused this proposal after his decision in London. He also abandoned the idea of purchasing the ICI process that Torii had repeatedly advised through telegrams from Tokyo.[19]

At first glance, the decision made by Ishida, top manager, may look arbitrary and adventurous, adhering to coal chemistry. Ishida's decision, however, was premised upon technical specialist Nakajima's careful on-site assessment, which was based on knowledge accumulated in the introduction of Fischer process technology by Mitsui Mining in the pre-war period. Nakajima's selection itself was a result of steady efforts to collect information through written documents and dispatches of personnel. It was above all examined through internal company screening, comparing it with the ICI process. The other reasons for choosing the low- over the high-pressure process were lower costs and reliability (the Fischer low-pressure process had been used since pre-war days). The meeting with Ziegler came about by chance, but the decision to implement his process was deliberate.

Here, we find two kinds of continuity from the pre-war period. One is expressed in the fact that at the introduction of polyethylene technology Mitsui selected a low-pressure technology, the Ziegler process. Mitsui Mining had introduced the Fischer process in the pre-war era and became familiar with the low-pressure process for synthesizing oil. The other continuity from the pre-war period is expressed in capital relationships. Mitsui Mining approached its West German partners just as in the pre-war era through its connections with iron and steel companies in the Ruhr district.

(2) The establishment of Mitsui Petrochemical

On 6 January 1955, Ishida concluded a tentative license contract with Ziegler. The license fee including an option fee of 150,000 US dollars was 1,200,000 US dollars (approximately 432 million yen) to which royalties could be added later. This contract was monopolistic or exclusive, a so-called general license. The contract cost was twice that of each European firm. Moreover, because Ishida's instructions were "not to bargain down the price," the license fee agreement was reached with little "hard negotiating."[20] Torii, one of the leading engineers, recalls: "The option fee had not been paid yet, so we did not understand what the catalyst would be...President Ishida returned to Japan with a few documents, with which we proceeded blindly. At any rate, we had found polyethylene as a product, and we thought we could make something out of it."[21] Another manager, Hirayama, also recalls: "We had not paid the contract fees yet, and if things did not go well, we intended to appeal to the government for disapproval of our move."[22] They separated the option clause from the main contract and applied to MITI for approval. In April 1955, the option was approved and the option fee was paid.

Mitsui Chemical paid the option fee of 150,000 US dollars. For Ishida and Mitsui Chemical, this was no small amount; nevertheless, it was decided to pay the entire sum on its own, without relying on Mitsui Mining. Mitsui Chemical wanted to begin with the Ziegler process as its own business.[23]

When news of the January 1955 signing of the contract was relayed to other Japanese companies attempting to become petrochemical companies, it was both a great shock and a stimulus. Simultaneously, however, it raised the question of success in commercialization. As a manager of Mitsui Chemical, who accompanied Ishida to Europe, recollects: "Of course, the reaction of Mitsui Chemical's managers in Tokyo to this matter was extremely passive. They thought we had purchased something absolutely worthless, and our reputation dropped a notch."[24] The Ziegler process technology had not gone beyond the laboratory-testing phase and they lacked sufficient know-how for manufacturing. All they had received for their 1,200,000 US dollar purchase were the rights for use of the Ziegler process and two notebooks of experimental laboratory data.

Mitsui Chemical stopped the research already undertaken on Reppe chemistry and began the research necessary for an assessment of the Ziegler process technology as well as the research necessary for establishing manufacturing techniques. Much time was required for resolving technical problems, such as a brown discoloration caused by the remaining catalytic agent.[25] Mitsui Petrochemical purchased the manufacturing know-how established by Mitsui Chemical for 300 million yen and advanced to the construction of its Iwakuni plant.

Even after deciding to introduce the Ziegler process, whether to choose coal chemistry or petroleum chemistry was still to be decided within the company. Technical staff, led by Nakajima and Torii, favored considering a shift from coal chemistry to petroleum chemistry. Ishida, however, adhered to the coal chemistry idea. Having specialized in accounting, Ishida did not have a scientific background and found difficulty in understanding the prospects for petroleum chemistry. He had "the definite idea of paying a low cost and quickly recovering invested capital" and was inclined to the proposal for converting coal gas into ethylene that could be used as a raw material.[26] Moreover, according to Nakajima's recollection, the choice was "unclear even in West Germany, where a multitude of different debates raged among coal mining companies over whether to use petroleum to produce petrochemicals or whether to use coal to develop coal chemistry; most favored coal chemistry at a ratio of 7 to 3 or 8 to 2."[27]

At the end, the engineering staff, which strongly believed in petroleum chemistry and in the naphtha resolution process, managed to convince Ishida. This decision, which was made in March or April 1955, also put forward the idea of establishing a new company. "If the idea of producing ethylene from oil were adopted, then purchasing the equipment alone would be extremely costly and risky. It was therefore decided that Mitsui Chemical, instead of maintaining its independent operating unit, should create a separate company thereby garnering the Mitsui group's overall strength. Ishida's concept originated from this decision as well as from the concurrent strong request of Toyo Rayon (later Toray) for petrochemicals as raw materials for nylon 66 and Tetron through ICI's technology."[28]

In reality, the estimated capital expenditure for construction of the equipment specified in the first project was roughly 11 billion yen. It was impossible for Mitsui Chemical to raise sufficient capital alone. Mitsui Chemical had already undergone a series of rationalization moves that reduced its personnel size. Moreover, it was provided coal from Mitsui Mining by "bowing many times." Some, therefore, considered it strange that Mitsui Chemical involved itself in petroleum. In addition, Japanese government policy dictated that only business groups, not single companies, apply for sale of its properties. It was under these circumstances that Mitsui group finally decided to engage as a group in the project.[29]

Thus, in July 1955, a new company Mitsui Petrochemical Industry was founded. It had 250 million yen in capital. Seven companies affiliated with the Mitsui group (Mitsui Chemical, Mitsui Mining, Miike Synthetic, Mitsui Metal Mining, Toyo Koatsu, Toyo Rayon, and Mitsui Bank) had an investment of 87.5 percent, and Koa Petroleum had 12.5 percent. The cost of constructing the equipment for the first project alone was 11.15 billion yen, so the balance of 10.9 billion yen was provided as a loan. With Mitsui Bank as the managing bank, the Long-Term Credit Bank of Japan, Japan Industrial Bank, Mitsui Trust Bank, Nippon Kangyo Bank, and Kyowa Bank provided cooperative financing. The Japan Development Bank also provided a loan. Even in times of economic strain, funding procurement was uninterrupted.[30] A manager responsible for financing recollects: "Fund procurement was quite easily done."[31]

Meanwhile, MITI hesitated in its approval of the Ziegler process as there was no history of industrial applications, but finally ceded in November 1955. Having received approval, Mitsui Chemical then settled its formal contract with Ziegler. In May 1956, Mitsui Chemical provided Mitsui Petrochemical with the rights for licensing the Ziegler process through a sub-licensing agreement.[32]

Seizing the opportunity, Mitsui business group, despite its previous difficulties in concluding its arrangements, began to strengthen its ties. Ishida became president of Mitsui Petrochemical and, following the advice of Mitsui Bank president Kiichiro Sato, devoted himself exclusively to Mitsui Petrochemical's business affairs. Once this new company was founded, a formal application was made for the sale of land

and equipment of the former Japanese army's Iwakuni fuel depot, and the terms of purchase were specified in May 1956. In June, the Iwakuni factory began construction and in April 1958, operations began.[33]

After the start of operations, Mitsui Petrochemical ran into trouble with the Ziegler process. The Ziegler process was purchased when it was still in the experimental phases and, for that reason, troublesome. Polyethylene products produced by the process were "different from high-pressure polyethylene. They were hard in quality but difficult to process. It required great amounts of energy and work to develop applications for these products, which were initially so hard to sell." Interestingly, the first products were plates for beer bottles, and the first customer was Kirin Beer of the Mitsubishi business group. At first "we only sold 120 tons from our 1,000 ton plant." As a result, "the required capital was over 30 billion yen, and the monthly deficit was 250 million yen."[34]

To cope with difficulties in product development, it was vital to obtain technical assistance from Hoechst in West Germany where the Ziegler process was implemented earlier and had already been a success. At the end of 1955, Hoechst's monthly productive capacity had reached a scale of 2000 tons.[35] Later, in 1960, contracts for technological support relating to processing technology and others were concluded with Hoechst. Mitsui Petrochemical sent scientists to Hoechst a number of times to acquire technical knowledge for product development. Further, following a request from Mitsui Petrochemical, two Hoechst scientists were also sent to Japan for one year. The results were applied to the development of production know-how, particularly to the improvement of solvents.[36]

Let us sum up. Mitsui Petrochemical took the lead in Japan in establishing a general petrochemical company. The opportunity of becoming a general chemical company arose in January 1955, with the introduction of a polyethylene manufacturing technology, the Ziegler process. The introduction of this process, however, was neither directly linked to the shift from coal chemistry to petroleum chemistry, nor to the establishment of Mitsui Petrochemical as a general chemical firm. Initially the dominant plan was to convert coal gas to ethylene as a raw material. In other words, the main idea was to introduce the Ziegler process in developing a position in coal chemistry. Finally, the naphtha resolution process was adopted for ethylene production, thereby simultaneously leading to a new path toward a general petrochemical company.

The Ziegler process for low-pressure polyethylene was not only one of the first foreign petrochemical technologies to be introduced in Japan, but also the starting point for Mitsui Petrochemical as the first general petrochemical company.

2. Mitsubishi Petrochemical: A systematic development and the introduction of the BASF process

(1) The establishment of Mitsubishi Petrochemical

Mitsubishi Petrochemical's technology introduction was no exception to the general process as there were a variety of sources: ethylene came from Stone and Webster, while oxidized ethylene and ethylene glycol from the Scientific Design Company. Technology introduction from Shell, Mitsubishi's partner, was limited to styrene monomer during the initial phase. West German BASF's high-pressure polyethylene technology was the most significant to Mitsubishi Petrochemical among the technologies introduced. Mitsubishi Petrochemical was delayed in establishing itself as a general petrochemical company, particularly with polyethylene. The introduction of this technology, however, helped it recapture its position in a single stroke, forge ahead as a petrochemical company, and even realize high profits from the beginning.

The former Mitsubishi zaibatsu, now the Mitsubishi business group, also took an early interest in the petrochemical industry. Indeed it was 1951 that marked the beginning of the project of two companies of the group, Tokai Ammonium Sulfate Industry and Mitsubishi Petroleum, and Shell. In 1952, this was transformed into a cooperative project by Mitsubishi Chemical Industry and Shell. In June 1954, Mitsubishi Chemical and Shell planned to establish a joint-venture company, Mitsubishi Shell Petrochemical, on a fifty-fifty basis to produce isopropyl alcohol, acetone, and acetone derivatives. MITI, however, expressed disapproval, charging that this plan was focused on a single product and furthermore laid more importance on ethylene products than pro- pylene products. As a result, the project was delayed and allowed to drop.[37]

In 1955, the sale of the land at the fuel depots, which had until then caused such complications, suddenly took a new turn as a political solu- tion was reached. This solution provided the Mitsubishi-Shell group with the former navy fuel depot in Yokkaichi. A general petrochemi- cals complex, thus, could finally be build. Mitsubishi Chemical hastily abandoned its former single-product project and established another project for a general petrochemical industry in June of the same year. It was referred to as the "general project" within the company.

In August of the same year, when the decision to sell Yokkaichi facility to Showa Petroleum, in which Shell had a 50 percent share, became official, Mitsubishi Chemical began negotiations with Shell for cooperation. Shell, however, hesitated about initiating its general petrochemical industry operations in Japan. For that reason, Mitsubishi Chemical opted to begin operations not alone, but as a part of the Mitsubishi group. Probably this move was influenced by a decision of the Mitsubishi group, which in July of that year had striven to progress in the same manner by the concentration of a number of firms to form a new company, Mitsubishi Petrochemical. Finally the May 1955 "general project" was transformed into the "Prospect for Mitsubishi Petrochemical Industry" in December 1955. Kamesaburo Ikeda, pre-war Mitsubishi Chemical president and at that time vice-president of the Japanese Association of the Chemical Industry, would become the top manager of the new company. It is especially interesting to note that Ikeda was the very manager who led Mitsubishi Chemical's investigation team to IG Farben for the introduction of the Haber-Bosch process. It was in this way that the Mitsubishi group could "get on board," joining the commercialization of the petrochemical industry.[38]

Meanwhile, the "Prospect for Mitsubishi Petrochemical Industry" in December 1955 had already included the plan for a general petrochemical company. Moreover, it laid importance on ethylene products such as styrene monomer, oxidized ethylene, and ethylene glycol. So far as it went, it conformed to MITI's conception. This plan had various limitations, however. It still did not include polyethylene. In addition, the raw material to be used was refining waste gas. Important items, such as manufacturing processes, also lacked technical concreteness, and the funding plan was consequently just tentative. The so-called plan, therefore, was still very much in its conceptual phases.[39]

Problems still lingered as to how adjustments would be made with Shell concerning capital investment. Ikeda proposed "in the beginning that Shell should own 50 percent of Mitsubishi Petrochemical's stocks so that Mitsubishi could exploit Shell's technologies.[40] Nonetheless, as was touched upon earlier, Shell, like many other foreign, especially petrochemical, companies in those years, held passive attitudes toward the formation of general petrochemical companies. At one point Shell even almost abandoned the idea of making a capital investment.[41] Shell became anxious about Mitsubishi's commercialization plan and strove to avoid risk. In the end, in January 1956, the "Kato-Pratt Memorandum" was concluded between A. W. Pratt of Shell Petroleum and Takeo Kato, the former president of Mitsubishi Bank, as the representative of Mitsubishi group, in which both sides agreed in principle with a set of conditions for cooperation. The contents of the memorandum are not clearly known. The main point was that as compensation for supplying technology Shell would receive 15 percent of the new company's shares and that Showa Petroleum would additionally invest 10 percent in exchange for Mitsubishi's investment in Showa Yokkaichi Petroleum.[42]

In this way, at last in April 1956, Mitsubishi Petrochemical Co., Ltd was established with capital of 200 million yen through the joint investment of six companies of the Mitsubishi group: Mitsubishi Chemical, Mitsubishi Rayon, Asahi Glass, Mitsubishi Shoji, Mitsubishi Metal Mining, and Mitsubishi Bank (later nine companies with the addition of Tokyo Marine Insurance, Meiji Life Insurance, and Mitsubishi Mining). The establishment date was approximately nine months later than that of Mitsui Petrochemical. Shell officially decided to contribute capital later, at the time of the second capital increase in October 1957, after the contract concerning introduction of technology for ethylene and styrene monomer was concluded in February 1957.[43]

At the time of the new company's establishment, concrete measures were devised for how the company would be run. Its president, Ikeda, proposed to start afresh by thoroughly reexamining such issues as the priority of equipment construction, manufacturing processes, quantities produced, product supply and demand relations, production costs, and the revenue and expenditures budget. To accomplish this task, Ikeda headed the newly set up intra-company "Petrochemical Committee" which was to concentrate on its reassessment activities over the next several months.

(2) The introduction of the BASF process

At Mitsubishi Chemical, too, early emphasis was placed on polyethylene, and concern mounted especially in early 1955, when Mitsui Chemical publicly announced its project to introduce the Ziegler process. Mitsubishi Chemical gathered information on the Ziegler process from a wide variety of sources, including Mitsubishi Shoji, Monsanto, and others, and analyzed the data internally As mentioned above, however, even at the end of 1955, polyethylene had not yet been included in the business plans.

This occurred only after Mitsubishi Petrochemical had been established in April 1956. Directly after that, a Petrochemical Committee was set up within the company, as mentioned above, and the project was subjected to thorough reexamination. In the process, polyethylene at last was paid considerable attention as the most promising plastic.

Nonetheless, until then, competition was vigorous for acquiring the best foreign technologies, because other petrochemical companies had already incorporated polyethylene into their operations as a key product. Sumitomo Chemical had received the ICI high-pressure process, Mitsui Chemical used the low-pressure Ziegler process, and Showa Electric Industry used the Phillips process, leaving no other important processes available for Mitsubishi Petrochemical. Mitsubishi Petrochemical, therefore, had no choice but to consider the ICI process for small molecular weight, which would not conflict with Sumitomo Chemical's technology or the other low-pressure processes such as that of Standard Oil of Indiana. Nonetheless, the latter was acquired by Furukawa Electric Industry.[44]

In April 1956, the technical inquiry commission, headed by the technology department's head, Tokijiro Oka, was sent to the United States and Europe. It selected polyethylene as one of its points of interest. It focused its attention on the BASF technology.

At that time, BASF of West Germany had established a joint venture, Rheinische Olefin Werke (ROW), with Shell and had started commercialization of polyethylene. ROW, having acquired ICI's patent rights, undertook operations using BASF technology The commission acquired this information before its departure, from an article in a magazine. They thought that they could introduce technology from BASF or ROW at a lower price than from Shell or ICI, and that they could acquire technological information on raw material gas and product lines from ROW.[45]

Further, Mitsubishi Petrochemical predicted tremendous future expansion of the polyethylene market, and foresaw adequate room for a third company, even with the participation of Mitsui Petrochemical and Sumitomo Chemical which had already received approval. It was precisely at that time, in April 1956, that Showa Electric Industry announced a project, which seemed likely to be approved by MITI, for the production of 7,500 tons of polyethylene by the Phillips process and 90,000 tons of ammonium sulfate. Those at Mitsubishi Petrochemical grew impatient as they felt it was necessary to put a plan into action before the approval of the Showa Electric Industry project.[46]

Frequent meetings took place with Shell technology experts. Ikeda communicated his desire to produce polyethylene to Shell, a parent company of ROW; however, Shell's reaction was extremely passive. BASF was so cautious in supplying know-how that it conceded know-how to its joint enterprise, ROW, but not to Shell. Shell urged Ikeda to concentrate on styrene monomer in the first period project.[47]

Based on the information, Oka and others hoped to arrange a visit to ROW's factories through the arrangement of Mitsubishi Shoji. Although this request was denied, they did succeed in their contacts with BASF. The mediator was Reppe, who had already negotiated with Mitsubishi Chemical concerning the Reppe process. The patent department of BASF, the contact partner of Oka and others, was afraid that ICI's patent had already been established in Japan, because the BASF high-pressure process utilized the ICI patent. Mitsubishi Petrochemical, knowing that ICI's patent had not yet been approved in Japan, requested this technology to be introduced to Japan.

Following this, BASF replied that it intended to grant the use of the technology. Mitsubishi Petrochemical again sent Oka and others to West Germany to begin negotiations with Mitsubishi Shoji's support.

In August 1956, the results of these activities, including Oka mission's report, which was closely examined and was used as the basis for a new subject of reinvestigation, were incorporated into Mitsubishi Petrochemical's "Prospect for Undertakings" and submitted to MITI. Accordingly, polyethylene was at last added to the list of products. For the manufacturing technique, although BASF's name was not mentioned, it was clearly stated that a high-pressure process would be incorporated and that a contact was forthcoming. Furthermore, revisions were made on the scale of styrene monomer production, increasing it to 18,000 tons. The planned production scale of ethylene was also increased from the originally projected 6,000 tons to 22,000 tons. The original plan was to use only waste gas from petroleum refining as a raw material, but this was revised to make naphtha the principal raw material.[48]

Consequently, the addition of polyethylene made it possible for Mitsubishi Petrochemical at last to define itself as a general petrochemical company. Mitsubishi Petrochemical, having lagged behind Mitsui Petrochemical and Sumitomo Chemical showed a far more systematic development from the beginning. Its 22,000 tons of ethylene raced ahead of both Mitsui Petrochemical, which produced 20,000, and Sumitomo Chemical, with 12,000 tons.

Here, we find another example of continuity from the pre-war period in addition to the case of Mitsui Petrochemical. The continuity is expressed, first, in the fact that at the introduction of polyethylene technology Mitsubishi selected a high-pressure one, the BASF process. In the latter half of the 1930s, when Mitsubishi Chemical was established, it introduced the Haber-Bosch process, a high-pressure hydrogenation process for synthesizing ammonium. In addition, Mitsubishi Mining, of the same Mitsubishi zaibatsu, had approached the IG process for synthetic oil, which controlled reactions under high pressure. Mitsubishi Shoji also had pushed the introduction of this technology. Second, continuity from the pre-war period is also expressed in capital relationships: Mitsubishi Chemical was established in the pre-war era with the ambition to be "IG Farben in the Orient" and BASF was one of IG Farben's successors.[49]

On the other hand, while the "Prospect for Undertakings" was awaiting MITI's decision, it became clear that the Mitsubishi Petrochemical project was delayed and suffered from fierce competition, especially with Showa Electric Industry and Furukawa Chemical, for MITI's approval. Mitsui and Sumitomo, whose projects had already been approved, proposed to MITI a redoubling in scale to prevent the latecomers' projects from being realized. Though the internal examination at MITI's Light Industries Department concluded once that Mitsubishi Petrochemical's project should be given first preference, MITI as a whole never reached a definitive decision. The basis for MITI's hesitation over the approval of Mitsubishi Petrochemical's and others' new projects was the anticipated demand. Having estimated that the demand for 1960 was 25,000 tons, MITI had approved Mitsui Petrochemical and Sumitomo Chemical's projects of producing 12,000 tons per year each. Consequently, it decided that there was no room for new participants.

Mitsubishi Petrochemical insisted that there was room for new participants, using its own survey included in the "Prospect for Undertakings" where it estimated that the demand for 1960 would be approximately 50,000 tons. Since before the Second World War this sort of division had been a familiar process when applications or decisions for permission were made. Be that as it may, this clearly demonstrated Mitsubishi Petrochemical's need to further hasten its formal application for polyethylene technology introduction as well as its reason for seeking to establish a contract with BASF. This is precisely the reason it hastily pursued a contract with BASF.[50]

In October 1956, Mitsubishi Petrochemical and BASF concluded a contract to provide technological support for the construction of equipment and operations for an annual production of 10,000 tons. On the BASF side, its subsidiary in Panama, Transatlantica, negotiated the contract because of West German tax laws. Further, as ICI had already obtained patent rights in West Germany, BASF could only grant know-how. This was Mitsubishi Petrochemical's first experience with technology introduction.

In November, it applied for approval based on the Foreign Capital Law. As was mentioned above, however, MITI hesitated in granting approval due to its future demand estimates. Mitsubishi, again presenting its own more optimistic estimates of demand, continued negotiations with MITI. Finally, having revised its demand estimates, MITI simultaneously granted approval for the projects of Mitsubishi Petrochemical, Showa Electric Industry, and Furukawa Chemical in February 1957.[51]

The sum required for the Mitsubishi first period plan was 11.6 billion yen, of which 1.8 billion yen (16 percent) came out of its own capital reserves, while the rest was financed through the loans by Shell (11 percent) and Japan Development Bank (13 percent) as well as through cooperative loans by other commercial banks (60 percent). The cooperative loan providers were composed of thirteen banking institutions, including Mitsubishi Bank, Industrial Bank of Japan, Japan Long-Term Credit Bank, and Mitsubishi Trust Bank.[52]

Operations of the new company started smoothly. "While many other petrochemical companies were experiencing technical difficulties with producing polyethylene by the medium- and low-pressure processes...partly because the high-pressure product enjoyed unexpectedly greater demand in Japan, the company [Mitsubishi Petrochemical] acquired extremely high yields soon after the opening of operations."[53] Within the second period plan, production was increased twice from 1959 to 1960, and by the end 1960, annual production volume had reached 50,000 tons.

Mitsubishi Petrochemical's polyethylene production increased far beyond what had been forecast. This may have lead BASF to think that the payment for technology under the technology assistance contract had been too low; they proposed a research contract to fill this gap. Both companies concluded a contract, through which Mitsubishi Petrochemical received exclusive rights to the BASF process technology for three years until the end of 1959, when the contract expired. Next, after a non-contract period, both concluded another new research contract to acquire new know-how and to enjoy exclusive rights, which got approval in August 1961. Whereas the original contract had assured that improved technology should be offered without compensation, the new one obliged Mitsubishi to pay royalties on a production volume basis. As dissatisfaction mounted with the research contract as well as with BASF's technology, Mitsubishi Petrochemical inquired into the technology of an American company, Rexhall. Negotiations never reached fruition, however.[54]

3. Conditions, the government policies, business strategies, and the results of technology introduction

The above sections have concentrated on the establishment as general petrochemical firms and the technological development of the pioneering firms, Mitsui Petrochemical and Mitsubishi Petrochemical, especially their introduction of foreign production technologies, particularly of West German ones, taking the production technology for most important business resources for the companies at least in those years.

There were several conditional factors present in the inauguration of general petrochemical companies. The first is the opening of the petrochemical product market. This was brought about by development of the synthetic fiber, synthetic resin, vinyl chloride, synthetic rubber, and synthetic detergent so widely used today. In fact, the import of petrochemical products continued to increase in the 1950s, when the petrochemical industry in Japan started as a raw materials supplier for these industries. A second factor leading to its development was the worldwide assurance of lower cost for the raw material naphtha, which was in principle subject to open competition. Third, funding of equipment investment was assured by the Japan Development Bank and other long-term credit banks, while other methods were also available, such as joint establishment of new companies by group-affiliated companies, funding through affiliated financial institutions, and foreign capital allotments. Procuring large sums was necessary to enter the equipment-intensive petrochemical industry. Due to the fundamental necessity of large procurements, three of the four companies involved were from former general zaibatsu, and one was a subsidiary of a foreign company. Nonetheless capital restrictions were virtually nonexistent for these four companies, which had been selected according to MITI's "promoting policies." Fourth, having cooperative labor relations was indispensable, as can be exemplified particularly in the case of Mitsui, which had completed rationalization measures just before engaging in petrochemical operations. Finally, MITI and other governmental bodies certainly played a great role in industrial policy. First, MITI's policies of nurturing the synthetic fiber, synthetic resin, and later synthetic rubber industries created a market for petrochemical products. Second, the government gave auspicious sites to companies through selling land and facilities of former military fuel depots. With these sales, the petrochemical industry, just as the atomic industry, gave an opportunity for organizing business groups. Third, the government also gave favorable capital backing as well as tax incentives.

The foreign production technology was one of the most important business resources for the companies in those years.

The appearance in Japan of general petrochemical companies came about in various ways and with a variety of characteristics. In the case of Mitsui Petrochemical, the introduction of the key technology, the Ziegler process, led the project. In the case of Mitsubishi Petrochemical, the first real examination of technology began after having established a new company. In other words, Mitsui Petrochemical's persistence in coal chemistry led to an unexpected result, whereas Mitsubishi Petrochemical wished from the beginning to systematically establish a petrochemicals company. At the introduction of one of the focal technologies, polyethylene, the various characteristics of these two companies were clearly visible: a central difference between high- and low-pressure processes was visible. The difference led to the wide variety of processes offered, although the significance of this difference was not clearly recognized at the time.

Here, the emphasis should be placed on similarities in the creation of each petrochemical company, particularly the similarities in strategies. When companies without original technology depended on existing technology imported from abroad, their tendency toward adopting similar strategies was strong. On the contrary, one can observe greater dissimilarity or divergence when companies with their own capabilities develop new areas. For example, in West Germany, it is said that there were several tacit cooperative agreements among the big three, BASF, Bayer, and Hoechst. One such illustration in the area of polyethylene is that Bayer did not join until the late 1960s.[55] In the early days of general petrochemical companies, one sees similarities, rather than dissimilarities, in business strategy.[56]

(1) Japanese companies

Understanding the conditions, selecting the technology, and deciding on and undertaking investments in facilities were the tasks of companies.

The focal point of understanding the conditions was knowing the extent to which companies realized the inevitability of changing from coal chemistry to petrochemicals; in other words, it was a question of whether they could tear themselves away from an attachment to coal or coal chemistry. Once converted to petrochemicals, the next question was whether they could quickly achieve the technology essential to pursuing a transformation to generalization. On this point, the four leading general petroleum companies preceded other companies.

At first glance, it may look as though some companies did not recognize these points and indeed entered petrochemicals by pure chance. This was typical of Mitsui Petrochemical and its introduction of the Ziegler process, which was still in the experimental phases. The story of President Ishida's "arbitrary decision" as well as the elevated price are reminiscent of the introduction of the Casale process by Shitagau Noguchi of Japan Nitrogen Fertilizer Company in the pre-war period. In the mind of Ishida, this purchase meant progress in coal chemistry. His adherence to coal chemistry was linked with his consideration of the interests of Mitsui Mining and Mitsui Chemical when, unlike in West Germany, in Japan coal chemistry was insufficiently developed, let alone petroleum chemistry. As explained above, however, the decision was premised upon technical specialist Nakajima's assessment, not only on Ishida's "arbitrary decision." The adherence to coal chemistry, therefore, was soon remedied. Indeed, the technical assessment was based on knowledge accumulated in the introduction of Fischer process technology by Mitsui Mining in the pre-war period.

Efforts for collecting information took shape in variety of ways. Staff members, often executives, were sent to the United States and Europe to collect data. Written documents painstakingly collected from technical magazines were carefully examined. German chemical companies' technical documents, the so-called PB Reports, which were seized by the Allied powers and made public in the Hibiya CIE Library by the General Headquarters in Japan, were thoroughly exploited by many technical experts of Japanese companies. Information collected by trading companies was also important, although it became less important than in the pre-war period, when it often played decisive roles in technical assessments and the selection process. In short, technical specialists with insight into the necessity of conversion from coal chemistry to petrochemicals were readily available. For their insight, they became key persons in the new industry.

Key persons were present during the negotiations process. They were in some cases the same persons as in the process of assessment. They needed and possessed the abilities not only to recognize the necessity of conversion but also to make technical assessments of individual technologies. For most negotiations and contracts, executives and top managers were sometimes directly responsible, while managerial organizations for international business were comparatively simple. In the process of negotiations leading to the eventual settling of contracts, trading companies' roles had decreased in comparison to the ones they had held in the pre-war period.

Thus, we can assume a continuous process from recognition of need down to the decision-making. In the process we find a continuity from the pre-war period, which is expressed most clearly in the fact that at the introduction of polyethylene technology Mitsui selected a low-pressure technology, the Ziegler process, and Mitsubishi selected a high-pressure one, the BASF process.

In the transition from mere recognition to decision-making for entry, it is certain that some sort of leap in the manager's decision making developed. This leap developed regarding the type of technology, the time of introduction, or the purchase price, whereas in the same period West German companies constantly faced the choice of whether to create themselves or to purchase foreign technology.

(2) Western companies, especially West German ones

An important conditional factor concerning technology should be emphasized: the way the international market for technology functioned at that time. European and American companies conducted extremely vigorous sales campaigns to Japanese companies in the 1950s. They often approached Japanese companies on their own. This was particularly true with American chemical engineering companies that blossomed in the 1930s, Stone and Webster being just one example. It was not only these companies; giants such as ICI were also active in sales campaigns to Sumitomo and Mitsui. In addition, other factors for the advantageous position of Japanese companies to purchase foreign technologies freely at lower prices were a relatively loose working of the international patent system.

On the other hand, at the same time, European and American were generally uninterested in the idea of establishing general petrochemical companies in Japan, as illustrated by Shell in the case of Mitsubishi Petrochemical as well as Caltex in the case of Japan Petrochemicals. They considered creating ethylene centers in Japan to be unnecessary. They probably underestimated the future expansion of the Japanese market potential.

"At that time, the overwhelming opinion in the United States was that Japan could buy its products from the United States and should not be involved in petrochemicals. Nonetheless, there were engineering companies that were willing to sell any sort of needed technology."[57] In addition, the vice-president of Shell said, in 1953, during a speech made in Japan: "It is still premature; Japan should import American semi-manufactures for processing. Without a refinery capable of producing 100,000 barrels, it cannot operate internationally."[58] To Japanese companies, this magnified the opportunities for becoming involved.

(3) The government policies

MITI's authority to approve the introduction of foreign technology was a large factor, because the introduction was an absolute necessity in the transformation of petrochemical production into a real industry. We can mention the 1949 law on foreign exchange and foreign trade control (Foreign Exchange Law) and the 1950 Foreign Capital Law, in which government approval played such a great role. The foreign capital law guaranteed payment in foreign currencies by Japanese purchasers of foreign technologies. The two conditions required for the approval were: "It contributes to improvement of the international balance of payments or to the major industries or public works." Application of that clause was entrusted to the Foreign Capital Council, which administered its decisions under extremely stringent guidelines. "On the one hand, the government sought only to import foreign capital and technologies for strengthening its industries' international competitiveness by imposing strict examination rules. On the other hand, from a narrower point of view to protect national companies in important industries, foreign capital was in principal excluded, even when it was considered from a wider point of view to contribute to the development of the Japanese economy."[59] The petrochemical industry was an exception as import restrictions were not imposed, but foreign capital policies were the same. Thus government approval made possible technology introduction without management control by foreign ownership or capital.

Thus, MITI put its restrictive measures into practice at individual examination processes conducted by the Foreign Capital Council, based upon the foreign capital law. MITI intervened in the core business activity, investment in facilities, by intervening in the selection of particular technologies as well as of conditions, such as price and time period.

(4) Results

Under the conditions that Japanese petrochemical companies enjoyed, they could purchase almost all kinds of manufacturing technologies they wanted. Facilities costs and licensing fees were sometimes enormous; Japanese companies as purchasers did not have to bear overly great hardships, however. In the case of Mitsui's Ziegler process technology, the top manager, Ishida, advised representatives "not to bargain down the price." Moreover, as was often the case, they could purchase at a lower price, as exemplified in Mitsubishi Petrochemical's introduction of polyethylene technology from BASF.

They expressed anxiety over expensive technology from the early stage of commercialization of petrochemicals. A document, "On industrialization technology for petrochemicals," which was written by the Meeting of Petrochemical Technology in February 1955 and became a premise of MITI's promoting policies, repeatedly insisted that "it is best to pay a lump sum for technology introduction concerning important technologies such as ethylene technology."[60] This statement might be interpreted as anxiety or caution over expensive technology purchases. From that time on, complaints and criticism regarding expensive technology were often repeated. "It was 1% of sales in a pre-war tie-up. After the war, however, 3 to 5% was average. There were cases of taking such sums as $100,000 or $1 million as a down payment."[61]

Nonetheless, while competition existed among Japanese companies as purchasers, so did cooperation, as can be observed in the purchase of the S&W process by Mitsui Petrochemical and Sumitomo Chemical. It was possible to "cut the first price asked by 60%."[62] Though it occurred much later, it is true that the engineers from the four firms, which introduced the same S&W process met to analyze the licensing fee.[63]

Moreover, conditions in the international technology market at the time were fortunate for the start of a Japanese petrochemical industry. MITI also administered projects in such a way as to cut prices down.

During the process of technology introduction from the beginning to negotiations and contracts, MITI functioned as a data bank or think tank; furthermore, through discussions between as well as within the various sections, it coordinated individual companies and industries. One could say that through this strict individual inspection of technology introduction it served as a means of determining basic patent costs and downward adjustments and as a last resort to prevent unfavorable conditions for introduction. The most important factor, however, was the vigorous competition among European and American companies as sellers. This resulted in the freedom of Japanese companies to purchase good technologies at comparatively low prices.

Developments were quick, once the transition from coal chemistry to petrochemicals had begun. Consequently, even in comparison with West Germany, Japan was not far behind, and on a world level, it had made a quick start. For example, consider the West German company Hoechst. It was not until 1952 that Hoechst entered the petrochemical business in earnest. That same year it introduced the technology for ethylene from the United States and also undertook industrialization of the Ziegler process. Next, Hoechst resumed research on synthetic fibers such as Perlon and acrylonitrile, and forged further ahead by finally introducing technology from ICI. What should be noted here is that Hoechst valued strategically the implementation of its own technologies. President Winnacker, who had inspected the American chemical industry in 1954, was candidly admiring of the continuous, rapid advances in American petrochemical technology. He observed that advancing into synthetic fiber, synthetic resin, film, and detergent production, for example, through "mass production in the new chemical industry for which the base was synthetic resin and synthetic fibers" was an urgent need. He considered that "we should not neglect our traditional fields." As unconditional imitation was improper, he emphasized the value of original technology in pharmaceuticals, dyes, and other organic chemical areas.[64]

Japanese companies did not hesitate in changing from a preoccupation with their own technology to the introduction from abroad. Moreover, they had a great capacity to absorb technology. Of course, one cannot overlook the comparatively favorable conditions for the later introduction of manufacturing technologies and know-how. One of the differences between the technology introduced from manufacturers and that from engineering companies is that, with the former, manufacturing technology or know-how accompanies it, whereas with the latter this is not always guaranteed. Even in the latter case, however, it was possible at that time to acquire manufacturing technologies and know-how through visits from other licensees. Whether the providers of technology are manufacturing or engineering companies in the purchase of chemical plants conducted by market transactions, buyer-seller cooperation is pursued by means of the introduction of a variety of organizational principles. We could say that the conditions necessary for that sort of cooperation were more prevalent in the 1950s than they are today [65]

In the beginning, as we can see from the polyethylene example, MITI was generally cautious in its demand forecasts. In addition, it adopted the principle of equality in its approval of technology introduction. This combination of policies gave birth to too many companies whose production levels were too low by international standards. Indeed, from the beginning, MITI stressed export and international competitiveness, especially because the petrochemical industry was an exception to import protection. In reality, however, the production scale of ethylene at that time was only 25,000 tons in Japan, whereas it was between 40,000 and 70,000 tons in the United States.[66] Firms of small production scale on an international basis, and of about equal size began their activities on the same footing at about the same time.

The situation could have originally given rise to or promoted "excessive competition" or "regulated excessive competition," which was produced by administrative approval. "While the enforcement of the foreign capital law was restrictive to new entrants, it also pleased everyone allowing the presence of many companies."[67] In reality, however, as demand increased faster than MITI's forecasts,[68] regulations went to work and brought generally high profit ratios, though with discrepancies in the ratios. Therefore, after the petrochemical industry first period plan, competition for upsizing developed in the form of latecomers increasing their investments in equipment of larger scale than that of the leaders, what was realized in the 1960s.

III. DEVELOPMENT IN THE PERIOD 1960–1973

1. The sophistication of introduced technology and the development of domestic technology: 1959–1964

(1) The second period plan

In December 1959, MITI created a "policy for conducting future petrochemical industry commercialization projects," and with this came the so-called petrochemical industry second period plan. Next, in May 1960,

MITI established a standard for producing ethylene on a scale of more than 40,000 tons. Finally to add to this, it liberalized the importation of petroleum in October 1962. The main characteristics of this period were: first, increases in productivity and lowered costs through expansion of the market and increased scale; second, the general use of olefin, which had not yet been used, the commercialization of new products, and the replacement of previous processes, such as the one for acetaldehyde.

In the 1960s, the four forerunners were joined by five new companies that would form ethylene centers: Toa Fuel Petrochemical, Daikyowa Petrochemical, Chemical-Mizushima, Maruzen Petrochemical, and Idemitsu Petrochemical. The early four, especially Mitsui Petrochemical and Mitsubishi Petrochemical, also reinforced their investments in facilities.[69]

Thus, as shown in Table 9.4, a system of nine ethylene centers formed. Japan's ethylene production capabilities reached a total of 730,000 tons by 1964, the time the MITI second period plan was completed. In the following year, ethylene production rose to 800,000 tons, putting Japan in second place after the United States, which was producing 4,000,000 tons. In terms of company ranking, Mitsui Petrochemical was tenth. By about 1965, the ratio of imports of petrochemical products to their production was a negligible 5 percent, concluding the import substitution process.

Table 9.4 Nine Ethylene Centers

	Center Company	Location	Production Scale (tons per year)	Operation Start
Leaders	Mitsui Petrochemical	Iwakuni	20,000	Apr 58
	Sumitomo Chemical	Niihama	12,000	Apr 58
	Mitsubishi Petrochemical	Yokkaichi	22,000	May 59
	Japan Petrochemical	Kawasaki	25,000	Jun 59
Followers	Toa Fuel Petrochemical	Kawasaki	40,000	Mar 62
	Daikyowa Petrochemical	Yokkaichi	41,300	Jun 63
	Maruzen Petrochemical	Chiba	44,000	Jul 64
	Kasei Mizushima	Mizushima	45,000	Jul 64
	Idemitsu Petrochemical	Tokuyama	73,000	Oct 64

From a technical standpoint, machines continued to increase in size and scale as more were domestically produced. In 1959, the government approval standards for introducing technology changed from a negative list to a positive list, making technology introduction automatically approved in principle. Given these conditions, technology introduction aggressively continued even further. At that time Japan witnessed a battle to introduce polypropylene, the so-called trek to Montecacini. At least some twenty-five companies, twelve chemical and thirteen textile, were in contact with Montecacini at that time.

Moreover, endeavors increased to make introduced technologies more sophisticated and to develop domestic technologies. Domestic manufacturing of machinery and equipment increased. Cooperation with foreign companies through the establishment of joint ventures also flourished. Because these joint ventures preceded capital liberalization, the 50–50 line was maintained, and technology introduction with maintenance of managerial rights continued.

The first four companies, especially Mitsui and Mitsubishi, led in the sophistication of introduced technology, development of domestic technology, and tie-ups with foreign companies, responding effectively to the challenge of the latecomers.

(2) Mitsui Petrochemical

Concerning the investments in facilities, in August 1959, Mitsui Petrochemical submitted the Iwakuni second period plan; as the MITI policy mentioned above was issued in December 1959, Mitsui Petrochemical revised its plan in April 1960; the revised version planned to produce ethylene at a scale of 60,000 tons, the highest level at that time, and selected high-pressure polyethylene, acetaldehyde, and styrene as a new project for using ethylene effectively. To make more effective use of polypropylene and acetone, it devised the industrialization of MIBK. It also later added a project for increased production of phenol and expanded to the Otake area, which neighbors Iwakuni.[70]

Concerning the transition toward producing machinery domestically, being accompanied by the development of large-scale technology, at Mitsui Petrochemical's ethylene plant, constructed during the first period, all of the measuring machines were imported from Honeywell and Foxborough. During the second period, however, they were produced domestically by Yamatake and Yokogawa instead.[71]

One illustration of domestically produced technology is Mitsui Petrochemical's Ziegler polymerization process, air oxidation technology in terephthalic acid, and automatic oxidation technology in cumene-process phenol. Mitsui also developed polypropylene technology later.[72]

Mitsui was also representative in establishing a joint venture to produce polyethylene. For this area, it selected a low-pressure process to which it devoted all of its efforts; however, it also decided to promote high-pressure polyethylene. Mitsui chose Du Pont's technology, which was the top among technologies not yet imported. Nakajima and others visited Du Pont, but failed in negotiation, as Du Pont at that time had no policy for technological support. Nonetheless, defeating the other two Japanese competitors, Mitsui and Du Pont founded Mitsui Polychemical (today Mitsui-Du Pont Polychemical) with a 50–50 ownership ratio in December 1960. Du Pont had to compromise despite its unwritten law of greater than 50–50 ownership for providing a process it had already developed. For Du Pont, this was the first time they had ever established a foreign venture with a 50–50 ratio and had not had full management rights.[73]

(3) Mitsubishi Petrochemical

Concerning the investments in facilities, in December 1958, heading the leading four firms, Mitsubishi Petrochemical had already submitted its prospectus for a second period project just a year before MITI's second period plan. The plan's distinguishing characteristic was "the realization of lower ethylene costs by the effective use of residual constituent parts, coupled with a simultaneous venture of creating a true system of general petrochemical operations." As it needed to "devise countermeasures for the increase in demand and reinforce the management base," Mitsubishi Petrochemical revised the project and resubmitted a new plan to MITI in July 1959. In December 1959, according to the MITI policy mentioned above, Mitsubishi Petrochemical revised the plan again and at last got ratification to the second period plan in June 1960. The previous plans had set the second ethylene plant at the same level as in the first period plan, or 22,000 tons, but the second period plan raised it to 38,000 tons and increased the production of polyethylene and styrene monomer.[74]

In the case of Mitsubishi Petrochemical, too, the increases in machine size were a notable means of making the introduced technology more sophisticated. It was said that Mitsubishi Petrochemical's high-pressure polyethylene equipment excelled that of BASF in terms of large-scale technology. Sumitomo Chemical also surpassed its provider, ICI.[75]

Concerning the transition toward producing machinery domestically, all of Mitsubishi Petrochemical's machines were produced domestically except the pipes used for polyethylene production.[76]

Mitsubishi Petrochemical also created a joint venture with BASF in the field of styropol (foaming polystyrene). Taking notice of styropol as a way to consume styrene monomer, it considered introducing technologies from BASF. BASF, exporting styropol to Japan, was interested in producing it in Japan. Mitsubishi Petrochemical wanted to produce for itself because of its preferential acquisition right, but BASF insisted on having a 50–50 joint-venture arrangement. As a result of negotiations, they decided to operate as a joint venture. Later, when BASF lost its patent dispute with Sekisui Chemical, the price of patents dropped considerably, and a new contract was concluded. This contract was approved in December 1961. The Japanese government had not approved of the 50–50 ratio, however, so Yuka-Badische, a new joint venture, was set up in January 1962 with Mitsubishi Petrochemical possessing 51 percent and BASF, 49 percent. In December of 1967, the ownership ratio was 50/50.[77]

2. Quantitative development under the open system: 1964–1973

(1) The third and fourth period plan: 1964–1973

As Japan moved to become a clause eight nation of IMF and joined the OECD in 1964, the nation faced the task of trade and capital liberalization toward a more open system. Reinforcement of this industry's international competitiveness became an even more important task, as MITI's promotion policy had already stressed. This change led to the opening of the third period plan from 1964 to 1967. In December 1964, MITI established the petrochemical cooperation meeting. This aimed at the pursuit of a government industrial policy on a government-business cooperative formula, after the bill on provisional measures for promoting specific industries was rejected. For the petrochemical industry, which was in favor of the bill, government-business cooperative relations were not fundamentally altered. In January 1965, the cooperation meeting set approval standards for new ethylene facilities at 100,000 tons, and revised this to 300,000 tons in May 1967. The remedy devised by the cooperation meeting was that the prerequisite for reinforcement of international competitiveness was a unit ethylene production of 300,000 tons; in order to reach that level, companies themselves had to establish responsibility, to foster competition, including internal rivalry within the same business group, on one hand, and to cooperate by joint and rotating investments.

At that time, according to an engineering company's estimate, it was essential to reduce costs by reaching a unit scale of 300,000 tons. Plants that could produce 300,000 to 400,000 tons appeared on the world scene. For the majority of companies in Japan, it seemed difficult to clear the approval standard of 300,000 tons. Nonetheless, contrary to the cooperation meeting forecasts, nine companies announced their desire to set up ethylene centers.

The leading four general petrochemical companies eventually planned and accomplished the construction of a second ethylene center. Apart from the Mitsui Petrochemical and Sumitomo Chemical plants constructed in Chiba and the Mitsui Petrochemical plant in Kashima, a plant was constructed jointly by Japan Petrochemicals and Mitsui Petrochemical in Kawasaki for producing 300,000 tons. As a result, as shown in Table 9.5, also through joint investments and rotating investments, the nine companies were able to construct new ethylene facilities of 300,000 tons. Accordingly, six new complexes were added to the nine already in place, forming a new system with a total of fifteen.

Table 9.5 Projects for 300,000 tons of Ethylene

Company	Investment Form	Location	Completion Year
Maruzen Petrochemical	Sole	Chiba	1969
Ukishima Petrochemical	Joint	Kawasaki	1970
Sumitomo Chiba Chemical	Rotation	Chiba	1970
Osaka Petrochemical	Joint	Senpoku	1970
Mizushima Ethylene	Joint/Rotation	Mizushima	1970
Mitsubishi Petrochemical	Sole	Kashima	1971
Shindaikyowa Petrochemical	Rotation	Yokkaichi	1972
Toa Fuel Petrochemical	Rotation	Kawasaki	1971
Sanyo Ethylene	Joint/Rotation	Mizushima	1972

As illustrated in the case of ethylene, the pursuit of economies of scale, by increasing the size of facilities, peaked during this period. At the same time, the transition toward newer processes for vinyl chloride, the aromatic compounds, ammonia, and acetic acid were also promoted just as in the previous period.

On the other hand, after technology introduction was completely liberalized in 1968, importation continued to occur. In ethylene technology for example, Mitsubishi Petrochemical switched from the S&W process to the Lummus process, while Sumitomo Chemical and Japan Petrochemicals worked toward the introduction of an improved S&W process. Epoch-making products and processes ceased to appear, however. Technology introduction processes became rather routine work, as illustrated by the fact that executives were rarely sent abroad to negotiate and conclude contracts.

Commercial conflicts developed in 1965 between the United States and Japan and again in 1967 between Europe and Japan, which tended only to grow worse. They represented greater barriers to the introduction of technology. The first capital liberalization was achieved in July 1967. For that reason, it was predicted that unilateral introduction of technology would become problematic and that demands by foreign companies for cross licensing or joint ventures would strengthen. The questions this posed included enlargement of facilities and development of domestic technology. These were not the only problems. Following the enlargement of facilities, environmental pollution in industrial complexes caused diseases such as Yokkaichi asthma, and factory fire hazards became common. Technology to remedy such environmental or safety problems became a new question.

Companies endeavored to strengthen their research organizations as a way to find remedies for these problems. At that time, the leading companies competed to set up central or general research laboratories. Sumitomo Chemical established a central laboratory in 1965, Mitsui Petrochemical created a general laboratory in 1967, as did Mitsubishi Petrochemical in 1968.[78] Mitsubishi Chemical's Life Science Research Laboratory, established in 1971, had anticipated the bioscience boom in later years.

Concerning the domestic development of technology, Mitsui Petrochemical's polypropylene technology was a pioneering example.

Active technology exportation starting around 1970 was the fruit of these efforts to develop domestic technologies, as exemplified in the cases of Mitsui and Mitsubishi. Sumitomo Chemical had already exported vinyl chloride resin manufacturing technology and others to the United States and Europe, starting around 1964. It exported polyolefin technology to Du Pont in 1969 and supplied a Dutch company, DSM, with polyethylene technology in 1972. In 1971, Japan Petrochemicals exported petroleum resin manufacturing technology to a West German company, Reinhold Albert Chemie. Thus, technology was not only exported to developing countries, but also to a growing number of developed ones.[79]

(2) Mitsui Petrochemical

In the framework of the second ethylene plan, the Mitsui Petrochemical plants were constructed in Chiba. Moreover, a plant was constructed jointly with Japan Petrochemicals in Kawasaki for producing 300,000 tons.

Within the Mitsui business group, Mitsui Chemical and Toyo High-Pressure merged to establish a new firm, Mitsui Toatsu Chemical, in October 1968, which joined forces with General Petroleum to form an industrial complex in Osaka-Sakai Senpoku and to form an ethylene center. Torii of Mitsui Petrochemical recollects: "We were to have 180,000 tsubo (1 tsubo = 3.3 square meters) of the land adjacent to Oriental Oil, but even so Mitsui Chemical did not come." "Had Mitsui Chemical participated in the Chiba complex at that time, the greater Mitsui Chemical Industries would have been created." In this way, the two Mitsui group companies, Mitsui Petrochemical and Mitsui Toatsu Chemical, became rivals, as in the Mitsubishi group, where Mitsubishi Chemical and Mitsubishi Petrochemical had already become so.[80] On the other hand, while Mitsui Toatsu Chemical abandoned the low-pressure process for polyethylene in entering into the petroleum chemistry, Mitsui Petrochemical ceased oxidized ethylene and ethylene glycol in an effort to readjust their fields of production. The two companies also collaborated in the production of phenol. These demonstrate the cooperation between the two firms.[81]

Mitsui Petrochemical's polypropylene technology is an example of a domestically developed technology. President Ishida, considering relations with Mitsui Chemical, gave strict orders not to undertake the development of polypropylene for ten years. They finally decided to undertake it, however, having taken into consideration the gas balance for the effective use of propylene and the complementariness of polypropylene with low-pressure process polyethylene. At first, Mitsui

Petrochemical tried in vain to introduce the Montecacini process with Toray. Then it concluded a contract in October 1964 with Eastman Kodak in the United States to introduce technology. By that time, however, they had the prospect of commercialization of their own technology. Mitsui Petrochemical therefore dissolved the contract in May 1966 and decided to rely on its own technology. In December 1966, after the establishment of a mid-term test facility, they quickly included the undertaking in the Chiba first period plan and completed a full-fledged plant in February 1968.[82] "Numerous improvements were made in the Highzex (low-pressure process polyethylene) plants and in the polypropylene plants. The phenol plant was of a new and completely different type. EPT was also commercialized, based on our own technology. In addition, manufacturing technology for aniline was introduced from an American company, Halcon International, Inc., and with our company's know-how, we were the first in the world to commercialize it."[83]

The company also took the lead in technology export. The first technology exported by Mitsui Petrochemical was that for low-pressure polyethylene, which was exported to Rumania in 1970. In 1971, it exported polypropylene technology to Poland. In 1971, it exported technology to Hercules Powder Company in the United States to manufacture petroleum resin.[84]

(3) Mitsubishi Petrochemical

In the framework of the second period plan, the Mitsui Petrochemical plant was built in Kashima.

Concerning the technology introduction, Mitsubishi Petrochemical switched from the S&W process to the Lummus process for manufacturing ethylene. Lummus, an American engineering firm, had developed the technology together with BASF and had a good record in terms of performance and experience. It then enthusiastically promoted sales to Mitsubishi Petrochemical. Fujii and others conducted a study in the United States and Europe and visited BASF, which had already adopted the Lummus process and Shell, which was using the S&W process. As a result of their study, they determined that despite high construction fees for the Lummus process, all things considered, the overall manufacturing costs were lower than for the S&W process. Consequently, the company went so far as to cancel its contract with Stone and Webster, and though Mitsui Toatsu Chemical was the agent of Lummus in Japan, it set up a contract with Lummus. This led many other companies to adopt the Lummus process, later, with the advent of large-scale production of ethylene.[85] On the other hand, Mitsubishi Petrochemical exported benzene technology to the Soviet Union in 1970, and ethylene and polyethylene technologies to China in 1973.[86]

CONCLUSION

In the latter half of the 1950s, with favorable conditions, all the companies uniformly adopted the same type of strategy and began to manufacture ethylene and its derivatives. In the 1960s, this uniformity in strategies continued in the form of competition for upsizing, such as in building ethylene centers. In other words, in the 1960s, the scaling up mechanism of the 1950s was repeated on a larger scale.

From its start as a new industry in the 1950s to the end of the 1960s, the Japanese petrochemical industry steadily increased its markets and equipment capacities; this expansion, combined with high profit ratios, enabled the industry to achieve rapid growth. Companies experienced rapid expansion, and industrial complexes were formed in various parts of the country. Though new, petrochemicals quickly became a key industry. In the first fifteen years, seen from retrospective view point, the Japanese petrochemical industry enjoyed a tremendous growth or "smooth, fast sailing with the wind at our backs", as Yutaka Katayama, former President of Japan Petrochemicals, recalls, or the heyday of the Japanese petrochemical industry.[87]

Rapid technological progress was among the most important factors in the rapid growth of petrochemical companies. The role played by foreign technology was particularly decisive. Indeed, the chemical industry along with the electrical equipment industry was among those in which the post-war introduction of foreign technologies had been most prevalent. The fifteen years saw the introduction of foreign technology and its subsequent sophistication as well as domestic technology development and the implementation of large-scale equipment. The introduction of foreign technologies was a general success; by about 1970, the Japanese petrochemical industry had succeeded in catching up with Western front-runners, and even surpassed some nations including West Germany in terms of scale. In other words, it ranked beside its counterparts, the United States and Western Europe, at least in terms of scale. Thus, the second trial of Japanese chemical industry to catch up with Western leaders, after the suspension of international technological transfers from the end of the 1930s to the beginning of the 1950s and the consequent half-failed first trial, was this time successful in a clear contrast to the failure of the first one.

However, once more, the success had its limit. By the early 1970s, it became manifest that investments in equipment had been excessive. The 1971 international monetary crisis and the 1973 first oil crisis, especially the latter, struck a particularly hard blow to the petrochemical industry, which relied heavily on oil consumption. Moreover, barriers to technology introduction rose because of narrowing of the technology gap and because trade conflicts with the United States and Europe became more serious.

The Japanese petrochemical industry suddenly became a structurally depressed industry. As Katayama, former President of Japan Petrochemicals, recalls this period, "our ship sailed into storm and stress then ran aground in rough seas during the latter fifteen years."[88] From the 1970s to the early 1980s, bemoaning the pressures of the recession and all the while receiving government policy support, the industry increased its efforts to improve structurally or to pursue a drastic process rationalization.

Thorough process rationalization and other measures, however, had to be implemented to cope with a prolonged depression. The transition to high value-added products and fine chemicals also became a subject of great interest. After having at last felt relief around 1990, the petrochemical companies began to develop high value-added products and fine chemicals, exploiting the results of process rationalization as well as their special characteristics. The third trial for catching up had to be started.

The limit that the successful second trial for catching up faced was also of technological character.

It is true that the Japanese petrochemical industry changed from dependence on foreign technology to improvements upon existing foreign technology and finally to domestic development and invention of technology. Starting about 1970, Japan began to export its own technology to developing countries and later to developed countries as well. However, the task of this industry was to continue expanding the development of original technology, and it still now remains to be solved

To put it differently: vigorous technology introduction, which occurred at the time of the establishment of general petrochemical companies, continued. Technology introduction is a part of technology development, and in reality, technology introduction, its sophistication, and the development of Japan's own technology were a continuous process. In technology introduction in early years, one can recognize the beginnings of technological innovation. Selection of technology occurred after companies had clearly established their targets and decision-making criteria. Once technology was selected, even abandoning their efforts to develop their own technologies, they endeavored to study the introduced technologies thoroughly from scratch. They aimed at a higher level than that of technologies they had received from the United States or Europe, and for that reason, sometimes met hardships. They took pride in, and were particular about, their own strong technology.

Through their continual efforts in the period of technology introduction, not only continuous or incremental development was realized, but also innovations were even possible, although not guaranteed. One must clarify whether the process of foreign technology introduction provided a catalyst for spontaneous domestic technological innovations and if so, what that catalyst was. In other words, this question concerns measuring the range of technology introduction.

To put it differently once more: introduction of foreign technology is one form of imitation. All innovation begins with imitation, so we could therefore say that imitation and innovation are linked. Nonetheless, imitation does not guarantee innovation. Perhaps the concept of "imported" versus "domestic" technology is a static idea. Innovative technology depends on constant technology transfer. It is essential to grasp the dynamics at the heart of the choice between imported technology and domestic technology.[89]

Given the current situation of technology trade, without challenge for original technology, Japanese petrochemical companies cannot survive in the international arena. It was, and still is, crucial whether there will be differentiation among Japanese petrochemical companies' strategies.

Source: *German and Japanese Business in the Boom Years: Transforming American Management and Technology Models* (KUDŌ Akira, Matthias Kipping and Harm G. Schröter (eds)), London: Routledge, 2004, pp. 1–29 (co-authored with Matthias Kipping and Harm G. Schröter).

10

Americanization: Historical and Conceptual Issues

INTRODUCTION

Reappearance of Americanization in the 1990s

AMONG THE MOST important trends in the international economy during the 1990s was the tremendous influence of the American economy, which manifested itself globally. This has led to a renewed debate about a possible Americanization.[1] The argument for Americanization has been fiercely contested with counter argument. This controversy has been linked with that on globalization, which has developed along with Americanization. The debate on convergence or divergence has also developed, arguing whether or not each nation's capitalism with its own character will change through Americanization and globalization.[2] This debate has been continuing even after the prosperity that long-persisted in the United States began to decline after 2000. In spite of the economic downturn, Americanization itself seems not to have lost its dynamics. It is interesting to ask why it persists. Moreover, its consequences are still unclear.

The word Americanization itself has a long history. One of the earliest meanings of the word was nation building in the early history of the United States. Today it is used in a variety of contexts: politics, the economy, society, culture and civilization.[3] Here, we use the word for the transfer of technology, management ideas and practices as well as institutional frameworks from the United States. We call this influence

Americanization when institutions and organizations in other countries use the United States as a 'reference' for local changes. Thus, in our view, Americanization is not a model (or several models) of values and behavior as such, but a process. Its results are characterized by selection, transfer, change and adaptation to local, regional or national circumstances. Americanization does not mean that, after it had taken place, all organizations, institutions, values and behavior had become identical to those in the USA, although they were definitely closer to American models than before.

During the 1990s, re-unified Germany and Japan came under considerable pressure from Americanization and globalization. They were not exceptional in this respect, but these developments had a special meaning for both countries: during the immediate post Second World War period both had already been subject to a significant US influence. Subsequently, for about two decades, during the 1970s and 1980s, they came to represent alternatives to the United States as an example of successful capitalist economies.

Americanization in Germany and Japan

After the Second World War, West Germany, to which we often refer below simply as Germany, and Japan experienced rapid economic reconstruction and high growth-rates on their way to becoming economic powers. As regional powers in Western Europe and East Asia, both countries were important as support for the Pax Americana, economically as well as politically. Moreover, during the 1970s and 1980s, German and Japanese firms and types of capitalism achieved better performance than their American competitor, counterpart and teacher. They differed characteristically from the latter in such areas as owner-manager relations, industrial relations, inter-firm relations and business-government relations. Observers argued for the advent of a 'Rhenish' model of capitalism and Japanese-style management; and they often hailed these as new, even post American models for business management and for capitalism itself[4] The words Germanization and Japanization of business management and capitalism became fashionable. Some even argued that both countries were threatening the United States, referring to the then ongoing strategic alliance between Daimler-Benz and the Mitsubishi business group, bearing in mind the war-time alliance between the German Messerschmitt and the Japanese Zero fighter.[5]

Ironically, from the start of the 1990s, just after the era of German and Japanese success, firms and capitalism in unified Germany and in Japan deteriorated in their performance. They then again found themselves under the influence of the United States. Taking into account the history of Americanization in both countries after the Second World War, we can call this process during the last decade of the twentieth century a 're-Americanization'. It reminds us of a process of ups and downs like the tide: Americanization became strong and weak as time passed. It is because of this that we have suggested that Americanization in the 1990s had special meaning for both countries. Germany and Japan give us ample examples in discussing Americanization. At the same time, American influences need special attention in reviewing the development of capitalism and firms in both countries.

During the 1990s, the influence of American business and capitalism extended to all functions of firms and all aspects of capitalism. At the individual firm level, it was pronounced in owner-manager relations ('shareholder value') and industrial relations (lay offs), in corporate finance, accounting practices, corporate governance, etc. Such American influences in business were closely linked to parallel influences of US-style capitalism in fields such as the finance and insurance sector, business philosophy, business education and consulting. The principal routes for these types of influences were direct investment and multinational firms, but these were not all. Trade, technology tie-ups (licensing agreements), advertising, visits, consultancies and diverse other routes exist; we may also add indirect investment, currency and financial policy, and, recently, economic policy.

The American influence on the German and Japanese economies has therefore become a topic that deserves particular attention today. As mentioned earlier, this phenomenon of Americanization of firms and the type of capitalism in Germany and Japan did not suddenly begin in the 1990s. It was visible on a large scale during the post Second World War decades, and even further back. It was at hand at the end of the nineteenth and beginning of the twentieth century, as well as in the 1920s, as will be seen later in this chapter.

While looking back at the long-term history of Americanization, the contributions of this volume will focus on the post Second World War decades, especially on the 1950s and 1960s, the period when this phenomenon reached a peak. We will try to compare the German and Japanese experiences during these years of rapid economic growth or 'boom', based on questions such as: what are the processes and routes of the respective Americanization? What was its scale in both countries? How should we assess its results? Have both types of capitalism changed as a result of Americanization? If so, how have they changed? Which country has been more Americanized, Germany or Japan? If we see any difference in Americanization of both countries, then what are the reasons for the difference?

Previous research and the focus of this volume

The reasons for this special attention to both, to a certain period and to a German-Japanese comparison, are the following. First of all, research on the history of Americanization in Germany and Japan has so far largely ignored the 'boom' years. Thus, most recent studies of Americanization have focused more on the immediate post-war period, when both countries were occupied by the US army (and the other Allied powers in the German case). In this context, there has been a comparison between both of the occupied countries, Germany and Japan.[6] Second, if comparative studies exist for the era of rapid growth, they focus mainly on the level of the national economy. In Japan, research has been conducted on the comparison with Japan's former model, Germany, paying attention to a parallel history of alliance, defeat, occupation and rapid growth.[7] The 1950s and 1960s were indeed eras of rapid economic growth as well as of rapid business growth in both countries. But it is not enough to describe the rapid growth of economy and business only as phenomena under the American-centred international order or the cold-war order.[8]

It is an important task to clarify the reality of Americanization by entering into firms, the main players of this growth, and for explaining the reasons of high growth in the economy and in business. There is a large and growing number of historical studies on Americanization in each of the two countries. Comparison in the context of firm-level Americanization for the boom period, however, has so far hardly been developed.

Pioneering research on Germany has been carried out since the 1980s by Volker Berghahn.[9] Building on the work of Heinz Hartmann,[10] Berghahn suggested that German capitalism had undergone an Americanization from the 1960s onwards. He also examined the different aspects of this process. Berghahn himself concluded by highlighting the need for further work. Various aspects, such as the acceptance, rejection and revision of Americanization during the 1950s and 1960s, as well as the causes of Americanization, remained to be analyzed in more detail. Furthermore, he took heavy industry and its relations with the government as representative, while in fact other sectors were possibly more open to American influences.[11] Initially, Berghahn's book, which appeared during the period when German Rhenish capitalism was in its heyday, caused comparatively little impact. Perhaps it is not purely by chance that since the 1990s we have experienced a boom in the interest of Americanization, not only in Germany, but also in the whole of Western Europe.[12] Japan, in contrast, did not see any boom, although the discussion is now finally flourishing.[13]

However, there have not yet been any thorough attempts to look at the Americanization of Germany and Japan at the level of the firm in a comparative way.[14] It is therefore crucial to ask how German and Japanese firms showed their own features in this wave of Americanization, and whether these features imparted competitiveness and served as the driving force behind economic growth. If we pay attention to Americanization at the level of the firm, it is precisely during this period that American influence on German and Japanese business was at its strongest. During this period, management skills and technology flowed in a large stream from the United States into both countries. By focusing on the level of the firm we can demonstrate the features and advantages of the perspective of business history, especially since material from company archives about this period are more easily obtained compared to more recent periods.

The remainder of this chapter has three major aims: first, it will put the Americanization of German and Japanese firms into context, by providing an overview of the different 'waves' of Americanization at the level of the firm since the end of the nineteenth century. Second, it will briefly summarize the findings from the individual chapters in this volume. And third, on this basis, it will develop some conclusions from the German-Japanese comparison.

A BRIEF BUSINESS HISTORY OF AMERICANIZATION IN GERMANY AND JAPAN

We will now outline the history of Americanization of German and Japanese firms from the late nineteenth century. In doing so, we find four large waves of Americanization before the 1990s: the first in the period from the late nineteenth century to the beginning of the twentieth century; the second in the 1920s; the third in the immediate post

Second World War period; and the fourth during the 1950s and the 1960s. There is a fifth one during the 1990s, which may not yet have ended, and it seems too early to provide the specific point of view of historians on this latest wave.

The first wave: end of the nineteenth and beginning of the twentieth century

Throughout the nineteenth century, American firms accumulated investment in plant and equipment that was labor-saving and capital-intensive, against a background of an influx of funds, technology and management expertise that came from immigrants. These factors broke down old-style work-skills and gave rise to the so-called American system of manufacturing. This system had a universal character, especially in mass production and interchangeable parts, turned out with big machines, while at the same time it kept its American uniqueness.[15] This became the base for early Americanization or the first wave of Americanization.

The first wave of Americanization in Germany appeared at the end of the nineteenth and the beginning of the twentieth centuries. Large-scale, standardized, American-made machinery, including agricultural machinery and machine tools, appeared in a steady stream on the German market, and the transfer of American technology that went along with them moved ahead.[16] There was some interest in the scientific management techniques developed by Frederick W. Taylor and others. Early attempts to apply them in Germany, however, were not always successful – quite often resulting in strikes.[17] American influence was also visible in universities and research centres; the establishment of the Kaiser-Wilhelm-Research-Institute, today's Max-Planck-Institute, was a response to the American shock. The trust and merger movements in the turn-of-the-century United States also gave a considerable shock to Germany, and occasioned large-scale merger plans, such as those by August Thyssen in steel and Carl Duisberg in the chemical industry – plans, which were not always carried out, at least not immediately. Expressions indicating American influence appeared, such as 'American invasion', 'American danger (*amerikanische Gefahr*)' and '*Amerikanismus*'.[18]

During the same period, the influence of American business also became markedly stronger in Japan, although it did not reach the same scale as in Germany. Taylor's *Principles of Scientific Management* appeared in a Japanese translation in 1913; Japan's first attempts at introducing scientific management techniques happened at about the same time as those of Germany. However, American-made machinery did not make a substantial appearance in the Japanese market. Industrialization in Japan did not reach such a level as to realize an American threat. The trust and merger movements in the United States at the turn of the century did not evoke a notable reverberation in Japan, mainly because Japanese firms, including the zaibatsu-affiliated ones, had not yet grown sufficiently.

The second wave: the inter-war period

During the period following the First World War, American business was generating a new structure of mass production, mass distribution and mass consumption, and had developed forms of enterprise and systems of business management to conform to this structure. Ford's production system had been firmly established in the automobile sector, and General Motors' Alfred Sloan had developed his sales and business management systems. Scientific management techniques had matured. Out of these developments the second wave of Americanization was born. The American system of production and business management was seen to be of more universal character than before.

American firms stepped up their direct investment in Germany during the 1920s.[19] Led by GM, Ford and General Electric, US firms began to produce directly in Germany. This entailed Americanization: the introduction of US methods of production, organization, supervision, distribution, etc. GM's subsidiary Opel, for instance, introduced the production line format. The influence of American styles appeared not only in Opel's management: other firms tried to learn as well, especially in marketing and financial management.

The increasing direct investment of US firms, along with increasing American security investment in Germany, generated a fear of the power of the dollar. There was a fear that Americans would buy up German industry cheaply (*Überfremdung*), especially during the hyperinflation period, when the German currency became worthless. German companies developed their own form of Taylorism, 'industrial rationalization', which became the main response to the American threat.[20] Standardization continued with an eye towards establishing a mass-production system. After a certain time-lag, the shock of the turn-of-the-century American trust and merger wave was countered by a similar German one, which had its peak in the establishment of

Vereinigte Stahlwerke.[21] At the same time German firms established other forms of economic concentrations, such as cartels.[22] Cartels were seen as a general answer to the American method of organization. Thus we find both the take-over of American ideas and structures and the expansion of a competing model.

In the 1920s, the influence of American business, with its established modes of mass production, distribution and consumption, became markedly stronger on Japan, too. American firms also launched direct investment in Japan. Ford and GM started to assemble knock-down kits for cars, and the Ford system was transferred in part. This was one factor driving standardization in Japan. At the same time, it also provided the opportunity for GM to introduce its distribution through dealers, a system previously unknown in the country.

However, American firms' direct investment in Japan did not teach the scale of their investment in Germany. Transfer of production technology from the USA to Japan occurred primarily through technology licence agreements. Experimental application of Taylor's ideas and production techniques also occurred relatively early. Regular on-site application, however, was limited to military arsenals, the railroad ministry, and some private spinning and machinery firms.[23] The response to the trust and merger movements in the USA at the turn of the century did not appear in Japan until the mid-1930s, when steel firms did finally merge to establish Nippon Steel, and Mitsubishi Chemical was established in the chemical sector. However, it can be questioned to what extent these developments were due directly to Americanization or to the influence of industrial rationalization and the cartelization movement in Germany.[24]

The period from the 1930s through to the defeat in 1945 was an era in which Americanization was interrupted and then set aside in Germany and Japan. It indicated the extent to which Americanization had advanced, as well as what happened when the process stopped. American institutions and ideas were Germanized or Japanized, sometimes to the point of becoming caricatures. Consequently, there was a renewed attempt at Americanization in the post-war period.

The third wave: a new economic world order after the Second World War

In repelling Germany's second challenge for supremacy in Europe, and in repelling Japan's challenge for supremacy in Asia, the United States played a decisive military role during the Second World War. In doing so the USA deprived Britain of its leadership and established its own hegemony. In other words, the USA arrived at the position of hegemon, replacing Britain. Hegemon may be defined as a state that leads by overwhelming others not only in terms of political, military and economic power, but also in terms of capacity to enact rules and create order.

The United States established a world order with itself at the center, Pax Americana. The main economic institutional base for this order was the Bretton Woods System: the International Monetary Fund (IMF), the World Bank, and the General Agreement on Tariffs and Trade (GATT). The US established not just an overwhelming dominance in terms of political, military, financial and economic power, but rather established a monopolistic concentration of these, and exerted an overwhelming influence in making the rules for the world system. The existence of a second superpower, the Soviet Union, with an alternative, centrally planned macro-economic and communist political system, as well as the opposition to it, served to strengthen the leadership role of the USA.

Against the background of the emerging cold war order, both the defeated countries, Germany and Japan, became important to American regional strategy in Western Europe and East Asia, albeit important to different extents. For this reason, both received support from the US through the GARIOA- and EROA-programs, the Marshall Plan, as well as the special procurement for the Korean War. American aid helped them to advance on the road to recovery under the aegis of the occupation powers. However, the aid was not totally free but bound to certain steps in opening up the markets to competition. For Germany, the introduction of these steps was monitored by the Organization for European Economic Co-operation (OEEC), which was set up in 1948 to coordinate the allocation of US aid and economic policies in Western Europe. Should these steps not be fulfilled, the next tranche of goods or funds from the Marshall Plan would be withheld.

These programs became powerful instruments of US policy in reshaping the rules of economic proceedings for firms as well as for countries. The international organizations, too, had their set of rules, without which participation was excluded. Germany, and after a time lag of a few years, Japan, joined international organizations such as the IMF and GATT and were integrated into the post-war international economic order. Both countries, sometimes reluctantly, chose to apply American rules, focusing on liberalism and competition, especially in foreign economic relations.

Both countries had been placed under the power of occupation forces since 1945. The way in which that power was exercised brought about important differences. In Germany the occupation was direct while in Japan it was indirect. In fact, however, it was more important that West Germany was occupied jointly along with British and French troops, while Japan was occupied *de facto* exclusively by the USA. This point was decisive in particular for the scale of Americanization: the American coloration was less in Germany because of the joint occupation. Meanwhile, because of embryonic regional integration in Western Europe, the American influence was much weaker than was the case in Japan. The reforms brought about by the occupation forces were focused on the level of the national economy and the institutions. Americanization, including reconfiguration of the large-enterprise system, decartelization, management purges and reforms in industrial relations, proceeded decisively.[25]

The Allied Powers' occupation policy in Germany was to diminish that country as a political and military power. Reforms in the Western Zones advocated de-nazification, de-militarization and economic de-concentration. The US was most stringent on this point. Americanization in the economic system was fairly wide-ranging, from the break-up of large firms, through the relationship between enterprises and the state, to the relationship between firms. At the very least, this corrected the imbalances brought about by Nazi ideology and militarization and served to stimulate political and economic competition. The enterprise system may be viewed as typical cases of this pattern. Decartelization, in some ways, was a campaign to Americanize the German economic system from a mainly cooperative approach to a more competitive one. Labor reform was in part a recovery of the rights to organize and bargain collectively, which had been realized during the Weimar era. Overall, compared to the Japanese case, post-war Germany's economic system changed less than its Japanese counterpart.

For Japan, in contrast, the Allied Powers were in fact one country, the United States, and reform brought on by US policies was a great shock. Reform was thorough, embracing not only the political and economic sphere, but also education, culture, and even the spirit. It did not stop at mere reconstruction and could hardly be characterized as a return to the Taisho Democracy era. The bulk of pre-war systems and institutions were rejected. The US attempted to transplant American systems and institutions through the dissolution of the zaibatsu, democratization of labor, land reform, and other efforts. The flip side of this attempt was that most Japanese were caught up in a deep feeling of defeat, to the extent that defeat was considered not only in military and political terms, but extended to the systems of science and technology. It was even understood as a cultural defeat. The strength of feeling of defeat corresponded to the nature of post-war economic reconstruction.[26]

The fourth wave: Americanization at the firm level in the 1950s and 1960s

The central part of Americanization during post-war economic reconstruction in Germany and Japan was observed on the level of the national economy. While there was also Americanization on the level of the firm, via the occupation forces or American firms, it was more or less sporadic. Once recovery had ended and rapid economic growth had begun, the focus shifted to Americanization from the level of institutions to that of enterprise. This fourth wave is obviously closely connected to the previous one.

As seen above, the predominance of American business already existed in some branches of industry at the turn of the century, even before the US position as a political hegemon had been established. This indicates that the competitive strength of American business has been the foundation for the acceptance of American rules by other countries, in other words for Americanization.[27] The predominance of American firms, and the influence it generated, tended to increase, taking the form of waves – a dynamic which had already become clear during the Second World War. Added to this was the background that the US position as hegemon was established. It is quite natural, therefore, that the fourth wave of Americanization in the post Second World War era was substantially greater than the previous ones. American influence at the level of the firm was not purely a firm-level phenomenon. To a certain extent, American business management became the model precisely because the USA was the hegemon. It was this evidence of superiority that caused managers to take American ideas into their business. The desire to learn from the United States, even in the niche of a defined enterprise and its proceedings, cannot be understood without the general and widespread idea that it was in the USA and no other country that one had to look for improvement and modern solutions.

Under US hegemony, the scale of production recovered to peacetime levels in about 1950 in Germany and 1955 in Japan. Post-war economic controls were almost entirely removed. We may observe that around these years post-war economic reconstruction in both countries ended. 'The post-war period is already over' was the catchphrase in Japan. Up until this point in the post-war economic reconstruction era, the increase in production was understood to be due to the increase in capacity with a focus on quantity. The old processes simply had to be reconstructed and started again. Raw material and machinery, energy and financial means were needed, rather than foreign advice. After this initial reconstruction, however, it became necessary to increase that part of production associated with increasing productivity. The so-called 'productivity centres' were actually established in 1950 and 1955 respectively. The focus also shifted to include quality. This called for investment in modernization, which in turn required Americanization of both technology and management at the level of the firm.

The productivity gap between the USA and both national econo-mies, as well as in technology and management of firms, was obvious. Even German scientists, engineers and managers, insistent on tradition and confident of their own technology and management, became des-perate to absorb technology and management skills from the USA. It is even easier to understand how Japanese technicians and managers were keen to absorb these, even to the point of greed. The primary routes for this introduction were the campaigns to improve productivity, direct investment, and technology tie-ups (licensing). The campaigns to boost productivity initiated in 1950 and 1955 respectively, played a leading role in Americanization.[28] In Germany this campaign was seen as a continuation of the rationalization movement in the inter-war period and was seen to be rather independent from the USA, even if many ideas in the 1920s had actually been taken over from the USA.[29] In Japan, the movement was more clear cut from its tradition and related with Americanization. In both cases, it was not only individual firms that undertook activities directed at Americanization via the route of productivity campaign; business organizations in finance and in indus-try, labor unions, as well as government organizations undertook them as well.[30]

Individual firms, especially large ones, aimed to absorb advanced American technology and management skills through routes includ-ing direct investment and technology tie-ups (licensing).[31] Visits to the USA by leading technical experts and managers were often an impor-tant opportunity for Americanization. In Germany, direct investment was a major route for Americanization. Germany liberalized inward direct investment as early as 1952, and also prepared its legal system. American-owned firms constituted one-quarter of foreign firms at an early date. Japan, on the other hand, did not liberalize inward direct investment until about 10 years after Germany. In contrast to its high degree of dependence on the USA in trade (approximately 40 percent compared to approximately 10 percent in Germany), Japan had an almost negligible proportion of American-owned firms. To that extent, the development of Americanization was more marked in Germany. On the other hand, however, American technologies were widely introduced to Japan via many technology tie-ups (licensing) in the 1950s and 1960s or in the period before capital liberalization. Moreover, many Japanese managers eagerly absorbed American management skills exploiting the chances of technology tie-ups.

Having briefly outlined the longer history of Americanization in Germany and Japan and clarified the position of the 1950s and 1960s within that history, we can reconfirm that the issue of Americanization on the level of the national economy was supplemented and complemented by that of Americanization on the level of the firm. The survey even suggests that Americanization on the latter level became more important and lasted longer than that on the former level.

THE CONTRIBUTION OF THIS VOLUME

This reconfirmation gives rise to a number of questions. For example, what level of technology and management techniques did German and Japanese firms introduce? In other words, were they cutting-edge technologies or just mature ones? In such cases, with what perception, intent and strategy did German and Japanese firms make such choices? How did they perceive the American enterprise system that was itself under transformation in these decades?[32] What, and how, did German and Japanese firms try to learn from American ones? What was the relationship of those introduced with technology and management skills existing within the firm? How successful were firms at learning the technology and management skills that had been introduced? Did German and Japanese businesses have sufficient learning capacity and, moreover, sufficient learning desire? What did they select from the American 'offer'? What were the conduits that were used for the learning process? To what extent were American solutions changed and adapted to local needs?

In this volume, we are taking up five key industrial sectors: automobiles, electrical machinery and electronics, synthetic fibers and rubber, consumer chemicals and distribution. These sectors were growth sectors and modern ones at that time. We can therefore expect a readiness for change as well as a desire for learning in those sectors. We also look at the channels for the dissemination of American ideas in two introductory chapters.

The individual case studies will clarify the entire process of introducing American technology and business management techniques; they will focus particularly on acceptance and resistance in that process and the question about the extent to which Americanization was implemented by German and Japanese managers. They will examine actual Americanization across a variety of firm functions, such as production technology, research and development, employment, distribution, sales and finance. Where possible, the case studies will also look at each of these functions in detail. Finally, they will engage in a debate about whether introduction of American techniques resulted in the establishment of a type of German and Japanese production system and business management that differed from the American. We are, in short, tracing Americanization in German and Japanese firms during its high point in the 1950s and 1960s from a comparative, historical perspective. Through this process we aim to contribute to the understanding of the historical phase of Americanization in the 1990s.

Chapters 2 and 3 look at the different channels for Americanization in Germany and Japan from the 1940s to the early 1970s, corresponding to the third and fourth waves identified above. For the German case, Matthias Kipping argues that, contrary to a widely held belief, many of the American management models were 'imported' rather than 'exported' to Germany. This means that German companies and their representatives actively searched for new ideas and practices in the United States. Until the mid-1960s, much of this activity was conducted through a few semi-public as well as associative institutions. In general, the former went back to the inter-war period, whereas the latter were founded in the late 1940s or early 1950s. Due to their near monopoly in the importation of foreign, American management models, these institutions had a considerable influence on the selection and interpretation of these ideas and practices. Only from the mid- to late 1960s onwards did US multinationals and consulting companies of American origin become more active and influential as carriers of management models. They increasingly displaced the earlier associative channels, most of which only survived in certain 'niches' of the emerging market for management knowledge.

In Chapter 3 on the different channels for the diffusion of technology and management techniques and ideas from the United States to Japan between the latter half of the 1940s and the 1970s, Satoshi Sasaki also highlights that different channels dominated at different stages. At first, under the American occupation, American management systems were introduced through personal exchanges between the occupation authorities (GHQ) and Japanese superintendents with technological knowledge and experience. Technology transfer, especially related to electrical machines and electronics, became important during this, and even more so during the subsequent, stage. Since the Japanese government strictly controlled foreign capital and foreign exchange, many Japanese companies were eager to introduce advanced American technology. In a third stage, the Japan Productivity Center, founded in 1955, promoted the productivity movement, including the dispatch of many inspectors, foreign and domestic training, and the invitation of foreign specialists to Japan. At about the same time, management associations also became increasingly important, often playing a consulting role for companies.

The next two chapters deal with the US influence on technology, production, marketing and supplier relations in the German and Japanese automobile industries. In Chapter 4, Christian Kleinschmidt examines the Americanization of the West German automobile industry between the late 1940s and the late 1960s, focusing mainly on the case of Volkswagen (VW). The German car industry as a whole had followed the American model since the 1920s. Volkswagen pursued a similar strategy from its foundation in the late 1930s. After 1945 it maintained and even expanded its orientation towards the American example, regarding production technology, but also marketing, sales and advertising. Until the 1960s, the success of VW was based on mass production and marketing of the famous 'Beetle', which became a symbol for the emerging consumer society in West Germany and also sold well in the United States itself. But the story of the Beetle also shows how too rigid a focus on the US model and the American market could prove counterproductive. In West Germany, Volkswagen struggled to change its one-product strategy when sales of the 'Beetle' started to decline from the late 1960s onwards. At the same time, the car was no longer competitive in the American market, because a tightening of safety and exhaust emission standards significantly increased production costs.

For the Japanese case, Hirofumi Ueda shows in Chapter 5 how the car producers developed a specific Japanese method of mass production. At the beginning of the reconstruction process of the Japanese automobile industry, car manufacturers realized the necessity of Americanization in business and production systems to ensure rapid growth of production levels and to realize high productivity as in advanced Western countries. They understood that Americanization meant mass production. Their Americanization, however, was Japanese. That is, they established Japanese style assembler-supplier relations for mass production with less investment. Japanese automotive carmakers achieved mass production differently from US makers, who produced many parts in-house in large plants. The chapter examines in detail the cases of Toyota and Mitsubishi. It begins with the so-called Keiretsu Diagnosis in the early 1950s, which analyzed the lessons productivity missions took from their observations in the USA in the 1950s, and identifies differences between assemblers and part-suppliers. It then clarifies how the specific Japanese-style supplier relations emerged when mass production began in the late 1950s and the early 1960s.

The following two chapters focus on the drivers and limits of Americanization in the German and Japanese electrical and electronics industries. Based on the Siemens case, Wilfried Feldenkirchen argues in Chapter 6 that it would be erroneous to speak of an Americaniza-tion of the West German electrical industry. Rather, in the extremely difficult period following the Second World War and during the years of the country's economic miracle, Siemens, like many other West German companies, sought targeted support to compensate for the lack of know-how and competencies. The detailed study focuses on company organization, human resources policy, sales and marketing, as well as key fields of technology such as nuclear energy, semiconductor research and data processing. It shows how outside factors, such as the occupa-tion, economic and industrial policies of the USA after the war, and domestic factors, such as the generation change in management in the 1950s, led to an orientation towards American structures and opera-tional methods in parts of the West German electrical industry. In the end, this led to a mixture of American and German elements in the industry.

In Chapter 7, Shin Hasegawa examines the effects of Americaniza-tion on Japanese electronics firms from the 1950s to the mid-1970s. He looks in particular at the general-purpose computer and semiconduc-tor technologies. While most of the firms in these industries cooper-ated with American companies from the early 1950s onwards, there was a relatively large discrepancy among their absorptive capacity for the new technology. Thus, in computers the results of these technology partnerships varied significantly for each Japanese firm due to the understanding and policies of top management, as well as the conditions of human resources within the firm. In some cases the products of the American firms did not match the demands of the Japanese market, which drove their Japanese partners to produce small- and large-scale computers to complement the US firm's offerings. In the mid-1970s, Japanese firms introduced a variety of computer series to compete with IBM's machines. It was at this time that the Japanese computer firms were able to catch up in terms of accumulated hardware technology and software skills. In semiconductors, Japanese firms also started to absorb American technology beginning in the 1950s. In the 1960s, they successfully introduced a limited scope of independent research and development, even if American firms remained the predominant players in the worldwide market. Only during the 1980s did Japan come to dominate certain segments. The basis for their relative success in both industries during this period, the chapter argues, was laid in the 'Japanization' of technologies originating from America during the preceding decade.

Chapters 8 and 9 look at the reaction of several companies in the artificial fiber and, for the German case, rubber industries. Christian Kleinschmidt examines three German chemical firms, Hüls, Glanzstoff and Continental, which had played a leading role in the fiber and rubber industry worldwide up to the Second World War. The three companies had cooperated for example in the production of car tyres: Hüls produced the raw material 'buna' (artificial rubber), Glanzstoff produced tyre cord and Continental completed the tyre manufacturing. All three companies had been successful internationally but lost their ability to compete during the war and were overtaken by their American counterparts. After 1945 they therefore depended on American aid to produce 'nylon', which proved to be superior material in the fiber and tyre sector. While the adoption of US technologies was necessary to recover their former strength, the orientation towards the American model was less pronounced in the field of industrial relations. These companies tried to introduce American-style human relations, but the German model of co-determination, involving management and worker representatives, proved resilient.

In Chapter 9, Tsuneo Suzuki examines the reaction of the Japanese artificial fiber industry to the American challenge, focusing on the major producer Toray. He shows how changes introduced in four areas enabled the company to acquire a distinctive competitive advantage during the 1950s and 1960s. In most of these cases, Toray struggled with, resolved and assimilated the American model. The first area concerns efforts made by the top management of Toray to exploit the intervention of the occupation forces, which aggressively introduced American business practices into rayon factories in Japan. The second area is the SQC (statistical quality control) movement, which deeply penetrated into Toray and, together with job analysis, was applied in the chemical company to maintain the manufacturing process. The third area is marketing, which the top management of Toray saw as one of the most successful business practices in the USA. Toray managers dispatched their subordinates to the USA to collect information which could be applied to the Japanese market. The fourth area is Toray's introduction of nylon patents and know-how from Du Pont to consolidate its development from the late 1930s. By investigating these different but related areas, this chapter uncovers the relation of 'new technologies' at the time in the world and the attitude of Toray towards them.

The two following chapters also look at chemicals, but consumer chemicals, especially detergents based on the cases of Henkel in Germany and Kao in Japan. In Chapter 10, Susanne Hilger argues that the German company, which had been one of the biggest players in the European consumer chemical industries since pre-war times, embraced Americanization after 1945 only rather reluctantly. She sees as the main trigger for this change the massive expansion of Anglo-American competition into the West German and European markets. After the Second World War, the big American 'soapers' Colgate and Procter & Gamble, as well as the Anglo-Dutch Unilever group, restarted their pre-war business with tough profit considerations and aggressive marketing strategies. In the view of the Henkel executives, these companies showed no respect for the 'culture' and traditions of the European business world. The Henkel management reacted at first to maintain the traditional way of dealing with competition, i.e. the conclusion of market regulating arrangements. Against the background of increasing competitive pressure, however, Henkel had little choice but to establish new strategies. These included the diversification into new product areas (e.g. cosmetics or food), the implementation of new organizational structures and planning instruments, as well as the adoption of modern American marketing techniques.

In Chapter 11, Akira Kudō and Motoi Ihara demonstrate a profound American influence on the Japanese consumer chemicals producer Kao

Corporation. This concerned the introduction of American technology and management techniques; these were transferred by various modes, including visits of managers and engineers to the USA, product analysis, and also competition, and covered a wide range of business activities, such as marketing, production technology and labor management. The company, however, was not only an imitator. American firms, from Procter & Gamble to other firms, were both teachers and rivals to Kao. Through its relations with American firms, Kao widely introduced American practices, adapting them to the Japanese environment, especially to the lifestyle and taste of Japanese consumers. The authors argue that this explains how Kao became competitive in the Japanese market in the 1950s and 1960s, and also then after the 1970s, in overseas markets.

The final two chapters of the volume focus on distribution. In Chapter 12, Harm G. Schröter shows that the US example had a profound impact on the West German distribution system, especially on retail trade. In his view, it seems justified to speak about a 'revolution' since everything changed: rules, organizations, sites, relationships, values and behavior. In terms of retail concepts and formats, the major change concerned the introduction of self-service. Other American innovations, such as supermarkets, chain stores and discount-markets, were also adopted. A key issue in this respect was the use of cars for shopping, which became a common feature in West Germany during the 1960s. In some areas, for example frozen food, Americanization took quite some time to take hold. In others, namely processed food, it only happened towards the end of the boom period. The author also shows that the process of Americanization in the German distribution system was a reflected one. West German consumers discovered the advantages or disadvantages of the US innovations fairly quickly. By contrast, store owners and managers needed more time to become Americanized, mainly because of the mental changes required. They had to learn to think in terms of sales rather than supply, to offer choices rather than necessities to their customers, to compete rather than cooperate with each other.

For the Japanese case, Mika Takaoka and Takeo Kikkawa focus in Chapter 13 on the changes in the supermarket system from the 1950s to the 1970s. They divide the growth process of the system into two phases: an Americanization process in the 1950s and 1960s, and a Japanization process in the 1960s and 1970s. In their view of the process of Americanization, the following two facts were most significant: the appearance of supermarkets following American models, and the application of chain operation theories. In the subsequent process of Japanization, the following three factors stood out: first, the unique financing technique based on wholesalers activities; second, the development of general merchandise stores; and third, the system innovation in perishable food sales. Their analysis finds that, on the one hand, the impact of American trends on the Japanese distribution industry after the Second World War was large. On the other hand however, in almost all individual cases the Americanization gave rise to Japanization, which was a process of adaptation of American techniques to the unique conditions in Japan.

Of course, more research has to be done, both on Americanization and on the comparison between the different processes of Americanization in Germany and in Japan. However, some preliminary thoughts and results of the comparison, based on the studies in this volume, can be suggested here.

PRELIMINARY CONCLUSION: COMMONALITIES AND DIFFERENCES

We have summarized the findings from the detailed case studies under four headings: periodization, the scale of the American influence, the Americanization process and, finally, results.

Periodization: Americanization in the 1950s and 1960s

As explained above, there have been several waves of Americanization in both countries. We decided to concentrate on the fourth one in the 1950s and 1960s, considering it to be more substantial than the previous ones.[33] The chapters in this volume have clearly confirmed this hypothesis. They show that during the earlier wave, the initial phase of reconstruction immediately after the Second World War, no special advice from the USA was necessary or even desirable, since the old processes of production and distribution were best known by those who ran them. At the beginning it was more important for Germans and Japanese to reorganize everyday life, to reconstruct transport lines, to rebuild plants and to restart production. Firms and managers were confronted with American rulings such as the dissolution of cartels, zaibatsu, or large firms as well as the purges of top managers.

In addition, initially the Americans were not welcome in either country in 1945, although the hostility was less in Japan than in

284 THE JAPANESE AND GERMAN ECONOMIES

Germany. Their forces came as victors and occupants. True, in both countries the old systems of behavior and values were shaken to the core, and many economic actors looked for a reorientation. Obviously the USA appeared to command a superior system for economic life, but still there was reluctance on the side of the losers to accept it. Initially, defeat did not mean a preparedness to learn. Moreover, the USA ordered without consultation. Where new systems were pressed upon the vanquished with political or military threat, they lasted only as long as the threat lasted, because a precondition of all learning is the positive attitude of the actor, and Americanization is just another type of learning.[34]

The overall attitude towards the United States in West Germany changed only gradually. Public opinion definitely shifted during the blockade of Berlin, when in 1948 Soviet troops blocked all land transport to the capital, and the Americans supplied the Western parts of the city by air. In Japan, the antagonistic feeling against the victor was not as great as in Germany and, moreover, it diminished as early as the beginning of the US occupation.

With respect to firm-level Americanization, demand for a new orientation emerged after the immediate reconstruction of war damages, together with the qualitative change of improvement in production, distribution, management, industrial relations and the enlargement of firms. The productivity gap compared to the USA was found to be very wide and, thus, much could be learned. Now advice was sought after, and it was quite easily obtained. The Americans not only offered their expertise but also the means for the process of selection and transfer through the productivity campaign. Businessmen, labor union representatives and administrators were invited to travel to the USA and were shown around the sites the Americans wanted them to see. At the same time, in many reports the invited experts not only admired what they could learn, but also underlined the access and the openness with which their questions were met. Coming from more closed societies, they had expected much less.

Thus, a massive transfer of technology and management ideas and practices, although of course always selected and adapted, took place through the various channels mentioned above. In both countries, the bulk of such transfers cumulated in the 1950s and 1960s, first in Germany and then in Japan. Together with the economic boom, mass consumer markets emerged, first in Germany and then in Japan. Mass markets entailed issues that were unknown before in both countries, such as self service, discount markets, shopping by car, and here again the USA acted as a place from which to learn. Last, but not least, a new generation of managers, no longer connected to the war-economy, but eager to modernize and more open to learn from abroad, entered the field of decision making from the second half of the 1950s onwards. This situation could obviously not last forever. It was quite natural that this wave of Americanization began to ebb after the transfer process had been accomplished and a learning and transformation had taken place in both countries.[35]

Breadth and depth of Americanization: reasons for the differences

In the century-long history of Americanization Germany was ahead of Japan. Even if we limit our sights to the period after the Second World War, Americanization started earlier in Germany, whether on the level of the national economy during the post-war recovery period or on the level of the individual firm during the era of rapid growth in the 1950s and 1960s. But the scale of post Second World War Americanization, both at the level of the firm and the level of the national economy, was both broader and deeper in Japan than in Germany. The shock of American supremacy was far greater in Japan than in Germany.

Again on the level of the firm, both German and Japanese managers relaunched their businesses under the same initial conditions of defeat and occupation. In Germany the desire to introduce technology and management techniques from the USA was more limited, and the partial introduction often stalled at the point of trials. Japanese managers, by contrast, showed a desire to fully accept American technology and business management techniques. Both German and Japanese managers had a high capacity to learn or relearn from the USA, but Japanese managers clearly had a stronger desire to learn.

Germany's Americanization was not so thorough in the field of the productivity movement as in Japan. Links to tradition remained important. The attitude was to build on indigenous technology and management techniques and to add from the USA those that were necessary or seemed desirable. The Japanese productivity movement stood in contrast to this attitude. While it is certainly possible to confirm their continuity with pre-war campaigns, the extent of such continuity was not as great as in Germany. Japanese campaigns were filled with the desire to introduce American technology and management techniques. This desire existed to a degree not seen in

Germany. The productivity movements in Germany and Japan both yielded remarkable results, but their processes differed, particularly concerning the scale of Americanization and the control that indigenous institutions exercised over the selection and interpretation of US management ideas and practices, which was much higher in Germany than in Japan.

At the same time, German companies were subject to much stronger American competition and immediate challenges, mainly through direct investment by American firms. As mentioned above, Germany had liberalized inward direct investment in 1952. Direct American investment in Germany was thriving from that year on, and American ideas, technology and management techniques were also introduced via this route. Having said that, while many aspects of the on-the-ground situation are not well known, it appears that the scale of Americanization was not necessarily that great. This was true even in the cases of American firms' German subsidiaries, such as German Ford and Opel.[36] By contrast, American firms did not invest actively in Japan during the 1950s and 1960s. Inward direct investment was still regulated, and capital liberalization did not occur before the 1970s. American firms were still not regarding Japan as an important region for investment.[37] During the boom years, the primary route for Americanization in the sphere of technology was licensing. Technology tie-ups covered practically the whole range of industries and were concluded in large numbers. In the case of technology tie-ups most Japanese firms tried to introduce American technology and management to the full. Moreover, Japanese firms entered into licensing agreements in large numbers and across a broad range of fields. Technology tie-ups thus became the primary route for Americanization in Japan.

The differences between Germany and Japan in the scale of Americanization were caused by differences in the preparedness of learning as well as in the differences in the principal routes for the phenomenon. Among the major causes for the differences in the scale of Americanization is the difference in the magnitude of post-war reforms during the occupation and recovery periods. In Germany, the United States' ideas to reform the country met with resistance from German business managers. Germans partly successfully played the occupation forces against each other; for example, in the area of industrial relations where the USA had very different ideas for Germany compared to the British Labor Government. Furthermore, with the start of the Cold War the international environment changed during this period. Germany became a major field of confrontation and contest. This again enlarged the German room for manoeuvre against US policy.

Reforms were realized, but inconsistently, in comparison to Japan. The break-up of firms ended in a partial and inconsistent state, and some, such as the large banks, successfully started to reassemble from the first day. Germany also basically maintained the legislation on enterprise, so that, for example, the authority of the supervisory board was as strong as it had been before. The post-war reforms were in part a return to the Weimar system of the 1920s. The old generation of managers remained active to such an extent that Japan's case was not even comparable, although a new generation of managers also partly emerged as mentioned above. Some of them were the very embodiment of managerial control, while others were constrained by owners. Traditional family control remained over a broad range of firms. As a result, reluctance or even resistance to introduce American ideas, technology and management seems to have been much greater than it was in Japan.

In Japan, the United States implemented its reform plans relatively intact, partly because the USA carried out a single-handed occupation. Resistance on the part of political actors, managers included, was quite weak, and change did not occur in the East Asian political environment until relatively late. This fact caused the delay in Americanization in East Asia in comparison to Western Europe. Reforms in Japan were thus implemented in a thorough fashion. The break-up of firms was thorough, and the occupation authorities swiftly executed their plans for eliminating excessive economic concentration. Legislation on business was also drastically revised following the American model. While there was some degree of continuity between the pre-war and post-war periods, Japan implemented post-war reforms using the USA as a model. A new generation of managers grasped the reins of power as the old generation was swept away. Reforms extirpated family control and instituted wide-ranging managerial control. Japanese managers' resistance to the introduction of American technology and business management techniques was weaker as well as different from that in Germany.

The gap between Germany and Japan in technological and business development must be cited as another cause of the difference between the two countries in the scale of Americanization. Germany had already gained a prominent position during the Second Industrial Revolution as a leader in heavy, chemical and electrical industry. By 1950, the country had arrived at the mature stage in those industries. Germany was also entering the era of full-scale mass consumption. Through the 1950s and 1960s, technology and business management were quite literally rebuilt. In contrast, Japan in and around 1950 could not stop at mere rebuilding. Japan had to take on right away the task of heavy and chemical industrialization. The age of mass consumption had not yet arrived. For these reasons, technology and business management required substantial reform. This large gap in the development of technology and management gave rise to the different degrees of Americanization.

That Japan, through the 1950s and 1960s, also chose Germany as a subject for study in the productivity movement, and that Japan introduced various technologies from Germany chiefly through licensing agreements, shows how large the gap was between the two countries. The final reports of the studies conducted by the United States Strategic Bombing Survey after the end of the Second World War underlined the existence of this gap. The reports expressed awe for the level of technology Germany had attained and for its productive potential in principal industries, including aircraft, shipbuilding, chemicals and petroleum. At the same time, it clearly expressed its evaluation of the low level that Japan had reached relative to Germany.[38]

The process of Americanization: between rejection, selective learning and wholesale adoption

Even German managers and technical experts, who took pride in their own management and technological skills, recognized the gap between their own and the American expertise and were willing to absorb the latter. This absorption, however, was ultimately based on and filtered through their own command of technology and management. Thus, it represented the addition of American techniques and proceedings to their own, not a build-up from scratch. There were limits to the desire for Americanization; at a certain stage managers and technical experts felt they had learned enough.

In contrast, most Japanese technical experts and managers were desperate to introduce advanced American technology and management practices as a whole, for a moment even to the point of denying previous achievements and traditions. Learning and relearning became a firm-wide move, whether it occurred in the productivity movement or in licensing agreements. Managers and technologists aimed for the broadest and deepest introduction possible. But at the same time Japanese managers and technical specialists did not completely discard the technology and management standards their own companies had achieved. Through the process of introducing (learning and relearning) American technology and management techniques, they did not fully set aside their own firms' technology and management styles. The desire to revitalize their own technology and to act according to their own style of management was never completely denied.

If we turn to the level of society or the national economy, the difference between Germany and Japan in their acceptance or rejection of American technology and management practices was both a matter of degree and of style. There were pro- and anti-introduction factions among managers in both countries, just as there were factions within organized labor for and against changes in the American direction. This is the case even if we assume that the rejection faction was stronger in Germany than in Japan. If we look at the level of the individual firm, however, Japanese enterprises, which showed a hunger to introduce technology and management practices from the USA, at the same time showed strong resistance towards doing so. In other words, a strong desire to introduce technology and a strong resistance to doing so co-existed at the same time within the same firm. The strong desire shown by the total introduction of American technology and management practices was accompanied by resistance, which was stubbornly backed by the firm's own technology and management practices.

This acceptance-rejection antinomy dogged Japan's Americanization far more than that of Germany. Resistance also appeared in Germany, but the manner in which the acceptance-rejection antinomy manifested itself was different than in Japan. The clash of values between the adherence to tradition, on the one hand, and reform, on the other, was more pronounced in Japan. The strains, which enveloped Japan during the 1950s and 1960s, were exceptional even in terms of modern Japanese history. Those strains appeared most strongly at the level of the firm. Managers' desire not only to introduce technology and management practices from the USA, but also to make those things their own, was quite fierce. This differs from the German pattern of adding American technology and management techniques to one's own! And even while it was imitation, it often went beyond imitation. At certain times imitation itself failed, while at other times improvement led to innovation. Thus, while Japanese managers and technical experts tried to be good pupils of their American teachers, they were sometimes bad students at the same time. Opinions about the introduction of technology and management practices were not clear-cut along the lines of autonomous technology versus introduced technology. Thus, the policy formulation process concerning that choice ought not to be explained solely in terms of backwardness of a certain economy. It rather should be explained from the perspective of learning and relearning.

How can we explain the differences between Germany and Japan in their acceptance or rejection of Americanization? Differences in the scale of Americanization or in the necessity for it are each likely factors, but are probably not sufficient explanations in themselves. An alternative suggestion would stress the different paths Americanization took in the respective countries: associative channels and foreign direct investment in the case of Germany and technology tie-ups in the form of licensing agreements in the case of Japan. Other explanations worth examining include business-nationalism on the part of Japanese technical experts and managers or the formation of business groups. These developments, though, are not likely to be the decisive factors that explain the unique shape of acceptance and resistance in Japan. Rather the decisive factor is to be found in the continuity and discontinuity of management.

Historians of science and technology long ago established that any substantial transfer of technology and management techniques is bound to a transfer of culturally specific values. This includes basic and universal characteristics of American modes of thinking and ideas. It is because of these traits that resistance to technology and management practices arose at the same time as they were accepted. Such a transfer of values occurred through a German or Japanese filter. In the process of transfer of technology and management practices the most powerful filters were, of course, the managers themselves.

In post-war Germany, although such filters temporarily thinned, making them more permeable, they regained their solidity and capacity relatively quickly. As a result, connections with tradition in Germany were relatively clear.[39] Post-war Japan experienced the same thinning of its filter, but in the case of Japan it was decisive. While occupation policy also purged managers in Germany, the purge was implemented more strictly in Japan. In the latter case, recovery from the purge took relatively longer, and the new filters differed from the old. They were executed by a new generation of salaried managers.[40] Thus, if we compare both countries, we find that the continuity of management and managers' values in Germany was much more profound than in Japan. Such values were characterized by the survival, on the one hand, of the old generation of managers and, on the other, of family control in a large sector in Germany.

Results: emergence of new types of capitalism

Notwithstanding the breadth and depth of the differences of Americanization, the performance of the national economy and business management in both Germany and Japan was similarly favorable. That both countries, after experiencing defeat and occupation, showed a performance superior to all those who won the war, was certainly no accident. However, to what extent this superior performance during the boom period up to 1973 was due to Americanization is a subject for speculation.

The difference in performance between the German and Japanese national economies and firms can partially be explained by the gap in the stage of development between firms and economies in the two countries. More precisely, Japan had the space in which a more powerful late developer's advantage could work. This space was equivalent to the difference in the scale of Americanization. However, the connection might not be as straightforward as has been suggested above. We have to consider what connection exists between Americanization and the performance of a nation's economy and firms. This entails the suggestion that differences in economic performance may be connected to different degrees of Americanization. This would lead to the formula: the more Americanization, the better the performance, which, we underline again, can be understood only as a research-stimulating hypothesis. This hypothesis should be evaluated together with another, somewhat competing one: not the extent of Americanization, but the challenge of and response to the whole of the US model (or models) would explain the remarkable fact that both losers of the war economically performed better than the winners.

Let us assume for the moment that good performance occurs when there exists simultaneously both a strong desire to introduce and a strong resistance to introduction. This would correspond to both the German and Japanese cases. Management education serves as an example of resistance. American-style business schools were not popular either in Germany or in Japan, and so Americanization of management education did not appear on a large scale in either country. This fact led to an avoidance of 'Wall Street syndromes', such as short-termism, and to both countries' showing better performance than the USA.[41]

Especially after the large wave of economic Americanization had ebbed, German and Japanese characteristics became manifest in business management and technology in both countries. Own types of business management and systems of production technology, different from those of the USA and from the previous indigenous ones, established themselves. They emerged together with different types of political as well as industrial relations. Thus, after a period of incorporating American ideas, behaviour and values, their own and new types of capitalist systems took shape, during the 1960s in Germany and during the 1970s in Japan. These types of capitalist systems include the one later known under the brand name of Rhenish capitalism in the case of Germany, which entered into serious (possibly terminal) crisis after the reunification of the two German states in 1990 and in the following decade. This later became famous as a Japanese style of management, which also lost its way, in the case of Japan, in the so-called bubble economy before the long stagnation in the 1990s. Of course these types could not be viewed merely as a return to tradition. These German and Japanese versions were largely a transformation of American models. They emerged under the impact of, as well as in contest with, American models. And this is exactly the meaning of Americanization.

Source: *German and Japanese Business in the Boom Years: Transforming American Management and Technology Models* (Kudō Akira, Matthias Kipping and Harm G. Schröter (eds)), London: Routledge, 2004, pp. 221–245 (co-authored with Ihara Motoi).

11

Emerging Post-war-type Managers and their Learning of American Technology and Management: The Consumer Chemicals Industry and the Case of Kao

DEFINING THE TOPIC

Typified by synthetic detergents, the consumer chemicals industry was one of the industrial sectors that helped advance the Second Industrial Revolution and establish a mass consumption society.[1] In Japan, the consumer chemicals sector traces its history back to the end of the nineteenth century. Its full-scale development, however, arrived only after the Second World War with the full advent of a mass consumption society in Japan. In the post-war period, especially in the 1950s and 1960s, in this industry like many others in Japan, the gap in technology and management techniques between Japan and the West, especially the United States, was very large. Consequently, the impact from the United States was overwhelming. In the Japanese consumer chemicals manufacturing industry, firms actively learned from the United States and attempted to catch up.

This chapter examines this era of full-scale development in Japan's consumer chemicals industry during the 1950s and 1960s. It will focus on one of the leading firms in the sector, Kao Soap, currently Kao, and will clarify both the firm's strategy for catching up with American

293

industry and the firm's business activities. Since its founding in 1887 and its entry into soap manufacture in 1890, Kao has long occupied, along with its primary competitor Lion Soap, now Lion, a leading position in the Japanese consumer chemicals market. Currently, it is diversifying from soap and synthetic detergents into cosmetics, hygiene products, and so on. Even though Western firms like Procter & Gamble and Unilever have fully entered Japan, Kao continues to maintain its position. In recent years it has developed plans to expand actively into Western and Asian markets as well.[2]

In the 1990s Kao became one of Japan's outstanding firms, receiving high marks for its production technology, research and development, marketing and distribution, as well as both its management and its internal sharing and disclosure of information. In terms of information disclosure and corporate governance, Kao is regarded as riding the crest of the globalization wave. At the same time, however, the company also holds out a more singular management philosophy. The previous chairman of Kao, Fumikatsu Tokiwa, in pointing out and criticizing Japanese companies' enthusiasm for things American, most strongly insisted that Kao was a firm with a Japanese corporate identity. So, in fact, Kao also appears representative of a Japanese firm. The American influence in Kao's history, however, is apparent and may be traced back to the firm's inception. Particularly during the 1950s and 1960s, Americanization held great significance for Kao. The technology and management methods available to the present-day Kao are the products of a discordant history of accepting this massive influence from the United States, of resisting that impact, and of attempting consequently to establish its own identity. Because most observers have overlooked this history, they often tend to see Kao as a 'pure' Japanese-style firm.

While Kao was a company that thoroughly learned from American industry, at the same time it appeared completely Japanese. By recovering the history of the process and consequences of the Americanization process at Kao in the 1950s and 1960s, this chapter will attempt to clarify, from a business history perspective, this paradoxical situation.

INITIAL CONDITIONS AND POLICY PRECONDITIONS

Technological accumulation

The inter-war period was the dawn of a mass consumption society in Japan. During this period Kao achieved major expansion in both its product development and distribution.[3] On the product development side, Kao began selling a synthetic soap equivalent to Procter & Gamble's Ivory, as well as a synthetic detergent for industrial use (household detergents remained powders). On the distribution side, the existing distribution organization was restructured to accommodate the launch of the synthetic soaps. The company also improved the efficiency of its transaction relationships with local wholesalers which had grown increasingly complicated.[4] Kao began efforts to develop its own technology in the 1930s and the first half of the 1940s. The core of this technological development was a technique for manufacturing aircraft lubrication oil by hydrogenating high-grade alcohols produced from coconut oil. As applications, Kao developed production technology for sorbitol, styrene resin, paraffin oxidation and the like. This research prepared the way for Kao's subsequent developments in surface science and polymer chemistry. Kao also launched a research council called the Research Study Group which pioneered experimenting in the management of R&D in Japanese industry. In labor management, the company eliminated the apprentice system in favor of continued training of company personnel in technology and marketing.[5]

In this process of managerial and technological development, there were influences from both German and American firms. From 1928 to 1929, Tomiro Nagase, the second president of Kao, took a study tour, of Europe and the United States. The managerial and technological methods learned from Western corporations on this tour greatly influenced Kao. In the inter-war period, German corporations' influences exceeded those of American companies. During the 1930s Japan imported dye adjuvants for the textile industry from Germany. Stimulated by this opportunity, in cooperation with other Japanese companies Kao undertook the joint purchase of related German patents. This project provided the basis for Kao's successful domestic manufacture of industrial synthetic detergents.

Thus, prior to the Second World War, Kao had attained a certain level of technology and management. Although not the leader within the soap market, Kao did belong to the upper group. Its own development of hydrogenation technology for aviation lubrication oil manufacture marked the highest point in technological development. Ironically, limited supplies of raw materials other than coconut and fish oils provided the primary reason for the development of this own technology. At the same time, however, there were limits to how fully such technology could be realized in mass production. Still, as described later, these experiences in experimentation at an early stage became the preconditions for the quick, decisive and thorough subsequent introduction of technology. This hydrogenation technology became useful in the post-war production of synthetic detergents. Equipped with hydrogenation facilities, the Wakayama factory arose as the driving force in Kao's post-war factory system. The technologies accumulated during the pre-war period became the basis for business expansion in the post-war period.

Corporate merger

The immediate aftermath of the Second World War produced circumstances of resource scarcity and heightened demand for manufactured goods. The government implemented both controls on feedstock oils and fats and a quota system for soap. Later in the midst of the Korean war, the price of feedstock oils and fats dropped precipitously, leaving many companies that had purchased materials at high prices with severe operational difficulties. Most Japanese firms in the immediate aftermath of the Second World War experienced business difficulties or experienced profound labor conflicts; Kao fared similarly. By accelerating conversion from military to civilian goods production and by restructuring its labor management system, Kao overcame its operational problems and labor strife.[6]

Meanwhile, in 1954 Kao Soap and Kao Oils and Fats – two companies that had separated of their own volition immediately after the war – reunited. In the process of overcoming its business difficulties and uniting these two firms, the company renovated its ownership and management structure. Within the overall stock ownership profile the proportion of stocks held by the founding family drastically declined. Stock ownership became more broadly dispersed. Moreover, the founding family was driven from top management in favor of salaried managers, initially managers brought in from the outside, who took over management control.[7] Kao thus transformed – or at least began the transformation – from a family business into a managerial enterprise. Completed prior to the arrival of rapid economic growth, the merger – and the accompanying reforms of ownership and management – proved a timely event. At this point, Kao contrasted strongly with Lion. Established around the same time as Kao in 1891, Lion was Kao's longstanding competitor. The company subsequently split into Lion Abrasives and Lion Oil and Fats; their reunion only occurred much later in 1980. In the difficulties following the war, Lion's management continued to be drawn from its founding family. Similarly, the two companies undertook post-war business reduction and rationalization independently.[8]

Even during the difficult post-war period, Kao's research and development team remained very much alive. In research and development at Kao, the collection of information from overseas publications played an important role. The 'PB Report', a collection of German materials on chemical technology seized and disclosed by the American military, was the most important of these. The Kao technology team made frequent visits to the Hibiya Library run by the occupation authorities (GHQ). There they learned much from the PB Report on file there. For example, one such fruit of their study was the surfactant Levenol, coming to Japan from Germany via the United States.[9]

A supervising engineer's visit to the United States

Although Kao started learning from the United States during the prewar period, it did not proceed in earnest until after the war. The opportunity for this was a visit to the United States by one of Kao's supervising engineers.[10] Against a background dominated by a deepening cold war, GHQ distinctly changed its occupation policy towards Japan in order to aid the reconstruction of the Japanese economy. As part of this, through the Science and Technology Administration Council (STAC), GHQ sponsored a program for Japanese firms to dispatch first rate technical specialists and managers to American businesses, universities and other institutions. Founded in January 1949, STAC was responsible for GHQ's science and technology policy. It had authority to assign foreign exchange to fund research in specific fields and research trips to the West.

Eizo Ito, the president of Kao Soap before the merger in 1954, received news of this program and, despite the harsh business climate, enrolled managing director Yoshiro Maruta. Prior to the war, Maruta had played a central role in the technical team developing technology for aircraft lubricant manufacture using hydrogenation. Now, Maruta was the plant chief at Kao Soap's main plant at Wakayama, the same plant that drove Kao's fortunes following the merger. Graduating from a national college of technology and being a chemist, Maruta had advanced through the company to become Ito's right hand man as a salaried manager. After the merger and Ito's rise to president, Maruta also ascended to the top management positions of president and then chairman – which suggests something of his abilities. Having such a career, Maruta, as a manager, was able to observe both from a technical and from a management perspective. Maruta toured the United States from November 1950 to March 1951. Preceding the first delegation sent by the Japan Productivity Center by 5 years, Maruta's visit occurred very early in the post-war importation of American expertise to Japan.

From the start Maruta showed a deep interest in the American oil- and fat-based chemicals industry. For example, because non-branded bar soaps were the mainstay of the Japanese laundry soap market, there had been scant attention to quality as a basis for competition. Maruta held a critical view of this behavior. He noted how brand name products held a large share of the United States market, how firms gained consumer support and kept market prices stable through clever marketing, and moreover how they managed to strengthen their businesses by keeping costs down through thorough rationalization and high-volume production. Based on these insights, Maruta studied trends in the United States oil- and fat-based chemicals sector, especially in the surfactant and synthetic detergent industries.

His densely scheduled observation tour of the United States demanded concentrated mental effort. At a stop in Hawaii on the way over, Maruta's observations had already begun. There, Maruta picked up a package of Procter & Gamble's synthetic detergent Tide. The product's contents interested him. Launched in 1946, Tide was a heavy-duty synthetic detergent produced mainly from petroleum-based alkyl benzenes. As such, it was representative of the synthetic detergent products then becoming more popular in the United States.[11] Maruta sent the sample back to Kao's headquarters, attaching a note detailing how Tide was capable of cleaning not only wool but cotton clothing as well, how coconut oil was used as one of its ingredients, and how this detergent could be manufactured in Japan. By the time that Maruta returned to Japan, Kao's technical team had analyzed Tide's different components and projected that Kao would be able produce it with the company's current technology. Analysis of Tide led to the development of Wonderful, a synthetic household detergent that typified the future of Kao.

Once in the continental United States, Maruta inspected not only soap and detergent companies like Procter & Gamble, Lever Brothers and Colgate-Palmolive, but also petrochemical and electrical firms as well as universities and research laboratories. Most of what he learned, however, he learned from the soap and detergent companies, especially Procter & Gamble. Maruta observed production equipment for soap and synthetic detergents (Tide) at Procter & Gamble's Cincinnati plant. The firm's high technological standards and rational business management techniques strongly impressed him. The highly automated, continuous, high-volume production equipment left an especially deep impression. For example, the moulding and packaging of soap, which in Japan still depended upon manual labor, had been automated using moulding and heat sealing machines connected by conveyor belt. Maruta learned much from Procter & Gamble, and, above all, learned about equipment modernization, automation, mass production and quality control.

Maruta also learned about business methods, such as sales techniques, from Procter & Gamble. An example of these was the '10 days 2 percent' cash transaction system, which later enabled Kao to revise transaction practices among its existing Japanese domestic distributors. In addition, at Procter & Gamble, Maruta learned various other aspects of business management, including public relations, systematic market research and business accounting that allowed one month's profits or losses to be calculated at the beginning of the next month.[12] In this way, acting as both a supervising engineer and a manager, Maruta undertook an extremely thorough study trip by himself to the United States comparatively early. Maruta recognized America's overwhelming technological and managerial lead. This understanding became the starting point for Kao to overcome this gap. The trip provided an opportunity for Kao to develop new products in the future and a starting point for technology import from America. It was also the beginning of exchange between Kao and Procter & Gamble, exchange that became a valuable source of information for Kao. Although, after this, like many other firms, many other managers and engineers from Kao would visit the United States, there would never be a visit with quite the significance of the first.

There were a number of prerequisites to learning from the United States. First, an important initial condition at Kao itself was the accumulation of technology and the business development led to its dissolution and merger after the war from the pre-war era through the post-war reconstruction era. Second, during the early 1950s, visits to the United States by leading technical experts at Kao provided the point of departure for further learning from the United States. Finally, the Japanese government's prohibitive policies on foreign capital in the 1950s and 1960s provided the policy circumstances influencing Kao's corporate activities. We cannot ignore the last condition because of its considerable regulation of Kao's attitude towards introducing technology and management practices from Western companies. During the 1950s and 1960s the Japanese government adopted foreign capital policy that strictly controlled inward direct investment. These measures continued until the Japanese government implemented capital liberalization around 1970.[13] This contrasts with West Germany. There, already in 1961, inward direct investment had been fully liberalized, and West German firms were already encountering foreign capital in their domestic markets.

During this period, Western firms gradually became more interested in the Japanese market. In the petrochemical industry, chemical engineering firms and medium-sized chemical firms specializing in certain areas were the main players moving into Japan through licensing. The West's leading large firms in the consumer chemicals field, on the other hand, had less interest in the Japanese market. In the light of the subsequent expansion of the Japanese market, this reflected these companies' effective underestimation of both Japanese firms and their domestic market. Japanese firms worked to introduce advanced technology and management practices through product analysis (reverse engineering) and licensing. Kao conducted product analysis and copied management methods as well. Kao also became one of the most active Japanese firms in the introduction of technology and management techniques via licensing, as seen below.

Development of new products

To the technical accumulation from the war period was added the fruits of Maruta's observation tour of the United States and the information collected from overseas publications. The technology researchers at Kao – comprised of both Kao Soap and Kao Oils and Fats – took up the development of new products like synthetic neutral shampoo and synthetic detergents which had not yet been marketed in Japan.

The development process for these new products reflects both the changes and constancy in the characteristics of life in Japan. In the 1950s and 1960s a mass consumption society finally emerged fully in Japan. In textiles, as cotton goods became pervasive, chemical fibers and then synthetic fibers quickly became popular. Also, electric washing machines spread into general household use; a suitable powdered or liquid synthetic detergent for such electric washing machines was needed. In terms of the Japanese diet, the consumption of fresh vegetables began to become more commonplace once the consumption of salad oil and other vegetable fats and oil began to expand. As a consequence, kitchen detergents began to become more widespread.[14] Using seminars, films, pamphlets, and advertising through radio, television, and the newspapers, Kao worked to accelerate these changes. Differences in lifestyle compared to the West, however, remained. For example, whereas in the West warm water was preferred for washing, in Japan cold water was the norm. Also, in terms of water quality, the hard waters common in the West differed from the soft water widespread in Japan. Even consumer characteristics differed; for example, Japanese hair is sensitive and easily damaged. In the consumer chemicals industry, there remained special market qualities that could not be ignored. Kao's goal was to develop products conforming to a Japanese market that continued to change even as it retained many special qualities.

Synthetic neutral shampoo[15]

When Kao developed synthetic neutral shampoos, it drew directly on American-made products and analyzed them from a variety of perspectives. It does not need repeating that Maruta's observations from the United States were an important resource in this. By analysing products popular in the United States at the time, Kao's research and development team determined that, because they were compounded from petroleum-based alkyl benzenes, American-made shampoos were too irritating to the skin to suit Japanese tastes. Using technology that Kao itself had accumulated in the pre-war era, Kao's technical team decided to use as their chief shampoo ingredient a powdered surfactant (alkyl sulfate) for industrial use, Emal, that was itself based on coconut oil. Into this they mixed an agent to prevent dirt being redeposited and to yield a new shampoo with better foaming, rinsing, anti-dandruff and anti-split end qualities. For the packaging, Kao took a cue from a product produced by the American company Colgate-Palmolive and adopted aluminum foil, which protected against moisture. Because this was the first use of aluminum foil for packaging in Japan, Kao had to make extraordinary efforts to develop the in-house technology to print onto the aluminum foil and process it into a tube.

Following its launch in October 1955, the resulting product – named Feather Shampoo – became the product that typified Japanese shampoos. Though it took American products as its model, it was developed based on Kao's existing development capabilities and thoroughly in conformity with the tastes of Japanese consumers.

Synthetic detergent[16]

At the time of Maruta's inspection tour of America, synthetic detergents were coming to the fore in the United States. Because they did not use traditional soap raw materials, they were called soapless soaps. From Maruta's perspective, these products were made using the same principles that had been used to make Excelin, a synthetic powdered soap Kao had developed before the war on the basis of German patents.[17] Excelin used as its raw materials high-grade alcohols made from coconut oil. Although American soapless soaps represented some measure of advancement in that they employed petroleum-based alkyl benzenes, one-third of the raw materials was still derived by the sulfonation of high-grade alcohols. At the time, Kao did not lead the soap industry. It was rather pushing against the more powerful firms in the industry like Mitsuwa Soap and Miyoshi Oil and Fat. Many firms, however, had still not come to a firm conclusion whether to go with soap or detergent in the future. Kao forecast the arrival of an era of synthetic detergents and began development at once (see Figure 11.1).

Procter & Gamble's Tide detergent, the prototypical synthetic detergent or soapless soap, was chemically analyzed in detail by Kao's technology team and its make-up ascertained. At the time, electric washing machines had only recently begun to become popular and hand-washing remained the norm in Japan. There was little demand for powdered detergents.[18] Moreover, products based on higher alcohols were preferred because of the good tone and soft touch imparted to the cloth. Whether the Japanese market would broadly welcome a Tide-type synthetic powdered detergent made from petroleum-based raw materials was, therefore, a matter of some concern.

Figure 11.1 Production of soap and synthetic detergent in Japan, 1945–75

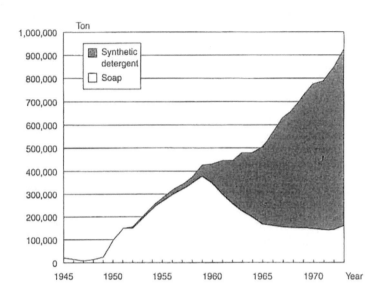

Source: *Nihon sekken senzai kogyokai nenpo* (Annual Reports of Japan Association of Soap and Detergent Industry).

In July 1951, Kao first launched a high-grade alcohol-based synthetic detergent, Emal. This only represented a name change to the synthetic detergent Excelin that had been introduced prior to the war. Emal's applications were limited to wool, silk and chemical artificial fibers. Unlike Tide, Emal could not be used on cotton products, which limited demand for the product. In October of the same year Kao embarked on the marketing of a Tide-type heavy duty detergent, Kao Laundry Powder, although 5 years behind Tide. Perhaps in order to appear American, the name was later changed to Wonderful. This helped boost sales, and Wonderful became Japan's prototypical household synthetic detergent. Unlike Emal, Wonderful could be used on all fiber products. Along with the adoption of the new name, Kao developed an original formula for compounding the product. Compared to Tide, which used primarily petroleum-based raw materials, Wonderful drew on the tradition of Excelin and contained a larger proportion of high-grade alcohol. The alkyl benzenes that comprised one ingredient in Wonderful were later ordered from California Chemical, a company which subsequently provided technology to Kao.

Wonderful did win consumer approval, but compared to Tide there were quality problems. Because it was an 'after-blend' type of product, its fine particles caused sneezing when used. For this reason, Kao's next objective was to establish production technology to dry already compounded raw materials to produce a granulated detergent.

Thus, sales of the newly-developed synthetics, Feather Shampoo and Wonderful detergent, grew, riding the wave of rapid growth in Japan. Feather Shampoo, the Tokyo plant's main product, and Wonderful, the Wakayama factory's primary product, each made major contributions to Kao's industrial performance. The success of both products matched the plan of Eizo Ito, the then vice president of the new Kao Soap after the 1954 merger, to 'move forward like Procter & Gamble at Wakayama and like Colgate in Tokyo'.[19] These products contributed to the fully-fledged development of a mass-consumption society in Japan.

Although the development of both products used knowledge that Maruta had gained in the United States, these products were not simply copies of American products. Both products achieved a certain level of quality using the existing stock of technology within the company. Also, they were developed with the aim of adapting this quality to specific Japanese consumer tastes. Nevertheless, problems remained. Compared to American products, quality was inferior. As before, the lack of mass-production technology remained a problem. In addition, the synthetic detergent industry was shifting to petroleum-based raw materials, whose price was lower and more stable. Consequently it was essential that Kao move to petroleum-based surfactants. For this reason, introduction of new technology was unavoidable. This led Kao to introduce technology from American firms

Introducing production technology

Continuous sulfonation: introducing technology from the Chemithson Corporation[20]

In 1956 Kao undertook a large-scale capital investment plan at its main Wakayama plant, with the goal of improving the quality of Wonderful detergent and increasing production. The plan was named the 'AW Plan' from the initials 'A' for alcohol and 'W' for Wonderful. Equipment for executing the plan could be procured domestically. Kao was dissatisfied with its performance and so purchased nearly everything from the United States. Purchases included continuous sulfonation equipment from the Chemithson Corporation and spray-drying equipment made by Industrial Engineering, Inc. Chemithson's continuous sulfonation equipment was used in the sulfonation of alkyl benzenes and high-grade alcohols. Industrial Engineering's spray drying equipment was used to address Wonderful's quality problems that were described above.

Kao received technical guidance from the American firms on how to set up the equipment and conduct trial runs. There was not enough budgetary slack to allow use of outside engineering firms, however, so Kao was forced to go it alone, depending on literature information on the overall engineering of the project. Still, since the construction of the pre-war hydrogenation equipment, Kao had accumulated little in the way of engineering experience. Therefore Kao hired a specialist in chemical engineering, Noboru Yasumura, from Mitsubishi Oil, and worked to foster its own engineering capacity by making him head of engineering. Kao's formula was, with the exception of civil engineering, architecture and electricity, to rely entirely on itself and in particular upon its supervising engineers. This approach called for capable supervising engineers that could largely decide plant efficiency. Great confidence resulted from the successful design, construction and testing of such comparatively high-level equipment.

This type of self-help in engineering capability led first to improvements in the technology introduced and subsequently to technological innovation. Spray dryer no. 2 was produced domestically through reference to the blueprints for spray dryer no. 1 bought from Industrial Engineering, Inc. Moreover, Kao added improvements. A little later, after efficiency and maintenance problems were noted in the sulfonation equipment from Chemithson, Kao designed improvements to the equipment. Kao solved these problems in the late 1960s by developing reaction equipment known as 'climbing film reactors.'[21]

Alkyl benzenes and lubricating oil additives: technology transfer from the California Chemical (Chevron Chemical) Company[22]

Kao introduced technology for manufacturing alkyl benzenes and lubricating oil additives from California Chemical (later Chevron Chemical), abbreviated Calchem below, a subsidiary of Standard Oil of California. Calchem was famous as a maker of lubricating oil additives.

At that time it was drawing up plans to manufacture lubricating oil additives in Japan through a joint venture. Kao announced its candidacy to be a partner in the joint venture. Both sides reached agreement, and in May 1961 the joint venture, Kalonite Chemical, was established. The capital shares were: Kao 45 percent, Calchem 45 percent and Nomura Company, the intermediator, 10 percent.

A broad division of responsibilities was worked out for the joint venture, with Kao in charge of overall management and Calchem in charge of technological development. Opinion was, however, divided as to production. Initially Calchem tried to have Kao manufacture on consignment; Kao objected to this arrangement, however, as it regarded production technology as critical. As a result, Calchem's production technology was installed, and an automatic control system modelled on Calchem's Oak Point plant was introduced to a new plant in Kawasaki. While Calchem was in charge of the basic design of this facility, Kao was responsible for the detailed design, under Calchem's guidance.

Various arguments went back and forth between the American and Japanese technology teams because of differences in design concepts. Understanding the difference in design concepts between Japan and the United States was in itself a form of learning for Kao. Of course, Calchem's efficient design methods based on technical standards, its management methods for project organization and so on, were not an inconsequential subject for study. Because of huge bodies of technical material and advanced engineering methods carried out at Kao, where initially the accumulated engineering capacity was poor, a passion for America spread among Kao's engineers. Through the cooperation with Kalonite, Kao's engineers had the opportunity to encounter genuine engineering practice. On the other hand, from the point of view of Kao's engineers, the design based on Calchem's technical standards appeared to raise the cost of construction materials considerably, because it assumed one size fits all applicability. The Kao team would have to consider thoroughly this point if they were to accept it.

For construction and operation, Calchem dispatched two engineers and Standard Oil of California sent one. Kao sent the manager for Kalonite Chemicals, Akira Numata, to visit the United States on an inspection tour of Calchem's factories. During construction, many engineers from Kao participated, assimilating the contents of huge amounts of technical standards, manuals, and so on. Simultaneously, to acquire operating technology, several people were dispatched to the United States.

Kalonite Chemicals reinforced its facilities after 1965. At that time the Kao technology team moved to domesticate production of its American equipment. At that point, they were provided with data on the analogous equipment at Calchem, which they analyzed and tested repeatedly. As a result, the quality of Kalonite's products garnered praise as the most outstanding among Calchem subsidiaries. Through this chain of borrowing and indigenization, the Kao technology team learned American mass-production technology and engineering techniques. The introduction of technology from Calchem was a response to the rise of petroleum-based synthetic detergents. After the introduction of this technology, it became possible for Kao to manufacture alkyl benzenes for petroleum-based surfactants without depending on imports from Calchem any more.

Surfactants and polyvalent alcohols: borrowing technology from Atlas Chemicals[23]

Kao also introduced production technology for non-ionic surfactants, polyvalent alcohols, polyurethane and other materials from Atlas Chemical, which originated at Du Pont. Atlas was a well-known producer of non-ionic surfactants like Tween and Span. Although Kao already possessed a stock of surfactant technology, the company was hoping to acquire from Atlas production technology for the superior non-ionic surfactants. Beyond surfactants, Kao also aimed for other production technologies for chemical products such as polyurethane.

Although Atlas had tried to initiate business in Japan through contacts with Nippon Oil and Fat, the negotiations had ended poorly. Kao was informed of the results of the contacts. In February 1962 Kao and Atlas held their first meeting and went ahead with contract negotiations. The foremost problem during the negotiation process was the product lines the joint venture would handle. Both Kao and Atlas were manufacturing surfactants. Because surfactants are quite diverse and because there was no method for classifying them perfectly, both firms found it difficult to separate their respective markets. As a last resort, in the joint-venture contract they agreed that the non-ionic surfactant 'scope of product' would be the 'contribution' of Kao-Atlas. Hard-to-classify products, clearly classifiable as non-ionic surfactants yet developed solely by Kao, came to market one after another. The cement dispersing agent Mighty, which was brought to market in the spring of 1966, was typical of these.[24] This product was recognized, on an exceptional basis, as a Kao product via an exchange of personal notes between Atlas Vice President Robert P. Barnett and the Kao technology team. Still, dissatisfaction at these limitations increased internally among members of the Kao camp.

Meanwhile, the Ministry of International Trade and Industry (MITI) issued instructions based on Japan's foreign capital regulations to the joint venture. The Ministry took a strict position towards Atlas. Noting that in the joint venture, the Japanese side should hold the majority of equity, MITI directed that Kao should have a 51 percent stake. In August 1963 the licensing agreement was approved, and the joint venture Kao-Atlas was established. Kao held a 51 percent capital stake, and Atlas 49 percent. The substance of the venture was 'the manufacturing and selling of surfactants, polyvalent alcohols, and polyester resins'. In February 1964 construction of facilities began at the Wakayama plant. Atlas was in charge of the basic plans and dispatched technicians; Kao was the main coordinator of the construction itself. For sales and research training Kao dispatched to the United States the five employees chosen for loan to Kao-Atlas.

How was Kao's introduction of technology from Atlas evaluated? Within the Kao technology group there were differences in this assessment. Initially, doubts existed at Kao concerning how much need there was for Atlas. When Kao-Atlas was established Kao expanded its central research and development facilities, the Industrial Science Research Laboratory, to absorb the Atlas technologies, and the research results generated at the laboratories were almost entirely Kao's original ones. In the 10 years following the start of the joint venture, hardly any new technology came from Atlas. What of the engineering methods as well as the marketing methods demanded by technical service requirements for chemical products? For Kao, which had already learned much engineering technology through its joint venture with Kalonite Chemicals, there was little new in the Atlas engineering technology. At this point, Kao learned little from Atlas.

From the start, however, Atlas' goal had been the expansion in the Japanese market of its Tween and Span products and subsequently Atlas' corporate headquarters had entered into the British ICI group. Thus, it should not necessarily be thought that Atlas' technological capabilities had declined. The secondary effects of technology introduction cannot be ignored. First, Kao developed experience in the manufacture of other products beyond surfactants such as polyester and sorbitol. Second, it found in Atlas' particular approach to surfactants a way to expand further its technical stock. Third, by undertaking exchange with American and British firms, Kao was able to receive foreign business know-how. If we include secondary effects like these, introduction of technology from Atlas led to the strengthening of Kao's surfactant and other industrial chemicals business and, indirectly, of its raw materials base for detergents and other household products.

Thus, the first case described learning stemming from the purchase of machine equipment. The next two examples demonstrated technology introduction based on licensing. Through this series of technology transfers from US firms, Kao acquired advanced technology for surfactants and other chemicals that were raw materials for synthetic detergents. When they turned to licensing, Kao adopted the joint venture format ultimately as an expedient for introducing technology. These transfers of technology played a major role in the sudden increase in the synthetic detergent business and in the fleshing out of the chemical products business at Kao. Not only that, they enabled Kao to learn advanced methods across the management spectrum, including engineering techniques, research and development, and marketing techniques, especially those for industrial chemicals for which technical service was central.

At the same time, an opposition of interests arose between Kao and the American firms. For Kao, it was desirable for the American firms to withdraw from Japan once a certain amount of learning had been achieved. The American firms, however, intended to expand their business in Japan. What allowed Kao to realize its own goals was the fact that Kao had created a system that eliminated the need for the American companies by accumulating its own stock of technology.

LEARNING MANAGEMENT TECHNIQUES

Marketing methods

A cash transaction system

Kao introduced the '10 days 2 percent' scheme, a cash transaction system that Maruta picked up from Procter & Gamble, for some products in 1960, and for their entire line in 1961. It replaced a transaction system based on credit and rebates.[25] Because the discount rate of 2 percent every 10 days was considerably higher than even contemporary bank loan interest rates, sharp merchants actively utilized the new cash transaction system. It rendered the previous, slow-moving bill clearance system unnecessary and shortened the transaction period. By doing so, capital turnover increased, thereby increasing business efficiency and allowing greater allocations for research and the like.

The cash transaction developed further and bore fruit in the 1970s as the exclusive sales company system. The formation of the exclusive sales company system needed the implementation of an additional condition, the Resale Price Maintenance Agreement System.[26] Based on the recognition that soap, detergent, cosmetics, medicine, books, etc. were exempt from the anti-trust law, the Resale Price Maintenance Agreement System aimed to maintain the wholesale and retail prices of these goods. This differed from the American anti-trust laws. Coming from America, the cash transaction system interacted with Japan's price maintenance system to produce Kao's particular distribution system.

Procter & Gamble's basic marketing strategy was to undertake price competition without regard for profit. At the launch of a new product, Procter & Gamble invested heavily in marketing to drive its competitors from the market. This approach featured aggressive promotional campaigns with distribution of free samples. In contrast, averting from a bold strategy to promote sales in response to competition from other companies, Kao considered of primary importance the establishment and maintenance of an efficient distribution system. Partially, the influence of Japan's distribution system, designed as it was to prevent 'excessive competition', limited sales promotion

Advertising techniques

Kao regarded an integrated marketing strategy as including not only distribution but also sales and advertising. Kao began advertising with radio spots in 1953. Around 1960, it quickly shifted focus to television. Throughout the 1950s and 1960s, advertising typically stood at approximately 10 percent of sales.[27] As an important component of Kao's active marketing strategy, advertising was strongly influenced by Procter & Gamble.

Kao's advertisements appear at first glance extremely local to Japan, as befits something so close to the lives of ordinary Japanese people. In reality, however, they were an attempt at modern marketing, and they were strongly influenced by Procter & Gamble's techniques. Rather than giving priority to image, they clearly demonstrate the quality of Kao products to the consumer. This sort of awareness already could be seen prior to the war. For example, in a Kao Soap advertisement the characters 'purity 99.4 percent' were reproduced on a figure of a traditional Japanese woman wearing a Japanese cook's apron. This followed Procter & Gamble's slogan '99.44 percent pure' extolling the virtues of its Ivory soap. Kao's language paralleled Procter & Gamble's catch phrase closely.[28] In the sponsorship of radio and television shows, Kao lagged behind Procter & Gamble (which had started sponsorship) and other American firms' methods by about 5 years.

Of course, this copying did not continue forever. Procter & Gamble's television advertisements unconsciously reflected the patterns of American life. Consequently, they were sometimes incompatible with Japanese consumers' sensibility. For example, the laundry detergent Cheer was described in a commercial as 'works the same in any temperature'. Because, unlike the American and European, the Japanese usually used cold water, this copy was not effective. Although Kao continued to emphasize clearly the quality of its products, Kao organized them to agree more with the patterns of Japanese life and the particulars of the Japanese market. Since the 1970s, when Procter & Gamble entered Japan, advertising became a sort of cultural barrier to entry.

An attempt to introduce the product manager system

In the 1960s, along with its chief rival Lion and other companies, Kao attempted to introduce an American-style product manager system, including a system of brand managers with much narrower authority. This movement was broadly visible in the consumer products sector. The product manager system had been driven by the notion of product management, in which the profits for products and brands were tracked individually. Japanese firms recognized the effectiveness of product management as a response to the need to unify marketing functions – for example. advertisements and sales – as well as to attain product diversification. Procter & Gamble was viewed as the model firm typifying product management. But ultimately, at least in the 1960s, product management did not take root in Japan.

In the case of Kao, already in 1960 a goods planning department, responsible for market research and design improvements, had been established. In 1967, Kao set up a marketing department to strengthen its market research. At the same time, it introduced a brand manager system. In 1970, Kao created product managers to supervise the brand managers for each product line. With the organizational changes of 1973, however, the product managers disappeared, although the brand managers remained as they were.[29] At Kao, the exclusive sales company system took the place of product managers. With the establishment of sales companies at the start of the 1970s, the front line for Kao's sales division moved from traditional wholesalers to the sales companies. In short, as a seller Kao moved into a closer relationship with the consumer and became able to grasp market movements with a higher degree of sensitivity. Because sales companies could recognize the movements of individual brands, Kao was able to have a more fine-grained product line-up.[30]

However, despite this sort of learning, in this most American field, Kao was clearly inferior in comparison to Procter & Gamble, a company that had developed and accumulated marketing theory since the 1920s. In 1970 Maruta saw marketing, rather than research and development, production technology or distribution, as the point where there was the largest gap between Kao and the likes of Procter & Gamble and Colgate-Palmolive.[31] One reason for this was that, despite an overwhelming desire to discover more, opportunities for learning were limited. One of a few exceptions was the continuing exchange of information with Procter & Gamble, which had continued following Maruta's 1951 visit to the United States, and which provided a valuable opportunity for such learning. The acquisition by Kao of a Procter & Gamble subsidiary in Taiwan provided another such opportunity.[32]

Personnel management methods

In the 1950s, American style personnel management based on ability pay was enthusiastically introduced into Japan. Although examples of an American style function pay existed, from the combination of meritocracy with Japanese circumstances, an ability-based grade system soon became widely spread.[33] Under the ability-based grade system, the employee was graded on their ability to carry out their duties and performance. The grading was used in promotion and wage decisions. As a system, the ability-based grade system was a certain kind of meritocracy. Its primary characteristic was that even though work might not change, wages could still increase. As a result, this system became a mechanism for promoting the development of capabilities in the work force.

Kao was one of the first companies to adopt the ability-based grade system. In January 1956 the company outlined the 'New Grading System'. Unlike its predecessor which was based on educational achievement, work tenure, and age, Kao implemented a grading system based primarily on workers' ability and performance to carry out their duty.[34] The nucleus of Kao's personnel system based on meritocracy was its evaluation system. Although ability, performance, character and behavior had been important under its previous evaluation system, and was aimed at strengthening the development of employee capabilities, Kao added self development and individual enhancement plans under the new system. In 1965, Kao introduced specialist work systems and discontinued compensation by post. This raised the status of staff employees as opposed to line employees. Although Kao's personnel management based on meritocracy was pioneering, it was pioneering in that it allowed space for compromise with its previous system. Of course, in that it lacked the possibility of demotion, there were areas where this meritocracy was not always fully applied. However, in its regard for the development of capability and flat organization to name only a few characteristics, the larger structure of Kao's current personnel system was created in this period. In addition, in 1960, Kao expanded the previous management sections, establishing an integrated planning department staffed to collect external data, establish operational plans, and so forth.[35]

Thus, American companies, especially Procter & Gamble, appear to have influenced Kao strongly in various management areas. In marketing, however, because of limits on the learning process, Kao's learning was less. Instead, the company developed its own system of exclusive sales companies. In personnel management methods, consideration was given to the continued introduction of meritocracy in the previous management system.

CONCLUSIONS

Outline

In a protected Japanese market, fierce inter-firm competition developed. Kao dominated the early market for Tide-type heavy-duty detergents and also led in the process for softening detergents. (This was linked to a change in raw materials from hard alkyl benzene ABS to soft alkyl benzene LAS.) In kitchen detergents, however, in 1956 Lion released and subsequently led the market for neutral detergents. Although Lion was overwhelmingly strong in the market for toothpaste products, Kao held one corner of it.[36]

From the 1960s to the early 1970s, Kao stood at the head of the synthetic detergent market, consistently ahead of Lion in market share (see Figure 11.2). By the end of this period, Kao had acquired, along with its chief rival Lion, the status of a leading firm in Japan's consumer chemicals industry.

Figure 11.2 Market share of synthetic detergent in Japan, 1960–76

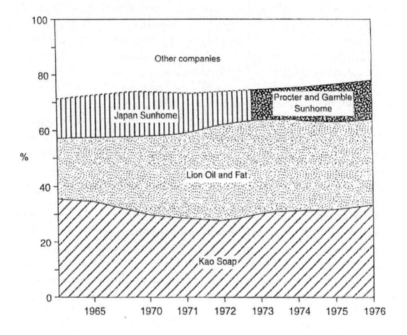

Source: *Yushi (Fats and Oils)*, 1977, vol. 30, no. 13, p. 28.

Note: 'Procter & Gamble Sunhome' has now been renamed 'Procter & Gamble Far East, Inc.'; similarly, 'Lion Oil and Fat' is now 'Lion Corporation', 'Kao Soap' is now 'Kao Corporation'.

Most of this success was based on Kao's ability to learn from American firms. Even in places where, looking from today's perspective, Kao seemingly felt little American influence, it is possible to discern real effects on the firm's management and technology resulting from Kao's knowledge gained from the United States. Behind this outcome lies Kao's aim, in every facet of management to copy thoroughly American corporations, beginning with Procter & Gamble.

Beginning with Procter & Gamble, what did Kao learn from the American firms? How did it learn these things? What level of American technology and management methods did Kao introduce? Alternatively, what did Kao dare *not* to learn, assuming that 'unlearning' is also a learning technique? How did the results of Kao's learning from Procter & Gamble and other American firms contribute to shrinking or eliminating the technological and management gap *vis-à-vis* American firms? In the conclusion to this paper, we would like to provide some answers to these questions.

Shape and medium of learning

Visits by managers to America provided the opportunity for the introduction of technology and managerial methods; subsequently Kao undertook active learning through technology introduction based on licensing. Kao adopted methods like the acquisition of technical standards materials and the dispatch and exchange of engineers and managers to do this. During product development, reverse engineering was also practised. Almost no learning occurred through internal direct investment.

Fields of learning

The content of the learning was multi-faceted, extending from product development, through production technology and marketing to personnel management and other fields.

Their partners in learning

Kao's partners in learning were likewise diverse. While Procter & Gamble's influence was probably greatest, Kao learned from many American and European firms.

Depth of learning

The opportunity to learn from the United States saw rapid increases in the levels of technology and management methods. Good examples are product development based on reverse engineering and learning through engineering technology, Kao did not, however, simply introduce these American firms' technologies and management methods, but rather adapted them to the requirements of the Japanese marketplace and labor relations. Kao did not adopt products that would be difficult to accept in Japan. This stemmed from Kao's understanding of the Japanese market and from possession of its own stock of technology. Examples of this were the development of synthetic detergent and shampoo in product development, the introduction of the exclusive sales companies system in distribution, and the introduction of the ability-based grade system in personnel management.

Subject of learning

What sustained this kind of technological borrowing was the powerful desire of engineers and managers to learn. The salaried managers who headed Kao in the post-war era believed that, having been isolated from the technologies developed by the advanced nations during the Second World War, they found themselves technologically blinkered. For people who thought this way, the fastest way to rebuild the company was to absorb advanced foreign technology, especially from the US, even if that meant some sacrifice.

Outlook: during and after the 1970s

Despite widespread and thorough learning from the United States in the 1950s and 1960s, today Kao can be regarded as a Japanese company mainly because it carried out product development closely tied to the needs of the Japanese consumer and established its own distribution systems and advertising methods. The Japanization of these technical and managerial methods occurred in earnest in the period of capital liberalization at the beginning of the 1970s, when Procter & Gamble changed from teacher into competitor.

Having nearly completed its program of trade liberalization from 1967 to 1973, the government changed its foreign capital policy and embarked on gradual capital liberalization. Oil and fat-based products such as soaps and detergents were marked for liberalization in the third stage from September 1970 onward.[37] Around this time, at long last, leading Western firms made clear their interest in the Japanese market. Among these firms, Procter & Gamble had the greatest presence.[38] Prior to capital liberalization and following Maruta's visit to the United States, Kao had chosen Procter & Gamble as its instructor. Kao tried to learn thoroughly American technology and managerial methods from Procter & Gamble. By allowing tours of its factories and research laboratories to Kao employees visiting America, Procter & Gamble became an important source of information to Kao for technological development. Kao also offered up information by providing factory tours and the like to Procter & Gamble personnel visiting Japan.

Prior to capital liberalization Procter & Gamble was an excellent instructor to Kao, although, at the same time, little by little both sides came to regard each other as their future competitor. Following capital liberalization, this latter aspect became clear. On the Kao side, Yoshiro Maruta, who was appointed President in 1971, saw Procter & Gamble as both Kao's best teacher and its strongest competitor.[39] In Maruta's words, one can see a love-hate relationship in Kao's relationship towards Procter & Gamble. In the spring of 1970, Procter & Gamble sounded out Kao regarding cooperating in the synthetic detergent business. This plan collapsed before the two companies had entered into earnest negotiation. Subsequently, in 1972 by making a capital investment in Japan Sunhome, Procter & Gamble formed Procter & Gamble Sunhome and entered the Japanese market for real. The company's main products were the heavy-duty detergent Cheer and the disposable diapers Pampers.[40]

Other Western firms followed into the Japanese market. Colgate-Palmolive attempted a tie-up with Kao. This cooperative relationship was to have sold Colgate products through Kao's sales companies, and it seemed that selling toothpaste and other Colgate products would have the advantage for Kao of increasing the number of products that its sales companies handled. Without an agreement about overlapping products, however, the cooperative relationship never materialized.[41] Unilever also created a joint venture with Honen Refineries called Honen Lever in 1964. In 1972, Unilever created a joint venture called Japan Cosmetic Soap between Honen Lever and Mitsuwa Soap; Honen Lever provided 70 percent of the capital with the balance coming from Mitsuwa. It entrusted soap production to Mitsuwa Soap. In 1973, Unilever made its own independent investment with the formation of Japan Unilever. Like other Western firms, Henkel showed interest in the Japanese market. By the late 1960s there had been contacts between Henkel and Kao. They too bore no fruit. Henkel's full-scale move into Japan happened during and after the 1970s, and the partner Henkel selected was not Kao but Lion instead.[42]

Kao met this assault of foreign capital. In the face of continuing severe competition for a share in the detergent market, Kao aimed to diversify away from its core detergent business. One component of this was the launch in 1968 of the base cosmetic Nivea built upon technology imported from the West German company Beiersdorf.[43] This goal of diversification became especially strong during the 1980s.[44] Kao further promoted the development of products in response to the Japanese consumer, the construction of an independent distribution system and the development of advertising methods. Thus, since capital liberalization, at least within Japan's domestic market, Kao has resisted the onslaught of Western corporations.

Kao has also earnestly expanded its international business operations through overseas direct investment.[45] Since 1990, however, in both its increasingly internationalized domestic market and its overseas markets, Kao has reportedly tough games. Because the conditions for competition have changed, using only its current competitive advantages, Kao is increasingly less able to compete. Various recent attempts at Kao to improve management reflect this problem. Although the particulars have changed, the attempts at self-reform from the 1950s and 1960s continue.

Source: *Approaches to Corporate Governance* (Kudō Akira (ed.)), Institute of Social Science, University of Tokyo, Research Series, No. 3, 2002, pp. 5–15.

12

An Introduction:
Approaches to Corporate Governance

I. LOCATING THE PROBLEM

JAPAN'S ECONOMY, WHICH became the object of international attention and admiration after the two oil crises of the 1970s, experienced a bubble, epitomized by stock and real estate speculation, during the latter half of the 1980s. It then experienced the collapse of that bubble in 1990–91. During the 1990s, the Japanese economy faced an extended period of stagnation, evidenced by low growth rates and rising unemployment rates (although there were, of course, alternating up and down phases). For Japanese firms, too, the 1990s were a difficult decade. The decade saw the deteriorating performance of many firms, and failures affected not only small and medium-sized firms but large firms as well. In the retail sector, supermarket chain operator Yaohan and the Sogo department store chain failed, while in the financial sector, Hokkaido Takushoku Bank, Yamaichi Securities, and the Long Term Credit Bank of Japan went under one after another. In the industrial sector, or, more pointedly, the core automobile sector, in which Japanese firms had become leading global players, Nissan fell into business difficulties, consequently looking to France's Renault for rescue and becoming affiliated with the French carmaker. Recently, Mitsubishi Motors has also fallen on hard times and requested German-American DaimlerChrysler to bail it out.

Japanese firms, which had swept the world with their direct investment offensive during the 1980s, faced a severe situation and often failure in their overseas projects during the 1990s, pulling out one by one. The Japan that had risen so rapidly as an investment and creditor superpower during the 1980s soon hit a massive wall in the 1990s. There was a feeling that Japan might experience in only one generation a rise to the status of investment and creditor power and subsequent fall, a history that in Great Britain had taken more than one hundred years to unfold.

In the past generation, we have observed the following changes in the Japanese economy and enterprises:

(1)   rapid success in the ten years following the first oil crisis,
(2)   a bubble economy in the latter half of the 1980s, and
(3)   a decade-long stagnation in the 1990s.

Examining the reasons for the stagnation in the last decade, while focusing on enterprises, we therefore have to raise the following three issues:

(1)   the causes for the success of Japanese firms in the ten years following the first oil crisis in 1973;
(2)   the causes for the bubble economy; and
(3)   the causes for the genuine failures of Japanese firms in the 1990s.

The first question relates to the success of Japanese firms. We must investigate the causes for the phenomenal achievements of Japanese firms after the Second World War and especially in the ten years following the first oil crisis in 1973. Hidemasa Morikawa, who has been at the forefront of research in business history in Japan, has written on this point in a review of Alfred Chandler, Jr.'s *Scale and Scope*:

> I cannot support the Professor's view that the cause for the stalling of American capitalism lies in the excessiveness of global oligopolistic competition after the 1960s. Was not oligopolistic competition the condition that forged organizational capabilities? It was not the intensification of oligopolistic competition that caused American industrial firms to stall but rather their defeat by Japanese managerial enterprises in that competition. But why were they beaten? We must ask why Japanese managerial firms won. . . . We must study separately how organizational capabilities at large American, German, British, and Japanese firms, as well as these firms' interrelationships, shifted and how they were transformed after the 1960s. In so

doing, might we not find that the flaws - the vestiges of personal capitalism - which link the period of American competitive managerial capitalism's greatest prosperity with its current defeat are immanent in that system? Were Japanese managerial enterprises able to achieve victory exploiting these flaws because they, painstakingly and over many years, forged and accumulated organizational capabilities that focused on human skills? It is necessary to shed light on these kinds of problems.[1]

This was published in 1991. Around this time, besides Chandler's book, the English version of Morikawa's book on zaibatsu and other important literature also appeared.[2] At that point, however, firms in Japan were already intoxicated with the bubble economy, and, by curious coincidence, the bubble economy went bust immediately thereafter. As a precautionary postscript, it should be noted that Morikawa's raising of these questions in no way loses its importance because of this recessionary state of affairs. Both then and now, such questioning is important and appropriate.

Second, then, we must ask why the bubble economy occurred. It was a phenomenon that clearly demonstrated the deterioration of Japan's economy, but did Japanese firms bear any responsibility for it? Was the bubble economy a necessary consequence of Japanese managerial capitalism, or was it, rather, an undesirable deviation? Most centrally, did it demonstrate the failure of the Japanese firm?

Third, we must inquire into the causes for the genuine failures of Japanese firms. Because speculative activity will necessarily lead to collapse at some point, the collapse of stock and real estate speculation was inevitable, as was the demise of the accompanying bubble economy. But one must inquire again into the causes of the subsequent decade-long stagnation.

The Japanese economy and firms have, of course, experienced crisis conditions numerous times, even if we limit our discussion to the postwar era. One might, therefore, argue that this period of long-term stagnation really should not be a cause for surprise, is merely a psychological problem, or is something normal for a capitalist economy. With even a bit of investigation into the scale and character of the long-term stagnation, though, it is safe to view these sorts of arguments as based upon rather excessive optimism or as showing a thick headedness unbecoming a crisis.

Where, then, are the causes for the long-term stagnation to be found? Should factors external to the firm be considered? Even in that case, should we point to international factors (globalization or Americanization) or to the Japanese government's failures in fiscal, trade, currency, industrial, or competition policies? Or were there some sorts of problems within firms themselves? Even if one is inclined toward this sort of judgment, there is likely a divergence between those who see the cause in, for example, a late response to international changes (these explanations are linked to an emphasis on changes in international conditions, such as globalization or Americanization, although they probably do not absolve firms of responsibility) and those who see the cause first and foremost as problems inherent in the enterprise system or in business management (these are the hardcore Japanese-firms-as-guilty-party arguments).

Taken in this way, all of these arguments (excepting those which trace everything to government failure) may be seen as placing responsibility more or less with the firm. In fact, inter-firm relations (cross-holdings of stock, keiretsu), the main bank system, and government-business relations (industrial policy, competition policy) are made the target of attack in treatments of the Japanese firm in the disciplines of economics and business management. The management system and industrial relations have also come under fire, and even the nature of the production and research and development systems has been called into question. The tone of the debate has become increasingly strident, even as people observe that the changes at Japanese firms have not in fact been quite so dramatic.

We must step back and calmly seek the causes rather than casually joining the fray. That task requires a new explication of the causes for the generation of the bubble economy, of course, and of the causes for the success of Japanese firms (even if there is no attempt here to touch on firms' growth prior to the Second World War). In this sense, the three foregoing questions are inextricably linked. In other words, the history of the success and failure of Japanese firms requires a consistent explanation. If industrial relations are emphasized as a factor in success, they may also have to be emphasized as a factor in failure.[3]

II. APPROACHES

These three issues regarding Japanese firms can be tackled through the application of various approaches. Here, the following three approaches are to be reviewed:

(1)   corporate governance debate;
(2)   convergence-divergence debate; and
(3)   globalization and Americanization discourse.

(1) Corporate governance debate

First, if we turn our attention to the ownership and management of firms (by examining shareholder-management relations) and also to their financial affairs (by examining creditor-management relations), a consideration of the corporate governance debate would seem to be a most effective approach. This approach, which traces its origins to the United States, has spread to Western Europe and East Asia.

In the case of the United States, where the corporate governance debate originated, we can see that it was the product of a historical process that began in the 1960s to 1970s.

Starting in the 1960s, a movement for the rehabilitation of stockholders emerged. Someone has called it 'the stockholders' anti-revolution', meaning a reaction against the managerial revolution. As factors for its emergence, Moriaki Tsuchiya, a management scholar, points to the following two facts, besides the beginning of pension funds' intervention in the boards of directors: 'The changing attitude of society in general toward stockholders, as a result of the increasing weight of pension funds as stockholders', and 'the fact that the stormy M&As in the first half of the 1980s had changed corporate behavior toward placing much importance on stockholders'.[4]

As Tadahiko Takaura, a business historian, notes, it was not until the 1970s that the term corporate governance began to be frequently used in literature and documents on corporate law in the United States.[5] As background to the phenomenon, Tsuchiya points out the fact that, from the latter half of the 1970s, lawyers called into question the discrepancies between the laws and the realities related to joint stock companies, and launched a movement for reforming the board of directors in order to adapt the realities to the laws. According to Tsuchiya, what in turn mobilized lawyers and resulted in reform of the board of directors included the citizens movements in the first half of the 1970s. From the end of the 1960s, the citizen movement against the Vietnam War criticized the managers of some chemical companies in the general meetings of stockholders on the one hand, while Ralph Nader began to attack General Motors on the other. The latter movement, the 'Campaign GM', organized by militant one-share holders, which investigated the social responsibilities of GM at the beginning of the 1970s, had a more direct impact. The movement made concrete proposals for the establishment of outside directors and a monitoring committee in the general meeting of GM.[6]

Hiroshi Shibuya, a scholar of public finance, also cites the following background in the 1960s: some members of the Diet, who belonged to the liberal group among the Democrats, argued that the 'establishment' was formed through mutual stockholding relations and mutual director-despatching relations among large financial institutions and large firms, and criticized the custom of transactions behind closed doors by the 'establishment' as anti-'free enterprise society'.[7]

It was following a series of dismissals and resignations of CEOs in the United States at the beginning of the 1990s that the term corporate governance became widely acknowledged, as Takaura points out.[8]

In the 1990s, US firms recovered rapidly through the implementation of thorough restructuring and reengineering, while Japanese firms that sang the praises of the so-called Japanese style of management in the 1980s became embroiled in a series of irregularities from this time on and numerous problems came to light. The competitiveness gap between US and Japanese firms narrowed rapidly and some industries saw a reversal once more.[9] This contrast between the US and Japan was one of the main reasons why corporate governance theory took root in Japan.[10]

Moreover, the following point that Takaura raises is worthy of note: The fact that John Smith, who came from the financial department, took the post of CEO at GM was not evidence of the revival of a financial-management-led type of enterprise. John Smith was not a mere financial person; in 1982 he had come to Japan to negotiate with Toyota on the establishment of the joint-venture NUMMI as a director of world-wide product planning and as a mission leader; he had also managed to restructure GM Europe as its president from 1987 on; he was familiar with operations and also had an understanding of Japanese management.[11]

Examination of these individual cases in the United States suggests that we need to focus not only on issues of ownership and management, but also on industrial relations. It has become evident that, in practice, the reorganization of owner-management relations requires, directly or indirectly, the reorganization of industrial relations.

In Japan today, the following observation by Shozo Kono, a management scholar, is widely adhered to: since the collapse of the bubble economy in 1990–91, various kinds of illegal behavior and irregularities are revealing themselves among financial institutions and other companies. While in the 1980s, Japanese firms had boasted of their global superiority in *corporate management* under the banner of a

Japanese style of management, they had totally lacked *corporate gover-nance* as a system for monitoring the adequacy of management.[12]

Kono further points out:

(1) In Japan, generally speaking, business management lays more importance on ROI (return on investment) than ROE (return on equity). Therefore, it is observed that managers are keen to promote the growth and development of companies themselves.

(2) In Japan, labor unions are organized not according to industry, but on a company basis. Therefore, the interests of labor are included in individual companies, and, as a result, it is in fact impossible for labor to monitor managers.

(3) In the managerial control [of Japanese firms], various functions and authority are concentrated within a representative director and president (or the committee of managing directors, with him as a core member, or other bodies) and excessive discretionary rights are given to a top manager. For example, a top manager has the right to ask certified public accountants to audit the company and to appoint outside directors and inside auditors. It is no exaggeration to say that those who are required to check have no power to do so.

(4) Thus, the only feasible avenue left is to strengthen the rights of stockholders.

    (4a)   The 1981 revision of the commercial law approved the right of stockholders to propose issues and the agenda at stockholders' general meetings.

    (4b)   The 1993 revision of the commercial law implemented the right of stockholders to sue management (Article 267 of the commercial law) , which was taken up also in the Strategic Structural Initiative between Japan and the US, and strengthened the right of stockholders to revise audits.[13]

This was a common observation by researchers at the end of the 1990s in Japan.

In journalism, too, the following kind of article was frequently seen: According to 'A questionnaire to 100 top managers' (92 responded), it is worthy of note that these firms are attaching more importance to stockholders by way of providing sufficient information to stockholders at general meetings of stockholders, holding round-table conferences on their products and services, and raising the prices of their own stocks through the depletion of their stocks. As much as 37% of them have already introduced or are considering introducing an executive director system in order to divide the decision making function of management and the execution of business. Management reform is also progressing rapidly toward the establishment of corporate governance by way of strengthening the auditors' function and appointing outside directors.[14]

The observations and research referred to above seem to be, however, too normative, setting aside the question of whether they are agreeable or not. The following research, based on questionaires, indicates that the reality is a mixture of change and the *status quo*:

(A) Business management and corporate governance:

    (Al) The following five reforms are to be observed:

        (1) Making clear the responsibiliy of management and strengthening consolidated management as a business group;

        (2) Promoting a personnel system, at the executive level, based on meritocracy and promoting efficiency through the centralization of management execution;

        (3) Shifting the emphasis from sales volume to ordinary profit;

        (4) Shifting from indirect financing to direct financing; and

        (5) Attaching importance to interfacing with stockholders.

    (A2) On the other hand, the following aspects of the *status quo* can be observed:

        (1) Attaching importance to prior stakeholders (subordinates, stockholders, and managers);

        (2) Attaching importance to good relations with stable stockholders;

        (3) No say by stable stockholders about management organization and management behavior; and

        (4) Insider promotion at the level of executive personnel management and a strong authority of a top manager regarding executive personnel management.

(B) Employment practices and industrial relations:
    (Bl)   Changing aspects:
        (1)   Employment management based on individuals;
        (2)   'Regression' of seniority orders and a shift towards multi-dimensional labor-conditions decisions;
        (3)   Increasing employment opportunities for older people;
        (4)   Growing importance of personnel management at the level of business groups;
        (5)   Reforming the methods of running of corporate pension systems; and
        (6)   Diluting the presence of company unions.

    (B2)   Unchanged aspects:
        (1)   Life-time employment or long-term stable employment;
        (2)   The corporate pension system; and
        (3)   Company-based industrial relations.[15]

Moreover, in a symposium held by academics as well as researchers in business, both changes and the *status quo* were pointed out.[16] Hideaki Miyajima, the organizer of the symposium, writes:

> The Japanese type of enterprise system that established itself in the high-growth era was characterized by long-term relations in such areas as firm-bank relations, transaction relations, stockholding relations, and industrial relations. In the 1990s, enormous changes began, although the degree of progress and the orientation differed from area to area. On the other hand, however, changes in other aspects of the Japanese type of enterprise system, especially in manufacturing sectors, were not necessarily big, despite the enormous changes in economic circumstances. Skills acquisition based on long-term employment, which had been supporting the Japanese economy, remained an unchanging aspect. Under such conditions, the efficiency and competitiveness of manufacturing sectors does not decline. In corporate governance, too, the role played by subordinates in Japanese firms remains important. Firms seem to make employment adjustments based on a relatively long-term perspective, responding to their external circumstances.[17]

However, one fact needs to be mentioned as a changed aspect, which the literature referred to above does not clearly point out. That is the rapid increase in the share of stocks held by foreigners. The share of stocks held by foreigners (companies and individuals) in the total market value of stocks in Japan increased sharply throughout the 1990s and almost reached the level of 20% at the end of the decade, catching up with the share of stocks held by Japanese individuals.[18] The share of stocks held by foreigners in all issued stocks of companies at the March 1998 account settlements was: Sony 44.9%, Hitachi 27.1%, Matsushita 21.4%, Bridgestone 21.3%, Honda 19.6%, Toyota 8.8%, Murata Seisakusho 36.2%, Orix 35.4%, Omron 29.5%, and Kyocera 26.0%. Moreover, some companies are rapidly reforming themselves: Sony decreased the number of its directors from 38 to 10, including 3 outside directors, in July 1997, and established an incentives committee and a nomination committee in May 1998.[19] The cases of Nissan, which came under the umbrella of Renault, and Mitsubishi Motors, which entered the DaimlerChrysler group, are also worthy of observation.

The corporate governance debate is, so to say, a kind of domestic-based approach. However, just as the fact that the corporate governance of some firms such as Sony is influenced by foreign stockholders' voices, we also have to apply a more international approach.

(2) Convergence-Divergence Debate as a means for international comparison

The focal points lie in owner-manager relations as well as in creditor-manager relations on the one hand, and in industrial relations on the other. The inclusion of such issues, then, causes a widening of the debate to cover business management as a whole: R&D, production technology, production management, quality control, sales policy, financial policy, and others. Furthermore, inter-firm relations and business-government relations need to be considered: concentrations, cartelization, business groups, long-term continuous relational transactions, financial keiretsu, distribution keiretsu, and subcontractor relations as inter-firm relations; and industrial policy and competition policy as business-government relations.[20]

Moreover, we have to include in our observation the wide range of stakeholders, as corporate governance theory in its wider meaning calls them, such as subordinates, suppliers, customers, and local communities. Something that might provide a clue for furthering our understanding of this broadened debate is the so-called convergence-divergence debate, which examines the convergence or divergence of national economies amid economic globalization.

Both the convergence camps and divergence camps possess a hard-line element and a soft-line one, and the former, naturally enough, comes across as holding sway in either camp.

Examples of convergence arguments are too many to enumerate, but let us look at some. Robert Boyer points to four types of capitalism: market-led (the United States), company-led (Japan), social-democratic regime led (Northern European nations), and state-led (France); Germany is located between the social-democratic regime led type and the state-led type. He stressiss the robustness of those four types.[21] Michel Albert argues that Germany is only one example of the Rhine type of capitalism, with which Northern European countries, Switzerland, and Japan have similarities.[22] Yusuke Fukada and Ronald Dore note: There are a number of streams of capitalism in the world. One is the Anglo-American type centring around the United States and Britain, while another type is different from the Anglo-American type in various ways and is found in the cases of Germany, Sweden, Norway, Denmark, the Netherlands, Switzerland, Japan, and so on. If we are to classify those various streams into two types, we will have the Anglo-American type and the Japanese-German type.[23]

However, this convergence-divergence debate is inevitably inclined to be normative. Convergence arguments are similar to globalism discourse, while divergence arguments are similar to anti-globalism discourse. For example, Albert, a divergence advocate, says: We have proved the economic and social superiority of the Rhine type of capitalism. We can, therefore, expect also its political victory. Unexpectedly, however, the opposite is happening.[24]

In evaluating this convergence-divergence debate, there is another, and more important point, i.e. it is necessary to return to the roots of the debate and evaluate economic globalization itself, rather than becoming mired in a static comparison of various national economies. In order to tackle this task, it is imperative that we consider international factors or international relations. To put it another way, we should address ourselves to a more dynamic debate, one that evaluates globalization and Americanization.

(3) Globalization and Americanization Discourse as a means for examining international relations

The origins of the dynamics of globalization, that is, its causes, the process thereof, and its result, must be discussed. In doing so, we must take into account the transformation of the international political, military, and economic systems as evidenced by, for example, the end of the Cold War, the frequent outbreak of local or regional conflicts, and the advance of regional integration; and such issues as technological progress (particularly in the fields of information and communications); the huge amount of international debt of the United States and the international monetary systems; and the sharp contrast between the US economy and the economies of Western Europe and East Asia. We would also do well to consider so-called global issues such as the environment and safety.

In order to examine the structure of globalization, we need to pay attention to an asymmetry, that is, the United States' unique position at the heart of that structure. Therefore, it is of necessity and importance to consider Americanization as well as globalization[25]

At least for Japan, a considerable part of globalization has been Americanization.[26] During the 1970s and 1980s, firms in Japan differed from their American counterparts in such areas as owner-management relations, inter-firm relations, and industrial relations. Observers argued for the advent of Japanese-style management, and often hailed this as a new model for business management and for capitalism itself. Ironically, however, just after that era, firms in Japan experienced the conditions of a bubble economy, its collapse, and a decade-long stagnation. Thus, in the 1990s, the formerly trumpeted Japanization of American business was driven to the verge of oblivion, and a much talked about Americanization of Japanese firms has now come to take its place. While the term Americanization indicates the influence of the United States in general, here it is being used to mean the economic influence of the US, especially in the areas of business management and technology. While the principal routes for this influence are direct investment and multinational firms, trade, technology tie-ups (licensing agreements), and diverse other routes exist, among which may be counted indirect investment, currency and financial policy, and, recently, economic policy.[27]

The influence of American business extended to various corporate functions but was especially pronounced in corporate finance and accounting practices and in corporate governance. This American business influence was closely linked to the influence of American-style capitalism in areas such as finance and insurance, business philosophy, business education, and business consulting.

III. THE TASKS OF THE WORKSHOP

This workshop, therefore, taking the three questions regarding Japanese firms as its starting point and applying, for the time being, an approach based on corporate governance theory, must concern itself with the issues and with the broader debate referred to above, in order to get to grips with the points of contention in corporate governance theory. Moreover, it must, as a matter of course, afford the same weight to industrial relations as it does to ownership issues (owner-management relations) and financial affairs (creditor-management relations).

Furthermore, rather than discussing in greater detail what ought to be done next, we must address ourselves to a thorough investigation of what exactly has taken place with regard to corporate governance during the last decade. This question must first be answered with respect to the United States, and we must be clear on whether a connection existed between corporate governance and the robust performance of the US economy, and, if so, its extent and the process thereof must also be clarified. We should then similarly address the situation in Japan and Western Europe. Regarding international relations, ties between Japan and neighboring Asian nations are also important, although this workshop neglects to focus on this point. In Japan's case, the discussion will, most likely, focus on whether or not there has been any transformation in the business groups that have traditionally secured cross share-holding, or in industrial relations that have traditionally aimed at co-operation between the two sides; if there has been any change, what kind of shift has occurred, and what relation these points have had to the prolonged economic stagnation of the past decade also need to be examined.

Source: *Business History around the World at the Beginning of the 21st Century* (Franco Amatori and Geoffery Jones (eds)), Cambridge: Cambridge University Press, 2003, pp. 271–297.

13

The State of Business History in Japan: Cross-National Comparisons and International Relations

JAPAN'S ECONOMY EXPERIENCED a bubble, epitomized by stock and real estate speculation, during the second half of the 1980s. It then experienced the collapse of that economic bubble in 1990–91. During the 1990s, the Japanese economy faced an extended period of stagnation evidenced in low growth rates and increased unemployment rates (although there were, of course, alternating phases of good times and bad, i.e. a business cycle). For Japanese firms, too, the 1990s were a difficult decade. The decade caused deterioration in the performance of many firms, and failures affected not only small and medium-sized enterprises but large firms as well. In the retail sector supermarkets and department stores failed, while Hokkaido Takushoku Bank, Yamaichi Securities, and the Long Term Credit Bank of Japan failed one after the other in the financial sector. In the industrial sector or, more specifically, the core automobile sector in which Japanese firms had made world-class achievements, Nissan fell into business difficulties, looked to France's Renault for rescue, and consequently became affiliated with the French automaker.

Japanese firms, which had swept over the world with their direct investment offensive during the 1980s, faced stalemate and failure in their overseas projects during the 1990s and successively pulled back. The Japan that had risen so rapidly as an investment and creditor superpower during the 1980s hit a massive wall in the 1990s. There was a feeling that Japan might experience in only one generation the rise to and fall from the status of investment and creditor power that in Great Britain had taken two centuries to unfold. This drastic change in a relatively brief period of time seems to have baffled Japanese business historians.

There are three problems concerning the Japanese firm that must be worked out for the field of business history, a field of historical research that, like Minerva's owl, always makes its appearance late. These three problems overlap in layers. The first problem relates to the success of Japanese firms. This problem is the explication of the causes for the phenomenal achievements of Japanese firms after the Second World War and especially in the ten years following the first oil crisis in 1973. Hidemasa Morikawa, who has spearheaded research in business history in Japan, has written on this point in a review of Alfred Chandler's *Scale and Scope*:

> I cannot support the Professor's view that the cause for the stalling of American capitalism lies in the excessiveness of global oligopolistic competition after the 1960s. Was not oligopolistic competition the condition that forged organizational capabilities? It was not the intensification of oligopolistic competition that caused American industrial firms to stall but rather their defeat by Japanese managerial enterprises in that competition. But why were they beaten? We must ask why Japanese managerial firms won…. We must study separately how organizational capabilities at large American, German, British, and Japanese firms, as well as these firms' interrelationships, shifted and how they were transformed after the 1960s. In so doing, might we not find that the flaws – the vestiges of personal capitalism – which link the period of American competitive managerial capitalism's greatest prosperity with its current defeat are immanent in that system? Were Japanese managerial enterprises able to achieve victory exploiting these flaws because they, painstakingly and over many years, forged and accumulated organizational capabilities that focused on human skills? It is necessary to shed light on these kinds of problems.[1]

This was published in 1991. By curious coincidence, the bubble economy burst immediately thereafter. As a precautionary postscript, it should be noted that Morikawa's raising of these questions in no way loses its importance because of this recessionary state of affairs. Both then and now, such questions are important and appropriate.

Second, then, we must ask why the bubble economy occurred. It was a phenomenon that clearly showed the deterioration of Japan's economy, but did Japanese firms have any responsibility for it? Was the bubble economy a necessary consequence of Japanese managerial capitalism or was it rather undesirable deviation? Most centrally, did it demonstrate the failure of the Japanese firm?

Third, we must inquire about the causes for the genuine failures of Japanese firms. Because speculation will necessarily collapse at some point, the collapse of stock and real estate speculation was inevitable, as was the demise of the accompanying bubble economy. But one must ask again about the causes of the subsequent decade-long stagnation.

Japan's economy and enterprises, of course, had experienced crisis conditions numerous times before, even if we limit discussion to the post-war era. One might therefore argue that this period of long-term stagnation really is not worthy of surprise, but is merely a psychological problem or a normal condition for a capitalist economy. With even a bit of investigation into the scale and character of the long-term stagnation, though, it is safe to say that these arguments are based upon either excessive optimism or a thickheadedness unbecoming a crisis.

Where, then, are the causes of long-term stagnation to be found? Should factors external to the firm be named? Even in that case, should we point to international factors – globalization or Americanization – or to Japanese government failures in fiscal, trade, currency, industrial, or competition policies? Or were there problems within the firms themselves? Even within these possible explanations, there is likely room for divergence. For example, was a late response to international changes – such as globalization or Americanization – to blame, or was the cause first and foremost problems inherent in the enterprise system or in Japanese business management?

Taken in this way, all of these arguments – excepting those that trace everything to government failure – may be seen as placing responsibility more or less with the firm. In fact, interfirm relations, the main bank system, and government-business relations (including industrial policy and competition policy) are the main targets of attack in treatments of the Japanese firm by the disciplines of economics and business management. The management system and industrial relations have also come under fire, and even the nature of the production and research and development systems has been called into question.

BUSINESS HISTORY'S UNIQUE CONTRIBUTION

In business history, we must step back and calmly seek the causes rather than casually join the fray. That task requires a new explication of the causes for the generation of the bubble economy, of course, and the causes of the success of Japanese firms. In this sense, the three foregoing questions are piled up in layers. In other words, the history of success and failure of Japanese firms requires a consistent explanation. If industrial relations are emphasized as a factor in success, they may also have to be emphasized as a factor in failure. Taking on this set of three overlapping questions is the task imposed on scholars of Japanese business history.

It is not odd that various explanations should rise and fall with the rapid and dramatic transformation in the facts on the ground. Although uncritical applause under the influence of the success of Japanese-style management was rare in the field of business history, a fair amount of research rapidly grew stale. Business history research in Japan has been unable to respond adequately to this rapid transformation in the Japanese firm and its environment.[2] Hidemasa Morikawa, who has taken the lead in business history research in Japan, has also been a pioneer on this point. He has been quick to propose answers to sets of questions like these, especially on causes for the failure of the Japanese firm.[3] He has pointed out the deterioration of managerial capitalism in Japan and has found the chief cause for that deterioration to be the deterioration in top management. This explanation is not sufficiently persuasive, but the attempt at explanation should itself be highly praised. Japanese business historians have been called upon to continue in Morikawa's footsteps.

This essay takes as its task the description of the current state of business history in Japan as it relates to the Japanese firm. In this case, the current state will be taken to mean the period from the 1970s through to the end of the 1990s. Naturally, I will touch on research from before this period, research conducted outside Japan and research related to foreign firms as needed. Conversely, and due to my own narrowness of perspective, there will certainly be research that I will fail to touch on, even though it is important. For this I make my apology in advance.

This task is extremely difficult, even if we set aside the multilayered problematization of the three issues previously described. By way of excuse, I note that there is a tremendous volume of business history research in Japan, and this research is extremely varied in its quality. As of the year 2000, the Business History Association (BHA) had more than 850 members. The papers and publications produced by business history scholars (both members and nonmembers) have reached a prodigious volume, as even a glance through the year in review column in the *Keiei shigaku* (the journal of the Business History Association) shows. Moreover, these publications cover various aspects of business history both in Japan and abroad and from the seventeenth century to the present. The yearly review column in the journal has come to be divided among a number of authors each year. That scale of current research is something that I alone could not possibly cover.

So, I will first try to give as objective as possible an overview of the current state of the discipline. Even so, some subjectivity is unavoidable, but at least that part focused on institutionalized aspects will be objective. Next, I will sacrifice objectivity and draw the discussion toward my own interests. That is, I will narrow the focus to the fields of comparative and international relations history, which I think are the most important currents, and then select and introduce several works considered to be representative in those fields (here too I have had no choice but to abandon comprehensiveness). This essay can only hope to introduce in a brief way the current state of business history in Japan.

A SERIES THAT SETS THE RESEARCH STANDARD FOR JAPANESE BUSINESS HISTORY

There is probably no objection to suggesting that the five-volume series *Nihon keieishi* (Japanese Business History) (Tokyo, 1995) is the publication to pick up first in order to gain an overview of the current state of Japanese business history research in Japan. This series consists of the following volumes with their editors: Volume 1 - *Kinseiteki keiei no hatten (The Development of Early-Modern Business)* (Shigeaki Yasuoka and Masatoshi Amano, eds);[4] Volume 2 - *Keiei kakushin to kōgyōka (Business Innovation and Industrialization)* (Matao Miyamoto and Takeshi Abe, eds);[5] Volume 3 - *Dai kigyō jidai no tōrai (The Arrival of the Age of Large Enterprise)* (Tsunehiko Yui and Eisuke Daitzō, eds);[6] Volume 4 - *"Nihonteki" keiei no renzoku to danzetsu (Continuities and Discontinuities in "Japanese-Style" Management)* (Hiroaki Yamazaki and Takeo Kikkawa, eds);[7] and Volume 5 - *Kōdo seichō wo koete (Beyond High Growth)* (Hidemasa Morikawa and Seiichirō Yonekura, eds).[8]

A number of compilations of business history research have already been produced in Japan. One representative thereof is the six-volume series supervised by Mataji Miyamoto and Keiichirō Nakagawa, *Nihon keieishi kōza (A Course in Japanese Business History)* (Tokyo, 1976–77). The five-volume series *Nihon keieishi (Japanese Business History)*, published twenty years later, is not only the most current work but also demonstrates the present level of business history in Japan. Comprehensive reviews have naturally pointed out a number of flaws in this series; however, by and large, they praise it highly.[9] The series is not merely an overview but also contains a large number of laboriously crafted pieces with original content.

ACTIVITIES OF THE BUSINESS HISTORY ASSOCIATION

As these organized publishing activities show, research in business history in Japan has been relatively well institutionalized. If one were to trace the development of business history, one would arrive back at the pioneering findings of Yoshitarō Wakimura, Mataji Miyamoto and others prior to the Second World War. The institutional foundations of business history as a discipline belong to the post-war period, though. The BHA was established in 1964. This constituted a landmark in the institutionalization of the discipline. The association has published the journal *Keiei shigaku* since 1966. As noted earlier, membership in the BHA as of 2000 exceeded 850, which makes the association among the largest academic organizations in the field of business history in the world. Over 300 business history professors (including associate professors) are affiliated with universities throughout Japan. There are approximately forty chairs of business history (including Japanese business history, Western business history, foreign business history, and general business history) in departments of economics, commerce, and business management at universities across Japan. Moreover, courses in business history are as numerous in business management departments and business information sciences departments as courses in marketing.[10]

Initially, the specialties of BHA members included (and still do) disciplines such as economic history, social history, labor history, history of technology, business management, and sociology, in addition to business history. The association came to foster the shared interest in business history among these fields. One factor that contributed to this growth, and that merits special mention, was the energetic introduction of overseas research trends. These exercises in comparative business history by Keiichirō Nakagawa, Yasuo Mishima, Shin'ichi Yonekawa and others in the initial period exerted a profound influence on subsequent work.[11] By dint of efforts such as these, business history established its significance as an independent discipline. The downside of this process was the lack of a broad-ranging debate on method in business history, with the result that the discipline went on without a clear consensus. The overall theme of the 1999 annual nationwide BHA conference was methodology, and that was probably the first time that an attempt had been made to deal with the topic in the history of overall conference themes at the national meeting.

The activities of the BHA focus on the publication of its journal, *Keiei shigaku,* but also cover a number of other areas. Aside from sponsoring an annual national conference, the association has active regional blocs in Kantō, Kansai, Kyūshū, Chūbu, and Hokkaidō. The activities of the BHA from its founding through 1984 have been assembled in a volume, *Keiei shigaku no 20-nen: Kaiko to tenbō (Twenty Years of Business History: Retrospect and Prospect)* (Tokyo, 1985), which was a pioneering attempt even in international comparative perspective.

The BHA has been engaged in international activities from its establishment. Since 1974 it has sponsored an annual international conference on business history, known as the Fuji Conference, that has enriched the comparative business history approach. The results of the research presented at the conference have been published by the University of Tokyo Press (volumes 1–20) and, from the fifth series (1994–98) on, by Oxford University Press. The sixth series, starting in 1999, is currently in process. One of the ripple effects of the Fuji Conference has been the start of bilateral conferences. Starting with a Japanese–German meeting and then adding Japanese–British and Japanese–French meetings, these bilateral conferences have each been held a number of times. The BHA has played a leading role on this front as well, and the bilateral conferences have each yielded a book.[12] Since 1984, the BHA has also published the English-language annual *Japanese Yearbook on Business History*. Its book review columns are probably the most suitable guides for English-speaking readers. In terms of international activities, then, the BHA may be placed in the active category, relative both to learned societies in the humanities and social sciences in Japan and to associations related to business history worldwide. I would like to acknowledge in particular the Taniguchi Foundation's long-standing interest and assistance in this area.

TEXTBOOKS, CASEBOOKS, AND COMPANY HISTORIES

I will now leave the BHA and return to my overview, limiting myself to the institutionalized dimension. A number of textbooks on business history have been published. Those that have an established reputation or have come to be regarded as standards include Tsunehiko Yui and Johannes Hirschmeier's book in English. Yōtarō Sakudō and others and Yoshitaka Suzuki and others have also produced respected textbooks, as has Akio Ōkouchi.[13] A relatively recent work that probably sets the current research standard has been produced by Matao Miyamoto and others.[14] Takeshi Yuzawa and others have produced a work that sets the current academic standard and covers the United States, Britain, and Germany, in addition to Japan.[15] Finally, Masaru Udagawa and Seishi Nakamura have crafted a textbook designed to attract the interest of beginning students.[16]

Although it is not a textbook, *Kindai Nihon keieishi no kiso chishiki: Meiji ishin ki kara gendai made (Fundamentals of Modern Japanese Business History: From the Meiji Restoration to the Present)* (Tokyo, 1974; expanded edition, 1979), edited by Keiichirō Nakagawa, Hidemasa Morikawa and Tsunehiko Yui, is a handy, reliable encyclopedia even today. The three-volume series *Sengo Nihon keieishi (Post-war Japanese Business History)* (Tokyo, 1990–91), edited by Shin'ichi Yonekawa, Kōichi Shimokawa and Hiroaki Yamazaki, is a full-scale treatment of post-war business history. Although research on the post-war period increased by leaps and bounds during the 1990s, especially among younger scholars, this series remains the touchstone of that movement.

In recent years, the publication of casebooks has become prominent. Typical of these works are a four-volume series edited by Hiroyuki Itami, Tadao Kagono, Matao Miyamoto and Seiichirō Yonekura, *Keesubukku Nihon kigyō no keiei kōdō (Casebook on the Business Behavior of Japanese Firms)* (Tokyo, 1998), and a book edited by Masaru Udagawa entitled *Keesubukku Nihon no kigyōka katsudō (Casebook on Entrepreneurial Activity in Japan)* (Tokyo, 1999).

The publication of company histories is closely related to business history research, and publication of company histories is flourishing in Japan. The *Kaisha shi sōgō mokuroku (General Index of Company Histories)* (Tokyo, 1986; expanded and revised edition, 1996), edited by the Japan Business History Institute, lists more than 8,000 company histories. In some cases, business historians participate in the writing of company histories, which then feed back into business history research. These company histories are especially valuable for the post-war period, for which there are problems of access to internal company materials and thus little case-study research on individual firms. Of course, company histories often have a tendency to turn into hagiographies of the firm or its top management and, as such, have drawn appropriate criticism. Even so, the quality and quantity of company histories in Japan are at a high standard internationally, and Japan can take pride in being one of the several company history superpowers in the world. Some academically important works related to company histories are *Gaikoku kigyō oyobi kigyōsha keieisha sōgō mokuroku (General Index to Foreign Company, Entrepreneur, and Manager Histories)* (Tokyo, 1979), edited by the Japan BHA Tenth Anniversary Project Committee; Nobuhisa Fujita, ed., *Shashi no kenkyû (Research on Company History)* (Tokyo, 1990); and *Nihon kaisha shi kenkyû sōran (Compendium of Japanese Company History Research)* (Tokyo, 1996), edited by the BHA.

THE FLOURISHING OF FOREIGN BUSINESS HISTORY

One of the characteristic features of the study of business history in Japan is vigorous research on foreign business history. The United States, Britain, Germany, and France are the principal subjects of research. In the background of this focus lies Japan's late-developer perspective, wherein the Western firm has traditionally served as the model. Starting from that perspective, comparison with the Japanese firm came to be attempted repeatedly. After 1970 or so, when Japan's economy had finished catching up, changes became apparent in the perspective of foreign business history research and the perspective of comparison with Japanese firms. A more explicit comparison came to be emphasized, and the previous standards, vantage point, and rigours of comparisons were called into question.

Here, limiting myself to monographs, I will introduce only a very small portion of foreign business history research. A number of works on the United States have been published, but here I will limit myself to Haruhito Shiomi, Seigo Mizota, Akitake Taniguchi and Shinji Miyazaki's book on the formation of American big business, *Amerika biggu bijinesu seiritsu shi (History of the Formation of Big Business in America)* (Tokyo, 1986). Several books on Britain may be noted – Keiichirō Nakagawa's comprehensive studies, Takeshi Yuzawa's book on railroads, Yoshitaka Suzuki's book on entrepreneurial activities in the age of the Industrial Revolution, Etsuo Abe's book on steel companies, Chikage Hidaka's book on the cotton industry, and Takashi Iida's book on the securities market.[17] Works on Germany include Hisashi Watanabe's book on industrialization, Sachio Kaku's book on the chemical industry, Sachio Imakubo's book on the electric giant Siemens, and Akira Kudō's book on the chemical industry.[18] Works on France include Isao Hirota's work on the economy and society in the inter-war period, Jun Sakudō's book on the chemical industry, and Terushi Hara's recent work on the economic history in the inter-war period.[19] On Europe in general, there is a collection on contemporary business history, *Gendai Yōroppa keieishi (Contemporary European Business History)* (Tokyo, 1996), which focuses on regional characteristics, edited by Hisashi Watanabe and Jun Sakudō. The foregoing works are just the tip of the iceberg in the thriving field of foreign business history.

Research on developing countries, and especially on Asian business history, has finally come into its own in recent years against a backdrop of economic and business development in that region. Two works that show some of the achievements in this area are Atsushi Mikami's work on family business in India and Fumikatsu Kubo's work on the Japanese sugar industry in colonial Formosa.[20] Asian business history is indispensable for contextualizing Japanese business development in the non-Western European world, providing, for example, comparative materials for generalizing Japanese *zaibatsu* firms as a case of family enterprise.

JAPANESE LARGE-FIRM BUSINESS HISTORY

Business history research on Japanese firms has concentrated on large firms. Thus, *zaibatsu* firms have been the focus of research on the pre-war period, and firms belonging to business groups have been the center of research on the post-war era.

One comprehensive survey of pre-war *zaibatsu* firms has been produced: *Nihon zaibatsu keieishi* (*The Business History of Japanese Family Business Groups*), a seven-volume series. It is also worthwhile to mention Yasuo Mishima, Yasuaki Nagasawa, Takao Shiba, Nobuhisa Fujita and Hidetatsu Satō's book on the Mitsubishi *zaibatsu* during the Second World War, *Dai 2 ji taisen to Mitsubishi zaibatsu* (*The Second World War and the Mitsubishi Zaibatsu*) (Tokyo, 1987). Regarding the research on the pre-war *zaibatsu*, I would like to focus especially here on the research of two authors who made great use of a cross-national comparative perspective.

One of these authors is Shigeaki Yasuoka, whose results are collected in several books by him on cross-national comparative history of *zaibatsu*-owned enterprises in Japan and family business in the world. It is his focus on the relationship between ownership and management in the *zaibatsu*-affiliated large enterprises, his attempt at specific cross-national comparisons between the *zaibatsu*-affiliated large enterprises and family-owned enterprises in Asia as well as in the West, and his proposal of the *Gesamteigentum* (whole ownership) concept that have set a new standard.[21] The other author is Hidemasa Morikawa, whose work is collected in a book on the business history of *zaibatsu* in Japanese[22] and an English book: *Zaibatsu: The Rise and Fall of Family Enterprise Groups in Japan* (Tokyo, 1992). While Morikawa accepted Chandler's results from *The Visible Hand* and *Strategy and Structure*, he pushed for a revision of those books' fundamental arguments. Morikawa proposed a perspective that emphasizes individual managers rather than the hierarchical

organization of managers. From this perspective, Morikawa
clarified empirically the dynamism of competition and cooperation
between family owners and salaried managers over the right to manage *zaibatsu* enterprises (*Business History Review* 64, no. 4 [1990]:
716–25).

Research, even on the pre-war era alone, naturally extends to various issues, including the differences among *zaibatsu* – such as those
between old and new *zaibatsu* or those due to the industrial sector
– and the argument that juxtaposes the idea of the *Konzern* (concern)
to the *zaibatsu* concept. On this score, I offer only one recent work,
Shōichi Asajima and Takeshi Ōshio's book on Shōwa Denkō, *Shōwa
Denkō seiritsu shi no kenkyū (Research on the Formative History of Shōwa
Denkō)* (Tokyo, 1997).

There is also a great deal of research on post-war business groups
and the large firms affiliated with them. A small sampling of such
works includes a volume on business groups before and after the Second World War edited by Jurō Hashimoto and Haruhito Takeda; a
book written by Masahiro Shimotani on *keiretsu* and business groups;
a volume on some relevant industries' development edited by Haruhito Takeda; Takeo Kikkawa's work on the continuity-discontinuity
debate; a volume on the post-war enterprise system edited by Jurō
Hashimoto; a volume from a Fuji Conference on business groups
edited by Takao Shiba and Masahiro Shimotani; and a volume on
interfirm competition edited by Masaru Udagawa, Takeo Kikkawa
and Junjirō Shintaku.[23] Each of these books works from the premise
that there is an issue in the continuities and discontinuities between
the pre-war and post-war eras. Further, this problematization is shown
quite clearly, especially in Kikkawa's work and in the volume edited by
Hashimoto and Takeda.

AN EXAMPLE OF EXPLICIT CROSS-NATIONAL COMPARISON

As noted previously, the study of business history in Japan has from
the outset shown a strong awareness of cross-national comparison.
The study of large enterprises has also taken such an awareness as
a given. Cross-national comparative business history has been a
powerful thread in two recently published collections of essays, a
volume edited by Keiichirō Nakagawa and another edited by Hidemasa Morikawa and Tsunehiko Yui.[24] Hiromi Shioji and T. D.
Keeley have provided a direct comparison of distribution systems

in Japan and the United States in *Jidōsha diiraa no nichi-bei hikaku (A Comparison of Automobile Dealers in Japan and the United States)* (Fukuoka, 1994).

With the partial exception of Yasuoka and some others, however, most of these works (including those coming out of the Fuji Conference and bilateral conferences) stop at implicit comparison. Most important at the present stage are attempts at explicit cross-national comparison. Implicit cross-national comparison tends more or less to assume existing methods and frameworks. If we desire methodological breakthroughs we must actually attempt, with our own hands, explicit cross-national comparison, even if we are hindered by our lack of knowledge. Akio Ōkouchi and Haruhito Takeda's edited volume, *Kigyōsha katsudō to kigyō shisutemu: Dai kigyō taisei no nichiei hikaku shi (Entrepreneurial Activity and the Enterprise System: A Historical Comparison of Large Enterprise Systems in Japan and Britain)* (Tokyo, 1993), which approaches this issue head on, is one of a small number of such works. Let us enter this collection of essays and introduce and evaluate them.

The book selects Japan and Britain as its objects of comparison and limits itself approximately to the period between the two world wars.[25] Comparison is clearly in mind in almost all of the chapters, which are then paired neatly. The book is a meticulously constructed comparative business history. Two chapters that make particularly worthwhile reading are Ōkouchi's comparison of Nakajima Aircraft and Rolls-Royce and Fujimoto and Tidd's Japanese–British comparison on the introduction of the Ford system. The former chapter relates how Rolls-Royce made ground-breaking achievements in aircraft engine development while Nakajima Aircraft failed to do so, stressing hypothetically the existence or lack of excellent managers as a factor in differentiating performances. The latter chapter traces and compares the history of the transfer and introduction of the Ford system into Britain and Japan in the automobile industry, the sector that is the prototype for American-style mass production and the large-firm system. Both chapters are attempts at extremely desirable forms of comparison that emphasize the importance of comparison in light of international relations.

The book is an attempt to generalize the individual cases at the level of business histories of the respective Japanese and British firms. Even viewed apart from the task of comparison, the book has been put together so that, by reading each chapter, one can obtain an overall picture of Japanese and British firms between the two world wars. The

reason for this is that the five themes the book takes up basically cover
the whole of business management.

I would like to add some critical evaluations on two points. The first
has to do with comparisons with the United States. Ōkouchi notes in his
preface, "Viewed globally, the development of American business society was a single, special experience, and while the Chandlerian understanding of the firm and image of history that took the US as a model is
one prototype, it is not history's royal road." In the same space Takeda,
too, says "The large enterprise system is itself a historical presence. The
various features that the system shows must be contextualized and taken
up along with the special characteristics of the United States." I would
have liked the comparisons with the United States, especially those with
the American large-enterprise system, to have been executed that clearly
throughout the entire book. Above all, whether the subject is production
technology or marketing, one cannot talk about business management
in any country in the twentieth century, including the inter-war period,
if one leaves out the transfer of technology and management skill from
the United States. It is impossible to proceed without comparison vis-à-
vis the United States, not because of Chandler, but because America was
America. In this book, too, there is certainly full awareness of this point
in the individual chapters. The thought pieces by Suzuki and Wada are
particularly aware of this, and such overtones are also strong in other
sections. But it seems as though comparison with the United States has
been suppressed in the book as a whole.

The other evaluation has to do with the time period this book has
covered. The book has been limited to the inter-war period and after,
when Japan's large-enterprise system might finally be worthy of comparison with that of Britain. In actuality, though, the handling of the
time period varies from chapter to chapter. One feels the relative dynamism of the chapters by Suzuki and by Fujimoto and Tidd, in which
the inter-war period and the period after the Second World War are
given equal treatment. Ironically, the book's strength lies in those places
where coverage was not strictly limited to the inter-war period. This is
probably not a chance outcome. The inter-war period was an exceptional one, in which the environment of the firm moved from world
war to world depression to the formation of blocs in the world economy. It was an exceptional period in the history of the large-enterprise
system as well, in which the international cartel was becoming the prototypical organization. The various peculiarities of the period are thus
impressed upon the activities of entrepreneurs and upon the enterprise

system, and the book pays attention to this important facet. In order to contextualize these peculiarities, the preceding and subsequent periods should be brought into range clearly. By expanding the time period and thus pursuing explicit cross-national comparison more effectively, this book could have been an even more significant work.

RESEARCH THAT PROVIDES
METHODOLOGICAL SUGGESTIONS

Explicit cross-national comparison is needed especially due to the keenly felt need for methodological breakthroughs in the field of business history. Conversely, however, it is extremely difficult to do explicit cross-national comparison without a methodologically coherent study. The work of two scholars is suggestive on this point.

One, Shin'ichi Yonekawa, proposed the "contemporary absolute comparison" perspective, from which he actively implemented explicit cross-national comparisons. In the process of pursuing a cross-national comparison of business management in the cotton industry, Yonekawa asserted the importance not of comparison at the same stage, which has traditionally been the method chosen in Japan, but of comparison only in the same era. He gave as his reason for this stance that "Each country's firms participate in the formation of the world market, and what determines their future is nothing other than competition in that market." Yonekawa noted that "They interactively take part and make rules through the world market. This is none other than the realistic base for contemporary cross-national comparison."[26] His long-term study of the management of firms in the cotton industry based on this perspective was recently compiled in a series of volumes.[27] This body of empirical research provides the punch to demolish the methodological discussions that smack of empty theory, and it provides important suggestions for future cross-national comparative research in business history.

The other scholar is Yoshitaka Suzuki. By expanding the Chandler model, Suzuki made cross-national comparisons of the hierarchical structure of large enterprises in the twentieth century and situated the Japanese firm among them. He argued that the firm first internalizes those business resources for which the transaction costs in the market are highest. The firm is then constructed so that it is able to monitor, adjust, and distribute those business resources. Using this perspective, Suzuki attempted to make a typology of business organization. The typology characterized the Japanese enterprise organization as a direct control organization that developed from the internalization of labor markets, as opposed to the American functional organization, in which goods markets had been internalized, or the British holding company organization, in which primarily capital markets had been internalized.[28] This expansion or universalization of the Chandler model has the potential to bring about the development of a cross-national comparative business history that incorporates national and historical differences in labor and capital markets.

HISTORY OF INTERNATIONAL BUSINESS RELATIONS

As the overseas direct investment of Japanese firms became regularized and business management became more internationalized or globalized during and after the 1970s, attention in the business history field turned to the international expansion of Japanese firms. When inward direct investment finally became regularized in the 1990s, research on the activities of foreign firms in Japan also finally started to become animated. Finally, as some multinational firms transformed themselves into more global firms, there arose a full-scale awareness that research should clarify the activities of Japanese firms in the context of international relations.

The notion that business management should be understood in an international context has a long tradition in Japan. The research of Yoshitarō Wakimura in the pre-war period was a pioneering effort in this area.[29] In the post-war era, there were already calls for such awareness at the beginning of the 1960s. By the early 1980s, at least the following three important research agendas, and the empirical research based upon them, had already come into being.

First, Keiichirō Nakagawa proposed a history of international business relations as well as a methodology. In order to clarify international differences in advanced capitalism, Nakagawa held that it was not enough merely to clarify the economic and social conditions within each country. Rather, he wrote, "We compare American and British capitalism not simply for our convenience in understanding American capitalism; we compare them because American capitalism itself is not a historical reality unless it is in the context of international relations with British capitalism."[30] Later, he went so far as to term this sort of research "business history based on international relations theory." At that point, Nakagawa understood international relations as especially meaning relations among organizations. More concretely, Nakagawa tried to explain the genesis and development of the general trading company in Japan in the context of the special international relations embodied in unequal treaties. Nakagawa also carried out a number of projects in the history of international business relations, most notably on the shipping industry.[31]

Shin'ichi Yonekawa then proposed a "contemporary absolute comparison" approach. This has already been introduced as a call for cross-national comparative business history, but it is also clearly a proposal for an international relations perspective. In developing a business history for the cotton industry, Yonekawa started with the recognition that British, American, Indian, and Japanese firms were placed in a competitive relationship in a single world market during and after the last quarter of the nineteenth century. On Yonekawa's research, Nakagawa stated insightfully at an early point, "It opens the way for research based on international relations theory, and I await its findings."[32]

One more methodological suggestion was Sakae Tsunoyama's invocation of world system theory. Tsunoyama wrote, "If dealing structurally with international economic history through the framework of world capitalist system theory is an influential approach, then how international relations theory-based business history ought to respond will be a future topic for discussion."[33] When he took up this issue in his own work, he used Japanese consular reports as source material, and organized research on the information-related interrelationship of firms and governments in the context of international relations.[34]

INVIGORATION OF RESEARCH ON THE HISTORY OF INTERNATIONAL BUSINESS RELATIONS

With the exception of the pioneering work of the preceding three authors, there was little research on the history of international business relations through the mid-1980s. After that, however, research activity rapidly grew. The BHA established a project on the history of international business relations at its annual conference, a history of international business relations category was set up in the yearly review column in *Keiei shigaku,* and the *Japanese Yearbook on Business History* put together a special issue on the subject. Individual pieces of empirical research dealing with international relations head on became prominent, even if they were not labelled as history of international business relations.

Research was first concentrated on the business activities of foreign firms in Japan in the first half of the twentieth century. Hisashi

Watanabe, making free use of internal company materials, wrote a pioneering series of works that clarified the Siemens Corporation's direct investment in Japan.[35] Masaru Udagawa did pioneering work on foreign companies' direct investment in Japan.[36] Other scholars who made significant contributions in the area of foreign firms in Japan were Tōru Takenaka on Siemens and Meiji Japan; Akira Kudō on the German chemical giant, IG Farben and other German large enterprises in inter-war Japan; Takeo Kikkawa on foreign oil companies' pre-war enterprises; and Bunji Nagura on Japanese–British relations in the arms and steel industry.[37] Two valuable collections of essays on the subject are the volume on foreign companies in pre-war Japan edited by Takeshi Yuzawa and Masaru Udagawa, *Foreign Business in Japan Before World War II* (Tokyo, 1990), and Erich Pauer, ed., *Technologietransfer Deutschland–Japan von 1850 bis zur Gegenwart* (München, 1992) on Japanese–German transfer of technologies.

On the expansion of foreign firms into Japan as well as Japan's response to it, it is possible to name a number of monographs covering the time period from the end of the Edo shogunate regime and the Meiji Restoration or early Meiji. Chief among these monographs are Kanji Ishii's work on Jardine Matheson and modern Japan; Kazuo Tatewaki's history of foreign banks in Japan; Shin'ya Sugiyama's monograph on a British merchant, Thomas Glover, and Meiji Japan; Toshio Suzuki's English book on Japanese government loan issues and the London capital market; and Naoto Kagotani's book on the Asian international trade network.[38] Tetsuya Kuwahara compiled a useful literature survey on foreign companies' direct investment in pre-war Japan.[39] Business activities of foreign firms in Japan in the post-war era remain an item for future study in the business history field.[40]

Works on foreign direct investment and overseas business expansion on the part of Japanese firms include Nobuo Kawabe's monograph on Mitsubishi Trading in the pre-war United States; Tadakatsu Inoue's paper on early foreign direct investment; Tetsuya Kuwahara's volume on the business activities of Japanese textile companies in China; Fumio Kaneko's studies of Japanese investment in Manchuria; and Fumikatsu Kubo's study on Japanese business activities in Formosa.[41] Tetsuya Kuwahara's survey in English of the literature on overseas business activities of Japanese firms in the pre-war era is also useful.[42] Overseas expansion by Japanese firms in the post-war era remains a topic for future study. Although it does not fall within the framework of business history, one such work that provides suggestions for the direction of future work in business history and that merits mention is Hiroshi Itagaki's edited collection on Japanese direct investment in Eastern Asia, *Nihonteki keiei seisan shisutemu to higashi Ajia: Taiwan, Kankoku, Chūgoku ni okeru haiburiddo kōjō* (*The Japanese-Style Management and Production System and East Asia: Hybrid Factories in Taiwan, Korea, and China*) (Kyoto, 1997). This volume explains the business activities of Japanese firms, especially in the automotive and electric machinery sectors, in East Asia, with a focus on the international transfer of technology. The book locates research questions in what aspects of the Japanese-style management and production system have or have not been transferred, to what extent transfer has occurred, and the factors that determine the extent to which that transfer has occurred. In other words, this collection looks at the tension between the direct application of the Japanese system and its flexible adaptation to the local environment.

The most recent comprehensive collection of essays is Hidemasa Morikawa and Tsunehiko Yui, eds, *Kokusai hikaku kokusai kankei no keieishi* (*Business History in Cross-National Comparative and International Relations Perspectives*) (Nagoya, 1997).[43] Each essay has its own distinct shading of the notion of international relations, and each tests its own approach to the issue in its concerns, methodology, and source materials. The essays also test cross-national comparisons at every turn. The essays by Kikkawa and Takaoka (on the transfer of the supermarket system between the United States and Japan) and by Yuzawa (discussing Japanese–British cotton industry talks) are examples of this.

The highest achievement in the history of international business relations at the present stage of the discipline may be Haruhito Shiomi and Ichirō Hori, eds, *Nichi-Bei kankei keieishi: Kōdo seichō kara genzai made* (*Japan-U.S. Relations Business History: From High Growth to the Present*) (Nagoya, 1998). Japanese–U.S. economic relations after the Second World War have been the most important basic relationship for the Japanese economy and for the world economy, and this volume makes a valuable contribution to its analysis from the perspective of business history. In comparison to research on Japanese–British and Japanese–German relations, which has stalled at the pre-war period, this book is quite significant as well.

In the preface, Shiomi observes that Chandler's model, which had broadly influenced the world of business history, met with a "phase shift" in the 1980s, and its utility came under suspicion. While maintaining the "from market to organization" viewpoint that undergirds the Chandler model, Shiomi holds that a new direction, oriented either explicitly or implicitly towards a post-Chandler model approach, has become visible in business history research. Focusing on Yoshitaka Suzuki and Akira Kudō, Shiomi catalogues the history of research in this field in Japan. He then asserts the usefulness of the history of international business relations, because it breaks through the limits of the Chandler model, which has been constructed within the framework of single-country histories.

In addition, the book discusses global firms in twelve key industries and emphasizes the analysis of the global competitive strategies of Japanese and American firms. The authors share three common premises: the establishment of a global, oligopolistic market that entails a "multi-layered global network"; the emergence of global firms of Japanese descent; and the Americanization of Japanese firms and the Japanization of American ones. The book then observes the interrelationships between the Japanese and American firms that are representatives of the global firms in the twelve key industries.[44] The book clearly shows not only the relationships between Japanese and American firms but also the shape of Japanese and American global big business. As such, it is a great step forward in contemporary business history. There are, however, points that warrant criticism. One such point is the considerable difference among the chapters in the shape or denotation of the interfirm relations that are the object of analysis. The shape or denotation of interfirm relations is, of course, multidimensional and includes trade, technology tie-ups, strategic cooperation, and foreign direct investment. If we also add the notion of competitor firms, the application of competitive strategies, and choice qua object of learning, then interfirm relations becomes an even more variegated concept. Also, the nature of the relations between Japanese and American firms differs by sector, and the authors' respective interests, perspectives, and agendas also differ. The availability and accessibility of materials and documents is also a consideration. Thus, it is natural that the aspects that come under study also differ in response to these conditions. But if the book had been given a somewhat more unified perspective, its claims would probably, as a whole, have had more of an impact.

If I were to venture a suggestion, my one additional request would be a characterization of relations between Japanese and American firms in the 1990s. The book tries to narrow its focus to the "phase shift" that took place from the 1970s to the 1980s. One wonders how the authors understand the shift from the 1980s to the 1990s. Based on this book's position – expressed in its afterword – with "the mid-range perspective that ought to be characteristic of business history," how should we characterize the 1990s? Do we move to the "retrading places between Japan and the United States" and "continuing 'almighty America'" perspectives? Or do we emphasize the information technology revolution or the services innovation perspective?

Research on the history of international business relations has finally become regularized. But methodological consideration has been insufficient, and many points have been left in an imprecise state. Even in the comprehensive collection edited by Morikawa and Yui, the reader finds no essays dealing with method. What scholars are looking for now is clear methodology. Serious thought needs to be given to how arguments that expressly assume Japan's special international context can acquire cross-national universality. The discipline must address a necessary question: is the history of international business relations methodologically independent, or is it rather just a subfield of business history? In the future, scholars must redouble their methodological search in parallel with their empirical work.

TOWARDS A GREATER INTERNATIONAL CONTRIBUTION

As I wrote at the outset, Japanese business history scholars have been given the challenge of answering a three-layered set of problems: the success that prevailed until the mid-1980s, the bubble economy of the late 1980s, and the failure of the 1990s. We must coolly observe what actually happened and what sorts of changes actually occurred. In order to do this, it is necessary to locate this single generation within a longer history and to observe from a long-term perspective. It is for precisely this reason that we look forward to business history's unique contribution to knowledge.

What such a turn requires is not a mindset that seeks to explain even as it is fixed within the existing theoretical framework but rather a mindset that seeks, through accumulated observations, to repeat attempts to propose universal frameworks. To assert out of the blue the uniqueness of Japanese business management or, alternatively, to assert *a priori* its universality ultimately assumes some sort of existing theoretical framework. Terminology, too, should not be a provincial jargon that is bandied about, but should rather express the results of observation using a universal vocabulary. In so doing, new terms should be proposed only when existing ones render expression impossible. This is one of the preconditions for Japanese business history if it is to make more of an international contribution.

The need for an international contribution on the part of Japanese business history is the same as it ever was or even greater. For example, the word *keiretsu* has been used to express a certain type of inter-firm relationship – in most cases, a vertical business group. This term, though, may run the risk of misleading readers on the issues surrounding *keiretsu*. It may also run the risk of interfering with the formation of a universal framework through the observation of Japanese cases.

KEY WORKS

Morikawa, Hidemasa. *Zaibatsu: The Rise and Fall of Family Enterprise Groups in Japan.* Tokyo, 1992.

Morikawa, Hidemasa and Tsunehiko Yui, eds *Kokusai hikaku kokusai kankei no keieishi (Business History in Cross-National and International Relations Perspectives).* Nagoya, 1997.

Nakawaga, Keiichirō, ed. *Kigyō keiei no rekishiteki kenkyû (Historical Research on Business Management).* Tokyo, 1990.

Nihon keieishi (Japanese Business History). 5 vols. Volume 1 – *Kinseiteki keiei no hatten (The Development of Early Modern Business)*; Volume 2 – *Keiei kakushin to kōgyōka (Business Innovation and Industrialization)*; Volume 3 – *Dai kigyō jidai no tōrai (The Arrival of the Age of large Enterprise)*; Volume 4 – *"Nihonteki" keiei no renzoku to danzetsu (Continuities and Discontinuities in Japanese-Style" Management)*; and Volume 5 – *Kōdo seichō wo koete (Beyond High Growth).* Tokyo, 1995.

Ōkouchi, Akio and Haruhito Takeda, eds *Kigyōsha katsudō to kigyō shisutemu: Dai kigyō taisei no nichiei hikaku shi (Entrepreneurial Activity and the Enterprise System: A Historical Comparison of large Enterprise Systems in Japan and Britain).* Tokyo, 1993

Shiomi, Haruhito and Ichirō Hori, eds *Nichi-Bei kankei keieishi: Kōdo seichō kara genzai made (Japan-US Relations Business History: From High Growth to the Present).* Nagoya, 1998.

Suzuki, Yoshitaka. *Japanese Management Structure, 1920–80.* London, 1991.

Yasuoka, Shigeaki. *Zaibatsu keiseishi no kenkyû (Studies on the Formative History of the Zaibatsu).* Kyoto, 1970; expanded edition, 1998.

Yonekawa, Shin'ichi. *Bōsekigyō no hikaku keieishi kenkyû: Igirisu, Indo, Amerika, Nihon (A Comparative Business History of the Spinning Industry: Britain, India, America, Japan).* Tokyo, 1994.

PART III

Japanese and European Business and Economics

Source: *The Internationalization of Japanese Business: European and Japanese Perspectives* (Malcolm Trevor (ed.)), Frankfurt am Main: Campus Verlag, 1987, pp. 63–72.

14

From Commercial Controversy to Industrial and Technological Cooperation between Japan and the EC: The New Role of Japanese Direct Investment in the EC

THE PURPOSE OF this report is to describe the history of the economic relations between Japan and the EC from the commercial controversy to industrial and technological cooperation, and to point out the influences of the development of industrial and technological cooperation on Japanese direct investment in the EC.

THE PAST AND PRESENT OF THE COMMERCIAL CONTROVERSY BETWEEN JAPAN AND THE EC

Lessons of the past

As is commonly assumed, at the official level, there have been four culminations in the commercial controversy between Japan and the EC: in 1976–77, 1980, 1982–83 and 1985, although the controversy itself has never been interrupted since the beginning of the 1970s.

The first conflict of 1976–77 is symbolized by the 'Doko-Shock'. In 1980, the second conflict occurred immediately after the second oil crisis, and so-called voluntary restrictions on exports to West Germany were introduced by the Japanese car and TV industries. The third conflict of 1982–83 rapidly compelled the new government of Mr Nakasone to place restrictions on exports in several industries.

355

At present, tension is so high that we can find ourselves at the fourth and perhaps highest culmination of controversy. The EC requires from the Japanese government 'a clearly verifiable commitment to a significant, sustained increase in imports into Japan of manufactured and processed agricultural products'.[1] The Japanese government thinks that it is endeavoring to increase imports and wishes its endeavor to be recognized enough by the EC. There is a great gap between them.

It is beyond the scope of this report to describe the details of the history of these conflicts.[2] Here I would like to confirm only one point: After the second oil crisis, the European economies, including the West German economy, have been suffering secular stagnation and high unemployment rates. Trade inbalances with Japan are persistent. Consequently, in 1982–83 and 1985, the attitude of the EC toward Japan has become stronger than before. But both sides have learnt from experience in the history of commercial controversies and are now exploring a new phase of industrial and technological cooperation.

STEPS TOWARDS INDUSTRIAL AND
TECHNOLOGICAL COOPERATION

The expression 'industrial and technological cooperation' or 'industrial cooperation' or 'technological cooperation' or 'scientific and technological cooperation' is relatively new and is often applied to relationships among developed countries, but it has different meanings depending on the situation. The meaning should be clear in the context of the controversy between Japan and the EC.

The idea of industrial and technological cooperation is said to date back to May 1979, when Etienne Davignon, the vice-president of the EC Commission talked with Masumi Esaki, Minister of MITI, in Tokyo.[3] Viscount Davignon was aware of the structural problems of European industries and so was the other vice-president, Wilhelm Haferkamp, who required moderation from Japan and effort from Europe,[4] and he intended to revitalise European industries through industrial and technological cooperation with Japan. On the other hand, it is certain that MITI also had this kind of idea and used the words 'industrial cooperation' before their talk.[5] In the year 1979, the well known secret report of the EC Commission, which became notorious in Japan, featured Japanese as workaholics in rabbit hutches, but the atmosphere between Japan and the EC was still good in comparison to that in later years. Anyway, the idea of industrial and technological cooperation has not actually been realized. It is worth noticing that in September 1979, four months after Viscount Davignon's visit to Japan, the EC Council took the first step toward the ESPRIT Program (European Strategic Program for Research and Development in Information Technologies).[6] It may not be entirely coincidental.

Through 1980 and 1981 few steps were taken towards cooperation.

In October 1981, during his visit to Europe as leader of an economic mission, Yoshihiro Inayama, president of Keidanren, opened his talks everywhere by calling on his European hosts to explore together the promise of 'industrial cooperation', the two-way flow of investment and technology. The European governments and industrial leaders in general, however, responded negatively. They concentrated on their own most pressing topic, that is, the menacing growth of Japan's export surplus in Europe and the urgency of holding it in check.[7]

In May 1982 the German electric company Grundig opened a campaign for industrial cooperation within the EC and made contact with the EC Commission.[8] In October, the Battle of Poitiers took place. Meanwhile, senior EC officials in Tokyo tried to agree with the Japanese government on industrial cooperation in such fields as nuclear fusion, solar energy, nuclear waste disposal and the application of a remote sensing technique for pollution control.[9]

In January 1983, the second Japan-EC Symposium in Brussels brought a new phase in the acceleration of industrial cooperation. Sadanori Yamanaka, Minister of MITI and Viscount Davignon agreed to hold regular consultations on this theme. At this time the commercial controversy became overheated. The well known drastic disposition of Mr Nakasone, which was unexpected by the European side, dated from February 1983, one month after this agreement. Only three months after, in May 1983, the EC Commission made a proposal to require a decision from the Council on the ESPRIT Program.[10] At the same time, the EC Commission was seeking the approval of EC member governments to open negotiations with Japan for a new cooperation agreement in such sectors as thermonuclear fusion, nuclear safety, environmental protection and the development of new energy resources.[11]

Consultations have been held twice since then, in November 1983 and December 1984. The Japanese side was represented by vice-ministers from MITI and the Science and Technology Agency, and the European side by the General Directors of Directorates-General III (Internal Market and Industrial Affairs) and of DG XII (Science, Research and Development). They took a 'pragmatic approach'.[12]

The first consultation was held in November 1983 in Tokyo. It is interesting that, in October of that year, Nissan's top management definitely decided to produce cars in Britain.[13] Both sides, Japan and the EC, exchanged statistical information on research and development with each other, especially in 'high-tech' industries, and on industrial policy, especially in depressed industries such as steel, shipbuilding and textiles. The EC side recognized that the purpose of the consultation was not to negotiate but to exchange information, and that decisions on direct investment depended on private initiatives. However, it hoped for an increase in mutual direct investment, especially in Japanese direct investment in 'high-tech' industries. At the second consultation held in December 1984, they did not only exchange information but also discussed some problems, such as the barriers against direct investment, for example the complicated formulae of the Japanese authorization system, and the lack of harmonization in company law and labor law in Europe. MITI proposed to establish a data bank on technologies, which was welcomed by the EC side. It should also be noted here that the ESPRIT Program rapidly took concrete shape after March 1983, and that the EC Council of ministers for research agreed with the 1985 work program for the ESPRIT Program during the second consultation in December 1984.[14] It does not seem to me that it was an entire coincidence.

THE PRESENT STATE OF INDUSTRIAL AND TECHNOLOGICAL COOPERATION

The commercial controversy between Japan and the EC became much sharper in 1985. After a series of Trade Expansion Committee meetings in February and May, Mr Nakasone's campaign to encourage people to buy more foreign products in March, the High Level Consultation in June, the announcement of the Action Program and Mr Nakasone's visit to Europe in July, some hopes on the European side in the first half of this year were disappointed in the second half. The disappointment was greater than before because of increased expectations.

The response of the EC Commission to the Action Program was negative. An EC press release said, 'The tariff changes now announced are unlikely to bring an immediate or sustained relief to the trade inbalance'.[15] The President's conclusions of the EC summit in Milan in June included one item specially relating to the critique of 'Japanese Trade'. In October, the EC Commission published a comprehensive and detailed document relating to 'Japanese Trade' and the Japanese government made quite a tough response.

Regretfully we have to say that this development was unfortunate. In these circumstances, however, the tempo of industrial and technological cooperation is now apparently being accelerated.

First, in May they reached agreement on cooperation in the telecommunications industry.[16] Secondly, in the Japan-EC Symposium from the end of September to the beginning of October, Keijiro Murata, MITI minister, made a proposal for industrial and technological cooperation in such fields as electronics, space, atomic energy and aircraft as follows:

(a) MITI would support Japanese enterprises in establishing research institutes in Europe.
(b) MITI would receive researchers from Europe.
(c) MITI would encourage Japanese enterprises to take part in EUREKA.
(d) MITI would cooperate in fostering the European components industries for cars and electronics.[17]

Furthermore, industrial and technological cooperation was a topic at the first Japan-EC Economic Forum in October and during the visit of the Keidanren mission led by Mr Inayama in the same month.[18] Lastly, at the Ministers' conference held in Tokyo in November, they agreed on the folowing points:

(a) to conclude an agreement for cooperative development in nuclear fusion;
(b) to promote cooperation in the research of biotechnology and new materials;
(c) to promote the exchange of young researchers in the field of advanced technologies; and
(d) to establish a 'Center for Industrial Cooperation' (a language training center for European engineers) in Tokyo.[19]

In the relations between Japan and the EC countries, we can also find acceleration in the movement towards cooperation. For example, in November, Japan, France, West Germany and the US agreed on cooperation in the field of fine ceramics.[20] Japan and West Germany had already reached agreement on scientific and technological cooperation in October 1984. With Great Britain, France and Belgium, Japan has regular consultations. JETRO has already established commissions for industrial cooperation in five EC Countries (Great Britain, France, West Germany, Italy and Belgium).[21]

To summarise, the history of discussions about industrial cooperaiton is not long, and concrete steps towards the realization of cooperation only began after the culmination of the commercial controversy in 1982–83. Until 1982 there were only discussions at the governmental level. In the course of repeated commercial conflicts in 1982–83, it became insufficient for both sides to depend on the measures used before. There is little room for negotiations and compromises, especially on the Japanese side, but industrial and technological cooperation has become an important way of resolving commercial conflicts.

SOME FACTORS AFFECTING THE PERFORMANCE OF INDUSTRIAL AND TECHNOLOGICAL COOPERATION BETWEEN JAPAN AND THE EC

Interest in cooperation

We consider the following factors as affecting the performance of industrial and technological cooperation: circumstances, interests and capability. Circumstances have changed due to the increased tension in the commercial controversy, and both sides are in circumstances appropriate for cooperation.

Furthermore, it is clear that cooperation can advance the interests of both sides. The Japanese authorities were somewhat indifferent to cooperation in comparison with the EC Commission. They estimated European potential in research and development as lower than that of the US. The Japanese authorities were sceptical about the capability of the EC in mobilising European potential for cooperation with Japan. Therefore, they regarded cooperation with the EC Commission as secondary, and attached more importance to cooperation with individual EC countries.

By now, the Japanese have more interest than scepticism, because they became conscious of the vulnerability of basic research in Japan: the share of the public sector in R & D costs is only one quarter, and the barriers for technology transfer into Japan are becoming higher.

On the other hand, the EC Commission has also become eager to cooperate with Japan at the governmental level, and it has been rather irritated by the slowness of consultation.

Power of mobilising the potential for cooperation

MITI and the Science and Technology Agency (STA) on the Japanese side have many science and research institutions under their control. The newest one is the Center for the Promotion of Basic Technology Research established in October 1985.

The importance of the government sector in Japan's scientific and technological development is yet to be investigated. Perhaps it is bigger than most Japanese observers assume, and smaller than foreigners usually estimate.

Anyway, MITI and the STA play more important roles in basic studies than in the applied field. They promote basic research that has a future but which is usually financially impossible for private enterprises to support. They have been applying the so called 'big project method' to the promotion of basic research since 1966; that is, MITI plays the role of coordinator, and gathers and systematises knowledge and know-how which has been accumulated in the public sector and by private enterprises. In 1985 MITI started a new 'joint research system of the public and private sectors' (*Kanmin rentai kyodo kenkyu seido*) and selected six research themes. They mapped out as new lines in joint research:

(a) exchange of research results
(b) joint use of equipment, and
(c) joint ownership of industrial property resulting from this joint research.[22]

Another example: the Ministry of Post and Telecommunications and the Center for the Promotion of Basic Technology Research has also decided to promote five projects in the field of telecommunications as 'national projects'.[23] MITI and other ministries have a tradition of and competence in mobilising private research potential and these systems have been efficient.

The EC had 67 internal projects within the framework of industrial and technological cooperation as of November 1984, in all industries from agriculture to space, in addition to ECSC and EURATOM.[24]

In these projects, the EC plays the role of coordinator and financier. Some of them are financed by the EC, some are financed privately and others are financed both by the EC and private companies. For example, in the case of the ESPRIT Program, private companies choose the technologies to be developed, and the R&D costs are financed by the EC and the private companies on a fifty-fifty basis. This is somewhat different from the 'big project method' in Japan. The EC Commission is now searching for a new way of cooperation.[25] Cooperation between Japan and the EC at the governmental level can develop further in the future.

There are, however, some uncertain factors. Among them, one is to be mentioned: the promotion of cooperation within the EC aimed at manufacturing and strengthening European competitiveness against the US and Japan. It is symbolic of the strategy of the EC that the President's conclusions at the EC Milan Summit included the items 'New Technology' and 'Japanese Trade' side by side. This conception of a certain type of technology community can increase the centripetal force of the EC. Only after consolidating cooperation within the EC, can the EC be prepared for cooperation with Japan and the US, as suggested several times before. For example, in the autumn of 1983, when the EC began consultations on cooperation with Japan, the EC also had the strongest will to establish internal cooperation.

On the other hand, EC countries are competing with each other for cooperation with the US and Japan. They cannot wait for the completion of internal cooperation.

European cooperation goes beyond the institution of the EC, for example the Airbus and Eurofighter, or beyond the territory of the EC, as in EUREKA and the Reunion Round Table.[26] These projects are mostly 'Eurocentric'. The first two are apparently closed. Although Mr Nakasone announced the possibility of Japan's participation in EUREKA,[27] this possibility seems to be slight. The Reunion Round Table is entirely exclusive. It may be suggestive that an American enterprise, IBM Europe, is participating in the ESPRIT Program, while no Japanese enterprise is yet doing so.[28]

The following scenario is most probable: France and West Germany will get closer to each other, either in the framework of the EC or beyond it. On this Paris-Bonn Axis, the EC will approach Japan for industrial and technological cooperation despite commercial conflicts. Cooperation between Japan and the EC will follow close on that between Japan and each EC member country. It will take, so to say a, '*de jure* approach', like cooperation between Japan and France.[29] If EC projects become more centripetal than centrifugal, the participation of Japanese business in EC projects will be limited.

CONCLUDING REMARKS: THE NEW ROLE OF JAPANESE DIRECT INVESTMENT IN THE EC

We have mainly seen a certain type of industrial and technological cooperation, that is, cooperation at the governmental level. Direct investment, the supply of technical licenses and know-how, etc. belong to another type of cooperation. Governments cannot promote this type of cooperation under their direction. They find this type of cooperation inadequate but are willing to facilitate it. We now consider the influences of the changes in Japan-EC economic relations on the future course of direct investment, especially on Japanese investment in the EC.

JETRO's second survey of Japanese investment in Europe says: 'In conclusion, the survey result indicates that local manufacturing in Western Europe is not without inherent problems, but that management flexibility has helped smooth out rough corners. In the process, Japanese managers have learned how to deal with local differences and gained confidence in their future in Europe'.[30] In reporting this result, most of the Japanese press laid emphasis on the successful introduction or penetration of the Japanese style of management into Japanese enterprises in Europe.[31] The EC Commission, on the other hand, criticises Japanese direct investment as follows:

(a) Japanese enterprises are being established mostly in tertiary industries in order to sell Japanese products or to finance Japanese producers, not in order to produce in Europe.

(b) The share of local procurement is considerably lower than the Commission wishes. The often mentioned 'difference in the quality of locally produced parts' is nothing but an excuse.

(c) Transfer of technology from Japan to the EC is insufficient, as seen from Japan's deficit balance of technology.

(d) All in all, Japanese investment in the EC is threatening European industries more than contributing to prosperity, employment and technological development in Europe.[32] Reportedly, the EC Commission (DG IV - Competition) is now examining the possibility of laying down guide lines in order to prevent the excessive dominance of joint ventures in the market.[33]

How and to what extent can Japanese enterprises in the EC respond to these criticisms by host countries? As one part of industrial and technological cooperation, Japanese direct investment in the EC can and should not only decrease the potentiality of commercial conflicts, but also contribute to the economic prosperity and political stability of Europe through the creation of employment and the transfer of technology to the EC. Here we can realise a new role for Japanese direct investment in the EC.

Source: *Japanese and European Management: Their International Adaptability* (Shibagaki Kazuo, Malcolm Trevor and Abo Tetsuo (eds)), Tokyo: University of Tokyo Press, 1989, pp. 107–117.

15

Kao Corporation's Direct Investment and Adaptation in Europe

INTRODUCTION

In this chapter, I wish to examine the motives and strategies of Kao Corporation Limited in its entry into Europe and discuss the problems of adaptation which may be encountered in this process. Kao was one of the first soap manufacturers in Japan. It has a history of almost one hundred years and is a leader in marketing and advertising. Moreover, it has been a keen investor in research and plant equipment in the areas of oil and fat, surface, and polymer sciences and has proceeded with a rapid diversification to cover the production of detergents, cosmetics, disposable nappies, toners, floppy disks, etc. The change of the official company name in 1985 from 'Kao Soap Company' to the present 'Kao Corporation' is, incidentally, one sign of this strong diversification drive.

My primary reason for examining the case of Kao was the strong impression made, while I was engaged in completing the company's centennial history, by the marked development in international activities recently set against the general managerial development of the company. Another reason was the easy facility to information sources. But these were not my sole reasons. The entry of Japanese chemical firms into European markets is less apparent than that of electric appliance or car manufacturers. Consequently, chemical firms are not yet at the center of the trade conflict, and problems in adaptation have not yet become evident. However, since Kao actually represents the case of a firm which is making an entry on the strength of its managerial as well as its technological superiority, it is likely that the adaptation problems discussed below will prove to be even more significant. Kao, in this sense, provides interesting material as a case study of localization and of the adaptation attempts of Japanese firms in Europe.

WHY EUROPE? THE DEVELOPMENT OF OVERSEAS ACTIVITIES

From the periphery to the center and diversification

Already before the Second World War, Kao had set up manufacturing centres throughout East and Southeast Asia. However, these were lost with the Japanese defeat and bear no direct relation to present development. The new starting point after the war dates from 1955 with the resumption of exports of household products to Southeast Asian markets. Direct investment began in 1961 when joint venture enterprises were begun in Thailand and Taiwan. During the sixties, joint ventures were successfully created throughout the Southeast Asian area. Development policy in the sixties centred on domestic products (personal care products, household products, hygiene products, cosmetics) and chemical products (fatty and specialty chemicals) and on the creation of these joint ventures in Asia.

Only towards the end of the sixties did Europe finally enter the company view. First, in 1968, a liaison office was opened in Brussels for exporting and marketing chemical products and for the collection of sales and technical data. At the same time, the British chemical corporation Bibby Chemicals, Ltd., was acquired and polyurethane production started. Further, in 1970 a joint venture in Spain was started and manufacture of the chemical product amine began. However, of these activities only the production of amine in Spain was continued; the Brussels office was closed in 1972 and the British subsidiary was sold off to ICI in the same year. In 1979, another joint venture was begun in Spain to manufacture a surfactant. We can sum up these developments in Europe in the seventies as being a failure in Northern Europe, while only the stronghold gained south of the Pyrenees remained.

Finally, in the eighties, Kao established a firm stronghold in Northern Europe. In 1979, Kao, in collaboration with the West German company Beiersdorf AG, acquired Guhl, manufacturer of such hair care products as shampoo, rinse, and hair dye. However, this subsidiary was formally in Beiersdorf's 100 percent ownership until 1986, when a 50–50 division of rights with Kao was formalized. Sales of the subsidiary increased steadily after acquisition, and it established a leading position in sales of shampoo to the commercial hairdressing network. It established its own subsidiaries in Holland, Austria, and Switzerland.

The strong yen after the G5 Conference of September 1985 created a very favorable context. Developments proceeded rapidly. In 1986, Kao took a 60 percent capital participation in a toner manufacturer and established a 100-percent-owned floppy disk sales subsidiary in West Germany, and in Düsseldorf, a sales subsidiary for cosmetics was set up. Also, sales of cosmetics in Europe began from June 1987, and at the same time localization of research and development began with the establishment of a research laboratory for cosmetics and hair-care products in Berlin. This had the double aim of the accumulation of technical and sales know-how and of using the appeal to Japanese consumers of the brand image of products sold in Europe.

A similar pattern of development was evident in North America. In Canada, a 70 percent capital participation was taken in a floppy disk manufacturer; in the USA, a research institute was established in Los Angeles. The sales of cosmetics began, and in the summer of 1987, the American manufacturer of surfactants, High Point Chemical Corporation, was acquired.

The developing pattern of Kao's overseas activities, with regional development in Southeast Asia in the sixties, expanding to Europe around the seventies, followed by a period of stagnation from the seventies to the mid-eighties, after which activities moved to Northwestern Europe and North America, shows an overall movement from the periphery to the center of the world economy. Investment activities in the first half of the sixties to the early seventies and in the early eighties roughly match the overall pattern of direct investment by Japanese firms. Moreover, the sequence of regional development is also typical of Japanese firms.

One of the characteristic traits of Kao's developing overseas activities at present is diversification. Apart from soap products, dating back to the pre-war years, Kao, starting from a line of household (detergents, etc.) and chemical products, has recently diversified to include cosmetics, hair-care products, and information-storage media. This is clearly related to the regional expansion of its international activities. However, it is especially interesting that the hypothesis of product cycles à la Vernon does not seem to be applicable in this case.[1] As can be seen from the basic chronology outlined above, both multinationalization and diversification were proceeding simultaneously. In any case, any time lag between domestic and international developments in diversification would seem to have been much smaller than Vernon postulates. In the field of cosmetics, floppy disks, and toners, Kao has not saturated the domestic market to the excess of creating an oligopolic system. While establishing its domestic position in the fields of household and chemical products and information storage media, it is simultaneously following a similar program in each of the three main areas of its overseas activities: Asia, Western Europe and North America.

Summing up, the overseas activities of Kao can be characterized as showing a movement from the periphery to the center in geographical terms and towards diversification in terms of product lines.

Idealism in strategy of diversification and multinationalization

The central strategy behind the overseas activities outlined above was an idealistically motivated multinationalization. This was the result of a strong desire to do business somehow or other in Europe and North America. In September 1982, a very critical moment in hindsight, President Maruta stated that 'our real aim . . . is, in one way or another, to become an international company'. Of course, considering the future competition with international companies like Procter and Gamble or Unilever, it was not possible for Kao to content itself with the Asian market. Moreover, particularly in the fields of cosmetics and hair-care products, the Euro-American market is the trendsetting market from the consumer's viewpoint, and the market size and scale of management resources make it very attractive. There is no doubt, then, that significant incentives existed for entry into the Euro-American market.

Further, a factor making entry possible was Kao's early establishment of its own independent technical base in the field of surfactants. Its technical standard was so high that a joint venture undertaken in Japan in the immediate post-war period could be summed up as 'not up to expectation in terms of production technology'. Kao, therefore, quickly set its aim on direct overseas investment while introducing new technology. Incidentally, Kao's first partner in a joint venture, Atlas Chemicals, an American surfactant manufacturer, was a mentor for Kao's overseas development activities, providing know-how on capital participation, take-overs, and the marketing of specialty chemicals, as well as being an invaluable information source and liaison with world markets.

However, when considering Kao's strategies of multinationalization, diversification, or vertical integration, it is the constant presence of this idealistic managerial philosophy that is most striking. It is impossible to separate its managerial philosophy from the person of President Maruta, who combines an un-Japanese thoroughness in his technical rationalism with personal charisma and who epitomizes the strategic style of management. President Maruta, who has exercised forceful leadership since 1971, has been the major driving force behind both Kao's multinationalization and diversification policies.

In accordance with this idealistic strategy of multinationalization in the late sixties and early seventies, Kao entered the Euro-American market, but then withdrew, not having found a suitable product to sell. In the seventies, when its overseas activities were stagnant, a series of trial-and-error attempts at co-operation, licensing, take-overs, joint ventures, etc., took place in Northwestern Europe and North America. To explain the failure of these attempts would require a wide-ranging examination, including the advent of the international money and the oil crises. However, it is clear that Kao's multinational policy was not reluctant.[2] Rather, during the seventies it could be said that the desire to enter foreign markets was unmatched by a sufficient ability to realize that desire. With the eighties, this desire became even stronger, and thanks to the favorable climate created by the strong yen, this desire was rapidly realized.

Incidentally, the trial-and-error attempts mentioned above influenced the parent company's structure. In July 1982, that is, after the launching of the Sofina cosmetic line, the Main Office for Overseas Activities was disbanded, and separate offices for the European American, and Pacific sectors were created. In 1983, with the exception of the American Office, these area offices were elevated to division status and were put under the direct supervision of the company vice-presidents. At about the same time, branch offices were opened in Düsseldorf, New York, and Singapore. Since then, structural reforms have taken place almost annually, and the employment of local managers in Düsseldorf and Paris was tried out. At present, the main division for each particular product is in charge of its own overseas activities so that company organization is a matrix of 'sales field x sales region'. Further, in Germany and America regional head-quarters are being set up. Given the tardy reform of Kao's Main Office structure, it would seem appropriate to see the eighties as the beginning of Kao's full-scale move towards the center of the world economy.

In this sense, we can say without exaggeration that the policy of multinationalization preceded product diversification and developed as technical and capital resources accumulated.

Adaptation and localization

Now let us turn to a brief examination of the questions of adaptation and localization. Applying to companies the concept of adaptation in its original biological sense, we might say that those will survive which are capable of adapting to their environment. However, following this line of thought we reach the conclusion that adaptability to surroundings equates with a firm's competitiveness. But the recent question of a firm's international adaptability cannot adequately be accounted for by its international competitiveness alone. Put simply, such an account underestimates the conflict involved.

Conflicts can be classified into those originating within a firm, that is, arising from the firm's internal decision-making process, and those arising between a firm and its external environment, for example, with other firms, the local society, and governments. Of course, these two categories are closely related, as in the case of an internal conflict about labor conditions which is taken to a labor tribunal. However, a firm's efforts to adapt to the environment are generally more effective in the internal rather than the external sphere. In internal affairs, its leeway for an active response is relatively greater, whereas with external conflict, it tends to be more passive. In psychological terms, the resistance to adjustment is greater in the latter case. Further, adaptation to external conditions tends to be more decisive. Put rather extremely, while it is possible for a firm having internal conflicts to continue its regular achievements, its continued existence becomes impossible if it is ordered by a government to leave the country.

Consequently, when discussing adaptation, I take this to include relations between the parent company and its local subsidiaries, and not only in the sense of a firm's internal problems.

Now let us examine localization. The three main alternatives for international development open to a firm – export, licensing, and direct investment – entail in that order an increasing necessity for localization. Aspects of localization include ownership and management localization, production technology, research and development, and labor relations. With direct investment, these issues become more likely to arise and require greater consideration.

Even if localization has taken place, this does not mean that adaptation is immediately possible. Localization does not equal adaptation. The solution to the problem of adaptation would be much simpler if this were the case. But any attempt to examine adaptation leaving out a consideration of localization would be extremely narrow. It is fair to say that most Japanese firms making direct investment abroad test out the possiblity of international adaptation through localization. Kao is no exception to this general pattern.

When localizing, Japanese firms see the European environment as more problematic than other areas because differing approaches elicit a greater variety of response. Of course, this impression is partly due to the small size of the Japanese entry, but also to the strength of Europe's socio-economic structure and cultural traditions. The existence of the Common Market is another influence. Gilpin's neo-mercantilist model more adequately accounts for the economic relations of Japan and the Common Market than either Vernon's liberalist model or Hymer's dependency model.[3] Japan's direct investment in the Common Market, even if unintentionally, is inevitably influenced by the motive of Euro-Japanese co-operation in industrial technology. For this reason, more so than in other regions, such as North America or Southeast Asia, the question of international adaptability is more pressing than that of international competitiveness.

KAO'S LOCALIZATION ATTEMPTS

Now let us examine the four main aspects of Kao's localization policy in Europe: ownership, management control, technology, and labor relations.

Localization of ownership

Kao, having judged it impossible to localize the quality control of household products with a policy of exportation and making it a principle of company policy not to license out key chemical products or technology, decided in its international activities on a strong commitment to direct investment. For direct investment, Kao chose total ownership instead of joint ventures, whether through a new investment or by acquisition (between these two methods there was no systematic preference). The joint venture enterprise in Spain, established in 1970, later came under total ownership, and the joint venture set up in 1979 was in actual fact totally owned by Kao.

One reason for this policy was the awareness from previous experience that joint-venture ownership limits the functioning of decision making in questions of profit use, plant and equipment investment, and sales. This was stated as follows: 'Effectiveness is lost while discussions take place between joint venture partners having differing managerial cultures. An equal division of ownership would mean that we could only realize half our ideas. So we decided to continue with our chosen policy of 100 percent ownership, which is what management à la Kao entails.'

Further, while it had been previously felt that managerial resources, such as technology, experience, human resources, and capital, had been insufficient, it was judged that these were now sufficient. Another regional factor was the fact that whereas in Asia total control had been virtually impossible for legal reasons, this was quite possible in Europe.

Localization of managerial control

Although it is difficult to characterize the Kao management style simply, any outline would include the principles of rapid decision making, prominence given to research and development, a marketing philosophy that whatever quality improvements might be made, no changes are made to brand names, prices, or packaging, and finally the principle of in-house information sharing.

As long as these aspects are seen as essential to Kao's managerial style, attempts to localize the managerial function will meet considerable difficulties. Whereas localization entails a large transfer of authority to local managers, it is unlikely that they would put into practice the managerial style outlined above. Rather, localization of this aspect would probably have to be postponed until management of the local subsidiaries had reached a level of smooth running practice.

Localization of technology

Kao had already gained experience in localizing research and development facilities and production technology with the amine plant in Barcelona and with the production of surfactants. In these cases, research centres for production technology were set up in the plants, and a desire to localize was strongly present from the start. At present, the Barcelona plant supervisor is Spanish, and of the 30 to 40-strong research team, only one Japanese is stationed in the research and development division and one is employed in production technology. Further, since Barcelona is pursuing product development in line with the needs of the European market, this contributes to sales experience. It is the policy of Kao's Head Office that development of the Spanish venture be done with the Spanish system constantly in mind and that capital and technology transfer from the parent company take place only when necessary.

The localization of research and development was a particular aim in the establishment of the research laboratory for perfumes and cosmetics set up in West Berlin in 1987. Its main aim was local research and development of products suited to local market particularities arising from conditions of climate or consumer habits. Actually, some 12 different types of products have been developed, and furthermore, a phase-two plan has been set up, including the establishment of further research centres in Düsseldorf and Paris.

In the case of West Berlin, the research staff is divided into two groups; each group consists of one Japanese researcher, one German researcher having a doctorate, two to three German laboratory assistants, and a number of German secretarial staff. As the venture is of recent date, it is on a small scale with the localization of research staff still in its development stage. For reasons of seniority and experience, the team leaders are, in fact, Japanese. As occasion demands, extra researchers are dispatched from Japan, and regular research results are available to the research institute in Tokyo through on-line information sharing. The Head Office in Tokyo centralizes authority over such administrative aspects as the setting of research targets, decisions on research planning policy, allocation of resources, and use of research results.

Localization of labor relations

Localization of labor relations is generally inevitable, and this is particularly so in Europe because of the strict legal limitations in operation. In Kao's case, local production is confined to Spain, where no significant problems have arisen to date because of the small scale of operations.

CONCLUSION

In summing up the above examination, I think we may make the following hypotheses.

If direct investment is taken to be based on some superior aspect possessed by a firm, we may suppose this superiority to be either technical or managerial. When direct investment takes place on the strength of technical superiority, one would suppose that localization of technology would present the biggest obstacle. Where managerial superiority is the basis, then the localization of ownership and management are the biggest problems. This is because where technical superiority is the basis of investment, it is difficult for the investor to decide on the localization of production technology and research facilities, since these will ultimately undermine the parent company's special superiority, and where investment is based on managerial superiority, the parent company is reluctant to localize ownership and management.

An examination of Japanese firms to date will show the majority as being examples of direct investment based on technological superiority, whereas only a small number belong to the latter type of investment on the basis of managerial superiority. Kao to date has in general proceeded with direct investment on the strength of its technological superiority in either production technology or marketing. This has been true in both Southeast Asia and in Spain. However, the pattern of foreign activities from the eighties can be seen as an attempt to change to an entry strategy based on managerial superiority. This is a clear manifestation of the drive to realize the Kao style of management with its central principle of 100 percent ownership. This is a strategic rather than an incremental style of management, inseparable from the forceful leadership practised by the company's president, Mr Maruta.

At present, the company's local production is confined to the periphery of Europe, and it will require time to evaluate the results of the research laboratory in Berlin. However, Kao's desire to expand its local production in Europe is very strong.

Given this change in emphasis from its technological to its managerial superiority, Kao will be faced with the question of how it can adapt to the firmly rooted European managerial environment, resistant as this tends to be to efforts of Japanese firms to effect change. Kao seems to have embarked on a pioneering course which will take it off from the beaten track, down a little travelled path of uncertain issues.

Source: *Managerial Efficiency in Competition and Cooperation: Japanese, West and East-European Strategies and Perspectives* (Sung-Jo Park (ed.)), Frankfurt am Main: Campus Verlag, 1992, pp. 327–343.

16

The United Germany and the Future of German Firms: A Japanese View

INTRODUCTION

IN JAPAN, THERE are two types of pessimism on the future of the united Germany. One is as to the political integration of the united Germany in the wider Europe. For example, Kiichi Miyazawa, one of the faction leaders of the Liberal Democratic Party and one of the most intellectual politicians in contemporary Japan, recently expressed his doubts as to whether either the CSCE (Conference on Security and Cooperation in Europe) or the EC (European Community) could control the stronger united Germany.[1] He may have good reason to be anxious about the potential power of Germany. He, however, underestimates certain developments in Europe in the 1980s: the role of the CSCE after the collapse of the NATO-WTO system and the EC's function in the political integration of Europe. It may only reflect his own anxiety on Japan which has no equivalent organizations with the Asian countries.

The other type of pessimism concerns the economic integration of the eastern part of Germany into the united Germany, that is, the integration of the planned economy into the "social market economy". It looks upon the deteriorating current indicators, such as the increasing number of bankruptcies and the rising rate of unemployment in Eastern Germany, as well as the increasing burden to the fiscal and monetary policy with fear. There is every reason to worry about failure in integrating the two different economic systems into one. It seems to me, however, that this type of pessimism also underestimates the developments in the 1980s and the socio-economic strength of the united Germany.

This paper aims at providing an optimistic prospect for the economic integration of the united Germany through a medium-range observation of a series of changes in the economic development of the two halves of Germany in the 1980s, especially those changes in industrial and firm-related conditions: industrial structure, the concentration of firms, industrial relations, ownership and management, and the attitude of business managers.

1. INDUSTRIAL STRUCTURE

The West German economy, as most other industrial economies, has exhibited a tendency towards a maturing service society since the 1970s, showing a declining percentage of primary and secondary industries and a rising percentage of tertiary industries.[2] It differs, however, from other industrial economies in that its secondary sector, especially manufacturing, is much more dominant, as shown in Table 16.1.

On the one hand, this fact seems to reflect the strong competitiveness of West German industry, represented by chemical, electrical and automobile manufacturers. On the other hand, this fact implies a lagged maturity in the West German economy in developing a service society, as compared to other developed countries.

The East German economy shows a similarly high percentage of secondary industry as the West German one. Its manufacturing industry, including productive handicraft, accounted for 40.5% of the labor force in 1988, the same as in West Germany. The share of secondary industry reached 64.9% of the national income and 61.6% of total investment.[3] Apart from the differences in classification of industry and from the disposition of the government and the military sectors, the industrial structure of East Germany without doubt revealed a significant dominance of the secondary sector and the corresponding lagged maturity as a service society. There are some causes for it: Berlin and the southern part of East Germany such as Saxony and Thuringia have been among the most industrialized regions since the nineteenth century and saw an accelerated development of heavy and chemical industry during the 1930s. In fact, after the Second World War, the eastern part of the divided Germany maintained more than half of the production capacity of sectors such as textiles, machinery, electrical, paper and precision industry in the old Germany. Given such a background, East Germany rushed into industrialization in the investment goods industry at the cost of the consumer goods industry.[4]

Table 16.1 Industrial Structure

Distribution of Employed by Industry (1987)

Industry	Primary	Secondary	Manufacturing	Tertiary
West Germany	5.1	40.5	33.0	54.4
United States	2.9	26.0	18.6	71.2
Japan	8.3	33.3	24.1	58.5
United Kingdom	1.5	29.1	23.6	69.4
France	7.0	29.4	21.8	63.6
Italy	10.3	32.0	22.1	57.7

Domestic Incomes by Industry (1988)

Industry	Primary	Secondary	Manufacturing	Tertiary
West Germany	1.6	11.2	32.4	57.3
United States	2.3	26. 4	20.1	71.3
Japan	2.3	34.9	25.9	62.8
United Kingdom	1.2	33.9	18.7	64.9
France	3.4	30.8	21.0	65.8
Italy	3.7	34.3	23.8	62.0

Source: The Bank of Japan, *Comparative Economic and Financial Statictics, Japan and Other Major Countries,* Vol. 27, 1990, pp. 49–50, 143.

The economic integration of these two economies is to proceed after the unification of the two halves of Germany. First, the integration process of two differently managed economies should certainly meet all kinds of trouble. The less developed Eastern economy will inevitably experience a profound structural change. However, the integration process of these two economies with almost the same industrial structure should advance rather smoothly. Secondly, the unified Germany will show an above-average dominance of the secondary sector, this being the reason for the lag in the developing service sector. The East German economy will add to the burden on the road to a service society.

Thirdly, however, the integration can provide a wider room for the service society in Germany and an incentive to its development. In West Germany, a catching-up process has already started. In the tertiary sector, the service industry, as defined in narrow sense, enlarged faster than other industries such as commerce and transportation which are closely related to manufacturing. In the secondary sector, industries which stand close to the tertiary sector developed faster than other industries. As for East Germany, a bank manager from West Germany has observed that service industries including hotels, restaurants, cinemas and petrol stations began to develop even before the monetary unification in July 1990.[5]

2. CONCENTRATION OF FIRMS

A booming concentration of firms characterizes the West German economy in the latter half of the 1980s. Figure 16.1 shows the increasing number of mergers notified under section 23 of the Act Against Restraints of Competition (ARC) from 506 in 1983 to 887 in 1987, the largest to date.

The figure also shows the fluctuation in the relative number of various types of mergers. It was the horizontal merger without product extension that increased most rapidly and contributed mostly to the increasing total number of mergers in recent years. This type of merger entails acquiring enterprises which involve the same markets as the enterprises acquiring them, and thus tends to be chosen through a defensive business strategy to maintain one's hold on the market. Conglomerate, non-production-related diversification extending to various industries and enterprises, also increased in the last decade, especially since 1987, and fluctuated above the level of 100. The increasing num

Figure 16.1 Type of the Merger (1970–87)

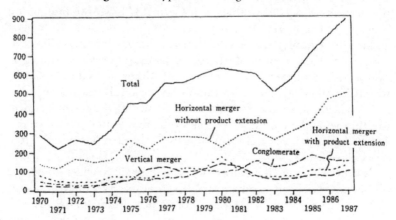

Source: *Hauptgutachten der Monopolkommission V 1982/1983*, p. 213: Deutscher Bundestag, *Drucksache 10/3550, p.131: 11/554,* p.119: OECD, *Competition Policy in OECD Counlries, 1987–1988*, p, 126: Hironori Yamaguchi, *Nishi Doitsu no Kyodai Kigyo lo Ginko(Big Business and Banking in West Germany)*, Tokyo, 1988, p. 64.

ber of conglomerates is primarily due to the 1980 amendment of the ARC which restrains horizontal mergers more restrictively than before and secondly due to the unprecedented boom in the stock market since 1983. Many big enterprises preferred conglomerates to the more restrictively regulated horizontal mergers in restructuring their business.[6] The series of mergers and acquisitions undertaken by the Daimler Benz Co. are among the most representative cases.

Figure 16.2 shows the numbers of each form of merger. A considerable increase is found in "acquisition of shares" and "acquisition of assets", particularly since 1985, which can be taken as being equivalent to "mergers and acquisitions" (M&As). The number of M&As did not decline even after the stock market crash in the fall of 1987 and reportedly increased further in 1988 and 1989. The scale of M&As has also been growing recently. German enterprises have been more frequently involved in international M&As than before, with the purpose of strengthening their international competitiveness on the eve of the completion of internal market integration within the EC. In short, we can observe a dynamically changing big business system in West Germany.

Figure 16.2 Form of the Merger (1973–87)

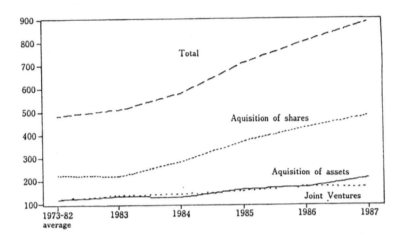

Source: OECD, *Competition Policy in OECD Countries, 1983–1984*, pp. 96–97:
1984–1985, p.110; *1985–1986*, p. 123: *1986–1987*, p. 125: *1987–1988*,
p. 126.

In East Germany also, the concentration of firms has reached a considerable level. In 1987, manufacturing firms with production value over one million marks totalled 88, or 2.6% of the total number of firms and accounted for 20.2% of the total labor force and 37.0% of total production value. Firms with production value over 500 millions marks totalled 225, or 6.6% of the total number, and concentrated 54.3% of total production value.[7] The East German economy showed at least the same level of firm concentration in manufacturing as did the West German one. The same can be seen in sectors other than manufacturing.

We can therefore observe highly concentrated business systems in both halves of Germany, and, moreover, an active M&A movement in West Germany. These two will be conditions which enable economic integration within the united Germany to proceed easier than otherwise. A key factor to economic integration would be a continuing concentration movement among big business in both parts of Germany.

Already on the eve of the monetary unification, large East German firms, all state-owned, entered fierce competition for survival. They are now under the ownership and control of the Treuhandanstalt

(Trust Institutution), which was established in order to take care of revitalization of those firms. Some of them were threatened with bankruptcy. Some others became targets for privatization. Some tried further to link with foreign big businesses, most of which were West German, through joint ventures and the like. The monetary and state unification apparently promoted this movement. The concentration movement in West Germany in a sense spilled over to the eastern part of the united Germany, in particular in the type of horizontal mergers without product extension and of conglomerates, as well as in the form of acquisition of shares and assets.

The rising level of concentration tends theoretically to restrict the dynamic activities of firms. The actual movement, however, apparently increases international competitiveness of German firms in the markets of the united Germany, the more integrated EC and the liberalized Eastern European countries.

The West German economy also experienced the revival of small business in the 1980s: the emergence of venture businesses in high technology, industries on the one hand, and the booming establish-ment of alternative cooperatives, which aim at reforming life style, on the other hand. West German medium and small-sized enterprises have maintained their traditional competitiveness. These vital medium and small-sized enterprises are also correctly expected to be pivotal in inte-grating the two economies.

3. OWNERSHIP AND MANAGEMENT

As has been shown above, in both parts of Germany, it is big business that should play a decisive role in completing economic integration.

The "socialization" of East German big firms was completed in all economic sectors through the beginning of the 1970s. A larger part of these firms became "volkseigen" (people-owned) and a smaller part of them became "genossenschaftlich" (cooperative). In this way, they were nationalized and controlled by the government and the governing party.[8]

Most state-owned East German firms, now under the ownership and control of the Treuhandanstalt, show little competitiveness. Most of them should be privatized in the long run and/or merged with their counterparts in the old West Germany, if they are to survive. The revi-talization of those firms depends mainly on the willingness and capa-bility of their West German counterparts.

We have good reason to be anxious about such willingness and capability, at least on the following points: (a) a small number of joint stock companies, which eventually means the limited financial capability of big business; (b) a small percentage of big business with diversified ownership structure, which also means in many cases limited financial capability; and (c) the profound influence on industrial enterprises' strategies used by big banks. All these points relate to the restriction of dynamic business strategy. There is, however, every reason to quell these anxieties as well, if we examine recent developments in ownership structure.

(a) It is true that relatively very few joint stock companies are registered in Germany (approx. 2,000) and listed on the market (approx. 230 on the Frankfurt stock exchange), while the number of limited private companies registered is increasing. Even among the 100 largest companies, only two thirds of them are joint stock companies. Recently, however, the number of joint stock companies has been growing faster than before and faster than the number of limited private companies, particularly due to the 1986 amendment of the Company Law according to the Directive of the EC Company Law, and also because of the amendment of laws aiming at promoting joint stock markets and consolidating owned capital of companies.

(b) Another characteristic of ownership structure in West German enterprises is found in the low level of distribution among big companies. Table 16.2 shows that only one quarter of the 100 largest companies are classified as "Distributed ownership of more than 50%." On the other hand, family business ("Mehrheit in Besitz von Eigenpersonen, Familien oder Familienstiftungen") also takes up a full quarter of the 100 largest companies. Observing Table 16.2 more closely, however, reveals the increasing number and production share of companies with dispersed ownership through the 1980s.

(c) It is well known that large industrial enterprises have close relationships with big banks through the so called universal banking system. They build enterprise groups ("Finanzgruppen"). It may be true that big banks use wide influence on business strategies of industrial enterprises through direct ownership, the use of voting rights on behalf of deposited stocks, and the appointment of directors. But

Table 16.2 Ownership Structure of the Largest 100 Companies (1978–86)

	1978		1980		1982		1984		1986	
	a	b	a	b	a	b	a	b	a	b
Distributed ownership more than 50%	22	39.2	23	39.5	23	39.4	23	41.1	25	43.9
Family-owned	18	12.0	18	11.8	25	16.2	24	16.0	23	13.7
Foreign-owned	20	16.3	22	15.5	16	12.9	19	13.1	18	12.6
Public-owned	11	8.5	8	8.1	11	9.3	10	8.5	14	9.9
Labor Union-owned	2	1.4	2	1.3	2	0.8	2	1.2	2	0.6
Other ownership	2	0.8	3	1.2	3	1.2	4	1.4	2	0.9
No majority	25	21.8	24	22.6	20	20.3	18	18.7	16	18.5
Total	100	100.0	100	100.0	100	100.0	100	100.0	100	100.0

Source: *Hauptgutachten der Monopolkommission IV 1980/1981*, p. 128: *VI 1984/1985*. p. 145: *VII 1986/1987*, p. 143.

a.   Number of Firms.
b.   Percentage of Production share.

it is incorrect to interpret that those industrial enterprises and enterprise groups are controlled or dominated by these big banks. The M&A activities of the Daimler Benz Co. can be realized less from the Deutsche Bank's strategy than from its own strategy, although the bank gave financial assistance to it. In fact, we can confirm that the self-financing ratio of industrial enterprises as a whole tended to rise since the first oil crises of 1973, and that they cover most of their gross investment through funds on hand. Enterprise groups or Finanzgruppen in Germany consolidate the management control of each member enterprise so that the overall management is effectively able to oppose intervention from outside such as from foreign investors. Therefore, enterprise groups in Germany can be seen as an equivalent to business groups in Japan which consist mainly of mutual ownership of industrial, commercial and financial joint stock companies.

Insofar as we observe the recent developments closely, we can conclude that ownership does not restrain management in West German enterprises, and that West German big businesses, including banks, have to a considerable extent the will and capability to take initiatives in revitalizing big East German firms. Besides, it is not difficult for West German enterprises to take the initiative in reconstructing their East German counterparts and even to merge with them, now that the Federal Republic *de jure* as well as *de facto* merged with the Democratic Republic.

4. LABOR MARKET AND INDUSTRIAL RELATIONS

The weak competitiveness of big firms in the old East Germany gives us good reason to fear massive unemployment in the eastern part. Most pessimistic observers predict 3 or 4 million unemployed within a few years. It is true that the situation in the eastern part is too severe to be optimistic in the short run; however, the medium and long term observation gives us a rather optimistic prospect.

First, although the West German labor market suffered from massive unemployment since the beginning of the 1980s and even in the business recovery and prosperity process after 1983 (see Figure 16.3), it recently experienced a slightly declining rate of unemployment. This prosperity reportedly even brought about a partial shortage in the labor force, such as managers, engineers, qualified, skilled labor. For example, information engineers, such as system engineers, are in serious shortage, which occasionally results in a bottleneck in the expansion of the information industry.

Figure 16.3 Labor Market (1970–88)

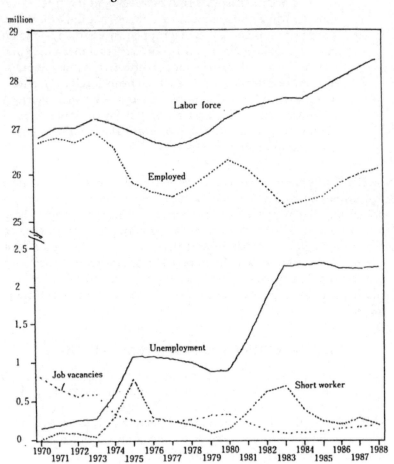

Source: Sachverständigenrat zur Begutachtung der gesamtwirtschaftlichen Entwicklung, *Weichenstellung für die Neunziger Jahre, Jahresgutachten 1989/90,* Stuttgart, 1989, p. 63.

Some structural factors promoted cyclical improvement in the labor market. The changing industrial structure caused a partial shortage of the labor force. Likewise, the changing structure of the population, mainly caused by the declining birth rate, will aggregate the labor shortage in general in the future. Shorter working hours will also add to demand for a larger labor force. The improved situation in the Western labor market can reduce the burden of unemployment in the Eastern part directly or indirectly, and will in the long run give a rather optimistic prospect for economic integration.

Secondly, industrial relations have also experienced a change in the last decade.

After the maladjustment of the West German economy at the beginning of the 1980s, employers became more dissatisfied with industrial relations. They criticized the high level of wages and social insurance charges, and complained of the rigidity of lay-off regulations as well as labor protection, and of the decreasing morale of employees. They further perceived a varying value system as well as the generation gap in the affluent society as unpleasant. They criticized in particular the new law on the "Mitbestimmung" (workers' participation), which they thought was too rigid a framework for them. Conflicts occurred at the Mannesmann company and on the amendment of the "Mitbestimmung" law in the coal and iron industry. Employees also became critical of industrial relations, given the massive unemployment and the decreasing rise of the wage rate. In 1984, the conflict over shortening working hours became acute, and the "social partnership" temporarily cracked.

In the latter half of the 1980s, however, industrial relations became rather eased and stable. Employers became more tolerant to the "Mitbestimmung" because of business recovery and continued prosperity. Trade unions also apparently became more ready to accept further introduction of microelectronics and further robotization.

The integration of industrial relations is to be pursued by introducing the western system into the eastern part of Germany. The realized reconstruction of the "social partnership" in West Germany in the latter half of the 1980s is to be the basis for the integration. Moreover, the integration should be accomplished without great difficulties, because the "socialistically" disciplined employees in the eastern part are potentially ready to accept the "social" industrial relations of West Germany: collective bargaining, the Mitbestimmung and participation at shop. Possible conflicts in the integration process will be no more serious in the integration of workers than in the integration of managers. The most decisive factor for the reconstruction of the eastern part lies not in industrial relations, but in management.

5. ATTITUDES OF MANAGERS: FROM PESSIMISM TO OPTIMISM

The maladjustment of the West German economy at the beginning of the 1980s made business managers uneasy. They criticized, on the one hand, present industrial relations and the Mitbestimmung law, yet on the other hand, were themselves criticized by observers. Some of them suffered from a loss of self-confidence. In those days, the export of Japanese industrial products such as automobiles and electric consumer goods to West Germany grew rapidly. A larger part of these managers criticized Japanese management as well as suddenly increased exports from Japan. A smaller part of them were interested in the Japanese style of management, and even considered it as a model for their own companies, although the Japanese style of management was only an additional factor to the "Americanization" of German management, which started late in the 1960s in Germany, much later than in Japan.[9]

One example of the criticism prevailing against West German management and lauding Japanese management is found in a West German book written by journalist Dietrich Strasser.[10] He criticizes all aspects of the business strategy of German companies as follows. With respect to production strategy, German managers and engineers are not well market-oriented and too often ignore consumers' tastes and technical standards on distant foreign markets. In marketing, they lack long-term points of view which make Japanese rivals so competitive. Strasser also points out the reluctance of adept businessmen to work abroad. As to personnel and labor policies, he points out the problems such as "internal hidden lay-offs", the lack of motivation, the lack of downward information flow, the shortage of "personnel inventory" and the negligence of directors responsible for personnel policy. In research and development, the negligence of application and product development reseach is criticized. As for financial policy, German managers are condemned for being too timid to curb dividends and to increase retained profits.

All in all, Strasser accuses West German managers of risk-avoiding management and of the lack of imagination and originality. Not all of the points may be true, and some of them obviously exaggerate the situation, but this is only one sample of the type of pessimism about German management which prevailed in the first half of the 1980s.

In the course of business recovery, the self-confidence of managers also recovered, as illustrated in a book by Peter Zürn.[11] He certainly admires Japanese management and society, rather stereotypically characterizing them as "consensus oriented" or "Gemeinschaft (community) oriented". He recommends "consensus oriented corporate culture", which consists of the "seven Ks": Konzeption, Kommunikation, Koordination, Kooperation, Kontrolle, Konzentration, and Konstitution. He does not, however, criticize German management, management by the seven Ks being a universal ideal. We can find here an optimistic view of German management.

The changing attitude of managers and observers – from pessimism to optimism – in the 1980s is an additional condition which enables economic integration to advance rather smoothly in the medium term.

CONCLUSION

Despite anxiety in the short term, the medium-range observation here leads us to an optimistic prospect for further economic integration in the united Germany. German business took a favorable turn in the 1980s in all aspects of industrial and firm-related conditions for economic integration which were investigated here: industrial structure, the concentration of firms, ownership and management, industrial relations and the attitudes of business management. Integration can fortunately exploit these favorable conditions. The most probable scenario is a smooth integration in the medium term. I believe that it would be time-saving to start from this scenario in speculating about, for example, what position the united Germany would and should take in the greater Europe and what kinds of strategies Japanese business would and should choose towards the united Germany and the greater Europe.

Source: *Annals of the Institute of Social Science, University of Tokyo*, No. 36, 1995, pp. 57–91.

17

A Partnership of Imbalance: Changes in Japanese-European Economic Relations

I. INTRODUCTION

IN THE LATTER half of the 1980s, and especially with the dissolution of the borders between West and East Germany in the autumn of 1989, the whole of Europe plunged into a period of tumultuous changes in the social, political, and economic regimes. The upheaval sent shock waves across the globe, even affecting Japan. In fact, the collapse of the Japanese political regime of 1955, which used to pivot around the rivalry between two major political parties, may be seen as part of the chain reaction to the European upheaval. This was not the first time that Japan was shaken by an upheaval in Europe. More specifically, the conclusion of the Soviet-German Nonaggression Pact in the summer of 1939 led to the wholesale resignation of the Hiranuma government, and the outbreak of war in Europe shortly thereafter as well as the outbreak of the war between Germany and the Soviet Union two years later became one of the factors that caused Japan to take a wrong turning.

There are, of course, a number of differences between the historical experience and the present turn of events. For one thing, unlike the previous occasion, Europe today is moving toward a Europe-wide regional integration. For another, the relations between Japan and Europe are now radically different from those in the late 1930s. Previously, Japan was on the receiving end of the shocks coming from Europe, and affected unilaterally by them; it was possible (though perhaps not appropriate) to explain social and economic developments in Europe without any reference to developments in Japan. Now, however, the Japanese

388

economy has grown too large to be neglected in explaining the present socioeconomic upheaval in Europe. On the contrary, Japan's economic power has been one of the important factors responsible for triggering the upheaval. In fact, European efforts to unify the European Community (EC) market by the end of 1992 might be said to have been undertaken primarily as a European response to the economic challenge posed by Japan. One might also say that the collapse of the socialist systems of the former Soviet Union and Eastern Europe was prompted, to a large extent, by the weakening of their economies under the overwhelming impact of the rapidly growing economies of East and Southeast Asia with their close links with Japan's economy and private firms. Thus, the relationship that exists between Japan and Europe today, unlike that of the late 1930s, is characterized as one of interdependence, in which influence and impact flow in both directions.

This paper attempts to analyze recent developments in Japan-Europe relations by looking at the interdependent nature of these relations. At the outset, however, some precautionary remarks must be made about the scope of this paper. For one thing, the following discussion is focused on Japan's relations with Western Europe, and in particular with the EC.[1] Among the many aspects of Japan's relations with Western Europe, or with the EC, this paper limits itself to dealing with economic aspects, because these, for good or bad, have been pivotal to the relations between Japan and Europe. Among various aspects of the economic relations, moreover, those pertaining to trade and direct investment are at the focus of analysis. The author hopes to present a holistic picture of the relations in trade and direct investment, by placing them in a long-term perspective, and interpreting them from a standpoint somewhat different from the conventional view.

II. CONFRONTATION AND COOPERATION: TRADE

1. The Cycles and Structure of the Trade Conflict

Since the early Meiji era, Japan has continued to learn technologies and managerial methods from Western Europe. Its relationship with Western Europe began as a "teacher-student relationship" and remained so for many years, but within this framework, it managed by the 1930s to raise itself to the position of a competitor to Western European countries. After World War II, Japan resumed the "teacher-student relationship" with Western Europe, while emerging also as a competitor. In other words, from the outset of its resumption after the war, the relationship entailed a latent conflict of interests between the two parties. Almost concurrently with its comeback in the arena of international politics, Japan re-established bilateral trade relations with West European countries based on the mutual granting of most-favored-nation treatment. This process unfolded as part of a larger process – that is, the process of Japan's participation in the Bretton Woods system, the system for managing the post-war world economy which upheld the principles of freedom, multilateralism, and non-discrimination. More specifically, the latter process unfolded as Japan's participation in the two core organizations underpinning the Bretton Woods system: the International Monetary Fund (IMF) and the General Agreement on Tariffs and Trade (GATT). Japan won admission into the IMF in 1952, concurrent with West Germany.

A conflict of interest between Japan and West European countries came to the fore for the first time over the question of Japan's participation in the GATT. Unlike West Germany, which was granted full membership as early as 1951 when it was still under Allied occupation, Japan's participation – after climbing the ladder from the status of an observer to that of a provisional member – was delayed until 1955. The delay was caused primarily by the concerted action of Western European countries, spearheaded by Britain, to prevent or limit Japan's participation in the GATT. Faced with these hostile actions, Japan was obliged to make a number of concessions, including acceptance of a safeguard clause, agreement to the establishment of a list of sensitive commodities, and pledges to practice voluntary export restrictions and to purchase specific commodities. As a result of these concessions, fourteen of the GATT member countries, including the United Kingdom, France, and the three Benelux countries, continued to discriminate against Japan by invoking Article 35 of the GATT. It was not until the Japanese-British Treaty of Commerce and Navigation took effect in 1963 that the UK stopped discriminating against Japan. France and the three Benelux countries also did the same in 1963, the year Japan became a full-fledged GATT member with its reclassification as an Article 11 country (one prohibited from restricting trade for reasons of balance of payments difficulties). It was in the following year that Japan became an IMF Article 8 country (one prohibited from restricting foreign exchange transactions for reasons of balance of payments difficulties), and was admitted to the OECD.[2]

In Western Europe, meanwhile, the European Economic Community (EEC) came into being following the conclusion of the Treaty of Rome in 1957. Despite the establishment of the regional organization, economic transactions between Japan and Western European countries continued to be carried out on a bilateral basis throughout the 1960s. With the termination of its initial transitional period at the end of 1969, the EEC began to take steps toward attaining a higher degree of integration by devising common policies. When the EEC actually began to devise its Common Commercial Policy (CCP) based on Article 113 of the Treaty of Rome, and identified a total of ten countries as the proposed targets of the CCP, Japan was singled out as the most formidable target.

The basic policy of the EEC (hereafter referred to as the EC, to avoid confusion) toward Japan called for consolidation of the member countries' Treaties of Commerce with Japan into a unified treaty, liberalization of trade with Japan, and introduction of a reciprocal and comprehensive safeguard clause applicable to the all EC member countries in their relations with Japan. In contrast, Japan's basic policy toward the EC put primary emphasis on the liberalization of trade, while asserting, with regard to the safeguard issue, that the use of safeguard measures in accordance with Article 19 of the GATT (the escape clause) alone should be allowed as an emergency action. In other words, Japan found the safeguard clause proposed by the EC utterly unacceptable.

Negotiations on the issue took place between 1970 and 1973. Within the EC, the Council authorized the EC Commission to negotiate with Japan on the issue; at the same time, however, the Council decided to allow the existing bilateral policies and treaties to remain in force (through extension and renewal), and also to allow the discriminatory practices against, and the quotas on imports from, Japan to remain in effect. This development gave the Japanese negotiating team the impression that the bargaining authority entrusted to the EC Commission was very ill-defined. In fact, negotiations were held at two different levels, the Japan-EC level and the bilateral level. Japan and the EC reached agreement on the need for trade liberalization as a matter of principle, but their opinions were divided on the safeguard clause. At one point, the EC contemplated a compromise proposal to make the safeguard clause effective for a finite period, but the proposal failed to win approval of member countries other than West Germany and thus was never formally presented to Japan. On the Japanese side, too, there was a significant difference in opinion between the Federation of Economic Organizations (Keidanren) and the Ministry of International Trade and Industry (MITI). Eventually, the negotiations failed, due primarily to the two parties' sharply divided opinions about the safeguard clause. Underlying the EC's antagonism toward Japan on this issue, one might say, were several factors: the memory of the fierce conflict the European countries had with Japan over trade back in the 1930s, a memory which must have remained fresh at the time; the growing anxiety the EC was entertaining about Japan's rapid economic growth and its increasing trade surplus with the EC (see Table 17.1); and the violent shakeup and collapse of the IMF-administered system of fixed exchange rates in the wake of the "Nixon shock" of August 1971. Subsequently, the safeguard clause was brought up for deliberation in the arena of the GATT, and was put on the agenda for the GATT's Tokyo Round negotiations (1973–79).[3]

Table 17.1 The EC's Trade with Japan (1)

Unit: million ECU

	Export to Japan	Import from Japan	Trade balance with Japan
1958	211	258	-47
1960	313	397	-83
1965	531	798	- 267
1970	1,426	2,090	-663
1975	2,345	5,599	- 3,253
1983	7,710	21,940	- 14,230
1984	9,364	25,668	- 16,304
1985	10,475	25,586	- 18,111
1986	11,399	33,215	- 21,816
1987	13,618	34,757	- 21,139
1988	17,020	41,618	-24,598
1989	21,130	46,337	- 25,207
1990	22,721	46,224	- 23,503
1991	22,155	51,818	- 29,663
1992	20,507	51,511	- 31,005

Source: *Eurostat, External Trade*, 1992, pp. 4–5, 7.

Not only did the "Nixon shock" bring an end to the IMF-administered system of fixed exchange rates, but it also brought down the post-war world economic regime with its manifested commitment to liberalism, nondiscrimination, and multilateralism. The first oil crisis of October 1973 shook the very material bases that had been sustaining the rapid economic growth of Japan and West European countries. Japan performed far more superbly than its European competitors in rebounding from the confusions caused by the shock, and thus sowed the seeds for commercial and trade conflicts with the EC.

The first of a series of commercial conflicts between Japan and the EC popped up in the period from 1976 to 1977, when the world was still in the process of recovery from the first oil crisis. Unlike the previous conflicts, which were of a bilateral nature, this conflict was the first of its kind, taking place between Japan and the EC. Imports from Japan against which the EC lodged its complaints included steel, ships, and bearings. The EC's commercial policy toward Japan at the time purported to seek some form of *ad hoc* settlement, pending the conclusion of a unified treaty of commerce between the EC and Japan. With this policy objective, the EC demanded that Japan start practicing orderly exports and taking voluntary export restrictions, as well as opening up its import markets to EC products. The conflict was resolved with the announcement of the joint Japan-EC statement of 1978, in which Japan pledged to open its import markets to foreign commodities and to stimulate effective demand domestically, in order to play the more active role of a "locomotive" for the world economy in response to the expectations expressed at the Bonn Summit.

The second conflict erupted in 1980, immediately following the outbreak of the second oil crisis in 1979. The EC's complaints this time were mainly targeted at Japanese exports of cars and color television sets. The composition of Japanese exports was changing so dramatically that trade conflicts with the EC began to take place in a cyclical manner, accompanied by a fairly rapid shift in the focus for each conflict from one group of commodities to another.[4]

The commercial conflict between Japan and the EC constituted part of the trilangular conflict among Japan, the United States, and the EC. It also had much to do with the GATT Tokyo Round negotiations, and later with the Uruguay Round negotiations. Thus, when Japan made some concessionary moves in response to its conflict with the US – pledging, for instance, to restrict its exports voluntarily – the EC felt dissatisfied with those moves, condemning Japan for placing disproportionate emphasis on its relations with the US. Such dissatisfaction sometimes led the EC to demand the same concessions from Japan as had been offered to the US, giving rise to further conflict between Japan and the EC. One might see a general tendency for a conflict erupting first between Japan and the US to be duplicated subsequently as one between Japan and the EC. One conspicuous feature common to Japan-US conflict and Japan-EC conflict was Japan's passive attitude. On the other hand, there was one significant difference: a conflict between the US and the EC, while entailing a very tough negotiation process, tended to reach an early and fairly straightforward settlement; a Japan-EC conflict tended to be characterized by the EC's aggressiveness and Japan's passivity, and its negotiation process by many turns and twists. Moreover, Japan-EC conflicts began to spread regionally into Asia, as the EC came to face increasing conflicts of interests with East and Southeast Asian countries as well.

The year 1986 saw a surge of Japanese exports to the EC. As shown in Table 17.1, the EC's trade deficit with Japan, which was ECU18.1 billion in 1985, jumped to ECU21.8 billion, topping the ECU20 billion mark. One important factor underlying this sudden upsurge of the EC's trade deficit was the fact that Japanese companies, in the face of the upward revaluation of the yen following the 1985 Plaza Accord among the G5 countries, redirected much of their exports to the US to the EC, and began to compete fiercely in the EC market. This led to the eruption of yet another commercial conflict. The tension continued until around 1989, when the "imbalance" in trade began to show signs of "improvement." It was asserted at the time that as the Japanese economy was picking up momentum, the economy was becoming less dependent on sales abroad to stimulate growth, or that the economic boom was now being led by domestic demand rather than by export demand. The booming domestic market was a combined product of the expansionary fiscal policy, measures for market liberalization, and the yen's soaring value. Even the "van Gogh effects" – imports of paintings and other objects of fine art at exorbitantly high prices with the surplus funds generated by the "bubble" economic boom – made a contribution to reducing the Japan-EC trade imbalance. On the other hand, the EC's exports to Japan showed increases beginning in 1987, centered around such products as wine and other alcoholic beverages, passenger cars, medical equipment, cosmetics, and pharmaceuticals. The EC Commission assessed this improved export performance as having been achieved by the export promotion efforts of the individual industrial sectors concerned. As demonstrated by Table 17.1, the deficit the EC incurred in its trade with Japan in 1989 was ECU25.2 billion, only a small increase over the previous year, and in 1990 it dropped to ECU23.5 billion. By the spring of 1989, the commercial conflict began to calm down.[5]

Toward the end of 1990, the EC's trade deficit with Japan suddenly began to increase at a rapid pace again (see Table 17.1). Japan's trade surplus with the EC in FY1992 exceeded the $30 billion mark and reached $31.2 billion. (Japan's total trade surplus in FY1992 was $136.1 billion, while its current account surplus, $126.1 billion, was in excess of the earlier record figure of $94.1 billion attained in FY1986.) The expanding trade deficit with Japan, occurring as it did when all the EC countries but the UK were suffering from protracted recessions and increasing unemployment rates, was sufficient to give rise to another conflict. The collapse of the "bubble" blew away the Japanese government's efforts to "improve" the "imbalance." The governments and industries of the EC countries grew ever more irritated by the expanding "imbalance" in their trade with Japan.[6]

The central issues of the Japan-EC commercial conflict, as in the case of the Japan-US conflict, are the balance of trade unfavorable to the EC and the expanding size of the imbalance. In the words of the EC authorities, the "serious and continuing deficits" incurred by the EC constitute the origin of the conflict. A significant "imbalance" in trade between any two partners can become a cause for dispute, especially when the international institutions for multilateral clearing headed by the IMF and the GATT are malfunctioning as they are today. There is no objective standard for judging what constitutes an imbalance in trade, to be sure; but, especially in times of recession, a country enjoying a trade surplus is regarded as an exporter of unemployment to its trade partners, and an "imbalance" in the balance of trade is instantly associated with unemployment.

As is evident from Table 17.2, which shows the breakdown of Japan's export to the EC by commodity, three commodities – i.e. general machinery, electrical equipment, and transportation equipment – account for approximately 25% each, or a combined share of approximately 75%, of the total. It is also these categories of goods that are earning the lion's share of Japan's trade surplus with the EC. According to the EC's argument, approximately half the EC's trade deficits are accounted for by four industrial sectors: automobiles, data-processing equipment, electric communication equipment, and electronics parts. The trade deficits sustained by the EC in the four sectors in 1991 were: ECU8.8 billion for automobiles, ECU4.6 billion for data-processing equipment, ECU 1.2 billion for electric communication equipment, and ECU2.5 billion for electronics parts. In fact, the EC has begun to demand, on the strength of these figures, that Japan take steps to attain balanced trade on a sector-by-sector basis.

Table 17.2 Japan's Trade with the EC Broken Down by Commodity, 1992

Units: $ million and %

	Japan's export to EC		Japan's import from EC	
	Amount	% of total	Amount	% of total
Textile and textile products	130	0.2	—	—
Foodstuffs	956	1.5	3,451	11.5
Chemicals	3,491	5.6	844	2.7
Nonmetal ore products	484	0.8	120	0.4
Metals and metal products	1,296	2.1	6,304	20.2
General machinery	15,581	24.9	2,426	7.8
Electric equipment	14,987	24.0	1,166	3.7
Transportation equipment	15,413	24.7	1,065	3.4
Precision equipment	4,507	7.2	11,009	35.2
Miscellaneous	5,631	9.0	4,752	15.2
Total	62,474	100.0	31,280	100.0

Source: *Tsusho Hakusho (Whitepaper on International Trade)*, 1993 edn., Volume on Particulars, pp. 4–7.

Note: Due to rounding up, percentage figures do not necessarily add up to 100.

On the other hand, 35% of the EC's export to Japan is accounted for by precision machinery, and 20% by metals and metal products. According to the EC's explanation, its export to Japan is concentrated on those consumption goods which are sensitive to the trend of the economy and disposable income (e.g. passenger cars, textile products, and alcoholic beverages), and these exports are growing at a faster pace than exports of organic chemicals, pharmaceuticals, nonferrous metals, and other capital goods. The EC is concerned, moreover, about the less-than-satisfactory performance of exports to Japan by some of the sectors which it believes to be internationally competitive, e.g. office equipment, communications equipment, and foodstuff.

Table 17.3 The EC's Trade with Japan (2)

Units: million ECU, %

	Export to Japan			Import from Japan		
	Amount (million ECU)	% of total export	Japan's standing	Amount (million ECU)	% of total import	Japan's standing
1980	4,810	2.2	11	13,698	4.9	4
1988	17,020	4.7	5	41,618	10.7	2
1989	21,130	5.1	5	46,337	10.4	2
1990	22,721	5.4	5	46,224	10.0	2
1991	22,155	5.2	4	51,818	10.5	2
1992	20,507	4.7	5	51,511	10.6	2

Source: *Eurostat, External Trade*, 1992, p. 8.
Note: The total amounts of export and import are exclusive of intra-regional trade.

One might say that the EC has grown more seriously concerned about its trade deficits with Japan. In part, this is due to the growing significance of Japan as its trade partner. As shown in Table 17.3, Japan's share in the EC's external trade was only about 2% in 1980, but jumped to around 5% in the decade since then, with the result that Japan now ranks as the fourth or fifth largest export market for the EC. Japan's share in the EC's import market also grew twofold during the 1980s to reach around 10%, making Japan the second largest exporter to the EC after the US. Thus, the position of Japan as the EC's trade partner has grown ever more important,[7] and trade deficits with Japan are becoming a matter of increasingly serious concern.

Several other factors are inducing the EC to take an increasingly serious view of its trade deficits with Japan. Not only the absolute size of the deficits with Japan, but their relative size compared with the trade volume is seen as unacceptable. Moreover, it finds it also problematic that, unlike its trade balance with the US, which oscillates between surpluses and deficits from time to time, it is chronically incurring deficits in its trade with Japan. Another source of the dissatisfaction felt by the EC is that, as shown in Figure 17.1, its trade balance in manufactured goods sustains huge excess imports only in relation with Japan. Glancing at this figure, one will naturally have an impression, whether well- or ill-founded, of the Japanese market as something "extraordinary" that stubbornly refuses to import fine manufactured goods from the EC.

Figure 17.1 EC's Trade in Manufactured Products in 1992 by Major PARTNER

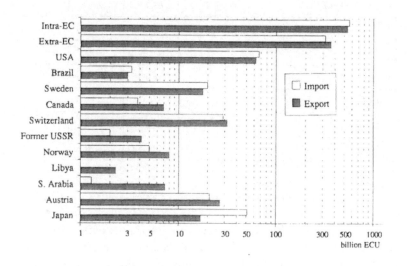

Source: Based on Eurostat, *External Trade – Statistical Yearbook*, 1993, p.xxxiii.
Note: Manufactured products consist of those listed under SITC 5, 6, 7, and 8.

Table 17.4 Japan's Trade with the EC in 1992, by Country

Unit: $ million

	Export to the EC	*Import from the EC*	*Trade balance with the EC*
Denmark	916	1,436	-520
United Kingdom	12,287	4,890	7,397
Ireland	1,166	1,078	88
The Netherlands	8,098	1,316	6,782
Belgium & Lux-embourg	4,855	1,294	3,561
France	6,312	5,412	900
Germany	20,310	10,739	9,571
Portugal	805	188	617
Spain	2,863	664	2,199
Italy	3,899	4,157	- 258
Greece	965	108	857
Grand total	62,474	31,280	31,194

Source: Eurostat, Tsusho Hakusho, 1993 edn., Volume on Particulars, p. 427.
Note: Figures entered in each column do not necessarily add up to the grand total.

A closer look at Japan's export to the EC broken down by country of destination will shed light on another important aspect. As shown in Table 17.4, Japan has been enjoying trade surpluses with almost all the EC countries, and has garnered especially large surpluses of $23.8 billion – or 76% of its total surplus with the EC – in its trade with three of the member countries, Germany, the UK, and the Netherlands. These three countries, with their imports from Japan far in excess of those of the other member countries, are regarded as the leading proponents of free trade within the EC. In contrast, the sizes of Japanese surpluses with France and Italy, the leading advocates of protectionism among the EC members, were much smaller, and even dropped into the negative (in the case of Italy) in

1992, the year of focus for this table. The latter two countries are maintaining protectionist policies, such as the imposition of import quotas on automobiles. Thus, Japan's trade relations with the two groups of EC countries, one advocating the principle of free trade and the other taking a protectionist stance, cut a sharp contrast. Even though strong correlations between the two groups' attitudes toward external trade relations and their respective balance of trade positions with Japan are not immediately discernible, there is no denying that the protectionist group's position has been manifested more straightforwardly than the free-trade group's position in the Japan-EC negotiations.[8]

2. The Present State of the Japan-EC Trade Negotiations

At the Japan-EC negotiations of high-ranking administrative officials in November 1989, the EC representatives pointed to the structural issues lying between the two parties. At the periodical ministerial conference in May the following year, bitter words were exchanged over trade issues, but the two parties agreed to the establishment of a joint working group that would meet periodically to deliberate on measures for resolving the trade issues. The first meeting of the Japan-EC Joint Working Group on Trade Problems was held in July the same year; at it the EC representatives proposed a total of 18 issues for inclusion in the Group's agenda, the Japanese representatives a mere 3 issues. As is evident from the wide discrepancy in the number of problem areas perceived by the two sides, there emerged a framework of negotiations quite similar to that in the Japan-US negotiations, in the sense that the EC representatives took the initiative and put the Japanese negotiators on the defensive. As a matter of fact, discussions at the first meeting of the Joint Working Group pivoted mainly around the need for opening up Japanese import markets. The EC representatives were particularly insistent on Japan's opening its markets to leather products, leather shoes, processed foods, and marine products from the EC. The second meeting of the Joint Working Group was held in October the same year, and the progress of the deliberation became the topic of discussion at the negotiations between high-ranking administrative officials that were held shortly thereafter. The EC officials expressed their strong dissatisfaction with the slow progress made by the Joint Working Group.

Subsequently, during then Prime Minister Kaifu's tour of Europe in July 1991, the first Japan-EC Summit meeting was held in the Hague, the Netherlands. The summit meeting concluded with the adoption of a joint statement in which the two sides reaffirmed their sharing of the basic values concerning freedom, democracy, human rights, and free trade, and their determination to work toward common purposes in political and economic fields, by holding more lively dialogues and stepping up cooperation and partnership in various fields of activities such as politics, economics, science, and culture. The summit meeting also agreed on holding similar meetings at the rate of once every year.

The joint statement could have marked a new beginning in Japan's relations with the EC, which had been centered excessively around economic relations. In reality, however, economic issues were by far the most serious topics of discussions between the Japanese and European leaders. For example, an argument that took place in the course of negotiations over the wording of the joint statement very eloquently revealed that there was a wide discrepancy between the lofty ideals spelled out by the statement and the realities of Japan-EC relations: during the drafting of the statement, the Japanese delegation staunchly opposed the French proposal to include in the statement a phrase "the equilibrium of interests"; the Japanese insisted that the proposed phrase, with its strong snynonymity with "the equality in results," be replaced by words more synonymous with "the equality in opportunity"; adopted in the final version was a phrase closer to the Japanese counterproposal, i.e., "equitable access."

The second summit meeting, in July 1992, reached an agreement on expansion of the EC's exports to Japan and the furthering of industrial cooperation. Subsequently, the third Japan-EC summit meeting was held during the G7's Tokyo Summit of July 1993, with then Prime Minister Miyazawa representing Japan. The third meeting, too, put trade problems at the top of its agenda. Given the climate of the time, when Japan's balance of current accounts was showing an expanding surplus and its trade surplus with the EC was at an all-time high, the leaders of the EC countries severely criticized the Japanese government's failure to stimulate the internal markets.

These meetings were preceded by the periodical ministerial conference of January 1993, which agreed to establish a joint Japan-EC meeting of specialists on trade statistics, or a Trade Assessment Mechanism (TAM), for jointly collecting and analyzing trade statistics to identify the causes underlying the growing "imbalance" in trade. In accordance with the EC's insistence that the TAM be specifically charged with the task of identifying product areas in which the EC's exports were being inhibited by Japanese "structural barriers," it was agreed that the TAM would convene a meeting in June the same year to study measures for expanding EC exports to Japan on a commodity-by-commodity basis.[9]

In the meantime, a wide array of measures had been adopted by the EC in response to imports from Japan; especially important among them were the discriminatory quantitative restriction (QR) on imports from Japan, a regulation for the prevention of dumping, and regulations concerning places of origin applicable to manufactured goods.[10] As of January 1993, as many as 20 commodities were subject to the QR. The anti-dumping regulation was also invoked frequently, targeting imports from Japan. The finished Japanese products that were subjected to the EC Commission's anti-dumping investigations during the 1980s were: electronic typewriters, bearings, electronic weighing scales, copy machines, outboard motors, hydraulic earth-moving shovels, couplers for forgeable pig-iron pipes, semiconductors (EPROMs [erasable programmable read-only memories] and DRAMs [dynamic random access memories]), printers (the daisy-wheel type and the dot-matrix type), video tape recorders (VTRs), cellular phones, microwave ovens, CD players, small-sized hydraulic earth-moving shovels, wheel loaders, audio cassettes and tapes, and halogen lamps. The products locally manufactured by Japan-affiliated firms in the EC that were similarly subjected to investigations were: electronic typewriters, electronic weighing scales, hydraulic earth-moving shovels, bearings, printers (the dot-matrix type), VTRs, and copy machines.

In 1988, Japan appealed to the GATT's Dispute Settlement Panel, condemning the EC's imposition of parts-dumping tariffs on these Japanese products; in its March 1990 ruling, the Panel declared the EC's practice as running counter to the GATT's regulations. Despite the GATT's ruling, the EC continued to take recourse to the same practice. Take the case of semiconductors, for instance. As the European market plunged into a recession beginning in 1990, the performance of European manufacturers of semiconductors deteriorated, with the French companies Bull and Thomson and the Dutch company Philips posting deficits for the accounting year 1990. The European manufacturers pressed hard for the imposition of high-rate tariffs and anti-dumping tariffs on semiconductors imported from Japan. Similarly, August 1992 saw the imposition of anti-dumping tariffs on copy machines imported from Japan.

The EC Commission's annual report on its anti-dumping policy, published in November 1993, reported that as of the end of 1992 a total of 158 product items imported from outside the community were subjected to the imposition of anti-dumping tariffs or to the minimum price regulations. Products made in Japan formed the largest group, accounting for 27 of the 158, and included semiconductors, DRAMs, EPROMs, printers, and audio cassette tapes. In terms of money values, Japan accounted for 70% of the imports on which anti-dumping tariffs were imposed. This was indicative of the fact that the EC's anti-dumping policy was targeted primarily against Japan. It should be pointed out, however, that the EC did not institute any new anti-dumping inquiries about imports from Japan in 1992 (while in the previous year new inquiries had been instituted about five product items imported from Japan). Manufactured imports from East Asia dominated the list of 158 product items subjected to the anti-dumping measures, with Japan's 27 product items followed by China's 20, and South Korea's 13.

In the year 1993, a new product item came under anti-dumping investigation. Almost concurrently with the publication of the afore-mentioned report, the EC Commission announced that it would tentatively impose an anti-dumping tariff at the maximum rate of 97% on television cameras imported from Japan for use by TV stations. In response, Japanese manufacturers restricted their exports voluntarily, so to speak. Japanese manufacturers of television sets, such as Sanyo and Sharp, which were exporting from their production bases in Asia to the EC (Sanyo from its Singapore plant, Sharp from its Malaysian plant), anticipated that the imposition of similar anti-dumping tariffs would be unavoidable, and made plans to completely terminate these exports from the Asian platforms to the EC. (An estimated total of one million TV sets were thus withdrawn from exports.) The two manufacturers planned to relocate some of their manufacturing operations to the EC. Given the fact that Matsushita and Sony have already relocated production from Asia to the EC, these new shifts will bring all the major Japanese electric appliance makers onto the European manufacturing scene.

The imposition of the anti-dumping tariffs was one of the issues debated by the GATT's Uruguay Round negotiations. When the negotiations were concluded in December 1993, it was decided that after an interval of a certain number of years the imposition of the tariffs would be reviewed in a restrictive way. The conclusion of the Uruguay Round negotiations, with its expected effect of stepping up imports, prompted the EC to intensify its anti-dumping measures, most likely targeted against Japan, among other countries. The EC's Council of Foreign Ministers had already decided to revise the procedure for the institution of an anti-dumping tariff, changing the previous requirement of a 70% majority vote to a simple majority vote. The decision will make the imposition of an anti-dumping tariff much easier.

Among the steps adopted by Japan to resolve Japan-EC trade conflicts is export monitoring, a measure for voluntary export restriction. This measure, adopted by Japan's MITI in response to the EC Commission's request, began to be implemented in 1986 with regard to automobiles, VTRs, color TVs, NC lathes and other machine tools. Export monitoring is so named because MITI monitors changes in the amounts of exports from one month to the next on the basis of export statistics compiled by industrial associations; in the event a certain export item is found to have increased excessively, it asks the companies concerned for explanations and advises them to curb their exports.

To illustrate how the export monitoring system has been at work, let us take the case of automobiles. The year 1980, when Japanese cars began to flow into the European market, and especially into the German market, marked the first year of increased imports of Japanese cars into the EC. After that Japan's car exports to the EC continued to increase by leaps and bounds, becoming the focal point of the Japan-EC trade conflict. One measure adopted by Japanese automakers in response to the conflict was to make direct investments in Europe. Another was the adoption in 1986 of *de facto* voluntary export restriction in the form of export monitoring on an EC-wide basis.

Subsequently, in December 1989, the EC Commission announced the basic principles of its common automobile policy in preparation for the market integration scheduled for 1992, and started to establish, in line with these principles, a unified measure for restricting automobile imports from Japan which would replace the restrictive measures adopted by the individual member countries. From the autumn of 1990 on, the EC Commission began to negotiate on the question with MITI in earnest. The negotiations involved many twists and turns, which were not always reported in full detail by the media. In any event, the two parties agreed on setting up a "transition period" of several years beginning in 1993, a period when the existing monitoring of quantities would continue to remain in place. As to the length of this "transition period," however, opinions were divided between the EC, which insisted that the period should last for six years, and MITI, which argued for a shorter period. More important points in the dispute were the question of whether the market share or the sales volume should be the monitoring standard, and the question of whether automobiles manufactured in the EC should also be monitored. The EC Commission insisted upon the use of the market share as the monitoring standard, and upon the inclusion of locally manufactured cars in the Japanese share. In contrast, MITI argued for a method that would take into account the increment in the number of Japanese cars sold in the EC, instead of their market share. It also refused to agree to consider locally manufactured cars as part of Japanese sales.

Press reports appeared at the end of September 1990 which cited sources in the EC as saying that the two parties had reached a basic agreement on extending the monitoring practice for several years after the 1992 market integration, until the end of 1997 or 1998, and on setting a 18% limit to the share of Japanese cars in the EC market at the end of the extended period. Of the 18% share, 9% was to be allocated to cars imported from Japan, and the remaining 9% to cars manufactured by Japanese transplants in the EC. (Note that in 1989 Japanese cars sold in the EC market, not including those manufactured inside the EC, numbered 1.23 million, approximately 9% of the market.) Judging from subsequent developments, however, the press reports were inaccurate on several important points.

On the part of the EC, there was an internal conflict of opinion. The auto manufacturers inside the EC were divided into two opposing camps, one in favor of free trade and a policy of appeasement toward Japanese competitors, the other in favor of protectionism and a stringent policy; the EC Commission stood in between. The rift developed into a split in the CCMC (European Community Manufacturers' Committee), a European-wide association of 12 major automakers, with eleven of the members – all but the French maker Citroën-Peugeot, the toughest proponent of protectionism and anti-Japanese stance – withdrawing from the association to establish a new one.

It was not until September 1991 that MITI and the EC Commission reached an agreement on the framework of monitoring to be put into effect after the 1992 market integration. The contents of the agreement were as follows: first, France, Italy, Spain, and Portugal would pledge to abolish their quantitative restrictions on Japanese car imports, and to refrain from imposing restrictions on cars manufactured by Japanese transplants in the EC; consequent upon this pledge, a monitoring ceiling for the number of Japanese cars exported to the EC would be established for each of the seven years from 1993 to 1999, based on the forecast of the demand for cars in the EC; MITI would guide the Japanese automobile industry so that the exports of Japanese cars would not exceed this ceiling (thus the monitoring ceiling, in effect, would be the same as the maximum limit of allowable exports); concurrently with the establishment of the monitoring ceiling, Japan would establish bilateral export ceilings with France, Italy, Spain, Portugal, and the United Kingdom; the monitoring ceiling would be established through negotiations between MITI and the EC Commission; according to the EC's understanding, the monitoring measure to be in effect during the "transition period" was meant to prevent the abolition of the existing restrictive measures from adversely affecting the ongoing restructuring efforts of the EC automakers. The agreement having these contents was different from what was reported in September 1990 in several respects. For one thing, exports were to be restricted not in terms of percentage share but in terms of the number of units exported, and cars manufactured locally by Japanese transplants would be exempted from restriction. For another, the duration of the "transition period" was much longer than what the EC Commission was reported to have insisted upon.

The concrete ceiling figure agreed upon for calendar year 1992 was 1,185,000 vehicles, a decrease of 6% from the previous year. The figure for 1993, the first year for the application of the new rule, was 1,089,000 units, down 8.1% from the previous year, resulting in decreases in Japanese car exports to the EC for two consecutive years.[11] Underlying these decreases was the growing dissatisfaction harbored by the European, especially German, automakers against the Japan-EC agreement on automobile trade, as they grew apprehensive about the increasing share of the EC market taken by Japanese cars at a time when the deepening recession was narrowing the European auto market and forcing European automakers to suffer from deteriorating performance. Not only the European manufacturers of small-sized cars, but also the manufacturers of luxury cars like Daimler-Benz had to lay off large numbers of their workers because of deteriorating performance. Ford Europe, for instance, was compelled to shut down its Dagenham and Southampton plants in the UK, and to start restructuring its operations throughout Europe.

Immediately following the conclusion of the first agreement on the monitoring ceiling, the EC offered to start a new round of negotiations on the grounds that auto sales in the EC were forecast to decrease by a far greater margin than had been expected. As a result of the renewed negotiations, it was agreed that the monitoring ceiling would be reduced from the original figure by 109,000 units to 980,000 units (or a reduction of 17.3% from the previous year). The renewed negotiations, the first since the establishment of the monitoring ceiling in 1986, also led to an agreement that, should the actual demand in the market deviate from the projected demand level by more than a certain amount, the two parties would renew negotiations. This latter agreement has the implication of keeping the percentage share of Japanese cars in the European market at a more or less fixed rate. To put it differently, the dispute over whether Japanese car exports should be monitored and restricted in terms of their market share or in terms of their actual number was settled essentially in line with the EC's argument.

Although some Japanese automakers had begun to invest directly in the EC in the mid-1980s, the establishment of the monitoring ceiling and its subsequent lowering have given further impetus for expanded production by Japanese transplants. Nissan, Toyota, and Honda are moving in this direction, while the manufacturers with no transplants in the EC, such as Mazda and Mitsubishi Motor, are having greater difficulty in responding to the new turn of events.

The expanding operations of the Japanese automobile transplants are meeting with the growing dissatisfaction of many European automakers, especially those of France, which are voicing the demand that the sales of Japanese cars in their entirety – regardless of whether imported from Japan or manufactured locally – ought be restricted. These latter makers consider that if the cars turned out by Japanese transplants are added to those imported from Japan, Japanese cars are actually garnering an increasing share of the EC market, and they are thus demanding that intra-regional exports of cars manufactured by Japanese transplants be included in the monitoring ceiling. Some of the European automakers, including those in Germany, are opposing this demand, but the issue is still in dispute. At any rate, one might say that the trade conflict over car exports, by giving rise to an expansion in direct investment and in local production by Japanese automakers, is increasingly taking on the appearance of a conflict over direct investment.

III. EXPECTATIONS AND CRITICISMS: DIRECT INVESTMENT

1. From a Rapid Increase to a Slowing or Decline

The 1950s and 1960s saw the deepening of economic relations between Japan and the countries of Western Europe, not simply in trade but also in direct investment, technological tie-ups, and various other economic activities. During the two decades, these relations still preserved much of the vestiges of the prewar days, enabling European countries to enjoy a favorable balance, whether in direct investments or in the export of technology.[12] In the early 1970s, however, Japan emerged as a net exporter of capital, expanding its foreign direct investment, including that destined for Western Europe. During the 1980s, offshore direct investment continued to increase and portfolio investment grew at an accelerated paces, making Japan the world's foremost capital exporter and creditor nation by the end of the decade. Already by 1985, Japan's net external assets of $129.8 billion put it in the world's top position, outpacing even the UK; and in 1988, it also replaced the UK as the world largest holder of gross external assets by increasing its holding of these assets to $1,469.3 billion. This staggering sum was seen at the time to carry immense significance, not merely for Japan but also for the world economy, almost comparable to the weight American outstanding gross external assets once had when they were at their peak.[13]

Japan's actual direct investment as recorded in its balance of international payments was $7.5 billion in 1985; it increased rapidly in the subsequent years, bringing Japan into third place after the US and the UK by 1987, and to second place by 1988. Then in 1989, with a 29.0% boost over the previous year to $44.1 billion, Japan jumped for the first time to the top. In terms of cumulative outstanding direct investment, Japan in 1989 ranked third following the US and the UK, with its sum of $154.4 billion, or 12.2% of the world total. Japan's foreign direct investment destined for Europe saw quick increases. Investment in offshore production facilities showed a strong increase, but far more conspicuous was a rapid increase in property investment in the UK and elsewhere, a phenomenon which took place as much of a vast sum of surplus funds generated by the "bubble economic boom" in Japan flew offshore in search of lucrative investment opportunities.

Beginning around 1990, however, there was a sea change in the flows of direct investment. In tandem with the world's total foreign direct investment, which peaked in 1990 at $234.0 billion and then began to subside, Japan's direct investment, too, tapered off. The actual amount of direct investment as reported to the Ministry of Finance (MOF), which peaked in FY1989 at $67.5 billion, continued to decrease for four consecutive fiscal years, declining to $34.1 billion, or approximately half the FY1989 figure, in FY1992. The reductions occurred in both manufacturing and non-manufacturing industries. Broken down in terms of forms of investment – securities acquisition, money-lending, and the establishment or expansion of branch offices or subsidiaries – the peak occurred in 1989 or 1990 in all areas; afterwards there were continuous declines. As for the national and regional breakdown, Japan's direct investments in the US, the major destination, showed a significant drop (Table 17.5). Underlying this decline were not only America's economic woes and the

Table 17.5 Japan's Foreign Direct Investment, by Major Region

	FY 1990			FY1991			FY1992			Cumul. total for FY1951–92		
	No. of cases	Amt. in $ million	% of total	No. of cases	Amt. in $ million	% of total	No. of cases	Amt. in $ million	% of total	No. of cases	Amt. in $ million	% of total
Europe	956	14,294	25.1	803	9,371	22.5	617	7,061	20.7	8,845	75,967	19.6
North America	2,426	27,192	47.8	1,714	18,823	45.3	1,258	14,572	42.7	27,197	169,580	43.9
Central & South America	339	3,628	6.4	290	3,337	8.0	307	2,726	8.0	7,794	46,547	12.0
Asia	1,499	7,054	12.4	1,277	5,936	14.3	1,269	6,425	18.8	21,180	59,880	15.5
Near East	1	27	0.0	10	90	0.2	16	709	2.1	366	4,231	1.1
Africa	70	551	1.0	76	748	1.8	23	238	0.7	1,557	6,813	1.8
Oceania	572	4,166	7.3	394	3,278	7.9	251	2,406	7.0	4,602	23,782	6.2
Total	5,863	56,911	100.0	4,564	41,584	100.0	3,741	34,138	100.0	71,541	386,530	100.0

Source: Ministry of Finance statistics.

deteriorating performance of Japanese firms within Japan, but also the worsening performance of Japanese transplants in the United States. On average, Japan-based concerns in the US have chalked up continuous years of losses. Japan's direct investment in Europe, too, decreased by large margins, even though Japanese-owned firms in Europe were not performing so poorly as those in the US. In stark contrast, Asia's share in Japan's direct investment has shown a rapid increase.[14] The net increase in Japan's foreign direct investment (i.e. the amount of new investment minus the amount of investment withdrawn) as recorded in the country's balance of payments was $17.2 billion in FY1992 – an amount which, equal to merely about one third of the peak of $49.1 billion reached in FY1989, represented a return to its mid-1980s level. Not only did new investment decline, but this was accompanied by a significantly large increase in the amount of investment funds withdrawn from abroad – consequent upon the shutting down of offshore transplants by manufacturing companies, the withdrawal by construction and real estate firms of their real estate investments from abroad, and the withdrawal by parent companies of their paid-up capitals in and long- to medium-term loans to their overseas subsidiaries.

Despite these setbacks, Japan remains a major capital-exporting and creditor country, ranked fourth in terms of foreign direct investment in 1992. Moreover, Japan's net external assets (external assets minus foreign debts) – inclusive not simply of direct investment, but also of indirect investment, as well as of external loans of the government in addition to the assets held abroad by private firms – continued to increase as the decade 1990s proceeded, reaching $513.6 billion by 1992.[15] Japan has since 1985 continually held first place in terms of net external assets, except for one year, 1990, when it was overtaken by the unified Germany, which boosted its direct investment in and loans to Eastern Europe and its direct investment in other EC countries. Japan's performance here cuts a striking contrast to that of the United States, which, ever since its becoming a net debtor country in 1986, has continued to pile up external debts.

Let us have a closer look at Japanese investments in Europe. Japan's direct investment in Europe showed rapid increases in the latter half of the 1980s. The amount, which in 1980 was a mere $600 million, accounting for 12% of the country's total foreign direct investment, reached the $8 billion mark by 1988, representing an increase in the relative share to 18%. The following year, 1989, witnessed a dollar-value increase of 62% to $14.8 billion, and an increase in the share to 22%. The year 1989 also saw the number of M&A activities by Japanese concerns in Europe double the previous year's level to 101 instances, which remains the peak figure to date. Many Japanese companies scrambled to establish European regional headquarters, often preferring the Netherlands as the site for such headquarters.[16] Real estate investment in 1989 also showed a significant jump of 75% over the previous year. Much of this increase was attendant upon direct investment in Europe by Japanese manufacturing, marketing, and other businesses, but it was also caused by a rush for real estate acquisition as part of *zaiteku* (financial engineering) money games. This phenomenon, which was propelled by the aggressive financing by Japanese banks, was most conspicuous in Great Britain, followed by France and then West Germany.

The sudden expansion of Japanese direct investment in Europe in the 1980s, particularly the latter half of the decade, was caused, at least to some extent, by the "bubble" economic boom in Japan; but the more substantive underlying factor was that Japanese companies had gained a competitive edge over their European counterparts in terms of financing and technological capabilities. Another factor that triggered the investment surge was the revision in the EC's trade policy toward Japan – that is, the adoption of new measures such as the imposition of antidumping tariffs and the monitoring of imports from Japan. The appreciation of the yen also helped, even though the yen's up-valuation relative to the European currencies was not great. On top of these, an additional factor of importance appeared on the horizon toward the end of the 1980s: the unification of the European markets scheduled for 1992. The anticipation that competition in the unified and expanded European market would grow harsher must have prompted the investment decisions of some Japanese companies. There seems no denying, however, that the investment boom was caused, to a far greater extent, by a combination of three factors: strong apprehension about the unified EC's becoming a closed fortress; Japanese companies' propensity for doing whatever their rivals would do; and the booming of the bubble economy. As a matter of fact, large firms were not alone in actively investing in Europe at the time; medium- and small-sized firms, too, were on an investing spree – in their efforts to adapt themselves to increased import tariffs, unified industrial standards, local content requirements, and anti-dumping tariffs, or to comply with the requests of larger firms to establish offshore supply bases in Europe.

Thus, Japanese direct investment in Europe boomed in the latter half of the 1980s, but there was a dramatic change in the picture with the opening of the 1990s, as investment began to stagnate and then decline. The yen's upward march resumed; but in contrast to its effect on investment in Asia, it does not appear to have propelled investment in Europe. The amount reported to MOF remained flat in FY1991 and showed a decline in FY1991, and in FY1992 it posted a 24.7% decline from the previous year to $7.06 billion (see Table 17.5). The tempo of this decline matches that of investment in the US. As is shown in Table 17.5, the regional shares of North America and Europe in Japanese direct investment dropped by significant margins in FY1992 to 42.7% and 20.7%, respectively. In contrast to these developments, Asia's share in Japan's investment rose to 18.8% in the same year, as the region's expanding market and low-cost labor, as well as the sudden upsurge of the yen, helped to attract Japanese investment there. If this trend continues, Europe will soon lose its second-place position (behind North America) to Asia on both an annual and a cumulative basis. For the time being, the environment for Japanese companies' investment in Europe is unlikely to become promising. Investment activities of Japanese companies aimed at gaining footholds in the market by establishing local manufacturing and marketing platforms have run their course; and these firms' concern now is how best they should reorganize or restructure these platforms and accommodate them to the integrated market and to the ongoing recession.

While Japanese investment in Europe has switched from the trajectory of rapid growth to that of zero growth, and then to that of decline, it is still in its infancy. As demonstrated by Table 17.5, the cumulative sum of investment in Europe as reported to and approved by MOF by the end of FY1992 stood at $75.7 billion, or less than half of the $169.6 billion invested in North America. Cumulative investment in Europe by manufacturing firms as reported to MOF by the end of FY1988 amounted to a mere $4.5 billion, as against $22.5 billion invested in North America. Given the fact that Europe in 1989 had a combined GNP of $4,811 billion, which was more or less comparable to the United States's $5,176, one might conclude that Japan's cumulative direct investment in Europe is still disproportionately small and leaves considerable room for expansion. Another comparison also points to the availability of such room for expansion: Japan's share in Western Europe's aggregate manufactured imports had by 1989 expanded to 55% of the share held by American products; but Japanese direct investment in Europe in the same year amounted to less than one quarter of investment from the US.[17]

2. Japan's Direct investment in Europe Broken Down by Destination and Industrial Sector

Table 17.6 displays the breakdown of Japan's direct investment in Europe by destination. The UK is by far the largest European receiver of investment from Japan, taking a 7.5% share in the cumulative total of Japan's direct investment in the period from FY1951 to FY1992, followed in descending order by the Netherlands (4.2%), and then by three countries with a share of between 1 and 2% each – Germany, Luxembourg, and France. As for the trend at work in the early 1990s, the dollar values of investment as reported to MOF in FY1992 were $2.95 billion for the UK, $1.45 billion for the Netherlands, $770 million for Germany, $460 million for France, and $330 million for Spain. The UK's front-rank position remains unchanged. Also noteworthy is that, despite former French Prime Minister Cresson's condemnatory claim that "Japan's next target is undoubtedly Europe," France was making a phenomenal gain in its receipt of Japanese investment, even surpassing Germany in the number of cases of investment. This seems to reflect the importance accorded by Japanese investing firms to France's policies of welcoming foreign capital and maintaining the exchange parity of the franc, and also to its leadership role in the EC. Spain, which had joined the EC as recently as in 1986, is also making significant gains in the inflow of investment from Japan.

On the whole, the relative importance of the Netherlands, Luxembourg, and other smaller countries as the destinations of Japanese direct investment has been in eclipse, in contrast to the larger countries, which have grown relatively more important, and the countries of Southern Europe, which have also made gains in their relative shares in Japanese investment.

Now let us focus attention on direct investment by manufacturing firms. In 1989 there were, in the whole of manufacturing sectors of Europe, a total of 403 Japan-affiliated firms (i.e. those owned at least 10% by Japanese parent firms), with the UK leading other countries as the home for these Japan-affiliated firms. By 1993, the number of such firms had increased to 713, of which 198 were located in the UK, 121 in France, and 107 in Germany.[18] The relative standing of the UK has not changed, as it remains the most attractive site of investment for Japanese firms. Here again, it is noteworthy that France overtook Germany in 1989, not only in the amount invested by Japanese firms but also in the number of Japan-affiliated firms it hosts.

Table 17.6 Japan's Foreign Direct Investment in Europe, by country

	FY 1990			FY1991			FY1992			Cumul. total for FY1951–92		
	No. of cases	Amt. in $ million	% of total	No. of cases	Amt. in $ million	% of total	No. of cases	Amt. in $ million	% of total	No. of cases	Amt. in $ million	% of total
UK	270	6,806	12.0	222	3,588	8.6	197	2,948	8.6	2,553	29,134	7.5
The Netherlands	138	2,744	4.8	118	1,960	4.7	84	1,446	4.2	982	16,222	4.2
Germany	134	1,242	2.2	119	1,115	2.7	65	769	2.3	1,371	6,574	1.7
Luxembourg	7	224	0.4	6	266	0.6	3	68	0.2	159	5,941	1.5
France	171	1,257	2.2	132	817	2.0	82	456	1.3	1,542	5,429	1.4
Switzerland	16	666	1.2	5	62	0.1	14	144	0.4	323	2,701	0.7
Spain	43	320	0.6	34	378	0.9	27	332	1.0	381	2,577	0.7
Belgium	39	367	0.6	17	222	0.5	19	281	0.8	372	2,222	0.6
Italy	52	217	0.4	45	322	0.8	34	216	0.6	386	1,438	0.4
Norway	19	138	0.2	29	169	0.4	12	86	0.3	112	903	0.2
Ireland	10	49	0.1	8	102	0.2	10	113	0.3	118	829	0.2
Total Europe	956	14,294	25.1	803	9,371	22.5	617	7,061	20.7	8,845	75,697	19.6
Total	5,863	56,911	100.0	4,564	41,584	100.0	3,741	34,138	100.0	71,541	386,530	100.0

Source: Ministry of Finance statistics.

There had been much talk about a forthcoming eastward shift in the center of gravity of Japanese direct investment, away from the UK to the Continent, and in particular to Germany; but such a shift has not yet taken place. One might say that the hopes entertained for the 1992 market integration and for the opening up of the largest remaining untapped market, which would result from the political changes in the former Soviet Union and East European countries, have thus far been disappointed. At the level of individual firms, however, some changes are taking place in the choice of investment sites, as part of the efforts at reorganizing operational bases. Thus, from the long-term perspective, the prospect of an eastward shift in the locus of investment activities still retains some plausibility and cannot be completely abandoned.

Let us next turn to the sectoral breakdown of Japan's direct investment in Europe in FY1992 as reported to MOF. Among manufacturing industries, the top four positions were occupied by machinery ($500 million), electrical equipment ($430 million), transport equipment ($390 million), and chemicals ($370 million). The three leaders in the non-manufacturing industries were finance and insurance ($1.39 billion), real estate ($1.25 billion), and commerce ($970 million).[19] When compared in terms of the cumulative totals invested in FY1951 to FY1992 (as shown in Table 17.7), all seven industries mentioned above stand out prominently, even though their relative positions, in both the manufacturing and the non-manufacturing sectors, are not exactly the same as in the comparison for FY1992. If we compare the pattern of investment in the EC with that in North America, there are some differences, including the proportionately larger shares held by the finance and insurance industries; but the industrial breakdown of investment in Europe is basically similar to that in North America, while it cuts a stark contrast to that in Asia.

Let us briefly overview the development of the investment activities of Japanese manufacturing industries in Europe. In the period before the mid-1980s Japanese manufacturers' direct investment in Europe was embryonic, and was aimed primarily at making inroads into and capturing larger shares of the markets of individual European countries and their neighbors. It was not until the mid-1980s that the manufacturers began to step up their investment activities in Europe in earnest. Triggered as it was by the EC's invocation of stringent trade policies against Japan as a means of dealing with intensifying competition, this upsurge of investment was geared to promote export substitution. And the number of Japanese companies aiming to enter the European market as an important link in their global strategies increased. Toward the end of the 1980s, investment skyrocketed as a number of Japanese manufacturers found it necessary to prepare themselves for the forthcoming market integration. The number of Japan-affiliated firms in Europe jumped from 117 in 1983 to 282 in 1987, and to 630 in 1991.[20]

Table 17.7 Japan's Foreign Direct Investment, by Sector and Region (Cumulative Totals for Fiscal Years 1951–1992)

	Europe		North America		Asia		Total	
	No. of cases	Amt in $ million	No. of cases	Amt. in $ million	No. of cases	Amt. in $ million	No. of cases	Amt. in $ million
Manufacturing								
Foodstuffs	122	597	704	2,587	853	1,396	1,983	5,234
Textile	362	1,130	232	1,058	1,553	2,312	2,387	5,043
Lumber/pulp	30	124	207	2,508	526	611	941	3,711
Chemicals	256	2,006	558	5,923	1,258	4,282	2,285	14,558
Steel and non-steel	400	734	446	5,027	1,147	3,310	2,268	12,040
Machinery	373	2,858	840	4,723	1,156	2,117	2,565	10,320
Electrical machinery	369	5,257	1,050	12,707	1,973	5,587	2,582	24,473
Transport vehicles	125	3,003	440	6,312	502	2,061	1,201	14,065
Others	385	1,623	1,082	9,524	2,282	3,016	3,975	14,537
Subtotal	2,422	17,331	5,559	50,367	11,250	24,691	21,187	103,981
Non-manu-facturing								
Agri./forestry	21	34	254	510	485	372	1,376	1,773
Fishery/marine products	24	33	105	189	339	285	849	900
Mining	102	1,811	420	2,484	313	7,980	1,460	18,812
Construction	51	285	342	1,556	596	1,001	1,194	3,353

	Europe		North America		Asia		Total	
	No. of cases	Amt in $ million	No. of cases	Amt. in $ million	No. of cases	Amt. in $ million	No. of cases	Amt. in $ million
Commerce	3,040	9,296	7,817	21,074	3,430	5,259	15,867	40,268
Finance/insurance	905	28,598	584	22,661	573	5,711	2,748	74,869
Services	928	5,039	3,273	27,801	1,603	6,731	6,926	46,610
Transportation	140	365	340	769	384	1,530	4,839	21,652
Real estate	545	9,457	5,104	38,326	850	3,608	7,916	59,895
Others	234	1,056	957	2,225	532	1,639	3,146	7,533
Subtotal	5,990	55,974	19,196	117,595	9,105	34,115	46,321	275,666
Branch estab./ expansion	253	2,354	437	1,133	663	1,038	1,495	6,289
Real estate	180	38	2,005	485	162	37	2,538	595
Total	8,845	75,697	27,197	169,580	21,180	59,880	71,541	386,530

Source: Ministry of Finance statistics.

Electronics and electrical appliance producers began to establish transplants in Europe relatively earlier than other Japanese manufacturers. At present, their investment is focused on the production of five products: color televisions, VTRs, copy machines, semiconductors, and computers. To take the semiconductor sector as an illustration, the growth trajectory of Japanese direct investment in this sector has been characterized by the following sequence of developments. The EC took recourse to anti-dumping tariffs as a means of countering the flooding imports from Japan, and at the same time took increasingly critical views of the Japan-US Semiconductor Agreement. In their efforts to dodge the growing criticisms directed at their export activities, Japanese semiconductor manufacturers, including NEC and Fujitsu, began to make direct investments in Europe. The opening of Japanese transplants offended the indigenous manufacturers of the EC, which blamed their respective governments for subsidizing the Japanese transplants to their own disadvantage. Against this backdrop, the EC Commission proceeded to impose antidumping tariffs on semiconductor parts, and not simply on finished products, which in turn induced many of the Japanese companies to start undertaking the pre-manufacturing process (i.e., the processing of wafers) locally in Europe. Even though the March 1990 ruling of a GATT panel found unsustainable the EC's antidumping tariffs targeted at imports of finished semiconductors and semiconductor parts from Japan, the trend toward growing Japanese direct investment in the sector continued. In another move, the EC Commission planned to establish a 45% local content requirement, for application beginning in 1992, on circuit boards (the product of the pre-manufacturing process) to be imported from outside the common market. The proposed establishment of the local content rule led Japanese manufacturers to proceed in earnest with plans for localizing the pre-manufacturing operations. In addition to NEC, which had already started production, Fujitsu, Mitsubishi Electric, and Hitachi began construction of plants for pre-manufacturing operations, and Toshiba, Oki Denki Industries, Sony, and Matsushita Electronics began deliberating on their respective plans for localizing pre-manufacturing operations. However, the EC withdrew the proposed local content ratio in the face of strong opposition from American firms and the US government. Hence Japanese firms revised their plans for local production in the EC.

In the automobile manufacturing sector, Japanese automakers, as has been pointed out, began to think about making direct investment in Europe in around 1980, when the rapid increase in Japanese car exports to the EC led to the establishment of an EC-wide system for monitoring car imports. Having already begun to look into the possibility of establishing a transplant in the UK, Nissan led this drive for local manufacturing by beginning to manufacture passenger cars in its Sunderland plant in Britain in 1986. Not only did Nissan's British operation become a focus of hot debate within Britain. It also aroused an objection from France, which demanded that Nissan cars assembled in Sunderland be subjected to local content requirements. Eventually, France agreed to regard locally-assembled Nissan cars as products of the EC, but demanded that these cars satisfy local content ratios of as high as 70%. Having market integration in view, Toyota and Honda followed in Nissan's footsteps, beginning local manufacturing in 1992 at their Derby and Swindon plants, respectively. These two manufacturing undertakings, too, aroused a protest, this time from the EC Commission. Mazda has a plan to establish a transplant in Germany in partnership with Ford, but at the moment the plan is at a standstill. Similarly, Mitsubishi Motor's plan to start local production in the Netherlands jointly with Volvo remains at the blueprint stage. On the Eastern European front, Isuzu has made direct investment in the Czech Republic, and Suzuki in Hungary.

The stagnant European economy and the collapse of Japan's bubble caused the number of Japan-based firms in all areas of Western Europe to stop increasing in 1991, bringing the number in 1993 to 713. As many as 76.4% of these firms admit being affected by the recession, and think that they will have to overhaul their reinvestment and employment plans. 21.9% of the firms sustained minor deficits in FY1991, and 25.2% significant deficits, which means that a total of 47.1% – or nearly half of the Japan-based firms – were in the red. Further, 44.1 % of the firms had lower earnings than in the previous year.[21]

Announcements of production cutbacks and outright withdrawals have been made one after another. The deepening of the recession in Europe's car market forced Nissan to readjust the output of its Sunderland plant by slowing the assembly line speed beginning in the summer of 1993. This was followed in the autumn of the same year by a switch from the two-shift to the day-shift system. 1993 production of passenger cars at the plant was expected to decline by 9%, from 270,000 to 246,000 units. This production cutback was indeed unprecedented for Nissan's British plant, with its previous record of uninterrupted production increase, and for all the Japan-based car makers in Europe as well. In the electric equipment sector, too, Hitachi announced its decision to close its VTR plant in Bavaria, Germany, because the protracted recession in the European market for audiovisual products and the rise in the value of the German mark relative to other European currencies had seriously undermined the German operation's profitability. The closure of an offshore VTR plant owned by a leading Japanese household electronics appliance maker was also unprecedented.

Not all the Japanese transplants in Europe are cutting back production or being shut down. There are also reports of scaled-up local production and establishment of new transplants. One might say that behind the mixture of these cutbacks of local production and pullouts, on the one hand, and expansion and new undertakings of direct investment, on the other, Japanese companies operating in Europe are restructuring their production, marketing, and R&D facilities on a Europe-wide basis. Such restructuring efforts may represent early signs of their full-fledged responses to changes in their competitive positions, to changes in market conditions, and to the European integration.[22]

3. Investment Conflict

As noted already, the increase in Japan's direct investment in the EC, to the extent it was facilitated by trade frictions, was aimed at substituting exports by local production. Government officials involved in negotiations to settle trade problems saw dwindling room for working out new negotiated concessions and compromises, and began to count increasingly on direct investment as a more effective solution. In fact, EC officials pinned hopes on and welcomed increased Japanese direct investment in Europe as a solution to the trade frictions. Needless to say, not all the new Japanese transplants were welcomed with open arms: some investment plans, such as Nissan's plan to locate in Great Britain, aroused much suspicion and hostility. The EC Commission took an especially critical view of the tendency for Japanese firms to establish "screwdriver" operations in Europe, which simply assembled a complete package of parts and components imported from Japan. This was why it set up a number of regulations on investment and local production, such as parts-dumping tariffs, rules on the place of origin, and local content ratios.

When Japanese companies' direct investment in Europe boomed in the latter half of the 1980s, there was much anxiety that the pendulum would swing from a strong welcoming mood to a renewed mood of hostility, and that there would be new tensions. Though originally expected to help solve the trade conflict, Japanese direct investment quickly outgrew this role and began to threaten to trigger a new conflict, i.e. one over investment.

The picture changed dramatically with the dawning of the 1990s. Direct investment stopped increasing, and then began to decline. Among the Japanese companies with direct investment in Europe surveyed in 1991, those still foreseeing a growth in friction were a minuscule 3.1%. The companies with strong anxieties were concentrated in the assembly and processing industries, such as transportation equipment and general machinery. The causes for their concern included the antipathy of indigenous competitors against the excessive presence of Japan-owned transplants, stepped-up activities of popular movements for environmental conservation and consumer protection, and frictions arising from the insufficient localization of management and production. Compared with the findings of the survey one year earlier, there was a significant decrease in the number of firms feeling uneasy about the hostile attitude of labor unions and employees toward "Japanese management practices" and about the friction in the high-technological areas. In other words, investment conflicts were judged to have become dormant.[23]

It should be remembered, however, that insofar as the investment imbalance remains unresolved, with Japanese companies making direct investment in Europe on a far greater scale than their European counterparts are doing in the Japanese market, the fact that investment conflicts are becoming dormant and invisible does not mean that they have been eliminated.

European companies' investment in Japan picked up momentum in the latter half of the 1980s in parallel with Japanese investment in Europe. The amount of European direct investment in Japan in FY1991 as reported to MOF showed an increase of 56% over the previous year to $4.3 billion, the largest amount on record. The investment was channeled into a wide array of activities, including the establishment of facilities for production, marketing, and R&D, the buyout of distribution firms, and the purchasing of warehouses and wholesaling and retailing facilities. The drop in land and stock prices at the time created a very favorable climate for these purchasing operations. The successful consolidation by the German luxury car maker BMW of a dealer network under its direct management is a case in point. With the establishment of a marketing system under its direct control, BMW managed to take fuller advantage of its high-quality cars, expanding sales in Japan dramatically.[24] The number of cases of purchasing of and capital participation in Japanese firms by European firms in FY1992 totaled 43, or 2.4 times the previous year's number. Targeted for acquisition and capital participation were firms belonging to a wide cross-section of industries, such as pharmaceuticals, chemicals, computer, electrical machinery, and electronics. In fact, M&A is becoming European companies' preferred form of making direct investment in the Japanese market.

Despite its recent dramatic increase, European companies' investment activity in Japan remains at best one tenth the level of Japanese companies' investment undertakings in Europe. Explanations of why European firms' investment in Japan remains relatively limited are still a subject of debate. Among the different explanations, those often referred to are institutional barriers – such as high land prices in Japan and cross-shareholding practices among Japanese firms – and cultural barriers. Some observers have pointed to five factors as responsible for obstructing direct investment in Japan: prohibitively high land prices, the relatively low rate of expected earnings, high corporate taxes, the difficulties faced by foreign-owned firms in recruiting competent Japanese staff, and the difficulties involved in taking over Japanese firms. These factors, except for the fourth, are also applicable to Japanese firms, and are thus not acceptable. It is possible that these factors, and especially those concerning the cultural barriers, may be referred to by European firms as a convenient excuse for the failures of investment undertakings in Japan. The full implications of these various barriers cannot be grasped unless they are analyzed in close relation to European firms' business strategies toward Japan. At any rate, there is no denying that European direct investment remains relatively small.

This constitutes another "imbalance" that is annoying the EC. Here, too, as is the case with the trade imbalance, there is no objective standard available with which to judge the existence of an investment imbalance. Even so, efforts at rectifying the "imbalance" will have to be made, so long as one of the parties to the investment relations is making a complaint about it. Given the fact, moreover, that Japanese investment in the EC is of crucial importance in mitigating trade frictions with the EC, and that its curtailment is not a viable option, the only choice left open is to beef up European investment in Japan. It is to this end that the EC is demanding abolition of the barriers obstructing European investment in Japan.

Were Japanese investment in the EC more or less on a par with the EC's investment in Japan, the trade conflict would not be a matter of serious concern as it is today. Japan's trade surplus would not discomfit the EC deeply, because the EC would ascribe a portion of Japan's surplus to exports by European-owned firms in Japan. The same argument applies to Japan-US economic relations. If US companies were able to expand their direct investment in Japan by sufficiently large margins, the Americans would be more tolerant of Japan's trade surplus with the US. This seems to suggest that investment frictions can have far more serious implications than trade frictions in the long run.

Conversely, in the event that no significant progress toward the narrowing of the Japan-EC investment imbalance is forthcoming, there is even a likelihood that the EC may place Japan's investment in Europe under severe controls. In the light of a prospect such as this, it is important to keep in mind that the investment conflict has not been dissolved, but has merely become dormant. What is needed now is to perceive the conflict and face it squarely at the deepest level of consciousness. Summing up the foregoing observations, it is possible to conclude that the focus of Japan-EC negotiations is shifting from trade to investment issues, from the question of opening up the Japanese import market to that of opening up its investment market.

Source: Institute of Social Science, University of Tokyo, Discussion Paper Series, F-73, 1998, pp. 1–37.

18

The Trajectory of European Integration: Possibilities for Substituting Hegemony

INTRODUCTION

ONE OF THE noteworthy phenomena of the second half of the twentieth century has been the progress of regional integration. For the time being, we may think of regional integration as the communal management or exercise of power – for example, where two or more sovereign states transfer a portion of their sovereignty to a communal agency. The characteristics of such communal agencies will depend on the level of communal surrender of rights, the most extreme case being a supranational form of government. In any case, regional integration is something more than a form of mutual dependence.[1]

Incidentally, if we look at the economic aspect of regional integration, we may take its general objective as being the creation of a greater economic sphere, whether through the creation of free trade areas or common markets, or through cooperative or communal economic policy-making. In Western Europe, the European Community and its successor the European Union fit this model, while North America has seen the emergence of the North America Free Trade Agreement (NAFTA) and South America the Southern Common Market (Mercosur). In Asia, the Association of South East Asian Nations (ASEAN) has both expanded and strengthened, and – while the member nations are only loosely tied, and it can not perhaps be seen as a form of regional integration – there is also an accelerating move to cooperation at the pan-Pacific level in the form of the Asian Pacific Economic Cooperation (APEC). In the late 1980s and early 1990s, in spite of substantial differences in the scale and character of such agreements, regional integration has expanded on a global scale.[2]

The trend towards regional integration has progressed at much the same pace as the decline of United States hegemony. By hegemony, I am referring to leadership by the US across a broad sphere of activities, including not only the economic, but also the political, military, and ideological. The first half of the twentieth century saw the decline of British hegemony accompanied, amidst great turmoil, by the rise of the United States, and the second half of the century saw the establishment of US hegemony through the suppression of German and Japanese aspirations, and its consolidation against a background of confrontation with the Soviet Union.[3]

However, US supremacy began to decline at the beginning of the 1970s, after a reign of less than 30 years. The decline of the dollar supremacy began with the collapse of the IMF fixed exchange rate system, followed by the first oil crisis, which brought to a close the era of US-dominated oil market supremacy. Subsequently, America's withdrawal from Vietnam indicated that US military supremacy had also passed its peak.

Then in the 1990s, the Soviet Union, which had represented the focus of US rivalries in the economic, political, and military spheres, collapsed, ending the Cold War and leaving the US without a rival. These events further hastened the decline of US hegemony. At the same time that US hegemony was a response to the Soviet political, economic, and ideological threat, US hegemony also depended on that threat. The Cold War was, indeed, one manifestation of US hegemony. Therefore, the end of the Cold War brought a weakening of American economic, political, and ideological dominance. Moreover, during this same period the economic power of the US continued to weaken. This became apparent at the time of the 1991 Gulf War. Without the financial support of its allies, the United States was unable to undertake even a regional war.

Thus, undermined by the collapse of the Cold War system, American hegemony weakened even further. There is a view that, since the collapse of the Soviet Union left the US as the world's only superpower, American hegemony actually strengthened. But that view is mistaken, I think. Certainly no successors have emerged in terms of political power, military power, or information-based power. Even in the economic field, the US retains its paramount position. However, it is hard to escape from the fact of American economic decline – more precisely, of American economic excess as evidenced by the transition to debtor-nation status. The foundations of US hegemony have clearly been undermined.[4]

What, then, is the relationship between the establishment and decline of hegemonies on the one hand, and the movement towards greater regional integration on the other? How do we explain the phenomenon of increased regional integration against a background of US hegemonic decline? And what significance does this phenomenon have for the collapsing system of US hegemony? Further, will regional integration go so far as to create a successor of hegemonic system?

In this paper, I will examine these issues, taking the example of European regional integration as a case study. Europe was the first to attempt regional integration in the wake of the Second World War. European regional integration has also attained a vast scale. The 15 nations in the EU have a combined area of 3.24 million square kilometers, or 1/3 the area of the United States. The EU population of 370 million and 1995 nominal GDP of $8. 4 trillion both surpass the US. With total trades of $1.5 trillion, the EU also represents the world's largest trading entity, accounting for 40% of world trade. Moreover, questions of scale apart, the EU is also pre-eminent in the level of its integration. The EU is more integrated in terms of trade, capital, currency, technology, people, and information than NAFTA or any other economic integration. In this sense, too, the EU is the most advanced example available. Moreover, the EU continues to expand across a variety of formats including increased membership, quasi membership, or cooperative agreements in the whole of Europe and association agreements such as those with the Mediterranean states and the African, Caribbean and Pacific states. The EU also has a significant impact on other regional unions, and indeed has become a model for others, and thus is the leader in the global wave of regional integration. For all these reasons, the EU provides excellent material for a study of the issues outlined above.

If we restate those issues in the light of the European integration, they are as follows.

First is the question whether there is any causal relationship between the progress of the European integration and the decline of American hegemony. Was the decline of US hegemony the cause of the progress of European integration? Or, conversely, did the integration of Europe hasten the decline of American hegemony?

Second, in the light of the decline of US hegemony, what was the aim in undertaking the integration of Europe, and how should we evaluate the results? This issue is especially relevant from the mid-1980s on.

Third, what significance does European integration have in the political context of the decline of US hegemony and the collapse of the cold war system? Was it just a product of the inertia of cold war thinking? If so, then perhaps it is no more than an anachronism and hence doomed to failure. Or can we perhaps see it as the first experiment in the post-cold-war construction of a new kind of cross-nationalties? In this context, the word "experiment" has two meanings: first, the passive meaning of a response to a period of systemic change following the decline of American hegemony; and second, assuming that America's was the last hegemony, the more active meaning of experimenting in forging a new system for the post-hegemonic world. This issue, then, is one of measuring the projectile range of the European integration.

All of these are difficult issues. In particular, the third issue is problematic because it involves forecasting the future during the current period of rapid change in the European situation. Our observation of the European integration is limited to the events up to the summer of 1997. Thus, in this last section in particular, I can do little more than make some speculative comments.

I. CHANGES IN THE MEANING OF EUROPEAN INTEGRATION

(1) From a self-protecting organization to an oppositional organization

European integration was originally a product of American hegemony. Europe was during the course of this century twice the locus of global wars; while the First World War was fought over the re-division of the world among the European great powers, the Second World War was fought over the division of Europe itself. The result of this war was that European nations virtually ceased to be colonizing imperial powers, and Europe was transformed from a sphere of expansion to one of contraction. Moreover, the nations of Europe were almost destroyed economically, becoming dependent on the United States for their economic reconstruction. With the establishment of the cold war system, America accepted the role of provider of assistance, but in order to maximize the efficiency of its aid – or, to put it another way, to economize the hegemonic cost – America demanded the creation of a Western Europe-wide cooperative system. This was the motive force behind the creation of the European Payment Union (EPU) and the Organization for European Economic Cooperation (OEEC). This was, then, a form of regional integration under American auspices, but that does not mean that it was necessarily linked to the present European integration.

In addition to responding to the prodding of a hegemonic America, European nations also embraced their own independent philosophies of cooperation or integration, and acted on those ideas. From an economic point of view, the philosophy of integration envisioned the creation of a huge common market, while from a political point of view, it aimed for the "containment" or "Europeanization" of West Germany. It was this independent line of thinking which resulted in the signing of the Treaty of Rome in 1957 and the launch of the European Economic Community (EEC) in the following year. America permitted this arrangement – in spite of its conflict with the GATT system – in the interests of preserving the cold-war order.[5]

Thus, regional integration first came into being under the aegis of the powerful influence of a hegemonic America. This kind of regional integration can be seen as an organization aimed at the self-defense of a contractionist Europe. Western European nations enjoyed high economic growth through the 1960s, and both accompanying and supported by this growth, the EEC was came into being in the form of a customs union. In this way, Europe was able to confront the "American threat" of large-scale direct investment by US multinationals. Thus, what began as a self-defense organization naturally evolved into an economic cooperative body.

At the beginning of the 1970s, American hegemony clearly entered the path to decline. The collapse of the IMF fixed exchange rate system, the first oil crisis, and then the defeat in the Vietnam War, were all major turning points on the path to decline. One cause was the late-developer growth of the European economy. It is ironic that just at the moment that Europe took its first step towards economic and monetary union, the collapse of the IMF fixed exchange rate system and the move to floating exchange rates caused the nascent movement to collapse. And as the world moved from the high growth era to low economic growth, the Western European economy also experienced inconsistent fluctuations based on low economic growth.

In retrospect, one result of this transformation was the liberalization of trade and capital and the intensification of international competition. Another was the arrival of the so-called "third industrial revolution" – also known as the microelectronics revolution – in which semiconductors and computers replaced steel as the staple of industrial development, the electronic and machinery industries were fused into one, and the software-based information and communications industries rapidly developed.[6] This "third industrial revolution" was the main element of the competition between developed capitalist economies based on trade and capital liberalization. In this process, the Western European economies fell behind America and Japan. Inflation, high unemployment, and falling investment rates resulted in declining international competitiveness, which in turn dulled economic growth. The stagnation of investment and technological innovation in high-tech industries, and the decline of competitiveness, led Europe to fall behind in the transition to a low-energy-based industrial structure. This stagnation was particularly apparent in the early 1980s, when it came to be known as "European arteriosclerosis."[7]

During this period, having struggled against the "American challenge", Europe also faced the challenge of the newest economic great power, Japan. This challenge was first manifested in the surge of Japanese imports, which resulted in trade conflicts. Later, in an effort to solve the trade problems, Japanese firms began a rapid program of direct investments in Europe.

In this situation, the European economies made many attempts to stimulate economic development. At the national level, European companies made concerted efforts to introduce American and Japanese technologies and methods of management. They also experimented with the privatization of government-owned companies and the introduction of industrial policies. There were also a number of initiatives at the pan-European level. An example is the "1992 market integration." This initiative emerged from the EC Commission's "Internal Market White Paper" produced for the June 1985 European summit in Milan. Based on this, in February 1986 the EC member nations signed the Single European Act, which was ratified by member nations and came into effect in July 1987. The primary goal of this act was the creation of a integrated market by the end of 1992, eliminating physical barriers such as border controls and custom controls, technical barriers such as differences in product standards, technology regulations, company laws, and public procurement rules, as well as breaking down technology and tax barriers, particularly differences in the value added tax (VAT) and national consumption taxes.

The enthusiasm generated by this market integration immediately produced calls for economic and monetary union and even political union. In this wave of integration, successive measures were introduced aimed at furthering market integration. In the interest of breaking down internal barriers, the EC Commission launched a number of initiatives which then, via the European summits and ministries councils, achieved the consent of the various European nations and were passed into laws by the EC Commission as well as by the member nations. With the exception of tax-related laws, this process worked smoothly for the most part. As of the end of 1992 – that is, around the eve of the European market integration – as many as 95% of proposed measures and regulations had been adopted. Then on January 1, 1993, the market integration got under way. Internal boundaries were reduced, and companies became able to overcome national boundaries with relative freedom. Trucks and passenger vehicles were able to travel freely throughout Europe.[8]

In this way, from the late 1980s, as American hegemony entered its decline, and under the influence of new circumstances including the "third industrial revolution" and the "Japanese challenge", Europe progressed towards integration. The nature of the European integration changed from an organization primarily aimed at defense, to an organization aimed at taking on the economic threat of America and Japan. In other words, it acquired the characteristics of an oppositional alliance. This was symbolized by the communiqué of the European Milan summit that launched the 1992 European market union: for the first time, this summit clearly stated the need to take on the challenge of Japan.

What, then, was the effectiveness of this "oppositional" integration? To what extent did it stimulate the economies of Western Europe, and to what extent did it succeed in narrowing the gap versus America and Japan in the "third industrial revolution" industries? To what extent did European companies recover their competitiveness? And what was the contribution of the progress of regional integration to this recovery?

It is impossible to be very affirmative in responding to these questions. The history of the oppositional alliance extends only over the 10 years or so since the mid-1980s, and so it is certainly difficult to evaluate its effectiveness. Moreover, evaluation is rendered even more difficult by the events which have since swept Europe, including German unification, the turmoil in the former Soviet Union and East European bloc, and the progress towards economic, monetary and political union in Europe. But it is difficult to point to any clear signs of economic stimulation. Ironically, it was in the latter half of the 1980s, during the build-up to market integration, that the Western European economy experienced substantial growth, aided by the global economic boom as well as by the surge in stocks as well as by mergers and acquisitions in the prevailing environment of "casino capitalism." By contrast, since the market integration the Western European economy has moved into recession, and since then it has lacked the strength to stage an effective recovery.[9]

Moreover, it is hard to see clear signs of improved competitiveness in the Western European firms on whom economic recovery depends. And indeed the term "European firms" is hardly appropriate, since in spite of the harmonization of corporate laws and related laws and regulations, corporations continue to display a strong sense of national identity, so that rather than "European" firms, they have developed as national firms operating on a Europe-wide basis. Moreover, the opportunities created by European integration apply equally to companies based inside and outside the region. Finally, industrial policies have been implemented both at the national and at the EU level, but they have not produced any clear results.

Thus, a large gap has emerged between the expectations for an integrated European market and the reality that it has produced. It is indeed hard to see any effect from the market integration. In the current circumstances of slow growth and, particularly, high unemployment, nations have focused on their own interests, while at the European level, efforts are now focusing not only on integration, but also on growth and employment. In December 1993 the European Commission produced a "Growth, Competitiveness, and Employment White Paper" for the European summit.

(2) Going beyond an oppositional organization

Even as it has failed to produce results as an oppositional organization, the European integration has begun to reveal a development that goes beyond that *raison d'être*. In this way, in the midst of its development from defense alliance to oppositional organization, the European integration has added an entirely new significance.

Already in the latter half of the 1980s, under the umbrella of the 1992 market integration, the first steps were taken along the path to economic and monetary union and political union. In June 1988, the

Hanover European summit reached agreement on the "deepening" of integration via an Economic and Monetary Union (EMU). In April 1989, the EC Commission released the "Report on EC Economic and Monetary Union", known as the Delors Report, which was subsequently ratified at the Madrid summit in June of the same year. At around the same time, the Soviet-East European socialist bloc entered a period of profound systemic turmoil, which resulted in German unification and, ultimately, in the restructuring of the entire Soviet bloc. Amidst this collapse of the cold war system, and with its development closely related to those events, European integration embarked on a new course.

At the December 1990 Rome summit, EC members studied revisions to the Treaty of Rome aimed at economic, monetary, and political union. On that occasion, the first intergovernmental conference was held. At the December 1991 Maastricht summit, agreement was reached on the revision of the Treaty of Rome and on the conclusion of a treaty of European Union (the Maastricht Treaty). The latter was signed in February 1992. Thus, the process of European integration emerged from a long period of confusion dating back to the early 1970s, and entered a new period of buoyancy. That buoyancy was severely tested by the process of ratification of the treaty by each member nation. In Denmark, ratification of the treaty was defeated in a national referendum. Even in France, the leading pro-Europeanist nation, the treaty was only ratified by a narrow majority in a referendum. Denmark only ratified the treaty when a second referendum was held which specifically excluded participation in a monetary union or a common defense policy. In this way, the Maastricht Treaty came into force in November 1993. The European Community now became known as the European Union.[10]

The process of integration displayed two markedly opposing trends. One was an internal "deepening" exemplified by the move to economic, monetary and political union. The other was an external "expansion" exemplified by the addition of new members or quasi-members to the Union. The process of "deepening" was particularly linked to German unification. One of the primary motive causes of the member nations other than Germany behind the signing and ratification of the Maastricht Treaty was to further the "Europeanization" or "containment" of the regional economic, political, and military giant, Germany. In 1993, unified Germany had a population of 81 million or 20% of the entire EU, and GDP of $1. 9 trillion, or 30% of the EU total. Even in the midst of its worries about low investment and high unemployment, Germany shone as the giant of Europe. And with the restructuring of the former Soviet states, German economic influence in the former East European bloc was powerful indeed. Indeed, one might say that a "mark bloc" had already come into existence. Even if Germany, in light of the failure of its hegemonic endeavors in the first half of the twentieth century, genuinely abhorred the notion of establishing even a limited regional hegemony, German economic, political and military might was undoubtedly threatening to the EU member nations.

The Maastricht Treaty aimed at establishing a system that would control Germany. The motivation for "containment" was particularly clear in the case of neighboring France. On the other hand, for newly unified Germany, monetary union, involving as it did the abandonment of the Deutsche mark, became a test of the unified Germany's loyalty to European integration. Since the Deutsche mark must be considered symbolic of German national identity, passing that test was a precondition for general acceptance of unification. In this way, the EU came to signify the containment of Germany, and at the same time the unification of Germany became a vital force in the "deepening" of European integration.[11]

The expansionist aspect of European integration is closely linked to the collapse of the former Soviet bloc in Eastern Europe. The turmoil and change experienced by the Soviet Union and Eastern European nations brought about this "expansion" of the integration. In early 1995 Austria, Finland and Norway joined the EU, bringing the number of member states to 15. This was a direct consequence of the weakening of the European Free Trade Association (EFTA), but it was also not unrelated to the changes taking place in the former Soviet Union. Moreover, the former East European Comecon members struggled successively to resurrect their former trade pact, and then to pursue independent trade structures, but in each case in vain. As a result, East European states also rushed to apply for EC/EU membership. The EC/EU was unable to permit immediate membership, but Poland, the Czech Republic, Slovakia, and Hungary were granted associate member status. It is hard to imagine Russia itself joining the EU, and indeed it is unlikely that Russia would apply, but the EU has nevertheless extended invitations to Russia to participate in its summits, and has engaged in economic cooperation with Russia, indicating endeavors to locate Russia in its periphery. Of course, in the case of Russia, political and military relations are at least as important, if not more so, than economic relations.

The collapse of the Warsaw Pact has seen a variety of efforts aimed at structuring new defensive alliances, including the expansion of NATO eastward and the gaining of Russian acceptance of that expansion; the substantialization of the Conference for Security and Cooperation in Europe (CSCE) and its successor the Organization for Security and Cooperation in Europe (OSCE); and the strengthening of the Western European Union (WEU). Taking place as they have against a background of declining US hegemony and the collapse of the Soviet bloc, these initiatives have had the effect of drawing Eastern Europe further into the EU embrace.[12]

Taking the two aspects of "deepening" and "expansion," "deepening" first preceded "expansion" and then the latter became vitalized in the first half of the 1990s. The shift to "expansion" has been slowed down by the economic and political circumstances of the East European candidate states, and indeed the EU recognized that "deepening" was necessary to further "expansion." Thus, from 1995, the emphasis returned once again to "deepening." Negotiations with East European nations were temporarily suspended, as the EU concentrated on revisions of the Maastricht Treaty. In March 1996, the first intergovernmental conference was held in Turin. This was aimed at both the full implementation of the Maastricht Treaty and at reviewing the Treaty. The meeting laid particular emphasis on clarifying the key issues affecting the Treaty, including employment, internal competition, terrorism, drug smuggling, international crimes, immigration, and the environment. In addition, the structure and procedures for adding new members to the EU were also raised as an issue. The meeting pointed to the development of a more democratic and efficient structure, as well as the strengthening of external activities, as key issues for study.

A number of IGC meetings have followed, and negotiations over Maastricht have also continued at the regular EU summits. The process of negotiations has been complicated by major political changes in two member states: the election of a Labor Government in Great Britain, and the appointment of a Socialist cabinet in France. In spite of its initial stance affirming the former Conservative government's resistance to joining the monetary union from the start, Britain's Labor Government has brought a new commitment to European integration, announcing for example its intention to participate in the Social Charter. On the other hand, the French Socialist cabinet, which came to power on the strength of popular discontent over efforts to reduce the fiscal deficit for the sake of participation in the monetary union, expressed reservations about that union. Ultimately, however, final agreement was achieved on schedule at the June 1997 Amsterdam summit, and the second treaty of integration (Amsterdam Treaty) was adopted. The movement for integration finally emerged from the confusion hanging over it since the efforts to ratify the Maastricht Treaty, to reach a new peak. However, it is undeniable that there is a lack of confidence or congratulation about this development.

Setting aside differences of opinion, this new treaty achieved agreement on the main issues, including monetary union, the deepening of market integration and freedom of movement for citizens, judicial cooperation, employment policy (a unified policy aimed at preserving a high level of employment), the establishment of a common diplomatic and security policy, and the expansion of a common trade policy (embracing services and intellectual property rights). The treaty – for the sake of efficiency – expanded the scope of application of the designated multiple decision system and also introduced a new constructive abstention-method decision-making procedure, allowing decisions to become irrevocable even if made in the face of abstention by designated member states. In order to promote integration, the treaty also introduced a system of differing speeds of integration, with accelerated integration for designated member states. The EU seemed not to wait for ratification to use the treaty in order to hasten membership negotiations with the former East European nations, the three Baltic nations, Malta, Cyprus and others. The process of "expansion" of integration is building on "deepening."

In this way, both the "deepening" and the "expansion" of European integration have been promoted by the systemic changes in the former Soviet Union and Eastern Europe, including the unification of Germany. On the other hand, European integration, bringing as it did an opportunity for East European participation, also helped accelerate the collapse of the former East European system.

In this process, German-French relations, which lie at the center of European integration, have suffered repeated fractures. France was of course deeply concerned by the unification of Germany, and France also felt strong reservations about the dispatch of German troops outside the NATO arena. On the other hand, the Chirac government's "anti-integration" stance excited concern in Germany. But these fractures were patched up. French-German relations have been re-established on the basis of French political leadership and German economic leadership, an arrangement that reflects both long-term strategic consensus and historical and ethical reflection. The boom and bust " integration cycle" as well as the meandering path integration has taken are undeniable, but in the long term the trend towards integration is surely irreversible.

The integration of Europe has in turn stimulated trends towards integration in other regions. The European integration is the most advanced, and, in spite of the admitted distance between stated goals and actual achievements, Europe has nevertheless reached a fundamentally high level of integration. Moreover, even without harking back to the Roman Empire, the strong historical ties from the Treaty of Westphalia to the Vienna System have added both depth and weight to the post-war integration, which is based on the two participating conditions of prosperity and democracy. Even for those participating citizens with little historical consciousness, the goal of a single Europe is surely not a new one. Therefore, it is not surprising that in today's post-cold war era of inter-regional rivalries Europe should be setting the pace for the world in terms of regional integration.

Seen in this way, it is natural to wonder if European integration has not taken on a meaning that goes beyond its just being a reaction to American hegemony. Even while it may retain some characteristics of an adversarial or defensive league, is it not also possible to see the European integration as at the beginning stages of developing into an existence substituting hegemonic system?

If that is the case, the possibilities for Europe emerging as a substitution of hegemony can perhaps be examined from two perspectives: the internal and the external. Internally, the issue is what significance integration has for the economic, political, and military stability of the region. Externally, the question is whether European integration supports American hegemony or it hastens the decline of American hegemony. A further important consideration is whether Europe could acquire the prosperity and systemic stability either to take on the role of hegemonic power in succession to America or to substitute hegemonic system in general.

I propose to examine the case of monetary union in order to study the question of Europe's potential to emerge as a substitution of hegemony. This is because monetary union was the focus of the Maastricht Treaty as much as, or even more than, political union. After briefly reviewing the history of the monetary union process to the present day, I will then consider the issue whether the monetary union represents simply a common use and management of sovereign rights, or whether it represents a decisive step towards the establishment of a supra-national organ of government. In addition, I will attempt to evaluate the prospects for Europe to emerge as a substitution of hegemony both from an internal and an external perspective.

II. THE POSSIBILITIES FOR EMERGENCE OF A NEW HEGEMONY – THE CASE OF MONETARY INTEGRATION

(1) Changes in the Meaning of Monetary Integration

If we take the launch of the European Payment Union (EPU) as the starting point of European monetary integration, then the integration began as a part of a defensive alliance. But if we are to look for a direct line to the present monetary integration, then we must look not at the EPU but at the 1970 Economic and Monetary Union Plan. This plan was, however, quickly abandoned in the face of the turmoil and systemic changes accompanying the collapse of the IMF fixed exchange rate system. In the 1970s, as the world moved to a floating exchange rate system, the EC experimented with the common floating exchange rate (the "Snake"), but this, too, offered only meager results. Based on this experience, the European Monetary System (EMS) was introduced in 1979. This was a measure centered on France and Germany, aimed at countering the collapse of the IMF fixed exchange rate system, turmoil in the floating rate system, and the "benign neglect" of the US government towards the depreciation of the dollar. The EMS had the goals of stabilizing regional currencies, expanding trade and investment, and stabilizing economic growth. As such, it can be seen as an "oppositional" framework for monetary integration.

However, the road to the present monetary union aimed at a single European currency began at the end of the 1980s. At that time, plans for monetary integration overlapped with the wave of market integration plans sweeping the continent. Following the agreement on "deepening" of integration at the Hanover summit in June 1988, the EC Commission produced the "Report on an EC Economic and Monetary Union", the so-called Delors Report, in April 1989. This report was approved (with the exception of the United Kingdom) by the June 1990 Madrid summit. With this approval, the movement towards creation of an economic and monetary union was launched. This movement toward monetary union had three stages, from complete freedom of capital movement within the region, and cooperation on monetary policy, to the establishment of a European Central Bank system, and to the introduction of a single currency. The movement was supported by the policies toward the economic union, including common market and competition policies, a common structural policy, and cooperation on macro-economic policies.

In October 1990, the EC Commission released a detailed research report on "The Benefits of a Single EC Currency Circulation." Based on the assumption that all 12 member nations would join the single currency area, the report summarized the benefits as follows. (1) Savings on currency exchange costs would total 13.1 to 19.2 billion ECU (0. 5% of EC GDP). (2) Interest rates would decline with the elimination of currency market instability (cumulative effect would equal GDP growth of 5%). (3) With the reduction of inflation and elimination of national financial deficits, economic growth would be enhanced by reduction of the high real interest rates paid by high-inflation economies (2–5% of GDP). (4) Higher resistance would be expected to external shocks such as oil shocks. (5) With a single ECU currency, the EC nations would reduce the need for holding foreign currency reserves, and the ECU would profit from the issuance of currency for foreign nations' reserves.[13] Thus, the main benefits foreseen by the report were cost reduction effects (regional exchange transaction costs, interest costs, and foreign reserves), and, related to some extent, the elimination of regional currency market instability.

The first step towards the economic and monetary union envisioned by the Delors Report was initiated in July 1990, when both long and short-term inter-regional capital transfers, including current and capital transactions, were completely liberalized. At this time, the United Kingdom joined the EMS exchange rate mechanism (ERM). In December 1990, at the Rome summit, EC leaders studied revisions to the Treaty of Rome in order to establish an economic and monetary union. On that occasion, the first intergovernmental conference was convened for the purpose of political union and the economic and monetary union. Then in December 1991, at the Maastricht summit, ministers reached agreement on the revision of the Treaty of Rome and the conclusion of the European Union treaty (Maastricht Treaty), which was signed in February 1992.

The provisions of the Maastricht Treaty relating to monetary union were as follows. First, at the beginning of 1994, the second stage of monetary union would begin, with the establishment of the European Monetary Institute (EMI), forerunner of a European Central Bank.

Second, by the end of 1996, EMI would realize a European System of Central Banks (this would be composed of member nations' central banks and a new European Central Bank, which should be independent from any national or European government agency). Then a summit meeting would decide whether at least half of the member nations meet the necessary conditions for the introduction of a single currency, and whether it would be appropriate to move to the third stage. If the decision were to be negative, the third stage would be launched automatically at the beginning of 1999, to include only those member nations meeting the necessary conditions. Third, by the launch of the third stage, both the European System of Central Banks and the European Central Bank would be created, and the European Monetary Institute would be liquidated.

According to clause 109j and the Appendixes of the Maastricht Treaty, the following conditions were to be met for the launch of a single currency and entry into the third stage of the plan. (1) Price stability – during the one year to the cut-off point, consumer prices must not have risen more than 1.5% points above the level of price increases in the lowest three countries. (2) Government fiscal position – the annual fiscal deficit must not exceed 3% of GDP, and government debts outstanding must be within 60% of GDP. (3) Stability of currency markets – the currencies of concerned states must have remained within their regular permitted boundaries within the EMS for the past two years, and they must not have carried out any devaluations during that period. (4) Market interest rates – during the one year to the cut-off point, the yields on long-term government bonds of the concerned states must not exceed those of the 3 EU states with the lowest price inflation by more than 2%.[14] Thus, the four major criteria were price stability, the fiscal position, currency market stability, and the level of long-term interest rates. These were also known as the "convergence criteria."

In the process of ratification of the Maastricht Treaty, considerable controversies erupted in some member countries, especially in Denmark and France. This was connected to concurrent currency problems. In September 1992, amidst turmoil in the currency markets, the British pound and the Italian lira withdrew from the main vehicle of the European Monetary System, the Exchange Rate Mechanism (ERM). In July 1993, the French franc plunged against the German mark, and the EMS was once again thrown into turmoil. At the beginning of August, the band of fluctuation permitted by the ERM was increased from 2.25% up or down (with 6% permitted in some cases) to 15% up or down. With this development, the EMS in reality became little more than a floating market system or at best a "managed floating market system." Hopes for monetary union were also dampened. Indeed, with the deterioration of the key Franco-German relationship, European integration itself was endangered by these developments. In the midst of these disturbances, the Maastricht Treaty came into effect in November 1993. The European Community now became the European Union. The United Kingdom and Denmark gained the right to abstain from the third stage of monetary union.

Following the provisions of the Maastricht Treaty, the second stage of monetary union came into effect at the beginning of 1994. The EMI was established in Frankfurt, which was also the location of the German Bundesbank. The role of the EMI included promoting cooperation between central banks and the development of cooperative monetary policies, as well as the development of both a structural and managerial framework for the European System of Central Banks, for which the EMI was to be precursor. In the third stage, under the direction of the European System of Central Banks, the primary task of a European Central Bank would be the launch of a single European currency.

This was the form that endeavors took for the creation of a single European currency. However, as the European economies struggled to recover from economic slowdown, it became increasingly unlikely that enough member states would clear the four basic conditions for introduction of a single currency - particularly those conditions relating to fiscal balance. In early 1995, the dollar fell steeply amidst the Mexican monetary crisis, while the pound and lira, still outside the EMS, came under selling pressure. The EMS itself also fell into turmoil, with the franc weakening against the mark, and, in March, the Spanish peseta and Portuguese escudo were forced to devalue. The Madrid summit in December 1995 abandoned plans for moving to the third stage at the beginning of 1997. Thus, according to the provisions of the Maastricht Treaty, a new schedule was established in which only those countries meeting the provisions would adopt a single currency, at the beginning of 1999. The participant countries would be decided based on 1997 statistics, at a special summit to be held early in 1998.

At the Madrid summit, the decision was also made to change the name of the single currency, from the "ECU" designated by the Maastricht Treaty, to the "euro." The Madrid summit also decided that the 1999 introduction of the euro would only be in a limited, non-cash format, with the circulation of euro currency coming only at the beginning of 2002. By July of that year, the euro would finally become the only legal tender of the participating nations.[15]

In this way, the prospects for monetary union have achieved or exceeded the goals originally established in 1970. Then, is this integration countering the collapse of dollar hegemony and acquiring the potential to substitute the dollar as the main global currency?

(2) The Situation of Supra-nationalism

a) Precedents and Gaps

A precondition underlying the progress of monetary integration in the 1990s was the existence of the European Monetary System (EMS), launched in 1979. This was a common floating exchange rate system based on fixed intra-regional exchange rates (within a plus or minus 2.25% band) and floating rates versus the rest of the world. What, then, was the connection between this system and the current status of monetary integration?

The prior history of the EMS has been studied in detail in a volume edited by Tanaka Soko, *EMS: The European Monetary System*. According-ing to this book, the connection between the "success of the EMS" in the 1980s and the monetary union is as follows. "As a result of the ability of the EMS to prevent changes of parities during the 'period of stability,' at least the core nations gained confidence in their ability to progress towards monetary union. The currency market was stable, and economic performance converged, so most nations came to believe that they would be able to achieve monetary integration by extend-ing the EMS a further stage."[16] Tanaka also notes the following: "The third achievement of the EMS is monetary union. The stability of the EMS led to the prospect for the second economic and monetary union, or the planning of monetary union was based on the 'stable period EMS.'.... Discussion of the euro is still premature, but it is undoubt-edly one outcome of the EMS."[17]

However, we cannot ignore the successive EMS crises of 1992, 1993 and 1995. With respect to these, Tanaka comments as follows: "... The program for the first-stage strengthening of the EMS not only failed to be achieved, but also a regression occurred. However, this was only a statement of broad goals, and from 1994 the second stage of monetary union was implemented on schedule, leading to the present situation."[18]

Thus, Tanaka maintains his assertion of the connection between the "success" phase of the EMS and monetary union.

However, Tanaka also states the following: ".... From our perspective of examining the future shape of the international monetary system, ... the 'flexible fixed exchange rate plus free capital movement' EMS system should be seen as the achievement of an EC/EU experiment in currency market cooperation. For in today's world of massive free movements of speculative capital against the background of capital liberalization, such a system of narrow fixed bands could never withstand the explosion of speculation.... This was the lesson of the 1992–3 EMS crisis."[19] This "flexible fixed exchange rate plus free capital movement" clearly refers to the EMS system after the 1992 and 1993 crises, The expansion of the fluctuation band to plus or minus 15% was in reality nothing more than the ruination of the fixed-rate system. Setting this fact aside, Tanaka indeed traced the path from the post-1993 EMS to European monetary union. In other words, Tanaka acknowledges the lack of a direct link between the 1980s "success" period of the EMS and monetary union.

It is at first sight hard to reconcile these conflicting interpretations of the link between the EMS and monetary union. Is the monetary union aimed at a single currency built directly on an extension of the experience of the 1980s EMS? In other words, has monetary union come about due to the "success" of the EMS in the 1980s, and in spite of the crises of the 1990s? Or does the monetary union build on the crises of the 1990s? When it comes to specifying the links between the EMS and a single European currency, *EMS: The European Monetary System* is less than clear.

In fact, the Delors Report, which acted as the basis for the present monetary union, correctly forecast the impact of capital liberalization and large-scale intra-regional capital transfers on the EMS fixed-exchange, narrow-band system. The Report theorized that since the EMS system would be very difficult to maintain, the introduction of a single unified currency would be necessary. And indeed, with intra-regional capital liberalization in 1990, large-scale capital movements became the norm, and these in turn triggered successive currency crises. The scale of capital movements significantly exceeded the funds available to national monetary authorities for stabilizing market intervention. Thus, the national authorities had no choice but to increase the band of fluctuation, effectively entrusting prices to the movements of the market. Of course it is questionable whether the Delors Report correctly forecast the scale of the EMS crisis. However, the report clearly spelled out the link between the EMS crises of the 1990s and subsequent developments. "In the event that, as a result of regional market planning, the exchange control should be abandoned, and particularly in the event that large amount of speculative capital movement should put pressures on foreign exchange markets, only three policy choices would be available in response. First would be to abandon efforts to stabilize currencies, and to entrust currency movements to the markets. Second would be for monetary authorities to intervene actively in currency markets in order to stabilize currencies, and third would be for the member nations to cooperate on macro-economic policy in order to stabilize currency prices, even going as far as monetary union...... The Delors Report indicated the third option as the basic policy for overcoming this problem."[20]

The first plan for monetary union in the early 1970s was abandoned due to the global move to a floating exchange rate system. In this second case, the effective abandonment of a fixed exchange rate system actually sustained the plan for monetary union. The effectiveness of the EMS during the 1980s was certainly available as a historical precedent for the monetary union of the 1990s, but between the two there is clearly a gap. I will return later to the fact that this gap had a distinctly political character.

A further historical precedent for monetary union was the effective creation of a mark bloc throughout Western Europe. "Within Western Europe, the German mark has already acquired the status of a exchange intermediary currency, and it is indeed driving out the US dollar as a exchange intermediary currency. It has reached the point where not only interregional currency transactions, but also interbank transactions between the US dollar and Western European currencies, and even yen-European currency interbank transactions are now denominated in German marks... Similar to the former dollar-pound axis, there is now an international mark alongside the international dollar. These developments began in the second half of the 1980s."[21] "In this way, with the transition of the mark to an exchange intermediary currency, it has become possible for Western European nations to conduct intra-European transactions (with the exception of swap transactions) without using the dollar. For both foreign exchange and security transactions, independence from the dollar within the "European currency bloc" has become a reality."[22]

As for the relationship between the creation of this effective mark bloc and monetary union, if we look once again at *EMS: the European Monetary System*, we find the following comments. "We may term the entire system of using various European currencies instead of the dollar in trade and capital transactions, the focus on the mark as an exchange intermediary currency in the foreign exchange market and particularly the interbank

market, and the use of the mark as the currency of intervention and reserve
in the EMS system which supports those transactions, the 'European
finance and currency bloc.' From its origins in the mid-1960s, this 'European finance and currency bloc' grew rapidly until reaching maturity in
the early 1990s, and after successfully withstanding the 1992–3 European
currency crises, it became the basic precondition for the third stage of
monetary union (introduction of a single currency) planned for 1999. ...
Looking only at the use of European currencies in investments and the use
of the mark as an exchange intermediary currency, compared with the first
plan for an economic and monetary union in the 1970s, we may conclude
that the current monetary union plan is far more realistic."[23]

Certainly, against a background of the decline of US hegemony, the
emergence of West Germany and a unified Germany as an economic
giant, and the progress towards European integration, a *de facto* mark
bloc has emerged. And we may take that as an extension of the historical precedent of the monetary union plan once abandoned in the early
1970s, only this time with a higher degree of realism. However, is it
not also clear that the existence of a mark bloc in no way makes the
emergence of a single currency inevitable, nor does it assure the success
of that currency? There is, once again, a substantial gap between the
emergence of a mark bloc and the introduction of a single currency.
mark bloc countries are more or less forced to use the German mark,
but the pressure forcing them to do so is economic. Although undeniably some political decisions are involved, as in the case of the central
EMS participants, for the most part the forces at work are economic.

By contrast, the decision whether or not to participate in the single
currency is essentially a political one. Even the four conditions stipulated
for member states to join the single currency could best be seen as economic pressures arising from political decisions. Moreover, if member
states once make the decision to participate in the single currency, it is
extremely hard, if not actually impossible, to withdraw. Since a "bail-out"
would throw not only the member state but also the entire economic and
monetary union into a crisis, it would be an extremely difficult choice to
make politically. There is an issue here of the transfer of national sovereignty. Thus, the United Kingdom and Denmark, while exercising their
national sovereignty, are being forced into extremely difficult decisions.

The authors of *EMS: the European Monetary System* compare the
creation of a single European currency and the monetary union of
Germany as follows: "In 1990, West Germany forcibly absorbed the
economically very weak East Germany, and unified the currencies.

The difference in productivity between the core EU member states is much smaller than that between the former East and West Germanys, and therefore the introduction of single European currency should be much easier than the mark unification."[24] Certainly, if differences in productivity were the only problem, this theory would be justified. However, the unification of the German currency was based on the decision to unify two nations. On the other hand, in the case of a single European currency, the political decision to transfer sovereignty remains in doubt, and even once the single currency is introduced, national sovereignty will by no means be eliminated.

b) National Sovereignty and Supra-nationality

The problem of national sovereignty in an integrated Europe has emerged repeatedly from the very beginning. The central issue is the extent to which nations will transfer sovereignty, or, to put it another way, the strength of supra-nationality. Thus, the progress of the integration movement to date has taken place through confrontation and compromise between the opposing desires to promote supra-nationality and to protect national sovereignty. It is a very broad view that the Maastricht Treaty provided a strong and unprecedented boost for supra-nationality, and that monetary union is one aspect of this new trend. However, this issue requires considerable further consideration.

In the first place, if we should see monetary union, or the introduction of a single currency to that end, as a common management and exercise of national sovereignty, we may take the following example of this kind of understanding: "Incidentally, if we ask what is the political thought behind the deepening of integration, we could define its special characteristic as the 'sharing of sovereignty' or the 'common use of sovereignty.' ... The second pillar of political thought behind 'sharing of sovereignty' is the conceptualization of economic and monetary union and the systemization of policy to that end."[25] Monetary integration involving a union or a single currency should, according to this view, be seen as a common management and exercise of national sovereignty. However, this view makes too light of the fact that it is hard to see monetary union as a simple extension of regional integration to date. If we explain the introduction of a single currency in traditional terms, it does indeed mean a transfer of currency issuing rights, which currently reside within the sphere of sovereign powers to a greater or lesser extent, to the European Central Bank. Moreover, concealed in that action is the possibility of a more generalized move towards the common management and exercise of national sovereignty. In other words, the creation of a single unified currency should perhaps best be seen as theoretically including the creation of a single national sovereignty. This type of sovereignty transfer is different again from that involved in the integration of diplomatic or security policy. Certainly, if we look at the current circumstances of monetary union, the present common floating market system does indeed involve to some extent a common management and exercise of sovereignty, but there is a decisive difference between this situation and the introduction of a single currency.

If we call that difference one of supra-nationality, then the supra-nationality involved in the creation of a single currency is, compared to prior efforts at economic, diplomatic, and security integration, comparatively high.

The problem is the establishment of that supra-nationality. For all that it is referred to as a supra-national single currency, within the limits outlined by the plan for the third stage of monetary union, it only occupies a small place within the broad structure of the common management and exercise of sovereignty. What, then, is its position within that overall structure? And how does it fit with the retention of sovereign rights in other areas?

The following comments are relevant to the "inherent limits" of the Maastricht Treaty.

"Basically, corresponding to the extent that the EU itself will hold the function of supra-nation, the single currency would effectively circulate in the overall economy, becoming a common currency. However, the Maastricht Treaty does not attempt in any positive way to invest the EU with the function of supra-nationality. Together with financial sovereignty, common diplomacy, defense and so on are vital factors in indicating the level of confidence in the nation in regard to the financial and capital markets. The current conditions of instability in Europe are immediately reflected in the financial conditions and capital markets of the issuing nation. Unless this circuit can be broken, it will be impossible to prevent differing developments in the financial and capital markets of each participating nation. In that case, no matter how clearly the Maastricht Treaty calls for an economic and monetary union, the realization of that program is in jeopardy. This must be seen as the inherent limits of the Maastricht Treaty."[26]

This discussion refers to the conditions after the introduction of a single currency. The author raises the concerns about inequalities, given the retention of national sovereignty, between currency circulation and values in various member nations, and about the viability of private and general circulation of a single currency. These concerns, as I will now show, are already casting their shadow even before the introduction of the single currency.

In contrast to the arguments raised to this point, there is also a view that the purpose of European integration is to re-strengthen the sovereign rights of each member nation, and that monetary union is also aimed at the same end. One might call this the soberest view of European integration. One proponent of this view argues as follows: "It would be easy to call their plan reckless. The problem is that in the wake of the demise of the ERM – which is essential to the realization of monetary union – the European leaders have no reason not to wave the flag of 'reckless' monetary union, which is contradictory with national sovereignty. Behind the decisions of the leaders is undoubtedly the following wily calculation as to national advantage. First, Europe has already in reality become a German mark bloc.... In that case, the only option left to the European leaders is to force the mark under common management, and to make it a *de jure* single currency, thus preserving at least some voice in the matter for each member nation. Secondly, the decision to form an economic and monetary union comes not from the European bureaucracy, but directly from the leadership of each member nation.... Third, the European Central Bank will, following the strident demands of Germany, retain the same independence from political pressure that the German Bundesbank currently enjoys.... In sum, far from meaning a loss of national sovereignty – that is, of the monetary authorities of each country falling under the guns of a 'Eurocrat financial Mafia' – the plan will actually mean nothing less than a restoration of the national right to respond appropriately to the circumstances of economic integration."[27]

These comments in part offer a correct explanation. Within the process aimed at achieving a single currency, there were indeed movements aimed at the restoration and strengthening of national powers, and policies have been adopted which certainly lend themselves to such an interpretation. However, the common management and exercise of national sovereignty has already to some extent been realized, and building on that, the introduction of a clear supra-nationality is being aimed at. Indeed, for the very reason that the transfer of a large amount of national sovereignty is on the agenda, it is not surprising that strident voices are being raised in support of national sovereignty.

(3) The Political Process Towards a Single Currency

Since entering the second stage of monetary union at the beginning of 1994, and in particular since the beginning of 1996, the transition to stage three has, under German and French leadership, been a top priority. One symbol of this was the Bundesbank's placing monetary union as one of its major objectives.

The member nations became all striving to meet the four conditions laid down by the Maastricht Treaty. Among the four, the stabilization of prices and the achievement of an appropriate level of long-term interest rates were relatively easy, and in 1996 from nine to eleven out of the fifteen member nations had cleared these hurdles. However, the condition relating to the fiscal position was difficult, and the only state to have cleared this was Luxembourg.[28]

Since the decision whether or not to participate was based on 1997 data, all the member states attempted to reduce their budget deficits in the 1997 budgets. Specifically, they aimed at meeting the condition that their budget deficits should not exceed 3% of GDP. In order to reduce their deficits, they resorted both to spending cuts such as reductions in social welfare spending, civil service cuts, and promotion of privatizations, and revenue-enhancing measures such as tax increases. The 1997 budgets also contained various forms of "window-dressing." Italy's "euro tax" is the most famous example. This was a new tax, which came with a promise that the money would be partially returned to taxpayers after the introduction of the euro. Even Germany, which had consistently stressed the need for strict adherence to the conditions, tried to resort to the same sort of window-dressing when it became apparent in May 1997 that there would be a severe shortfall in tax revenues. The finance minister attempted to resort to deficit reduction measures such as promotion of privatizations and freezing of some budgeted expenditures, and revaluation of the Bundesbank's holdings of gold to current market prices, with the profit accruing to the national treasury. This plan was loudly criticized as "window-dressing" both within and outside Germany, and the Bundesbank's refusal to acquiesce in particular forced its revision, so that ultimately it was decided that even though the gold holdings would be revalued, the accrual of profits to the public purse would be delayed one year.

The result of these efforts, which were mainly aimed at reducing expenditures, was a sudden drop in the fiscal deficits of most member countries. But even with these measures, few members were able to meet the requirements of the treaty.

With regard to the foreign exchange markets, membership in the ERM was a precondition for participating in the monetary union, and to this end, too, member states made great efforts. Denmark and the three Benelux states, the core members of the ERM, held tenaciously to the ERM, while France adopted a strong franc policy at the behest of Frankfurt (known as the "franc fort"). Italy, which had withdrawn from the ERM in September 1992, adopted a high interest rate policy and rejoined the mechanism, expressing the desire to participate in monetary union from the beginning. Finland also joined the ERM, leaving only the United Kingdom, Greece, and Sweden outside the system.

Among the various efforts aimed at smoothing the path to introduction of a single currency, the most noteworthy is the conclusion of so-called stable agreements. The purpose of these agreements is to place obligations on participants in the single currency to meet fiscal standards in order to assure the stability of the euro once it is launched. In other words, these agreements call for an (albeit partial) transfer of fiscal sovereignty to the EU, and one can see this as an attempt to circumvent the "inherent limitations" of the Maastricht Treaty, referred to above. For that reason alone, these agreements are noteworthy.

The originator of the idea behind these agreements was Germany. The European Commission reviewed this idea and drafted a plan, which called for financial sanctions against member states with fiscal deficits in excess of 3% of GDP after monetary union. Thereafter, work proceeded on the details of sanctions, but opposition was expressed at the finance ministers council to the rules relating to exceptions to the sanctions. Germany had emphasized a strict statistical standard, but other members pressed for a looser standard of interpretation. The negotiations were protracted, but agreement was formally concluded at the June 1997 Amsterdam summit. France's new socialist cabinet had requested revision of the plan, but in the end the plan was passed without revision.

The final provisions for sanctions were as follows. (1) In the event that any member state has a budget deficit in excess of 3%, up to 0.5% of GDP will be claimed as a penalty, to be placed on deposit without interest. (2) If the deficit is not reduced within two years, the money will be forfeited and placed at the disposal of the EU for the benefit of the member states. (3) Exceptions: when the real growth rate of a member state is below minus 2%, the sanctions will not apply. When the real growth rate is between minus 0.75% and minus 2%, the finance ministers council will decide whether or not to apply the sanctions. In all other cases, the sanctions will in principle apply. However, in exceptional circumstances such as war or natural disaster, the finance ministers council will have the right to waive sanctions.

The June 1997 Amsterdam summit also came to formal agreement on the fate of the ERM after the introduction of a single currency. It devised this agreement in order to control fluctuations in the exchange rate between the euro and the currencies of non-participating EU members to within a specified range. However, the agreement expressly stipulated that EU member central banks, and the European central bank, do not have an unlimited obligation to intervene in currency markets to maintain exchange rates.

During this period, the designs were also announced for the euro banknotes and coinage. The EU commission also released an optimistic forecast on meeting the conditions for participation in the euro. According to this forecast, 13 out of the 15 members (the exceptions were Italy and Greece) would meet the condition for holding the deficit to within 3% of GDP in 1997. The European Commission made a number of other attempts to stir up enthusiasm for the single currency, announcing that the euro would enjoy a similar share of foreign reserves and trade settlements as the dollar, and forecasting that the euro would become an international currency similar to the dollar.

However, these efforts, particularly those at window-dressing and at optimism by the European Commission, actually serve to reveal the opaqueness of the monetary union. Since the EU recorded real growth of minus 0. 6% in 1993, efforts at recovery have consistently lacked strength. Policy efforts aimed at meeting the conditions for membership in the single currency, particularly those polices aimed at fiscal retrenchment, have had the effect of delaying economic recovery. Meanwhile, employment has failed to recover, and unemployment has remained at high levels. In 1997, both France and Germany had the highest level of unemployment since the Second World War (12.2% for Germany in January-February, 12.7% for France in May). For this reason, political and social tensions have increased throughout the region. In Germany, civil servants went on strikes, and the Deutscher Gewerkschaftsbund organized massive demonstrations. Opposition to monetary union was strongest not only in West Germany, for which the mark was an expression of national identity and which had been dragged into national unification, but also in the former East Germany. In France, too, there were repeated long-term strikes by public employees and others. Spain and Italy, in spite of their professed desires to participate in monetary union, were no exceptions to this unrest.

Fiscal restructuring was originally a common topic of the advanced capitalist economies, and Japan, the US and Europe were competing to promote such restructuring. Monetary union, with the accompanying need to clear the conditions for participation, imposed a great moral duty such as was not seen in Japan or the US. Because of this moral duty, even in the midst of high unemployment and social tensions, the governments of member countries were able to press on with the retrenchment of fiscal expenditures, particularly social welfare expenditures, and the shrinking of the public sector.

With the escalation of political and social tensions, the Chirac government lost the May 1997 elections after campaigning on a platform of placing the euro on a par with the dollar and the yen, resulting in the creation of a socialist cabinet. Although the new cabinet has not demanded a revision of the 1999 time schedule, it has attempted to fulfill its election promises by requesting a relaxation of the conditions for participation in the interests of relieving the employment situation. The impact of these actions immediately became apparent. Although the stability agreement regarding fiscal management after the introduction of a single currency was passed without revision, based on French insistence, a new agreement was concluded on employment policy, and was included in the final release of the European council. Moreover, it was also decided to use the European Investment Bank and other funds aimed at promoting low-cost funds for small and medium-sized as well as high-tech businesses. And a section concerning employment was, again, inserted in the Amsterdam Treaty, with a concurrent decision to hold a temporary European council on the employment issue. These measures had no particularly new flavor, and there was a strong sense of deadlock in them. Moreover, employment measures were understood to depend not on fiscal outlays, but on structural reforms. However, it is undeniable that even these limited measures acted to some extent as a break on endeavors to meet the criteria for participation in a unified currency.

In addition to this new focus on employment policy, another noteworthy point is the changes in the planned operations of the European central bank after introduction of a single currency. The final statement of the Amsterdam summit, based on the initiative of France, provided for the finance ministers council and the European Commission to have some voice in the policy of the European Central Bank, to the extent that inconsistencies did not arise with the bank's independence and its primary duty of maintaining price stability. Interpretations of this rule differ between France and Germany, but the revision could potentially be of great importance.

Based on the belief that a delay in introducing the single currency would invite confusion and might be tantamount to the death of the initiative, the EU member states have been rushing to complete their preparations by 1999. If the schedule is immovable, then in the event of difficulties in meeting the required conditions, the only choices available are relaxation of the conditions or a flexible interpretation of them.

As I have already mentioned, the fact that even the German government, which had been so active in leading the calls for a strict interpretation of the conditions, should have considered a measure such as revaluing the Bundesbank's gold reserves, speaks eloquently of the anxiety felt about meeting the conditions. Since monetary union has been the focus of "deepening," and since "deepening" is, as already discussed, a measure for the "containment" of Germany, Germany has no moral grounds on which to oppose the monetary union. Moreover, for German companies a single currency bloc would have the advantage of representing a vast market. However, in order to capture voters who are opposed to abandoning the strong mark, it is not enough simply to assert that the future European Central Bank is modeled on the German Bundesbank and that the euro is the successor to the mark. The government must promise that the single currency euro will be at least as strong as the mark, if not more so. The emphasis on a strict interpretation of the conditions for participation is thus also aimed at domestic consumption. Even under these circumstances, the German government was forced into adopting makeshift measures to circumvent the conditions.

Already in the Maastricht Treaty, there were stipulations allowing the relaxation of the conditions or flexibility in their interpretation. The task of preparing the reports that would decide which nations would participate in the third stage is in the hands of the European Monetary Institute and the European Commission. Since those agencies prepare the report, they at least have the possibility to be flexible in their interpretation. The same applies to the ministers councils which will decide by a specified majority based on the results of the report. In addition, the European Parliament will also study the issue, and will be able to voice its opinion on the matter, thus adding to the overall pressure for a flexible interpretation. And finally, it is up to the European council to decide on the participating nations.

In this event, it is of course unclear whether the leader nation Germany will carry out the strict interpretation and application of the conditions. The maintenance of the value of the euro is not only a posture for the benefit of voters. It is also economically called for. However, on the other hand, if as a result of a strict interpretation Italy, for example, should be excluded, the maintenance of the exchange rate between the euro and the lira would also become a difficult issue. A cheap lira would bring with it the threat of an export drive by Italy. Thus, whether from the beginning or later, it is necessary to plan for the inclusion of the nations south of the Alps, including Italy, Spain and Portugal. If this is to take place, then in some form or another it may ultimately be necessary to relax the conditions. Even the Bundesbank has begun pointing to the existence of exception clauses that permit participation even for those countries with deficits in excess of 3%, provided that there is a clear tendency for the deficit to decline.

Therefore, it is unclear at this point which nations will be permitted to join the single currency. The conclusion with regard to Italy and Spain is unclear, and there is also the issue of when the United Kingdom and Denmark will join. On the surface, it seems unlikely that all fifteen member countries will join, so for those new member countries who have followed the path of "expansion" following "deepening," there is little prospect for early participation. Moreover, it is likely that the relations between the single currency and the nations not participating in monetary union will be regulated by a new ERM, but since there is no obligation for the relevant central banks to intervene without limit in the currency markets, the effectiveness of such a system is also by no means assured.

The problem, therefore, is how strict the application of the conditions will be, and which nations will participate. It becomes in short a problem of the value of the single currency euro. The initial price level will be influenced by the conditions for participation, and subsequent price levels will fluctuate depending on the fiscal management of each nation, or, to put it differently, on the effectiveness of the stability agreements. The possibility of a currency crisis prior to the introduction of the euro, or of a mark crisis, is by no means absent.

Moreover, in the beginning we may assume that an objective of the "deepening" of integration through monetary union was to increase the dynamism of the European economy versus those of Japan and the US and to nurture and strengthen the competitiveness of European and EU firms in the age of the "third industrial revolution." However, monetary union might almost be seen as for its own sake. There has been a move towards emphasizing employment, but that lacks any new flavors or prospects. Even the success of market integration as an oppositional organization meets with little acknowledgement today. As yet, the market integration has shown no appreciable results. And as in the case of market integration, monetary union offers opportunities not only to European companies but also to those from outside the region, including Japanese and American companies. As long as no measures are taken to restrict those endeavors, the euro has little prospect of assuring an increase in the competitiveness of European companies.

Both before and after the introduction of the euro, the old-fashioned process of clashes and compromises over national sovereignty, including new issues such as the common management and execution of national sovereignty, and the rapid growth of supra-nationality, are likely to continue.

CONCLUSION

The ultimate prospects for monetary union, one of the focal points of European integration, remain unclear. However, based on the considerations outlined above, the following points may be asserted with some confidence. First, the collapse of the IMF fixed exchange rate system, accompanied by the declining value of the dollar and the lack of any attempt by the US government to reverse that decline, brought about European monetary integration in the form of the EMS, and, linked to the EMS, the formation of a *de facto* German mark bloc. Second, that monetary union then took on the characteristics of a measure in opposition to the supremacy of the dollar. This became all the more evident as European nations began planning the introduction of a single currency. The goal was for the euro to become an international currency competitive with the dollar and the yen. However, third, if we ask whether the progress of monetary union has succeeded in creating a potential substitute of the dollar, we must answer that it has only partially, at best. The dollar has undeniably been in a long-term decline concurrent with the decline in American hegemony, but the dollar's status as an international currency remains as firm as before.

After the introduction of a single European currency, uncertainties abound. It is unclear even which countries will participate, and it is also unclear whether attempts to coordinate fiscal policy under the stability agreements, which are an essential component of the management of the single currency, will meet with success. Moreover, it is most unlikely that smooth progress will be made in policy coordination in non-financial areas, in the transfer of sovereign rights, or in steps towards political union. Internally, given the high level of dependence on intra-regional trade, a single currency should reduce the disturbances caused by the dollar in the regional currency market. Externally its substitutability for the dollar will be partial at best, and it is likely that the status of the dollar will continue. Even the rosy projections of the European Commission go no further than envisioning equal status for the Europe versus the dollar. Unless other regions opt to follow the example of the euro and pursue monetary union, it is hard to foresee the downfall of the dollar.

The final problem is to what extent the European monetary union will have a positive meaning for the world in the aftermath of American hegemony, or indeed of hegemony in general. Unfortunately, the considerations contained in this paper so far offer almost no material to answer this question. However, the following speculations may perhaps be advanced.

The first question is whether, if the European monetary union is to progress as a substitute of the dollar, the progress to date in establishing common management and exercise of sovereignty is adequate, and whether it is necessary to introduce a supra-national single currency. A single market will only be achieved by the introduction of a single currency. However, why does it have to be a totally single market? The revitalization of the European economy has come to be seen as possible through a common market even in the absence of a single market. Will a single market make possible what the common market could not make reality? Or, reversing this question, perhaps it is necessary to recognize a little more the fact that even the present level of economic integration has, from a global perspective, reached an extremely high level. Certainly, Europe is aiming for a high standard of market integration through the introduction of a single currency, and, as we have already seen, there has been intense pressure to that end since the liberalization of intra-regional capital movements. However, even before that event, the EMS up to that point represented, in spite of its failures, a rare experiment in global terms. If we consider the matter in this light, then perhaps the experience of developing a currency bloc within Europe independent of US hegemony, and the techniques of common management and exercise of national sovereignty developed in the process of maintaining that integration, will be a priceless asset in the development of a currency system for the post-hegemonic world.

Source: *The Political Economy of Japanese Globalization* (Glenn D. Hook and HASEGAWA Harukiyo (eds)), London: Routledge, 2001, pp. 120–136.

19

Americanization or Europeanization?: The Globalization of the Japanese Economy

INTRODUCTION

THE INTERNATIONALIZATION OF the Japanese economy has been proclaimed repeatedly even if this observation is limited to the post-war era. The specific meaning of internationalization has varied with each successive wave, but generally speaking, up to the end of the 1980s, the trend was from internal internationalization – the internationalization of the Japanese economy itself – to external internationalization – the international influence of the Japanese economy. The latter can be referred to as 'international Japanization'. Considering the growing status of Japan in the global economy, such a trend was only natural (Ozawa 1995; Kudō 1994a, 1995a).

From the beginning of the 1990s, however, a reversal has occurred: 'internal internationalization' has once again become the focus of debate. For example, major topics have included the opening of allegedly closed markets, the elimination of barriers to FDI in Japan, and an emphasis on international cooperation in economic policy. Certainly, debate about 'external internationalization continues', but its focus is less on the active international role of the Japanese economy than on its passive impact. Take, for example, the debate on the chaos that might accompany the widespread sale by Japan of US treasury bills (short-term government bonds). Why the debate has shifted in this way requires analysis, but it is undeniable that the shift has in fact taken place.

These issues have certainly taken on a new coloration in the 1990s, but basically they remain variations on a theme that has repeatedly appeared in the past. The older term 'internationalization' has also largely given way to the term 'globalization', but that is surely little more than a question of terminology. So does that mean that the question of the internationalization or globalization of the Japanese economy in the 1990s and early twenty-first century is unworthy of academic scrutiny? Two reasons suggest otherwise. First, the Japanese economy of the 1990s follows the unprecedented experience of the 'bubble economy' of the late 1980s. The present economy is marked with the scars the 'bubble' inflicted, which cut to the very heart of the economy's structure. Second, after a period in which the decline of US hegemony was widely forecast, the 1990s have witnessed the re-emergence of a powerful US influence, or at least the feeling of such influence.

The 'bubble economy' and its aftermath

The boom of the late 1980s – the so-called 'bubble economy' – was a phenomenon unprecedented in Japanese economic history. This is clear from the unparalleled rise in stock and land prices, as well as from the many scenes of people and institutions both leading and being led in this sordid dance. The unsavory facts are still emerging today, and, even more disturbing, some of the activities are actually being repeated. It is no exaggeration to say that the scars of the bubble era remain the guiding force of the Japanese economy in the 1990s and early twenty-first century, and they may be seen as the basic condition underlying the internationalization or globalization now taking place. Thus, we must perforce clarify the underlying causes of the bubble economy. Scholars have so far failed to reach a consensus on that point, and many issues remain unresolved. Such an attempt at clarification is therefore doomed to failure at present; but at least it is necessary to specify the basic issues that still need to be resolved.

It is apparent that one of the pillars supporting the boom of the late 1980s was the international competitiveness of Japan's manufacturing industries. In this sense, to refer to the 'bubble economy', which evinces an image of rising stock and land prices, is to point to only one aspect of that phenomenon. Nevertheless, as the peculiar characteristic of that phenomenon was the extraordinary speculation in stocks and land, the term 'bubble economy' remains the preferred expression.

What caused the 'bubble economy'?

If the above term is to be retained, then above all the causes of that speculation need to be elaborated. Where, and how, was the speculative capital generated? And why was that capital directed towards speculation and not towards other investments? Behind the speculation lie various financial institutions, including the so-called non-banks. These institutions engendered the speculation, spurred it, and then ultimately were brought down by it. Thus, the credit created by these institutions was a major cause of the bubble phenomenon. But what caused this credit creation in the first place was the accumulated capital of manufacturing industry. This capital became excess to the needs of the manufacturing sector, and was used for speculative purposes via the medium of the above financial institutions, or else was invested directly. In the latter case, the investments took the form of equity financing or real-estate lending. At the time, the fashionable term to describe this was *zai-tech* (zai = finance). Nowadays the term has fallen into almost total disuse, but at the time large numbers of companies (as well as individuals) rushed into *zai-tech* activities. Indeed, only an exceptional minority failed to participate. Today, those companies are almost without exception industry leaders. Just why these companies did not participate is a fascinating as well as an important question.

In any event, if the location and mechanism for the creation of excess capital were as described above, then the conclusion must be that the birth of the bubble economy lay above all in the following causes. First, the international competitiveness of Japanese manufacturing industry grew throughout the 1970s and the early 1980s in spite of – and partly as a result of – the two oil crises afflicting the global economy. The greatest reason for this competitiveness was manufacturing technology at the factory level, while the *keiretsu* system of inter-corporate ties, which also encompassed smaller companies, was another important factor. The Japanese economy of this period has been aptly described as 'collective capitalism' (Lazonick 1990, 1991) or the 'Japanese enterprise system' (Fruin 1992). This competitiveness resulted in enormous trade surpluses, and caused Japan to accumulate huge amounts of capital. The industries that showed particularly strong international competitiveness were limited to production and assembly industries such as automobiles, electronics and related industries, but these represented global products – hence, large-scale capital accumulation occurred.

Second, the capital accumulated by manufacturing industry, as well as other capital, was recycled through the credit-creating mechanism of the financial institutions to create still more capital, and much of this was directed into stock and real-estate speculation. However, the financial system itself was not at the time sufficiently developed to deal with this phenomenon. There was a huge imbalance between the expansion of capital and the underdeveloped technical and management skills of the financial institutions. This phenomenon closely parallels the US financial system at the time of the 1929 stock market crash. Indeed, the imbalance extended to the entire Japanese service sector.

In other words, we must view the cause for the emergence and subsequent collapse of the 'bubble economy' in the imbalance between the 'bright side' represented by the skills of Japan's manufacturing industry, and the 'dark side' represented by the administrative ineptitude of financial institutions and other service industries (including, incidentally, the administrative functions of manufacturing industry) (Yoshihara 1989).

But in searching for the fundamental causes of the 'bubble economy', it is important not to be limited solely to the location and mechanism bringing about the emergence of excess capital. It is also necessary to consider why this capital was not directed towards investments other than stock and real-estate speculation. This is related to the question why, after the collapse of the bubble in the 1990s, domestic capital was directed not towards the reconstruction of the Japanese economy and society, but instead was invested overseas, particularly in US securities. It would be narrow-sighted to treat this simply as an issue of interest rates. For it is, at heart, a policy issue: the problem lies in the deficiency in, or even lack of, a will or strategy to reform Japan's economy and society, as well as a similar lack of will or strategy to contribute to the global economy.

Unresolved issues in the bubble economy's wake

To develop this point a little further, the bubble economy can be said to have left the following unresolved issues for the Japanese economy and society. First, the Japanese manufacturing system, which as we have seen has been termed 'collective capitalism' or the 'Japanese enterprise system', needs to be reformed. The strength of that system's international competitiveness was built on the sacrifice of the individuality of employees as autonomous members of society – a phenomenon sometimes termed 'enterprisism' (Baba 1991). Indeed, the apostle of the Japanese 'knowledge-creating organization', Nonaka Ikujirō, has pointed precisely to the physical 'exhaustion' of Japanese workers as the system's greatest defect (Nonaka and Takeuchi 1995). Again, Ronald Dore, who has praised the high efficiency of Japanese capitalism, says that he would prefer not to live in Japan (Fukada and Dore 1993). The reform of the Japanese enterprise system would probably have the effect of reducing the international competitiveness of Japanese manufacturing industry. That is unavoidable. Indeed, it is even desirable: first it will promote the 'humanization' of the domestic economy and society; and, second, it will reduce Japan's trade surplus, which has been the cause of endless disputes with the US and elsewhere.

Next, the financial sector – and, subsequently, the entire service sector – needs to be made more transparent in order to transform that 'dark side' of the Japanese economy. In particular, the imbalance between the quantitative expansion of the financial system and the underdevelopment of its qualitative technical and management skills needs to be addressed. In order to achieve this, internationalization or globalization is necessary, too. Globalization is not a meaningful objective in and of itself. Great harm would be caused by an unprincipled rush into globalization as a result of fears about the 'hollowing out' of the Tokyo financial market, itself caused by the transfer of massive sums of capital overseas. There are many speculative markets around the world today. It would be foolish to compete against them. The globalization of financial markets is in fact a means for the improvement of the Japanese financial sector. This process should contribute to the development of appropriate incentives for capital.

Third, and related to the above two points, reform of the Japanese economy and society is necessary. For a long time, policy-makers and critics have argued that Japan must develop from an 'economic great power' to a 'lifestyle great power'. Despite these calls both inside and outside the circles of power, however, little progress has been made. The current debates and policy initiatives on domestic reform do not adequately link the reform of the domestic economy with the reform of the Japanese enterprise system. There is lots of talk of the downsizing of government, privatization and deregulation. Lest we forget, however, the leading players in these initiatives are precisely those companies which form part of the much praised 'collective capitalism' or 'Japanese enterprise system' – in other words, the background against which these initiatives are taken is hardly a textbook fair market in which investors could place their trust. Unless the corporate system is reformed, trust in the market will fail to rise, and there will be no way to reform the economy and society. The fundamental platform for reform must surely be how to restore the fruits of the international competitiveness of Japanese manufacturing industry to the domestic economy and society. Indeed, this is the real significance of the present Japanese focus on corporate governance as a key aspect of those reforms. But under the present condition of the Japanese economy, what is occurring is a strengthening of 'enterprisism' and a concurrent decline in the much-touted 'knowledge-creating organization' at the corporate level. That, to be sure, is one of the major reasons for the deadlock over reform at the national level.

Fourth, the rebuilding of Japan's international economic relations is necessary. Japan still commands vast capital resources, with individual savings said to total some ¥1,200 trillion. The fact that much of this capital is currently invested overseas, and in the US in particular, is testimony to the undeveloped state of the Japanese financial system. It also highlights how the 'economic superpower' remains unable to understand its international responsibilities. This point was made abundantly clear by the 1997 East Asian financial, currency and economic crises. True, as the 'bubble economy' was an exceptional phenomenon, the 1990s can be seen as a period of returning to normality. But such normalization will only be possible through reform in the twenty-first century.

GLOBALIZATION OR 'AMERICANIZATION'?

The reform of the Japanese economy and society must be generated internally, but one problem remains. That is the phenomenon of *gaiatsu* or international pressure, specifically pressure from the US, which is referred to in this chapter as 'Americanization'.

In the 1990s, there was constant talk about the internationalization or globalization of the Japanese economy. Behind this theme lies the development of a global financial market in which capital, particularly speculative short-term capital, can be moved at will around the world. As seen above, there is certainly some logic to such a development. Nor is this simply a domestic concern: the capital cities of the US, Europe and Asia, as well as global financial institutions themselves, constantly harp on the same theme. This, in itself, is a form of *gaiatsu*. More specifically, however, the strongest and most effective calls for reform of the Japanese system have come from the US, which in the late 1990s enjoyed a period of great prosperity. In other words, what is currently taking place is actually 'Americanization' under the name of globalization.

The economic crisis in East Asian countries following the 1997 depreciation of the Thai baht bolstered this trend. The Federal Reserve Board (FRB) Chairman, Alan Greenspan, referred to the 'collapse of Asian mercantilism', which he compares to 'eighteenth-century British mercantilism', and has emphasized the 'excellence of American-style market capitalism' (*Nikkei* 17 January 1998). This is a cry of victory for the US.

Forms of 'Americanization'

'Americanization' is progressing on a large scale both at the corporate level and at the level of the national economy. At the corporate level, for instance, bold restructuring and the elimination of unprofitable divisions are moving rapidly forward regardless of the unemployment spawned as a result. Or, at least, these trends are being loudly proclaimed. Rapid management decision making, symbolized by bold take-overs, is lavishly praised. At the same time, emphasis on profits (return on equity (ROE), return on assets (ROA), etc.), shareholder returns and, to that end, management transparency and the establishment of corporate governance, are all being positively touted. The emphasis on profitability, which then Sony Chairman Morita Akio stressed several years ago, is now, on the basis of the US corporate model, becoming an accepted dogma. By contrast, Japanese technology, management and labor relations, which were lavishly praised in former times, are now held up as a model of ossification. The auto-maker Mazda is symbolic of this reversal: the company, which supports no less than 10 percent of the population of Hiroshima prefecture where it is based, has fallen completely under the Ford umbrella, and it is now attempting to fight its way out of its difficulties by introducing Ford-style management.

At the national level, 'Americanization' is even more evident. With the US as a model, intercorporate relations and corporate–government relations are being transformed through the relaxation or abolition of regulations, and through the promotion of competition. US companies and the US government are now able to intervene effectively in this debate with, for example, calls for the abolition of the Large-scale Retail Establishment Law. In the fields of society, lifestyle, culture, speech and research, US influence is strengthening before our very eyes.

The paradox of 'Americanization'

In this way, the impression has been created that, in the 1990s, US influence on Japan – 'Americanization' – has grown even stronger than in the past. If 'Americanization' is examined in its historical context, however, this impression is wide of the mark. The history of 'Americanization', even if the discussion is limited to relations with Japan, has a history of at least a century, although the first great wave did not hit Japanese shores until the 1920s (Sasaki and Nonaka 1990). Following this, in the aftermath of the Second World War, the influence of the reforms carried out by the occupation forces in politics, the economy and society continued to reverberate throughout the 1950s and 1960s. Following the post-war reconstruction, the US was in every way a model for the Japanese economy and society, which was struggling to work its way up the developmental ladder. The productivity movement was a typical example (Sunaga and Nonaka 1995). Indeed, the 1950s and 1960s were the high-water mark of US hegemony, a fact which increased US influence. In the 1970s and 1980s, moreover, the decline of US supremacy, accompanied by the economic ascent of Japan, resulted in a weakening of the pressure for 'Americanization'.

Thus, the rise in US pressure in the 1990s (or at least, the impression of such a rise) may be seen as a reversal in the context of the overall history of 'Americanization'. What is more, during this period US hegemony, particularly as manifest economically, was continuing to decline (Tateyama 1995). Seen in this light, this historic reversal appears paradoxical. Why has 'Americanization' recovered – or, at least, given the appearance of recovering?

One argument is that, following the end of the Cold War, the US has become the world's only superpower. It continues to wield ever greater political and military power, and no signs can be found of any other hegemonic power emerging to take its place. Second, US corporate competitiveness has recovered owing to the strength of the US information technology sector, which is in the vanguard of the Third Industrial Revolution. Third, with the current crisis of the West European welfare economies, the low level of welfare provision in the US no longer causes undue comment.

The reason for the recovery of 'Americanization', however, must be seen primarily to lie in the situation of Japan itself. In the aftermath of the 'bubble economy', many managers and bureaucrats remain unable to find a way out of their troubles independently – hence, the US success story appeals as a model. At the corporate level, profitability, corporate governance and 'economies of speed' are the current catchphrases, while at the national level, the mantra is deregulation.

Problems of 'Americanization'

Nevertheless, problems with this kind of 'Americanization' abound. To some extent, of course, it is necessary in order to promote reforms and a return to normality after the 'bubble economy'. In some cases, too, 'Americanization' should be welcomed. It forms an indispensable part of the learning process in the development of corporate management and the national economy. In no way should the Japanese adopt a narrow-minded nationalism.

Indeed, inflexible adherence to those once-praised models – 'Japanese-style management', 'Japanese-style capitalism' and so on – will lead Japan to its doom. The path to recovery does not lie in clinging to these outdated models. In this sense, it is necessary to return to the Japanese tradition of learning from foreign models. In the past, Japanese companies and bureaucrats exhibited a fervent desire to learn fully the technological, management and social systems of the advanced economies of Europe and the US. To this end, both the business and bureaucratic elite boosted their learning capabilities, aiming for innovation through imitation followed by improvement (Kudō 1995b). For 'Japaneseness' implies a process of constant learning and enhancement. In this sense, the fundamental cause of the 'bubble economy' is straightforward: companies and the government forgot their habit of learning, and relied too much on their own prior successes. To that extent, 'Americanization' offers a golden opportunity for the renewal of learning.

In the longer term, however, the sacrifice of employees in favor of profits and shareholder value in pursuit of the US model clearly endangers the special features of Japanese management. Moreover, at the national level, 'Americanization' can potentially spawn a high level of long-term unemployment, a squeeze on wages, and the growth of inequalities in income and assets, thus tearing at the nation's social fabric. There is also a danger that indiscriminate deregulation not only will result in excessive competition and market chaos, but also may threaten the environment and overall security. The US at present may truly be said to illustrate these sorts of dangers. Post-war Japan has often been labelled a land of 'public weakness and private flooding', and certainly it has failed to achieve a national consensus on the relationship between the public and private spheres. If under this condition Japan adopts unadulterated US-style deregulation, then the nation faces the danger of ending up with even more troubles than the US presently faces.

Until now, learning from the US by Japanese companies and the government appears partial and selective. Toyota, for example, has publicly adopted the stance that 'we will protect our workforce at all costs', and 'we will not undertake hostile takeovers' (*Nikkei* 17 December 1997). Companies are selectively introducing US methods on top of their own technology and management. Moreover, companies which have undertaken such experiments seem to be for the most part restricted to a few corporate giants. However, if the current reforms do not bring results, and if the reason is seen to be an incomplete adoption of the US model, then 'Americanization' may make inroads on a much larger scale. At that time, associated problems will surely increase in salience.

This is by no means a groundless fear. In recent Japanese-US relations (and this is by no means a new phenomenon), Japan has fended off the US 'self-centred hegemony' (Tateyama 1995) and 'aggressive unilateralism' (Sasaki 1997) through a series of *ad hoc* measures (Ozawa 1995). Seen in this light, concern should indeed be raised.

Comparison with Europe

In Western Europe, too, France and Germany – which are the nucleus of regional integration – have also been swept by waves of Americanization, but in those countries 'Americanization' has been a topic of academic debate since the 1970s (Berghahn 1986), and it is currently being openly attacked in journalistic circles (Albert 1991). In Japan, on the other hand, few critical voices have been raised. Although it has been possible for some time to engage in comparatively objective discussion of the US presence, such debates have begun in academic circles only recently. In the media, the following comment by Iida Tsuneo is an exception:

> We Japanese have come to assume that 'somewhere over the mountain' lies an ideal system and set of rules. This 'somewhere over the mountain' has so far meant Europe and the United States, and particularly the United States. But recently, we have come to realize that that is nothing more than an illusion. That must be a sign of Japanese people's 'maturation'. But very recently, that 'maturity' has disappeared somewhere.
>
> (*Mainichi Shinbun* 24 November 1997)

And 'Without Japanese-style capitalism, what Japan?' (Fukada and Dore 1993): such remarks are already being seen as mere blustering.

Where this difference between Europe and Japan should come from is itself an interesting question. It may come from the difference in regional integration and in socio-economic maturity, or it perhaps lies in the difference in historical relations with the US, which results in US pressure being more formidable in Japan. The history of Japanese-US relations from the black ships of Commodore Perry (1853) to the post-war occupation (1945–52) has certainly served to breed an inferiority complex. What remains a far more serious problem, however, is that this pressure has not been sufficiently recognized or subject to criticism. Perhaps this is related to the fact that there has been insufficient recognition of the need for reform.

'EUROPEANIZATION' AS AN ALTERNATIVE

Since the US model suffers from a range of problems, there is ample reason to look also to Europe (by which is meant Western Europe, including the UK) when considering social and economic reform in post-bubble Japan. This statement immediately raises questions. Why must the Japanese learn from Europe? If an examination is made of the present state of corporate management and technology, or the condition of the national economy and welfare society, can we really learn anything from Europe? Surely Europe itself is undergoing the same flood of 'Americanization' as Japan. What is more, can it not be said that Europe itself has lost the desire and wherewithal to teach anything to Japan? These are all reasonable questions.

'Europeanization', as discussed here, is not mere romanticism. What kind of meaning does, or should, 'Europeanization' entail? And is 'Europeanization' possible, or, more precisely, how can it be made possible? The current state of Japanese–European economic relations in their historical context is examined below in order to throw some light on these questions.

Regional integration as a reason for 'Europeanization'

Since before the Second World War, Euro-Japanese economic relations have been characterized by a one-way flow of knowledge from Europe to Japan. However, even before then, a competitive relationship also existed (Kudō 1998a). This competitive relationship became stronger after the war. Then, following the first oil crisis, it developed into actual trade conflicts. At that time, the European economies were falling behind in the microelectronics (ME) revolution and the Third Industrial Revolution. They became the target of the economic endeavors of Japan, which was ahead in these areas. The long-term trade imbalance which emerged gave rise to repeated trade conflicts. The cause of this, in the final analysis, was the gap in competitiveness between Japanese and European manufacturers. This gap did not appear in all products, but only in those that formed the nucleus of global trade. In aerospace, cosmetics and foodstuffs, for example, Europe was the more competitive. As a result of these trade conflicts, as well as of the superiority of Japanese technology and management in the key fields of global trade, Japanese direct investment in Europe grew by leaps and bounds. Moreover, strategic alliances and industrial technology cooperation between Japanese and European big business also increased. Finally, at the government level, industrial, scientific and technological cooperation forged ahead (Kudō 1995a, 1995b).

Behind these trade conflicts was continuing European integration. The 1992 market integration, the Maastricht Treaty, the deepening of political and monetary union, as well as the expansion of the EU to include former Eastern Europe and other countries, were to some extent a response by Europe to the economic prosperity and economic challenge posed by Japan. Increasingly, however, it came to represent rather a European economic challenge to Japan (Tanaka 1996; Schulz 1998; Kudō 1998b). For example, the monetary union towards which Europe is currently advancing is also a challenge to the future of the yen as a vehicle for international payments and reserves (Schulz 1998).

European integration has spurred regional integration around the world, perhaps most strongly in the case of Malaysian Prime Minister Mahathir's brainchild, the EAEC, as well as the US-led APEC, where both recognize the challenge of Europe. Although Japan occupies a predominant economic position in this contested region (Hook 1996), from the perspective of regional integration it remains in isolation. Caught between the two organizations, Japan is desperately searching for a way forward. The 1997 currency, financial and economic crises in East Asia have certainly once again confirmed Japan's confusion in this area.

At present, Japan is seeking an appropriate response to the European challenge. The issue is, above all, the need to rectify the imbalance in Japanese–European economic relations, particularly the trade imbalance. Also at issue are the expansion and strengthening of political ties, and Japan's commitment to East and Southeast Asian integration. To that end, a deepening and expansion of Japan's understanding of European integration – or, to put it more generally, learning from Europe or 'Europeanization' – is essential.

Company–society relations as a reason for 'Europeanization'

'Europeanization' is not only necessary in the field of foreign relations, however. European companies and the European economy and society must also be the subject of Japanese learning. For a long time these were indeed models for Japan, but as the relationship between Japan and Europe became more competitive, at some point the tendency to disregard 'learning from Europe' became deep rooted. Amidst repeated trade conflicts, however, Europe has repeatedly been sending important messages to Japan – for example, in regard to working hours and market openness. It should be borne in mind, of course, that not all of these demands were justified, but surely there was a problem in the way that Japan has to this day piled up remedies in response to these complaints. In conflict, self-knowledge can be sought through the recognition of differences between the two parties. In essence, was not Europe asking Japan what kind of companies it should have, what kind of labor, what kind of liberalism, what style of management, and what kinds of relations between individuals and companies, companies and society, and companies and the government?

Today, above all, as Japan struggles to come up with social and economic reforms to help it recover from the post-bubble crisis, and move it away from 'enterprisism' and towards a 'lifestyle great power', the nation needs to learn from Europe's companies and its socio-economic system, particularly the latter. The standards of living, welfare, environment, safety, and land planning in Europe represent vital learning materials. One representative index is working hours. Each European country's, as well as the EU's, published goals may also be adopted as goals for Japan.

The fact that European companies and the European economy and society are by no means always successful in achieving their results is no reason to abandon learning from them. On the contrary, the very fact that the countries of Europe – particularly continental Europe – are struggling to maintain their standards of living in the face of low economic growth and high unemployment, while being swept by the same wave of 'Americanization' as Japan, provides ample common ground to ensure learning from Europe is even more meaningful.

Again, the fact that Europe is itself by no means enthusiastic about learning from Japan is not a reason to avoid 'Europeanization'. Certainly, Europeans are reluctant to take Japan as a model. While it is true that, at the corporate level, 'even those stubborn German companies have fairly seriously studied the Japanese system and actually adopted it in part with quite good results' (Abo 1993), at the national level Japan continues to be the subject of sharp criticism (long working hours, export-led growth, closed *keiretsu* relationships, structural impediments, producer privileging, etc.), and hardly anyone argues that they should learn from Japan for the sake of improving the economy and society. It could even be said that the basis for European understanding of Japan lies with those who see Japan as representing the challenge of nineteenth-century barbarism to twentieth-century civilization (Hager 1984). The ideal situation of mutual learning between Europe and Japan seems a long way off. Nevertheless, rather than using the situation of the other side as a reason for abandoning learning from Europe, it would be better for Japan and, indeed, for the relationship between the two, if Japan were to take a close and objective look at what can be learned from Europe. Such learning would also help Japan to take a more objective stance towards the process of 'Americanization'.

EUROPEAN DIRECT INVESTMENT
AS A WAY OF 'EUROPEANIZATION'

How, then, and by what means, should learning from Europe, or 'Europeanization', take place? The focus here is on corporate and economic reforms, although these are not unrelated to the fields of scientific and cultural studies. Even limiting ourselves to the economic field, individuals, corporations, the government and others can benefit from such learning, which may take place through a variety of means. Corporate direct investment may be the most powerful and appropriate of such means, because, in the context of direct investments, the contacts between people are the closest and widest ranging both at the factory and the administrative level.

In that case, European companies' direct investment in Japan is the most effective. Of course, the opposite channel of Japanese investment in Europe can play a similar role. A lot can be learned by teaching; cases also exist where the desire for technologies and management skills unavailable within the company act as a catalyst for direct investment in Europe. In such a case the program of learning is clear cut. However, this kind of Japanese direct investment in Europe is a round-about way of learning from the point of view of Japanese companies collectively, even more so of the economy and society in general. It should be possible to learn more directly from European companies' direct investments in Japan. FDI is an effective means of protecting employment and incomes, stimulating the regional economy and preventing 'hollowing out'. That is the same for Japan as for Europe. But that is not the only significance of direct investment. Its significance as a means of learning is perhaps even more important.

History and current problems of European FDI in Japan

European FDI in Japan dates from before the Second World War (Yuzawa and Udagawa 1990), but with the passage in 1949 of the Foreign Exchange and Foreign Trade Control Law, and the 1950 Foreign Capital Law, which between them constituted Japan's new system for dealing with foreign investment, European investment dropped off for some time. The reasons include the Japanese market's lack of appeal, and the lack of a management environment favoring acquisitions. While Japanese companies were anxious to import technology and management skills, few were willing to contemplate handing over management control to foreign companies. Further, the Japanese government's policy towards investment was restrictive and even prohibitive. Japan did not need capital, so companies acquired technology unaccompanied by management control by US companies. As a result, entrepreneurial skills remained in the hands of the Japanese (Gilpin 1975).

The turning point came in 1967. The Japanese government's comprehensive capital liberalization measures from 1967 to 1976 resulted – particularly from the mid-1980s – in the growth of foreign, including European, investment in Japan. After peaking in 1992, investments began to decline (Kudō 1994a, 1995a). The leading European investors were the UK, Germany and Switzerland, and the leading industries were pharmaceuticals, chemicals, computers, electrical equipment and electronics. The motivation for investment was generally to establish a local base for manufacturing and marketing, as well as for research and development. Also notable was the acquisition of warehousing and wholesale and retail facilities by foreign distributors. The most common method of investment was acquisition of, or investment in, existing Japanese companies.

A representative case from this period is German luxury car maker Bayerische Motor Werke's (BMW's) investment in the establishment of a dealership network. BMW increased its investment in Japan in order to create a direct sales system, enabling it to communicate directly with its customers in order to convey information on the excellence of its product. It resulted in greatly increased sales. Following that success story, both Daimler-Benz and Volkswagen established sales networks in Japan. During this period, European car makers' share of total auto exports to Japan grew, with Volkswagen-Audi, Mercedes-Benz, BMW, Rover and Volvo coming to command almost 70 percent of the import market. An example of investment in Japan for the sake of research and development is German chemical company Bayer's setting up of a research center. Examples in the service industry include many investments by finance and insurance companies, as well as investments by the UK's Wembley (events and leisure planning and management) and the Virgin retail groups.

European investment in Japan during this period was second only to the US. Nevertheless, on a flow basis, Japanese companies were investing ten times as much in Europe. The inequality between Europe and Japan in direct investment mirrored that in trade. Considering the size of the Japanese economy, inward direct investment remained particularly low.

In Europe, this inequality, or excessively small investment level, became a political issue. Of course, just as with trade, no absolute objective standard exists of what constitutes 'inequality'. However, as long as one side continues to make an issue of it, 'equalization' can only be ignored at peril. Moreover, since the expansion of Japanese investment in Europe is unavoidable as a means of averting trade conflicts, the only way to resolve the inequality is to expand European investment in Japan. For that reason, Europe is demanding the abolition of barriers to investment.

Agenda for future study

'Inequality' is a problem not only on the European side. It is also a problem for learning from Europe – 'Europeanization' – by the Japanese side. The too-low level of European investment in Japan also means a too-low level of opportunities for learning. The first issue needing to be examined is, therefore, why European investment in Japan is so low. There are a variety of theories about this issue. Frequently mentioned are the geographical and psychological distance between Europe and Japan, although this is hardly an adequate explanation as Japanese investment in Europe remains high. In addition, high land prices, relatively low expected profitability ratios, high corporate taxes, the difficulty of hiring good-quality Japanese staff, and the difficulty of acquiring Japanese firms can be cited. The causes of this last point include a Japanese business culture which militates against acquisitions, cross-shareholdings between big companies, and Japanese companies' consistent adherence to licensing rather than a willingness to give up management rights. All of these difficulties, though, with the exception of the hiring of good-quality staff, apply also to Japanese companies investing in Japan. It is therefore difficult to accept them as powerful explanations for the low level of European investment. Moreover, the hiring problem appears to have improved considerably in recent years.

Incidentally, pre-war European companies which expanded in Japan also recognized barriers related to business culture (Kudō 1996). At the same time, the question still needs to be asked: how did Japanese companies investing in Europe deal with similar issues of business culture? Examples include the need for quality in response to high purchasing power (the push towards high quality and refined goods, the advance in taste and fashion, and strict delivery requirements); strict environmental protection (e.g. the obligation to recycle packaging materials); strict safety standards both for workers and consumers; and the existence of a specialist mentality with clear job descriptions in the workplace (Kudō 1994b). To some extent we may understand Japanese business culture as the reverse of these characteristics.

In any event, as yet no theories are able to explain adequately the low level of European investment in Japan. We must look to a future analysis that includes not only the existence of barriers on the Japanese side, but also the motivations of European companies – for example, the relative excellence of European companies, their understanding of Japanese companies and the Japanese market, their Japan strategies, and their desire to learn from Japan. To that end, the analysis of individual case studies is indispensable.

A second issue, related to these individual cases, is whether or not they really represent an opportunity for learning or 'Europeanization' and, if so, to what extent and in what way. Case studies might include the background and motivation for expansion in Japan; global strategy and the place of the Japanese market in a global and Asian context; methodologies of expansion (product exports, licensing, direct investment, as well as market research, negotiations with government and strategic allies, and decision making); choice of location; business, functional and competitive strategies; organizational development; relations with parent company; and others. From the perspective of this author's research, a more important topic is the question of what impact these factors exert in each case on Japanese corporate management, markets, economy and society. In particular, the influence on distribution, marketing organization, technology, labor relations and management philosophy are crucial.

A third issue for study is the willingness and ability of Japanese companies to learn from Europe. It can be assumed, from the limited impact of the much larger-scale Japanese investment in Europe, that the impact of European companies on the Japanese market and management is less tangible (Kudō 1994b). Therefore, if investment in Japan by European companies is to represent an opportunity for 'Europeanization', the active endeavor of Japanese companies is required. We must also look at what companies, central and regional government, and regional NGOs are doing to increase the attractiveness of Japan as an investment market, and removing barriers to inward investment. This will provide some indication of the willingness and ability of the Japanese side to learn.

Looking at existing studies from the perspective of these concerns, a few observations are in order. First, existing case study research is not totally absent. However, for the most part these are practical, 'how-to' case studies. Moreover, most look only at the management side and do not deal with the factory or administrative line level. Among these, the most sophisticated is that by Yoshihara (1994). However, the purpose of this work is to understand the reasons for the success of foreign-associated companies, and it does not necessarily address itself to the concerns expressed in this chapter. Research specifically on these concerns still remains to be undertaken.

CONCLUSION

It has become clear to a wide range of observers that the Japanese economy and society must be reformed as a result of the 'bubble economy' and its collapse. At the same time, the 1990s were also the period of the Japanese economy's globalization. Theoretically, at least, reform and globalization are linked. However, for the most part globalization has actually meant 'Americanization'. To the extent that the need for 'Americanization' is allied to a domestically generated need for reform, it must be accepted. However, 'Americanization' does have clear demerits. Therefore, the Japanese economy and society must also look to alternative models of globalization. 'Europeanization' is one such alternative. Much can be learned from Europe in the cause of reform. This chapter has attempted to contribute to – or at least to suggest an agenda for – the study of 'Europeanization' through its most effective means, direct investment by European companies in Japan.

REFERENCES

Abo, T. (1993) 'Kaigai kigyō wa ima-demo "Nihongata" wo manandeiru' (Overseas firms are still learning 'Japanese style'), *Economisuto*, 25 May: 24–7.

Albert, M. (1991) *Capitalisme contre capitalisme*, Paris: Editions du Seuil.

Baba, H. (1991) 'Gendai sekai to Nihon kaishashugi' (The contemporary world and Japanese companyism) in Institute of Social Science, University of Tokyo (ed.) *Gendai Nihon Shakai* 1: *Kadai to shikaku* (Contemporary Society 1: Problems and viewpoints), Tokyo: University of Tokyo Press.

Berghahn, V. R. (1986) *The Americanisation of West German Industry 1945–1973,* Leamington Spa and New York: Berg.

Fruin, M. (1992) *The Japanese Enterprise System: Competitive strategies and cooperative structures,* Oxford: Clarendon Press.

Fukada, Y. and Dore, R. (1993) *Nihongata Shihonshugi nakushite nan no Nihon ka* (What Japan without Japanese-style capitalism?), Tokyo: Kōbusha.

Gilpin, R. (1975) *U.S. Power and the Multinational Corporation: The political economy of foreign direct investment,* New York: Basic Books.

Hager, W. (1984) 'Free trade means destabilization', *Intereconomics,* January/February: 28–31.

Hook, G. D. (1996) 'Japan and the construction of Asia-Pacific', in A. Gamble and A. Payne (eds) *Regionalism and World Order,* London: Macmillan.

Kudō, A. (1994a) 'A partnership of imbalance: changes in Japanese–European economic relations', *Annals of the Institute of Social Science,* No. 36: 57–91.

—— (1994b) 'Ninon kigyō no chokusetsu tōshi to Yōroppa no keiei fūdo' (Japanese direct investment in Europe and the European business climate), in Japan Center for International Finance (ed.) *Tai Ōshū Chokusetsu Tōshi no Genjō* (Current situation of direct investment in Europe), Tokyo: Japan Center for International Finance.

—— (1995a) 'Nichiō keizai kankei no henbō' (Changes in Japanese–European economic relations), in A. Kudō (ed.) *20 Seiki Shihonshugi: Haken no henyō to fukushi kokka* (Twentieth century capitalism: changing patterns of hegemony and welfare states), Tokyo: University of Tokyo Press.

—— (1995b) 'Japan's technology transfer and business management: an analysis from the standpoint of business history', *Annals of the Institute of Social Science,* No. 37.

—— (1996) 'Cultural barriers facing exporters to Japan: German business in the inter-war period', in A. Godley and O. M. Westall (eds) *Business History and Business Culture,* Manchester: Manchester University Press.

—— (1998a) *Japanese–German Business Relations: Co-operation and rivalry in the inter-war period,* London: Routledge.

—— (1998b) 'Yōroppa tōgō no shatei: haken daitai no kanōsei' (The range of European integration: possibility of substituting hegemony), in Institute of Social Science, University of Tokyo (ed.) *20 Seiki Shisutemu: 6 kinō to henyō* (Twentieth century system 6: Functions and changes), Tokyo: University of Tokyo Press.

Lazonick, W. (1990) 'Organizational capabilities in American industry: the rise and decline of managerial capitalism', *Business and Economic History,* Second Series, vol. 19.

—— (1991) *Business Organization and the Myth of the Market Economy,* Cambridge: Cambridge University Press.

Nonaka, I. and Takeuchi, H. (1995) *The Knowledge-Creating Company: How Japanese companies create the dynamics of innovation,* New York and Oxford: Oxford University Press.

Ozawa, K. (1995) 'Nichi-Bei kankei no gyakuten' (The reversion in Japan–US relations), in A. Kudō (ed.) *20 Seiki Shihonshugi: Haken no henyō to fukushi kokka* (Twentieth century capitalism: changing patterns of hegemony and welfare states), Tokyo: University of Tokyo Press.

Sasaki, S. and Nonaka, I. (1990) 'Nihon ni okeru kagakuteki kanrihō no dōnyū to tenkai' (Introduction and development of scientific management in Japan), in T. Hara (ed.) *Kagakuteki Kanrihō no Dōnyū to Tenkai: Sono rekishiteki kokusai hikaku* (Introduction and development of scientific management: its historical international comparison), Kyoto: Shōwadō.

Sasaki, T. (1997) *Amerika no Tsūshō Seisaku* (US trade policy), Tokyo: Iwanami Shoten.

Schulz, M. (1998) 'The EMU and Japan: economic policy during globalization', Unpublished manuscript.

Sunaga, K. and Nonaka, I. (1995) 'Amerika keieikanri gihō no nihon e no dōnyū to henyō' (Introduction of American business management skills and their transformation in Japan), in H. Yamazaki and T. Kikkawa (eds) *Nihon Keieishi 4: 'Nihonteki' keiei no renzoku to danzetsu* (Japanese business history 4: Continuity and discontinuity of 'Japanese' management), Tokyo: Iwanami Shoten.

Tanaka, S. (ed.) (1996) *EMS, Ōshu Tsūka Seido: Ōshu tsūka tōgo no shōten* (EMS, European Monetary System: Focal point of European monetary integration), Tokyo: Yūhikaku.

Tateyama, Y. (1995) 'Pakusu Amerikaana no kōzō' (Structure of Pax Americana), in A. Kudō (ed.) *20 Seiki. Shihonshugi: Haken no henyō to fukushi kokka* (Twentieth century capitalism: Changing patterns of hegemony and welfare states), Tokyo: University of Tokyo Press.

Yoshihara, H. (1989) 'The bright and the dark sides of Japanese management overseas', in K. Shibagaki, T. Malcolm and T. Abo (eds) *Japanese and European Management: Their international adaptability,* Tokyo: University of Tokyo Press.

—— (ed.) (1994) *Gaishikei Kigyō* (Foreign-affiliated enterprises), Tokyo: Dōbunkan.

Yuzawa, T. and Udagawa, M. (eds) (1990) *Foreign Business in Japan before World War II,* Tokyo: University of Tokyo Press.

Source: *Strategies towards Globalization: European and Japanese Perspectives* (Sung-Jo Park and HIROWATARI Seigo (eds)), Berlin: Institute for East Asia Studies, Freie Universität Berlin, 2002, pp. 309–340.

20

A Note on Globalization and Regional Integration

THROUGHOUT THE 1990s, both within Japan and abroad, the doctrine of economic globalization has been advocated with such intensity as to seem the very spirit of the age. "Globalism," as the discourse advocating globalization may be called, has grown conspicuously extreme in its claims, asserting in various ways that a unitary, undifferentiated world has or will in the near future become reality. At the same time, arguments opposing or wary of that prospect have also been put forward on various fronts.

In the final decade of the twentieth century, indeed, the process of economic globalization has advanced remarkably, supporting these claims for globalism's ascendency. The advance is most striking in the instantaneous transfer of large sums of money in the international financial market.

The tide of globalization did not swell all of a sudden in the 1990s, however. The groundwork for swift, international transfer of enormous quantities of funds was laid in the 1970s when trade and capital liberalization also gained momentum in developed capitalist countries, in parallel with the transition of the international monetary system to a floating rate system. By the 1980s, this wave of trade and capital liberalization had extended to semi-developed capitalist countries that had experienced sustained economic growth, and with this came the establishment of a global, open-economy system. This, too, spurred the international transfer of funds. This period was also characterized by dramatic growth on a global scale of not only American- but also European- and Japanese-based large corporations, and by an increasing trend toward corporate multinalionalization. Multinationalization became another factor accelerating the international movement of funds. The 1980s also saw this rise of "neo-liberalism," represented by "Reaganomics" and "Thatcherism," which may be regarded as the precursor of today's globalism.

Looking further back in history we find the establishment of the Bretton Woods System at the end of World War II, followed by its maturation in the 1950s and 1960s. This system was the cornerstone of post-war globalization growing out of the disintegration of the inter-war period world economy. Traced back even further to before World War I, we can see that Britain's advocacy of free trade and free-trade imperialism in the nineteenth century was also a kind of globalism, and that that age was one of globalization as well. Capitalism, in other words, arose in the sixteenth and seventeenth centuries literally as a world-unifying system. Globalization, it may therefore be said, is as old as capitalism.

However, globalization seems to have reached its peak in the 1990s. The unprecedented vigor and dynamism the doctrine of globalism now displays, indeed, reflects the new realities ensuing from the demise of the socialist bloc, the dissolution of the Soviet Union, and the collapse of the Cold War order; and presumably is in part due to a kind of rapt celebration of capitalism's recovery, after some seventy years, of a unified field of action. Yet even if we ignore such overreactions and focus only on the realities of globalization, it still seems that the process is proceeding more vigorously than ever before. The history of capitalism has included a number of periods of swift international transfer of funds in large amounts. The most recent precedent of such a period was in the 1920s, although in terms of the scale and speed of monetary flow, the situation in the 1990s may be regarded as exceeding rather than duplicating that of the 1920s.

The international transfer of funds was based on trade and capital liberalization worldwide and on the establishment thereby of an open-economy system. It was also affected by the emergence of large-scale, organized groups of investors and speculators. This international transfer of funds increased in scale and speed to an unprecedented level, until the logic of investors/speculators overwhelmed the logic of producers. This shift had enormous impact. It threatened the very foundations of Western European welfare states as well as the competitiveness of the Japanese corporate state. In responding to that impact, companies in Western Europe and Japan were faced with the urgent necessity to reform their business management practices, labor relations, and inter-company relationships. In the economies of Southeast Asia, celebration of sustained economic growth was abruptly ended by the currency and financial crisis. Capitalist countries, developed and semi-developed alike, were plunged into a scramble for funds – in the competition for which winners would enjoy blissful prosperity while losers fell over an abyss of economic decline. With globalization continuing at a breakneck pace, the situation has taken a rather convoluted and farcical turn. Now the former champions of globalization are pointing to a crisis in global capitalism – a crisis, needless to say, that has been fueled by their own massive financial losses – and, having reconciled with their anti-globalist opponents, are warning that the brakes must be applied to globalization.[1]

Americanization in the Guise of Globalization

The globalization that enveloped the world in the 1990s was far from homogeneous in all countries and regions. Even setting aside the very poor countries that do not participate in international transfers of funds, the scale and impact of that flow of funds varied considerably among the developed and semi-developed countries vying to attract them. We may even take this a step further and say that the process of globalization exhibits a kind of pyramidal or hierarchical structure. The most salient aspect of this hierarchy, furthermore, is the unique position of the United States.

This uniqueness is born out in the phenomenon of rapid and large-scale international transfer of funds, the acceleration of which has been driven primarily by the absorption of funds in the United States. Naturally, a major factor has been the United States' long-running economic boom. That prosperity encouraged the flow of funds to the United States from countries all over the world – most notably Japan – which in turn helped to sustain favorable conditions in the US economy through brisk stock market activity and other effects. In this way, the United States came to occupy the apex of the pyramidal/hierarchical structure of globalization.

At the same time, of course, the United States' perennial balance-of-payments deficit continued and its accumulated debt went on increasing. The United States is still the world's top debtor nation and top creditor nation at the same time. It is difficult to predict how long it will remain in this position. What is certain is that the global economy will reach a major turning point when there is an end to this long-term US boom fueled by the influx of international funds. Though we may not know how long it will continue, the boom cannot continue indefinitely.

The liberalization of trade and capital among the capitalist countries paved the way for increased international transfer of funds. This liberalization, particularly of capital, has been effected largely through American advocacy, persuasion, and application of pressure. Furthermore, international standards for industrial goods, financial products, and systems, and so on – which in Japan are called "global standards" – have often actually been US standards in disguise.

This pyramidal/hierarchical order in the globalization process, and the United States' peculiar position in that order, means that, ironically, nation-states have not relinquished their role as the main protagonists in the world economy even under the current conditions of globalization. The environment of the nation-state has changed markedly in recent decades. One source of this change was the emergence of multinational companies. Although the multinationals that appeared in the 1960s and 1970s posed a threat to the very existence of the nation-state, at the time nation-states had some leeway with which to resist or counter that threat. But as multinational companies developed further and became global corporations, the nation-state faced an even greater challenge. Nonetheless, even today nation-states continue to tenaciously resist the effects of multinationalism; they intend to maintain their welfare-state systems and protect the losers and underdogs of the free market. In response to the large-scale transfer of funds, the efforts of nation-states to attract those funds, such as through strict adherence to austere fiscal and monetary policies, can also be seen as proof of the tenacity of nation-state identity in the face of changing conditions. The question of whether or not the nation-state will survive is no longer an issue, as nation-states are now an integral part of the world economy.[2]

My concern here, however, is not with nation-states in general, but with one nation-state, the United States, and its influence. For the present purposes I will call the effects of American influence on other nation-states and regions "Americanization." Much, although certainly not all, of what constitutes globalization may more accurately be termed Americanization. This refers to the distortion that has developed whereby what is peculiarly American appears to be universal.[3] We may also term the discourse that promotes Americanization "Americanism." The relationship of Americanization to Americanism corresponds to that of globalization *vis-à-vis* globalism,

Americanization is hardly a recent phenomenon. Though it may not be as old as globalization, Americanization has grown along with the rise of the American hegemony and has a history going back more than a century. Though the word "hegemony" in this context may be replaced by "leading power" or "key state," the great breadth of US dominance not only in economic but in various other areas, political, military, and ideological, suggests that we may reasonably venture to refer to it as hegemony.[4]

The Paradox of Americanization

The maintenance of hegemony requires economic surplus. As the hegemonic power of the nineteenth century, Britain derived its economic surplus from colonization. In sustaining its twentieth-century hegemony, the United States, having no such constant source of economic surplus, has had to generate its own. This is the distinguishing feature of American hegemony by contrast to that of Britain. When the United States depletes that self-generated surplus, it will go into decline.[5]

The first half of the twentieth century witnessed a troubled but progressive transition involving the final decline of the British and the emergence of the American hegemony. In the latter half of the century, the American hegemony was confirmed in the face of challenges by Germany and Japan and reinforced during the period of tense relations with the Soviet Union. As the US hegemony reached its peak in the 1950s and 1960s, so did the process of Americanization.

By the 1970s, however, the US hegemony, though still not thirty years old, had already begun to drift toward decline. This was due largely to the abolition by the International Monetary Fund (IMF) of the fixed exchange rate system, which marked the beginning of the end of US dollar dominance; and to the first oil shock, which cast a pall over the market supremacy of major American oil companies. Meanwhile, the United States' effective defeat in the Vietnam War meant that US military influence had also passed its peak. Then came the 1990s. The Soviet Union, which until then had challenged US hegemony through competition in the areas of economic growth, political influence, military buildup, and lifestyle, forfeited that contest, relinquished its position as challenger to world hegemony, and was dissolved, thus bringing an end to the Cold War order.

This spurred the decline of US hegemony, which had been sustained, even more than it had been threatened, by the presence of the Soviet political, military, and ideological rival. The Cold War structure had been one of the mainstays of US hegemony. With its disappearance, therefore, the political, military and ideological unifying power of the American hegemony weakened. At the same time, the United States continued to lose economic strength and its economic surplus had almost dried up. This became apparent with the Gulf War of 1991, when the United States, could not afford to fight even such a local war without financial contributions from its allies.

The American hegemony was thus further weakened by the collapse of the Cold War order. Revival theories have been put forward according to which, with the United States now the sole superpower, its hegemony has been strengthened, but this view appears to be mistaken. Certainly there have emerged no rivals to the United States in terms of military power, political influence, or intelligence, and it also remains the greatest economic power. It is obvious, however, that its economic surplus has been depleted, as is indicated by its having become a debtor nation. The foundations of US hegemony have clearly been undermined.[6]

But it is difficult to deny the revival of the United States' power of influence – or at least the feeling that such an arrival is at hand. This is due to Americanization in the guise of globalization. A paradox has arisen whereby, despite the waning of the US hegemony itself, the process of Americanization has waxed. One factor behind this is obviously the United States' long-running economic boom, and another, it is fair to say, is the stagnation of the Western European and Japanese economies, particularly the latter. Western Europe and Japan have been outdone by the United States. History shows us, furthermore, that hegemonies have always encouraged globalization, and that this insistence on globalization has always grown more strident as the hegemony begins to weaken. Thus the current situation can be seen as a manifestation of hegemony in decline.[7]

REGIONALIZATION AS AN UNDERCURRENT

The Progress of Regionalization

The other major trend in the world today alongside globalization is regionalization. The term "region" has various meanings.[8] For the present purposes I use it to signify an entity encompassing and transcending nation-states, and potentially including hegemony, which is one kind of nation-state. Although the imperialist powers also sought to subsume and unify the various regions of the world that had remained relatively separate from each other, it was with the rise of modern capitalism that deeper ties were forged between such regions and the world became one. The regions did not disappear, however. On the contrary, they have tenaciously continued to preserve and assert their identity. The term regionalization describes this tenacity of identity. The doctrine of promoting that advance is regionalism.

The development of regionalization has come to attract considerable attention, especially since US hegemony began to wane. Although varying in scale, character, and significance from region to region, regionalization progressed on a worldwide scale from the latter half of the 1980s through the first half of the 1990s. The economic aspect of regionalization may be described as efforts to form free-trade zones and – through the creation of common markets, the coordination of economic policies and the implementation of joint economic policies – to form even larger economic zones. In Western Europe this trend is represented by the European Community (EC) and the European Union (EU); in North America by the North American Free Trade Agreement (NAFTA); and in South America by the Mercado Común del Cono Sur (MERCOSUR). In Asia, meanwhile, the Association of Southeast Asian Nations (ASEAN) has been enlarged and consolidated, and efforts have even been made toward integration at the pan-Pacific level in the form of the Asian Pacific Economic Cooperation (APEC).[9]

Like globalization, regionalization has had an enormous impact on the environment of nation-states. By extension, regionalization has also had a strong impact on the prevailing hegemony as one kind of nation-state, as will be discussed below. Regionalization has further had a regulating effect on multinational companies through measures such as company laws, competition policies, and labor policies. In some cases this effect has taken the form of actual resistance to and retaliation against multinational companies by groups of nations. Meanwhile, relations between regional organizations – that is, interregional relations – have become important as a facet of international relations.

Regionalization as Alignment Opposing Globalization/Americanization

Among the significant aspects that regionalization has come to assume, I would like to consider its relation to hegemony. How has the progress of regionalization fared in relation to the prevailing hegemony, that is, the American hegemony? And how should we interpret its relation to globalization/Americanization?

First, let me reiterate that hegemony has not caused the regions to disappear. Apart from being impossible to achieve, such a phenomenon has not been necessary. In order to gain sway, hegemony has had only to accept the existence of multiple regions as given, and to promote stable relationships among them. Such efforts have taken the forms of mercantilism, liberalism, and imperialism. In the nineteenth century, Britain, the hegemonic power at the time, recognized the existence of multiple regions worldwide – though, of course, it reorganized some of those regions to suit its own interests – and forged relationships among them through its navy, merchant marine, and trade in industrial products. Similarly, even when the United States, the hegemony of the twentieth century, achieved for a time a level of preeminent wealth and military power in no way inferior to that once enjoyed by Britain, it sanctioned the existence of regional groupings, rather than seeking to eliminate them.

However, hegemony in its ascendancy stands in a different relation to regions from hegemony in decline. From an observation of history we may hypothesize that regionalization progresses when hegemony is on the wane. The period following the start of the British hegemony's decline in the latter half of the nineteenth century was a period of modern, competitive imperialism that also saw the progress of a kind of regionalization. The final quarter of the twentieth century has been a period of decline of US hegemony during which regionalization has advanced more or less in step with that hegemony's retreat. The United States itself has shifted direction toward the formation of an "Amexicana" region under the NAFTA banner, which corresponds to what the British Empire once was to Britain.

We may infer from this that regionalization progressed in a tense relationship to waning hegemony. This has a bearing on and has the power to change hegemony. We may therefore identify regionalization as a form of alignment opposing hegemony. More specifically, regionalization can be significant as alignment in opposition to globalization and/or Americanization.

The nature of regionalization must be examined in terms of its relationship to hegemony. In general, discussions of regionalization in relation to nation-states have examined the supranational nature of regionalizing organizations. Furthermore, given that regionalizing organizations have developed to the point of being, along with nation-states, main actors in the shaping of the world order, debate has also focused on their relationships to one another and to the global economic system. Particular attention has been paid to the question of whether such organizations are open or closed. An example still fresh in memory is the furor over the threat of "Fortress Europe" at the time of the EC's market integration in 1992.

The degree of openness is also evaluated in relation to multinational companies. In such inquiries, too, it would be difficult to gain an accurate understanding of the actual pyramidal/hierarchical structure of regionalization without giving due consideration to regionalization's relationship to the prevailing hegemony. For the moment, the 1992 EC market integration may be deemed an open-door style of regionalization rather than one aimed at the formation of a 1930s-style closed bloc.[10] This evaluation must be reconsidered, however, in terms of the relationship between the EC market integration and the American hegemony. In working toward such a reconsideration, let us now examine the case of the EC/EU in more depth.

REGIONALIZATION/REGIONAL INTEGRATION IN WESTERN EUROPE

High Level of Integration

The EC/EU is an example of regionalization and also, as closer examination of its form and content reveals, of regional integration. In terms of its relations with nation-states, regional integration takes the form of collective management and exercise of sovereignty by nation-states through such means as the transfer of partial sovereign power to a joint organization.[11] The term may be taken to imply a collective organization superior to its constituent nation-states or a movement toward an entity occupying such a position. The nature of such collective organizations varies according to the degree of joint management and exercise of sovereign power achieved; those in which the transfer of sovereignty is most advanced become supranational entities. Regional integration is thus not merely the increase of interdependence among nations. It may be described, rather, as an advanced form of regionalization. Regional integration in Western Europe has been the most conspicuous phenomenon of the post-World War II trend toward regionalization. As is evident in the supranational nature of the EC and EU, and in their orientation toward supranationality, regional integration in Western Europe has been the most advanced form of regionalization. This alone makes it the most suitable case for observing the phenomenon of regionalization with particular reference to its relation to US hegemony. Furthermore, the fact that the progress of regional integration in Western Europe has attracted increased attention since US hegemony began to decline also makes it a useful subject for scrutiny.[12] The advanced nature of regional integration in Western Europe – it is advanced in terms of regionalization as well, because regional integration is the spearhead of regionalization – will be briefly proven below.

Regional integration in Western Europe was the first case of regional integration to begin after World War II and the one that developed most rapidly. There is also its outstanding record of actual achievement up to the present day. As for scale, the total land area of the fifteen-nation EU is 3.24 million square kilometers, roughly one third the size of the United Stales. Its total population is roughly 370 million, and in 1995 its nominal GDP reached 8.4 trillion US dollars, in both respects surpassing that of the United States. The EU also accounts for some 40 percent of world trade, with imports and exports totaling 1.5 trillion US dollars. In addition to its scale, the EU also stands out in terms of degree of integration attained. Whether viewed in terms of trade, capital, currency, technology, people or information, the EU is far more integrated than NAFTA or any other economic zone.

Also noteworthy is the EU place as a key player in international relations. Apart from the obvious influence of the currency union, we may also point to the effect of international technical standardization: the EU, drawing on a record of experience and success in intra-regional coordination, is now influencing global technical standardization to such a degree as to prompt a Japan's Ministry of International Trade and Industry official to talk of "technological imperialism." In the area of development assistance, the EU has applied comparatively small amounts of funding to a remarkably successful effect. It is also the world leader in such areas as environmental protection, human rights, democracy, and security.

The EU is a longstanding member of the world summit conference of advanced nations, but at the same time it continues to create a diverse and progressive network of cooperative ties with developing countries such those of the Mediterranean and those of Africa, the Caribbean, and the Pacific (the ACP countries). In addition, it is developing various forms of cooperation with the countries of Eastern Europe – "Eastern" here being meant in the purely geographical sense – such as toward their membership or provisional membership to the EC or for other kinds of partnership. The EU has an immense impact on, and has even become a model for, regionalization efforts in other parts of the world. It leads the worldwide trend toward regionalization.

While the preceding overview has highlighted mainly the economic aspects of the advanced level of EU regional integration, its integration on the political side must not be overlooked either. Although such political integration is still at a low level in comparison with economic integration, it is, for better or worse, more advanced than similar efforts in other regions. It is ironic that Western Europe, the very birthplace of the international political system based on nation-states, is now the home of the most highly developed instance of what may be regarded as a rejection of that system, that is, regional integration.

Why does Western Europe stand out so far in the area of regionalization? It would be ambitious to attempt a ready answer to this question here. Looking back on the history of research in this area we find that, as the tide of integration temporarily ebbed – "temporarily," that is, from the hindsight of today –, certain theories attempting to explain the phenomenon of regional integration in Western Europe – especially that of neofunctionalism, which was considered the most compelling – were gradually abandoned; and that this was followed, ironically, by a resurgence of efforts toward integration. This illustrates the difficulties in identifying the reasons for the advance of regional integration in the case of Western Europe.

On the other hand, the political and economic factors that promote regional integration are relatively well understood. In previous studies of the history of regional integration in Western Europe in relation to the American hegemony, I have proposed that such integration began as an organization aimed at defense against US hegemony, transformed into one opposing that hegemony, and then evolving further as a force seeking to replace that hegemony. In this way, I presented a viewpoint highlighting the role of regional integration as a form of alignment opposing globalization and/or Americanization. Regardless of how successful that kind of explanation may be, it is fair to say that post-World War II political and economic factors are the most important factors contributing to the advent of regionalization in Western Europe.[14]

Social factors should also be included in this account. If we recall the activity surrounding the EU Social Charter, we should probably judge the level of social integration achieved in Western Europe to be far below that of economic integration and quite low in comparison with that of political integration. Even so, however, social integration cannot be overlooked. Though it progresses at a slower pace than that of either economic or political integration, it may be regarded as their basis and foundation, and as that which has prevented their regression. This may be inferred because, had integration been for only a certain social, class or political faction, presumably sooner or later it would have reached an impasse.[15]

Regarding the time-frame of the development of regional integration in Western Europe, it is necessary to go back to times before World War II, which may be sketched in the following broad brushstrokes. Developing along with the heyday of European maritime exploration and trade, European expansionism reached its peak toward the end of the nineteenth century in the form of modern imperialism, with the European powers vying with one another for supremacy. Following the two imperialist world wars, a socio-economically exhausted Western Europe abandoned expansionism and reaffirmed itself in policies of downscaling. This was a process of regional integration, manifested outside the region through the relinquishing of colonial rule and the adoption of a "small Europe" doctrine, and pursued within the region through efforts to prevent confrontation and promote coopera- tion. This is the form in which Western European identity has asserted itself in the latter half of the twentieth century. Even if this cannot be regarded as a return to earlier forms of European international order – to the system devised at the Congress of Vienna after the Napoleonic Wars; to that of the Peace of Westphalia, which established the sys- tem of modern nation-states; or to that of the medieval Holy Roman Empire – it is nonetheless useful to view the evolution of regional inte- gration in Western Europe in a time-frame of this breadth.[16]

In any case, what I would like to establish here is that, in efforts toward regionalization in Western Europe – that is, the regional inte- gration of Western Europe – it cannot be denied that there has been a long-term increase in levels of integration, as is suggested even by the cursory examination above of the reasons for the advanced nature of European integration. From the 1957 Treaty of Rome, when it began in earnest, that integration movement proceeded in alternating cycles of progress and stagnation, surviving a number of crises. The history of its market integration, likewise, did not progress along a straight- forward, linear path but underwent cycles of integration and disinte- gration. Yet even while repeating these historical cycles, the European Common Market, a diverse entity from the outset, has continued to move toward integration in the long run and as an overall trend. The same may be said, to a greater or lesser extent, for the other aspects of integration. Even when integration occasionally regressed, it did not regress to its former level. Thus a kind of transfer effect has arisen, resulting in an overall tendency toward integration.

My purpose here is to elucidate, in the context of this long-term, overall trend toward integration, the significance of Western European regional integration as a form of alignment opposing globalization and/or Americanization. This trend toward integration coincides with the fact that the decline of the American hegemony has already had a generation-long history that is likely to continue from now on for a relatively protracted period. When observed from this perspective, the progress of market, currency, financial and other forms of economic integration; of political integration; and of social integration in such areas as the labor market and labor relations, should appear in more detailed relief.

Multi-dimensional Elements

Naturally, however, regional integration in Western Europe cannot be fully understood solely in terms of the simple schema of cycles and over-all trends just described. The integration movement currently emerging in Western Europe – and throughout Europe as a whole – displays more complex aspects, namely, increasing depth, expansion, and, in parallel with integration, a process of differentiation. These aspects add various nuances to the role of Western European regional integration as an alignment opposing globalization/Americanization.

The deepening and expansion aspects are well known. The former is evident in the metamorphosis of the EC into the EU. The latter can be seen, even without looking back to the history of EC expansion, in the expansion in recent years of the EU within Western Europe itself through the inclusion of the remaining EFTA (European Free Trade Association) countries; in its anticipated expansion on a pan-European scale through the inclusion of Eastern European countries; and in the changing nature of NATO.

The process of differentiation paralleling that of integration is also quite widely understood thanks to advances in research on this subject in fields such as political science and sociology. Studies addressing this phenomenon are also beginning to appear in economics.[17] In addition to the sense in which I have been using it so far, the term "region" can also refer to an independent movement or organization involving elements within or in certain segments of the nation-states involved. In this sense it may denote a region composed by and for a certain population group, or what may be called a "community zone." With an even closer focus on the component and target population, the term is also understood as referring to independent movements or organizations for ethnic identity. This trend may be called sub-regionalism, a term that has already gained widespread currency. More so than the commission of the EC or the EU, the Strasbourg-based European Parliament has become the focus of attention as the principal agent of recent integration efforts. This focus may be interpreted as one expression of the decentralization of European power *vis-à-vis* its centralization in Brussels, and furthermore as an aspect of the trend toward differentiation. This kind of differentiation was also evident at the time of Germany's unification. The unification was effected through a procedure whereby the former East German administrative units were abolished and replaced by newly created – or in some cases revived – states which then joined the German national federation. While this was, of course, prescribed by the fact that West Germany had a federal system, we may also see in it the reawakening of local identity in regional communities, as in the case of Germany's Sachsen (Saxon) ethnic group.

While regional integration among nation-states proceeds at one level, at another, aspirations toward community-zone or ethnic autonomy are intensifying among certain component parts of individual or multiple nation-states. It may even be said that, once the confrontation between capitalism and socialism lost its crucial significance, community-zone identity and ethnicity replaced nationality as the new symbols of integration. The hard shell of the nation-state is thus being gnawed away at not only from outside in but from inside out.

The integration currently in progress in Western Europe and on a pan-European scale is a multi-tiered form of integration that includes elements of differentiation, pluralization, and diffusion. For the time being it is likely to continue unfolding at three levels: regional integration, integration within the nation-states, and community-zone or ethnic integration. We may even venture to suggest the prospect of European integration taking place ultimately as the integration of minutely differentiated community-zone or ethnic units. In any case, for the time being attention will remain focused on how the interaction among the three levels of integration has developed so far – a significant level of interaction has already been achieved – and how is likely to further develop from now on. The so-called principle of subsidiarity, a concept proposed in theoretical discourse on the integration process, is interpreted and applied variously by different analysts. Those variations are related to the realities of integration's three-tiered structure. In attempting to confirm that the integration of Western Europe has reached an advanced level, we must take into consideration these multi-dimensional elements.

Beyond National and Supranational Frameworks

Until now, many analysts – myself included – have considered regional integration in Western Europe in terms of the relationship between national sovereignty and supranational organizations, or of that between nationality and supranationality. Although different scholarly trends have been more influential in sociology and other disciplines, this framework of understanding has been widely applied at least in the fields of economics and political science.

Monetary union appears to provide an ideal case in point for this framework of understanding. That is, the EU's single currency unit (euro) is clearly the product of a supranational organization and embodies supranationalism in every respect. Accordingly, the issue has been presented in terms of whether or not the EU will move in the direction of further supranationality. The introduction of a single currency not only requires a single financial and monetary policy but also necessitates that fiscal policy be coordinated and ultimately unified. The same may be said for structural adjustment policy, regional policy, industrial policy and so on. Projecting from this chain of unified policies, we inevitably arrive at the prospect of unified sovereignty. Is the EU really proceeding down that path? The Maastricht Treaty, which provided for the introduction of a single currency and for the establishment of the EU itself, includes no rigorous provisions regarding coordination or unification of fiscal policy. In this respect, a contradiction inherent in the Maastricht Treaty is manifest and its treaty's internal limitations made evident.[18]

If, however, integration that includes monetary union in the form of introduction of a single currency has progressed in parallel with the process of differentiation as discussed above, then our interpretation of the introduction of a single currency may have to be altered. That is, if we, while considering the autonomous development of community-zone and ethnic sub-regions, view the process of monetary union, even what appeared to reveal the inherent contradictions and limitations of the Maastricht Treaty may present a different aspect. Indeed, it may reveal, to begin with, the inherent contradictions and limitations of understanding regional integration in terms of the transfer of national sovereignty, the understanding that was the premise of the nationality-supranationality frame of reference.

Once we experience such difficulty in perceptions, we can begin to see ways to develop new approaches.[19] One of the most compelling of those efforts at the moment centers around the "new medieval ages" theory.

Proposed by Hedley Bull, the view based on the notion of the "new medieval ages" uses medieval Europe as a metaphor in examining the diversity of actors in the Western European international scene today. While naturally acknowledging the various differences between the "old" and "new" forms of "medieval ages," this approach focuses particularly on Western Europe and regards the EU as a test case.[20]

This kind of thinking is not entirely unique in this field of debate. Even within the scope of my own knowledge, among Japanese scholars in regional studies Yamakage Susumu has proposed an approach focusing on the overlapping rather than the multi-layered nature of regions. This approach is developing a view of regions in terms of their inter-relatedness rather than resemblance. Although this view does not explicitly refer to the "new medieval ages," the thinking is similar, albeit presented in a different context and with different terminology.[21] It should be noted here that in the "new medieval ages" theory the application of the "medieval ages" metaphor is limited to Western Europe. Another view, expounded by Tanaka Akihiko, removes this limitation. While acknowledging that the features of the "new medieval ages" are most prominent in the relations among the countries of Western Europe, Tanaka identifies North America and Japan, for instance, as another zone that has plunged into the "new medieval" period. His reason for this is that these countries share the same fundamental values. Other zones he characterizes as either "modern" or "chaotic."[22]

This view is a *re-interpretation* rather than an interpretation of the original "new medieval ages" theory. While I would not reject the validity of the re-interpreted version entirely, for my present purposes I would like to adhere to a crucial point of the original theory, which is that it is limited in application to the "medieval ages" metaphor of Western Europe. This is because I affirm Western Europe's advanced status in regional integration and so in regionalization as well. While regrettably there is not enough space to elaborate on this point here, I concur with Andrew Gamble in highlighting the usefulness of the metaphor.

REGIONALIZATION IN EAST ASIA

Low Level of Regionalization

When we shift our attention from Western Europe to East Asia, we see contrasting developments. The term "East Asia" is used here in the broad sense to include Northeast and Southeast Asia. "East Asia" and indeed "Asia" are designations bestowed from outside, and so do not, of course, vouch for any kind of inherent identity or unity among the countries referred to. The same is true, however, of the terms "Western Europe" and "Europe." There is little point in overlooking this fact and then speculating about the meaning or meaninglessness of East Asia as a unit for observation. In any case, it is essential in considering regionalization to acknowledge that, if we are to observe the expanse called Western Europe, then it is only natural that, by way of comparison, we also observe the expanse called East Asia.

The question at hand is how far regionalization in East Asia has progressed. The most salient example of East Asian regionalization on the economic side is the Association of Southeast Asian Nations (ASEAN), which began as an organization for political cooperation. As it evolved into an entity for economic cooperation, ASEAN also gained in both size and depth. It also created various regional cooperation organizations with ASEAN itself as their core, such as the ASEAN Industrial Cooperation scheme, the ASEAN Free Trade Area (AFTA), and the ASEAN Regional Forum (ARF). ASEAN has also forged ties with external countries and regions, including its relations for extra-regional dialogue (which later became the Expanded ASEAN Foreign Ministers Conference); its agreement on cooperation with the EEC (later lapsed); the ASEAN Plus 3 forum; and the Asia-Europe Meeting (ASEM).[23]

In this way, we can confirm, a certain degree of progress in efforts toward regionalization centering around ASEAN. At the same time, however, we must acknowledge the disparity between this and the level of regionalization attained in Western Europe. According to Yamakage, although it is possible to discern a striking resemblance between the EC/EU and ASEAN in the circumstances of their establishment, in the tempo of their development – stagnating in the 1980s, flourishing in the 1990s – and in their intent, in terms of actual results ASEAN compares poorly.[24] Taking the comparison further, we find no situation in the ASEAN case that corresponds to the transfer or limitation of national sovereign power, and therefore no supranationality in that sense.[25] On that basis we may assert that, by the definition applied in the present discussion, ASEAN does not qualify as a case of regional integration, and that therefore it has necessarily been limited in the degree of regionalization it has attained.

In Northeast Asia, meanwhile, no efforts toward regionalization even equivalent to those of ASEAN in Southeast Asia are apparent. Accordingly, the level of regionalization in East Asia as a whole is markedly lower than that in Western Europe.

It is also necessary to give due consideration to APEC, as it has attracted considerable attention as one aspect of regionalization in East Asia. One immediately apparent point about APEC in this regard is that in terms of composition/membership a comparison with the EC/EU is pointless from the outset. Furthermore, APEC is a very loose cooperative association; although it can be regarded as one type of regional framework, and although comparison with the EC/EU as regional integration is, of course, possible, there is little to be gained from such comparison – that is, as long as the comparison is based on the conventional nationality-supranationality frame of reference.[26] In addition, APEC is not significant in terms of my present concern, namely, the potential for an alignment in opposition to globalization and/or Americanization.

Furthermore, although the trend toward differentiation so clearly evident in Western Europe has also appeared in East Asia, it is not as vigorous. We must also acknowledge the gap between the two in terms of sub-regionalization and sub-regionalism.

While the causes of this disparity with Western Europe in terms of regionalization should, of course, be explained, such explanation is likely to be even more difficult than explaining the causes of regional integration in Western Europe. Generally – albeit with the particular case of Western Europe in mind – a precondition for regional integration – not regionalization – is intra-regional commonality identified in terms of economics (level of prosperity, as indicated by per-capita income), politics (maturation of democracy), and, as a hidden factor, religion (in Europe's case the spread of Christianity). From this perspective it would appear that similar conditions have long been almost nonexistent in Northeast and Southeast Asia.

Looking at the matter more in terms of actual history, we may point to differences in the settlement of responsibilities and issues arising out of World War II. The settlement of such war issues involving Japan, at least as far as Northeast Asia was concerned, differed markedly from that of Western Europe as illustrated by the Franco-German reconciliation. While the Franco-German reconciliation provided the basis for the subsequent development of regional integration in Western Europe, there has been little hope for regional integration in Northeast Asia. Alternatively, we may consider the matter from the perspective of the abovementioned schema explaining regional integration in Western Europe in terms of a shift from self-defense against, to opposition to, and finally to replacement of the prevailing hegemony. In Northeast Asia – and in Southeast Asia as well – the American hegemony has been so direct and immense as to leave little strategic leeway for either self-defense against or opposition to it.

Implications for Japan of Regional Integration in Western Europe

On the basis of the foregoing outline of the state of progress of regionalization in East Asia, let us now consider the implications for Japan of regional integration in Western Europe.

As we have seen, a clear disparity has arisen between the level of regionalization achieved in East Asia and that achieved in Western Europe. Regionalization in Southeast Asia has progressed without Japan's direct participation. In Northeast Asia regionalization remains undeveloped and there are not even incipient signs of regional integration, which would pave the way for regionalization. From this we see that Japan's involvement in regionalization in East Asia remains at an extremely low level.

A number of responses to this situation, or to this perception of the situation, are possible. One response we have seen is simply the bemoaning of the low level of Japan's – or East Asia's – progress in regionalization, and envy at the progress made in Western Europe. This response is obviously naïve. From 1998 through 1999, Japan produced a veritable flood of literature about the euro. It was a phenomenon, however, that highlighted the transformation of Japanese interest in Western Europe's regional integration, which had been on the decline, into an idealization. One wonders to what extent this literature about the euro was free of such naïveté. Without due reflection on the reasons behind the disparity, attempts to emulate Western Europe as a model would be futile.

Taking the opposite position, one argues in support of the *status quo*. One such argument is the extreme one that equates China with the EC/EU. This view identifies China as the East Asian organization for regionalization or regional integration equivalent to the EC/EU. In other words, while interpreting the EU as a kind of federal system, this view similarly regards China as a kind of federal nation. Contrary to its apparent eccentricity, and given the traditional geographical comparison of Japan and Britain – both island nations close to continents –, this is in fact a rather straightforward understanding. It also includes some surprisingly keen perceptions, such as in exploring the reality of China as a multiethnic nation and the fiction of a "Greater China." However, this argument remains open to the criticism of detachment from history.

Another, more moderate argument rooted in approval of the *status quo* may be summarized as follows. In reality, economic interchange centering around Japan and Japanese companies is advancing in East Asia. The development of trade, licensing, and direct investment in East Asia has been sustained by export of capital goods, direct investment, business management and technology transfer via Japanese companies, and by development assistance provided by the Japanese government. These efforts have met with success, the clearest evidence of which is East Asia's record of economic growth.[27] From this perspective, proponents of this argument doubt that East Asia should rush toward regionalization, or that regionalization is necessary at all.

Regionalization in the above sense implies institutionalization. The issue may therefore be rephrased, emphasizing the advance of regionalization in practical terms but not taking institutional form. Naturally, it also emphasizes that Western Europe and East Asia differ in the preconditions for regionalization and regional integration. This presentation of the argument includes some convincing points. An EU-like system is not the only form of regionalization conceivable, nor is it the only possible model to imitate. It may be impossible to transplant the EU model to East Asia, or at least unnecessary. It is conceivable that East Asia, which has a different history and different preconditions from those of Western Europe, could develop its own distinctive form of regionalization. The important thing is to maintain a calm, level-headed scrutiny, free from naïve wishful thinking, of the way in which regionalization is actually progressing.

Whatever the case, and leaving aside the overall underdevelopment of regionalization in East Asia, surely the problem of Japan's low level of involvement is one of the key difficulties. Corporate-led exchange is limited in terms of variety of actors, so that opportunities for the diverse forms of mutual exchange, understanding and learning that should be entailed in regionalization are being lost. There is insufficient breadth of exchange, apart from economic. Even personnel exchange is taking place mainly through economic exchange. The absence, or at least inadequacy, of institutionalization is hindering the progress of stable and irreversible regionalization. Surely my uneasiness about Japan's isolation in East Asia in terms of human relations is more than just a personal illusion.

Japan's low level of participation in regionalization may be regarded as the flip side to its high degree of Americanization – high, that is, in comparison with Western Europe. Of course, comparison of the two in terms of degree of Americanization is itself an immense task. There is also the problem of the dubiousness of thus comparing a single country, Japan, with an entire region, Western Europe – a point I will return to below. In Japan, American influence is strong, and it is as if, in its journey across the Pacific, the prevailing wind of American reality gains force and becomes idealized. One factor behind this is the tendency on the Japanese side to hold up the example of the United States as a justification for reform. In Western Europe, meanwhile, American influence is comparatively weak, the current of Americanization appearing to wane as it crosses the Atlantic. The distorted perception whereby Americanization appears in the guise of globalization and American particularity takes on the look of universality is more difficult to discern in Japan than it is in Western Europe.[28]

What are the reasons for this disparity between Japan and Western Europe in terms of degree of Americanization? One possible factor is the difference in their levels of regionalization; the higher level of regionalization in Western Europe may work to weaken the effect of Americanization and the lower level of regionalization in Japan to strengthen it. In Japan, opposition to the United States has such a strong tendency to be linked to various agendas of national reempowerment that little regard is given to the question of how Japan should relate to neighboring countries.[29]

Another crucial point for Japan concerning the low level of regionalization in East Asia is the effect of various imbalances in its relations with the EC/EU. While there have been imbalances of trade and direct investment between Japan and the EC/EU for some time, an even more important one has been the imbalance in the number of nation-states involved due to the progress of regional integration in Western Europe. At first the relation was between Japan and six EC nations, but the latter number has increased to fifteen. The problem with this imbalance is not limited to the fact that it makes relations between the two sides especially complicated. Among the factors contributing to the groundswell of regional integration in Western Europe in the first place were the economic development of Japan and other East Asian countries and their expansion into Western and Eastern European markets. Regional integration in Western Europe has been advanced as a response to this challenge. At the same time, it has represented a new challenge to East Asia by Western Europe. Japan now faces the question of how to respond to that challenge. Whether it realizes it or not, Japan is no longer in a passive position in its relationship with Western Europe, but rather is becoming a force which can influence and reshape that relationship. The question is how Japan should respond to the consequences of that change.[30]

Japan's Options

Let us now consider the options available to Japan in light of the preceding economic perspective on the trend of regionalization and comparison of Western Europe and East Asia in terms of regionalization.

One option would be a form of regionalization including the United States. This would involve placing greater emphasis on relations with the United States than on those with neighboring countries in East Asia, and becoming more closely tied to the United States. In its most extreme form, this option would lead to the creation of an "Amerippon" economy. A moderate version of this option already exists in the form of APEC. In such a case, it is unlikely that any organization that includes the United States among its members would serve as an alignment for opposition to Americanization or as a vehicle for negotiation with the EU.

A second option would be to pursue regionalization in East Asia. Although efforts have already been made in that direction in the form of the East Asian Economic Caucus (EAEC) and East Asian Economic Group (EAEG), these may be regarded as having all but failed. Attracting attention more recently is the ASEAN Plus 3 group, though this has yet to achieve any concrete results. This option could bring about, and in fact has brought about, some degree of opposition to the United States. Efforts in this direction could provide a period of distance from the processes of globalization and/or Americanization, or even lead from there to the formation of an alignment opposing them. This option has even greater potential for providing a vehicle for negotiation with the EU.

Which option will Japan take, or which is it in the process of taking? At present Japan is a member of APEC, is at the same time pursuing the ASEAN Plus 3 scheme, and is also placing its hopes on ASEM. Japan is thus taking a wait-and-see stance. It may maintain this position for the time being, though it is also possible that it will commit to one path or the other unexpectedly soon.

Let us briefly consider the scenario of the second, perhaps more difficult option. The first question is whether or not Japan wants or intends to take that path. If so, then there is the question of whether the conditions necessary for acceptance of that choice exist. Yamakage has pointed out that Japan's failure to take a leadership role in international affairs has been because it was unable rather than unwilling to do so.[31] Although this view was advocated in the mid-1990s, fundamentally it still applies today. Apart from the question of Japan's desire for or inclination toward the second option – regionalization in East Asia – the prospects for that option are generally limited by the lack of preconditions for its success. Careful consideration must be given to how to bring about conditions suitable for that course of action.[32]

In closing, I would like to point out one more difficulty that may arise should Japan take the second option. The implications of the Western European challenge are twofold. That is, Western Europe has presented Japan with a challenge not only through its regionalization/regional integration but also in its firm adherence to the principles of social welfare, or to "social Europe." Against Japan's and East Asia's

economic challenge – and against the US hegemony – Western Europe
has preserved its welfare state and "social Europe" systems, and this
is another reason for its determination to pursue regional integration.
Japan, one of the instigators of the economic challenge to Western
Europe, lacks an adequate understanding of this point. Far from being
unrelated, the determination of an international stance and the shaping of social policies are inextricably bound up with one another. Japan
must keep that connection in mind when considering which option to
take in regionalization. If Japan meets this twofold challenge squarely
and chooses the option of integration in East Asia, it would also face
the problem of how to preserve or reconstruct its own welfare society
within that region. One aspect of this problem is the question of what
position it will take with regard to foreign workers in Japan.

These are not the only challenges Japan must face, however. The countries of East Asia are pursuing the course of developmentalist state, and
there is little indication of a shift in their direction in the foreseeable
future. If Japan prompts East Asian nations to focus only on develop-
mentalism while itself working toward becoming a welfare state, this will
result in the consolidation of a structure of relations based on a developmentalist state-welfare state division of roles. Is that a desirable contin-
gency? Rather, what is required is a structure of relations that will promote a shift toward the creation of welfare states throughout East Asia,
and it is there that Japanese leadership in the region can be exercised.

This is a formidable challenge. In terms of economic relations it
means Japan must deepen its ties with the developmentalist states of
East Asia – that is, actively transfer and open up Japanese-developed
technology and management expertise to other parts of East Asia, and
support the development of the region's "catch-up"-style systems of
production and management – while at the same time promoting the
metamorphosis of those countries into welfare states. Although this is
no easy task, it would appear that the only way Japan can squarely meet
the challenge put to it by Western Europe is to find a way to overcome
those difficulties so as to forge a course toward the creation of a "social
Japan" and, at the same time, a "social Asia."[33]

<h2 style="text-align:center">REFERENCES</h2>

Albert, Michel (1991) *Capitalisme contre Capitalisme,* Paris: Seuil.
Baba Hiroji (1995) "Sekai Taiseiron to Dankairon," [The World System
Theory and the Stages Theory] in: Kudō Akira (ed.) *Nijusseiki Shihonshugi*

II: Haken no Hen'yō to Fukushi Kokka [Twentieth-Century Capitalism II: The Changing World Hegemony and the Welfare State] Tokyo: University of Tokyo Press.

Bull, Hedley (1977) *The Anarchical Society: A Study of Order in World Politics*, New York: Columbia University Press.

Fujiwara Kiichi (1998) "Hegemonî to Nettowâku: Kokusai Seiji ni okeru Chitsujo Keisei no Jōken ni tsuite," [Hegemony and Network: Conditions for the Formation of Order in International Politics] in: University of Tokyo, Institute of Social Science (ed.) *Nijusseiki Shisutemu 6: Kinō to Hen'yō* [The Twentieth-Century Global System 6: Function and Transformation], Tokyo: University of Tokyo Press.

Fukada Yusuke and Dore, Ronald (1993) *Nihon-gata Shihonshugi naku-shite nan no Nihon ka* [There Can Be No Japan Without Japanese-style Capitalism], Tokyo: Kobunsha.

Gamble, Andrew (1998) "Globalisation and Reginalisation: Theoretical Approaches," paper presented to the University of Sheffield Symposium on "Japan, Asia Pacific, and Regionalism: Global and Regional Dynamics into the Twenty-first Century," 21–22 September.

Hosono Akio (1995) *APEC to NAFTA* [APEC and NAFTA], Tokyo: Yuhikaku.

Itagaki Hiroshi (ed.) (1997) *Nihonteki Keiei Seisan Shisutemu to Higashi Ajia: Taiwan, Kankoku, Chūgoku ni okeru Haiburiddo Kōjō* [Japanese-style Management and Production Systems and East Asia: Hybrid Factories in Taiwan, South Korea, and China], Kyoto: Minerva Shobo.

Kaelble, Hartmut (1987) *Auf dem Weg zu einer europäischen Gesellschaft. Eine Sozialgeschichte Westeuropas 1880–1980*, München: C.H. Beck.

Kaneko Masaru (1997) *Shijō to Seido no Seiji-Keizaigaku* [The Political Economy of Markets and Institutions], Tokyo: University of Tokyo Press.

Kaneko Masaru (1999) *Han-gurōbarizwnu: Shijō Kaikaku no Senryaku-teki Shikō* [Anti-globalism: Strategic Ideas of Market Reform], Tokyo: Iwanami Shoten.

Kanemaru Teruo (ed.) *EU towa nanika: Ōshū Dōmei no Kaisetsu to Jōyaku* [What Is the EU?: Commentaries on the European Union and Treaties], Tokyo: Japan External Trade Organization (JETRO).

Kikkawa Takeo (1998) "Keizai Kaihatsu Seisaku to Kigyō: Sengo Nihon no Keiken," [Economic Development Policy and Corporations: Post-war Japan's Experiences] in: University of Tokyo, Institute of Social Science (ed.) *Nijusseiki Shisutemu 4: Kaihatsu-shugi* [The Twentieth-Century Global System 4: Developmentalism], Tokyo: University of Tokyo Press.

Kudō Akira (1995) "Nichi-Ō Keizai Kankei no Henbō," [Transformation of the Japanese-European Economic Relations] in: Kudō Akira (ed.) *Nijusseiki Shihonshugi II: Haken no Hen'yō to Fukushi Kokka* [Twentieth-

Century Capitalism II: The Changing World Hegemony and the Welfare State], Tokyo: University of Tokyo Press.

Kudō Akira (1998) "Yōroppa Tōgō no Shatei: Haken Kōtai no Kanōsei," [Range of European Integration: Possibility of Substituting Hegemony] in: University of Tokyo, Institute of Social Science (ed.) *Nijusseiki Shisutemu 6: Kinō to Hen'yō* [The Twentieth-Century Global System 6: Function and Transformation], Tokyo: University of Tokyo Press.

Kudō Akira (forthcoming) "Americanization or Europeanization?: The Globalization of the Japanese Economy," in: Hook, Glenn D. and Hasegawa Harukiyo (eds) *The Political Economy of Japanese Globalization,* London: Routledge.

Nakamura Naofumi (1998) "Kōhatsukoku Kōgyōka to Chūō Chihō: Meiji Nihon no Keiken," [Industrialization of a Less Developed Country and the Central and Local: Meiji Japan's Experiences] in: University of Tokyo, Institute of Social Science (ed.) *Nijusseiki Shisutemu 4: Kaihatsu-shugi* [The Twentieth-Century Global System 4: Developmentalism], Tokyo: University of Tokyo Press.

Nakamura Tamio (1998) "Amusuterudammu Jōyaku no Dai-ni Dai-san no Hashira no Hōteki Danmenzu: Shinka? Shinka? suru EU," [A legal cross section of the Second and Third Pillars of the Amsterdam Treaty: Deepening? or Evolving? EU] in: *Nihon EU Gakkai Nenpō,* vol. 18, 1998.

Ozawa Kenji (1995) "Nichi-Bei keizai kankei no gyakuten," [A Reversal of Japan-US Economic Relations] in: Kudō Akira (ed.) *Nijusseiki Shihonshugi II: Haken no Hen'yō to Fukushi Kokka* [Twentieth-Century Capitalism II: The Changing World Hegemony and the Welfare State], Tokyo: University of Tokyo Press.

Pomian, Krzysztof (1990) *L'Europe et ses nations,* Paris: Gallimard.

Saeki Keishi (1998) *"Amerikanizumu" no Shūen: Shivikku Riberarizumu Seishin no Saihakken e* [The End of "Americanism": Toward Rediscovering the Spirit of Civic Liberalism], enlarged edition, Tokyo: TBS Britannica.

Sasaki Takao (1991) "Shohyō Robato Girupin, Ōkurashō Sekai Shisutemu Kenkyūkai yaku, *Sekai Shisutemu no Seiji-Keizaigaku: Kokusai Kankei no Shindankai,"* [Book Review: Robert Gilpin, Ministry of Finance World System Study Society trans. *Politial economy of International Relations*], Toyo Keizai Shinposha, 1990, Hosei University, *Keizai shirin,* 59:1.

Soros, George (1998) *The Crisis of Global Capitalism: Open Society Endangered,* New York: Public Affairs.

Tanaka Akihiko (1996) *Atarashii Chūsei: Nijuisseiki no Sekai Shisutemu* [New Medieval Ages: The World System of the Twenty-first Century], Tokyo: Nihon Keizai Shinbunsha.

Tanaka Toshiro (1996) "Yōroppa Tōgō," [European Integration] in: The Historical Science Society of Japan (ed.) *Kōza Sekaishi 11: Kiro ni tatsu Gendai Sekai Konton wo osoreru na* [Lectures on the World History 11: The Contemporary World at a Crossroads – Chaos Is Not to Be Feared], Tokyo: University of Tokyo Press.

Tanaka Toshiro (1997) "ASEM (Ajia Ōshū Kaigō): Atarashii Taiwa no Tanjō," [The Asia-Europe Meeting (ASEM): Birth of a New Dialogue], *Nihon EU Gakkai Nenpō*, vol. 17, 1997.

Tateyama Yutaka (1995) "Pakusu Amerikaana no Kōzō," [The Structure of Pax Americana] in: Kudō Akira (ed.) *Nijusseiki Shihonshugi II: Haken no Hen'yō to Fukushi Kokka* [Twentieth-Century Capitalism II: The Changing World Hegemony and the Welfare State], Tokyo: University of Tokyo Press.

Tsunekawa Keiichi (1996) *Kigyō to Kokka* [The State and Private Enterprise], Tokyo: University of Tokyo Press.

Watanabe Hisashi and Sakudō Jun (eds) *Gendai Yōroppa Keieishi* [Contemporary European Business History], Tokyo: Yuhikaku.

Yamada Makoto (1996) *Doitsu-gata Fukushi Kokka no Hatten to Hen'yō: Gendai Doitsu Chihō Zaisei Kenkyū* [The Development and Transformation of German-type Welfare State: A Study of Local Finance in Contemporary Germany], Kyoto: Minerva Shobo.

Yamakage Susumu (1991) *ASEAN: Shinboru kara Shisutemu e* (ASEAN: From Symbol to System), Tokyo: University of Tokyo Press.

Yamakage Susumu (1994) *Tairitsu to Kyōzon no Kokusai Riron: Kokumin Kokka Taikei no Yukue* [Conflict and Coexistence: A Theoretical Approach to International Relations], Tokyo: University of Tokyo Press.

Yamakage Susumu (1997) *ASEAN Pawā: Ajia Taiheiyō no Chūkaku e* [ASEAN Power: Growing as the Core of the Asia-Pacific Region], Tokyo: University of Tokyo Press.

Source: *Japanese Responses to Globalization: Politics, Security, Economics and Business* (Glenn D. Hook and HASEGAWA Harukiyo (eds)), Basingstoke: Palgrave Macmillan, 2006, pp. 131-150.

21

The Response of Japanese Capitalism to Globalization: A Comparison with the German Case

INTRODUCTION

THIS CHAPTER EXAMINES the response of Japanese capitalism to globalization or Americanization in the 1990s and into the early twenty-first century, comparing the Japanese with the German case. We start by considering the reasons why the German case is taken into account in examining Japan's response to the intertwined processes of globalization and Americanization. Consideration is also given to the methodology of comparison, where we suggest that capitalism is defined and institutionalized by the state. We next move on to provide a historical Japanese–German comparison in relation to globalization and Americanization. Our third point is a comparison focused on the two central features of capitalism, namely, the enterprise system and international orientation.

METHODOLOGY

To start with, questions may be raised methodologically with regard to the reason for making a comparison with Germany (West Germany and unified Germany) in examining the response of Japanese capitalism to globalization. Under the Cold War system before 1990, there was certainly valid meaning in making a Japan–Germany comparison. Its basis lies, more than anything, in their common or parallel historical experiences, as illustrated by their defeat in the war, the occupation and the post-war reforms pushed forward by the Allied Powers, as well as their economic growth and rise to economic superpower status following the reforms.

However, with the end of the Cold War around 1990, a large divergence occurred in the paths charted by the two countries. West Germany achieved unification with East Germany and concretely experienced the end of the Cold War, one of the essential causes of which was the unification itself. As Europe's political, military, economic and social integration progressed, unified Germany's capitalism became greatly 'Europeanized'. Indeed, following the introduction of the single currency euro, some might argue in favor of discussing European capitalism rather than German capitalism. In contrast, Japanese capitalism exists within an international environment centring on East Asia where the Cold War system still persists as illustrated by the existence of divided states, the system of some bilateral security treaties, the presence of the US military, and the lack or underdevelopment of regional integration. Thus, there is no possibility to talk about the 'Asianization' of Japanese capitalism or Asian capitalism at the institutional level.

In this way, in the post-Cold War world, the paths of Japan and Germany have diverged, suggesting that, as long as we simply probe the meaning of comparison in the similarity or parallel characteristics of their historical experiences, we need to acknowledge that the comparison now has somewhat less meaning than before. Even if this is the case, however, at the very least the meaning of the Japan–Germany comparison can still be elucidated. In a sense, the comparison made in this volume might turn out to be the last chapter in the long history of comparing the two countries, but compared with the overwhelming tendency to compare Japanese capitalism with American capitalism, new insights should nevertheless come to light. In short, we need to compare Japanese capitalism not only with American capitalism, but also with German and other European capitalisms, as this helps to shed light on the question of whether Japanese or, in fact, American capitalism is distinctive. Herein lies the main reason for the approach taken in this chapter.

Next, a few words are needed on comparison as a way of understanding, while touching on the reasoning and meaning of the comparison. Whether our purpose is to analyze Japanese or German capitalism, both exist only within the context of the structure of the international system. Therefore, understanding based on the comparative method forms only one part of our understanding in terms of their dual position within the whole structure of the international system. In other words, understanding using comparison as the means of analysis will always provide only a partial abstract of the whole structure – that is, the relation between the two specific forms of capitalism, rather than a simple comparison between the two, is central to the methodology adopted in this chapter.

Identification, discrimination and characterization based on comparison are useful tools for understanding, especially in cases where the comparison is carried out in accordance with established criteria. That being said, the main point to be stressed here is that the comparison should be based on relations: on the one hand, this points to how the comparison should be contemporaneous; on the other, contemporaneous comparison inevitably amounts to comparison based on relations. On the contrary, non-contemporaneous comparison tends to have an *a priori* or arbitrary model or notion of stages as the premise of comparison. Of course, even if a comparison on the basis of relations is to be carried out, methodological problems still remain, such as how to define contemporary and how to take into account relations.

There are direct and indirect relations between the objects of comparison in carrying out a comparative study. First, in the case of the Japan–Germany comparison, particularly that in the post-Cold War era, no substantial research yet exists based on direct Japanese–German relations. Second, as far as comparison based on indirect relations is concerned, comparison based on the two countries' relations with the USA is most meaningful. Here the closest work conducted so far compares both nations' relations with the industrializing nations (see for example Kato, 2002). After the Second World War, direct relations between Japan and Germany became less important than previously, as both nations strengthened relations with the USA. The purpose of this chapter lies here.

In carrying out this kind of comparison, we need to decide the target of comparison – the enterprise, industry, the national economy or capitalism – and our focus is placed squarely on the latter. The reason is straightforward: it is certainly possible to compare an enterprise with another; however, this does not in itself amount to a comparison of Japanese and German enterprises. For instance, would it be possible to classify Japanese enterprises or German enterprises? Toyota and Nissan differ. Matsushita and Sony are different. Indeed, Matsushita is perhaps more similar to Siemens than Sony. Again, does Japanese-style management exist? Successful businesses (as well as failed) are often said to have similar characteristics regardless of nationality. Or, again, can enterprises be characterized simply by their nationality, or is there something more than just nationality? Large enterprises in particular are becoming increasingly internationalized in terms of ownership, making their nationality difficult to determine. Finally, the management of large enterprises as well as the managers themselves are internationalized, as are their activities. Both Japan and Germany are only a part of the potential market place for these enterprises.

Thus, if we were to compare enterprises with enterprises, we are not necessarily comparing Japan with Germany, whereas comparing Japanese capitalism with German capitalism would lead to comparing both nations, as capitalism includes enterprises, and further incorporates the markets and their institutions, customs and conventions. As capitalism is divided by national borders, moreover, comparing capitalism will amount to an international comparison, at least as a starting point, as national borders and the framework of the nation-state have become less transparent.

JAPAN–GERMANY COMPARISON OF AMERICANIZATION

So far we have discussed the importance of relations when carrying out comparison, the meaning of Japan–Germany comparison, the meaning of comparing Japanese and German capitalism, and the meaning of comparing both nations' relations with the USA. Here let us compare their relations with the USA by focusing on Americanization.

For the first decade after the end of the Cold War around 1990, both Japanese and German capitalism were concerned with the revival of Americanization or re-Americanization for the first time since the post-war occupation and the era of high growth (Kudō, Kipping and Schröter, 2004). Behind the development of re-Americanization, besides the US's extraordinary military and diplomatic power, were the liberalization of trade and capital led by the USA, the expansion of international financial markets, the boom of the American economy, the stagnation of the Japanese and German economies, and so on. Although as soon as we entered the twenty-first century the American economy faced the collapse of the bubble economy, the potential of re-Americanization will not disappear completely, even if it lessens (Kudō, 2002b). This re-Americanization (hereafter, the re-Americanization of the 1990s will simply be referred to as Americanization) is alternatively known as globalization. Of course, certain aspects of globalization are not the same as Americanization, as illustrated by such slogans as securitization, 'shareholder value' and corporate governance, which in essence are related to the development of stockmarkets and their international integration. At the same time, whereas Americanization in the early post-war years had occupation policies and the transfer of technology and management as the conduit, ideas are at the heart of Americanization today. That is why Americanization or globalization now takes the form of Americanism and globalism, even if the question of how deep-rooted these ideas are still needs further investigation.

As far as Americanization is concerned, Michel Albert's 1991 book, *Capitalisme contre Capitalisme,* which was a prescient examination of this problem, albeit not the first, is the most memorable for the way he analyzed German-type capitalism as a contrast to Anglo-Saxon capitalism. He pointed out the difference between the Anglo-Saxon principle of insurance and the German-Swiss version and further highlighted the differences between Anglo-Saxon capitalism and German or Rhenish capitalism. He added that Japanese capitalism is of the same category as German. What is more, he was concerned that Rhenish capitalism, with better performance than Anglo-Saxon capitalism, was not given just praise, being critical of the way Anglo-Saxon capitalism seemed to be used as a world model. Although this work is not necessarily academic and Albert's understanding of Japanese capitalism leaves much to be desired, the work is useful, especially in a comparative analysis based on relations.

Ronald Dore followed Albert along the same lines shortly afterwards with Dore and Fukada's 1993 book *Nihongata shihonshugi nakushite nan no nihon ka* (Without Japanese-style capitalism, what kind of Japan is it?), which similarly made a comparison based on relations. Their conclusion is that Japanese capitalism, not German, is the main rival to the Anglo-Saxon model, although the poor performance of both economies throughout the 1990s in comparison with Anglo-Saxon capitalism took much of the sting out of their analysis. Therefore, whether we take Albert's call for the good economies not to follow the bad or Dore and Fukada's call to maintain Japanese-style capitalism, albeit with poor performance seemingly giving no good reason to do so, both books were overtaken by the slow down of the two economies. It is no surprise, then, to find an increasing number of Japanese and German voices calling for the adoption of the Anglo-Saxon model of capitalism.

The recent publication by Dore in 2000, *Stock Market Capitalism: Welfare Capitalism. Japan and Germany versus the Anglo-Saxons* was written based on his ability to look back on the experience of the past decade of economic stagnation. Here Japanese and German capitalism are treated as rivals to Anglo-Saxon capitalism and positioned in the same camp. Americanization is characterized as 'marketization' and 'financialization'. Despite the fact that Japanese and German capitalism hardly marked up success during the previous decade, he praised them and placed value on maintaining their distinctive styles, suggesting he is not affected in his evaluation by short-term trends. The fact that the US bubble economy collapsed and the so-called new economy faced a setback at about the time his book was published does not necessarily prove the success of Japanese and German capitalism. It does not necessarily support Dore's observation either. For Dore's perspective is more long-term: the constitution of Japanese and Germany capitalism in respect of 'marketization' and 'financialization' over the long term.

It goes without saying that the analysis of Japan in this work is much deeper than in Albert's earlier effort, as in the case of Germany. There are three strengths. First, this work grasps the fundamental meaning of globalization or Americanization, as illustrated by the book title: *Stock Market Capitalism: Welfare Capitalism*. Second, the comparison of Japan and Germany is based on relations: a comparison of their relations with the USA or, more precisely, Americanization. Third, the comparison is made not only from the perspective of the enterprise system but also from the viewpoint of international orientation – the other aspect of capitalism of interest to us in this chapter. In short, while Dore's 1997 work does not make a comparison based on relations, and examines Japanese capitalism in comparison with Anglo-Saxon capitalism, omitting German capitalism, his later effort in 2000 makes an important contribution to our understanding in terms of both relations and international orientation.

Let us keep in mind Dore's observations as we now turn to examine the response of Japanese capitalism to globalization or Americanization. Space does not permit a comparison of Japanese–German capitalism, as our main concern is to shed light on the characteristics of Japanese capitalism (for the Germany case, see Kudō, 1999; Tohara, Katō and Kudō, 2003).

ENTERPRISE SYSTEM

Similarities and differences between Japan and Germany

As far as the comparison of Japanese and German capitalism from the viewpoint of Americanization is concerned, both are naturally seen as self-proclaimed representatives of capitalism rivalling the American model, particularly in the post-Cold War era of the 1990s. At the same time, both are seen in terms of their similarities rather than their differences, with commentators tending to view Americanization not as an ideal but as a process to be resisted by these allies in capitalism. It is precisely due to this tendency to see them in a position of rivalry or opposition to the US model that, whatever their differences, critics tend to want to see them to be similar, as illustrated above by Albert.

Thus, in comparing Japanese and German capitalism, the similarities between the two have always been discussed, despite the salient differences that have existed from the 1960s, when the form Americanization took in the two economies became clear, as illustrated by differences in their industrial relations and business–government relations. In the 1970s and 1980s, when Japan and Germany achieved economic superpower status second only to the USA and when managerial capitalism in the USA fell into disarray, talk even emerged of the Japanization and Germanization of American capitalism as illustrated by the American introduction and learning from Japanese and German systems of production. In the process, the salient, individual characteristics of capitalism in Japan and in Germany became even more salient, as did the differences between the two (Kudō, Kipping and Schröter, 2004). Of course, the two are similar; however, their differences should not be ignored as the differences are just as important as, perhaps more than, the similarities.

WHAT IS CORPORATE GOVERNANCE, AND WHY IS IT AN ISSUE?

As discussed by Albert, capitalism mainly refers to the enterprise system and the main aspects of the system, such as ownership–management relations, creditor–management relations, industrial relations, inter-firm relations, and business–government relations. There are many theories concerning the enterprise system, and so we can make a Japan–Germany comparison in these terms. The most representative theories are probably those related to convergence and divergence as well as corporate governance. If the theoretical dispute over convergence and divergence is used with regard to the enterprise system, then we inevitably need to deal with corporate governance theory. On the other hand, in order to discuss the ownership–management relations and industrial relations at the heart of the theory of corporate governance, we need to expand our perspective to the entire enterprise management system, taking into account stakeholders such as workers, suppliers, customers, local society, and so on. In this way, the theory of corporate governance is related to the convergence-divergence dispute and the two theories thereby overlap. And as these two theories are the core ones used in relation to the dynamics of Americanization (or globalization), even when only used as a method of classifying capitalism, all three theories can be said to overlap. It goes without saying that the theory of corporate governance is most directly related to the enterprise system (Kudō, 2002a). So let us move onto the question of corporate governance.

To start with, the discussion of corporate governance frequently begins with an investigation into the definition of the concept and the acceptance of the universal meaning of the word based specifically on the American case. As early as the 1970s the term corporate governance started to be used regularly in the literature and documents related to US corporate law. The reason is that members of the protest movement against the Vietnam War took up the issue of collaboration in the war by the managers of a number of chemical companies in the general stockholders meetings, on the one hand, while Ralph Nader began to attack General Motors, on the other. 'Campaign GM', which was organized by militant one-share holders, had a more direct impact on corporate governance as it sought to investigate the social responsibilities of GM at the beginning of the 1970s. The campaign made concrete proposals for the establishment of outside directors and a monitoring committee at GM's stockholder meeting. It was against the general background of a series of chief executive officers (CEOs) being dismissed or resigning in the USA in the early 1990s that, once again, brought the spotlight on corporate governance (Kudō, 2002a). Two points are clear from this brief discussion: first, corporate governance is an American concept born out of the USA's anti-big business and populist tradition; second, it places importance on the value of shareholders as individuals.

Here corporate governance is understood in the context of the demands of the country and society in a much wider sense than above, with its specific meaning differing according to the state or the society. The stress laid in the specific case of the United States will therefore be different to countries operating under a different mode of capitalism, as historically American capitalism possessed a strong speculative element not necessarily present elsewhere. On top of that, as Haruta Motoo argues, the security market is unusually well-developed in the USA, as

> ... each state has a different banking law and the geographical expansion of the banks' branches was restricted until recently. Therefore, a mosaic of segregated banking regulations was created and the nationwide organization of the financial system could not be well achieved by the banking sector. Thus the formation of a system that unifies the whole was, so to say, on the surface, achieved by the development of the securities market and this is dissimilar to other main capitalist countries such as the UK, Germany and Japan. The banking sector was not 'fully matured' and the securities sector

became 'fatter' in the US… [and] the financial order in the modern world in which cross-border dealings are fast-increasing is, so to say, of the same type as that in the US. (Yamaguchi et al., 2001: 243)

In short, the USA has a banking system that is divided by state and it was the securities market that served to integrate the system across the whole country. In Japan and Germany, in contrast, the security market has traditionally been relatively underdeveloped, the banking system was integrated across the whole country, and therefore the main form of corporate financing was indirect. It is true that the securities market developed to a certain extent in Germany in the 1990s, but not to the same level as in the USA. As for Japan, the securities market has seen a well-known stagnation since the collapse of the bubble at the beginning of the 1990s.

In this way, the demands of the country and the society implied by the word corporate governance in the wider sense used here differed fundamentally in the USA in comparison with Japan and Germany. It was thus based on the narrow premise of American-type capitalism that, during the 1990s, 'corporate governance' spread around the globe. As we have seen, its premise is a developed securities market and so it is no surprise that the worldwide spread of 'corporate governance' took the form of securitization and the importance placed on shareholder value.

While corporate governance is thus an American concept right from the outset, why did this specific concept of corporate governance begin to diffuse in Japan and Germany, despite their different institutional settings? One of the main reasons for the increased salience of corporate governance in Japan was 'irregularities', as was the case with East Asian capitalism as a whole in the aftermath of the currency and economic crises of 1997. The same can be said for German capitalism and, after the Enron incident, the USA, too. Provided that such 'irregularities' were the core reason for corporate governance becoming an issue, we should be able to go even further back in time, apply it to the 'bubble economy' of the late 1980s, and ask why manufacturing enterprises as well as financial institutions pursued speculative activity in the name of 'zaiteku', thereby creating the source of 'irregularities' faced by Japan later on. Without addressing this point, the theory of corporate governance lacks persuasive power.

As far as the economic performances of Japan and Germany is concerned, both experienced poor performance during the 1990s, with Japan the worst of the two mainly as a result of the 'bubble economy' of the late 1980s. Germany experienced the 'reunification boom' as a result of the reunification of the two Germanies in 1990, but neither the characteristic, scale, nor effect of the boom is in any way comparable with the Japanese 'bubble economy'. From the present-day perspective, the bubble economy cannot be seen to represent good performance (there were, of course, people who knew this then), so it would be wrong to say that the Japanese economy was on form until the 1980s and simply lost momentum in the 1990s. This means problems existed at the time of the 'bubble economy', as illustrated by the fact that, in the wake of the bubble's bursting in 1990–91, 'irregularities' and a range of illegal behavior among financial institutions and other companies have been exposed (Kudō, 2001).

Conventional wisdom tells us that, while in the 1980s Japanese firms had boasted of their global superiority under the banner of Japanese-style 'corporate management,' 'corporate governance' as a system for monitoring the adequacy of management was nowhere to be seen. This distinction between corporate management and corporate governance suggests the need to establish corporate governance through the stock market. What needs to be taken into account, however, is the governance of the stock market *per se,* as this is where the 'zaiteku' and 'bubble' actually occurred. This is where the conventional view of Japanese corporate governance needs to be investigated, as the call for corporate governance now being made is precisely because of the failure of corporate governance during the 'bubble' era. Yet insisting on the need for securitization or the development of the stock market on the grounds that the level of Japanese securitization is far below the USA misses the central point – namely, that the 'bubble economy' was born during securitization. It is for this reason, in particular, that the conventional view of corporate governance in Japan lacks persuasiveness (Kudō, 2002a).

Nevertheless, since the Enron incident this conventional view lives on in the form: shareholder value (and its maximization) is different from the principle of share supremacy; and it is the maximization of shareholder value that is important (*Nihon Keizai Shimbun,* morning edition, 11 August 2002). No matter what efforts are made to maintain this sort of view, however, no one can deny that the share price is the ultimate measure of shareholder value.

CORPORATE GOVERNANCE: REALITY IN THE 1990S

While Dore points out that in 1990s Japan conceptual rethinking of corporate governance took place, as illustrated by heated debates, he perceptively observes that little, if anything, changed in terms of the institutional setting of corporate governance (Dore, 2000: 71–132, especially 128). He is certainly right in terms of changes brought about in the understanding of corporate governance, as testified to by the frequent journalistic references to reform at the level of the enterprise in the face of Americanization or globalization. Expressions such as American system of business accounting, current price accounting system, admission of adversarial merger and acquisition (M&A), and stock options, seemed to pop up everywhere. The academic world is no different, with 'corporate governance' rather than Americanization or globalization, the order of the day. Finally, reform of the commercial law and the Securities and Exchange Act went forward taking account of governance issues in the face of Americanization or globalization.

Thus, while as we noted earlier the main conduit for previous Americanization was occupation policies and the transfer of technology and management, at present it is the call for a conceptual change. We need, therefore, to investigate the extent of Americanization or re-Americanization in terms of the depth of real change, if any. Dore's point is here pertinent as he clearly sees little change has taken place at the institutional level, as indicated by a number of surveys. For example, in a survey carried out by Inagami et al. (2000) we find both elements that changed and those that did not:

(A) Business management and corporate governance
(A1) The following five reforms are observed:
     Making clear the responsibility of management and strengthening consolidated management as a business group;
     Promoting a personnel system, at the executive level, based on meritocracy and promoting efficiency through the centralization of management execution;
     Shifting the emphasis from sales volume to ordinary profit;
     Shifting from indirect financing to direct financing; and
     Attaching importance to interfacing with stockholders.

(A2) On the other hand, the following aspects of the *status quo* can be observed:
     Attaching importance to prior stakeholders (subordinates, stockholders, and managers);
     Attaching importance to good relations with stable stockholders;
     No say by stable stockholders regarding management organization and management behavior; and

Insider promotion at the level of executive personnel management and the strong authority of top managers regarding executive personnel management.

(B) Employment practices and industrial relations:
(Bl) Changing aspects:
Employment management based on individuals;
Weakening seniority system and a shift towards decisions based on multi-dimensional labor-conditions;
Increasing employment opportunities for older people;
Growing importance of personnel management at the level of business groups;
Reforming the methods of running the corporate pension system; and
Diluting presence of company unions.

(B2) Unchanged aspects:
Life-time employment or long-term stable employment;
The corporate pension system; and
Company-based industrial relations.

Employee Value: Present state and future prospects

As can be suggested from the above, the Japanese enterprise system did not go through much structural change in the 1990s. What actually occurred in the process of change was the unfavorable performance of many enterprises and a series of failures of large enterprises. These failures arose in all kinds of industries – manufacturing, construction, distribution and finance – and the economy experienced long-term stagnation even through the business cycle. Deficit public financing increased enormously compared with other industrially developed nations. Monetary policy was paralysed. Now, at the beginning of the twenty-first century, the Japanese enterprise system, especially its monetary system, is facing a systemic crisis.

Two conclusions can be drawn from the unchanged structure of the enterprise system, on the one hand, and worsening business performance, on the other, and often are by journalists, business leaders and academics. The first is to suggest that, because the enterprise system failed to respond or adapt to Americanization or globalization, Japanese enterprises performed poorly and the economy became sluggish. The other is that, now more than ever, the enterprise system ought to change into a more Americanized type in order to respond to Americanization or globalization. Yet if we expand the point of view from within the enterprise to the whole of society, other changes have clearly been underway, as in the decline in equality (Dore, 2000: 63–70, 128–32).

When the Japanese enterprise system is viewed from the perspective of corporate governance, employee value is given more weight than shareholder value in most Japanese enterprises, illustrative of cooperative industrial relations and the acceptance of egalitarianism in society. Yet throughout the 1990s, inequality in the distribution of income and wealth increased, as seen in the dissolution of the 'middle-class myth' and the increasing bipolarization of society (Tachibanaki, 1998). If we now clarify the implication of increased inequality by comparing Japan and Germany, we find that, although in both countries greater emphasis is being placed on employee value than shareholder value, the difference between Japanese and German capitalism in respect of corporate governance in the wider sense used here can be seen in the demands of the country and society. In short, the demands of the country and society are expressed more strongly and are institutionalized by law in Germany. At the root of this kind of institutionalization lie ideas of economic order such as the 'social market economy'. In Japan, in contrast, the demands placed on enterprises by the country and society are relatively weak, and thus the level of legal institutionalization is low, giving a greater role for institutionalization through custom rather than law.

If we now turn to industrial relations, then cooperative industrial relations are institutionalized by law such as double-layered, co-determination in Germany. While Dore finds class conflict in German society (Dore, 2000: 182–206), he does not mean this in the classical sense, as social democracy is strong and the public is embedded in institutions beyond narrowly understood social democracy, such as in determining environmental policies and Atomausstieg. And such built-in social democracy and the embedding of the public in policy-making is not simply a German phenomenon: it is occurring all around Europe as the EU penetrates different levels of European life. In addition, the enactment of EU company law and European works council law will not only take account of the demands of different countries and the societies, but different European regions, too. On the other hand, cooperative industrial relations in Japan are still largely dependent on custom and social democracy remains weak. In the institutionalization of the public, Japan is one step behind Germany, and cooperative industrial

514 THE JAPANESE AND GERMAN ECONOMIES

relations are always flexible – that is, easily changed and subject to considerable deviation depending on the workplace in question.

To put this another way, since the level of institutionalization in industrial cooperation in Japan is lower than in Germany, resistance to external pressure, as in the case of Americanization (or globalization) as well as in an economic downturn, is ineffective as a means to maintain the importance placed on employee value. In Germany, the phrase 'flexibilization' of industrial relations is a slogan trotted out by employers for their benefit, not that of the workers, with the Japanese model of industrial cooperation being clearly at the back of their minds. In fact, throughout 1990s Japan the custom of attaching importance to employee value was beginning to crumble, as dismissals in the name of restructuring took place not only in small and medium-sized enterprises, but even in large-scale enterprises, too, where the mainly middle to older age groups and non-union members were shown the door. What is more, the mainstream labor unions sought to protect employment by accepting management's stop of pay rises or even a cut in wages. The young unemployed also increased rapidly, including a new category of young unemployed called 'no-hopers' *(shitsubō sha,* not *shitsugyō sha* or unemployed) who have no hope of gaining a job. Many of the others have become part-timers or 'freeters' who stay outside of the mainstream enterprise system, some spontaneously, others half-forcefully or still others with no choice but this type of limited employment. While it is unclear at this time whether these changes mean the death of long-term continuous employment ('life-long employment'), which became a customary pattern of employment as a result of large-scale labor conflicts after the war and then took root in the high-growth era, it is obviously under strain.

Another example of a characteristic difference between Japan and Germany is work sharing. In Germany, the originator of the system, this has been a labor-side demand, which often requires introduction without a drag on wage levels. This is where Dore's 'class conflict' is manifested, as employers are naturally reluctant to implement such new arrangements and the workers are therefore forced to resort to industrial action such as strikes. On the contrary, in Japan, work sharing is not particularly widespread, and employers, along with the government, are often the originators of such proposals. Needless to say, these are pushed forward on the basis of a reduction in the salaries of the workers. What is striking, too, is how these measures do not necessarily lead to the stand off between the two sides, as in Germany, but rather their acceptance by the workers, illustrating just how 'cooperative' industrial relations are in Japan.

The difference in the level of institutionalization in Japan and Germany with regard to corporate governance, then, not only suggests a difference in terms of the importance in employee value, but also in terms of the resistance of management to the pressures of Americanization or globalization. In Germany, the greater degree of institutionalization acts as a barrier to Americanization in terms of both the management system and management methods, that is barriers to the introduction of external directors, stock options, and so on. Of course, German management sees this as problematic. In Japan, on the other hand, as a result of the way the custom of placing more importance on employee value is flexible and changes in light of circumstances, industrial relations are not a major impediment to the Americanization of the management system and management methods.

INTERNATIONAL ORIENTATION

Stratified dynamics

The other aspect of capitalism alongside the enterprise system is international orientation. If we focus on the dynamics of the international environment in relation to the international orientation of Japanese and German capitalism, then it is not only Americanization or globalization that needs to be addressed, but also the dynamics of regionalization, such as regional integration. Add to that the move toward localization as illustrated by support for 'the region within sight,' and the dynamics of strengthened nationalism, which often rivals the power of Americanization or globalization, and we can see how the ending of the Cold War and the structural change this implied has released or intensified latent forces. In this way, dynamics such as regionalization, localization, and nationalism, as well as Americanization or globalization, are intertwined in a much more complex way than in the period before the collapse of the Cold War system. It is thus not enough to examine the international orientation of Japanese and German capitalism in terms of Americanization and globalization alone. It needs to be understood in the context of these three other dynamic processes.

Similarities and differences between Germany and Japan

When we take these three processes into account, a number of differences between Japan and Germany become clear. First of all, there is the difference in regionalization. In the 1990s, Germany was actively involved in the regional integration of Europe, especially in the development of the monetary union. Monetary union can be seen as a method of avoiding the disadvantage caused by the appreciation of the deutschmark for Germany. More than anything, it enables the EU internal market to be a stable and giant market without fear of currency fluctuations, suggesting how the monetary union and the creation of the euro acts as a rival to Americanization, although European integration has aspects of competing against and cooperating with Americanization or globalization.

On the other hand, although Japan was involved as an outsider in the regionalization of Southeast Asia throughout the 1990s, regionalization in Northeast Asia has not seen much progress and its future is far from clear. Japan lacks both the intention and the ability, and more than that, the qualification to be able to play a critical role in the regionalization of Northeast Asia. The difference in the level of regionalization that exists between East Asia (Southeast Asia and Northeast Asia) and Western Europe is patently clear, and the fear of a rising China in Japan may act as an obstacle to further regional integration on an East Asian scale.

In this way, Japanese capitalism lacks a buffer zone against Americanization or globalization through the dynamics of regionalization. As a result, not only has Japanese capitalism been open to the full force of Americanization, rivalry has also created among neighboring countries with low wage costs. Although the strong yen following the Plaza Accord of the mid-1980s had little effect in the 'bubble' era (more precisely, the strong yen helped hasten the bubble), it reduced the international competitiveness of Japanese industries in the post-bubble era. From the perspective of East Asia, and even from the West European point of view, maintaining manufacturing industries in Japan, in spite of the appreciated of the yen and associated costs, is nothing but surprising. Clearly, at least some part of the long-term stagnation of the economy can be explained in terms of the weakening of location advantage or the hollowing out of industry caused by the strong yen.

As far as the level of integration with East Asia is concerned, the international orientation of Japanese capitalism will no doubt increasingly turn to the region, in line with the increase in regional interdependence. But regional interdependence should not be confused with either regional integration or regionalization. It is even different from regionalization. For although regional integration is premised on interdependence, institutionalization is a necessary condition of integration, as is the transfer of national sovereignty, at least to some degree.

Secondly, while the difference between Japan and Germany is thus quite clear in terms of regionalization, with Germany integrated into the EU and Japan part of a region with increased interdependence, differences also can be found in terms of localization. Germany traditionally has been a federal system, and even strengthened the basis of this system in the 1990s through the unification of the two Germanies, especially because the unification itself took the form of newly born states in the former East Germany taking part in the Federal Republic of Germany or West Germany. In this system, equalization of economy and life between the east and the west has been promoted via the federal system. On the other hand, Japan traditionally has been a highly centralized state, which has not changed since the Meiji era in the middle of the nineteenth century. The decentralization of power to the localities, whether right or wrong, has not made much headway, as in the case of discussions to move the capital city, or at least some of the functions of the capital, to other parts of Japan. In short, little chance seems to exist at present for a major increase in local autonomy in Japan.

Thirdly, differences exist in terms of nationalism, which in a sense is just the reverse of the above. In Germany, the central government or the state forms one part of the three-tiered structure constructed out of the EU, the federation of states and the states. Whereas three-quarters of legislation is said to be controlled through Brussels, the German states have been traditionally strong. This is in marked contrast to Japan, where the central government is strong due to the lack of regionalization within Northeast Asia, on the one hand, and the weakness and small size of the prefectures, on the other.

We cannot expect those Japanese voices raised against the USA to take up the call in resisting either the US definition of corporate governance or Americanization. That would be to give too much power to nationalist sentiment. In fact, resistance to Americanization in post-war Japan was weak relative to Germany and other EU countries. With the gradual rise of nationalism in the post-Cold War era, what is of most importance is to understand what implications this more nationalist orientation will bring for the future of the international orientation of Japanese capitalism.

CONSEQUENCES OF THE GROWTH SUPREMACY PRINCIPLE

The case of economic policy may help to shed some light on this question, as economic policy with the goal of growth has always fitted well with nationalist sentiment. The rise of nationalism in Japan is in clear contrast to the case of Germany, where the development of European integration has all but smothered the embers of German nationalism. Whether we examine foreign trade and the division of labor as well as integration in East Asia on the one hand, or the independence and stability of local economies on the other, we find not much more than neglect, except for the usual methods of Keynesian fiscal policies and easy-money policies as in the past. Even more problematically, a change of government has repeatedly led to a zigzag between financial expansion and financial consolidation. In looking to grow, based on the long-standing 'growth first' principle, government policy has simply worsened the actual situation by the repetition of financial expansion and calls for austerity.

Even in the twenty-first century, therefore, the Meiji goal of development and the growth supremacy principle introduced in the post-war period continue to hold sway among the policy-making elite. None seems to question the idea that financial consolidation should be carried out in order to stimulate business recovery and even the voters seem to persist in their fascination with growth, although such an attitude is perhaps more suitable as an object of psychology orientation than of economic policy. What is more, government after government has made an international pledge to recover, without seemingly considering whether or not this pledge is in line with their other commitment to the principles of the market economy.

Dore looks at the problem of economic 'efficiency', arguing that Japan seems to need to increase its growth rate and express superiority in the economic field in order to compete against Anglo-Saxon type capitalism (Dore, 2000: 225-6). But this need not be the best choice for Japan, as the spread of 'efficient' convenience stores, trucks filling the road and worsening traffic jams testify: economic 'efficiency' may create an 'inefficient' society, never mind the question of whether the achievements of economy and society should be measured in terms of 'efficiency'. If the yardstick is the stability of society, then doubts must be raised about whether even the USA performed well under this criterion.

This kind of growth supremacy principle is a hindrance to Japan playing a critical role in the regionalization of East Asia as well as to the international orientation of Japanese capitalism. The Bank of Japan's possible policy of pursuing a weak yen as a way to promote economic recovery may not only lead to conflict with the USA and Europe, but also with other East Asian nations, who are now often competing directly with Japan in the US and European markets. This possible situation is in stark contrast to the policy pursued by the German government and the Bundesbank in the run up to the introduction of the single currency, after both had sought to maintain the external value of the German mark.

Of course, the 'growth-first' principle has not yet completely disappeared even in Germany, although nationalism does seem to have been overcome, suggesting how economic policy does not need to be swayed by extremes. Fiscal policy is set under the Maastricht criteria and currency and monetary policies are kept in the hands of the European Central Bank. Chancellor Gerhard Schröder publicly declared that 0.1 percent difference in growth rate really did not matter at all. And even some German philosophers are groping with the question of abandoning the aim of full employment, accepting unemployment as the natural state of affairs, and how both the employed and unemployed can coexist together. Needless to say, the situation in Germany is quite different to that in Japan.

CONCLUSION

The above discussion of the response of Japanese capitalism to Americanization or globalization from the viewpoints of both the enterprise system and international orientation has shed light on a number of important points that the comparison with Germany helped to clarify. To start with, although changes in the concept of corporate governance took place in the 1990s, little change took place in the enterprise system of Japanese capitalism. There was some change in the custom relating to the emphasis placed on employee value, in tandem with a decrease in equality in Japanese society, but major change was not witnessed. As far as international orientation is concerned, Japanese capitalism was weak in responding to both regionalization and localization and instead became more nationalistic. From this point of view, it may be possible to interpret the changes in the enterprise system such as the decrease of employee value as well as of social equality, on the one hand, and the appearance of increased nationalism, as seen in the international orientation of Japanese capitalism, on the other, as linked to each other. In this sense, we might conclude by saying that Japanese capitalism might now have begun to strengthen the weaker enterprise system through the promotion of nationalism.

REFERENCES

Albert, M. (1991) *Capitalisme contre Capitalisme* (Paris: Seuil).
Dore, R. (1997) 'The distinctiveness of Japan', in C. Crouch and W. Streeck (eds), *Political Economy of Modern Capitalism. Mapping Convergence and Diversity* (London: Sage).

—— (2000) *Stock Market Capitalism: Welfare Capitalism. Japan and Germany versus the Anglo-Saxons* (Oxford: Oxford University Press).

Dore, R. and Fukada, Y. (1993) *Nihongata shihonshugi nakushite nan no nihon ka* (Without Japanese-style capitalism, what kind of Japan is it?) (Tokyo: Kōbunsha).

Inagami, T. and Rengō Sōgō Seikatsu Kaihatsu Kenkyūjo (eds) (2000) *Gendai nihon no kōporêto gabanansu* (Corporate governance of contemporary Japan) (Tokyo: Tōyō Keizai Shimpōsha).

Kato, K. (2002) *The Web of Power. Japanese and German Development Cooperation Policy* (Lanham, Md.: Lexington Books).

Kudō, A. (1999) *20-seiki doitsu shihonshugi: Kokusai teii to daikigyō taisei* (German capitalism in the 20th century: international position and the large-scale enterprise system) (Tokyo: University of Tokyo Press).

—— (2001) 'Americanization or Europeanization? The Globalization of the Japanese Economy', in G.D. Hook and H. Hasegawa (eds), *The Political Economy of Japanese Globalization* (London: Routledge).

—— (ed.) (2002a) *Approaches to Corporate Governance. ISS-Sheffield Workshop on Corporate Governance in Asian-European Perspective* (Tokyo: Institute of Social Science, University of Tokyo).

—— (2002b) 'A Note on Globalization and Regional Integration', in S.-J. Park and S. Hirowatari (eds), *Strategies Towards Globalization. European and Japanese Perspectives* (Berlin: Institute for East Asia Studies, Freie Universität Berlin).

—— (2003) 'The State of Business History in Japan. Cross-National Comparisons and International Relations', in F. Amatori and G. Jones (eds), *Business History around the World at the Turn of the Twenty-First Century* (Cambridge: Cambridge University Press).

Kudō, A., Kipping, M. and Schröter, H.G. (eds) (2004) *German and Japanese Business in the Boom Years. Transforming American Management and Technology Models* (London: Routledge).

Tachibanaki, T. (1998) *Nihon no keizai kakusa:Shotoku to shisan kara kangaeru* (Economic gap in Japan: a consideration in terms of income and assets) (Tokyo: Iwanami Shoten).

Tohara, S., Katō, E. and Kudō, A. (eds) (2003) *Doitsu keizai. Tōitsu go no 10-nen* (German economy: 10 years after integration) (Tokyo: Yūhikaku).

Yamaguchi, S., Ono, E., Yoshida, S., Sasaki, T. and Haruta, M. (2001) *Gendai no Kinyū shisutemu: Riron to kōzō* (Modern financial system: theory and structure) (Tokyo: Tōyō Keizai Shimpōsha).

NOTES

Foreword

1 *Nichi-Doku kōryū 150 shūnen ni atari Nichi-Doku yūkō kankei no zōshin ni kansuru ketsugi* (The promotion of friendship between Japan and Germany on the celebration of the 150th anniversary of the amity treaty between Japan and Prussia in 1861) in the 177th Diet.

2 For example, Ronald P. Dore, *Stock Market Capitalism: Japan and Germany versus the Anglo-Saxons*, Oxford: Oxford University Press, 2000; Kozo Yamamura and Wolfgang Streeck, *The End of Diversity? Prospects for German and Japanese Capitalism*, Ithaca, NY: Cornell University Press, 2003.

3 There are numerous publications on the 'hired foreigners' in Japanese and in English. One of the typical books in Japanese is UMETANI Noboru, *O-yatoi gaikoku-jin gaisetsu* (Overview on the 'Hired Foreigners'), Tokyo: Kajima Shuppan Kenkyū-kai 1975; for the English version, see UMETANI Noboru, *The Role of Foreign Employees in the Meiji Era in Japan*, Tokyo: Institute of Developing Economies 1971; also H.J. Jones, *Live Machines, Hired Foreigners and Meiji Japan*, Tenterden, Kent: Paul Norbury Publications, 1980.

4 Lit. '*Fukoku, kyōhei*'; the phrase originated from an ancient Chinese text for war. The Meiji government used this phrase as a national slogan.

5 For details, see Georg Kerst, *Jacob Meckel, sein Leben und sein Wirken in Deutschland und Japan*, Göttingen: Musterschmidt-Verlag, 1970. "*60-nen no Ayumi*" (Sixty Years of the Society), in *Political Economy & Economic History*, March 2008.

6 For this, see E. Kraas and Y. Hiki (eds), *300 Jahre deutsch-japanische Beziehungen in der Medizin*, Berlin/Heidelberg: Springer Verlag, 1992.

7 For details, see the biography written by his son: Toku Bälz, *Erwin Bälz. Das Leben eines deutschen Arztes im erwachenden Japan*, Stuttgart: J. Engelhorns Nachf., 1930.

8 Published by J.G. Cottasche Buchhandlung Nachfolger, Stuttgart, 1900; a reprint is available from Kessinger Publishing, 2010.

9 DOHI Tsuneyuki, 'Taishō-ki no Ōshū keizai-shigaku to Fukuda-gakuha' (The 'Fukuda School' and European Economic History Studies in Taishō Japan), in *The Hitotsubashi Review*, vol. 132 (2004), no. 4.

10 HIRANUMA Yoshirō, "Shakai-keizai shigaku no sōkan ni saishite" (Some Remarks on the Publication of the Journal of the Social and Economic History Society), *Shakai-keizai shigaku (The Quarterly Journal of the Social and Economic History Society)*, vol. 1 (1931), no. 1. The journal was originally issued once every two months, but recently changed to publishing five issues per year. The Society published a centenary edition every decade, which includes a history of the Society and an outline of the principle debates engaged in by its members.

522 THE JAPANESE AND GERMAN ECONOMIES

[11] *'60-nen no Ayumi'* (Sixty Years of the Society), in *Political Economy & Economic History*, March 2008.

[12] Currently, although FBHC is working hard to secure financial support, it is now impossible to realize the size and regularity of conference and publication activity as before, and the Society is trying to maintain its tradition of international conference by gathering various funds including governmental grants for scientific research.

[13] KUDŌ Akira, Matthias Kipping and Harm G. Schröter (eds), *German and Japanese Business in the Boom Years: transforming American management and technology models* (Routledge International Studies in Business History), London: Routledge Chapman & Hall, 2003.

[14] His works were published in ŌTSUKA Hisao, *Ōtsuka Hisao chosaku-shū* (Collected Works of Ōtsuka Hisao), Tokyo: Iwanami Shoten, 1969.

[15] For this, Kudō, Footnote 11.

[16] James C. Abbegglen, *The Japanese Factory: Aspects of its Social Organization*, The Free Press, 1958.

[17] ABO Tetsuo (ed.), *Hybrid Factory: The Japanese Production System in the United States*, Oxford University Press, 1994.

[18] SHIOMI Haruhito and HORI Ichirō (eds), *Nichi-Bei kankei keiei-shi* (Competition between Japanese and American Companies*)*, Nagoya: Nagoya Daigaku Shuppan-kai, 1998.

[19] SHIOMI Haruhito and KIKKAWA Takeo (eds), *Nichi-Bei kigyō no gurōbaru kyōsō senryaku* (Competitive Strategy for Globalization between Japanese and American Companies), Nagoya: Nagoya Daigaku Shuppan-kai, 2008.

[20] NAGURA Bunji, *Heiki tekkō-kaisha no Nichi-Ei kankei-shi* (Anglo Japanese Relations in the Case of Vickers and Armstrong), Tokyo: Nihon Keizai Hyoron-sha, 1998.

[21] In the early 1910s when Japan was strengthening her naval power by importing foreign advanced equipment, German and British armaments makers were hard selling their goods. When Vickers tried to sell a battleship and approached the high ranking naval officers offering a 25 % kickback to them, it was revealed that Siemens had already bribed the naval authorities to sell wireless equipment by giving a 15 % kickback. This developed to a big political issue and resulted in the dissolution of the current cabinet. See NAGURA Bunji, YOKOI Katsuhiko and ONOZUKA Tomoji (eds), *The Nichi-Ei heiki sangyō to jiimensu jiken. Buki iten no kokusai keizai-shi* (Japanese and British armament industry in the naval race-economic history of arms transfer and the Vickers Kongo case in 1910), Tokyo: Nihon Keizai Hyōron-sha, 2003.

[22] WATABANABE Hisashi, 'Fuji Denki seiritsu katei', in *Kigyōsha katsudō no shi-teki kenkyū* (Historical Studies on Entrepreneurship – Festschrift for NAKAGWA Keiichirō), Tokyo: Nihon Keizai Shinbun-sha, 1981. This article was translated into English as 'A History of the Process Leading to the Formation of Fuji Electric', in *Japanese Yearbook on Business History*, 1984.

[23] WATANABE Hisashi, 'Fuji Denki no sōritsu katei – dai2, dai3 dankai wo chūshin to shite' (The Creation of Fuji Electric – Its Second and Third Stages), in *Kigyo keiei no rekishi-teki kenkyū* (Historical Studies on Business and Management – Festschrift for WAKIMURA Yoshitarō), Tokyo: Iwanami Shoten, 1990.

[24] The study has been translated into German and published as *Siemens in Japan: Von der Landesöffnung bis zum Ersten Weltkrieg*, Stuttgart: F. Steiner, 1996.

25 This three-volume-series includes twenty articles, focusing on the time between 1890 and 1945. The books were reviewed by Professor Watanabe in *Shakai keizai-shigaku*, vol. 75 (2009), no. 2. He proposed the critical turning point to consider the relation between two countries is not the Mukden Incident of 1931, but rather the Treaty of Versailles in 1919. It will be important to answer the question of when Japan graduated from its German teacher, and became instead an equal partner with Germany. The series has been partially translated into English and expanded and edited by Kudō Akira, Tajima Nobuo and Erich Pauer (eds), *Japan and Germany: Two Latecomers to the World Stage*, Folkestone: Global Oriental, 2009.

Prologue [1]

1 *Nichi-Doku kigyō kankei-shi* (A History of Japanese-German Business Relations) (Yūhikaku) and *Ii-Gee faruben no tai-Nichi senryaku: senkanki Nichi-Doku kigyō kankei-shi* (IG Farben's Japan Strategy: A history of Japanese-German business relations in the inter-war period) (University of Tokyo Press). Subsequently, in the field of the history of Japanese-German relations, I have also produced: *Japanese-German Business Relations: Cooperation and Rivalry in the Inter-war Period* (Routledge, 1998), Kudō Akira and Tajima Nobuo (eds) *Nichi-Doku kankei-shi, 1890–1945, zen sankan* (Japanese-German Relations, 1890–1945, 3 vols), (University of Tokyo Press, 2008), and Kudō Akira, Tajima Nobuo and Erich Pauer (eds), *Japan and Germany: Two Latecomers to the World Stage, 1890–1945*, 3 vols (Global Oriental, 2009).

2 These examples have all been taken from *Nijusseiki Nichi-Doku keizai kankei-shi* (A History of Japanese-German Economic Relations in the Twentieth Century) (2 vols: (1) *Kokusai teii* (International Orientation); (2) *Kigyō taisei* (Business System) currently in preparation.

Chapter 1

The author acknowledges with gratitude the assistance of Fumiaki Moriya for translation and Lynn Cornell for retyping.

1 This is a revised, English version of an earlier paper prepared in German and presented at a symposium on the History of Japanese–German Technological Transfer held in Tokyo in July 1990 by the German Institute of Japan Studies. The proceedings of the symposium was published as E. Pauer (ed.), *Technologietransfer Deutschland–Japan von 1850 bis zur Gegenwart* (München, 1992). A Japanese version of the paper, with some revisions, was included in the author's book, *I.G. Farben no Tainichi Senryaku: Senkanki Nichi-Doku Kigyo-Kankei-shi* (*I.G. Farben's Japan Strategy: A History of Japanese–German Business Relations during the Inter-war Period*) (Tokyo, 1992). The English version was first published in *Annales of the Institute of Social Science*, University of Tokyo, No.34, 1992.

2 For an overview of German technology and management transfer to Japan, see E. Pauer, 'German Companies in Japan in the Inter-war Period: Attitudes and Performance', in T. Yuzawa and M. Udagawa (eds), *Foreign Business in Japan before*

World War II: The International Conference on Business History, 16 (Tokyo, 1990). As for Japanese technology and management transfer to Germany, see A. Kudō, 'Japanese Enterprises in Germany: Attempts at Technical-Industrial Cooperation prior to the Second World War', in H. Pohl (ed.), *Der Einfluss ausländischer Unternehmen auf die deutsche Wirtschaft vom Spätmittelalter bis zur Gegenwart* (Stuttgart, 1992).

3   Beziehungen der BASF zu Japan, BASF-Archiv; Bayer Japan Kabushiki Kaisha, *Nihon to tomoni 75-nen (75 Years Together with Japan)* (Tokyo, 1986), p.12. See also E. Verg *et al., Meilensteine: 125 Jahre Bayer 1863–1988* (Köln, 1988), p.586.

4   Documents housed in Hoechst-Archiv.

5   R. Miwa, '1926-nen Kanzei Kaisei no Rekishiteki Ichi' (Historical Implications of the Revised Tariff of 1926), in T. Sakai et al. (eds), *Nihon Shihonshugi: Tenkai to Ronri (Japanese Capitalism: Its Development and Logic)* (Tokyo, 1978), pp.176–8 and 181–2; M. Udagawa, Business Management and Foreign-Affiliated Companies in Japan before World War II', in Yuzawa and Udagawa (eds), *Foreign Business in Japan,* pp.2–3. See also T. Hara and A. Kudō, 'International Cartels in Business History', in A. Kudō and T. Hara (eds), *International Cartels in Business History: The International Conference on Business History, 18* (Tokyo, 1992).

6   Protokoll über die Besprechung der Firmen Ludwigshafen, Leverkusen und Hoechst üder das Japan-Geschäft am 11 Dezember 1923; Protokoll über die Sitzung der Japan-Kommission am 13 Mai 1924, etc., Hoechst-Archiv.

7   H. Morikawa, *Zaibatsu no Keieisliiteki Kenkyu (Studies in the Business History of Zaibatsu)* (Tokyo, 1980), pp.168–75.

8   Bosch (BASF) an die Herren des Gemeinschaftsrates, 19 Juni 1925, etc., Hoechst-Archiv.

9   I.G. Farben an CMC, Geigy und Durand & Huguenin, 2 Mai 1929; Ciba an Geigy, 27 Mai 1929, Firmenarchiv Geigy VE/IGK 15, Ciba-Geigy-Archiv.

10 Auszug aus der Niederschrift über die Sitzung des Arbeitsausschusses, 23 Nov. 1926, Hoechst-Archiv, etc.

11 Doitsu Senryo an die Abteilung Export 1, 21 Juni 1926, etc., Hoechst-Archiv.

12 Dokkoku Dai-13 Go (Document No.13 on Germany), Gaimusho Gaiko Shiryokan Shozo Joyakusho 6 (File of Treaties, No.6, housed in the Archive of the Japanese Ministry of Foreign Affairs).

13 J. Hashimoto, 'Ryuan Dokusentai no Seiritsu' (The Emergence of a Monopoly in Ammonium Sulphate), *Keizaigaku Ronshu* (Journal of Economics, University of Tokyo), Vol.45, No.4 (1980), pp.59–63.

14 I.G. Farben Control Office of the Decartelization Branch, Economics Division, of the Office of Military Government for Germany (US), *Activities of I.G. Farbenindustrie AG in the Dyestuffs Industry,* 1946, p.15, Hoechst-Archiv.

15 I.G. Farben Control Office of the Decartelization Branch, Economics Division, of the Office of Military Government for Germany (US), *Activities of the Former 'Bayer' I.G. Farbenindustrie AG in the Pharmaceutical Industry,* 1946, pp.90 and 134, Hoechst-Archiv.

16 Udagawa, 'Business Management', pp.2–3.

17 I.G. Farben Control Office of the Decartelization Branch, *Activities of I.G. Farbenindustrie AG in the Dyestuffs Industry,* pp.86–7 and 90–1, Hoechst-Archiv.

18 K. Suzuki, 'Senji Keizai Toseika no Mitsui Bussan, III' (Mitsui Bussan under Wartime Economic Control, III), *Mitsui Bunko Ronso (Journal of the Mitsui Research Institute for Social Economic History),* No.20 (1986), pp.211–12 and 221.

[19] I.G. Farben Control Office of the Decartelization Branch, *Activities of I.G. Farbenindustrie AG in the Dyestuffs Industry*, pp.88–9.

[20] H. Ahrens & Co. Nachf., 29. März 1934 mit 2 Anlagen: Agreement, M. Kobayashi and H. Bosch, 23 March 1934, T74/11 CIA Internationale Konventionsverträge 1923–34; Exposé über die internationale Stickstoff-Verständigung, 25 März 1935, T74/10, BASF-Archiv.

[21] Doitsu Senryo seems to have engaged in the following intelligence activities beginning in 1928: submission of summary reports of travels to Ludwigshafen every two months; submission to the headquarters of one copy each of complete reports, that were judged to be of possible interest to the headquarters; and compilation of biannual reports giving overviews of Doitsu Senryo's performance in dyestuff business and important developments in the dyestuff market (such as the trends in competition, changes in fashion, effects of business cycles, and the performance of local dyestuff manufacturers). In order to ensure that these activities be performed satisfactorily, a proposal was made to make the pre-existing system of information gathering, under which German employees had been responsible for collecting and handling information on specific items of expensive dyestuffs, also applicable to the low-priced items which had become subject to the Saito–Waibel Agreement. It was also decided that Doitsu Senryo should file with the headquarters a report each year on its judgement as to whether each product introduced during the year would be marketable or not. Moreover, for any dyestuff that it found unfit for the market, Doitsu Senryo was to specify why not, and to propose viable measures for making it acceptable in Japan. Waibel, Voigt, Bericht über die Besprechung über das Japan-Geschäft, 31 Aug., 1–3 Sept. 1927, Japan China 1920–36 Allgemein. Habers Reise nach Japan 1924 84, Hoechst-Archiv.

[22] The report briefly surveyed the political, economic, social and cultural situations of each area or country of the region. Volume one was devoted to the discussion of the situation in Japan and Manchuria. M. Ilgner, 'Bericht über eine Reise nach Ostasien 1934/35', n.p., n.d. Even though the date of compilation of the report is unknown, it is certain that it was compiled by the middle of 1936, at the latest. '1934–1935 Dr Max Ilgner Ostasien 81' in 'IG AG Marktforschung T52/11', BASF-Archiv.

[23] Die Chemiewirtschaft Japans, BASF-Archiv.

[24] Rundschreiben Leverkusen, 2 Juli 1934, Hoechst-Archiv.

[25] Besprechung über Auslandsprojekte, 9 Juni 1939, BASF-Archiv.

[26] I.G. Farben Control Office of the Decartelization Branch, Economics Division, of the Office of Military Government for Germany (US), *Activities of I.G. Farbenindustrie AG in the Nitrogen Industry*, 1946, pp. 116–17, Hoechst-Archiv. However, the name of Taki Seihisho is missing from this document. Moreover, what this document regards as a contract signed with Mitsubishi Shoji was actually technological licensing granted to Dainippon Tokkyo Hiryo.

[27] A. Kudō, 'I.G. Farben's Japan Strategy: The Case of Synthetic Oil', in *Japanese Yearbook on Business History*, No.5 (1989).

[28] Contract; Stickstoff-Besprechung, 15 Juni 1935; Vertrag, 17 Feb. 1936, BASF-Archiv.

[29] H. Ahrens to Taki Seihisho (Taki Fertiliser Works), 11 Sept. 1937, housed in the Archive of Taki Kagaku (successor to Taki Seihisho); Akira Kudō, 'Japanese

Technology Absorption of the Haber-Bosch Method: The Case of the Taki Fertiliser Works' in D.J. Jeremy (ed.), *The Transfer of International Technology* (Aldershot; 1992).

[30] A recollection by Mr Genzo Ema, a young engineer at that time.

[31] Waibel, Voigt, Bericht über die Besprechung über das Japan-Geschäft, 31 Aug. 1–3 Sept. 1927, Japan China 1920–36 Allgemein. Habers Reise nach Japan 1924 84, Hoechst-Archiv.

[32] Bayer Japan Kabushiki Kaisha, *Nihon to tomoni 75-nen,* op. cit., pp.7–8 and 13; Harada, *Senryo (Dyestuffs)* (Tokyo, 1938), p.211.

[33] J. Hirschmeier and T. Yui, *The Development of Japanese Business, 1600–1973* (1975), pp.179–80; Y. Suzuki, E. Abe and S. Yonekura, *Keieishi (Business History)* (Tokyo 1987), pp. 196–7. Also note the following point made in K. Toba, 'Nihon no Marketing: Sono Dentosei to Kindaisei nitsuiteno Ichi Kosatsu' (Japanese Marketing: An Analysis of its Traditional Nature and Modern Nature), *Keiei shigaku (Japan Business History Review),* Vol.17 No.1 (1982), p.5: 'One significant difference with the American marketing system was that Japanese manufacturing firms were undertaking marketing activities only on a very limited scale by themselves, and their inaction in this regard was made up for by wholesalers, inclusive of trading firms, who were performing extremely active roles in the country's distribution system'.

[34] Nihon Senryo Seizo Kabushiki Kaisha ('Nissen' for short; Nihon Dyestuff Manufacturing Co. Ltd), *Nissen 20-nenshi (20 Years History of Nissen)* (Osaka, 1936), p.65.

[35] Osaka Enogu Senryo Dogyo Kumiai (Osaka Paints and Dyestuff Manufacturers' and Dealers' Association) (ed.), *Enogu Senryo Shoko Shi (History of Manufacturing and Transactions of Paints and Dyestuffs)* (Osaka, 1938), pp.1201–2.

[36] The only legal provision existing at the time that addressed itself to the procedure of discharging workers was Clause 2, Article 27 of the Ordinance concerning the Enforcement of the Revised Factory Law of 1926, which stipulated that a worker to be discharged should be either given at least 14 days' notice, or be paid at least 14 days worth of wages. This provision is regarded as having paved the way for the establishment of a retirement allowance system in Japan. See M. Numagoshi, *Taishoku Tsumitatekin oyobi Taishoku Teate Ho Shakugi (Annotation of Laws concerning Retirement Compensation Reserve Funds and Retirement Allowances)* (Tokyo, 1937), p.38. It was, however, not until the late 1930s that the payment of a retirement allowance for a discharged worker was explicitly written into law.

Chapter 2

[*] The following abbreviations are used: BAP, Bundesarchiv Abteilungen Potsdam; BASFA, BASF Archiv; FG, Firmenarchiv Geigy of the Firmenarchiv Ciba-Geigy; HA, Hoechst Archiv; I.G.FC, I.G. Farben Control Office of the Decartelization Branch, Economics Division, of the Office of Military Government for Germany (U.S.).

[1] This article is a summary of the main points I made in my book *I.G. Farben no tainichi senryaku: Senkanki nichi-doku kigyo kankei-shi (I.G. Farben's Japan strategy:*

A history of Japanese-German business relations during the inter-war period) (Tokyo, 1992). It takes the perspective of "I.G. Farben and Japan," or I.G. Farben's Japan strategy, whereas my previous summary took the perspective of "I.G. Farben in Japan," or the influence of its technology and management transfer into Japan. See A. Kudō, "I.G. Farben in Japan: The transfer of technology and managerial skills," *Business history, 36:1* (1994), esp. 172–9.

2 T. Nakamura, *Senkanki Nihon keizai seicho no bunseki (An analysis of the Japanese economy in the inter-war period)* (Tokyo, 1971), 3.

3 For tariffs, see R. Miwa, "1926-nen kanzei kaisei no rekishiteki ichi" (The 1926 revision of tariffs in a historical perspective), in T. Sakai et al. eds, *Nihon shihonshugi: Tenkai to ronri (Capitalism in Japan: Development and reason)* (Tokyo, 1978); for foreign capital policies and foreign direct investment in Japan, see M. Udagawa, "Business management and foreign-affiliated companies in Japan before World War II," in T. Yuzawa and M. Udagawa eds, *Foreign business in Japan before World War II* (Tokyo, 1990).

4 For the Japanese strategies of international cartels, the challenge of the Japanese firms to them, and the response of international cartels, see T. Hara and A. Kudō, "International cartels in business history," in A. Kudō and T. Hara, eds, *International cartels in business history* (Tokyo, 1992), 8–22. Also see A. Kudō, "Western multinationals in Japan: Missed opportunities and lessons from inter-war business history," *Asia pacific business review, 2:1* (1995).

5 T. Suzuki, "Kyushu ni okeru kagaku sangyo no hatten" (Development of chemical industry in Kyushu) in T. Kojima ed., *Kyushu ni okeru kindai sangyo no hatten (Development of modern industries in Kyushu)* (Fukuoka, 1988), 221–2.

6 I.G.FC, *Activities of I.G. Farbenindustrie AG in the dyestuffs industry* (Frankfurt am Main, 1946), 15, HA.

7 I.G.FC, Activities of the former "Bayer" I.G. Farbenindustrie AG in the pharmaceutical industry (Frankfurt am Main, 1946), 90, 134, HA.

8 A. Kudō, *Gendai Doitsu kagaku kigyo-shi – I.G. Farben no seiritsu, tenkai, kaitai (A history of modern German chemical enterprise – emergence, development, and dissolution of I.G. Farben)* (Kyoto, 1999); also H. Takeda, "Kokusai kankyo" (International environment) in 1920-nendaishi Kenkyukai, ed., *1920-nendai no Nihon shihonshugi (Japan's capitalism in the 1920s)* (Tokyo, 1983), 23.

9 G. Plumpe, *Die I.G. Farbenindustrie AG. Wirtschaft, Technik und Politik 1904–1945* (Berlin, 1990), 51, 455.

10 Die Chemiewirtschaft Japans, BASFA; BAP 80 I.G. Farben 1, Vowi. Abteilung. There are some differences between the German and Japanese statistics.

11 Plumpe (ref. 9), 51.

12 Ibid., 439, 446, 448.

13 Ibid., 562.

14 See the concept of the "half developed nation" in T. Nakaoka ed., *Gijutsu keisei no kokusai hikaku – kogyoka no shakaiteki noryoku (Technology development in international comparison – social capability of industrialization)* (Tokyo, 1990).

15 Bosch an die Herren des Gemeinschaftsrates, 19 June 1925, etc., HA.

16 Auszug aus der Niederschrift über die Sitzung des Arbeitsausschusses, 23 November 1926, HA.

17 Doitsu Senryo an die Abteilung Export 1, 21 June 1926, HA.

18 Udagawa (ref. 3), 2–3.

[19] BAP 80 I.G. Farben 1, A1305, A73, A125, A1270; A4963, A4964, A2031, A2032; A1066, A4921, EKB32/334.

[20] Protokoll über die Besprechung der Firmen Ludwigshafen, Leverkusen und Hoechst über das Japan-Geschäft am 11 Dez 1923: Protokoll über die Sitzung der Japan-Kommission am 13 Mai 1924, HA.

[21] BAP, 80 I.G. Farben 1, A1270, Bl. 9–10.

[22] 1934–1935 Dr. Max Ilgner Ostasien 81, I.G. AG Marktforschung T52/11; BAP, 80 I.G. Farben 1, Vowi. Abteilung.

[23] Die Chemiewirtschaft Japans, BASFA; BAP 80 I.G. Farben 1, Vowi. Abteilung.

[24] For more details, see Kudō, *Farben tainichi* (ref. 1), Chapters 1–4.

[25] Compiled from a document held in HA. See also Kudō, *Farben tainichi* (ref. 1), p. 24.

[26] For details, see ibid., 29–31.

[27] For details, see ibid., 61–3.

[28] For details of the conclusion of the Saito-Waibel Agreement, see ibid., 80–6.

[29] A. Kudō (ref. 8). For details, see V. Schröter, *Die deutsche Industrie auf dem Weltmarkt 1929 bis 1933: Außenwirtschaftliche Strategien unter dem Druck der Weltwirtschaftskrise* (Frankfurt am Main, 1984), 295–8; H.G. Schröter, „Kartelle als Form industrieller Konzentration: Das Beispiel des internationalen Farbstoffkartells von 1927 bis 1939," *Vierteljahrschrift für Sozial- und Wirtschaftsgeschichte, 74:4* (1987), 488–94; H. Schröter, "Cartels as a form of concentration in industry: The examples of the international dyestuffs cartel from 1927 to 1939," *German yearbook on business history 1988* (1990), 122–8. Also see H. Schröter, "The international dyestuffs cartel 1927–1939 with special reference to the developing areas of Europe and Japan," in Kudō and Hara, eds (ref. 4).

[30] Nihon Senryo Seizo Kabushiki Kaisha, *Nissen 20-nenshi* (20 *years history of Nihon Senryo*) (Osaka, 1936), 67; Japanese Association of Tar, ed., *Nihon tar kogyo shi - hokozoku seisan no shiteki tenkai* (A *history of the tar industry in Japan – historical development of the production of aromatic compounds)* (Tokyo, 1965), 391–2. On the anxiety of the Swiss companies, see Vertretung von Sandoz, Kobe an Sandoz, Basel, 8 November 1928, FG VE/I.G.K 15.

[31] Ciba an Sandoz, 19 Feb 1929; I.G. Farben an Ciba, 6 March 1929, FG VE/I.G.K 15.

[32] I.G. Farben an CMC, Geigy und Durand & Huguenin, 2 May 1929, FG VE/I.G.K. 15.

[33] Ibid.; Ciba an Geigy, 13 May 1929; Geigy an I.G. Farben, CMC und Durand & Huguenin, 15 Mai 1929; Ciba an Geigy, 27 May 1929, FG VE/I.G.K. 15.

[34] For details, see V. Schröter, "Industrie" (ref. 29), 300–302; H. Schröter, „Kartelle" (ref. 29), 498–9, 504–7, 511; H. Schröter, "Cartels" (ref. 29), 130–1, 135–8, 142.

[35] For details of the process of European re-penetration in the United States, see Ito, "Kokusai senryo karuteru to Du Pont" (International dyestuffs cartels and Du Pont), *Osaka City University management studies*, 28:2 (1977), 6–17; V. Schröter, "Participation in market control through foreign investment: I.G. Farbenindustrie AG in the United States: 1920–38," in A. Teichova, M. Lévy-Leboyer and H. Nussbaum eds, *Multinational enterprise in historical perspective* (Cambridge, 1986), 171–184; H. Schröter, „Kartelle" (ref. 29), 485, 508; H. Schröter, "Cartels" (ref. 29), 118, 138–9.

[36] H. Schröter, „Kartelle" (ref. 29), 501–4; H. Schröter, "Cartels" (ref. 29), 133–5.

[37] Osaka Paints and Dyestuffs Manufacturers' and Dealers' Association, eds, *Enogu senryo shokoshi* (*History of manufacturing and transactions of paints and dyestuffs*) (Osaka, 1938), 1498, 1685.

[38] Auszug aus der Niederschrift über die Sitzung des Arbeitsausschusses, 17 February 1932, HA

[39] I. Harada, Senryo (Dyestuffs) (Tokyo, 1938), 294; Osaka Paints, et al. eds (ref. 37), 1703.

[40] Nihon Senryo (ref. 30), 76; Y. Yamashita, "Wagakuni ni okeru senryo kogyo no sosei" (Emergence of the dyestuffs industry in Japan) (3), Chuo University *Journal of commercial science, 5:5/6* (1964), 95–6; I.G.FC (ref. 6), 15, HA; H. Schröter, „Kartelle" (ref. 29), 511; H. Schröter,."Cartels" (ref. 29), 141.

[41] Waibel, Voigt, Bericht über die Besprechung über das Japan-Geschäft, 31 August, 1–3 September 1927, HA.

[42] I.G. Farben an Geigy und CMC, 22 April 1931, FG VE/I.G.K 15.

[43] I.G. Farben an Geigy und CMC, 29 June 1931; I.G. Farben an Geigy und CMC, 4 July 1931, FG VE/I.G.K 15.

[44] Ciba an Geigy, 27 Okt. 1930; Geigy an Ciba, 24 April 1931; Ciba an Geigy, 27 April 1931, FG VE/I.G.K 15.

[45] I.G. Farben an Geigy und CMC, 30 December 1937; I.G. Farben an Geigy und CMC, 29 December 1938, FG VE/I.G.K 15–1; I.G.FC (ref. 6), 90–1.

[46] I.G. Farben an Schweizer, Französische und Englische Gruppe, 28–29 October 1936; I.G. Farben an Geigy und CMC, 22–24 January 1938; I.G. Farben an Schweizer, Französische und Englische Gruppe, 1 December 1938, FG VE/I.G.K 15/1; I.G.FC (ref. 6), 88–9.

[47] For details, see M. Shimotani, *Nihon kagaku kogyoshi ron (Historical treatise on the Japanese chemical industry)* (Tokyo, 1982), 196–216; T. Suzuki (ref. 5), 257–9, 288. The original sources are in Mitsui Mining's unpublished history of the company.

[48] K. Suzuki, "Senji keizai tosei kano Mitsui Bussan" (Mitsui Bussan under wartime economic control), III, *Journal of the Mitsui Research Institute for social economic history, 20* (1986), 211–12. The original sources are unclassified documents of the institute.

[49] BAP 80 I.G. Farben 1, A1305, Bl. 54–5; I.G. Farben an Schweizer, Französische und Englische Gruppe, 29 May 1935, FG VE/LG.K 15/1.

[50] I.G. Farben an Schweizer, Französische und Englische Gruppe, 29 May 1935; 12 July 1935; 16 July 1935, FG VE/I.G.K 15/1; K. Suzuki (ref. 48), 211–13.

[51] Schweizerische Gesellschaft für Chemische Industrie an Mitglieder, 1 July 1936, FG VE/I.G.K 15/1.

[52] I.G. Farben an Geigy und CMC, 5 December 1931, FG VE/I.G.K 15; I.G. Farben an Schweizer, Französische und Englische Gruppe, 18/20 June 1936; 15 April 1937; 16 June 1939, FG VE/I.G.K 15/1.

[53] For details, see Kudō, *Farben tainichi* (ref. 1), 127–8.

[54] For details, see ibid., 128–9, 147–9.

[55] Memorandum of 16 March 1931, FG VE/I.G.K 15; Minutes of the special meeting of the four-party cartel held in Frankfurt of 26/27 August 1937, re Far East, FG VE/I G.K 15/1; I.G.FC (ref. 6), 77–85; V. Schröter (ref. 29), 310.

[56] K. Suzuki (ref. 48), 216–17, 239.

[57] I.G. Farben an Schweizer, Französische und Englische Gruppe, 24 April 1935; Proposed cable from I.G. Farben to Du Pont, no date, attached to ICI to German, Swiss and French Group, 30 April 1935, FG VE/I.G.K 15/1.

58 ICI to German, Swiss and French Group, 30 April 1935; I.G. Farben an Schweizer, Französische und Englische Gruppe, 24 April 1935; 3 May 1935; 16 Mai 1935; Ciba an Deutsche, Französische und Englische Gruppe, 26 April 1935, FG VE/I.G.K 15/1.

59 Agreement, 14 May 1935, FG VE/I.G.K 15/1.

60 I.G. Farben an Schweizer, Französische und Englische Gruppe, 2 May 1938; 4 June 1938, FG VE/I.G.K 15/1; K. Suzuki (ref. 48), 217–19.

61 Farben an Französische und Englische Gruppe, 2 July 1938; 5 December 1938; 28 December 1938; Minutes of the meeting of the board of directors of the four-party cartel held in Paris, 3 Nov 1938, FG VE/I.G.K 15/1; K. Suzuki (ref. 48), 219.

62 Aktennotiz, 8 March 1939, FG VE/I.G.K 15/1.

63 Minutes of the special meeting held at Frankfurt on Main, 8 March 1939; I.G. Farben an Schweizer, Französische und Englische Gruppe, 14 March 1938; 5/6 June 1939; Minutes of the meeting of the board of directors of the four-party cartel held in Basle, 30 March 1939, FG VE/I.G.K 15/1.

64 I.G.FC (ref. 6), 86–7; K. Suzuki (ref. 48), 219.

65 H. Schröter, „Kartelle" (ref. 29), 512–13; H. Schröter, "Cartels" (ref. 29), 142–3

66 For more details, see Kudō, *Farben tainichi* (ref. 1), Chapters 5 and 6.

67 L.F. Haber, *The chemical industry, 1900–1930: The international growth and technological change* (Oxford, 1971), 90–1, 219.

68 Besprechung in Leuna über Auslandsprojekte, 9 June 1939, BASFA, Nachlaß Pier, 1 Japan 1936–45. This engineer undertook the licensing in Japan of the I.G. process relating to synthetic oil. See A. Kudō, "I.G. Farben's Japan strategy: The case of synthetic oil," *Japanese yearbook on business history 1988* (1989), 94–5.

69 With reference to the activities for the Haber-Bosch process in Japan in the 1920s, refer to T. Watanabe ed., *Gendai Nihon sangyo hattatsushi XIII kagaku kogyo (jo) (History of modern Japanese industrial development, Chemical industry, 13:1* (Tokyo, 1968), 312–18 (written by T. Suzuki); H. Morikawa, *Zaibatsu no keieishiteki kenkyu (Studies in the business history of zaibatsu)* (Tokyo, 1980), 168–75; J. Hashimoto, "Ryuan dokusentai no seiritsu" (Establishment of the ammonium sulphate monopoly), *University of Tokyo's Journal of economics, 45:4* (1980), 48–9. In connection with technology transfer and the investment boom in the 1920s, refer to ibid., 49–55; T. Suzuki, *Nihon ryuan kogyoshi ron (Treatise on the history of the Japanese ammonium sulphate industry)* (Kurume, 1985), 62–108.

70 Hashimoto (ref. 69), 59–63.

71 H. Ahrens & Co. Nachf., 29 March 1934 mit 2 Anlagen: Agreement, M. Kobayashi and H. Bosch, 23 March 1934, T74/11 CIA Internationale Konventionsverträge 1923–34; Exposé über die internationale Stickstoff-Verständigung, 25 March 1935, T74/10, BASFA.

72 T. Yui and M. Fruin, "Nihon keieishi ni okeru saidai kogyo kigyo 200 sha" (The largest 200 Japanese firms in Japanese business history), *Japan business history review, 18:1* (1983), 41–5.

73 English translation of the words addressed to Mr Taki by Dr Münzing on the occasion of the transfer of the Haber–Bosch ammonium sulphate plant to Japanese management, Taki Chemical Co., Ltd. (descendant of Taki Fertilizer Works), Historical archives, file box, Ammonium Sulphate Plant – H. Ahrens.

74 Taki Chemical, *Taki kagaku 100–nenshi (A hundred years' history of Taki Chemical)*, (Kakogawa, 1985), 83; also Taki Chemical, plant report tables from 1933 to 1947.

[75] Yui and Fruin (ref. 72), 41–5.

[76] In detail, see Kudō, *Farben tainichi* (ref. 1), Chapter 5.

[77] For details, see ibid., Chapter 7.

[78] Kudō (ref. 8). Very little consideration was given from the beginning to exports. Aside from cost and shipping problems, the firm had difficulty predicting where a profitable export market might be. Part of the reason for this was no doubt the fact that developing a synthetic fuel production capability and sustaining a production capability therein were crucial elements in achieving economic autarky and military self-sufficiency. Fuel could be stored, but any demand arising from such action would be extremely limited and in any case, importing synthetic fuel could be considered inherently contradictory.

[79] In August 1928, a report issued by a fuel committee made up of representatives from the various ministries called for "helping industries that develop alternative fuels to oil and encouraging research in this area," and for "undertaking research in coal liquefaction." The report did not go beyond simply encouraging such work, however. In May 1930, a Ministry of Commerce and Industry commission of inquiry called for measures to encourage research into coal liquefaction as part of a national fuel policy, but it went no further. In September 1933, a liquid fuel committee, composed of ministry representatives, drew up a set of guidelines for a national fuel policy. One of the four main proposals was for the promotion of alternative fuel development. The committee directly called for industrial development in this area and cited the need to complete research on coal liquefaction and then develop concrete plans for large-scale production. In a rider to the Oil Industry Law of March 1934, the Lower House of the Diet attached a resolution calling for the government to develop as quickly as possible a basic policy for the acquisition and development of oil resources and the production of alternative fuels. See H. Takeda, "Nenryokyoku sekiyu gyosei zenshi" (An administrative history of the early years of the fuel bureau), in Sangyo Seisakushi Kenkyusho ed., *Sangyo seisaku kenkyu shiryo* (*Research material on industrial policy*) (Tokyo, 1979), 205–8, 213, 221–2 and 226. See also M. Miwa, "Jinzo sekiyu seizo keikaku to sono zasetsu – senzen Nihon no ekitai nenryo mondai" (Synthetic oil production planning and the failure thereof – pre-war Japan's liquid fuel problem), (unpublished master's thesis, Tokyo Kogyo Daigaku, Faculty of Engineering), Chapters 2 and 3, 1985.

[80] Takeda (ref. 79), 236.

[81] Jinzo Sekiyu Jigyoshi Hensan Kankokai ed., *Honpo jinzo sekiyu jigyoshi gaiyo* (*A summary history of Japan's synthetic oil industry*) (Tokyo, 1956), 3–5. See also Japan Association of Tar, ed. (ref. 30), 305–307; and Ministry of Trade and Industry, ed., *Shoko seisakushi 20 kan, kagaku kogyo (jo)* (*A history of commercial and industrial policy, 20: chemical industry, 1* (Tokyo, 1968), 277–8 (by C. Nakamura).

[82] R. Enomoto, *Kaiso 80-nen (An 80-year retrospective)* (Tokyo, 1976), 191, 194.

[83] Preliminary calculations by government officials (c. 1937) estimated that gasoline produced by direct liquefaction would sell for 74 to 75 sen per gallon. For synthetic fuel, the figure was 67 to 68 sen. Compared with gasoline produced from natural oil, these figures were 22 to 30 sen higher. Thereafter, however, profitability was not an issue. See A. Okabe, *Sekiyu (Petroleum)* (Tokyo, 1986), 85.

[84] Jinzo Sekiyu Jigyoshi Hensan Kankokai (ref. 81), 7.

[85] Enomoto (ref. 82), 177.

[86] Aus Besprechungen mit Tillmann und Vigeveno, 18 July 1938, BASFA.

[87] See Kudō, *Farben tainichi* (ref. 1), Chapter 7.

[88] Aus Besprechungen (ref. 86).
[89] Toa Fuel Industry Co., Ltd., *Tonen 30-nenshi (ge) (A thirty-year history of Toa Fuel,* Vol. 2) (Tokyo, 1971), 355–6.
[90] Bosch an Krauch, 21 February 1936, BASFA.
[91] Rundschreiben Leverkusen, 2 July 1934, HA.

Chapter 3

[1] On culture as a barrier, see Shuji Hayashi, *Culture and Management in Japan,* Tokyo, 1988, Chapter 3.
[2] See, for example, D. S. Landes, 'French business and businessmen in social and cultural analysis', in E. M. Earle (ed.), *Modern France,* Princeton, 1951.
[3] On the relationship between culture and competitiveness, see M. Casson, 'Entrepreneurial culture as a competitive advantage', in M. Casson, *Enterprise and Competitiveness,* Oxford, 1990.
[4] On Western firms in pre-war Japan, see Takeshi Yuzawa and Masaru Udagawa (eds), *Foreign Business in Japan before World War II. The International Conference on Business History 16,* Tokyo, 1990. Erich Pauer's 'German companies in Japan in the inter-war period: attitudes and performance' in that collection is particularly relevant to this chapter; see also Akira Kudō, *A History of Japanese-German Business Relations,* Yuhikaku, 1992 (in Japanese).
[5] On the story of IG Farben's dyestuffs business in Japan, see Akira Kudō, *IG Farben's Japan Strategy. A History of Japanese-German Business Relations during the Inter-War Period,* Tokyo, 1992 (in Japanese) and Akira Kudō, 'IG Farben in Japan: the transfer of technology and managerial skills', *Business History,* 36: 1, 1994, pp. 159–83.
[6] Kudō, 'IG Farben in Japan'.
[7] For example, see Johannes Hirschmeier and Tsunchiko Yui, *The Development of Japanese Business, 1600–1973,* London, 1975, pp. 179–80.
[8] On the history of the German dyestuffs distribution system in Japan, see Kudō, 'IG Farben in Japan'.
[9] *IG Farben's Japan Strategy,* p. 109.
[10] Kudō, 'IG Farben in Japan'.
[11] Ibid.
[12] Kudō, *IG Farben's Japan Strategy.*
[13] Kudō, *Japanese-German Business Relations,* Chapter 6.
[14] See Akira Kudō and Terushi Hara (eds), *International Cartels in Business History. The International Conference on Business History 18,* Tokyo, 1992.
[15] Kudō, *Japanese-German Business Relations.*
[16] Kudō, 'IG Farben in Japan'; Kudō, *IG Farben's Japan Strategy.*
[17] Akira Kudō, 'IG Farben's Japan strategy: the case of synthetic oil', *Japanese Yearbook on Business History,* 5, 1989 and Kudō, *IG Farben's Japan Strategy.*
[18] Kudō, *IG Farben's Japan Strategy,* Chapters 5 and 6 and Akira Kudō, 'The Japanese technology absorption of the Haber-Bosch method: the case of the Taki fertilizer works', in D. J. Jeremy (ed.), *The Transfer of International Technology: Europe, Japan and the USA in the Twentieth century,* Aldershot, 1992.
[19] At this time Yataro Nishiyama was the head of one of Kawasaki Shipyard's steel works. He was to become the president of the company and one of the most

entrepreneurial of Japan's top managers in the post-war era. See Seiichiro Yonekura, 'The post-war Japanese iron and steel industry: continuity and discontinuity', in Etsuo Abe and Yoshitaka Suzuki (eds), *Changing Patterns of International Rivalry. Some Lessons from the Steel Industry. The International Conference on Business History 17*, Tokyo, 1991, especially pp. 211–20.

[20] Kudō, *Japanese-German Business Relations*, Chapter 4.

[21] Ibid., Chapter 6.

[22] Kudō, *IG Farben's Japan Strategy* and Kudō, 'IG Farben in Japan'.

[23] See note 13.

[24] Kudō, *Japanese-German Business Relations,* Chapter 6.

Chapter 4

[1] After the Second World War, in 1947, English notation for the Fuji in Fuji Electric was changed to Fuji from Fusi, which had been used before that. "Fu" stands for Furukawa, and "Si" for Siemens. "Fuji" is used herein.

[2] Toru Takenaka, *Siemens to Meiji Nihon* (Siemens and Japan in the Meiji Era), Tokyo, 1991, Chapter 8. See also, do., Siemens in Japan: von der Landesöffnung bis zum Ersten Weltkrieg, Stuttgart, 1996.

[3] For details of the establishing Fuji Electric, see Hisashi Watanabe, A History of the Process Leading to the Formation of Fuji Electric, in *Japanese Yearbook on Business History 1984*, 1984. See also a brief reference in Wilfried Feldenkirchen, Siemens 1918–1945, München and Zürich, 1995, pp. 242–4.

[4] Akira Kudō, Western Multinationals and Japan: Missed Opportunities and Lessons from Inter-War Business History, in *Asia Pacific Business Review*, Vol. 2, No. 1, 1995.

[5] Akira Kudō, *Japanese-German Business Relations: Cooperation and Rivalry in the Inter-War Period*, London, 1998, pp. 18–30.

[6] Akira Kudō, *I.G. Farben no Tainichi Senryaku: Senkanki Nichi-Doku Kigyo Kankei-shi* (I.G. Farben's Japan Strategy: A History of *Japanese-German Business Relations* during the Inter-War Period, Tokyo, 1992. See also, Kudō, *Japanese-German Business Relations*, Chapters 2, 4, 6 and 7; do., Dominance through Cooperation: The Japan Strategy of I.G. Farben, in John E. Lesch (ed.), *The German Chemical Industry in the Twentieth Century*, Dordrecht and Boston, 2000.

[7] Kudō, I.G. Farben's Japan Strategy, pp. 57–8, 248–61.

[8] Kudō, *Japanese-German Business Relations*, pp. 26–7.

[9] Ibid., pp. 27–8.

[10] Ibid., p. 28. For details, see ibid., pp. 26–30.

[11] Ibid., pp. 165–6.

[12] Ken'ichi Yasumuro, *Kokusai Keiei* (International Management), Tokyo, 1993, p. 138.

[13] Ibid., pp. 135, 139.

[14] Kudō, *Japanese-German Business Relations*, Chapter 9. This chapter is an English translation of Akira Kudō, *Nichi-Doku Kigyo Kankei-shi* (A History of Japanese-German Business Relations), Tokyo, 1992, Chapter 6, which depends on the documents in Siemens AG, Siemens-Archiv-Akte.

[15] Fuji Denki Seizo Kabushiki Kaisha (Fuji Electric Manufacturing Co., Ltd), *Fuji Denki Shashi 1923–1956* (The History of Fuji Electric 1923–1956), Tokyo, 1957, pp. 12–13.

[16] Kudō, *Japanese-German Business Relations*, p. 187.
[17] Fuji Electric, p. 30.
[18] Ibid., p. 30.
[19] Ibid., p. 30.
[20] Ibid., pp. 28, 29.
[21] Ibid., pp. 31, 36.
[22] Kudō, *Japanese-German Business Relations*, p. 198.
[23] Ibid., p. 196.
[24] Ibid., p. 194.
[25] Ibid., p. 195. For details, see ibid., pp. 187–95.
[26] Ibid., p. 199.
[27] Fuji Electric, p. 40.
[28] Ibid., p. 39.
[29] Ibid., p. 41.
[30] Kudō, *Japanese-German Business Relations*, p. 206.
[31] Fuji Electric, p. 43.
[32] Kudō, *Japanese-German Business Relations*, pp. 215–17.
[33] Ibid., p. 217.
[34] *Fuji Electric*, p. 47.
[35] The volume of orders placed by China for heavy electric equipment from Siemens China Co. dropped to a mere 130,000 reichsmark in 1937/38 from 3,860,000 reichsmark in 1935/36 and 7,640,000 reichsmark in 1936/37. The orders placed by Japan and Manchukuo, on the other hand, increased dramatically, from 2,410,000 reichsmark in 1936/37 to 8 million reichsmark in 1937/38.

Chapter 5

[1] United Nations, Department of Economic Affairs, *International Cartels* (New York, 1947), p. 1.
[2] Ibid., p. 1.
[3] The following are some of the works on international cartels that concern our viewpoint. P. Kypriotis, *Les Cartels Internationaux* (Paris, 1936); Laurence Ballande, *Essai d'Etude Monographique et Statistique sur les Ententes Economiques Internationales* (Paris, 1937); E. Hexner, *The International Steel Cartel* (Chapel Hill, N.C., 1943); idem, "International Cartels in the Postwar World," *Southern Economic Journal* (October 1943); a study made for the Subcommittee on War Mobilization of the Committee on Military Affairs, United States Senate, *Economic and Political Aspects of International Cartels* (Washington, D.C., 1944); G.W. Stocking and M.W. Watkins, *Cartels in Action: Case Studies in International Business Diplomacy* (New York, 1946); International Chamber of Commerce, *Competition and Business Agreements,* brochure no. 162 (Paris, 1952); A. Teichova, *An Economic Background to Munich: International Business and Czechoslovakia, 1918–1938* (Cambridge, 1974); E.S. Mason, *Controlling World Trade: Cartels and Commodity Agreements* (Cambridge, Mass., 1946), which was translated into Japanese by Hiraoka Kinnosuke, Kanagawa Tōru, and Motomura Teruo (1977); A. Teichova, M. Lévy-Leboyer and H. Nussbaum (eds), *Multinational Enterprises in Historical Perspective* (Cambridge, 1986); A. Teichova, M. Lévy-Leboyer and H. Nussbaum

(eds), *Historical Studies in International Corporate Business* (Cambridge, 1989); and C.A. Wurm, *International Cartels and Foreign Policy* (Stuttgart, 1989).

4   Frederick Haussmann and Daniel Ahearn, "International Cartels and World Trade: An Explanatory Estimate," *Thought, Fordham University Quarterly,* series no. 1, vol. 19, no. 74 (September 1944): 429, 434, cited by the United Nations, op. cit., p. 2.

5   Ervin Hexner, "International Cartels in the Postwar World," *Southern Economic Journal* (October 1943): 124, cited by the United Nations, op. cit., p. 2.

6   According to the account given in the United Nations, op. cit., pp. 2–3.

7   Ballande, op. cit., pp. 312–13.

8   Kypriotis, op. cit., pp. 39–40.

9   This explanation is according to Ballande, op. cit., chapter 13 (pp. 324–31) and chapter 14 (pp. 332–41).

10 International Chamber of Commerce, op. cit., p. 22.

11 United Nations, op. cit., pp. 10–13.

12 This classification into three types is according to the United Nations, op. cit., pp. 12–22.

13 Ibid., pp. 12–22.

14 Nakamura Takafusa, *Senkanki Nihon Keizai Seichō no Bunseki* (An Analysis of the Japanese Economy in the Inter-war Period) (Tokyo, 1971), p. 3.

15 Miwa Ryōichi, "1926-Nen Kanzei Kaisei no Rekishiteki Ichi" (The 1926 Revision of Tariffs in a Historical Perspective), in Sakai Takahito et al. (eds), *Nihon Shihon Shugi: Tenkai to Ronri* (Capitalism in Japan: Development and Reason) (Tokyo, 1978); Masaru Udagawa, "Business Management and Foreign-Affiliated Companies in Japan before World War II," in Takeshi Yuzawa and Masaru Udagawa (eds), *Foreign Business in Japan before World War II* (Tokyo, 1990).

16 Hoshimi Uchida, "Western Big Business and the Adoption of New Technology in Japan: The Electrical and Chemical Industries 1890–1920," in Akio Okochi and Hoshimi Uchida (eds), *Development and Diffusion of Technology* (Tokyo, 1980).

17 Within the steel industry, we have an actual example of this type of agreement: namely, the extraordinary agreement concerning exports to Japan of the international wire rod cartel, which was under the jurisdiction of the international crude steel cartel. See the historical data in the possession of Haniel-Archiv, 400 003/4 Walzdraht Japan-Export, 1928–33.

18 Kudō Akira, "I.G. Farben no Tainichi Senryaku: Senryō no Keesu" (I.G. Farben's Japan Strategy: The Case of Dyestuffs), Tokyo Daigaku, *Shakai Kagaku Kiyō,* no. 36 (1987): 14–93. The original historical data is in the Hoechst Archives.

19 Harm G. Schröter, "Cartels as a Form of Concentration in Industry: The Example of the International Dyestuffs Cartel from 1927 to 1939," *German Yearbook on Business History 1988* (1990): 123–8.

20 Kudō, op. cit., p. 166.

21 I.G. Farben an Geigy und CMC vom 4 Juli 1931, Firmenarchiv der CIBA- Geigy; FAG VE/IGK 15; I.G. Farben Control Office of the Decartelization Branch, Economics Division, of the Office of Military Government for Germany (U.S.), *Activities of I. G. Farbenindustrie A G in the Dyestuffs Industry* (1946): 90–1.

22 Ibid., pp. 88–9.

23 I.G. Farben an Schweizer, Französische und Englische Gruppe vom 18/20 Juni 1936, Firmenarchiv der CIBA-Geigy; FAG VE/IGK 15/1; Suzuki Kunio, "Senji Keizai Tōseika no Mitsui Bussan, III" (Mitsui & Co. under the Control of the Wartime

Economy, III), *Mitsui Bunko Ronsō*, no. 20 (1986): 211–12, 221. The original
material is contained in historical data in the possession of the Mitsui Library.

[24] I.G. Farben Control Office, op. cit., pp. 77–85.

[25] Suzuki, op. cit., pp. 216–17, 239.

[26] Agreement of May 14th, 1935, Firmenarchiv der CIBA-Geigy; FAG VE/ IGK 15/1.

[27] I.G. Farben Control Office, op. cit., pp. 86–7.

[28] Ōshio Takeshi, "Fujiwara-Bosch Kyōteian to Nihon no Ryūan Kōgyō" (The Fujiwara-
Bosch Agreement Proposal and the Japanese Ammonium Sulfate Industry), Meiji
Gakuin Daigaku *Keizai Kenkyū*, nos. 49–50 (1978); Hashimoto Jurō, "Ryūan
Dokiusentai no Seiritsu" (The Establishment of the Ammonium Sulfate Monopolistic
System), Tokyo Daigaku *Keizaigaku Ronshū*, vol. 45, no. 4 (1980); Kudō Akira, "I.G.
Farben no Tainichi Senryaku: Chisso no Keesu" (I.G. Farben's Japan Strategy: The Case
of Nitrogen), Tokyo Daigaku *Shakai Kagaku Kenkyū*, vol. 39, no. 2 (1987); Suzuki
Tsuneo, "The Foundation and Amalgamation of Miike Nitrogen Industries Inc. and
Toyo Koatsu Industries Inc.," in *Japanese Yearbook on Business History 1987* (1987).

[29] Suzuki Tsuneo, "Senkanki Waga Kuni ni Okeru Sōda Kōgyō no Hatten: Asahi Garasu
Wo Chushin ni" (The Development of the Japanese Soda Industry in the Inter-war
Period: Asahi Glass Co., Ltd.), *Fukuoka Kenshi Kindai Kenkyū Hen Kakuron (1)*
(Fukuoka Prefecture History, Research on Modern Age, Particulars, vol.1), 1989.

[30] Kudō Akira, "I.G. Farben's Japan Strategy: The Case of Synthetic Oil," in *Japanese
Yearbook on Business History 1988* (1989); I.G. Farben Control Office, op. cit., pp.
135–6.

[31] Nihon Denkyū Kōgyōkai (ed.), *Nihon Denkyū Kōgyōshi* (A History of Japanese
Electric Lamp Industry) (Tokyo, 1963).

[32] Hasegawa Shin, "Satsukikai (Jūdenki Karuteru)" (Satsuki Association, the Heavy
Electric Equipment Cartel), Hashimoto Jurō and Takeda Haruhito (eds), *Ryōtaisen
Kanki Nihon no Karuteru* (Japanese Cartels in the Inter-war Period) (Tokyo, 1985);
Yoshida Masaki, "Senzen ni okeru Waga Kuni Denki Sangyō no Kigyōsha Kōdō"
(Activities of Japanese Entrepreneurs in the Electrical Equipment Industry in the Pre-
war Period), *Mita Shōgaku Kenkyū*, vol. 22, no. 5 (1979); Wilfried Feldenkirchen,
"Zur Unternehmenspolitik des Hauses Siemens in der Zwischenkriegszeit," in
Zeitschrift für Unternehmensgeschichte, vol. 33, no. 1 (1988).

[33] *Nippon Denki Kabushiki Kaisha Nanajūnenshi* (A Seventy-Year History of NEC
Corporation) (Tokyo, 1962), pp. 45–50.

[34] Takenaka Tōru, "Siemens-sha no Tokyo Dentō e no Yūshi Keikaku" (Siemens' Plans
for Investment in the Tokyo Electric Lighting Co.), *Shirin*, vol. 71, no. 2 (1988): 108.
See also idem, "Die Tätigkeit der Firma Siemens in Japan vor dem Ersten Weltkrieg,"
in *Vierteljahrschrift für Sozial- und Wirtschaftsgeschichte*, vol. 76, no. 3 (1989).

[35] Aussprache am 22 November 1924 über die künftige Behandlung des
Telephongeschäftes in Japan, Siemens Archiv-Akte 20/La 216; *Nihon Denki
Kabushiki Kaisha Nanajūnenshi*, op. cit., pp. 174–5.

Chapter 6

The earlier version of this paper was read at Reading, Gilleleje and London in 1992–93.
I express my gratitude to Professors Geoffrey Jones, Howard Cox, Charles Harvey,
Lauge Stetting and Stefan Kaiser for their kind help.

1   Terushi Hara and Akira Kudō, 'International Cartels in Business History', in Akira Kudō and Terushi Hara (eds), *International Cartels in Business History. The International Conference on Business History, 18* (Tokyo 1992).

2   Harm G. Schröter, 'Cartels as a Form of Concentration in Industry: The example of the International Dyestuff Cartel from 1927 to 1939', *German Yearbook on Business History 1988* (1990); H.G. Schröter, 'The International Dyestuffs Cartel, 1927–1939, with Special Reference to the Developing Areas of Europe and Japan', Kudō and Hara (eds), *International Cartels*.

3   Leonard A. Reich, 'General Electric and the World Cartelization of Electric Lamps', Kudō and Hara (eds), *International Cartels;* John Kenly Smith, Jr., 'National Goals, Industry Structure, and Corporate Strategies: Chemical Cartels between the Wars' in Kudō and Hara (eds), *International Cartels.*

4   Takafusa Nakamura, *Senkanki Nihon Keizai Seicho no Bunseki (An Analysis of the Japanese Economy in the Inter-war Period) (Tokyo, 1971).*

5   R.P.T. Davenport-Hines and Geoffrey Jones, 'British business in Japan since 1868', in R.P.T. Davenport-Hines and Geoffrey Jones (eds), *British Business in Asia since 1860* (Cambridge, 1989); Erich Pauer (ed.), *Technologietransfer Deutschland–Japan von 1850 bis zur Gegenwart* (München, 1992).

6   Ryoichi Miwa, '1926-nen Kanzei Kaisei no Rekishiteki Ichi' ('The 1926 Revision of Tariffs in a Historical Perspective') in Takahito Sakai et al. (eds), *Nihon Shihon Shugi: Tenkai to Ronri (Capitalism in Japan: Development and Reason)* (Tokyo, 1978); Masaru Udagawa, 'Business Management and Foreign Affiliated Companies in Japan before World War II', in Takeshi Yuzawa and Masaru Udagawa (eds). *Foreign Business in Japan Before World War II. The International Conference on Business History, 16* (Tokyo, 1990).

7   Hoshimi Uchida, 'Western Big Business and the Adoption of New Technology in Japan: Electrical and Chemical Industries 1890–1920', in Akio Okouchi and Hoshimi Uchida (eds), *Development and Diffusion of Technology: Electrical and Chemical Industries. The International Conference on Business History, 6* (Tokyo, 1980).

8   Nihon Denki Kabushiki Kaisha, *Nihon Denki Kabushiki Kaisha 70-nen Shi (A Seventy Year History of NEC Corporation)* (Tokyo, 1962); Mark Mason, 'With Reservations: Prewar Japan as Host to Western Electric and ITT' in Yuzawa and Udagawa, *Foreign Business.*

9   Toru Takenaka, 'Die Tätigkeit der Firma Siemens in Japan vor dem Ersten Weltkrieg' in *Vierteljahrschrift für Sozial- und Wirtschaftsgeschichte, 76.* Band, Heft 3, 1989; T. Takenaka, *Siemens to Meiji Nihon (Siemens and Japan in the Meiji Period)* (Tokyo, 1991).

10 Siemens AG, Siemens-Archiv-Akte (hereafter referred to as SAA), 20/La 216; *Nihon Denki Kabushiki Kaisha.*

11 Fuji Denki Seizo Kabushiki Kaisha, *Fuji Denki Seizo Shashi 1923–1956 (A History of Fuji Electric Manufacturing Co. 1923–1956)* (Tokyo, 1957); Hisashi Watanabe, 'A History of the Process Leading to the Formation of Fuji Electric', *Japanese Yearbook on Business History 1984* (1984); H. Watanabe, 'Fuji Denki no Soritsu Katei: Dai 2, 3 Dankai wo Chushinni' ('Formation Process of Fuji Electric – with Special Reference to the Second and Third Stages') in Keiichiro Nakagawa (ed.), *Kigyo Keiei no Rekishiteki Kenkyu (Historical Studies on Business Management)* (Tokyo, 1990); Wilfried Feldenkirchen, 'Zur Unternehmenspolitik des Hauses Siemens in

der Zwischenkriegszeit' in *Zeitschrift für Unternehmensgeschichte*, 33. Jahrgang, Heft 1, 1988.

[12] *Nihon Denki Kabushiki Kaisha;* Oki Denki Kogyo Kabushiki Kaisha, *Oki Denki l00-nen no Ayumi (The 100 Years Course of Oki Electric Co.)* (Tokyo, 1981); Toshiaki Chokki, 'Japanese Business Management in the Prewar Electric Machinery Industry: The Emergence of Foreign Tie-up Companies and the Modernization of Indigenous Enterprises' in Yuzawa and Udagawa (eds), *Foreign Business.*

[13] SAA 11/Lf 480 Köttgen; Fuji Tsushinki Seizo Kabushiki Kaisha, *Shashi 1 (Company History* I) (Tokyo, 1964).

[14] SAA 20/La 216.

[15] SAA 20/La 219.

[16] Toshiharu Fujisawa, '1920-nendai niokeru Doitsu Denki Kogyo no Kigyo Kinyu' ('Corporate Finance in the German Electrical Equipment Industry in the 1920s'), *Niigata Daigaku Shogaku Ronshu (University of Niigata Journal of Commerce)*, Vol. 15, 1982; Feldenkirchen, 'Zur Unternehmenspolitik'.

[17] SAA 20/La 220; Fuji Tsushinki Seizo Kabushiki Kaisha, *Shashi I.*

[18] SAA 11 /Li 1 v. Buol.

[19] Nihon Denki Kabushiki Kaisha; Tokyo Shibaura Denki Kabushiki Kaisha, *Tokyo Shibaura Denki Kabushiki Kaisha 85-nen Shi (The 85 Years History of Tokyo Shibaura Electric Co.)* (Tokyo, 1963); Mason, 'With Reservations'.

[20] Fuji Tsushinki Seizo Kabushiki Kaisha, *Shashi I.*

[21] SAA 11/Lg 498 Jessen.

[22] Fuji Tsushinki Seizo Kabushiki Kaisha.

[23] Schröter, 'Cartels as a Form of Concentration in Industry'.

[24] Akira Kudō, *Nichi-Doku Kigyo Kankei Shi (The History of Japanese-German Business Relations)* (Tokyo, 1992); A. Kudō, *IG Farben no Tainichi Senryaku: Senkanki Nichi-Doku Kigyo Kankei Shi (IG Farben's Japan Strategy: The History of Japanese-German Business Relations in the Inter-war Period)* (Tokyo, 1992).

[25] Ciba-Geigy AG, Ciba-Geigy Archiv, Firmen Archiv Geigy (hereafter referred to as FAG), VE/IGK 15.

[26] Schröter, 'Cartels as a Form of Concentration in Industry'.

[27] Kudō, *Nichi-Doku Kigyo Kankei Shi;* and *IG Farben no Tainichi Senryaku.*

[28] FAG VE/IGK 15; I.G. Farben Control Office of the Decartelization Branch, Economics Division, of the Office of Military Government for Germany (US), *Activities of I.G. Farbenindustrie AG in the Dyestuffs Industry* (Frankfurt am Main, 1946).

[29] I.G. Farben Control Office, *Activities of I.G.*

[30] FAG VE/IGK 15/1; Kunio Suzuki, Senji Keizai Tosei kano Mitsui Bussan (III) (Mitsui & Co. under the Control of the Wartime Economy (III)) in *Mitsui Bunko Ronso (Journal of the Mitsui Research Institute for Social Economic History)*, Vol.20, 1986.

[31] I.G. Farben Control Office, *Activities of I.G.*

[32] *Suzuki, Mitsui Bussan.*

[33] FAG VE/IGK 15/1.

[34] Ibid.

[35] Ibid.

[36] Ibid.

[37] Ibid.

38 Ibid.
39 I.G. Farben Control Office, *Activities of I.G.*
40 Udagawa, 'Business Management'.
41 Harm G. Schröter, 'Risk and Control in Multinational Enterprise: German Business in Scandinavia, 1918–1939', *Business History Review*, No.62 (1988).
42 Yuzawa and Udagawa, *Foreign Business;* Akira Kudō, 'I.G. Farben in Japan: The Transfer of Technology and Managerial Skills', *Business History*, Vol.36, No.1 (1994).
43 Udagawa, 'Business Management'.
44 Robert Gilpin, *U.S. Power and the Multinational Corporation: The Political Economy of Foreign Direct Investment* (New York, 1975).
45 Shin'ichi Yonekawa, Koichi Shimokawa and Hiroaki Yamazaki (eds), *Sengo Nihon Keieishi I, II, III (The Business History of Japan after World War II, Vols. I, II, III)* (Tokyo, 1990–1991).
46 Nihon IBM Kabushiki Kaisha, *Nihon IBM 50-nen Shi (The 50 Years History of IBM Japan Co.)* (Tokyo, 1989).
47 Hideki Yoshihara, *Naze Fuji-Xerox ha Xerox wo koetaka? (Why Fuji-Xerox Has Exceeded Xerox?)* (Tokyo, 1992).

Chapter 7

Here and throughout this paper. East Asian names are given in the East Asian order, i.e. with the family names first, except in citing works in English where the authors' names are given in the reverse order

1 Earlier versions of this essay were presented at a workshop on "How to Locate Japanese Technology Development in World History?" (held in the City of Kawasaki, October 23–25, 1993, under the sponsorship of the Japan Science Foundation), and also at a conference on "Historical Patterns of Entrepreneurship and Management in Europe and Japan" (held at the European University Institute, Florence, in March 1995). I would like to acknowledge my indebtedness to the participants who commented on my papers at the two meetings. My special thanks are due to Professors Uchida Hoshimi (Tokyo Keizai University and the organizer of the 1993 workshop) and Okada Kazuhide (Senshu University), as well as to the three organizers of the Florence conference, Professors Hara Terushi (Waseda University), Albert Carreras (University of Pompeu Fabra), and Richard Griffiths (European University Institute). My thanks are also due to Mr Stephen Johnson for his translation of the earlier English version of the paper presented in Florence, and to Mr Moriya Fumiaki for his help in preparing the final English text presented here.
2 Alfred D. Chandler, Jr., *Scale and Scope: Dynamics of Industrial Capitalism,* Harvard University Press, 1990; see also the Japanese translated edition, *Sukeru ando Sukopu: Keieiryoku Hatten no Kokusai Hikaku,* Yuhikaku, 1993, especially "Nihongo-ban e no Jobun" (Introduction to the Japanese Edition).
3 Nakagawa Keiichiro (1981a and 1981b); Kudō Akira (1992a and 1992b).
4 For a case study on the Shimazu process for the manufacturing of lead powder for use in storage batteries, one of the rare cases of technology transfer from Japan to the West, see Kudō (1992a; Chapter 5).

5   Useful survey articles are: Uchida Hoshimi (1985); and Kiyokawa Yukihiko (1984). Another useful reference is "Nenkan Kaiko" (The Year in Review), which appears regularly each year in the Japan Association of Business History's organ, *Keiei shigaku* (Business History), although it does not list works of importance on technology transfer under the heading of "technology" or "technology transfer."

6   Keep in mind a penetrating remark of Kobayashi Tatsuya: "Japanese technologies were so fully devoted to imitation that ... it was tacitly understood in as early as the Meiji era that technologies are unrestricted by cultures." Kobayashi Tatsuya (1990, p. 39).

7   A 1931 survey by the Ministry of Commerce and Industry identified a total of eighty-eight firms owned totally or partially by foreign firms. As of 1941, the number of foreign-owned plants had reached 8,843. Not all of the latter were subject to licensing arrangements, and there were a number of licensing arrangements that were not based on patents. However, the latter figure may give us a rough idea of how licensing arrangements were preferred to foreign direct investment. See Kudō (1992a; pp. 24, 26–7).

To add in passing, it is accepted wisdom that technologies and management skills tend to produce more extensive and profound effects when these are introduced through licensing arrangements than through the importation of finished products, and when introduced through foreign direct investment than through licensing arrangements. Nonetheless, given the large number of licensing arrangements involved, we might say that "even if foreign direct investment could produce deep but narrow transfer effects, the importation through licensing produced shallow but extensive effects." See Kudō (1992a, p. 246).

8   In this regard, Uchida Hoshimi remarks as follows: "The new technologies of electricity, chemicals, petroleum, and internal combustion engines, which were developed in the second half of the nineteenth century, produced profound changes in the social and economic life of the advanced countries, changes so radical as to be befitting to be called the Second Industrial Revolution. These new technologies were invented in Britain, and to some extent in Germany and the United States, as well, but it was large firms of these countries that played a pivotal role in their diffusion across the national borders. The patent systems, which were successively established in each country since the beginning of the nineteenth century, were brought into closer coordination with each other by the signing of the Paris Treaty on patents, which set up an institutional framework for technology transfer among the advanced countries. A format of a contract on technology exchange with provisions on the royalty payment, the duration of the contract, and other matters became standardized. The institutionalization of international technology transfer, based on this international patent system, facilitated the transfer of new technologies. At the same time, it induced large firms, which were in possession of basic patents, either developed by themselves or purchases from individual inventors, to play the central role in such transfer."

"On the other hand, firms in the German and American electric machinery and chemical industries, which had begun to undertake in-house research and development programs since the early part of the nineteenth century, found it to their advantage not to apply the newly developed technologies to their domestic operations alone, but to go international and recover the development costs more promptly. They thus began to actively transfer their newly developed technologies abroad by establishing foreign subsidiaries of their own or by teaming up with overseas partners. By stepping up their technology transfer activities, these firms established themselves as multinational enterprises, each satisfying the defining attribute of a multinational firm, namely, its engagement in the transfer of its own technologies abroad. Thus, the emergence of multinational enterprises and international technology transfer were inseparably related to each other." See Uchida (1991a: p. 22).

9 For valuable discussions on this question, see Nonaka Ikujiro, *Chishiki-sozo no Keiei* (A Theory of Organizational Knowledge Creation), Nihon Keizai Shimbunsha, 1990; and Ikujiro NONAKA and Hiro TAKEUCHI, *The Knowledge-Creating Company*, New York: Oxford University Press, 1995. Nishikawa Koji's study (1993) is one of the pioneering works that try to apply the concepts developed in cognitive science to studies in business history, although the main topic of his discussion is quite different from that of this paper. See, in particular, Nishikawa (1993, p. 72), where he attempts to apply analytical concepts of cognitive science, such as semantic memory, episodic memory, declarative knowledge, and procedural knowledge, to his analysis of the Japanese plate glass industry in its embryonic stage.

10 For further discussions on salaried/professional managers, see Morikawa Hidemasa (1981, 1988, and 1991). For further discussions on Japanese engineers, see Uchida Hoshimi (1988 and 1991b).

11 See Okuda Kenji (1985); Morikawa Hidemasa (1988 and 1991); Sasaki Satoshi and Nonaka Izumi (1990, p. 245); and Imakubo Yukio, *19-seikimatsu Doitsu no Kojo* (German Factories at the End of the Nineteenth Century), Yuhikaku, 1995, pp. 436–63.

12 See Kudō Akira (1992a, Concluding Chapter), where I present my tentative view on how the "Yamamura Thesis" should be understood.

13 See Kobayashi Tatsuya (1990, pp. 46–7).

14 See Uchida Hoshimi (1991a, pp. 22–3).

Chapter 8

1 The literature on the dissolution of IG Farben is thin, compared to that on the steel industry, for instance. The work that has set the standard for research on the subject is Hans-Dieter Kreikamp, Die Entflechtung der I. G. Farbenindustrie A. G. und die Gründung der Nachfolgegesellschaften, in: *Vierteljahrshefte für Zeitgeschichte*, Jahrgang 25, Heft 2, 1977. Kreikamp chiefly uses unpublished documents in the collection of Bayer's company archives, and his work is at present practically the only research based on primary sources. It is also, in the main, convincing. This paper accepts in large part Kreikamp's suggestions, but more clearly sets out the research problem. It also utilizes sources from the BASF and Hoechst company archives, the Koblenz National Archives, and the Kiel University newspaper archives, that were not used by Kreikamp. The Japanese research is Teijiro Kanbayashi's piece in Kanbayashi, Kiyoshi Inoue and Soichiro Giga, eds, *Gendai kigyo keitai ron* (On Contemporary Enterprise Configuration), Minerva Shobo, 1962, pp. 181–202, although in terms of his sources Kanbayashi generally relies on Reichelt's work. Also making some mention of the IG Farben dissolution are Akira Hayashi, *Gendai doitsu kigyo ron* (The Contemporary German Firm),

Minerva Shobo, 1972, pp. 17, 19, and Ken Sasaki, *Gendai yoroppa shihonshugi ron* (Contemporary European Capitalism), Yuhikaku, 1975, pp. 36, 41–2. These have, in general, not gone beyond introducing or mentioning past research, have denied the significance of the dissolution, and have taken a strongly preachy tone asserting the simple reversion of IG Farben to its status as a monopoly. Tohara's argument focusing on post-war reform in West Germany, by contrast, sets the standard for Japanese research. While relying on Gross and Reichelt, Shiro Tohara also takes up the dissolution of IG Farben from the perspective of rational reorganization of the enterprise system. Shiro Tohara, Post-war Reform in West Germany, in: *Tokyo Daigaku Shakai Kagaku Kenkyujo*, ed., Sengo kaikaku 2: kokusai kankyo (Post-war Reform 2: International Environments), Tokyo Daigaku Shuppankai, 1974, pp. 145–7.

[2]   Hermann Gross, *Material zur Aufteilung der I. G. Farbenindustrie Aktiengesellschaft*, Kiel, 1950, S. 41–2, Anhang, S. 7. Plumpe gives rather different figures for this, based on internal sources. Gottfried Plumpe, *Die I. G. Farbenindustrie AG. Wirtschaft, Technik und Politik 1904–1945*, Berlin, 1990, S. 747.

[3]   Badische Anilin- & Soda-Fabrik AG (BASF), *Bericht über die Neugründung 1952–1953*, o. O., o. J., S. 27, 52–53; Carl Wurster, *Die Neugründung der BASF im Zuge der I. G.-Entflechtung und die Entwicklung der BASF 1945–1954*. Rechenschaftsbericht, erstattet anläßlich der ordentlichen Hauptsammlung der BASF am 15 Juli 1954, o. O., o. J., S. 3, BASF Archiv.

[4]   Erik Verg et al., *Meilensteine. 125 Jahre Bayer 1863–1988*, Leverkusen, 1988, S. 300–2.

[5]   Karl Winnacker, *Nie den Mut verlieren*, Düsseldorf, 1971, 2. erganzte Auflage, 1974, S. 124–7.

[6]   BASF, op. cit., S. 28.

[7]   Allgemeine Anordnung Nr. 2 zum Gesetz Nr. 52 der (US) Militärregierung vom 5 Juli 1945, in: Hoechst AG (Hrsg.), *Dokumente aus Hoechst-Archiven. Beiträge zur Geschichte der Chemischen Industrie 48. US-Administration. Die Verwaltung des Werkes Hoechst 1945–1953*, Frankfurt am Main, 1976 (hrsg. von Klaus Trouet), S. 30–1. This is one of the three-part materials collection concerning the post-war occupation period that has been published by the Hoechst archive. The materials collected therein are a part of the voluminous IG Farben historical materials that were seized by the U.S. military government after the war and later returned. See also I. G. Farbenindustrie AG in Liquidation, *Bericht über die Entflechtung und Liquidation*, Frankfurt am Main, 1955, Anhang, S. 1–2, Hoechst Archiv.

[8]   Gross, op. cit., S. 42–3.

[9]   Ibid., S. 43.

[10]   I. G. Farbenindustrie AG in Liquidation, op. cit., Anhang, S. 2–3.

[11]   The Kilgore Committee's view of IG Farben is reflected in, for example, Joseph Borkin, *The Crime and Punishment of I. G. Farben*, New York, 1978 (*Die unheilige Allianz der IG Farben. Eine Interessengemeinschaft im Dritten Reich*, Frankfurt am Main, 1979, 3. Auflage, Frankfurt am Main, New York, 1981); Josiah E. DuBois, Jr., *The Devil's Chemists. 24 Conspirators of the International Farben Cartel Who Manufacture Wars*, Boston, 1952.

[12]   Stellungnahme der Gewerkschaften zar Neuordnung der I. G. Farbenindustrie AG (November 1940), Bundesarchiv Koblenz, B 102/338.

13 Hoechst AG (Hrsg.), *Dokumente aus Hoechst-Archiven. Beiträge zur Geschichte der Chemischen Industrie 49. Der Hoechst-Konzern entsteht. Die Verhandlungen über die Auflösung von IG-Farben und die Gründung der Farbwerke Hoechst AG 1945–1953, Teil 1*, Frankfurt am Main, 1978 (hrsg. von Klaus Trouet), Einführung, S. 13. For the activities of the U.S. military government, its monthly report (OMGUS Monthly Report, Institut für Zeitgeschichte, Archiv) is the basic source. In the reports are numerous articles concerning IG Farben's overseas assets and the like, but pieces directly relating to the theme of this paper are nowhere to be found. For U.S. military government materials see also James J. Hastings, Die Akten des Office of Military Government for Germany (US), in: *Vierteljahrshefte für Zeitgeschichte*, Jahrgang 24, Heft 1, 1976, S. 75–101.

14 Request by Mr Martin for consideration of dispersal by industries, in: Hoechst, Der Hoechst-Konzern, op. cit., S. 19; Ausarbeitung der Werksleitung Hoechst für Sub Control Office Lt. Col. Percival, Ffm.-Hochst, 12 Februar 1946, in: Ibid., S. 21; Aktennotiz über den Besuch amerikanischer Sachverstandiger, Ffm.-Hochst, 18 April 1946, in: Ibid., S. 24–5.

15 Hessisches Wirtschafts- und Verkehrsministerium an die Betriebsleitung Hoechst, in: Hoechst, US-Administration, op. cit., S. 102.

16 *Rhein-Neckar-Zeitung*, 28 November 1949; *Handelsblatt*, 19 Oktober 1949; *Industriekurier*, 20 Oktober 1949, Institut für Weltwirtschaft, Universität Kiel.

17 Ernst Falz, *Aus der Treuhänder-Zeit der I. G. Farbenindustrie A. G. »in dissolution« in Hessen 1945 bis 1950*, Konigstein im Taunus, 1985, Hoechst Archiv.

18 Erich Ott, *Die Wirtschaftskonzeption der SPD nach 1945*, Marburg, 1978, S. 127–8.

19 *Hamburger Allgemeine Zeitung*, 24 Januar 1947, Institut für Weltwirtschaft, Universität Kiel.

20 Ott, op. cit., S. 128–32.

21 Stellungnahme der Gewerkschaften, op. cit.; Gross, op. cit., S. 44. On British occupation policy in Germany in general, see James P. May and William E. Paterson, Die Deutschlandkonzeptionen der britischen Labour Party 1945–1949, in: Claus Scharf und Hans-Jürgen Schröder (Hrsg.), *Politische und ökonomische Stabilisierung Westdeutschlands 1945–1949*, Wiesbaden, 1977. In addition, the literature on the socioeconomic history of the British zone of occupation has been moving forward at a rapid pace in recent years; principal examples include Werner Plumpe, Wirtschaftsverwaltung und Kapitalinteresse im britischen Besatzungsgebiet 1945/46, in: Dietmar Petzina und Walter Euchner (Hrsg.), *Wirtschaft und Wirtschaftspolitik im britischen Besatzungsgebiet 1945/1949*, Düsseldorf, 1984, S. 121–52; Friedrich Stratmann, Strukturen der Bewirtschaftung in der Nachkriegszeit. Das Beispiel der Chemiebewirtschaftung in der britischen und der Bizone 1945 bis 1948, in: ibid., S. 153–71; Horst Lademacher, Die britische Sozialisierungspolitik im Rhein-Ruhr-Raum 1945–1948, in: Claus Scharf und Hans-Jürgen Schröder (Hrsg.), *Deutschlandpolitik Grosbritanniens und die Britische Zone 1945–49*, Wiesbaden, 1979, S. 51–92; Dieter Scriverius, Die britische Demontagepolitik im Spiegel der Überlieferung des Hauptstaatsarchivs Düsseldorf, in: Ibid., S. 93–101. These works, though, make no mention of the IG Farben dissolution.

22 Winnacker, op. cit., S. 150, 151–2; Wemer-O. Reichelt, *Das Erbe der IG-Farben*, Düsseldorf, 1956, S. 132, 134.

23   *Rhein-Neckar-Zeitung,* 20 April 1948; *Der Tagesspiegel,* 27 April 1948, Institut für Weltwirtschaft, Universität Kiel.

24   Ott, op. cit., S. 134–6. Steininger especially emphasizes the effect of national security policy considerations as a reason why Britain bowed to American pressure. Rolf Steininger, Reform und Realität. Ruhrfrage und Sozialisierung in der anglo-amerikanischen Deutschlandpolitik 1947/48, in: *Vierteljahrshefte für Zeitgeschichte,* Jahrgang 27, Heft 2, 1979, S. 198–224, 239.

25   Gross, op. cit., S. 45; BASF, op. cit., S. 28. There are arguments that the French military government directly managed each plant (Stellungnahme der Gewerkschaften, op. cit.), but these will not be addressed here.

26   On French occupation policy in general, see Gerhard Kiersch, Die französische Deutschlandpolitik 1945–1949, in: Scharf und Schröder, Politische und ökonomische Stabilisierung, op. cit.; Claus Scharf und Hans-Jürgen Schröder (Hrsg.), *Die Deutschlandpolitik Frankreichs und die Französische Zone 1945–1949,* Wiesbaden, 1983.

27   Demontage-Vorhaben der BASF - Nach Mitteilung der französischen Militärregierung vom 21. 4. 49, 8 November 1949, Institut der Weltwirtschaft, Universität Kiel; Memorandam. Demontage-Vorhaben, Ammoniak-Synthese der BASF, 17 November 1949, Institut der Weltwirtschaft, Universität Kiel.

28   Reichelt, op. cit., S. 117–19.

29   Gross, op. cit., S. 45.

30   Teijiro Kanbayashi, History of the IG Farben Leuna plant: including the emergence history of the IG Farben Trust, in: *Keiei shigaku,* Vol. 2, No. 2, 1967, pp. 22–7.

31   Rainer Karlsch, Zwischen Partnerschaft und Konkurrenz. Das Spannungsfeld in den Beziehungen zwischen den VEB Filmfabrik Wolfen und der Agfa AG Leverkusen, in: *Zeitschrift für Unternehmensgeschichte,* Jahrgang 36, Heft 4,1991, S. 248.

32   This characterization of each of the three zones of occupation, which is also a summary of the above analysis, agrees in the main with that of Stokes. See Raymond G. Stokes, *Divide and Prosper. The Heirs of I. G. Farben under Allied Authority 1945–1951,* Berkeley, Los Angeles, London, 1988, Chapters 2–4, esp. pp. 63, 83, 103–4.

33   For example, see Alfred Grosser, *Deutschlandbilanz. Geschichte Deutschlands seit 1945,* München, 1970 (8. Auflage, *Geschichte Deutschlands seit 1945. Eine Bilanz,* München, 1980), S. 115–20.

34   The "myth" referred to here is the conventional wisdom that currency reform, along with the Marshall Plan and the ideal of a social market economy, made possible for the first time the rapid economic growth called "the economic miracle." The following work, however, casts doubt on this conventional wisdom. Werner Abelshauser, *Wirtschaft in Westdeutschland 1945–1948. Rekonstruktion und Wachstumsbedingungen in der amerikanischen und britischen Zone,* Stuttgart, 1975, S. 9. In the final analysis, Abelshauser bases his argument on the fact that industrial production had already been increasing prior to June 1948 and thus the currency reform did not consitute any sort of turning point (ibid. S. 35–63). Certainly, the belief that economic expansion first began after the currency reform has become the conventional wisdom, and one can find rather misleading statements, such as "a large increase in industrial production appeared at earliest in the second half of 1948" in the enlightened literature on Japan (Takashi Inoue's piece, in: Takeo

Onishi, ed., *Gendai no Doitsu 3: Keizai to sono antei* (Contemporary Germany 3: The Economy and Its Stability), Sanshusha, 1981, p. 28). There is a certain significance to Abelshauser's "demystifying" argument in terms of correcting the conventional wisdom. Problems remain, however. First, even according to the corrected estimates that are made by himself, the tempo of the expansion in industrial production picks up from the third and fourth quarters of 1948 (ibid., S. 59, Abbildung 10). Second, there are more basic problems with a method that takes industrial production alone as an indicator for the direction of the entire West German economy. It must be said that Abelshauser gives scant attention to addressing the currency reform in the context of incorporating the West German economy into the West's world economic system. One survey of the socioeconomic history of the post-war occupation that merits perusal is, Michael Geyer, Alliierte Militärregierungen: Okkupation, militarische Verwaltung, Staatsgründung, in: *Sozialwissenschaftliche Informationen für Unterricht und Studium*, Jahrgang 6, Heft 3,1977.

35 Gross, op. cit.., S. 45, 58.
36 *Handelsblatt*, 2 November 1948, Institut für Weltwirtschaft, Universität Kiel.
37 Arbeitsgemeinschaft Chemische Industrie des Vereinigten Wirtschaftsgebietes, Rundschreiben Nr. 5/49, 26 November 1949, S. 2–3, Bundesarchiv Koblenz, B 102/338.
38 Abschrift von BICO (Bipartite Control Office) an den Verwaltungsrat des Vereinigten Wirtschaftsgebietes vom 5 August 1948, in: Hoechst, *Der Hoechst-Konzern entsteht*, op. cit., S. 29–31; Abschrift von BICO an den Verwaltungsrat des Vereinigten Wirtschaftsgebietes vom 22 September 1948, in: Ibid., S. 42–4; I. G. Farbenindustrie Aktiengesellschaft in Liquidation, op. cit., S. 15.
39 Abschrift des Vorsitzenden des Verwaltungsrates des Vereinigten Wirtschaftsgebietes, Hermann Pünder, an BICO vom 6 September 1948, in: Hoechst, *Der Hoechst-Konzern entsteht*, op. cit., S. 36–7; Bericht von Stein (Arbeitsgemeinschaft Chemische Industrie des Vereinigten Wirtschaftsgebietes) vom 10 September 1948, in: Ibid., S. 38–41. Haberland was inaugurated as head of the Nordrhein-Westfalen unit of the Federation of German Industry (Bundesverband der Deutschen Industrie or BDI) in May 1950. Newman and his office had been on guard against this action turning into a rehabilition of former IG Farben managers. William A Acton to McDowell (US-High Commission), April 14, 1950, RG 260, Box 523, 17228–1 15 Resistance to Farben Program, National Archives, Washington, D. C.
40 Bericht von Stein (Arbeitsgemeinschaft Chemische Industrie des Vereinigten Wirtschaftsgebietes) vom 10 September 1948, in: Hoechst, *Der Hoechst-Konzern entsteht*, op. cit., S. 39–40.
41 *Industriekurier*, 30 Oktober 1948; *Handelsblatt*, 4 Dezember 1948; *Rhein-Neckar-Zeitung*, 1 Dezember 1948; *Die Welt*, 27 Januar 1949, Institut für Weltwirtschaft, Universität Kiel. In this connection, newspaper articles reporting on the issue of appointments to FARDIP were also closely analyzed by the French occupation authorities as a reflection of German public opinion. French study on FARDIP and German public opinion, by the French Decartelization Branch, September 1949, Institut für Zeitgeschichte, OMGUS-Unterlagen, 17/8248/6 (note: number is the index number in the OMGUS Schlagwortkatalog II).

[42] *Welt am Sonntag*, 12 November 1948; *Industriekurier*, 30 Oktober 1948, Institut für Weltwirtschaft, Universität Kiel.

[43] Hoechst, *Der Hoechst-Konzern entsteht*, op. cit., Einführung, S. 14; Abschrift von BICO an die Unabhängigen Einheiten vom 21 Februar 1949, in: Ibid., S. 45.

[44] *Wirtschaftszeitung*, 23 Februar 1949, Institut für Weltwirtschaft, Universität Kiel.

[45] *Die Welt*, 27 Januar 1949, Institut für Weltwirtschaft, Universität Kiel; Farbenfabriken Bayer Aktiengesellschaft, Geschäftsbericht für das Jahr 1952, o. O., o. J., S. 4. Möhn, however, was a chemist, and could not strictly be said to be a labor union representative. In addition, Kurlbaum from the Bavarian labor union was later named the second labor union representative, but Eberhard Esser, vice chairman of the Chemical Workers' Union, was dissatisfied at not having received advance notice of that appointment. Eberhard Esser an den Bayerischen Gewerkschaftsbund, 9 Mai 1949, DGB Archiv, Entflechtung/Neuordnung 1949.

[46] Wurster, op. cit.

[47] Control Commission for Germany (British Element), Douglas Fowles to R. H. Newman, 25 September 1950, Institut für Zeitgeschichte, OMGUS-Unterlagen, 17/8248/19; Gross, op. cit., S. 46. "The first asset to be put up for sale will be the Kalle Company of Wiesbaden." McCloy, n. d. (draft), RG 260 Box 331 11–3 2 IG Farben (TRIFCO), National Archives, Washington, D. C.

[48] Stellungnahme der Gewerkschaften, op. cit.

[49] Anweisungen von BICO an FARDIP vom 5 August 1948, in: Hoechst, *Der Hoechst-Konzern entsteht*, op. cit., S. 33.

[50] *Die Welt*, 7 August 1948, Institut für Weltwirtschaft, Universität Kiel. Kreikamp relies on Danek to make an argument with the same point as this. Kreikamp, op. cit., S. 223. Paul Danek, Zur Reaktionaren Rolle des staatsmonopolistischen Kapitalismus bei der Wiedererrichtung und Machtausweitung des IG-Farbenmonopols in Westdeutschland, (Diss. Halle) 1961. In any case, it is absolutely impossible to say "the Allies themselves did not have any concrete ideas about resolving the IG Farben problem," as Reichelt (op. cit., S. 67) does.

[51] FARDIP, Grundlinien eines Gesamtplanes zur Entflechtung der IG-Farbenindustrie AG i. A, 29 Juni 1950, Hoechst Archiv; Auszug aus dem FARDIP-Plan, in: Hoechst, *Der Hoechst-Konzern entsteht*, op. cit., S. 64–5.

[52] Kreikamp, op. cit., S. 224–5.

[53] 1. G. Farbenindustrie Aktiengesellschaft in Liquidation, op. cit., S. 19–20.

[54] Fowles to Newman, op. cit., Institut für Zeitgeschichte, OMGUS-Unterlagen, 17/8248/19. Conflict among the Allied powers developed first over the place of the German panel and later arose over the principles to be incorporated into High Commission Law Number 35. Although the United States, Britain, and France all agreed on the ultimate objectives for IG Farben's dissolution, there were differences of opinion over the methods and procedures needed to achieve them. In particular, both the U.S. and France asserted that the IG Farben Control Officer ought to bear responsibility for the entire process of liquidation and dissolution even while obtaining the assistance of an organization consisting of Germans (although there was a conflict between the U.S. and France over the status of the German organization; the U.S. asserted that the organization must obey the orders of the Allied IG Farben Control Office without being publicly granted status through legislation, while France held that such legal status should be granted). The British countered that official status should be

granted by law to the German body from the proposals for liquidation and dissolution to their implementation, and that authority should be delegated as much as possible to the German body even while reserving ultimate authority to the Allied powers. These differences of opinion "were based upon a fundamental conflict over principles," and "it would be impossible to find a point of compromise concerning this conflict of principle." H. Plumbly (Allied High Commission, Decartelization and Industrial Deconcentration Group) to Economic Committee, 4 April 1950, RG 260, Box 330 11 11–2 8 (no title), National Archives, Washington, D. C.

[55] On this point there are documentary constraints, and some uncertainty remains. Kreikamp also makes a similar argument, but he also stays in the realm of speculation. Kreikamp, op. cit., S. 222–3.

[56] Hermann-Josef Rupieper, *Der besetzte Verbündete. Die amerikanische Deutschlandpolitik 1949–1955*, Opladen, 1991, S. 37–8.

[57] Ibid., S. 15. He took office effective 13 June 1949. Harry S. Truman, Executive Order 10063. Defining Certain Functions of the United States High Commissioner for Germany, RG 466 Class. Her. Reds. McCloy Box 1, National Archives, Washington, D. C. For details on McCloy, see Rupieper, op. cit., S. 19–25. McCloy participated closely in U.S. goverment policies for managing the post-war world, including advising President Truman in the formulation of surrender conditions for Japan, and he had been pegged as a candidate for High Commissioner for Germany (Hochkommissar für Deutschland) by President Roosevelt as early as 1944. At that time McCloy had advised the president that the head of the goverment in occupied Germany should be a soldier, not a civilian, or, in other words, that a military government should be set up. He recommended General Lucius Clay to head that government. John J. McCloy, From Military Government to Self-Government, in: Robert Wolfe (ed.), *Americans as Proposals. United States Military Government in Germany and Japan 1944–1952*, Carbondale and Edwardsville, 1984.

It should be noted that, of the Allied High Commission's documents, some of the U.S. High Commissioner's documents were made open to the public in 1985 and were moved from the U.S. State Department to the National Archives. These were the so-called McCloy Papers, which had been collected in 53 boxes as Record Group 466 (RG 466: Records of the U.S. Allied High Commissioner for Germany, U.S. High Commissioner John J. McCloy) (McCloy Boxes: July 1949-July 1952). Some U.S. High Commission documents have been placed in the U.S. Military Goverment for Germany (OMGUS) papers. There are also published reports in the form of articles on the IG Farben dissolution. Amt des Amerikanischen Hochkommissars für Deutschland, 7. Bericht über Deutschland, 1 April-30 Juni 1951, o. O., o. J., S. 60–61; do, 11. Bericht über Deutschland, 21 September 1949–31. Juli 1952, o. O., o. J., S. 148–50; Erika J. Fischer und Heinz-D. Fischer, *John J. McCloy und die Frühgeschichte der Bundesrepublik Deutschland. Presseberichte und Dokumente über den Amerikanischen Hochkommissar für Deutschland 1949–1952*, Köln, 1985.

[58] Gross, op. cit., S. 46; I. G. Farbenindustrie Aktiengesellschaft in Liquidaton, op. cit., S. 12.

[59] Rupieper, op. cit.

[60] de Fouchier to Beaulieu, July 1949, RG 260 Box 331 11–3 2 IG Farben (TRIFCO); TRIFCO/P(49)20, 31 October1949; Maupin to Barron, 7 November 1949;

McCloy, n. d. (draft), RG 260 Box 331 11–3 2 IG Farben (TRIFCO), National Archives, Washington, D. C.

[61] Gross, op. cit., S. 47; I. G. Farbenindustrie Aktiengesellschaft in Liquidaton, op. cit., S. 15; Kreikamp, op. cit., S. 223–4.

[62] Andreas Hillgruber, *Europa in der Weltpolitik der Nachkriegszeit 1945–1963*, München, Wien, 1979, S. 57–8; Hans-Peter Schwarz, *Die Ära Adenauer 1949–1957* (Geschichte der Bundesrepublik Deutschland, Band 2), Stuttgart, Wiesbaden, 1981, S. 112–4.

[63] Allied High Commission for Germany, Press Release, No. 196, 17 August 1950, RG 466 McCloy Class. Her. Reds. Box 18, National Archives, Washington, D. C.; Allied High Commission for Germany, Press Release, No. 201, n. d, Institut für Zeitgeschichte, OMGUS-Unterlagen, 17/8248/15. The full text of this law (except attached tables) has been recorded in I. G. Farbenindustrie Aktiengesellschaft in Liquidaton, op. cit., Anhang, S. 3–10; Reichelt, op. cit., Anhang, S. 223–32.

[64] 1. G. Farbenindustrie Aktiengesellschaft in Liquidaton, op. cit., S. 13; Reichelt, op. cit., S. 69.

[65] On the reception for High Commission Law Number 27, see Tohara, op. cit., pp. 138–9.

[66] Staff Anouncement, No. 113, 30 June 1950, McCloy Staff Anouncements, RG 466 Box 1, National Archives, Washington, D. C.; Allied High Commission for Germany, Press Release, 30 June 1950; No. 407, 13 July 1950, Institut für Zeitgeschichte, OMGUS-Unterlagen, 17/8248/15.

[67] Letter of Grant W. Kelleher to Bowie, 15 June 1950, Institut für Zeitgeschichte, OMGUS-Unterlagen, 17/8248/15.

[68] Letter of Kelleher to Friedrich Ulrich, 17 July 1950, Institut für Zeitgeschichte, OMGUS-Unterlagen, 17/8248/15.

[69] Prentzel, Vermerk für Schalfejew, 18 Januar 1950, Bundesarchiv Koblenz, B 102/338. On Erlenbach, see also Karl Winnacker, Abschiedsworte, Hoechst Archiv.

[70] Prentzel had had experience working at IG Farben prior to his entry into the Economic Ministry. After he retired from the Economic Ministry, he became the chairman of the board of directors at a chemical firm, DEGUSSA (Deutsche Gold- und Silber-Scheideanstalt). He also served concurrently as a director at Hoechst and Metallgesellschaft AG. It is certain that he was a person extremely close to IG Farben. Working Group of Former Prisoners of the Auschwitz Concentration Camp of the Committee of Anti-Fascist Resistance Fighters in the German Democratic Republic (ed.), *IG-Farben, Auschwitz, Mass Murder*, n.p, n. d, pp. 56–7.

[71] Prentzel, Vermerk, 12 September 1950, Bundesarchiv Koblenz B 102/339.

[72] *Frankfurter Allgemeine Zeitung*, 29 September 1950, Institut für Weltwirtschaft, Universität Kiel; Stellungnahme zum I. G.-Gesetz Nr. 35, Hoechst Archiv 3/84; Stellungnahme zum I. G.-Gesetz Nr. 35, Bayer Archiv, Sekt. Haberland, Besatzung 1945–1951, Sigu. 271/1.1.10. Menne worked as the founding chairman of the Chemical Industry Association until 1956. From 1949 until 1968 he was also Vice Chairman of the Federation of German Industry. He was also named a director with the establishment, on a provisional basis, of the Hoechst company. Für die Presse. Dr. h. c. Alexander Menne wird 65 Jahre alt, Hoechst Archiv.

73   Wurster, op. cit., S. 5; *Handelsblatt*, 2 September 1950, Institut für
     Weltwirtschaft, Universität Kiel. Schmidt was named an auditor when
     BASF was established on a provisional basis. Upon Schmidt's death, BASF
     expressed its appreciation for his "continuous relationship" with the three big
     ex-Farben firms in his role as chairman of the Association of Private Securities
     Ownership Protection. BASF, Bericht uber das Geschäftsjahr 1954, o. O., o.
     J., S. 3, BASF Archiv.
74   Prentzel, Vermerk, 12 September 1950, Bundesarchiv Koblenz B 102/339;
     Wohlthat an Böker, 30 Oktober 1950, Bundesarchiv Koblenz B 102/405.
75   *Frankfurter Allgemeine Zeitung*, 31 August 1950, Institut für Weltwirtschaft,
     Universität Kiel; Telegramm, Schmid an Prentzel, 5 September 1950, Bundesarchiv
     Koblenz B 102/339; Reichelt, op. cit., S. 70–3.
76   *Frankfurter Allgemeine Zeitung*, 28 September 1950, Institut für Weltwirtschaft,
     Universität Kiel.
77   *Rhein-Neckar-Zeitung*, 2/3 September 1950, Institut für Weltwirtschaft,
     Universität Kiel. This newspaper is Ludwigshafen's local paper.
78   Chemical workers' unions formed in each of the three zones of occupation around
     1946, and the Chemical Workers Union became an organization uniting the
     three zones in October 1948. Its chairman was Wilhelm Gefeller. IG Chemie,
     Papier, Keramik (IG Chemie), Protokoll über die Verhandlungen des Gründungs-
     Verbandstages am 17 und 18 Dezember 1946 in Hamburg-Harburg; do,Protokoll
     des Vereinigungsverbandstages der IG-Chemie-Papier-Keramik am 14–16
     Oktober 1948 in Hannover, IG Chemie Archiv.
79   *Die Freiheit*, 4 September 1950, Institut für Weltwirtschaft, Universität Kiel.
80   IG Chemie, Papier, Keramik, Jahrbuch 1949–1950, o. O., o. J., S. 25.
81   Abschrift hergestellt vom Bundesverband des Deutschen Gewerkschaftsbundes
     und vom Hauptvorstand der Industriegewerkschaft "Chemie, Papier, Keramik"
     und an die Alliierte Hohe Kommission geschickt, gez. Böckler, 6. September 1950,
     Institut für Weltwirtschaft, Universität Kiel. This document was patterned after
     a document that the Chemical Workers Union produced and distributed under
     joint signature with the German Confederation of Labor in November 1949.
     Stellungnahme der Gewerkschaften zur Neuordnung der I. G. Farbenindustrie
     Aktiengesellschaft, o. O., o. J., Bundesarchiv Koblenz B 102/338. The Office
     Employees Union also made statements similar to these. DAG, Die Neuordnung
     der I. G. Farbenindustrie A. G., Eine Stellungnahme der Deutschen Angestellten
     Gewerkschaft, Hamburg, 1950, Hoechst Archiv. The Confederation of Labor,
     at its founding convention in Munich in October 1949, adopted the Munich
     program, which called for the conversion of basic industries to public ownership,
     full co-determination, and conversion of the national economy to central
     planning. Its chairman was Hans Böckler. Chu Hanami, *Rodokumiai no seijiteki
     yakuwari: Doitsu niokeru keiken* (The Political Role of Labor Unions: The German
     Experience)), Miraisha, 1965, pp. 324–40; Shigeyoshi Tokunaga, German
     capitalism and industrial relations, in: Hideo Totsuka and Shigeyoshi Tokunaga,
     eds, *Gendai rodo mondai: roshi kankei no rekishiteki dotai to kozo* (Contemporary
     Labor Problem: Historical Dynamics and Structure of Industrial Relations),
     Yuhikaku, 1977, pp. 290–1.
82   *Frankfurter Allgemeine Zeitung*, 5 September 1950, Institut für Weltwirtschaft,
     Universität Kiel. On the reaction of labor unions, see also *Die Welt*, 5 September

1950; *Hamburger Echo*, 5 September 1950, Institut far Weltwirtschaft, Universität Kiel.

83 *Gewerkschaftspost*, Nr. 19, 16 September 1950, IG Chemie Archiv. This newspaper is the house organ of the Chemical Workers Union.

84 Arbeitsgemeinschaft Chemische Industrie, Rundschreiben Nr. 5/49, 26 November 1949, Bundesarchiv Koblenz B 102/338; Auszug aus "I. G. Farbenindustrie AG. Beschleunigte Aufteilung statt Chemietreuhandverband", herausgegeben von der Arbeitsgemeinschaft der Schutzvereinigungen für Wertpapierbesitz, Dezember 1949, in: Hoechst, *Der Hoechst-Konzern entsteht*, op. cit., S. 54–6; *Die Welt*, 1 Juli 1950, Institut für Weltwirtschaft, Universität Kiel.

85 *Die Welt*, 18 August 1950, Institut für Weltwirtschaft, Universität Kiel.

86 Office of the U. S. High Commission for Germany, Incoming Message, Hays, 31 August 1950, RG 466 Box 18, National Archives, Washington, D. C.

87 Hans Booms (Hrsg.), *Die Kabinettsprotokolle der Bundesregierung*, Band 2, 1950, Boppard am Rhein, 1984, S. 663, 669.

88 *Die Welt*, 4 September 1950; *Düsseldorfer Nachrichten*, 4. September 1950, Institut für Weltwirtschaft, Universität Kiel.

89 Booms, op. cit., S. 716.

90 Prentzel, Vermerk, 12 September 1950, Bundesarchiv Koblenz B 102/339.

91 *Informationsdienst*. Wirtschaft, Nr. 157, 4 September 1950, Bundesarchiv Koblenz B 102/339.

92 *Frankfurter Allgemeine Zeitung*, 29 August 1950, Institut für Weltwirtschaft, Universität Kiel.

93 Clippings from or introductions to this article may be found in a number of archives. The Rhein-Ruhr Bank, one of the successors to the dissolved Dresdner Bank, reprinted this article and distributed it internally and externally to related agencies and firms. Bayer Archiv, Sekt. Haberland, Besatzung 1945–1951, Sigu. 271/1.1. 10.

94 *Handelsblatt*, 6 September 1950; *Die Zeit*, 7 September 1950; Herbert Gross, Im Schatten Morgenthaus, in: *Der Leitartikel*, Jahrgang 1, Nr. 53, 1 September 1950, Institut für Weltwirtschaft, Universität Kiel.

95 *Frankfurter Allgemeine Zeitung*, 15 September 1950, Institut für Weltwirtschaft, Universität Kiel.

96 Kreikamp argues that the foundations for non-political, specialized discussions between the Allied powers and Germany were laid by Law Number 35 (Kreikamp, op. cit., S. 244). He fails to mention, however, the nearly unanimous, violent reaction of the various German actors toward the law, the process by which this led to the initiation of negotiations, and the judgments and strategies of the various actors. For this reason his conclusions probably overemphasize the apolitical and specialized character of the negotiations. Plumpe criticizes Kreikamp's piece for "assuming that the interested parties accepted this law relatively affirmatively," and this paper makes essentially the same critique. Plumpe, op. cit., S. 757–8, Anm. 44.

97 Prentzel, Vermerk, 12 September 1950, Bundesarchiv Koblenz B 102/339.

98 Office of the U. S. High Commissioner for Germany, Incoming Message, Hays, 31 August 1950, RG 466 Box 18, National Archives, Washington, D. C.

99 C. E. Marshall (Chairman, Economics Committee of the Allied High Commission) to Erhard, 31 August 1950, Bundesarchiv Koblenz, B 102/339.

100 Prentzel, Vermerk, 12 September 1950, Bundesarchiv Koblenz B 102/339.

[101] Hillgruber, op. cit., S. 58–9.

[102] Minutes of the Twentieth Meeting of the Council of the Allied High Commission with the Chancelor of the German Federal Government, 23 September 1950, RG 466 Box 19, National Archives, Washington, D. C.

[103] Prentzel, Vermerk, 19 September 1950, Bundesarchiv Koblenz, B 102/339.

[104] Adenauer an Ivone Kirkpatrick (Geschäftsführende Vorsitzende, Alliierte Hohe Kommission), 2 Oktober 1950, Bundesarchiv Koblenz, B 102/342a. The model for the Adenauer letter is in Kolfen, Vermerk, 29 August 1950, Bundesarchiv Koblenz, B 102/338.

[105] Entwurf Vorschläge der Bundesregierung an die Alliierte Hohe Kommission zur Aufteilung der I. G. Farbenindustrie A. G., 18 Oktober 1950; Entwurf Aufteilung und Abwicklung der I. G. Farbenindustrie A. G., 18 Oktober 1950; Begründung zu Rechtsvorschriften über Aufteilung (und) Abwicklung der I. G. Farbenindustrie A. G., Bundesarchiv Koblenz, B 102/342a. The Federal Government proposal is also recorded in: Hoechst, *Der Hoechst-Konzern entsteht*, op. cit., S. 79–82; Booms, op. cit., S. 791–2.

[106] Protokoll über die Besprechung Erhards mit den Economic Advisers (Vorsitz-General McReady) am 19 Oktober 1950, 20 Oktober 1950, Bundesarchiv Koblenz, B102/405. Note that "McReady" is correctly spelled "Macready."

[107] Kirkpatrick an Adenauer, 26 October 1950, Bundesarchiv Koblenz, B 102/342a.

[108] U. S. Allied High Commisssioner for Germany, Press Release No. 240, RG466 Box 21, National Archives, Washington, D. C.; *Die Neue Zeitung*, 2 November 1950, Hoechst Archiv.

[109] For example, see *Industriekurier*, 11 November 1950; *Handelsblatt*, 15 November 1950, Institut für Weltwirtschaft, Universität Kiel.

[110] Erhard an Adenauer, 31 Oktober 1950, Bundesarchiv Koblenz, B 102/405.

[111] Memorandum by U. S. member of Legislative Drafting sub-committee, Dissolution, Liquidation and Dispersion of I. G. Farbenindustrie A. G., 4 April 1950; 9 May 1950; 10 May 1950, RG 260 Box 330 11 11 –2 8 (no title), National Archives, Washington, D. C.

[112] Macready to U. S. and French Economic Adviser, 23 August 1950; Draft Paper for Submission to the Council; Macready to U. S. and French Economic Adviser, 18 September 1950; Council of the Allied High Commission, Status of the TRIFCO (Tripartite IG Farben Control Office), 18 September 1950, Institut für Zeitgeschichte, OMGUS-Unterlagen, 17/8248/19.

[113] British Paper. Interpretation of Law 35, 21 September 1950; French/US Paper. Interpretation of Law 35, 22 September 1950; TRIFCOG (Tripartite IG Farben Control Group) to Economics Committee, 22 September Institut für Zeitgeschichte, OMGUS-Unterlagen, 17/8248/19.

[114] Fowles to Newman, 22 September 1950; Newman to Fowles, 26 September 1950; Newman, TRIFCOG Work: Past and Future, 5 October 1950, Institut für Zeitgeschichte, OMGUS-Unterlagen, 17/8248/15; Fowles to Newman, 25 September 1950; Newman to Fowles, 28 October 1950, Institut für Zeitgeschichte, OMGUS-Unterlagen, 17/8248/19.

[115] Newman, TRIFCOG Works: Past and Future, 5 October 1950, Institut für Zeitgeschichte, OGMUS-Unterlagen, 17/8248/15; Hoechst, *Der Hoechst-Konzern entsteht*, op. cit., Einführung, S. 14.

116 Slater to Dittmann, 23 November 1950, Bundesarchiv Koblenz, B 102/342a; Auszug aus dem ABD-Plan, in: Hoechst, *Der Hoechst-Konzern entsteht*, op. cit., S. 100–6.

117 Amick to Newman, 19 September 1950, Institut für Zeitgeschichte, OGMUS-Unterlagen, 17/8248/15.

118 Bücher an Adenauer, 9 Dezember 1950, Bundesarchiv Koblenz, B 102/414.

119 Alliierte Hohe Kommission für Deutschland an Blankenhorn (Bundeskanzleramt), November 1950, Bundesarchiv Koblenz, B 102/342a.

120 Günther, Vermerk über eine Besprechung mit den Wirtschaftsberatern und den Leitern der Decartelisation and Industrial Deconcentration Group der Alliierten Hohen Kommission am 22 November 1950, 23 November 1950, Bundesarchiv Koblenz, B 102/342a.

121 Erhard an Adenauer, (14) Dezember 1950, Bundesarchiv Koblenz, B 102/364.

122 Entwurf. Adenauer an Geschäftsführenden der Alliierten Hohen Kommission, (18.) Dezember 1950, Bundesarchiv Koblenz, B 102/342a, 102/364. See also Begleitschreiben und Memoranden (Auszüge) der Bundesregierung an die AHK vom 18 Dezember 1950, in: Hoechst, *Der Hoechst-Konzern entsteht*, op. cit., S. 126–30; *Frankfurter Allgemeine Zeitung*, 19 Dezember 1950, Institut für Weltwirtschaft, Universität Kiel.

123 J. E. Slater (Secretary General) to Dittmann, 23 November 1950, Bundesarchiv Koblenz B 102/342a.

124 Günther, Vermerk über eine Besprechung mit den Wirtschaftsberatern und den Leitern der Decartelisation and Industrial Deconcentration Group der Alliierten Hohen Kommission am 22 November 1950, 23 November 1950, Bundesarchiv Koblenz B 102/342a.

125 Entwurf Adenauer an Geschäftsführenden Vorsitzenden der Alliierten Hohen Kommission, Dezember 1950, Bundesarchiv Koblenz, B 102/342a.

126 *Frankfurter Allgemeine Zeitung*, 28 November 1950; 13 Dezember 1950, Institut für Weltwirtschaft, Universität Kiel.

127 *Frankfurter Rundschau*, 28 September 1950; *Wiesbadener Kurier*, 28 September 1950; Hilpert an Adenauer, 4 November 1950; Adenauer an Hilpert, 6 November 1950, Hoechst Archiv.

128 von Rospatt, Vermerk über die Besprechung am 6 Dezember 1950 mit den Vertretern der Wirtschaftsministerien der Länder (Hessen, Bayern, Rheinland/Pfalz, Württenberg-Hohenzollern), Dezember 1950, Bundesarchiv Koblenz, B 102/414.

129 Prentzel, Vermerk, 20 September 1950, Bundesarchiv Koblenz, B 102/339; Interpellation der Fraktion der CDU, FDP und DP (Entwurf), September 1950; Interpellation der Fraktion der CDU/CSU, FDP und DP, 21 September 1950, Bundesarchiv Koblenz, B 102/338; Interpellation der Fraktion der CDU/CSU, SPD, FDP, DP, BP, des Zentrums und der WAV, 5 Oktober 1950, Bundesarchiv Koblenz, B 102/339. Note that subsequently, also on 15 November, the aforementioned eight parties submitted the joint questionnaire. *Die Neue Zeitung*, 14 November 1950; *Die Welt*, 16 November 1950; *Handelsblatt*, 17 November 1950, Institut für Weltwirtschaft, Universität Kiel.

130 Prentzel an Erlenbach, 27 Oktober 1950, Hoechst Archiv.

131 Menne an Erlenbach, 4 November 1950; Erlenbach an Menne, 6 November 1950, Hoechst Archiv.

132 Stellungnahme zum I. G.-Gesetz Nr. 35, Hoechst Archiv 3/84; Bayer Archiv, Sekt. Haberland, Besatzung 1945–1951, Sigu. 271/1.1.10.

133 Menne an Erlenbach, 23 November 1950, Hoechst Archiv.
134 Stichwort für die Besprechung (Menne-McCloy), 11 November 1950, Bundesarchiv Koblenz, B 102/414.
135 BASF an Prentzel, 12 Dezember 1950, Bundesarchiv Koblenz, B 102/364.
136 Thiesing, Vermerk, 7 Dezember 1950, Bundesarchiv Koblenz, B 102/364.
137 *Der Tagesspiegel*, 6 Dezember 1950, Institut für Weltwirtschaft, Universität Kiel. In this newspaper reporting, however, the separation of Titanium Industies was to bring about "especially serious and alarming difficulties," an assertion which runs counter to the source cited in note 136.
138 Erlenbach an Menne, 6 November 1950; Karl Winnacker, Ansprache anläßlich der Hauptversammlung der Farbwerke Hoechst AG am 20 Juli 1950, S. 75; do, Eine neue deutsche IG ist nicht sinnvoll, 16 Januar 1970, S. 1600, Hoechst Archiv.
139 Menne an Erhard, 10 Dezember 1950, Bundesarchiv Koblenz, B 102/364.
140 Bücher an Adenauer, 9 Dezember 1950, Bundesarchiv Koblenz, B 102/414.
141 *Handelsblatt*, 13 Dezember 1950, Institut für Weltwirtschaft, Universität Kiel.
142 Erhard an Adenauer, (14) Dezember 1950, Bundesarchiv Koblenz, B 102/364.
143 von Rospatt, Vermerk (Entwurf), Betr.: Sitzung des Wirtschaftspolitischen Ausschusses des Bundestages am 9 Januar 1951, Januar 1951, Bundesarchiv Koblenz, B 102/414; Deutscher Bundestag, Kurzprotokoll aus der Sitzung des Ausschusses, Nr. 13 am 9 Januar 1951, 10 Januar 1951, Hoechst Archiv.
144 Aktennotiz. Besprechung mit verschiedenen Vertretern der Gewerkschaften (10 November 1950), Bundesarchiv Koblenz, B 102/397.
145 Aktenvermerk über eine Besprechung mit dem Bundesvorstand des DGB am 20 November 1950, 27 November 1950, Bundesarchiv Koblenz, B 102/397.
146 Gefeller an Erhard, 24 November 1950; IG Chemie, Stellungnahme zum Gesetzentwurf der Bundesregierung, Bundesarchiv Koblenz, B 102/405.
147 von Rospatt, Vermerk, Bter.: Besprechung mit Vertretern der Gewerkschaften am 6 Dezember 1950, Dezember 1950, Bundesarchiv Koblenz, B 102/397; vom Hoff (DGB) an Prentzel, 11 Dezember 1950, Bundesarchiv Koblenz, B 102/364.
148 Spaethen an Bundeswirtschaftsministerium, 29 November 1950, Bundesarchiv Koblenz, B 102/397.
149 Erhard an Adenauer, (14) Dezember 1950, Bundesarchiv Koblenz, B 102/364.
150 Richter (IG-Chemie), Petersen (Arbeitsgemeinschaft), Betr.: Unterredung mit Adenauer und Erhard am 20 Dezember 1950, Bundesarchiv Koblenz, B 102/405.
151 Gefeller, F. Brünger an Adenauer, 26 Januar 1951, DGB Archiv, 1951. See also *Welt der Arbeit*, 2 Februar 1951; IG Chemie, Papier, Keramik, Jahrbuch 1951, o. O., o. J., S. 24–25, DGB Archiv AIK/p/28.
152 *Frankfurter Allgemeine Zeitung*, 13 März 1951, Institut für Weltwirtschaft, Universität Kiel; IG Chemie, Papier, Keramik, op. cit., S. 25. Note that the legislation of co-determination for the coal and steel industries that was based on the January 1951 agreement was not completed until 21 May of that year. Hanami, op. cit., pp. 381–3; Tokunaga, op. cit., pp. 283–93.
153 Erste Stellungnahme des Bundesministeriums für Wirtschaft zu den Ausführungen in dem Bericht des Tripartite Untersuchungsausschusses (Amick-Gutachten) zum Komplex Leverkusen, 16 Januar 1951; Erste Stellungnahme des Bundesministeriums für Wirtschaft zu den Ausführungen in dem Bericht des Tripartite Untersuchungsausschusses (ABD-Gutachten) ohne den bereits

behandelten Komplex Leverkusen, 23 Januar 1951, Bundesarchiv Koblenz, B 102/342a.

[154] Akten-Notiz über die Besprechung betreffend Entflechtungsfragen der I. G. Farben am 23 Januar 1951, Bundesarchiv Koblenz, B 102/342a.

[155] Akten-Notiz über die Besprechung betreffend Entflechtungsfragen der I. G. Farben am 27 Januar 1951, Bundesarchiv Koblenz, B 102/342a.

[156] Vorschläge des Bundesministeriums für Wirtschaft für die rechtliche Form des Anschlusses der A G. für Stickstoffdünger (Knapsack) an die Maingruppe, 27 Januar 1951; Begründung des Bundesministeriums für Wirtschaft für eine Fusionierung der Sauerstoff-Gruppe mit der A G. für Stickstoffdünger (Knapsack), 27 Januar 1951, Bundesarchiv Koblenz, B 102/342a. See also *Handelsblatt*, 29 Januar 1951, Institut für Weltwirtschaft, Universität Kiel.

[157] Akten-Notiz über die Besprechung betreffend Entflechtungsfragen der I. G. Farben am 27 Januar 1951, Bundesarchiv Koblenz, B 102/342a.

[158] Kreikamp's work focuses on these negotiations (Kreikamp, op. cit., S. 234–42). It is affected by time biases in the sources upon which he relied in the Bayer archives. In other words, it seems that there were almost no documents to be found for the period from August through December 1950 in the archive. Perhaps for that reason Kreikamp's paper gives rather exaggerated praise to the January 1951 negotiations and assesses too lightly the negotiations through December 1950 as well as the significance of December's basic agreement concerning Farben's three-way division.

[159] Handley-Derry to Blankenhorn, 17 April 1951, Bundesarchiv Koblenz, B 102/371.

[160] Adenauer an Handley-Derry, 27 April 1951, Bundesarchiv Koblenz, B 102/371.

[161] *Die Welt*, 20 April 1951, Institut für Weltwirtschaft, Universität Kiel.

[162] Adenauer an Handley-Derry, 27 April 1951; McCloy an Adenauer, 17 Mai 1951, Bundesarchiv Koblenz, B 102/371; *Industriekurier*, 26 Mai 1951; *Frankfurter Allgemeine Zeitung*, 25 August 1951; *Die Welt*, 16 Januar 1952; *Frankfurter Allgemeine Zeitung*, 17 Januar 1952, Institut für Weltwirtschaft, Universität Kiel.

[163] Slater an Blankenhorn, 4 Mai 1951; Dittmann an Slater, 18 Mai 1951, Bundesarchiv Koblenz, B 102/371.

[164] *Frankfurter Allgemeine Zeitung*, 8 Dezember 1951; *Handelsblatt*, 21 Dezember 1951; *Frankfurter Allgemeine Zeitung*, 31 Januar 1952, Institut für Weltwirtschaft, Universität Kiel.

[165] Winnacker, op. cit., S. 171–4.

[166] Wurster, op. cit., S. 8–9.

[167] I. G. Farbenindustrie Aktiengesellschaft in Liquidation, op. cit., S. 21; Hoechst, *Der Hoechst-Konzern entsteht*, op. cit., Einführung, S. 16.

[168] Reichelt, op. cit., S. 80–1.

[169] I. G. Farbenindustrie Aktiengesellschaft in Liquidation, op. cit., S. 33.

[170] *Handelsblatt*, 5 Dezember 1952; *Frankfurter Allgemeine Zeitung*, 6 Dezember 1952; *Die Welt*, 6 Dezember 1952, 12 Dezember 1952, 24 Dezember 1952; *Handelsblatt*, 24 Dezember 1952; *Die Welt*, 29 Januar 1953; *Frankfurter Allgemeine Zeitung*, 19 März 1953; Winnacker, op. cit., S. 208–12. Note that there are discrepancies between Winnacker's memoirs and newspaper reports concerning the disposition of Kalle; this paper has followed Winnacker's account.

[171] Winnacker, op. cit., S. 213–16. I.G. Farbenindustrie in Liquidation made public its starting Deutsche mark balance sheet in June 1952 (Reichelt, op. cit., S. 82). With the establishment of this company, the successor firms were no longer

liable for any claims or retroactive demands in the subsequent rebuilding process (Winnacker, op. cit., S. 193).

I.G. Farbenindustrie in Liquidation continued to exist after this, and like a ghost emerged with the unification of East and West Germany in 1990. The company asserted its claims against former IG Farben assets that had become state-owned enterprises in the former East Germany. The object of these claims were 151 million square meters of land, buildings, factories, and 130,000 square meters of property in Berlin. At the end of November 1991, 400 out of an estimated 30,000 holders of interests in the company assembled in Frankfurt am Main to discuss changing the company's articles of incorporation to allow the production and sale of chemicals and pharmaceuticals and the execution of the necessary business for liquidation. The price of a share in the liquidation company rose from 8 to 28 Deutsche mark (*Der Tagesspiegel*, 22 November 1991). During the privatization process for former state-owned firms, though, ex-IG Farben assets did not fall into the hands of the liquidation company, notwithstanding that firm's request.

172 For details on what follows, see Hoechst, *Der Hoechst-Konzern entsteht,* op. cit., Einführung, S. 17, and Wurster, op, cit., S. 10; *Frankfurter Allgemeine Zeitung,* 21 März 1953.

173 I. G. Farbenindustrie Aktiengesellschaft in Liquidation, op. cit., S. 25. Based on the Business Organization Law enacted in July 1952, one third of the membership of the board of auditors must be occupied by employee representatives. On the Business Organization Law, see Hanami, op. cit., pp. 419–20, and Tokunaga, op. cit., p. 292.

174 Reichelt gives a somewhat different explanation of the allocation of shares in firms other than the four successor companies (Reichelt, op. cit., S. 93).

175 *Der Volkswirt,* Beilage: Chemische Industrie, 3 April 1954, Institut für Weltwirtschaft, Universität Kiel.

176 I. G. Farbenindustrie Aktiengesellschaft in Liquidation, op. cit., Anhang, S. 12–21; Hoechst, *Der Hoechst-Konzern entsteht,* op. cit., Einführung, S. 17; *Handelsblatt,* 4. Februar 1955.

177 I. G. Farbenindustrie Aktiengesellschaft in Liquidation, op. cit.

178 *Die Zeit,* 7 September 1950, Institut für Weltwirtschaft, Universität Kiel.

179 Karl Winnacker, Übertragung der Hoechst zugesprochenen Werke und Beteiligungen aus dem Vermögen der I. G. Farbenindustrie, 27 März 1953, S. 5–6, Hoechst Archiv; do., *Nie den Mut verlieren,* op. cit., S. 482–3.

180 Kreikamp, op. cit., S. 220. Again, see note 96 above.

181 Plumpe, op. cit., S. 758.

182 Wolfgang Heintzelner, Die Neugundung der BASF ma 28. 3. 1953, in: *Die BASF,* Jahrgang 3, 1953, BASF-Archiv.

183 Gross, op. cit., S. 48–9.

184 Ibid., S. 50. Note that measures prohibiting the repayment of old debt were again confirmed in September 1950.

185 Winnacker, op. cit., S. 168–9.

Chapter 9

1 Surveying the historical research dealing with the petrochemical industry, we observe a wealth of excellent studies in the fields of industrial and technological history. The

most representative works in industrial history are: Tsunetada Kawate and Mitsuo Bono, *Sekiyu Kagaku Kogyo* (The Petrochemical Industry) (revised edition) (Tokyo, 1970) and Tokuji Watanabe (ed.), *Sengo Nihon Kagaku Kogyoshi* (History of the Post-war Japanese Chemical Industry) (Tokyo, 1973). Readers may also consult Hiroaki Yamazaki's case study of industrial complexes including Japanese petrochemicals in the following work: "Kawasaki Fukugo Sekiyukagaku Konbinato no Seiritsu to Tenkai: Showa 30-nendai wo chushinni" (Formation and Development of Kawasaki Compound Petrochemical Complex: A Focus on the 1955–1965) in: *Kanagawa Kenshi Kakuronhen 2 Sangyo/Keizai* (Kanagawa Prefecture History. Particulars. Vol. 2: Industry and Economy) (1983). As for industrial history with the addition of policy history, we can find research of exceptional quality conducted by the Japanese Petrochemical Association in *Sekiyu Kagaku Kogyo 10-nenshi* (A Ten-year History of the Petrochemical Industry) (1971). In comparison, research on business or company history is scarce. Though companies are mentioned in industrial and technological histories, systematic research is limited. As for business or company histories containing technological history, readers should consult: Toshiaki Chokki, "Gijutsu Donyu no futatsuno Kata: Scale Merit Tsuikyugata to Kakushingata" (Two Types of Technology Introduction: Scale Merit-oriented and Innovation-oriented), in: Masaaki Kobayashi et al. (eds), *Nihon Keieishi wo Manabu 3 Sengo Keieishi* (Study of Japanese Business History 3 Post-war Business History) (Tokyo, 1976); Takashi Iijima, *Nihon no Kagaku Gijutsu: Kigyoshi ni miru sono Kozo* (Japan's Chemical Technology: The Structure Observed in Company Histories) (Tokyo, 1981).

[2]   Akira Kudō, *Japanese-German Business Relations: Cooperation and Rivalry in the Inter-war Period*, London, 1998, chap. 2. For more details about the fields of dyestuffs, nitrogenous fertilizer and synthetic oil, see Kudō, *IG Farben no Tainichi Senryaku –Senkanki Nichi-Doku Kigyo Kankei-shi* (IG Farben's Japan Strategy: A History of Japanese-German Business Relations during the Inter-war Period), Tokyo, 1992, chaps. 1–4. See also Kudō, Dominance through cooperation: I.G. Farben's Japan strategy, in John E. Lesch (ed.), *The German Chemical Industry in the Twentieth Century*, Kluwer Academic Publishers, 2000. This is an overall observation of the topic.

[3]   Kudō, *Japanese-German Business Relations*, chaps. 5, 6 and 7; further Kudō, *IG Farben's Japan Strategy*, chaps. 5–9. See also Akira Kudō and Motoi Ihara, Innovation through Thorough Imitation: The Consumer Chemicals Industry and the Case of Kao, Discussion Paper, Institute of Social Science, University of Tokyo..

[4]   See Final Reports of the United States Strategic Bombing Survey, National Archives, Washington, D.C., 1945–1947. For chemical industry as a whole, see Oil 109–114 (115–125), Rubber 129 (126–128), Propellants (130–133) for Germany and (Oil) 51–52, (Chemicals) 49–50. Chemicals in Japan's War. Report of the Oil and Chemical Division, February 1946 for Japan. Especially for synthetic oil industry, see Oil Division Final Report, First Edition 25 August 1945, Second Edition January 1947 for Germany, and Oil in Japan's War. Report of the Oil and Chemical Division, February 1946. Oil in Japan's War. Appendix to the Report of the Oil and Chemical Division, February 1946 for Japan.

[5]   Watanabe, 277–282.

[6]   Kudō and Ihara.

[7]   Yoshihiko Hirakawa, *Sekiyu Kagaku no Jissai Chishiki* (Actual Knowledge of Petrochemicals) (Tokyo, 1961) 160; Ministry of International Trade and Industry

(ed.), *Shoko Seisakushi 21: Kagaku Kogyo* (Ge) (Commercial and Industrial Policy History 21: Chemical Industry Vol. II) (Tokyo, 1969) 321–322.

8 Basic historical information collected at Mitsubishi Petrochemical Corporation and interviews with Mr Shigeru Fujii, 8 and 22 March 1988.

9 See Hoshimi Uchida, "Taisho Showa Shoki no Kagaku Kogyo niokeru Gijutsu Donyu to Jishu Kaihatsu: Kokusai Gijutsu Iten Katei toshite mita Gijutsu Katsudo" (Technology Introduction and Independently Initiated Development during the Taisho and Early Showa Periods: Technological Activities as seen in the Process of International Technology Transfer), in: *Keiei shigaku* (Japan Business History Review), Vol. 7, No.1, (1972) 69–70. By applying an almost identical method, Akira Kudō has attempted to analyze the process of technology transfer. Refer to Kudō, *Japanese-German Business Relations*; and Kudō, *IG Farben's Japan Strategy*.

10 Interviews with Mr. Yasuharu Torii on 1, 16, 29 October 1987. Also see Yasuharu Torii, "Gijutsu Kaihatsu no Keifu" (The Tracing of Technological Development), in: Kagaku Keizai (The Economy of the Chemical Industry) (May 1988) 30–41.

11 Yasuharu Torii's recollections, Hideo Edo, *Watashi no Mitsui Showa-shi* (My History of Mitsui during the Showa Period) (Tokyo, 1986) 177–178.

12 Noboru Nakajima, "Zadankai Kaisha Soritsu wo furikaette" (Round Table: Reminiscing on the Founding of the Company), in: Mitsui Petrochemicals internal publication, Ginto, No. 77 (1965) 15.

13 Endo, Round Table, 10.

14 Nakajima, Takeshi Hirayama, Round Table, 13. Interview with Mr Torii.

15 Nakajima, Round Table, 11; interview with Mr Torii.

16 Nakajima, Round Table, 11; interview with Mr Torii.

17 Nakajima, Round Table, 9, 11.

18 Hirayama, Round Table, 11.

19 Nakajima, Round Table, 11; interview with Mr Torii.

20 Hirayama, Round Table, 11–12.

21 Torii, Round Table, 12.

22 Hirayama, Round Table, 12.

23 Endo, Round Table, 10.

24 Endo, Round Table, 12.

25 Iijima, 274.

26 Endo, Round Table, 13.

27 Nakajima, Round Table, 9. See further Rolf Petri, *Revolution or Evolution: Competing technologies and raw materials in the synthetic rubber industry before the oil crises*, Milan, October 2000.

28 Torii's recollections, Edo, 181. Regarding Toyo Rayon's interest with nylon material phenol, also see Mitsui Petrochemical Company, *Mitsui Sekiyu Kagaku Kogyo 20-nenshi* (A Twenty-year History of Mitsui Petrochemical Corporation) (1978) 13–14.

29 Interview with Mr Torii.

30 A Twenty-year History of Mitsui Petrochemical Corporation, 33–4.

31 Endo, Round Table, 16–17.

32 A Twenty-year History of Mitsui Petrochemical Corporation, 32.

33 See A Twenty-year History of Mitsui Petrochemical Corporation, 10–14, 19–27.

34 Endo, Round Table, 17; Torii's recollections, 182; Interview with Mr Torii.

[35] Karl Winnacker, Nie den Mut verlieren. Erinnerungen an Schicksalsjahre der deutschen Chemie, Düsseldorf, 1974 (second edition) 243.

[36] A Twenty-year History of Mitsui Petrochemical Corporation, 48–49; interviews with Mr Torii. Also, ibid., 14–19.

[37] Mitsubishi Yuka KK, *Mitsubishi Yuka 30-nenshi* (A Thirty-year History of Mitsubishi Petrochemical) (1988) 34–35,40.

[38] Ibid., 68–73.

[39] Mitsubishi Yuka KK, *Nihon Sekiyu Kagaku Kogyo Seiritsushi Ko* (A Consideration of the History of the Formation of Japan's Petrochemical Industry) (1970), basic company history documents, and interviews with Mr Shigeru Fujii. I was also kindly granted an interview with Mr Yoshiro Tokuhisa, 19 October 1987, and given great assistance by being shown historical documents.

[40] Memoirs of Kamesaburo Ikeda Editing Committee, *Ikeda Kamesaburo* (Tokyo, 1978) 316; recollections of A.R.G. Raybern.

[41] Ibid., 230–231, recollections of Kanzo Tanaka.

[42] A Thirty-year History of Mitsubishi Petrochemical, 74–75. Later, however, witnessing an improvement in the results of Yuka's sales, Shell requested that its shares be increased to as much as 50%. As a result of the ensuing negotiations, as capital increased in 1960, Shell's ratio rose by 32.5%. Basic company history documents.

[43] A Thirty-year History of Mitsubishi Petrochemical, 77–78.

[44] Basic company history documents.

[45] Basic company history documents and interview with Mr Fujii.

[46] Basic company history documents.

[47] Ibid.

[48] Ibid., 78–79, basic company history documents.

[49] On this point, see Kudō, *IG Farben's Japan Strategy*, Chaps. 5, 6 and 7.

[50] A Thirty-year History of Mitsubishi Petrochemical, 80; basic company history documents and interview with Mr Fujii.

[51] A Thirty-year History of Mitsubishi Petrochemical, 81; basic company history documents and interview with Mr Fujii.

[52] A Thirty-year History of Mitsubishi Petrochemical, 105.

[53] Ikeda Kamesaboro, 148, Makoto Okuma's recollections.

[54] Basic company history documents and interview with Mr Fujii.

[55] Winnacker, 456–457.

[56] For questions of differentiation and homogeneity of business strategies in post-war Japanese business history, see "Dai 23 kai taikai toitsu rondai 'Sengo Keieishi wo kaerimiru' togi hokoku" (The Topic of General Debate at the 23rd Meeting: 'Reflecting on Post-war Business History' Report for discussion), in: *Keiei shigaku* (Japan Business History Review), Vol. 23, No. 1 (1988) 102–103.

[57] Nakajima, Round Table, 15.

[58] Hirayama, Round Table, 15.

[59] Toshimasa Tsuruta, "'Sangyo Seisaku' to Kigyo Keiei – 'Nihon Kabushiki Kaisha' no Keisei Katei no Bunseki," ('Industrial Policy' and Business Management: Analysis of the Formation of 'Japan, Inc.'), in: Kobayashi et al., 136–137.

[60] Commercial and Industrial Policy History: Chemical Industry, Vol. II, 317–320.

[61] Ibid., 224.

[62] Morikawa, 111.

63 Hirakawa, 80–81.
64 Winnacker, 236–247.
65 Interview with Mr Fujii; Junzo Ishii, Akihiro Okumura, Tadao Kagono, lkujiro Nonaka, *Keiei Senryakuron* (Management Strategies) (Yuhikaku, 1985) 136–137.
66 A Thirty-year History of Japan Petrochemicals, 29.
67 A Ten-year History of the Petrochemical Industry, 197.
68 Kawate and Bono, 146.
69 For further details, see A Ten-year History of the Petrochemical Industry, 97–101.
70 A Twenty-year History of Mitsui Petrochemical, 59.
71 Interviews with Mr Torii.
72 A Twenty-year History of Mitsui Petrochemical, 97 and interview with Mr Torii.
73 A Twenty-year History of Mitsui Petrochemical, 64–65.
74 A Thirty-year History of Mitsubishi Petrochemical, 94–95,116–118,124–125.
75 A Ten-year History of the Petrochemical Industry, 325–327.
76 Interviews with Mr Fujii.
77 Basic company history documents and interview with Mr Fujii.
78 See each company history.
79 History of Sumitomo Chemical Industries, document 17, A Thirty-year History of Japan Petrochemicals, 272.
80 Torii's Recollections, Edo, 184–185.
81 A Twenty-year History of Mitsui Petrochemical, 128–129, 159.
82 A Twenty-year History of Mitsui Petrochemical, 92, 109–110, and interview with Mr Torii.
83 Ibid., 130.
84 A Twenty-year History of Mitsui Petrochemical, 157–178.
85 Basic company history documents and interview with Mr Fujii. Regarding the example of Mitsubishi Petrochemical's development of its own technology, see A Thirty-year History of Mitsubishi Petrochemical, 259.
86 Ibid., 434.
87 Japan Petrochemicals KK, *Nihon Sekiyu Kagaku 30-nenshi* (A Thirty-year History of Japan Petrochemicals) (1987) 250.
88 Ibid.
89 See Barbara Molony "Innovation and Business Strategy in the Prewar Japanese Chemical Industry," in: Keiichiro Nakagawa and Tsunehiko Yui (eds), *Japanese Management in Historical Perspective. Proceedings of the 15th Fuji Conference,* (Tokyo, 1989); Akira Kudō Comment in: ibid.

Chapter 10

1 A. Kudō, 'Americanization or Europeanization? The Globalization of the Japanese Economy', in G.D. Hook and H. Hasegawa (eds), *The Political Economy of Japanese Globalization,* London: Routledge, 2001, pp. 120–36.
2 See, for example, R. Whidey (ed.), *The Changing European Firm: Limits to Convergence,* London: Routledge, 1996 and D. Held et al., *Global Transformations. Politics, Economics and Culture,* Oxford: Polity Press, 1999.
3 H.G. Schröter, 'What is Americanisation? Or About the Use and Abuse of the Americanisation-Concept', in D. Barjot, I. Lescent-Giles and M. de Ferrière le Vayer (eds), *L'Americanisation en Europe au XXe Siècle: Economie, culture, politique.*

Americanisation in 20th Century Europe: Economics, Culture, Politics, vol. 1, Lille: CRHEN-O, Universitè Charles de Gaulle-Lille 3, 2002, pp. 41–57.

4   M. Albert, *Capitalisme contre Capitalisme,* Paris: Seuil, 1991; Y. Fukada and R. Dore, *Nihongata shihonshugi nakushile nan no nihon ka* (What Japan without Japanese Style of Capitalism?), Tokyo: Kobunsha, 1993. Dore later modified his tone in his book: *Stock Market Capitalism: Welfare Capitalism. Japan and Germany versus the Anglo-Saxons,* Oxford: Oxford University Press, 2000.

5   K.S. Molony, 'Japanese and Germans as Business Partners: Should America Care?', *USJP Occasional Paper 94–07,* Harvard University, 1994.

6   See, for example, D. Yui, M. Nakamura and N. Toyoshita (eds), *Senryo kaikaku no kokusai hikaku: Nihon ajia yoroppa* (International Comparison of Reform under Occupation), Tokyo: Sansei Do, 1994.

7   See, for example, K. Demizu, *Nichi-doku keizai hikaku ron* (Comparative Studies on Japanese and German Economy), Tokyo: Yuhikaku, 1981.

8   See, for example, A. Forsberg, *America and the Japanese Miracle. The Cold War Context of Japan's Postwar Economic Revival, 1950–1960,* Chapel Hill: The University of North Carolina Press, 2000; L. Lindlar, *Das mißverstandene Wirtschaftswunder. Westdeutschland und die westeuropäische Nachkriegsprosperität,* Tübingen: Mohr Siebeck, 1997.

9   V.R. Berghahn, *Unternehmer und Polilik in der Bundesrepublik,* Frankfurt am Main: Suhrkamp, 1985; *The Amercanisation of West German Industry 1945–1973,* Leamington Spa: Berg, 1986; V.R. Berghahn and D. Karsten, *Industrial Relations in Germany,* Leamington Spa: Berg, 1987; V.R. Berghahn, 'Wiederaufbau und Umbau der westdeutschen Industrie nach dem Zweiten Weltkrieg', *Tel Aviver Jahrbuch für deutsche Geschichte,* 1990, vol. XIX, pp. 261–82; 'Technology and the Export of Industrial Culture: Problems of the German-American Relationship 1900–1960', in P. Mathias and J.A. Davis (eds), *Innovation and Technology in Europe: From the Eighteenth Century to the Present Day,* Oxford: Blackwell, 1991, pp. 142–61; 'Deutschland im "American Century"', 1942–1992. Einige Argumente zur Amerikanisierungsfrage', in M. Frese and P. Michael (eds), *Politische Zäsuren und gesellschaftlicher Wandel im 20. Jahrhundert. Regionale und vergleichende Perspektiven,* Paderborn: Schoningh, 1996, pp. 789–800.

10 H. Hartmann, *Authority and Organization in German Management,* Princeton: Princeton University Press, 1959; *Amerikanische Firmen in Deutschland,* Köln: Westdeutscher Verlag, 1963.

11 W. Link, *Deutsche und amerikanische Gewerkschaften und Geschäftsleute 1945–1975. Eine Studie iiber transnationale Beziehungen,* Düsseldorf: Droste, 1978.

12 M. Kipping and O. Bjarnar (eds), *The Americanisation of European Business. The Marshall Plan and the Transfer of US Management Models,* London: Routledge, 1998; M.-L. Djelic, *Exporting the American Model. The Postwar Transformation of European Business,* Oxford: Oxford University Press, 1998; H.G. Schröter and E. Moen (eds), 'Americanization as a Concept for a Deeper Understanding of Economic Changes, 1945–1970', *Enterprises el Histoire,* 1999, no. 19, pp. 5–13; J. Zeitlin and G. Herrigel (eds), *Americanization and its Limits: Reworking US Technology and Management in Post-War Europe and Japan,* Oxford: Oxford University Press, 2000; M. Kipping and N. Tiratsoo (eds), *Americanisation in 20th Century Europe: Business, Culture, Politics,* vol. 2, Lille: CRHEN-O, Université Charles de Gaulle-Lille 3, 2002.

13 J. Hashimoto (ed.), *Nihon kigyo shisutemu no sengoshi* (Japanese Enterprise System since 1945), Tokyo: University of Tokyo Press, 1996; J. Hashimoto, S. Hasegawa and H. Miyajima, *Gendai nihon keizai* (Modern Japanese Economy), Tokyo: Yuhikaku, 1998.

14 A first interesting attempt was made for the steel industry by G. Herrigel, 'American Occupation, Market Order, and Democracy: Reconfiguring the Steel Industry in Japan and Germany after the Second World War', in Zeitlin and Herrigel (eds), *Americanization and its Limits,* pp. 340–99; see also for the similarities between Germany and Japan, compared to France and South Korea, on the one hand, and the USA on the other, M. Kipping, 'How Unique is East Asian Development? Comparing Steel Producers and Users in East Asia and Western Europe', *Asia Pacific Business Review,* Autumn 1997, vol. 4, no. 1, pp. 1–23.

15 D.A. Hounshell, *From the American System to Mass Production, 1800–1932: The Development of Manufacturing Technology in the United States,* Baltimore: The Johns Hopkins University Press, 1984; N. Suzuki, 'Universal and Specific Character of Mass-production System: With Special Consideration of American Automobile Industry', in University of Tokyo, Institute of Social Science (ed.), *20-seiki shisulemu: 2 keizai seicho I kijiku* (The 20th Century Global System: 2 Economic Growth I Core System), Tokyo: University of Tokyo Press, 1998, pp. 122–56.

16 F. Blaich, *Amerikanische Firmen in Deutschland 1890–1918. US-Direktinvestitionen im deutschen Maschinenbau,* Wiesbaden: Steiner, 1984; *Der Trustkampf (1901–1915). Ein Beitrag zum Verhalten der Ministerialbürokratie gegenüber Verbandsinteressen im Wilhelmischen Deutschland,* Berlin: Duncker & Humblot, 1975; H. Kiesewetter, 'Beasts or Beagles? Amerikanische Unternehmen in Deutschland', in H. Pohl (ed.), *Der Einfluss ausländischer Unternehmen auf die deutsche Wirtschaft vom Spätmittelalter bis zur Gegenwart,* Stuttgart: Steiner, 1992, pp. 165–96; R. Koda, *Doitsu kosaku kikai kogyo seiritushi* (An Emergence History Of German Machine Tool Industry), Tokyo: Taga Shuppan, 1994; W. Fischer, 'American Influence on German Manufacturing before World War I: The Case of Ludwig Lowe Company', in Barjot et al. (eds), *LAmericanisation en Europe,* pp. 59–70.

17 H. Homburg, *Rationalisierung und Industriearbeiterschaft: Arbeitsmarkt, Management, Arbeiterschaft im Siemens-Konzern Berlin 1900–1939,* Berlin: Haude & Spener, 1991.

18 G. Feldman, 'Foreign Penetration of German Enterprises after the First World War: the Problem of "Überfremdung"', in A. Teichova, M. Levy-Leboyer and H. Nussbaum (eds), *Historical Studies in International Corporate Business,* Cambridge/Paris: Cambridge University Press, 1989, pp. 87–110; S.A. Marin, 'L'americanisation du monde?' Etude des peurs allemandes face au "danger americain" (1897–1907)', in Barjot et al. (eds), *L'Americanisalion en Europe,* pp. 71–92; Kiesewetter, 'Beasts or Beagles?', pp. 166–7.

19 For American direct investment in Germany in the inter-war period, see M. Wilkins, *The Maturing of Multinational Entterprise: American Business Abroad from 1914 to 1970,* Cambridge, Mass.: Harvard University Press, 1974; T. Abo, *Senkanki amerika no taigai toshi: Kin'yu sangyo no kokusaika katei* (American Foreign Investment in the Inter-war Period: The Process of Internationalization of Finance and Industry), Tokyo: University of Tokyo Press, 1984.

[20] Berghahn, *The Americanisation*, pp. 146–9; R. Koda and M. Ito, 'The Development of Scientific Management in Germany', in T. Hara (ed.), *Kagakuteki kanriho no donyu to tenkai: Sono rekishitehi kokusai hikaku* (Introduction and Development of Scientific Management: an Historical International Comparison), Kyoto: Showado, 1990, pp. 161–81; M. Kipping, 'Consultancies, Institutions and the Diffusion of Taylorism in Britain, Germany and France, 1920s to 1950s', *Business History,* October 1997, vol. 39, no. 4, pp. 67–83.

[21] It remains an open debate, however, whether these large German combines ever achieved the same level of integration as their US counterparts. See T. Welskopp and C. Kleinschmidt, 'Zu viel "Scale" – zu wenig "Scope"'. Eine Auseinandersetzung mit Alfred D. Chandlers Analyse der deutschen Eisen- und Stahlindustrie in der Zwischenkriegszeit, *Jahrbuch für 'Wirtschaftsgeschichte,* 1993, vol. 2, pp. 251–97.

[22] On cartelization, see A. Kudō and T. Hara (eds), *International Cartels in Business History,* Tokyo: University of Tokyo Press, 1992; M. Kipping, *Zwischen Kartellen und Konkurrenz,* Berlin: Duncker & Humblot, 1996; H.G. Schröter, 'Cartelization and Decartelization in Europe, 1870–1995: Rise and Decline of an Economic Institution', *Journal of European Economic History,* 1996, vol. 25, no. 1, pp 129–53.

[23] On the introduction of the Taylor system into Japan, see S. Sasaki and I. Nonaka, 'The Introduction and Development of Scientific Management in Japan', in Hara (ed.), *Kagakuteki kanriho,* pp. 235–8, 241–5, 258; S. Sasaki, *Kagakuteki kanriho no nihonteki tenkai* (Japanese Development of Scientific Management), Tokyo: Yuhikaku, 1998, chaps. 1–3; W.M. Tsutsui, *Manufacturing Ideology: Scientific Management in Twentieth-Century Japan,* Princeton: Princeton University Press, 1998.

[24] J. Hashimoto and H. Takeda (eds), *Ryotaisen kanki nihon no karuteru* (Cartels in the Inter-war Japan), Tokyo: Ochanomizu Shobo, 1985.

[25] The anti-cartel law in Germany met resistance from managers and politicians; see Berghahn, *Unternehmer und Politik,* pp. 155–81; Schröter, 'Cartelization and Decartelization in Europe'. In Japan, it was early in enactment, although it was revised as early as in 1953; Committee on the Compilation of a History of International Trade and Industrial Policy (ed.), *Tsusho sangyo seisaku ski* (A History of International Trade and Industry Policy), vol. 5, Tokyo: Tsusho Sangyo Chosa Kai, 1989, pp. 243–347 (written by H. Miyajima). Management purges seem to have been more rigorous in Japan than in Germany; see Berghahn, *Unternehmer und Politik,* p. 17; P. Erker and T. Pierenkemper (eds), *Deutsche Unternehmer zwischen Kriegswirtschaft und Wiederaufbau. Studien zur 'Erfahrungsbildung von Industrie-Eliten,* München: Oldenbourg, 1999; H. Joly, *Patrons d'Allemagne, Sociologie d'une élite industrielle 1933–1989,* Paris: Presses de Sciences Po, 1996; H. Miyajima, 'Establishment of professional managers', in H. Yamazaki and T. Kikkawa (eds), *'Nihonteki' keiei no renzoku to danzetsu* (Continuity and Discontinuity of 'Japanese' Management), Tokyo: Iwanami Shoten, 1995, pp. 96–105.

[26] For reforms in Japan during the occupation period in general, see R. Miwa, *Nihon sernyo no keizai seisakushi teki kenkyu* (Historical Studies of Economic Policy in Occupied Japan), Tokyo: Nihon Keizai Hyoron Sha, 2002; for the dissolution of large enterprises in particular, see Mitsui Bunko (ed.), *Mitsui jigyo shi: Honpen dai 3-kan ge* (History of Mitsui Business Activities: Main parts, vol. 3, no. 2) (written by K Suzuki), Tokyo: Mitsui Bunko, 2001, chap. 3.

[27] See, for example, P. Kennedy, *The Rise and Fall of the Great Powers: Economic Change and Military Conflict from 1500 to 2000,* New York: Random House, 1987.

[28] See, for Germany, A. Kudō, *20-seiki doitsu shihonshugi: Kokusai teii to daikigyo taisei* (The 20th-century German Capitalism: International Orientation and Big Business System), Tokyo: University of Tokyo Press, 1999, III, chap. 2; for Japan, Sasaki, *Kagakuteki kanriho,* chap. 5; K. Sunaga, 'American Technical Assistance Programs and the Productivity Movement in Japan', *Japanese Yearbook on Business History,* 1995, vol. 12, pp. 23–38; S. Sasaki, 'The Emergence of the Productivity Improvement Movement in Postwar Japan and Japanese Productivity Missions Overseas', op. cit., pp. 39–71; T. Saito, 'Americanization and Postwar Japanese Management. A Bibliographical Approach', op. cit., pp. 5–22.

[29] See M. Kipping, 'Consultancies, Institutions' and also his chapter 2 in this volume.

[30] M. Kipping and N. Tiratsoo, 'The "Americanisation" of European Companies, Consumers and Cultures: Contents, Processes and Outcomes', in Kipping and Tiratsoo (eds), *Americanisation in 20th Century Europe,* pp. 7–23.

[31] H. Kiesewetter, 'Amerikanische Unternehmen in der Bundesrepublik Deutschland 1950–1974', in H. Kaelble (ed.), *Der Boom 1848–1973. Gesellschaftliche und wirtschaftliche Folgen in der Bundesrepublik Deutschland und in Europa,* Opladen: Westdeutscher Verlag, 1992, pp. 63–81.

[32] For the case of automation in the car industry, see D.A. Hounshell, 'Planning and Executing "Automation" at Ford Motor Company, 1945–65: The Cleveland Engine Plant and its Consequences', in H. Shiomi and K. Wada (eds), *Fordism Transformed: The Development of Methods in the Automobile Industry,* Oxford: Oxford University Press, 1996, pp. 49–86.

[33] The most recent wave in the 1990s might have been more important, but we lack both the historical distance and sufficient evidence to make a qualified assessment about it.

[34] A parallel case, Sovietization pressed upon East Germany (GDR), showed the same mechanisms and the same ends. See H.G. Schröter, 'Zur Übertragbarkeit sozialhistorischer Konzepte in die Wirtschaftsgeschichte. Amerikanisierung und Sowjetisierung in deutschen Betrieben 1945–1975', in K.H. Jarausch und H. Siegrist (eds), *Amerikanisierung und Sowjetisierung in Deutschland 1945–1970,* Frankfurt am Main: Campus, 1996, pp. 147–65.

[35] A longer lasting flow of Americanization was to be observed only in t hose branches of industry where the USA kept its position ahead of the rest of the world.

[36] See D. Granick, *The European Executive,* London: Weidenfeld & Nicholson, 1962.

[37] On American firms in Japan, see M. Mason, *American Multinationals and Japan. The Political Economy of Japanese Capital Controls, 1899–1980,* Cambridge, Mass.: Council on East Asian Studies, Harvard University, 1992.

[38] For Germany, see Summary Report (European War), 30 September 1945; Overall Report (European War), 30 September 1945; Statistical Appendix to Overall Report (European War), February 1947. For Japan, see Summary Report (Pacific War), 1 July 1946, National Archives, Washington, D.C.

[39] Berghahn, *Unternehmer und Politik,* pp. 249–51; Hartmann, *Authority; Amerikanische Firmen.*

[40] Berghahn, *Unternehmer und Politik;* Miyajima, 'Establishment'.

[41] This argument was made most forcefully by R.R. Locke, *The Collapse of the American Management Mystique,* Oxford: Oxford University Press, 1996.

Chapter 11

[1]   A.E. Musson, *Enterprise in Soap and Chemicals*, Manchester: University of Manchester Press, 1965.

[2]   M. Ihara and A. Kudō, 'Technology Transfer and Adaptation to Local Condition: Multinationalization of the Japanese Chemical Industry and the Case of Kao', CIRJE Discussion Paper Series F-106, University of Tokyo, February 2001.

[3]   For the history of Kao in the pre-war period, see S. Hattori and Y. Kobayashi, *Kao sekken 50-nen shi* (*A 50 Year History of Kao Soap*), Tokyo: Kao Soap Corporation, 1940; and T. Yui, A. Kudō and H. Takeda, *Kao shi 100-nen* (*A Century of Kao History*), Tokyo: Kao Corporation, 1993 (subsequently referred to as Kao History).

[4]   L. Rubinfein, 'Ryutsu kakushin no kokoromi: Kao no keesu wo chushin ni' (An Attempt at Innovation in Distribution, with Attention to the Kao Case), in A. Okouchi and H. Takeda (eds), *Kigyosha katsudo to kigyo shisutemu: Daikigyo taisei no nichiei hikakushi* (*Entrepreneurial Activity and the Enterprise System: A Historical Comparison of Large Enterprise Systems in Japan and Britain*), Tokyo: University of Tokyo Press, 1993, pp. 154–82; S. Sasaki, 'Kao ni miru senzen nihon no ryutsu kakushin' (Innovation of Distribution in Pre-war Japan as Seen at Kao), *Keiei shiguku* (*Japan Business History Review*), 1994, vol. 28, no. 4, pp. 28–53; 'Keshohin-sekken gyokai ni miru gijutsu kakushin; Shiseido to Kao no jirei wo chushin ni' (Technological Innovation seen in the Cosmetic and Soap Business: Focus on the Cases of Shiseido and Kao), in T. Yui and J. Hashimoto (eds), *Kakushin no keieishi: Senzen sengo ni okera nihon kigyo no kakushin kodo* (*A Business History of Innovation: Innovative Activities at Japanese Firms in the Pre- and Post-war Eras*), Tokyo: Yuhikaku, 1995, pp. 115–34.

[5]   S. Sasaki, 'Kao ni miru senzenki shokuinso kogakurekika no hitokoma' (An Aspect of the Trend for White Collars' Higher Education in Pre-war Era seen from Kao's Case), in H. Kawaguchi (ed.), *Daigaku no shakai keizai shi* (*A Socio-Economic History of the University*), Tokyo: Sobunsha, 2000, pp. 209–26.

[6]   Kao History, pp. 165–212.

[7]   Ibid., pp. 212–23.

[8]   Lion Corporation: Company History Editing Committee, *Raion 100-nen shi* (*A Century of Lion*), Tokyo: Lion Corporation, 1992, pp. 1–7, 51–9, 202–11.

[9]   Kao History, p. 188.

[10] For more on Maruta's visit to the United States, see Kao Corporation Historical Compilation Room Archives (subsequently referred to as Kao Archives), Y. Maruta, 'Mite kita amerika' (The America I saw), Tokyo: Kao Soap Corporation, 1951; S. Ochiai, *Ito Eizo: Sono hito to jiseki (Eizo Ito: The Man and the Evidence)*, Tokyo: Kao Soap Corporation, 1973, pp. 181–8; T. Nomura, 'Kao: Sengo no tachi-naori to saisho no amerika shisatsu' (Kao: Post-war Comeback and the First U.S. Study Tour), in Japan Business History Institute, *Keiei to rekishi (Business and History)*, 1987, vol. 10, pp. 43–7; Kao History, pp. 203–8.

[11] After having marketed the first synthetic detergent Dreft in 1933, Procter & Gamble continued new product research and development and played a major role in the popularization of synthetic detergents in the United States. By 1957, synthetic detergents held over 90 percent of the American market for household detergents.

[12] This 'direct costing' method was implemented around 1962. Kao had formerly used total costing, or the so-called 'rolling formula' (see Kao History, p. 329),

whereby monthly accounts were settled around the 20th of the following month. By introducing direct costing, which calculated manufacturer costs solely on the basis of variable manufacturer costs, it became possible to settle accounts on the 10th of the succeeding month.

[13] On trade liberalization and the approval system for technology introduction, see Committee on the Compilation of a History of International Trade and Industrial Policy (ed.), *Tsusho sangyo seisaku shi (A History of International Trade and Industrial Policy)*, vol. 8, Tokyo: Tsusho Sangyo Chosa Kai, 1991, pp. 463–94.

[14] Japan Neutral Detergent Association, *Nihon chusei senzai kyokai 20-nen shi (A Twenty Year History of the Japan Neutral Detergent Association)*, Tokyo: Japan Neutral Detergent Association, 1983, pp. 11–35.

[15] For details on the development of shampoo, see Kao History, pp. 262–8.

[16] For details on the development of synthetic detergent, see ibid., pp. 230–3, 246–7.

[17] Ibid., p. 206.

[18] On the spread of the electric washing machine and its social influence, see J. Suzuki, *Shin gijutsu no shakai shi (Social History of New Technology)*, Tokyo: Chuo Koron Shinsha, 1999, pp. 241–61; S. Partner, *Assembled in Japan: Electrical Goods and the Making of the Japanese Consumer*, Berkeley: University of California Press, 1999.

[19] For details, see Kao History, p. 264.

[20] Ibid., pp. 248–55.

[21] Ibid., pp. 464–9. The climbing film reactor, however, was not based directly on research into how to improve the Chemithson equipment but rather was the product of a key part of the sulfonation research group's pure research and development activities at the Wakayama research lab.

[22] Ibid., pp. 276–80.

[23] For details, see ibid., pp. 280–3.

[24] On the development of Mighty, see ibid., pp. 534–42.

[25] Ibid., pp. 296–8.

[26] Ibid., pp. 365–72; I. Son, 'Kodo seichoki ni okeru ryutsu shisutemu no henka: Sekken, senzai gyokai wo chushin ni' (Change in the Distribution System During the High-speed Growth Era: Focus on the Soap and Detergent Sector), *Keiei shigaku (Japan Business History Review)*, 1993, vol. 27, no. 4, pp. 32–63.

[27] Kao History, p. 304.

[28] S. Ochiai, *Kao kokuku shi (A History of Advertising at Kao)*, Tokyo: Kao Corporation, 1989, pp. 98–101.

[29] ' "Awa" to kieta Kao sekken no purodakuto maneja' (The Product Manager at Kao Soap that Disappeared like 'Suds'), *Kindai keiei (Modern Management)*, December 1973, pp. 62–6; Kao History, pp. 422–7. A number of explanations have been offered for why product managers did not strike roots in Japan's consumer products sector: 1) Japanese enterprise organization was vertically divided on product lines and was not amenable to profit management for each product; 2) while in the US product changes were dramatic and the market was highly segmented, the Japanese market was homogeneous and had little necessity for product diversity. However, these explanations are rather impressionistic and cannot account for the important role that the product manager system played in the automobile industry.

30 S. Sasaki, 'Toiretari: 1960–70-nendai no ryutsu senryaku: Raion no tai kao senryaku wo chushin ni' (Toiletries: Distribution Strategy in the 1960s and 1970s: Focus on Lion's Kao Strategy), in M. Udagawa, T. Kikkawa and J. Shintaku (eds), *Nihon no kigyo kan kyoso (Inter-firm Competition in Japan)*, Tokyo: Yuhikaku, 2000.

31 Y. Maruta, *Waga jinsei kan waga keiei kan (My Life View, My Management View)*, Tokyo: Kao Soap Corporation, 1984, pp. 267–73.

32 Kao History, pp. 438–9.

33 On the ability-based grade system, see H. Sato, '*Nikkeiren noryoku shugi kanri: Sono riron to jissen* wo yomu' (Reading Japan Federation of Employer's Association *Meritocracy Management: Its Theory and Practice*), in *Dai 42-ki Hitotsubashi Foramu 21 (42nd Hitotsubashi Forum 21)*, Tokyo: Josuikai, 2000.

34 Kao History, pp. 314–23; Japan Federation of Employers' Association Workshop of Meritocracy Management, *Noryoku shugi kanri: Sono riron to jissen (Meritocracy Management: Its Theory and Practice)*, Tokyo: Japan Federation of Economic Organization, 1969, pp. 158–62.

35 Kao History, p. 325.

36 'Kao korugeto de hamigaki ni saichosen' (Kao Rechallenges Over Toothpaste with Colgate), *Yushi (Oil and Fat)*, 1977, vol. 30, no. 3, p. 27; Kao History, pp. 506–12.

37 On capital liberalization, see Committee on the Compilation of a History of International Trade and Industrial Policy (ed.), *Tsusho sangyo seisaku shi (A History of International Trade and Industrial Policy)*, vol. 8, Tokyo: Tsusho Sangyo Chosa Kai, 1991, pp. 363–494.

38 H. Yoshihara, 'Procter & Gamble Far East, Inc. Nihon kogaisha ga inobeshon no gensen' (Procter & Gamble Far East, Inc. The Japanese Subsidiary Company is the Origin of Innovation), in Yoshihara *et al.*, *Gurobaru higyo no nihon senryaku (Japan Strategy of Global Enterprise)*, Tokyo: Kodansha, 1990, pp. 238–82.

39 Maruta, *Waga jinsei kan waga keiei kan*, pp. 186–9.

40 A. Yoshioka, 'P&G nihon shinshutsu no 10-nen de okina tenki ka?' (Decisive Change in the Ten years after P&G's entry into Japan?), *Yushi (Oil and Fat)*, 1983, vol. 36, no. 10, pp. 24–7.

41 'Kao korugeto de hamigaki ni saichosen', pp. 22–7.

42 *Kagaku kogyo nippo (Chemical Industry Daily Report)*, 23 April 1987. The business tie-up between Lion and Henkel not only occurred with Japan's domestic market but also in Europe and Asia. For the development of international competition centring on Asia, see M. Ihara, 'Kagaku shohizai sangyo no ajia jigyo tenkai: Kigyo nai gijutsu iten to genchi tekio' (Consumer Chemicals Industry's Business Development in Asia: Intrafirm Technology Transfer and Local Adaptation), unpublished Ph.D. thesis, Graduate School of Economics, University of Tokyo, 2000.

43 On the manufacturer of Nivea, Beiersdorf, see H.G. Schröter, 'Erfolgsfaktor Marketing: Der Strukturwandel von der Reklame zur Unternehmenssteuerung', in W. Feldenkirchen, F. Schönert-Röhlk und G. Schulz (eds), *Wirtschaft Gesellschaft Unternehmen. Festschrift für Hans Pohl zum 60. Geburtstag (Vierteljahrschrift für Sozial- und Wirtschaftsgeschichte, Beiheft 120)*, 1995, pp. 1099–127. Also, see Kao History, pp. 512–17.

44 In terms of diversification, Kao trailed Henkel of West Germany. In 1966, the proportion of total product sales occupied by detergents (including soap) was 73

percent. It was not until 1977 that this dropped below 50 percent. In 1966, Henkel had already reached 43 percent. Cf. Kao History, p. 337.

45 See Ihara, 'Kagaku shohizai sangyo no ajia jigyo tenkai'; Ihara and Kudō, 'Technology Transfer and Adaptation to Local Condition'.

Chapter 12

1 Hidemasa Morikawa, 'Book review', *Keiei shigaku [Japan Business History Review]*, Vol. *26,* No. 2 (1991).

2 Hidemasa Morikawa, *Zaibatsu: The Rise and Fall of Family Enterprise Groups in Japan,* Tokyo: University of Tokyo Press, 1992; Mark Fruin, *The Japanese Enterprise System: Competitive Strategies and Cooperative Structures,* Oxford: Clarendon Press, 1992; William Lazonick, 'Organisational Capabilities in American Industry: The Rise and Decline of Managerial Capitalism', *Business and Economic History,* Second Series, Vol. 19 (1990).

3 See Akira Kudō, 'The State of Business History in Japan: Cross-National Comparisons and International Relations', in Franco Amatori and Geoffrey Jones, eds, *Business History around the World,* forthcoming.

4 Moriaki Tsuchiya, 'Formation Process of Modern Joint Stock Companies in the United States: From Division of Ownership and Management to Rehabilitation of Stockholders', in *Proceedings of the 34ᵗʰ Annual Conference of the Association of Business History,* Tokyo, 1998.

5 Tadahiko Takaura, 'History and Prospect of Corporate Governance: Focusing on Japan', in ibid.

6 Tsuchiya, 'Formation Process of Modem Joint Stock Companies in the United States'.

7 Hiroshi Shibuya, 'Institutional Investors and Corporate Governance in the United States: An Essay to Set a Viewpoint for Research', *Shoken keizai kenkyu [Journal of Security Economy],* No. 22 (1999), p. 27.

8 Takaura, 'History and Prospect of Corporate Governance'.

9 Ibid.

10 In Britain, Cadbury Committee, *Report of the Committee on the Financial Aspects of Corporate Governance,* London, 1992; and [Hampel] Committee on Corporate Governance, *Final Report,* London, 1998, were published. For East Asia, see Akira Suehiro, 'Asian Corporate Governance: Disclosure-Based Screening System and Family Business Restructuring in Thailand', unpublished paper, September 2000.

11 Tadahiko Takaura, 'GM and Corporate Governance: Focusing on the Resignation of President Stempel', *Rikkyo keizaigaku kenkyu [Rikkyo Journal of Economics],* Vo. 54, No. 1 (2000), pp. 138–9.

12 Business Management Group of Tohoku University, *Keesu ni manabu keieigaku [Business Management Studied through Cases],* Tokyo: Yuhikaku, 1998, p. 265.

13 Ibid., pp. 266–7.

14 *Nihon Keizai Shinbun,* 25 June, Morning edition, 1998.

15 Working Group on Personnel and Labor Management, Nihon rodo kenkyu kiko (JIL), *Shin seiki no keiei senryaku, koporeto gabanansu, jinji senryaku ni kansuru chosa kenkyu: chukan hokoku [Inquiry and Research on Business Management, Corporate*

Governance, and Personnel Strategy in the New Century: Interim Report], Tokyo: JIL, 1999, pp. 29–32.

16 Institute of Industry and Business Management, Waseda University, *Sanken akademikku foramu* [*IIBS Academic Forum*], No. 4, 1999.

17 Juro Hashimoto, Shin Hasegawa and Hideaki Miyajima, *Gendai nihon keizai* [*The Modern Japanese Economy*], Tokyo: Yuhikaku, 1998, p. 384.

18 *The Economist,* 17 February 2001.

19 Yoshiaki Takahashi, 'Comment', in *Proceedings of the 34th Annual Conference of the Association of Business History,* Tokyo, 1998.

20 A few examples of politic literature on this topic are Ronald Dore, 'Equity-Efficiency Trade-offs: Japanese Perceptions and Choices', in Masahiko Aoki and Ronald Dore, eds, *The Japanese Firm: The Sources of Competitive Strength,* Oxford: Oxford University Press, 1994; W. Carl Kester, 'American and Japanese Corporate Governance: Convergence to Best Practice?', in Suzanne Berger and Ronald Dore, eds, *National Diversity and Global Capitalism,* Ithaca, NY: Cornell University Press, 1996.

21 Robert Boyer, 'The Convergence Hypothesis Revisited: Globalization but Still the Century of Nations?', in Berger and Dore, eds, *National Diversity and Global Capitalism.*

22 Michel Albert, *Capitalisme contre Capitalisme,* Paris: Editions du Seuil, 1991, [p. 133].

23 Yusuke Fukada and Ronald Dore, *Nihongata shihonshugi nakushite nan no nihon ka* [*What Kind of Japan without Japanese Style of Capitalism?*], Tokyo: Kobunsha, 1993, p. 35.

24 Albert, *Capitalisme contre Capitalisme,* [p. 211].

25 Akira Kudō, 'Globalization and the Japanese Economy', in Hook and Hasegawa, eds, *The Global Meaning of Japan*; and idem, 'A Note on Globalization and Regional Integration', ISS Joint Research Project Discussion Paper, No. 1, 2000.

26 See the two papers referred to in note 25.

27 Akira Kudō, 'West Germany and Japan under Americanization: Problematizing the Concept', a paper presented at the Third Japanese-German Business History Conference, University of Tokyo, 24–25 March 2000.

Chapter 13

Mrs Takeo Kikkawa, Minoru Sawai and Takao Shiba read the manuscript and gave me their valuable comments. I deeply appreciate their kindness. It goes without saying that any errors and omissions are entirely my own responsibility.

1 Hidemasa Morikawa, book review, *Keiei shigaku* (*Japan Business History Review*) 26, no. 2 (1991): 65–8.

2 See, for example, the Kikkawa piece in Takeshi Yuzawa et al., *Erementaru keieishi* (*Elemental Business History*) (Tokyo, 2000).

3 Hidemasa Morikawa, *Toppu manejimento no keieishi: Keieisha kigyō to kazoku kigyō* (*A Business History of Top Management: Managerial Enterprises and Family Enterprises*) (Tokyo, 1996). Its English version is id., *A History of Top Management in Japan: Managerial Enterprises and Family Enterprises* (New York, 2001).

4 Volume 1 includes the following chapters with authors: Chapter 1 –
"Overview: From the Edo Period to the 1880s" (Shigeaki Yasuoka); Chapter
2 – "Merchant Wealth Accumulation and the Form of Enterprise" (Kenjirō
Ishikawa and Shigeaki Yasuoka); Chapter 3 – "Business Organization and
Business Management" (Masahiro Uemura and Matao Miyamoto); Chapter
4 – "The Employment System and Labor Management" (Shigeaki Yasuoka and
Akiko Chimoto); Chapter 5 – "Accounting Organization and Bookkeeping
Techniques" (Noboru Nishikawa); Chapter 6 – "Early-Modern Distinctiveness
of Business Ideals" (Shigeaki Yasuoka, Makoto Seoka and Teiichirō Fujita);
Chapter 7 – "Business and the Shift of an Early-Modern Paradigm" (Masatoshi
Amano).

5 Volume 2 includes the following chapters with authors: Chapter 1 – "Overview:
The 1880s to 1915" (Matao Miyamoto and Takeshi Abe); Chapter 2 – "Building
the Base for Business Development" (Kaoru Sugihara); Chapter 3 – "The Sudden
Rise of Enterprise, Modern Business, and Traditional Business" (Masayuki
Tanimoto and Takeshi Abe); Chapter 4 – "Industrialization, Trading Companies,
Shipping, and Finance" (Mariko Tatsuki); Chapter 5 – "The Heavy and Chemical
Industries and Engineers" (Minoru Sawai); Chapter 6 – "Meiji-Period Men of
Means and the Company System" (Matao Miyamoto and Takeshi Abe); Chapter
7 – "Establishment of the Factory System and Labor Management" (Kōnosuke
Odaka).

6 Volume 3 includes the following chapters with authors: Chapter 1 – "Overview:
1915 to 1937" (Tsunehiko Yui); Chapter 2 – "The Structure of Large Enterprise
and Zaibatsu" (Haruhito Takeda); Chapter 3 – "From Technology Introduction
to Technology Development" (Shin Hasegawa); Chapter 4 – "Modernization of
the Factory Management System and Organizational Capacity" (Satoshi Sasaki);
Chapter 5 – "Marketing and Distribution Mechanisms in the Inter-war Period"
(Eisuke Daitō); Chapter 6 – "Funding Procurement in Large Enterprise" (Shōichi
Asajima); Chapter 7 – "The Manager's View of Firm and Labor" (Tsunehiko Yui
and Masakazu Shimada).

7 Volume 4 includes the following chapters with authors: Chapter 1 – "Overview:
1937 to 1951" (Hiroaki Yamazaki); Chapter 2 – "Hegemony of the Salaried
Managers: The Emergence of the Japanese-Style Managerial Enterprise" (Hideaki
Miyajima); Chapter 3 – "The Formation of the Japanese-Style Production
System" (Kazuo Wada and Takao Shiba); Chapter 4 – "Japanese Introduction
and Transformation of American Business Management Techniques" (Kinsaburō
Sunaga and Izumi Nonaka); Chapter 5 – "The Formation of Japanese-Style
Employment Relations: Employment Regulations, Wages, and 'Employees'"
(Shinji Sugayama); Chapter 6 – "The Transformation of Intermediate
Organizations and the Formation of Competitive Oligopoly Structures" (Takeo
Kikkawa); Chapter 7 – "The Emergence of Post-war-Style Industrial Policy"
(Tsuneo Suzuki).

8 Volume 5 includes the following chapters with authors: Chapter 1 – "Overview:
1955 to the 1990s" (Hidemasa Morikawa); Chapter 2 – "Long-Term Relational
Connections and Enterprise Keiretsu" (Jurō Hashimoto); Chapter 3 – "Post-
war Top Management" (Hiroyuki Itami); Chapter 4 – "The Financial System in
Post-war Japan: Banks, Enterprises, Government" (Tetsuji Okazaki); Chapter
5 – "Internationalization and Japanese-Style Management" (Hideki Yoshihara);

Chapter 6 – "Enterprise and Government: The Third Hand" (Masaru Udagawa and Etsuo Abe); Chapter 7 – "The Appearance and Demise of the Japanese System as Shared Illusion" (Seiichirō Yonekura).

[9] Reviews by Yōtarō Sakudō, Kanji Ishii, Takeshi Ōshio, Satoshi Saitō and Kiyoshi Nakamura in *Keiei shigaku (Japan Business History Review)* 32, no. 1 (1997); and those by Masaharu Uemura, Tetsuji Okazaki and Satoshi Saitō in *Shakai keizai shigaku (Socioeconomic History Review)* 64, no. 5 (1998–9). An English translation of the former is found in the English journal *Japanese Yearbook on Business History* 15 (1998).

[10] See the papers and materials for distribution concerning the conference theme "The State and Issues of Business History Education" at the BHA 2000 annual conference.

[11] Keiichirō Nakagawa, *Hikaku keieishi kenkyū 1: Hikaku keieishi josetsu (Studies in Comparative Business History 1: Introduction to Comparative Business History)* (Tokyo, 1981); Yasuo Mishima, *Keiei shigaku no tenkai (The Development of Business History)* (Kyoto, 1961; expanded edition, 1970); Shin'ichi Yonekawa, *Keiei shigaku: Tanjō, hatten, tenbō (Business History: Its Birth, Development and Prospects)* (Tokyo, 1973).

[12] A few examples are: Keiichirō Nakagawa and Tsunehiko Yui, eds, *Organization and Management 1900–1930: Proceedings of the Japan-Germany Conference on Business History, 15* (Tokyo, 1981); and Etsuo Abe and Robert Fitzgerald, eds, *The Origins of Japanese Industrial Power* (London, 1995).

[13] Tsunehiko Yui and Johannes Hirschmeier, *The Development of Japanese Business, 1600–1973* (London, 1975) (also published in Japanese as *Nihon no keiei hatten* [Tokyo, 1977]); Yōtarō Sakudō et al., *Nihon keieishi (Japanese Business History)* (Kyoto, 1980), Yoshitaka Suzuki, Etsuo Abe and Seiichirō Yonekura, *Keieishi (Business History)* (Tokyo, 1987); and Akio Ōkouchi, *Keieishi kōgi (Lectures on Business History)* (Tokyo, 1991).

[14] Matao Miyamoto et al., *Nihon keieishi (Japanese Business History)* (Tokyo, 1995)

[15] Takeshi Yuzawa et al., *Erementaru keieishi (Elemental Business History)* (Tokyo, 2000).

[16] Masaru Udagawa and Kiyoshi Nakamura, eds, *Materiaru Nihon keieishi: Edo ki kara genzai made (Materials on Japanese Business History: From the Edo Period to the Present)* (Tokyo, 1999).

[17] Keiichirō Nakagawa, *Hikaku keieishi kenkyū 2: Igirisu keieishi (Comparative Business History 2: British Business History)* (Tokyo, 1986); Takeshi Yuzawa, *Igirisu tetsudō keieishi (Business History of British Railroads)* (Tokyo, 1988); Yoshitaka Suzuki, *Keieishi: Igirisu sangyō kakumei to kigyōsha katsudō (Business History: Industrial Revolution and Entrepreneurial Activities in Britain)* (Tokyo, 1982); Etsuo Abe, *Daiei teikoku no sangyō haken: Igirisu tekkō kigyō kōbō shi (The British Empire's Industrial Hegemony: The Rise and Fall of British Steel Firms)* (Tokyo, 1993); Chikage Hidaka, *Eikoku mengyō suitai no kōzu (The Decline of the British Cotton Industry)* (Tokyo, 1995); and Takashi Iida, *Igirisu no sangyō hatten to shōken shijō (The Development of Industry and the Securities Market in Britain)* (Tokyo, 1997).

[18] Hisashi Watanabe, *Rain no sangyō kakumei: Genkeizaiken no keisei katei (The Rhine Industrial Revolution: The Emerging Process of Economic Proto-Sphere)* (Tokyo, 1986); Sachio Kaku, *Doitsu kagaku kōgyō shi josetsu (An Introduction to the History of the German Chemical Industry)* (Kyoto, 1986); Sachio Imakubo, *19-seikimatsu Doitsu no kōjō (The Late-19th-century German Factory)* (Tokyo, 1996); and Akira Kudō,

Gendai Doitsu kagaku kigyō-shi: IG Farben no seiritsu, tenkai, kaitai (*A History of the Modern German Chemical Industry: The Establishment, Development and Dissolution of IG Farben*) (Kyoto, 1999).

[19] Isao Hirota, *Gendai Furansu no shiteki keisei: Ryōtaisenkanki no keizai to shakai* (*The Foundation of Modern France: Economy and Society Between the Wars*) (Tokyo, 1994); Jun Sakudō, *Furansu kagaku kōgyō shi kenkyū: Kokka to shakai* (*Studies in the History of the French Chemical Industy: State and Society*) (Tokyo, 1995); and Terushi Hara, *Furansu senkanki keizai shi kenkyū* (*Studies in French Economic History in the Inter-war Period*) (Tokyo, 1999).

[20] Atsushi Mikami, *Indo zaibatsu keieishi kenkyū* (*Business History Research on Indian Family Business Groups*) (Tokyo, 1993); and Fumikatsu Kubo, *Shokuminchi kigyō keieishi ron: "Jun kokusaku kaisha" no jisshōteki kenkyū* (*The Business History of Colonial Enterprises: Empirical Studies of "Parastatal Companies"*) (Tokyo, 1997).

[21] Representative are Shigeaki Yasuoka, *Zaibatsu keisei shi no kenkyū* (*Studies on the Formative History of the Zaibatsu*) (Kyoto, 1970; expanded edition, 1998); id., *Zaibatsu keiei no rekishiteki kenkyū: Shoyū to keiei no kokusai hikaku* (*Historical Research on Zaibatsu Management: A Cross-National Comparison of Ownership and Management*) (Tokyo, 1998).

[22] Representative are Hidemasa Morikawa, *Zaibatsu no keieishiteki kenkyū* (*A Business History Approach to the Zaibatsu*) (Tokyo, 1980); id., *Zaibatsu: The Rise and Fall of Family Enterprise Groups in Japan* (Tokyo, 1992). (The English-language work is not merely a translation of the Japanese.)

[23] Jurō Hashimoto and Haruhito Takeda, eds, *Nihon keizai no hatten to kigyō shūdan* (*Business Groups and the Development of the Japanese Economy*) (Tokyo, 1992); Masahiro Shimotani, *Nihon no keiretsu to kigyō gurūpu: Sono rekishi to riron* (*Japan's Keiretsu and Business Groups: History and Theory*) (Tokyo, 1993); Haruhito Takeda, ed., *Nihon sangyō hatten no dainamizumu* (*The Dynamism of Japanese Industrial Development*) (Tokyo, 1995), Takeo Kikkawa, *Nihon no kigyō shūdan: Zaibatsu tono renzoku to danzetsu* (*Japan's Business Groups: Continuity and Discontinuity with Family Business Groups*) (Tokyo, 1996); Jurō Hashimoto, ed., *Nihon kigyō shisutemu no sengo shi* (*Post-war History of the Japanese Enterprise System*) (Tokyo, 1996); Takao Shiba and Masahiro Shimotani, eds, *Beyond the Firm: Business Groups in International and Historical Perspective* (Oxford, 1997); and Masaru Udagawa, Takeo Kikkawa and Junjirō Shintaku, eds, *Nihon no kigyōkan kyōsō (Interfirm Competition in Japan*) (Tokyo, 2000).

[24] Keiichirō Nakagawa, ed., *Kigyō keiei no rekishiteki kenkyū* (*Historical Research on Business Management*) (Tokyo, 1990); and Hidemasa Morikawa and Tsunehiko Yui, eds, *Kokusai hikaku kokusai kankei no keieishi* (*Business History in Cross-National and International Relations Perspectives*) (Nagoya, 1997). Morikawa and Yui's edited volume contains a number of essays: Keiichirō Nakagawa, "Markets and Business Organization: A Three-way Typology of National Economies"; Yō Ten'itsu, "Cross-National Characteristics of Chinese Family Business"; Yukio Yamashita, "Some Thoughts on 'Motivation': From the Standpoint of Discovering Mankind"; Katsumi Tomizawa, "Specialized Managerial Technicians versus 'Civilian' Managers: The Contest of Two Ethos in Industrial Democracy in Post–World War I America"; Shin Gotō, "Merits and Demerits of Planned Shipbuilding: Its Role in the Post-war Recovery of Japan's Shipping Industry, 1948–1960"; Hidemasa Morikawa, "Government and Business: Suggestions for Cross-National Comparison"; Masaaki

Kobayashi, "Cross-National Comparison of Business Modernization: Looking at American Research on Japan."
[25] The constituent sections and their authors are as follows: 1 – "Enterprise Form and Holding Company Functions" (Yoshitaka Suzuki and Haruhito Takeda); 2 – "Interfirm Relations and the Business System" (Chikage Hidaka and Haruhito Takeda); 3 – "Distribution Mechanisms and Marketing" (Kazuo Wada and Louisa Rubinfein); 4 – "Production Rationalization and Labor Management" (Tomoji Onozuka and Eisuke Daitō); 5 – "Research and Development and Technological Innovation" (Akio Ōkouchi, Takahiro Fujimoto and Joseph Tidd).
[26] Shin'ichi Yonekawa, "The Road to Comparative Business History: Focusing on Industry History," *Hitotsubashi ronsō* 79, no. 4 (1978): 42–59; id., "Comparative Economic History," in *Shakai keizai shigaku no kadai to tenbō (Issues and Prospects for Socioeconomic History)*, ed. Shakai keizai shi gakkai (Tokyo, 1984), 354–61.
[27] Shin'ichi Yonekawa, *Bōsekigyō no hikaku keieishi kenkyū: Igirisu, Indo, Amerika, Nihon (A Comparative Business History of the Spinning Industry: Britain, India, America and Japan)* (Tokyo, 1994); id., *Tōzai bōseki keieishi (A Business History of Spinning: East and West)* (Tokyo, 1997); id., *Tōzai sen'i keieishi (A Business History of Textiles: East and West)* (Tokyo, 1998); id., *Bōseki kigyō no hasan to fusai (Bankruptcy and Debt in Spinning Firms)* (Tokyo, 2000).
[28] Yoshitaka Suzuki, *Japanese Management Structure, 1920–80* (London, 1991).
[29] Yoshitarō Wakimura, *Oil, Shipping, Shipbuilding*, vol. 3 of *Wakimura Yoshitarō chosaku shū (Collected Works of Yoshitarō Wakimura)* (Tokyo, 1980); and *Cotton, International Trade, Oil Tankers*, vol. 5 of ibid. (Tokyo, 1981).
[30] Keiichirō Nakagawa, "Comparative Economic History and International Relations," in *Hikaku keieishi kenkyū 1 (Studies in Comparative Business History 1)* (Tokyo, 1981), 101–16.
[31] Keiichirō Nakagawa, *Ryōtaisenkan no kaiungyō (The Shipping Industry between the Wars)* (Tokyo, 1980).
[32] Business History Association, ed., *Keiei shigaku no 20-nen: Kaiko to tenbō (Twenty Years of Business History: Retrospect and Prospect)* (Tokyo, 1985), 20.
[33] Sakae Tsunoyama, "Economic History," in ibid., 47–8.
[34] Sakae Tsunoyama, ed., *Nihon ryōji hōkoku no kenkyū (Studies in Japanese Consular Reports)* (Tokyo, 1986). See also id., "Japanese Consular Reports," *Business History* 23, no. 3 (1981): 284–7.
[35] Hisashi Watanabe, "A History of the Process Leading to the Formation of Fuji Electric," in *Japanese Yearbook on Business History*, vol. 1 (1984), 47–71; id., "The Process of Formation for Fuji Electric: Second and Third Phases," in Nakagawa, *Kigyō keiei*, 263–83.
[36] Masaru Udagawa, "Business Management and Foreign-Affiliated Companies in Pre-war Japan (Parts 1 and 2)," in *Keiei Shirin* 24, no. 1 (1987). 15–31; no. 2 (1987): 29–40.
[37] Tōru Takenaka, *Siemens to Meiji Nihon (Siemens and Meiji Japan)* (Tokyo, 1991); id., *Siemens in Japan: Von der Landesöffnung bis zum Ersten Weltkrieg* (Stuttgart, 1996); Akira Kudō, *Nichi doku kigyō kankei-shi (A History of Japanese-German Business Relations)* (Tokyo, 1992); id., *I.G. Farben no tainichi senryaku (IG. Farben's Japan Strategy)* (Tokyo, 1992); id., *Japanese-German Business Relations* (London, 1998); Takeo Kikkawa, "Business Activities of the Standard-Vacuum Oil Co. in Japan Prior to World War II," in *Japanese Yearbook on Business History*, vol. 7 (1990),

31–59; Bunji Nagura, *Heiki tekkō kaisha no nichiei kankei-shi: Nihon seikōsho to eikoku gawa kabunushi 1907- 52 (History of Japanese-British Relations in an Arms and Steel Company: Japan Steel Works and Its British Stockholders, 1907–52)* (Tokyo, 1998).

[38] Kanji Ishii, *Kindai Nihon to Igirisu shihon: Jardine Matheson shōkai wo chūshin ni (Modern Japan and British Capital: With a Focus on the Jardine Matheson & Co.)* (Tokyo, 1984); Kazuo Tatewaki, *Zainichi gaikoku ginkō shi (History of Foreign Banks in Japan)* (Tokyo, 1987); Shin'ya Sugiyama, *Meiji ishin to Igirisu shōnin: Thomas Glover no shōgai (The Meiji Restoration and a British Trader: The Life of Thomas Glover)* (Tokyo, 1993); Toshio Suzuki, *Japanese Government Loan Issues on the London Capital Market, 1870–1913* (London, 1994); and Naoto Kagotani, *Ajia kokusai tsūshō chitsujo to kindai Nihon (Asian International Trade Order and Modern Japan)* (Nagoya, 2000).

[39] Tetsuya Kuwahara, "Foreign Firms' Investment in Japan Before World War II: Based on a Survey of the Secondary Literature," *Keizai Keiei Ronsō* 26, no. 2 (1991): 17–51.

[40] For a pioneering work on foreign firms in Japan, see Hideki Yoshihara, ed., *Gaishi kei kigyō (Foreign-Affiliated Companies)* (Tokyo, 1994).

[41] Nobuo Kawabe, *Sōgō shōsha no kenkyū: Senzen Mitsubishi Shōji no zaibei katsudō (Research on the General Trading Company: The Activities of Mitsubishi Trading in the Pre-war United States)* (Tokyo, 1982); Tetsuya Kuwahara, *Kigyō kokusaika no shiteki bunseki (A Historical Analysis of Business Internationalization)* (Tokyo, 1990); Fumio Kaneko, *Kindai Nihon ni okeru taiman tōshi no kenkyū (Investment in Manchuria in Modern Japan)* (Tokyo, 1991); and Kubo, *Shokuminchi kigyō keieishi.*

[42] Tetsuya Kuwahara, "Trends in Research on Overseas Expansion by Japanese Enterprises Prior to World War II," in *Japanese Yearbook on Business History,* vol. 7 (1990), 61–81.

[43] The essays that may be considered attempts at a history of international business relations are Tsunehiko Yui, "Technology Transfer Between Japan and Europe in the Inter-war Period and Cumulative Innovation: The Case of Tōyō Rayon"; Kazuo Sugiyama, "The Establishment of the Gold Standard and the *Tōyō Keizai Shinpō*"; Takeaki Teratani, "The Establishment of the NBC Kure Shipyard: With a Focus on Hisashi Shindō"; Eisuke Daitō, "The Development of the Spinning Industry in Hong Kong: In the Context of Its Relationship with the Post-war History of the Japanese Cotton Industry"; Masaru Udagawa, "The Industrial Development Activities of Yoshisuke Ayukawa: With a Focus on Indigenization of Automobile Manufacture"; Takeo Kikkawa and Mika Takaoka, "The International Transfer of the Supermarket System and Its Japanese Transformation"; Hisashi Watanabe, "The Process of the Establishment of the Duisburg-Ruhrort Harbor Corporation"; Keizō Kawada, "The British Computer Industry and International Relations: From the Late 1950s On"; and Takeshi Yuzawa, "Japanese-British Economic Competition in the Inter-war Period."

[44] These are as follows: in steel, US Steel and New Japan Steel (Ichirō Hori); in automobiles, General Motors and Toyota (Haruhito Shiomi); in electrics, General Electric and Toshiba (Yasuyuki Kazusa); in oil, Exxon/Mobil and Tōnen/Idemitsu Kōsan (Takeo Kikkawa); in chemicals, Du Pont and Mitsubishi

Chemicals (Akira Morikawa); in aerospace, Boeing and Mitsubishi Heavy Industries (Seigo Mizota); in computers, IBM and Fujitsu (Keiji Natsume); in semiconductors, Intel and NEC (Hiroshi Koizuka); in telecommunications, AT&T and NTT (Shinji Miyazaki); in automobile franchise systems, the Big Three and Toyota and others (Hiromi Shioji); in sundries retailing, U.S. and Japan Seven-Eleven (Nobuo Kawabe); and in finance and securities, Merrill Lynch and Nomura Securities (Kazuko Kobayashi). To these chapters are attached a summing-up chapter (Ichirō Hori) and a chronological table (Akira Tanaka).

Chapter 14

[1] *EC Council Declaration on EC-Japan Relations*, 18 June 1985.
[2] See Akira Kudō, *Handelskontroverse zwischen Japan und der EG*, Occasional Papers, East Asian Institute, Free University of Berlin, 1985.
[3] *JETRO-Information, Sonderausgabe für industrielle und technische Kooperation*, March 1984.
[4] Wilhelm Haferkamp, 'Japan and the European Community: An Uneasy Partnership', *Intereconomics*, January/February 1981.
[5] *The Japan Times*, 19 June 1979.
[6] Yoshikiyo Minami, 'New Development of Research and Development Policy in Information Technologies in the European Communities', *EC Studies in Japan*, No.5, 1985 (in Japanese), pp. 202–3.
[7] *The Japan Times*, 20 October 1981.
[8] Minami, op. cit., pp. 212–13.
[9] *Financial Times*, 22 June 1982. See also *The Japan Times*, 22 June 1982.
[10] Minami, op. cit., pp. 215–16.
[11] *Financial Times*, 10 May 1983.
[12] The following description depends primarily on interviews held in June 1985 with some civil servants of the EC Commission and of Japanese Embassies in the EC. The records of these consultations are confidential.
[13] *International Herald Tribune*, 24 October 1983.
[14] Minami, op. cit., p. 227.
[15] EC Press Release.
[16] *Frankfurter Allgemeine Zeitung*, 13 May 1985. In March 1985, the EC Commission had made a proposal for RACE (R & D in Advanced Communications Technologies for Europe). Minami, op. cit., p. 226.
[17] *Nihon keizai Shinbun*, 29 September 1985.
[18] Ibid., 3 & 18 October 1985.
[19] Ibid., 17 & 19 November 1985.
[20] Ibid., 8 November 1985. Other examples: Japan, Great Britain, France and the US in the automatic translation telephone; Japan and West Germany in the space Lab project 'D2'; Japan and France in 'Aqua renaissance 90'. Ibid., 23 & 34 November 1985.
[21] JETRO, op. cit.
[22] *Nihon Keizai Shinbun*, 28 October 1985.
[23] Ibid.

24 *Die Forschungspolitik der Europäischen Gemeinschaft*, 2nd Edition, 1985, p.42.
25 Interviews in Brussels.
26 Participating enterprises are Volvo, Fiat, Olivetti, Philips, Petrofina, the National Coal Board, Awooa and R.T, The President of the EC Commission, Jacques Delors, and other members of the Commission are also participants. EC source.
27 *Frankfurter Allgemeine Zeitung*, 12 July 1985.
28 Minami, op. cit., p. 227.
29 Cooperation between Japan and each EC country is in progress. France is *de jure* oriented and Great Britain and West Germany are *de facto* oriented, for example, in the case of the fifth generation computer. *Frankfurter Allgemeine Zeitung*, 16 May 1984 and Nihon Keizai Shinbun, 15 October 1985.
30 *Japanese investment in Western Europe: a JETRO survey*, 1985.
31 JETRO materials.
32 Interviews in Brussels.
33 *Nihon Keizai Shinbun*, 16 November 1985.

Chapter 15

In the course of preparing this paper, several interviews were held with Mr Ikuo Nakamura, in charge of overseas activities in the presidential office of Kao. However, the author alone is responsible for compiling the present paper and for any mistakes that may have been made herein. The author gives his warmest thanks for the invaluable assistance received from Mr Nakamura, Mr Toshikazu Nomura, Head of the Editing Office for Company History, and from Ms Masumi Mori, researcher at the Institute for the Business History of Japan.

1 Cf. Raymond Vernon, *Sovereignty at Bay*, New York, 1971.
2 It can be a center-evidence to Trevor's thesis developed in Malcolm Trevor, *Japan's Reluctant Multinationals*, London, 1983.
3 *Robert Gilpin, U.S. Power and the Multinational Corporation: The Political Economy of Foreign Direct Investment*, New York, 1975; Vernon, *op. cit.;* Stephen Hymer, *The International Operations of National Firms: A Study of Direct Foreign Investment*, Cambridge, Mass., 1976.

Chapter 16

1 *Nihon Keizai Shinbun*, 10 September 1990.
2 Sachverständigenrat zur Begutachtung der gesamtwirtschaftlichen Entwicklung, *Weichenstellungen für die Neunziger Jahre, Jahresgutachten 1989/90*, Stuttgart, 1989, pp. 241, 245.
3 *Statistisches Jahrbuch der Deutschen Demokratischen Republik 1989*, pp.101, 105, 112.
4 Karl-Heinz Eckhardt, *Die DDR in Systemvergleich*, Reinbek bei Hamburg, 1986, p. 109.: *PLOETZ. Die Deutsche Demokratische Republik*, Freiburg, Würzburg, 1988, pp. 86–7.
5 *Nihon Keizai Shinbun*, 20 September 1990.

⁶ Hironori Yamaguchi, *Nishi Doitsu no Kyodai Kigyo to Ginko (Big Business and Banking in West Germany)*, Tokyo, 1988, pp. 66–7, 86.
⁷ *Statistisches Jahrbuch der Deutschen Demokratischen Republik 1989*, p. 139.
⁸ Eckhardt, op. cit., p. 224.
⁹ Volker Berghahn, *Unternehmer und Politik in der Bundesrepublik*, Frankfurt am Main, 1985, p. 326; do., *The Americanisation of West German Industry 1945–1973*, Leamington Spa, 1986, p. 328.
¹⁰ Dietrich Strasser, *Abschied von den Wunderknaben. Die Krise der deutschen Manager und Unternehmer*, München, 1985.
¹¹ Peter Zürn, *Vom Geist und Stil des Hauses. Unternehmenskultur in Deutschland*, the second edition, Landsberg, 1986.

Chapter 17

* Here and throughout this paper, East Asian names are given in the East Asian order, i.e. with the family name first, except in referring to published works in Western languages where the author's name is given in the reverse order (and in referring to such works, the author's family name is capitalized).

¹ With the signing of the Maastricht Treaty, the European Community changed its name to the European Union at the beginning of 1994. This paper, however, uses the old name (EC) as it deals with developments until the end of 1993.
² For further details on the Japanese-European negotiations on Japan's participation in the GATT, see Akaneya Tatsuo, "Saikeikoku Taigu wo Motomete" (In Search of Most-Favored-Nation Treatment), in Watanabe Akio (ed.), *Sengo Nihon no Taigai Seisaku* (Foreign Policies of Post-war Japan), Yuhikaku, 1985, pp. 117–18, 124–6. See also Akaneya, *Nihon no GATT Kanyu Mondai: Rejimu Riron no Bunseki Shikaku ni yoru Jirei Kenkyu* (Japan's Participation in the GATT: A Case Study from the Standpoint of the Regime Theory), University of Tokyo Press, 1992.
³ For further details on the Japan-EC negotiations in the early 1970s, see Ando Ken'ichi, "Oshu Kyodotai no Kyotsu Tsusho Seisaku no Seiji-keizaigaku: 1970–1973-nen no Tainichi Kyotsu Tsusho Seisaku no Tenkai wo Chushin ni shite" (Political Economy of the European Community's Common Commercial Policy: An Analysis with Emphasis on the Development of its Common Commercial Policy toward Japan in 1970–73), in Hokkaido University *Keizaigaku Kenkyu*, Vol.40, No.l, 1990. Published information about how the negotiations were carried out in 1970–73 still remains limited. Many of the major works dealing with the Japan-EC negotiations, such as the following, start their discussions from the year 1976: Masamichi HANABUSA, "Trade Problems between Japan and Western Europe," Royal Institute of International Affairs, 1979; Albrecht Rothacher, *Economic Diplomacy between the European Community and Japan 1959–1981*, Edward Elgar, 1983; and Kenjiro ISHIKAWA, *Japan and the Challenge of Europe, 1992*, London, 1990.
⁴ For further details on what circumstances led to the eruption of this conflict, what products and industries were at issue, how the negotiations proceeded, and what solutions were agreed upon, see: Muroi Yoshio, "Oshu Kyodotai" (The European Community) in Shibagaki Kazuo (ed.), *Sekai no Nakano Nihon Shihonshugi*

(Japanese Capitalism in the World), Toyokeizai Shimpo-sha, 1980; Akira Kudō, "From Commercial Controversy to Industrial and Technical Cooperation: The New Role of Japanese Direct Investment in the EC," in Malcolm Trevor (ed.), *The Internationalization of Japanese Business: European and Japanese Perspectives*, Frankfurt am Main: Campus Verlag, and Boulder: Westview Press, 1987; Kudō Akira, '"Nihon no Chosen' to EC" ("Japanese Challenge" and the EC), *Kokumin no Dokusen Hakusho* (People's White Paper on Monopolies), No. 10, Ochanomizu Shobo, 1987; and Uchida Katsutoshi and Shimizu Sadatoshi (eds), *EC Keizairon: Oshu Togo to Sekai Keizai* (The EC Economy: The European Integration and the World Economy), Mineruva Shobo, 1993, pp. 223–4, 231, 234–6, 241 (authored by Uchida).

5 Tanaka Sokoh, *EC Togo no Shintenkai: Togo Oshu Saihensei* (New Developments concerning the EC's Unification: Restructuring of Unified Europe), Toyokeizai Shimpo-sha, 1991, pp. 136–8; Ishikawa Kenjiro, *EC Togo to Nihon: Mohitotsu no Keizai Masatsu* (The Unification of the EC and Japan: Another Economic Friction), Seibunsha, 1991, p. 17.

6 Ishikawa, op. cit., Chapter 7.

7 Since approximately 60% of the EC's total trade takes the form of intra-regional trade, in terms of both imports and exports, Japan's shares in its overall imports and exports, inclusive of intra-regional transactions, are less than half the percentage figures mentioned here. In 1991, Japan accounted for 2.0% of its gross exports and 4.5% of its gross imports. On the other hand, the EC in the same year accounted for 18.4% of Japan's total exports, and 13.4% of its total imports. See *Tsusho Hakusho* (White Paper on International Trade), 1993 edn., Volume on Particulars, pp. 11 and 443.

8 Uchida and Shimizu (eds.), op. cit., p. 333.

9 The standpoint that underlay the EC's insistence on the establishment of the TAM was typically manifested by the following argument, for instance:

"The EC Commission is apprehensive of the existence of significant discrepancies between trade statistics of Japan and those of the EC. The statistics for 1989 are a case in point. According to the statistics on the Japanese side, the EC's trade deficits with Japan are supposed to have decreased in 1989 by 13.3% in the US dollar terms (or by $19.7 billion), and by 7.3% in the yen terms (or by ¥2.7 trillion), respectively. In contrast, the statistics on the EC side shows a 2% increase in its trade deficits with Japan to ECU25.0 billion."

"Several factors are mentioned to explain the discrepancies in the two series of trade statistics. These include, for instance, differences that arise at the time of currency conversions, differences in the viewpoints about purchasing of pictures (Japan is regarding its purchases of a picture as an import from the country where it was originally drawn), differences arising from the practice of using the FOB prices in the calculation of exports and the CIF prices in the calculation of imports, and effects of time-lags due to transportation. While it may be difficult to eliminate the statistical discrepancies in their entirety, it is necessary for both Japan and the EC to make efforts to arrive at a much clearer picture of the real situation. The crux of the problem is undeniably the immense trade deficits the EC is sustaining with Japan; but the negligence of the need for clarifying these problems will nurture misunderstandings, and render the grasping of the true situation difficult." The EC Delegation in Japan, Press and Information Service,

Gekkan EC (Monthly EC, currently *Gekkan Yoroppa* [Monthly Europe]), July-August 1991, p. 3. In describing the current developments in this and other sections of the paper, the author has drawn extensively on news stories published in the *Gekkan EC* (currently *Gekkan Yoroppa)*, as well as in the *Nihon Keizai Shimbun,* the *Financial Times,* and other news media, but chooses to avoid specifying the sources.

[10] For further treatment of the EC's import restriction measures, see Shimano Takuji, "EC no Taigai Tsusho Seisaku no Kaiko to Tembo" (The EC's External Trade Policies: An Overview and Future Prospects), *Nihon EC Gakkai Nempo* (EC Studies in Japan), No.8, 1988, pp. 12–14; and Ishikawa, *EC Togo to Nihon,* op. cit., pp. 20–1 and Chapter 8.

[11] For more detailed accounts of the rift within the EC Commission over the import restrictions on Japanese cars, the argument for a boycott of Japanese cars advanced by Carbet, board chairman of Citroën-Peugeot, and French Prime Minister Cresson's arguments, see Ishikawa, *EC Togo to Nihon,* op. cit., Chapters 9 and 10; and Tanaka Toshiro (ed.), *EC Togo to Nihon: Posuto 1992-nen ni Mukete* (The EC's Integration and Japan: Looking forward to the Post-1992 Era), JETRO, 1991, pp. 156–60, 187–96.

[12] A detailed analysis of the historical implications of the full-scale increase in Japan's foreign direct investment in manufacturing that has taken place since the early 1970s, and especially during the 1980s, is not undertaken in this paper, but is left for another occasion. With regard to Japanese direct investment in Europe in the prewar years, I have presented some case studies in Chapters 2 and 5 in my *Nichi-Doku Kigyo Kankei-shi* (A History of Japanese-German Business Relations), Yuhikaku, 1992.

[13] For a further discussion of this assessment, see Nihon Keizai Chosa Kyogikai (Japan Economic Research Council), *Senshinkoku ni okeru Toshi Masatsu to Nihon no Taio* (Investment Frictions among the Advanced Countries and Japan's Policy Response), 1991, pp. 23–42 (authored by Abo Tetsuo).

[14] The Japan Export-Import Bank's monthly *Kaigai Toshi Kenkyusho-ho* (Foreign Investment Research Center Report) (July 1993, pp. 73–4) offers the following explanations for the increasing Japanese direct investment in Asia: "(1) With large-scale investment undertakings, especially in the advanced countries, having almost run their course, the size of investment projects has grown smaller. (2) The advanced countries continue to be stuck in the mire of recessions, and their market trends remain uncertain. (3) On top of the bursting of the bubble economy in Japan, which has left many Japanese parent companies in financially bad shape, the generally poor business performance of Japanese offshore plants in the US and Europe is making Japanese parent companies additionally cautious about making new direct investment in advanced countries. (4) The practice of low-cost financing through massive flotation of share-linked bonds (such as convertible bonds and warrant bonds) – used widely in the latter half of the 1980s – has become difficult to use; BIS regulations and other factors have continued to force financial institutions to follow a cautious lending policy; and many companies are drained of disposable funds for investment as their share-linked bonds which they floated earlier began to reach maturity en masse in FY1992."

[15] Ministry of Finance, *Taigai Taishaku ni kansuru Hokokusho* (Report on the Balance of Capital Account).

[16] See Tanaka, op. cit., p. 151.

[17] See Uchida and Shimizu, op. cit., p.347; Ishikawa, op. cit., p. 256.

18 Japan External Trade Organization (JETRO), *Zaio Nikkei Kigyo (Seizogyo) no Keiei Jittai: Dai 9-kai Jittai Chosa Hokoku* (The Actual State of the Operations of Japanese Manufacturing Firms in Europe: Report on the Ninth Fact-finding Survey), JETRO, 1993, p. 5.
19 Ministry of Finance data.
20 Ibid., p. 5.
21 I.bid., pp. 4–5, 19, 21.
22 See Nihon Zaigai Kigyo Kyokai (Association of Japanese Businesses Overseas), *Waga Kuni Kigyo no Kaigai Jigyo ni okeru Manejimento Genchika no Konnichiteki Kadai: Genjo to Mondaiten* (Present-day Challenges Faced by Japanese Businesses Overseas in Their Attempts to Localize Management: Present Realities and Problems), Nihon Zaigai Kigyo Kyokai, 1992; Yasumuro Ken'ichi, *Gurobaru Keiei-ron: Nihon Kigyo no Atarashii Paradaimu* (Global Management: The New Paradigm for Japanese Companies), Chikura Shobo, 1992, pp. 214–22; and Kudō Akira, "Nihon Kigyo no Chokuselsu Toshi to Yoroppa no Keiei Fudo" (Japanese Companies' Direct Investment and the Business Climate in Europe), Japan Center for International Finance, *Taio Chokusetsu Toshi no Genjo* (Present State of Direct Investment in Europe), Japan Center for International Finance, 1994.
23 JETRO, op. cit., pp. 73, 76.
24 See Wada Mitsuo, "Meikaku katsu Kyoretsu na Kigyo Tetsugaku" (A Clear and Strong Corporate Philosophy), in Yoshihara Hideki, Wada Mitsuo, Ishida Hideo, Furukawa Kosei, Takagi Haruo and Suzuki Sadahiko, *Gurobaru Kigyo no Nihon Senryaku* (Japan Strategy of Global Firms), Kodansha, 1990.

Chapter 18

1 The following definition of regional integration may be helpful. "The origins of this kind of international political system with sovereign nations at its center may be traced to Europe. Put it differently, we may assert that the sovereign nation system developed in Europe has now spread to every region of the globe. Europe, meanwhile, is implementing a system of common management and execution of sovereignty, transcending national boundaries. This we call integration." Tanaka Toshiro, *"European Integration"* in The Historical Science Society of Japan, ed., *Lectures on the World History II: The Contemporary World at a Crossroads – Chaos Is Not to Be Feared,* University of Tokyo Press, 1996, pp. 77–8 (in Japanese).
2 Kanemaru Teruo, ed., *What is the EU? – An Interpretation of the European Union and its Treaties,* JETRO, 1994, Hosoya Akio, APEC and NAFTA, Yuhikaku, 1995 (in Japanese), and Yamakage Susumu, *ASEAN – From Symbol to System,* University of Tokyo Press, 1991 (in Japanese).
3 With reference to hegemony in general, Baba Hiroji, "World Systems Theory and Stage Theory" in Kudō Akira, ed., *20th Century Capitalism II - The Transformation of Hegemony and the Welfare State,* University of Tokyo Press, 1995, especially pp. 16–18 (in Japanese). In reference to US hegemony and the Pax Americana, Tateyama Yutaka, "The Structure of the Pax Americana", in ibid. (in Japanese).
4 See, Tateyama, op. cit., pp. 63–73. For a summary of academic debate surrounding hegemony, post-hegemony, the cold war, and the post-cold war, see Tanaka

Akihiko, *New "Medieval Ages" – the World System of the 21st Century*, Nihon Keizai Shinbunsha, 1996, chaps. 1–4 (in Japanese).

5 A detailed account is in Kudō Akira, "Post World War 2 Economic Growth and Regional integration" in Hara Terushi and Kudō Akira, eds, *An Economic History of Modern Europe*, Yuhikaku, 1996, pp. 248–59 (in Japanese) as well as the bibliography to that volume. The article examines the history of European integration in the second half of the twentieth century, paying particular attention to the links to economic growth.

6 For the "Third Industrial Revolution", see Masuda Yuji, "The Transformation of the World Economic System and the Third Industrial Revolution", in *International Politics*, No. 93, 1990 (in Japanese).

7 Kudō Akira, "The Economic Relations between a Unified Germany and Eastern Europe – Is the "Nazi Great Economic Sphere" Re-emerging?" in Sakai Eihachiro and Hosaka Kazuo, eds, *The Path Toward a Europeanized Germany – Current Conditions and Issues for a Unified Germany*, University of Tokyo Press, 1996, pp. 144–5 (in Japanese). In addition, Uchida Katsutoshi and Shimizu Sadatoshi, eds, *A Theory of the EC Economy – European Integration and the World Economy*, Minerva Shobo, 1993, Ch. 3 (by Maeda Keiichi) and Ch. 5 (by Tanaike Nobuyasu) (in Japanese).

8 See Kudō, "Post World War 2 Economic Growth and Regional integration", op. cit., pp. 259–66. For "Expansionist Europe" and "Contractionist Europe", see Hara Terushi, "The Formation of the European Economy" in Hara and Kudō, eds, op. cit. (in Japanese). For a recent general survey, see Tanaka Toshiro, op. cit. For a survey of economic relations with Japan, see Kudō, "Changing Pattern of Japanese-European Economic Relations" in Kudō, ed., op. cit. (in Japanese).

9 For a simple account of business cycles in Western Europe and unified Germany, see Kudō in Sakai and Hosaka, eds, op. cit., pp. 123, 130–2, 147–8.

10 Kudō in Hara and Kudō, eds, op. cit., pp. 120–5.

11 For Germany as a great economic power, see Kudō in Sakai and Hosaka, eds, pp. 132, 145–6.

12 See ibid., pp. 148–52. Sumiya Kazuhiko, Kudō Akira and Yamada Makoto have attempted an account of the similarities and differences between German unification and the changes in the former East European socialist bloc in *German Unification and East European Reforms*, Minerva Shobo, 1992 (in Japanese).

13 Tanaka Soko, ed., *EMS: The European Monetary System – Focal Point of European Monetary Integration*, Yuhikaku, 1996, p. 346 (in Japanese). For the history and current conditions of monetary integration, see also Peter B. Kenen, *Economic and Monetary Union in Europe: Moving beyond Maastricht*, Cambridge University Press, Cambridge (Mass.), 1995.

14 Tanaka, ed., op. cit., p. 322.

15 For details on the time schedule, see ibid., pp. 334–6.

16 Ibid., pp. 316–17.

17 Ibid., p. 361.

18 Ibid., p. 333.

19 Ibid., p. 360.

20 Ando Ken'ichi, "The Dynamics of Economic Integration" in Sasaki Takao and Nakamura Ken'ichi, ed., *The De-mythification of European Integration – The Study of the Post-Maastricht Political Economy*, Minerva Shobo, 1994, p. 132 (in Japanese).

21 Inoue Ichiro, The European International Currency and the Asian International Currency, Nihon Keizai Hyoronsha, 1994, pp. 230–1 (in Japanese).

22 Tanaka, ed., op. cit., p. 251.
23 Ibid., pp. 279, 316–17.
24 Ibid., p. 355.
25 Kamo Takehiko, "EC Integration and the New World Order" in Dentsu Soken, ed., *EC Integration and the New Europe*, Iwanami Shoten, 1993, pp. 5–6 (in Japanese).
26 Yamada Makoto, *The Development and Transformation of the German-style Welfare State - A Study in the Regional Finances of Contemporary Germany*, Minerva Shobo, 1996, p. 324 (in Japanese).
27 Osabe Shigeyasu and Tanaka Tomoyoshi, eds, *The Focal Point of Expanding Europe – Market Integration and the Composition of the New Order*, JETRO, 1994, pp. 30–1 (by Osabe and in Japanese).
28 Martin Schulz, European Monetary Union: Risks and Chances, unpublished lecture paper, 1996.

Chapter 20

1 Soros, George (1998) *The Crisis of Global Capitalism: Open Society Endangered,* New York: Public Affairs.
2 Tsunekawa Keiichi (1996) *Kigyō to Kokka* [The State and Private Enterprise], Tokyo: University of Tokyo Press.
3 Yamakage Susumu (1994) *Tairitsu to Kyōzon no Kokusai Riron: Kokumin Kokka Taikei no Yukue* [Conflict and Coexistence: A Theoretical Approach to International Relations], Tokyo: University of Tokyo Press, pp. 309, 318–19.
4 Regarding hegemony in general, see Baba Hiroji (1995) "Sekai Taiseiron to Dankairon" [The World System Theory and the Stages Theory], in: Kudō Akira (ed.) *Nijusseiki shihonshugi II: Haken no Hen'yō to Fukushi Kokka* [Twentieth-Century Capitalism II: The Changing World Hegemony and the Welfare State], Tokyo: University of Tokyo Press, especially pp. 16–18.
5 For US hegemony, see Tateyama Yutaka (1995) "Pakusu Amerikaana no Kōzō" [The Structure of Pax Americana] and Ozawa Kenji (1995) "Nichi-Beiei keizai kankei no gyakuten" [A Reversal of Japan-US Economic Relations], both in: Kudō (ed.). As for the characteristics of US hegemony, see Kaneko Masaru (1997) *Shijō to Seido no Seiji-Keizaigaku* [The Political Economy of Markets and Institutions], Tokyo: University of Tokyo Press, p. 175. With regard to the idea of hegemonic stability, see a critical study in Sasaki Takao (1990) "Shohyō Robato Girupin, Ōkurashō Sekai Shisutemu Kenkyūkai yaku, *Sekai Shisutemu no Seiji-Keizaigaku: Kokusai Kankei no Shindankai*" [Book Review: Robert Gilpin, Ministry of Finance World System Study Society trans. *Politial economy of International Relations*], Toyo Keizai Shinposha, Hosei University, *Keizai shirin,* 59:1, 1991.
6 See Tateyama (1995) pp. 63–73. As for a systematic study of theories and arguments concerning hegemony and post-hegemony as well as the Cold War and post-Cold War, see Tanaka Akihiko (1996) *Atarashii Chūsei: Nijuisseiki no Sekai Shisutemu* [New "Medieval Ages": The World System of the Twenty-First Century], Tokyo: Nihon Keizai Shimbunsha, chapters 1–4.
7 See Kudō Akira (forthcoming) "Americanization or Europeanization?: The Globalization of the Japanese Economy," in: Hook, Glenn D. and Hasegawa Harukiyo (eds) *The Political Economy of Japanese Globalization*, London: Routledge.

[8] For region in general, see Yamakage (1994), Part III, Chapter 3 "Kokusai Shakai no Chiiki Ninshiki" [Regional Perception in the International Society].

[9] Kanemaru Teruo (ed.) (1994) *EU towa nanika: Ōshū Dōmei no Kaisetsu to Jōyaku* [What Is the EU?: Commentaries on the European Union and Treaties], Tokyo: Japan External Trade Organization (JETRO), Hosono Akio (1995) *APEC to NAFTA* (APEC and NAFTA), Tokyo: Yuhikaku; and Yamakage Susumu (1991) *ASEAN: Shinboru kara Shisutemu e* (ASEAN: From Symbol to System), Tokyo: University of Tokyo Press.

[10] Gamble, Andrew (1998) "Globalisation and Regionalisation: Theoretical Approaches," paper presented to the University of Sheffield Symposium on "Japan, Asia Pacific, and Regionalism: Global and Regional Dynamics into the Twenty-First Century," 21–22 September, p. 11.

[11] Tanaka Toshiro (1996) "Yōroppa Tōgō" [European Integration], in: The Historical Science Society of Japan (ed.) *Kōza Sekaishi 11: Kiro ni tatsu Gendai Sekai Konton wo osoreru na* [Lectures on the World History 11: The Contemporary World at a Crossroads – Chaos Is Not to Be Feared], Tokyo: University of Tokyo Press, pp. 77–8.

[12] This point is discussed using monetary union as an example in Kudō Akira (1998) "Yōroppa Tōgō no Shatei: Haken Kōtai no Kanōsei" [Range of European Integration: Possibility of Substituting Hegemony], in: University of Tokyo, Institute of Social Science (ed.) *Nijusseiki Shisutemu 6: Kinō to Hen'yō* [The Twentieth-Century Global System 6: Function and Transformation], Tokyo: University of Tokyo Press. I reconsider the subject in a broader perspective in this paper.

[13] Yamakage (1994), p. 104 (first appearance in 1983).

[14] Kudō (1998).

[15] Especially, Kaelble, Hartmut (1987) *Auf dem Weg zu einer europäischen Gesellschaft. Eine Sozialgeschichte Westeuropas 1880–1980,* München: C.H. Beck.

[16] A study made in a super-long-term perspective is Pomian, Krzysztof (1990) *L'Europe et ses nations,* Paris: Gallimard.

[17] In the field of economics, see especially Watanabe Hisashi and Sakudō Jun (eds) (1996) *Gendai Yōroppa Keieishi* [Contemporary European Business History], Tokyo: Yuhikaku.

[18] Yamada Makoto (1996) *Doitsu-gata Fukushi Kokka no Hatten to Hen'yō: Gendai Doitsu Chihō Zaisei Kenkyū* [The Development and Transformation of German-type Welfare State: A Study of Local Finance in Contemporary Germany], Kyoto: Minerva Shobo, p. 324.

[19] Especially noteworthy are Nakamura Tamio (1998) "Amusuterudammu Jōyaku no Dai-ni Dai-san no Hashira no Hōteki Danmenzu: Shinka? Shinka? suru EU" [A legal cross section of the Second and Third Pillars of the Amsterdam Treaty: Deepening? or Evolving? EU], in: *Nihon EU Gakkai Nenpō,* vol. 18, 1998; and Fujiwara Kiichi (1998) "Hegemonî to Nettowâku: Kokusai Seiji ni okeru Chitsujo Keisei no Jōken ni tsuite" [Hegemony and Network: Conditions for the Formation of Order in International Potitics], in: University of Tokyo, Institute of Social Science.

[20] Bull, Hedley (1977) *The Anarchical Society: A Study of Order in World Politics,* New York: Columbia University Press, and Gamble (1998).

[21] Yamakage (1994), pp. 293–303 (first appearance 1988).

[22] Tanaka Akihiko (1996), p. 253.

23 Yamakage Susumu (1997) *ASEAN Pawâ: Ajia Taiheiyō no Chūkaku e* [ASEAN Power: Growing as the Core of the Asia-Pacific Region], Tokyo: University of Tokyo Press, pp. 8–10. For ASEM, see Tanaka Toshiro (1997) "ASEM (Ajia Ōshū Kaigō): Atarashii Taiwa no Tanjō" [The Asia-Europe Meeting (ASEM): Birth of a New Dialogue], *Nihon EU Gakkai Nenpō,* vol. 17, 1997.

24 Yamakage (1997), p. 318, and (1994), pp. 121–4.

25 Yamakage (1997), p. 318.

26 See Nakamura (1998) and Fujiwara (1998). The discussion of networks in Fujiwara (1998, pp. 318–33), while recognizing their elements in EU, is confined to the cases of ASEAN and APEC.

27 Concerning the fact of East Asian growth, views have been presented that emphasize economic interdependence within the region and that place more stress on the networks of overseas Chinese. I rather pay more attention to the role of Japanese corporations – their technology transfer and management transfer – in the technological and management development in the region. I would like to put forth an anti-Alice Amsden and anti-Paul Krugman hypothesis that the technological and management development in the region has a certain autonomy and has the potential of innovation in the future. As for facts in this connection, see Itagaki Hiroshi (ed.) (1997) *Nihonteki Keiei Seisan Shisutemu to Higashi Ajia: Taiwan, Kankokū, Chūgoku ni okeru Haiburiddo Kōjō* [Japanese-style Management and Production Systems and East Asia: Hybrid Factories in Taiwan, South Korea, and China], Kyoto: Minerva Shobo.

28 Recall how and how much two works were read in Western Europe and Japan: Michel Albert (1991) *Capitalisme contre Capitalisme,* Paris: Seuil; and Fukada Yusuke and Dore, Ronald (1993) *Nihon-gata Shihonshugi nakushite nan no Nihon ka* [There Can Be No Japan Without Japanese-style Capitalism], Tokyo: Kobunsha.

29 In Saeki Keishi (1998) *"Amerikaitizumu" no Shūen: Shivikku Riberarizumu Seishin no Saihakken e* [The End of "Americanism": Toward Rediscovering the Spirit of Civic Liberalism], enlarged edition, Tokyo: TBS Britannica, regionalization is not discussed, but I wonder if that is merely for argument's sake.

30 See Kudō Akira (1995) "Nichi-Ō Keizai Kankei no Henbō" [Transformation of the Japanese-European Economic Relations]. It is necessary to reconsider what can be seen and cannot be seen through the Arnold Joseph Toynbee schema of challenge and response.

31 "Japan has been criticized for not taking leadership in international society. Actually, it has not been unwilling to take leadership but has not been able to do so. It is not Asian countries alone that have been wary of Japanese leadership. Even in the 1980s, in the IMF and the World Bank, for example, some major industrial countries were opposed to capital increases that might be linked to an increase in Japan's voting power. Japan has behaved over the half century after the war within the framework of the will of the Allied powers system that suggests that Japan should 'pay up' but not interfere." Yamakage (1994), p. 318.

32 This point does not seem to be adequately discussed even in Kaneko Masaru (1999) *Han-gurōbarizwnu: Shijō Kaikaku no Senryaku-teki Shikō* [Anti-globalism: Strategic Ideas of Market Reform], Tokyo: Iwanami Shoten, pp. 105–10, although the book includes many valuable insights about the problems of globalization.

33 University of Tokyo, Institute of Social Science (ed.) (1998) *Nijusseiki Shisutemu 4: Kaihatsu-shugi* [The Twentieth-Century Global System 4: Developmentalism],

Tokyo: University of Tokyo Press, contains two essays on Japanese experiences: Nakamura Naofumi "Kōhatsukoku Kōgyōka to Chūō Chihō: Meiji Nihon no Keiken" [Industrialization of a Less Developed Country and the Central and Local: Meiji Japan's Experiences]; and Kikkawa Takeo "Keizai Kaihatsu Seisaku to Kigyō: Sengo Nihon no Keiken" [Economic Development Policy and Corporations: Post-war Japan's Experiences]. The inclusion of these essays is of great significance, going beyond the intention of the editors' emphasis on the difference between Japan's and other Asian nations' experiences.

Index